V&R Academic

Refo500 Academic Studies

Edited by
Herman J. Selderhuis

In Co-operation with
Günter Frank (Bretten), Bruce Gordon (New Haven),
Mathijs Lamberigts (Leuven), Barbara Mahlmann-Bauer (Bern),
Tarald Rasmussen (Oslo), Johannes Schilling (Kiel),
Zsombor Tóth (Budapest), Günther Wassilowsky (Linz),
Siegrid Westphal (Osnabrück), David M. Whitford (Trotwood)

Volume 30

Frances Luttikhuizen

Underground Protestantism in Sixteenth Century Spain

A Much Ignored Side of Spanish History

Vandenhoeck & Ruprecht

Bibliographic information published by the Deutsche Nationalbibliothek
The Deutsche Nationalbibliothek lists this publication in the Deutsche Nationalbibliografie;
detailed bibliographic data available online: http://dnb.d-nb.de.

ISSN 2198-3089
ISBN 978-3-525-55110-3

You can find alternative editions of this book and additional material on our Website: www.v-r.de

Typesetting by Konrad Triltsch GmbH, Ochsenfurt
Printed and bound by Hubert & Co GmbH & Co. KG, Robert-Bosch-Breite 6, D-37079 Göttingen

Printed on aging-resistant paper.

Contents

The research for this book was possible thanks to
Peter, who planted the seed,
David, who watered it, and
Alfredo, who brought the sunshine.

Acknowledgments

I recall with a profound sense of gratitude the many people who have assisted me with my research. I especially want to mention Dr. Bernard Aubert, who read the manuscript several times and made very helpful suggestions, and Elke Liebig and Christoph Spill, who were most helpful with the final editing process. I also wish to thank those who gave me financial support, such as Howard and Roberta Ahmanson, The Providence Forum, and CIMPE (Centro de Investigación y Memoria del Protestantismo Español).

I must also mention my father, Martin Luttikhuizen, from whom I inherited a love for history, a profound admiration for people who stand up for their beliefs, and an appreciation for textual ethics.

Likewise, I am also deeply grateful to Dr. Herman J. Selderhuis, of Vandenhoeck & Ruprecht Press, who was willing to incorporate the book in his Refo500 Academic Studies (R5AS) series.

Abbreviations

ADC Archivo Diocesano de Cuenca
AGS Archivo General de Simancas
AHN Archivo Historico Nacional
BNE Biblioteca Nacional de España
BMS Biblioteca Municipal de Sevilla
f. folio
doc. Documento [document]
lib. Libro [book]
leg. Legajo [file, bundle]

Timeline of Events

Year	Event
1478	Spanish Inquisition established
1479	Pedro de Osma's *De confessione* publicly burned
1490	Publication in Spanish of Jean de Gerson's *Menosprecio del mundo*
1492	Jews expelled from Spain
	Ximenez de Cisneros becomes Queen Isabel's confessor
1495	Cisneros becomes archbishop of Toledo
1497	Cisneros begins his reforms
1499	First statute of "purity of blood" (Toledo)
1502	Montesino translates *Vita Cristi* into Spanish
	Work begins on Complutensian Polyglot Bible
1504	Queen Isabel dies
1507	Cisneros becomes Inquisitor General
1508	University of Alcala opens its doors
1510	Bianda de Mendoza opens her beguine house in Guadalajara
1512	Isabel de la Cruz preaches mystical abandonment (*deixamiento*) in Guadalajara
	Montesino translates *Epistles and Gospels for the Liturgical Year*
1516	Erasmus's Greek-Latin New Testament arrives in Spain
	Translation of Erasmus's *Sermon* on the *Child Jesus*
	King Ferdinand dies
	Cisneros becomes regent
1517	Printing completed of the Complutense Polyglot Bible
	Charles V arrives in Spain as king of Castile and Aragon
	Cardinal Cisneros dies
1520	Publication of Erasmus's *The Education of a Christian Prince*
	Antonio de Baeza becomes governor of Escalona
	Comunero uprising in Castile
1521	Charles V meets Luther at Worms
	First official decree against Lutheran books
1522?	Juan de Valdes arrives in Escalona
	"Recogimiento" (withdrawal) practiced in Escalona

Year	Event
1523	Pedro Ruiz de Alcaraz leaves Guadalajara for Escalona
	Ruiz de Alcaraz and Francisco Ortiz of "recogimiento" movement part company
	Deixados meet in the palace of Diego Lopez de Pacheco (Marquis de Villena)
1524	Pedro Ruiz de Alcaraz incarcerated
1525	Juan Lopez de Celain organizes "The Twelve Apostles of Medina de Rioseco"
	Edict of Toledo against the *alumbrados-deixados*
	Translation of Erasmus's *Enquiridión, Manual of a Christian Knight*
1527	Valladolid Conference convened to examine the writings of Erasmus
1529	*Auto-da-fe* in Toledo against *alumbrados* (Ruiz de Alcaraz, Isabel de la Cruz)
	Publication in Alcala of Juan de Valdes's *Dialog on Christian Doctrine*
1530	Juan de Valdes flees to Italy
	Juan Lopez de Celain burned at the stake in Granada
1531	Publication of Erasmus's *Sermon on Two Psalms*
1532	Carlo de Sesso arrives in Spain
1534	*Auto-da-fe* in Toledo against *alumbrados*
1536	Erasmus dies; his works are prohibited in Spain
1538	First Index of Prohibited Books (Brussels)
1540	Rodrigo Valer called before the Inquisition in Seville
1542	Agustín Cazalla appointed personal chaplain of Charles V
1541	Juan de Valdes dies in Naples
1543	Francisco de Enzinas presents his New Testament to Charles V in Antwerp
1546	Council of Trent, "Decree Concerning the Edition of The Sacred Books"
1547	Charles V defeats Schmalkaldic League at the Battle of Mühlberg.
	"Purity of blood" decree applied to all ecclesiastical posts in Toledo
	Fernando de Valdes becomes Inquisitor General
1548	Constantino Ponce de la Fuente accompanies prince Philip through Europe
1550	Charles V decrees the "Edict of Blood" against heretics in Flanders
	Dr. Egidio incarcerated
	Luis Fernández, Luis del Castillo, Juan Perez de Pineda flee to Paris
	Carlo de Sesso returns to Spain from Italy with Protestant literature
1551	First "Index of Prohibited Books" printed in Spain
1552	Inquisition confiscates 300 Bibles in Seville
	Dr. Egidio brought to trial
	Francisco de Enzinas dies in Strasbourg
1554	Carlo de Sesso appointed *corregidor* in Toro
1555	Philip II (regent) extends statute of "purity of blood" to all official posts
1556	Charles V abdicates and retires to Yuste; Philip II ascends to the throne
	Perez de Pineda busy translating and editing Protestant literature in Geneva
1557	Twelve monks from the Santiponce monastery flee to Geneva
	Colporteur Julian Hernandez arrives in Seville and is incarcerated
1558	Members of the Protestant communities in Valladolid and Seville incarcerated
	Constantino Ponce de la Fuente incarcerated
	Fernando de Valdes publishes his Index of Forbidden Books
	Agustín Cazalla incarcerated
	Carlo de Sesso incarcerated

Year	Event
1559	*Autos-da-fe* in Valladolid against Lutherans (May 25; October 8)
	Auto-da-fe in Seville against Lutherans (September 24)
	Bartolome de Carranza incarcerated
	Cipriano de Valera translates Calvin's *Institutes* in London
	Philip II orders all Spanish students studying abroad to return
1560	*Auto-da-fe* in Seville against Lutherans (December 22)
	Constantino Ponce de la Fuente dies in prison
1562	*Autos-da-fe* in Seville against Lutherans (February; April 26; October 28)
1563	*Auto-da-fe* in Seville against Lutherans (July 11)
1565	*Auto-da-fe* in Seville against Lutherans (May 13)
1567	Duke of Alba establishes the "Court of Blood" in the Netherlands
	Reginaldo Gonzalez de Montes's *Artes de la Inquisición* printed
1569	Casiodoro de Reina publishes his *Biblia de Oso* in Basel
1571	Arias Montano's Expurgatory Index published
1572	*Biblia Regia* o (Antwerp Polyglot) published
1583	Index of Forbidden Books enlarged
1598	Philip II dies
1609	Philip III expels the *Moriscos* from Spain
1614	Juan Aventrot translates Heidelberg Catechism into Spanish
1631	Aventrot burned at the stake in an *auto-da-fe* in Toledo
1738	Freemasons and the Enlightenment-minded new targets of the Inquisition
1767	Jesuits expelled from Spain
1782	Ban lifted on vernacular translations of the Bible
1790	Last Index of Prohibited Books
1793	Felipe Scio's translation from the Vulgate printed in Valencia
1808	Napoleon abolishes Inquisition
1814	Ferdinand VII returns; Inquisition reestablished
1815	Jesuits readmitted
1820	Mobs storm Inquisition palace in Barcelona
1822	Juan Antonio Llorente publishes his *History of the Inquisition* in Paris
1826	Cayetano Ripoll executed in Valencia
1829	Thomas M'Crie publishes his *History of the Reformation in Spain* in Edinburgh
1834	Inquisition finally abolished
1836	British and Foreign Bible Society sends George Borrow to Spain
1844	Spanish National Historical Archives open to the public
1845–65	Luis Usoz y Rio rediscovers writings of Spanish reformers and publishes them in *Reformistas Antiguos Españoles*

Preliminary Remarks

> For it is the business and duty of historians to be exact, truthful, and wholly free from passion, and neither interest nor fear, hatred nor love, should make them swerve from the path of truth, whose mother is history, rival of time, storehouse of deeds, witness for the past, example and counsel for the present, and warning for the future.
>
> *Don Quijote*, Book I, Ch. 9

The story of underground Protestantism in sixteenth century Catholic Spain is a significant area of Spanish history—and Reformation history—that many scholars overlook. This neglect is due in part to the overwhelming, and well-deserved, attention given to the *Siglo de Oro* (Spanish Golden Age) with its exceptional contributions to the arts and to literature. The Spanish Golden Age, which covered nearly two centuries, from the publication of Antonio de Nebrija's *Grammar of the Castilian Language* in 1492 to the death of Pedro Calderon de la Barca in 1681, produced great poets, novelists, playwrights, and painters that are still celebrated today. It was the age of Cervantes, of Quevedo, Lope de Vega, Velazquez, Zurbaran, El Greco, and others. But parallel to this great outburst of artistic euphoria, two very negative sides of Spanish history were also under way: the severe dealings of the Inquisition with religious dissidents and the Counter-Reformation. Though this aspect of Spanish history is much less glamorous and gratifying, nevertheless, it is as much part of the country's history as the former and therefore deserves as much serious study.

The history of early modern Spanish spirituality carries with it connotations of devotion and mysticism associated with the writings of Santa Teresa de Avila, San Juan de la Cruz, Fray Luis de Leon, Francisco de Osuna, and others;[1] the impact of the Protestant Reformation on modern Spanish spirituality is associated with much lesser known authors such as Juan Perez de Pineda, Francisco de Enzinas, Casiodoro de Reina, Cipriano de Valera, and Antonio del Corro, whose writings were banned. The dearth of English literature on the contributions of these men and the circumstances that compelled them to leave their native country and seek refuge in places where freedom of conscience was allowed motivated me to undertake this area of research.

Several excellent studies exist in English regarding the activities of the Spanish Inquisition, but there is the tendency to pass over lightly the impact of the Protestant Reformation in the Iberian Peninsula, mainly because it was thought to be so short-lived. This book is an attempt to correct this assumption

---

1 See Rady Roldan-Figueroa (2010a).

and to provide English readers with an overall account of the arrival, reception, and suppression of Protestantism in sixteenth century Spain. The survey begins with the socio-political-religious context that prevailed, Cardinal Cisneros's reforms, the role of the *alumbrados-deixados* (Illuminati), and the Erasmian influence at the University of Alcala. It then goes on to deal with the severe persecution of the underground evangelical circles in Seville and Valladolid, and the exiles, whose names and writings remained virtually unknown until the mid-nineteenth century. Our study concludes with the abolition of the Inquisition and the tireless efforts of Luis Usoz y Rio to rediscover and reprint the works of these forgotten Spanish reformers.

Primary Sources

Because the main tool for the study of the Inquisition is found in the primary sources of the period, it was essential to resort to numerous contemporary Inquisition reports, dispatches, and trial records found in the archives. At the beginning of the twentieth century, the German historian Ernst H. J. Schäfer searched through these archives and published the trial records related to the evangelical movement in Valladolid. However, because Schäfer's work—*Beiträge* (Contributions)—was published in German, few researchers had access to it until recently, thanks to Francisco Ruiz de Pablos (2014) who translated Schäfer's work into Spanish and restored the *urtexte* and the current reference numbers. Our references to Schäfer are taken from Ruiz de Pablos's Spanish edition unless otherwise indicated. Likewise, reports and trial records found in the National Historical Archives related to the evangelical movement in Seville have also been collected and published recently by Tomas Lopez Muñoz (2011). Although these two publications still remain in Spanish, they nevertheless have greatly facilitated our research. Translations of these documents are mine unless otherwise indicated.

A second contemporary source was Reginaldo Gonzalez de Montes's *Sanctae Inquisitionis hispanicae artes aliquot detect* (1567). Montes's work, referred to hereafter as *Artes,* was translated into English the year after it was first published in Latin. Our references to Montes's work are taken from the second printing of the English version (1569), which includes several appendixes, hereafter referred to as *A Discovery.* Vincent Skinner, the translator, graduated from Trinity College (University of Cambridge) in 1564. After leaving Cambridge, he went on to Lincoln's Inn, a political finishing school for young lawyers and an extension of the court. Lincoln's Inn had developed a Protestant identity in the 1560s and it was within this confessional dimension that the idea of "active citizenship"—a philosophy espoused by educational institutions which advocated that citizens have certain roles and responsibilities to society—emerged. The main commitments of this movement were to purify the Church of England of all semblances to the Roman Catholic Church and to make their fellow citizens aware of the ensuing political consequences should Catholicism be restored. Spanish intervention in the Netherlands, just a few hours away from the English coast, was considered a real danger and a giant step in this direction hence the reception of any material describing the cruelties of the Spanish Inquisition was welcome.

Vincent Skinner's rendering is faithful to the original, but like all Elizabethan translators, he made profuse use of rhetorical devices such as puns, witty conceits, alliteration, and euphuistic doublets not always present in the original, nevertheless making the text a delight to read. He took special care to explain cultural references unfamiliar to his readers by incorporating clarifications. For example, "to talk by signs and watchwords, *like peddlers French* (Montes: 1569, f. 24r);"[2] "they are shut up in a narrow cell, where they have scarcely good elbowroom for cleanliness and light, *not much unlike Little Ease* (f. 5v);"[3] "[the Inquisitors] were blind *and yet as bold as Bayard* (f. 84v);"[4] "in civil causes even of small importance they will not admit a man's enemy, nor a liar, or a defamed person, or an idiot, or a *Bedlam* (f. 14v);"[5] and so on. Likewise, whenever Skinner suspected that his readers might not understand a given reference, he inserted a more familiar one. For example, where the original text states that the practice of not mentioning a witness by name is taken from the book of ancient mysteries of "Mother Eleusine,"—referring to the Eleusinian Mysteries of ancient Greece—, Skinner rendered, "This whim, I tell you, is taken out of their *Sancta Sanctorum* (f. 15v)."[6] Or, suspecting his readers did not know who the Cyclopes were, he used the term Termagants (f. 48v).[7] His clever use of alliteration can be found in added adjectives: "a *hungry* hunter," "a *curtaled* cur,"[8] a "*pelting* priest."[9] The best example of alliteration, however, is found in the Preface to the Reader, where he uses the expression "pield polling priest" as an euphemism to refer to Pope

---

2 The sort of slang language used by wandering beggars was known as "Peddlers' French."
3 "Little Ease" refers to the basement in the Tower of London. This chamber was built in the thickness of the wall and measured only four square feet.
4 Pierre Terrail, Lord of Bayard (1476–1524), was a French military hero known as "*le chevalier sans peur et sans reproche*" (the knight without fear or reproach).
5 An inmate of Bedlam, an insane asylum in London.
6 "*Sancta Sanctorum*" refers to a secluded, mysterious place held in the highest esteem.
7 Termagants were imaginary deities of a violent character often appearing in morality plays, which the majority of his readers would have been familiar with.
8 A short-haired dog.
9 "Pelting" was an adjective used often in the sixteenth century to mean "despicable, mean, wretched." In John Lyly's *Midas* (1592) we read, "attire never used but of old women and pelting priests."

Pius V:[10] "pield," a malapropism for "pied" (two colors)—the black cloak over a white soutane worn by the Dominicans—; "polling," one who shaves the top of his head—a tonsured friar.

A third primary source was Juan Antonio Llorente, a former secretary of the Inquisiton. Llorente's *Histoire critique de l'Inquisition d'Espagne* (1817–1818) was translated into English in 1826 as *A History of the Inquisition of Spain*. Llorente reaffirms many of the details revealed earlier by Montes, who he describes as a faithful reporter of events, and also provides new information regarding the persecution of Protestants. Our references to Llorente's work are taken from the English edition published in Philadelphia in 1843.

Historiographical Overview

The historiography of underground Protestantism in sixteenth century Spain begins with Reginaldo Gonzalez de Montes's *Sanctae Inquisitionis hispanicae artes aliquot detectæ* (1567). The English version, which appeared the following year, was barely off the press when, on July 3, 1568, the Spanish ambassador in London, Guzman de Silva, reported the publication to king Philip:

> A book has been printed here and has been sold publicly for the last three days and has even been fixed in certain public places in this city, a quarto nearly two inches thick, called *Declaracion evidente de diversas y subtiles astucias de la Sancta Inquisicion de Espana*. It was written in Latin by Reginaldo Gonzales Montano and has been recently translated into English, but the translator's name is not given. I have only been able to see the prologue, which speaks very shamelessly of the pope. (Calendar, 1894).

Within a year of its publication in Latin, *Artes* was translated into both English and French. The following year there appeared two German versions, three Dutch versions, and two abridged versions, one in Hungarian and the other in French.[11] One of the Dutch renderings was done from the Latin, the other two from French, one translator was Maulumpertus Taphaea, the other was done by Joris de Raed with a prologue by the Dutch theologian Petrus Dathenus.[12] The printers of the two German versions—Andreas Petri and Johannes Mayer—also deserve mention. Andreas Petri belonged to a family of German printers working at Basel. He was probably a nephew of Adam Petri, who after 1517 was

---

10 Pius V was a Dominican priest. His papacy—1566 to 1572—coincided with the publication of *Artes*.

11 The first Spanish version of *Artes* was published in 1851. See Appendix B for these publications.

12 Today Joris de Raed is remembered for his translation of Calvin's Institutes into Dutch and Petrus Dathenus for his translation of the Heidelberg Catechism.

primarily occupied with the publication of texts of the Protestant Reformers. Johann Mayer, the other German printer, is remembered as the publisher of the Heidelberg Catechism (1563).

In addition to the various translations of *Artes*, a reprint of the 1567 Latin version came off the Ernest Voegelin press in Heidelberg in 1603. This slightly abridged edition was compiled by Simon Stenius, professor at the University of Heidelberg. The curious title—*Seven brief essays on the Spanish Inquisition, based on Reinaldo Gonzalez Montes' report of 38 years ago*—suggests the existence of a 1565 edition. Could Stenius have meant XXXVI instead of XXXVIII—making it 1567, the date Artes was first printed—or was there actually an earlier manuscript edition of *Artes* in circulation in Germany? A few years later, in 1611, Joachim Ursinus [Beringer], a Lutheran pastor, published a bilingual Latin-German edition in Amberg, Bavaria.[13] In 1856, Luis Usoz y Rio reprinted the original Latin edition of *Artes* and included it as volume XIII in his collection *Reformistas Antiguos Españoles*. A new translation from the Latin, done by Francisco Ruiz de Pablos, appeared in 2008.

In the early years of the seventeenth century, with the growing tensions in northern Europe regarding the uncertain future of recently gained religious liberties, there was renewed interest in disclosing the "wiles and guiles" of the Spanish Inquisition. Both John Foxe and Jean Crespin mention the plight of the Spanish Protestants and the *autos-da-fe* in passing in their martyrologies, but in the enlarged edition of Crespin's *Histoire des Martyrs* (1608, VII, ff. 521–566), Simon Goulart inserted the anonymous 1568 French rendering of *Artes* in full together with a lengthy account of the *auto-da-fe* in Valladolid held May 21, 1559, which was not part of Montes's narrative, but which he interpolated between the second and third section. The inserted information includes a full description of the scaffolds, the names of the grandees and bishops that attended, and a brief biographical sketch of the thirty prisoners that were sentenced that day. Goulart states that he found the information regarding Valladolid in "certain letters sent to Germany." One of such letters, entitled *"breve relación"* (brief account), is reproduced in Schäfer (2014, III, 52–63). It was a rewrite, in German, of an official report entitled *"relación verdadera"* (true account).[14] Schäfer notes that the language employed in the *"breve relación"* suggests that the placard was translated into German by a somewhat inexperienced translator from southern Germany with strong Protestant leanings. It is interesting to note that whereas the opening line of the official Spanish report is a paraphrased version of Proverbs 1,32 [For the waywardness of the simple will kill them, and the complacency of fools will destroy them], the non-official German version com-

---

13 See Appendix B for these publications.
14 BNE, ms. 2058, núm. 91, fol. 230–239, in Schäfer (2014, III, 24, doc. 378).

mences with Matthew 5,10 [Blessed are those who are persecuted because of righteousness, for theirs is the kingdom of heaven].

Once the inquisitors realized that eyewitnesses of the *autos-da-fe* were sending reports abroad, they commissioned scribes to write up reports of the same events for broader circulation and to counteract what the others might be reporting. This was done because, as Montes (1569, ff. 53r–53v) points out,

> When they began to celebrate their Triumph upon the Lutherans (as they call them), they that were present at the sight and beheld the way things were done, would write to their friends both in the realm and abroad, detailed reports of all such things as there were done and seen, especially of those that did penance, also what sentences were pronounced upon them, with the causes and circumstances of all their other punishments and penalties. But the Holy House (as daily practice makes everyone master of his craft) grew so cunning in their affairs that straightway they began to smell out the matter that it might in time turn against them and that the doctrine which they so greatly detested and abhorred might be published and spread further than they would wish, so that many, who otherwise would have continued in their blindness, if they had never heard nor seen any such reports, should be occasioned thereby to open their eyes and understandings and to confess as well the doctrine itself and receive it, and also spy the wickedness of them that persecute it. Therefore, to remedy this mischief and inconvenience, the Holy House prepared and published similar reports, brief and as were not likely to do any great harm, so that whoever wanted to inform their friends of such matters, should follow those authorized reports. Indeed, they appointed certain great penalties for the transgressors that should make up their own reports in any other more exhaustive manner than was by their order prescribed. The manner whereof was this: that after they had told who and what manner of man he was that was punished or executed, they should add: "because he held Luther's opinions (without naming any), so and so was burned, or thus or thus punished or executed according to the truth of the matter."

Until the Inquisition was abolished and more documents were available, Montes's account was basically the only information in circulation regarding the procedures of the Spanish Inquisition against Protestants. In England, Skinner's translation was reprinted in 1625 by John Bellamie under a new grandiloquent title—*A full, ample and punctually discovery of the barbarous, bloudy, and inhumane practises of the Spanish Inquisition, against Protestants: with the originall thereof. Manifested in their proceedings against sundry particular persons, as well English as others, upon whom they have executed tyrannie*—and redrafted again fifty years later by Richard Dugdale (1680) in an abridged edition. Information taken from *Artes* appeared in the various re-editions of John Foxe's *Acts and Monuments*, in Philipp von Limborch (1816), in Johann Lorenz von Mosheim (1765), in Michael Geddes (1741), in Joseph Lavallée (1809), and John Joseph Stockdale (1810).

The general public, however, became aware of the impact of the Protestant

Reformation in the Iberian Peninsula thanks to the efforts of Juan Antonio Llorente and the Scottish historian Thomas M'Crie. Llorente, who had access to authentic documents, first published his work in French (1821). It was immediately translated into Dutch (1821), German (1823) and repeatedly into English (1826, 1827). Nevertheless, the Scottish church historian Thomas M'Crie's work (1829) became the standard text in English-speaking Protestant circles until John Stoughton published his *Spanish reformers, their memories and dwelling-places* (1883) and the American historian Henry Charles Lea produced his four-volume seminal work *History of the Inquisition in Spain* (1906–07). Thomas M'Crie had already made a name for himself as an historian with his *History of the Reformation in Italy* (1827), rapidly translated into German (1828), French (1831), and Italian (1835). His *History of the Reformation in Spain* (1829) was translated into German (1835) and Dutch (1838).[15] Whereas earlier authors rarely disclose their sources, M'Crie duly acknowledged, and referenced his primary sources, which included Llorente, John Strype (1709), and the 1569 printing of Skinner's *A Discovery*. M'Crie also frequently cites the German geographer-historian Anton Friedrich Büsching's *Commentatio De vestigiis Lvtheranismi in Hispania* (Traces of Lutheranism in Spain) (1755).

Other nineteenth century authors whose works appeared in English include Adolfo de Castro, Elizabeth R. Charles, and Cornelius A. Wilkens. Adolfo de Castro's *The Spanish Protestants, and Their Persecution by Philip II* (1851) and his *History of Religious Intolerance in Spain: or, an Examination of some of the causes which led to that nation's decline* (1853) met with great enthusiasm. Elizabeth R. Charles's novelized *The Martyrs of Spain and the Liberators of Holland* (1862) was often reprinted and translated into French (1866), Spanish (1871), Norwegian (1877), etc. Cornelius August Wilkens's *Die Geschichte des spanischen Protestantismus im sechzehnten Jahrhundert* (1888) enjoyed several reprints and in 1897 was translated into English and slightly abridged by Rachel Challice. All these pioneer studies became inspiration and source material for the American historian Henry Charles Lea at the turn of the century. Lea began by publishing *Chapters from the Religious History of Spain Connected with the Inquisition* (1890) and *The Moriscos of Spain, their Conversion and Expulsion* (1901). That same year, the Dutch historian Maximilian F. van Lennep published *De Hervorming in Spanje in de zestiende eeuw* (The Reformation in Spain in the Sixteenth Century) (1901; 1984), but it was Ernst H. J. Schäfer's three-volume *Beiträge* (1902) that enabled Lea to produce his four-volume *History of the Inquisition in Spain* (1906–07), as he duly acknowledged.

Unfortunately, authors such as Wilkens failed to document many of their

---

15 The first Spanish translation did not appear until 1950, translated by Adam F. Sosa. This rendering has recently been reprinted in Seville with an introduction by Doris Moreno.

statements, leaving the reader unsure of the validity of their conclusions. On the other hand, it must be remembered that although the Inquisition had been abolished, the official archives were not yet accessible to the general public until the end of the century. In this respect Schäfer's *Beiträge* was groundbreaking. Aware that too often "histories" were written that lacked the support of original documents, Schäfer basically limited his efforts to transcribing the original accounts kept in the national archives at Simancas and Madrid:

> Although much research has appeared in recent times regarding the suppression of the Reformation in Spain, which is of great value for those interested in the subject of the Reformation and its history, and among these I must mention M'Crie, de Castro, and Wilkens, nevertheless, in nearly all these studies I find a serious inconvenience, that is, the authors do not quote the original sources, which is of paramount importance for any serious historical survey, especially when trying to clarify such a dark period of history. (Schäfer: 2014, I, 198).

Whereas most of the research carried out before 1950 centers on the *autos-da-fe* that took place in Seville and Valladolid, historical scholarship during the 1960s and 70s sent many historians back to the archives. This methodology has continued and has encouraged the incorporation of large segments of authentic primary material. It has also given rise to a wider range of more specific topics. Classic studies such as those by Henry Kamen (1966) and Edward Peters (1989), and more recently Joseph Perez (2005) and Michael C. Thomsett (2010), as well as statistical studies such as those carried out by Gustav Henningsen (1986), mention the persecution of evangelicals in passing, but also address the practices of the Inquisition regarding crypto-Jews, Muslims, black magic, blasphemy, bigamy, etc. On the other hand, scholars such as Marcel Bataillon, John Longhurst, Antonio Marquez, Angela Selke, Alvaro Huerga, Arthur G. Kinder, Klaus Wagner, Jose C. Nieto, Jose Luis Gonzalez Novalin, Stefania Pastore, Helen Rawlings, Werner Thomas, Lu Ann Homza, Doris Moreno, Rady Roldan-Figueroa, Michel Boeglin, etc., have branched out into specific areas attempting to offer a more in depth vision of the Reformation in Spain by explaining the rise of the evangelical movement through the *alumbrados*, the Erasmians, the persecution of foreigners, etc.[16] The fact that only a few of the above authors have published in English, clearly evidences the lack of material regarding the outreach of the sixteenth century evangelical movement in Spain for English-speaking readers.

Current Historical Memory Studies have produced a renewed interest in the activities of the Spanish Inquisition above and beyond its persecution of crypto-

---

16 Abundant primary material regarding the *alumbrados-deixados* can be found in Longhurst (1969) and Homza (2006); primary material regarding the persecution of foreigners can be found in Thomas (2001a; 2001b).

Jews and Muslims. The two great seminal works in this area belong to Marcel Bataillon (1936; 1966) and Jose C. Nieto (1970; 1997). Since it is impossible to do justice to all the fine scholarship that has appeared, we must simply refer the reader to several comprehensive bibliographies: Emile Van der Vekene (1982–92); Arthur Gordon Kinder (1999); Klaus Van der Grijp (2005); and Frances Luttikhuizen (2009). Despite these efforts, the increase in the last decade of publications focusing on the sixteenth century evangelical movement in Spain require new up-dated bibliographies. The full-scale story of the outreach of the Protestant Reformation in Spain has not been written, nor will it ever be. As the nineteenth century English historian John Stoughton (2013,17) put it,

> When we have analyzed all the facts recorded in history, and have put together what serves to explain, so far as secondary causes are concerned, how it was that the Reformation failed in Spain, there is a residuum at the bottom of the crucible, as in many other cases, which must ever defy our attempts at explanation. Why the destiny of the movement in Spain was so different from that of the movement in England remains amongst the inscrutable mysteries of Providence.

Though we deal briefly with the plight of some of the men and women who adhered to the evangelical movement in sixteenth century Spain, the present study is an attempt to shed light on the social-political-religious context in which the movement emerged, developed, and was suppressed.[17] The reader may find the numerous, and sometimes lengthy, excerpts of original documents somewhat cumbersome, but as Rawdon Brown, the nineteenth century historian who spent twenty years in Venice researching the reports of Venetian ambassadors to England, and editor of what would become *Calendar of State Papers in the Archives of Venice* (1864–1886), states:

> For the general reader perhaps the greatest charm of original documents is that they present the actors in all the reality of life, and not as puppets danced before the reader's eyes in the plausible and measured narrative of the historian. (Calendar, 1864, Preface).

In sum, through the profuse use of primary sources, we hope to offer the reader fresh insights into an obscure chapter of Spanish history and allow the actors to speak for themselves. At all times, I have tried to abide by the facts as they appear in the official records, and to stay away from commonplace statements and attitudes that wish to suppress the ugly side of history:

> Long did old-fashioned English Protestants and other anti-Catholics put their attention upon words such as 'jesuitical,' 'popish,' 'jansenistic,' and 'inquisitorial' in their polemics. But possibly the most odious, and the most successfully repromoted, is the idea of the hated Inquisition as the cruel tool of the Catholic Church to crush its enemies...

---

17 Comprehensive lists of the men and women imprisoned and/or sent to the stake for their faith can be found in Leon de la Vega (2012).

American Know-Nothings and John Foxe's *Book of Martyrs* constantly reprinted, or
even the purveyors of the post-1968 sexual revolution or abortion-on-demand today,
bring up the ghost of the Inquisition to suit their diverse purposes. But what do they
know of its history? (Van Hove: 1992).

It is precisely this history that we propose to explore in the following pages and
in so doing I hope to clarify certain misconceptions regarding Inquisition history and to enlarge on other aspects that heretofore have been ignored such as
the literature confiscated, the significant role of women in the evangelical
movement in sixteenth century Spain, and the rediscovery of the writings of the
Spanish Reformers. Undoubtedly, if more primary material were available in
English, more scholars would be encouraged to explore these still rather unknown pages of Spanish history. This survey is another step forward in that
direction.

Chapter 1:
Socio-Political Background

> The confiscation of prisoners' goods is a prerogative that has always been defended
> most consistently by the inquisitors, as they have been persuaded by Paul's doctrine
> that the minister of the altar must live by the altar; consequently it is natural that those
> who persecute the enemies of the faith should live at their expense.
> *Manual de inquisidores* Ch. 10 (Montpellier, 1821).

The Spanish Inquisition was much more than an isolated event. It cannot be
studied by itself, but in the context of other events. The decade of the 1480s
brought great socio-political changes in the Iberian Peninsula. Reginaldo
Gonzalez de Montes (1569, Preface) describes the situation thus:

> After the wars were ended wherein Ferdinand and Isabella, of famous memory, expelled
> the Turks out of the territory and city of Granada,[1] and other places in Spain, which they
> had occupied for the space of 778 years, from the time of Rodrigo, the last king of Spain
> that was of the race and linage of the Goths, having restored their country into the
> ancient estate that it was in before, and gotten to themselves perpetual fame and
> renown, they turned from those continual troubles and tumults of war to reforming
> and purging of religion.

Implementing the Spanish Inquisition

One of the consequences of the violent anti-Jewish pogroms of the late fourteenth century throughout Spain was the mass conversion of Jews. These new
converts came to be referred to as *conversos* or "new" Christians. Many *conversos*, now freed from the anti-Semitic restrictions imposed on employment,
attained important positions, including positions in the government and in the
Catholic Church. It did not take long, however, before the ruling class and the
populace distrusted the "new" Christians. A commonly leveled accusation was
that they were false converts, secretly practicing their former religion as crypto-
Jews. When Alonso de Hojeda, a Dominican friar, convinced Queen Isabel of the
existence of crypto-Judaism among Andalusian *conversos* during her stay in
Seville in 1477, she decided to act. She appealed to the pope for permission to

---

1 The Granada War began in 1482 and lasted until 1492, when Boabdil, the last Muslim ruler of
the kingdom of Granada, surrendered the keys of the Alhambra Palace to the Castilian
soldiers.

create an ecclesiastical tribunal to punish backsliding *conversos*.[2] Papal consent came in 1478, when Pope Sixtus IV authorized the implementation of the Spanish Inquisition with the papal bull *Exigit sinceras devotionis affectus*, making it an arm of the Spanish monarchy. This bull gave the monarchs exclusive authority to name the inquisitors in their respective kingdoms: Ferdinand in Aragon and Isabel in Castile.

Initially, the Inquisition's main function was to ensure orthodoxy, but soon the concept of *pureza de sangre* (cleanliness of blood)—Christians with no Muslim or Jewish ancestors—was imposed. This status, which focused more on ancestry than on personal religion, placed a ban on *conversos* and their posterity from official positions. The case of Hernando de Talavera (1428–1507), a Spanish monk of *converso* origin, was an early example. Talavera, Archbishop of Granada from 1493 to 1507, was not keen on mass baptisms and "miraculous" conversions but was a believer in clear preaching and appropriate schooling of children, a line strongly disapproved by the inquisitors. This led to suspicions regarding his background and his attachment to his ancestors. In 1505, Diego Rodriguez de Lucero, inquisitor at Cordoba, sent orders of Talavera's imprisonment to Rome, along with genealogical enquiries into his ancestors, but Pope Julius II ordered the release of Archbishop Talavera in 1507. Another case is that of the Spanish humanist Juan Luis Vives (1493–1540), who was also of *converso* ancestry. Vives saw his family decimated by the Inquisition. His father, executed in 1524, was accused of Judaizing; his mother, who had died of the plague in 1508, was also accused of apostasy in 1530. As a result, her body was exhumed and her bones burned (Fantazzi: 2008, 25).

Tomas de Torquemada, who was then the inquisitor general, believed that as long as the Jews remained in Spain, they would influence the tens of thousands of recent converts to continue practicing Judaism. With the country's unification accomplished, the king and queen concluded that the Jews could be dispensed with and, on March 30, 1492, they issued an expulsion decree to take effect within four months. As a result, by July 30 of that year, the entire community— nearly two-thirds of the population—had left the country, putting an end to the largest and most distinguished Jewish settlement in Europe. Both Italy and Portugal benefited from this measure. According to Thomas M'Crie (1833, 59),

> In the literary history of Italy, during the early part of the fifteenth century, several persons are spoken of as Hebrew and Arabic scholars; the most distinguished of whom was Giannozzo Manetti, a Florentine, who drew up a triglot psalter, containing a Latin translation made by himself from the original. But the study of Hebrew in Italy, properly speaking, was coeval with the printing of the Hebrew Scriptures; and it was

---

2 By becoming Christians, they had come under the jurisdiction of the Church, and as such could be punished by its most powerful instrument of punishment, namely, the Inquisition.

facilitated by the severe measures taken by Ferdinand and Isabella, at the instigation of the inquisitors, against the Jews, which induced many of that people to emigrate from Spain to Italy, where, from lucrative motives, they were favourably received by the popes.

The Muslim population, or Moors as they are generally referred to, which constituted another large portion of society, did not fare much better. According to the terms of the treaty drawn up in 1492, when Boabdil surrendered the keys of the Alhambra Palace in Granada to the Castilian soldiers, the Muslims were allowed to preserve their mosques and religious institutions, to retain the use of their language, and to continue to abide by their own laws and customs. Within seven years these terms had been broken. When the moderate missionary approach of the archbishop of Granada, Hernando de Talavera, was replaced by that of Cardinal Cisneros, who organized mass baptisms and the burning of all religious texts in Arabic—one of the blackest pages in Cisneros's personal history—, the citizens of Granada rebelled. This gave the Catholic monarchs an excuse to revoke their promises and by 1526 the Moors were given a choice between conversion or exile. For the majority, baptism was the only practical option. In 1567, Philip II renewed an edict that had never been strictly enforced, making the use of Arabic illegal and prohibiting Islamic dress and customs. This edict resulted in a second uprising, which was brutally suppressed. By 1582 expulsion was proposed as the only solution to the conflict though the actual decree was not officially signed until April 4, 1609. On September 11 the expulsion order was announced in the Kingdom of Valencia, and the first convoy departed from Denia at nightfall on October 2. The *moriscos*[3] of Aragon, Castile, Andalusia and Extremadura received expulsion orders during the course of the following year.

Reginaldo Gonzalez de Montes (1569, Preface), whose first-hand report begins with an overall review of the "arts" employed by the Inquisition, lamented the methods employed to instruct the new converts:

> This Inquisition, you will say, was not brought in to the end that any should thereby be instructed in the principles of true religion, but only that heresy, by means thereof, might be abolished. So much we yield unto them indeed. For it appears plainly, by the zeal that was in those good princes, that they had a better understanding with them at first than that which through their wicked counselors afterward was put in execution. The Inquisition, being thus established for the same ends and purposes which I have before mentioned (as some affirm) before the battle at Granada, which in no way contradicts our purpose, the charge of instructing the people in the principles of religion was first referred to vicars and curates, and from them transferred to the

---

3 "New" Christians of Muslim background came to be known as *moriscos;* those of Jewish background were pejoratively called *marranos* (a play on "swine" and "filthy").

wardens of the church, and afterward to the clerks in every town and perish, who taught the simple abused people their Ave Maria, Pater Noster, their Creed, with Salve Regina, in Latin, shall I say, nay in a barbarous kind of Latin, and for sport and mocking the poor souls, without any devotion or zeal, nor reward either, but very dearly and at a high price; many times besides their common wages, they were paid with the good wife's honesty or the daughter's virginity.

The other five commandments of the Holy Church, which they said were necessary to salvation were: the hearing of mass on holy days and Sundays; the going to shrift and holy confession; the receiving of holy bread; the due observing of fasts required by the church; and the true paying of their tithes and church duties. These things, I warrant you, were beaten into their heads in plain words and mother tongue. By which kind of discipline, what other thing, I pray you, could seem to be sought than to bring men into a heap of perpetual errors. And the court of Inquisition being erected, on the other hand, for the reformation of errors, they might be sure, like good hunters, to lodge the deer and take their stand, and thus obtain a continual prey. But to proceed.

Let us grant them thus much, that the Inquisition was ordained to none other end than that they be two separate and distinct offices: to teach the faith and to root out heresies, yet, were it the duty of good and discreet counselors to provide that the authority committed to bishops by the Holy Scriptures of God should not thereby be taken from them, neither should any other persuasion enter into their heads that there were any other fire or sword to root out heresies but only the sword of God's word, both the which things the holy Apostle did most evidently teach in the Epistle to Titus, where among other qualities required in a bishop, he would have him embrace the word of God fit for instruction that he may be able to exhort by wholesome doctrine, and to convince the gainsayers and adversaries. For surely as a true and justifying faith cannot be forced on anyone (the nature thereof is such), no more can heresy be destroyed by the heretic's death. But the Word of God is most apt and fit for both purposes, for thereby faith is not only engendered but increased and multiplied marvelously, and whatsoever is not agreeable to true faith, if it be examined and tried by the light of this Word, shall soon be betrayed. Wherefore, they ought first to have resorted to the Scriptures and taken counsel of them, whether they had limited any punishment for such as should show themselves willful and obstinate against the truth, or the most cruel execution that can be by fire. For as concerning the confiscation of goods, what can be thought more wretched and covetous, or more unjust and shameless, or further from the profession of a Christian man? And to permit their open infamy, the stain thereof will hardly be sponged out again, who can worthily speak enough against them that use the same kind of punishment even against those poor wretches, whom they have persecuted, to recant from their errors?

The German historian Cornelius August *Wilkens* (1897, 1) begins his survey of the Protestant Reformation in Spain with the following words:

Although only Queen Isabella and a few others believed at first in the reports of the transatlantic voyagers, yet when the glitter of gold and the sight of home-brought treasures proved the fact that a new world had been found, public opinion soon followed in the wake. The king prostrated himself with thanksgiving before the Creator, in the presence of the discoverers, and the cathedral rang with the strains of the Te Deum! On the other hand, as regards the new world of thought, the golden treasures of such a discovery not being patent to the physical eye, its pioneers and their followers received no immediate gratitude for bringing such a blessing within the reach of Spain.

Whereas it is true that Queen Isabel, together with her husband Ferdinand, was responsible for the implantation of the Spanish Inquisition, which would in due course suppress the "golden treasures of the new world of thought," it is also true that she did show spiritual concern for her subjects and was responsible for putting into the hands of the common people—in their common language—a Harmony of the Gospels known as *Vita Cristi Cartuxano* (The Life of Christ by the Carthusian). Around 1500, she commissioned her court poet and preacher, the Franciscan monk Fray Ambrosio de Montesino,[4] to make a Spanish translation of *Vita Cristi,* a work that had been compiled some time in the fourteenth century by the German Carthusian, Ludolf de Saxonia.[5] Whether the idea to translate *Vita Cristi* into Spanish was Queen Isabel's idea, or Cardinal Cisneros's, or Fray Montesino's is unsure. The four-volume work was a sort of recast of the four Gospels, to which was added a series of texts borrowed from the Church Fathers. It was not just a biography of Jesus but a commentary, a series of dogmatic and moral dissertations of spiritual instructions, meditations, and prayers. The work had significant influence on the development of techniques for meditation. It introduced the concept of immersing and projecting oneself into a biblical scene. In the words of Marcel Bataillon (1966, 44–45),

> The masters of Spanish spirituality were imbued with its peculiar spirit of piety. The contemplation this book fostered reached the heart via the imagination: the pious reader could imagine the pebbles of the mountain path the Virgin took to visit Saint Isabel, the stark poverty of the Bethlehem stable, the scaffold of the cross, the nails, the crown of thistles, the sponge socked with bile, etc.

But to return to our query as to whose idea it was to translate *Vita Cristi* into Spanish. Although Cardinal Cisneros had been Queen Isabel's personal confessor since 1492, it was probably initially the queen's idea and it was she who asked Cisneros to find a translator, which he did in his fellow Franciscan and friend, Ambrosio Montesino.[6] She certainly did not want to appear less interested in the religious education of her subjects than her neighbor—and in-

---

4 "Fray" (brother) was a title applied to members of the four mendicant orders: Augustinians, Carmelites, Dominicans, and Franciscans.

5 The work, printed first in Alcala de Henares in 1502, was reprinted in Seville in 1520, 1530, 1531, 1536, 1537, 1543, 1544, 1551, etc. Montesino highlighted with special bold characters the passages that came directly from the gospels.

6 Fray Montesino and Fray Francisco Jimenez de Cisneros had coincided at the Franciscan monastery of San Juan de los Reyes, in Toledo, around 1484.

tellectual rival—the Portuguese queen, Eleanor of Viseu, who already in 1495 had commissioned a translation of the *Vita Cristi* into Portuguese.[7] It must be remembered that Portugal was already a world power at that time with colonies in Africa, Asia, and Brazil, and the undertakings of the much admired and well-read Portuguese queen were undertakings to be imitated. Moreover, the spiritual situation in Portugal was much the same as in Spain. At the Synod of Braga (1477), Archbishop Luis Pires declared:

> Due to the negligence of rectors, priests, and godfathers, there are many children, as well as older men and women, who do not know the Lord's Prayer, the Ave Maria, and the Creed, and consequently cannot recite them; they do not know the Ten Commandments and the works of mercy and therefore cannot fulfill them; they do not know the articles of faith, hence they do not know what they believe; they do not know which, or how many, are the mortal sins to keep from falling in them. Hence, the synod orders all abbots, priors, rectors and priests to teach their people in their churches the content of the Christian Doctrine. But, whereas the Lord's Prayer, the Ave Maria and the Creed should be taught in both Latin and Portuguese, the rest should be taught only in Portuguese. (Sánchez Herrero: 1986, 1059).

The *Vita Cristi* was the first work to come off a printing press in Alcala de Henares. The four large volumes came off the press at separate intervals between November 1502 and September 1503 in the city where Cardinal Cisneros had just founded the College of San Ildefonso, which later would become the University of Alcala. The printer, Estanislao Polono, had just recently come from Seville, but business must not have been what he expected because in 1504 he was back in Seville. The expensive four-volume edition was followed, in 1503, by a smaller, less luxurious edition of which only volumes 1 and 4 were printed in Alcala.[8] In 1505, Garcia de Rueda, the merchant who financed the printing of the *Vita Cristi*, sent Cisneros a proposal to print books for his newly founded college, but the proposal was turned down. There is no evidence that Cisneros was displeased with Polono's work, but liturgical books commissioned by the cardinal had been coming off Pedro Hagenbach's press in Toledo for several years and he may not have wanted to make any changes (Mendez Aparicio: 1981). Indeed, it seems that between 1504 and 1510 printing activity ceased completely at Alcala until the French printer, typesetter, and editor, Arnao Guillen de Brocar—invited by Cardinal Cisneros for the printing of his Polyglot Bible—opened a printing shop there in 1511.

Ambrosio de Montesino, who had earlier translated the *Vita Christi*, further

---

7 Queen Eleanor of Visue (1458–1525), wife of King Joâo II, owned several books of prayer, two small Bibles, four psalters, a *Vita Christi* in Spanish, *Meditaçôes* de Santo Agustinho, *De Consolaçam* by Boethius, an *Exposiçam de Evangelhos e Epistolas*, etc. See Pérez García (2014).
8 The set was completed in Seville in 1520 and 1521 at the shop of Jacob Cromberger, who bought up Polono's type.

contributed to making portions of the Scriptures known in Spanish when, commissioned by King Ferdinand, he revised an earlier Spanish version of the *Epistles and Gospels for the Liturgical Year.*[9] The work consisted of the passages of Scripture read in Latin in the churches each Sunday to which were interspersed commentaries and sermons by Hugo de Prato and Johann Herolt of Basel, Walafrid Strabo's "Glossa ordinaria," Anselm of Laon's "Glossa interlinearis," Nicholas of Lyra's "Postillas," etc. (Bustos Táuler: 2010). With continuous cross-references to the Old and New Testament in the *glossas*, the work became a well-rounded overview of the biblical message. In all likelihood it was Cardinal Cisneros, zealous for the importance of precision in the translating of biblical texts, who, taking advantage of his new post as Regent of Spain, urged King Ferdinand to commission this new translation. From his position as Archbishop of Toledo, Cisneros had set about reforming the Franciscan order in Spain, requiring the priests to reside in their parishes and to preach every Sunday. Many of them did not know Latin hence *Epistles and Gospels for the Year* gave them material for their sermons. Indeed, *Epistles and Gospels* was a sort of manual, in Spanish, of pastoral theology from which these priests, as well as devout lay persons who wanted to meditate on them in private—and in a language familiar to them—greatly benefited. In this respect, *Epistles and Gospels* can be considered the first printed edition of large portions of the Scriptures in the Spanish language available for the common people. It enjoyed many reprints until it was put on the Index of Prohibited Books in 1559 as a result of the decree that prohibited the printing of Scripture in the vulgar tongue.[10]

Catechizing the Populace

Nearly all the synods celebrated in Spain from the fourteenth century on expressed concern regarding the doctrinal ignorance of the masses and the need for their instruction. For a panoramic view of the spiritual situation in Spain in the sixteenth century, we must backtrack to the reign of Alfonso XI (1311–50). In order to solve the difficult socio-economic, political and religious situation of the country, Pope John XXII sent Cardinal Guillaume Pierre Godin, Bishop of Sabina, to Spain as papal legate with full powers to summon parliament in order to resolve political matters and to reform the Spanish church. In May of 1322, he convened a national synod at Valladolid to implement reforms. Being more

---

9   *Epistles and Gospels for the Liturgical Year* had been translated in 1485 by Gonzalo Garcia de Santa Maria, a lawyer from Zaragoza.

10 Toledo, 1512, 1532, 1535, 1549; Antwerp, 1512; Zaragoza, 1525, 1550, 1555; Seville, 1526, 1536, 1537, 1540, 1543, 1549; Antwerp, 1538, 1540, 1542, 1543, 1544, 1550. After 1586 the work was again reprinted but with corrections (*nuevamente visto y corregido*).

occupied with political affairs—mainly the reconquest—than ecclesiastical reform, the Spanish ecclesiastical authorities had ignored the agreements reached
at the II Council of Lateran (1139). One of Godin's first commitments was to
institute the doctrine of celibacy and to condemn the public concubinage of the
priests, which had become common practice in Spain and accepted by the
general public.[11] His second commitment was to enlarge the official manual of
instruction in the faith, known as the *Catecismo de Doctrina Christiana*, or
simply *Doctrina Christiana* (Christian Doctrine). The catechism used in Spain
until then contained basically only the Creed, the Ten Commandments, the
sacraments of the church, and the seven vices and virtues.[12] Cardinal Godin
inserted three additional articles, namely, the gifts of the Holy Spirit, the distinction between venial sins and mortal sins, and the seven works of mercy. He
also ordered all parish priests to have copies of the *Doctrina* in their churches, in
both Latin and Spanish.

The synods that followed reinforced what was approved at Valladolid with
occasional additional recommendations. For example, the Synod of Toledo
(1323) encouraged the priests to teach the people "in the vulgar tongue" the
articles mentioned in the catechism approved at the Council of Valladolid. The
Synod of Palencia (1345) required that the priest have these articles in writing,
"at least in Spanish." The Synod of Segorbe (1367) ordained that the children be
taught the fundamentals of the faith. The Synod of Cuenca (1399) was slightly
more aggressive:

> Since not only the faithful, but also the beneficiaries of the Church in the city and
> bishopric of Cuenca, ignore the fourteen articles of faith, the sacraments, the Ten
> Commandments, the seven virtues (3 theological and 4 cardinal), the seven mortal sins
> and the fourteen works of mercy, the Council requires that they learn them verbatim.
> (Sánchez Herrero: 1986, 1056).

The Synod of Oviedo (1382) complained of the same thing, namely, that the
beneficiaries of the church ignored the articles of faith, the sacraments, the Ten
Commandments, the virtues, etc., and that, due to this inadequacy, the priests
are unable to properly teach the people. Priests were given two months to
memorize them. At the Synod of Cuenca (1409), the bishop again censured the
clergy for not knowing the Creed, the Ten Commandments, etc. Bishop Pedro de
Castilla, at the Synod of Palencia (1440), not only required the priests to have the
articles of Christian Doctrine available in writing in the churches, but also
required them to bring a copy to the synod as proof. The Synod of Burgos (1474)

---

11 The I Lateran Council (1123) decreed clerical marriages invalid; the II Lateran Council
   (1139) confirmed the previous council's decree.
12 For a survey of the development of the Spanish church prior to the introduction of the Roman
   liturgy, see Thomas M'Crie (1829, 1–51).

alerted that it was pointless to have the Creed in writing if it was not preached to the people. The Synods of Alcala (1480), Avila (1481) and Plasencia (1499) ordered all the parish priests to post the Creed, the Ten Commandments, etc., in a visible place in the church, and to designate certain Sundays when they should be expounded "*en romance, con alta e inteligible voz*" (in Spanish, in a clear loud voice). Likewise, the archbishops were to reinstate the catechism classes (*escuelas-catequesis*) in all the parish churches. (Sánchez Herrero: 1986, 1060).

The synods held after 1480 showed a growing concern for the theological training of the clergy and for the need to preach the basic principles and doctrines of the Catholic faith, as listed in the *Doctrina Christiana*, from the pulpit. Despite this effort to train the clergy, popular religious literature continued to center basically on the lives of saints and the miracles of the Virgin Mary (Estrada: 2012, 120–126). For example, Gonzalo de Berceo's *Los milagros de Nuestra Señora* (The Miracles of Our Lady), a series of twenty-five miracles performed by the Virgin for her devotees, not only promoted Marian devotion but also, because it was in Spanish, it was easily expounded by priests who knew little or no Latin and even less theology. Indeed, *Los milagros de Nuestra Señora* was so popular that even Juan de Valdes mentions it in his *Dialog on Christian Doctrine* (1529):

ANTRONIO: I am very devoted to Our Lady.

ARCHBISHOP: As for the devotion you profess for Our Lady, that is good and I don't want to compete with you, but I wouldn't want you to do as many that I know do, who on the one hand pride themselves of being very devoted to her and on the other are her deadly enemies.

ANTRONIO: How is that?

ARCHBISHOP: I know many people who are entangled in a thousand vices and show not the slightest sign of Christianity, except that they say they are devoted to Our Lady. And with the trust they put in this their devotion, they think it's licit to do the wicked things they do. That's why I often say that those who love Our Lady the least are those that practice that type of devotion, for those who love her well, and are truly devoted to her, try, as far as they can, to imitate her humility, her chastity, her charity and her modesty. With this, which is good, she is more honored than by dedicating many masses to her or reciting many prayers or fasting many days for her. It is rash foolishness for me, being steeped in vice, to consider myself a devotee of Our Lady just because I recite certain prayers to her and I fast certain days. This is truly the greatest mockery and abomination in the world.

ANTRONIO: According to what you are saying, I don't think you have seen a book describing the miracles performed by Our Lady, written by a person who had the same sort of devotion to her as the people you have just reproved.

ARCHBISHOP: Yes, I've seen it and I've read most of it. And when I think of the opportunity this little book gives some fools for licentiousness, all I can say is "*mal *viaje*"[13] for the person who wrote it and the first to print it.

ANTRONIO: Why do you say that?

ARCHBISHOP: Because something so contrary to evangelical doctrine should not be printed among Christians.

ANTRONIO: In what is it contrary to evangelical doctrine?

ARCHBISHOP: St. Paul says, besides many other thing to this effect found in other passages, the evangelists, and he himself also say, that neither the lustful, nor the greedy, nor one sunk in sin will enter the kingdom of God and your little book tells of many who were all this that the apostle describes and even worse things, and yet when one of them died, because it was found that every day he said the Ave Maria, he went to heaven.[14] Have you ever seen a more absurd form of devotion? (Valdes: 2008, 185. Translation and notes mine.).

As the century came to a close, more emphasis was put on the instruction of the children. The Synods of Jaen (1492) and Zaragoza (1495) reminded parents, godparents and tutors to have their children learn the basic tenets of the *Doctrina Christiana*. In 1497, Cardinal Cisneros convoked a synod in Alcala, and another in Talavara de la Reina the following year, in which he addressed the issue of religious education. One specific constitution required that priests teach children the *Doctrina Christiana* according to a catechism that he himself had written.[15] The Synod of Badajoz (1501) required each church to have someone on hand willing and able to teach the children and that parents were obliged to send "all the children in their household—both theirs and those of their servants— under the age of twelve" to be instructed. The Synod of Tuy (Pontevedra) of 1528 introduced a new approach: besides posting the articles of the *Doctrina Christiana* at the entrance of the church, every parishioner was to have a copy in his/her house and each Sunday of the year these articles were to be read and taught to the congregation, together with the *Gospel and the Epistle*. The Synods of Plasencia (1534) and Orense (1539) specified that every Sunday a minimum of fifteen minutes had to be dedicated to this activity. The Synod of Coria (1537) not only required that the tables of the *Doctrina Christiana* be written on parchment and read every Sunday during mass, but also required that all priests be examined regarding their knowledge of the *Doctrina* before being licensed.[16]

Besides the official editions of *Doctrina Christiana*, several archbishops and theologians, such as Hernando de Talavera (1496), Juan de Valdes (1529), Constantino Ponce de la Fuente (1543, 1547, 1548), Domingo de Soto (1552), Diego Ximenez (1552), Felipe de Meneses (1554), and Domingo de Baltanas

---

13 "I don't wish him well."

14 This refers to Miracle VI, The Devout Thief (1997).

15 The articles taught to the children did not include the sacraments, which pertain to the catechism for adults (García Oro: 1992, 124–127).

16 For a full account of the decrees of these and more synods regarding Doctrina Christiana, see Sánchez Herrero (1986, 1051–1118).

(1555) published their own editions to which they added explanations and pedagogical guidelines (rhymes, question-answer format, etc.) to facilitate memorization. Hernando de Talavera was so intent on promoting the knowledge of Christianity among the Moors in Granada that he hired Pedro de Alcala, a Hieronymite monk, to draw up a grammar, vocabulary, and catechism in Arabic (in Spanish characters) containing the rudiments of Christian Doctrine for the use of parish priests and catechists (M'Crie: 1829, 70). Many of these catechisms were placed on the Index after 1559, or even before as was the case of Juan de Valdes's *Dialog on Christian Doctrine*, which, less than a year after it had come off the press at Alcala, was put on the Index of Prohibited Books. No one was beyond the reach of the Inquisition, not even an archbishop, as was the case of Bartolome de Carranza, Archbishop of Toledo and Primate of Spain. In fact, certain statements in Carranza's *Comentarios sobre el catecismo de Doctrina Cristiana* (1558) led to his arrest and incarceration in 1559. The Dominican theologian Melchor Cano, professor at Salamanca, who was one of Carranza's staunches opponents, described the book as being harmful because "it gives the common people, in the Spanish language, matters concerning theology and Holy Scriptures that are difficult and perplexing, things the common people cannot possibly digest due to their human frailty no matter how simply and clearly they are presented." (Sarrión Mora: 2003, 55). In 1559, all the copies of Carranza's *Catecismo* were confiscation together with all commentaries on the Christian Doctrine written in Spanish and printed abroad after 1550.

Chapter 2:
Cardinal Cisneros (1436–1517)

> The Spanish monks were diverted for a time from searching after the writings of
> Luther, by their anxiety to suppress those of Erasmus, from which they dreaded more
> immediate danger.
>
> Thomas M'Crie, *History of the Reformation in Spain* (1829)

From humble beginnings, Francisco Jimenez de Cisneros—better remembered
as Cardinal Cisneros—rose to the heights of power. As a young man he studied
canon and civil law at Salamanca. In 1459, he traveled to Rome to work as a
consistorial advocate where he attracted the notice of Pope Pius II.[1] He returned
to Spain in 1465 with a letter from Pope Paul II, who had just been elected pope,
giving him possession of the first vacant benefice in the diocese of Toledo, which
happened to be that of Uceda, in the province of Guadalajara. Alfonso Carrillo,
the archbishop of Toledo, refused to accept the letter, wishing instead to bestow
the benefice on one of his own favorites. For six years Cisneros persisted until
finally, in 1480, Carrillo gave in. Cisneros traded the benefice almost at once for a
chaplaincy at Sigüenza, under Cardinal Pedro Gonzalez de Mendoza, brother of
Diego Hurtado de Mendoza of Guadalajara. Cardinal Mendoza, impressed by
Cisneros's strength of character, shortly afterwards made him vicar general of
the bishopric of Sigüenza. When it seemed that he was on the sure road to
success, in 1484, at the age of forty-eight, Cisneros decided to become a Franciscan friar. He gave up all his worldly belongings and entered the Franciscan
monastery of San Juan de los Reyes in Toledo, and later transferred to the
Convent of La Salceda, near Tendilla, where he lived in extreme austerity for the
next ten years. Meanwhile Mendoza, now archbishop of Toledo, had not forgotten him and in 1492 recommended him to Queen Isabel as her confessor. The
post was politically important, for Isabel took counsel from her confessor not
only in private affairs but also matters of state. When Cardinal Mendoza died in
1495, Isabel procured a papal bull nominating Cisneros to Mendoza's vacant
archdiocese of Toledo. When in 1504 Isabel died, and her son-in-law ruling
consort Philip the Handsome died unexpectedly two years later, Cisneros set up
a regent government until Ferdinand returned from Naples. In return for his
loyalty, Ferdinand made Cisneros inquisitor general in 1507—a post he held
until his death in 1517—and prevailed on the pope to make him a cardinal.

---

1 At the time Cisneros was in Rome, there were only seven consistorial advocates proper,
forming the Consistorial College. Around 1480, Sixtus IV added five more, called juniors.

Ferdinand died in January of 1516 leaving Cisneros as regent again until Charles V's arrival from Flanders in September of 1517.[2]

Inquisitor General

Francisco Jimenez de Cisneros became inquisitor general of Castile in 1507, at a time when the conspiracy against the Holy Office was at its height in Cordova as a result of the uprisings against the former—extremely oppressive and abusive—inquisitor general, Diego Rodriguez de Lucero. Under Cisneros the tribunal became less savage. Indeed, this tardy act of justice resulted in liberating many who were still in prison, restoring their honor, reconstructing demolished houses at the expense of the treasury, etc. Nevertheless, although Cisneros deposed a number of agents who had abused their power, the number of victims increased, especially in Aragon. In short, whereas he was one of the most ardent partisans of reform of the convents while archbishop of Toledo, he became one of the most obstinate defenders of the greatest abuses by twice preventing modifications and by celebrating more *autos-da-fe* than his predecessor Diego de Deza (Llorente: 1826b, 122–126).

Reforms

Once installed in his new position as archbishop of Toledo in 1495, Cisneros set about reforming the Franciscan order in Spain, which at that time was experiencing a bitter conflict between the "conventuals," who had diverged considerably from the austere regulations of St. Francis becoming feudal lords and indulging in worldly pleasures, and the strict "observants." His strict reforms of the Franciscan convents did not leave the monks indifferent. Several hundred fled to North Africa with their concubines. Those that remained became very observant. The frenzy created by Cisneros's reform in the more radical, "observant" wing of the order—and in certain sectors of society—developed into impacting spirituality among the humanists that gravitated around Diego Hurtado de Mendoza in Guadalajara.

Among Cisneros's reforms was the requirement that Franciscan monks engage in one and a half hours of mental prayer daily. To make this experience meaningful, Cisneros commissioned Spanish translations of medieval mystical texts, including those of St. Augustine, St. Jerome, St. Bonaventure, John Cli-

---

2 On his way to meet young king Charles, Cisneros fell ill and died. For a comprehensive study of the life and times of Cardinal Cisneros in English, see Rummel (1999).

macus, Angela of Foligno, Santa Catalina of Sienna, and a popularized version of pseudo-Dionysius's mystic theology known as the *Sol de Contemplativos.*[3] It is interesting to note that Cisneros also encouraged the diffusion of the writings of Girolamo Savonarola even after the Florentine monk had been condemned and burned at the stake, in particular his commentary on Psalm 51, *Devotissima exposicion sobre el psalmo de Miserere Mei Deus* (1511).[4] Many of these authors, who admonished the reader that the path to salvation began with the acknowledgement of one's sins, were read by the *alumbrados-deixados.*

In the 1540s Savonarola works again became popular and were translated and printed throughout Spain.[5] In 1548, the Italian banker living in Valladolid, Juan Lorenzo Otavanti, translated Savonarola's *Triumph of the Cross.* All these works were collected and printed in Antwerp in one volume in 1558.[6]

The University of Alcala

Cardinal Francisco Jimenez de Cisneros's most notorious answer to the question of education was to establish a university in the town of Alcala de Henares. Cisneros's project to create a center of higher learning had several recent precedents in Spain. In Sigüenza, when he was canon of the cathedral in 1476, his friend Juan Lopez de Medina had founded the College of San Antonio de Portaceli. Cisneros played an active part in the design of this educational project.[7] When Cisneros became archbishop of Toledo, he saw this as the right moment to put his own project into practice. In 1498, he submitted his plan to Pope Alexander VI. The project began as the College of San Ildefonso and opened its

---

3 St. Augustine, *Las Meditaciones & soliloquio* (Valladolid: Gumiel, 1511; Valladolid: Brocar, 1515); St. Jerome, *Epistolas* (Valencia: Costilla, 1520); St. Buenaventure, *Estímulo de amor divino* (Toledo: Hagenbach, 1505); Juan Clímaco, *Escala del cielo* (Toledo: Hagenbach, 1504); Ángela de Foligno, *Libro de la bienaventurada santa Angela de Fulginio* (Toledo: Hagenbach, 1505); Catalina de Siena, *Epístolas y oraciones* (Alcala: Brocar, 1512); Hugues de Balma, *Sol de contemplativos: teologia mistica* (Toledo: Hagenbach, 1514).

4 Girolamo Savonarola, *Devotissima exposicion sobre el psalmo de Miserere Mei Deus* (Alcala: Brocar, 1511). This volume was reprinted in Valladolid by Diego de Gumiel in 1512, in Seville by Jacobo Cromberger in 1513, 1514, 1527, and in Cuenca by Francisco de Alfaro in 1532. For the strong influence of Savonarola on Cisneros, see Joseph Pérez (2014).

5 Girolamo Savonarola, *Exposicion del psalmo Inte domine speraui* (Astorga, 1547); *Reprobacion de la Astrologia judiciaria o diuinatoria* (Salamanca, 1546); *El Triumpho de la Cruz de Christo* (Valladolid, 1548).

6 *Las Obras que se hallan romançadas del excelente doctor fray Hieronymo Sauonarola de Ferrara* (Antwerp: Martin Nucio, 1558).

7 There were two others: the College of Santa Cruz in Valladolid founded in 1477 by Pedro González de Mendoza and the College of Santa Catalina in Toledo founded in 1485 by Francisco Álvarez Zapata.

doors in July of 1508. Most of the teachers had been recruited from Salamanca. The rector was to be chosen by the students (not by the professors, as was the custom at Salamanca). Besides theology and canon law, the plan of study included logic, metaphysics, ethics, medicine, anatomy, Hebrew, Greek, rhetoric, mathematics, and grammar. Demetrius Ducas and Nicetas Phaustus, two native Greeks, taught classical Greek; Alfonso de Zamora, Pablo Coronel, and Alfonso de Alcala taught Hebrew; Juan de Vergara, his brother Francisco de Vergara, and Lorenzo Balbo taught Latin literature; and Antonio de Nebrija—sometimes referred to as the Erasmus of Spain—taught grammar. From the beginning Alcala was different. Firstly, it had no faculty of civil law because Cisneros considered that legal studies were detrimental to the study of theology. Secondly, the university offered a three-fold approach to theology, with the teaching of Thomism, Scotism, and Nominalism.[8] Thirdly, Alcala emphasized the direct study of the Bible, with the help of ancient languages, and the study of patristic literature.

Cisneros's interest in biblical studies may have taken root during the time he spent in Italy as a young man. During his years in Italy, he could not have failed to notice the growing interest in Greek studies and ancient manuscripts. In early April 1438, a large Greek contingent had arrived at Ferrara to attend the 17th Ecumenical Council. The following year, the Council became even more international when a delegation of Coptic Christians joined the sessions. Greek classical literature was introduced by several of the delegates from Constantinople, including the renowned Neo-Platonist philosopher Gemistus Pletho. Western Europe had had some access to ancient Greek philosophy, but the Byzantines had many documents that the West had never seen before. One of the great contributions of the Italian Renaissance was to encourage the study of oriental languages. Even before the massive arrival of Byzantine scholars in Italy, with their ancient Greek scrolls under their arms, fleeing the advance of the Turks after the fall of Constantinople in 1453, the Italian humanist philosopher Lorenzo Valla (1406–1457) was busying himself with philological issues. In Rome, as secretary to Pope Nicholas V, Valla also translated Greek authors into Latin and applied his philological skills to revise the standard Latin Vulgate translation of the Bible. As a literary critic, he was a forerunner of Erasmus and the Protestant Reformers. His comparison of St. Jerome's Latin translation of the Bible—the Vulgate—with Greek manuscripts of the New Testament laid the foundations of critical biblical scholarship. The resulting "Annotations" on the

---

8 That is, the teachings of Thomas Aquinas and the scholastics, and John Duns Scotus, who commented extensively on Peter Lombard's *Four Books of Sentences*. Nominalism studies at Alcala were centered mainly on the texts of the German theologian Gabriel Biel, which were a combination of scholastic thought and the nominalist views of Wm. Ockham.

New Testament became his most influential work. Valla died two years before Cisneros arrived. Antonio de Nebrija (1441–1522), who after studying at Salamanca had gone to Italy to study theology in the Royal College of Spain in Bologna and who would later become a professor at Alcala and collaborate with Cisneros in his Polyglot Bible, also missed him by a few years. Nevertheless, Lorenzo Valla's approach to textual criticism influenced both Cisneros and Nebrija.

As stated above, the newly established University of Alcala opened its doors in July of 1508. The years prior to this were eventful in the life of Cisneros. There were serious matters of state to attend to. In 1504, Queen Isabel died and he had to organize the state funerals. In 1506, Philip the Handsome died suddenly and he became regent governor until Ferdinand's return. As inquisitor general, in the spring of 1508, he was in Burgos as head of a delegation of twenty-two illustrious citizens to discuss the misconduct of his predecessor. Despite all this, by 1508, Cisneros was back in Alcala to open of his new university and to reunite with the scholar-editors he had selected for his second pet project: the Complutensian Polyglot Bible.

The Complutensian Polyglot Bible

Cisneros's humanist interest in languages and his scholar's zest for disputation made him a key figure in Spain's transition from the Middle Ages to the Renaissance. As Erika Rummel (1999, 10) points out, "Anticipating Luther, he understood the necessity of a true reformation of church and religion. A contemporary of Erasmus, he promoted the humanities with the aim of reforming university studies." His founding of the University of Alcala cannot be separated from his other great project, namely, the publication—and financing[9]—of the first complete polyglot bible, the *Biblia Sacra Polyglota*, known today as the Ximenez Polyglot or the Complutensian Polyglot.[10]

---

9 Gomez [Alvaro Gomez de Castro], whose life of Ximenez is the chief authority for most of the existing information about his life, tells us that the Cardinal spent no less than 50,000 gold ducats upon the work. As an illustration of the lavish nature of the expenditure, he recounts how 4000 ducats were paid for seven Hebrew manuscripts alone. [...] How far these were used it is now impossible to say, and indeed one writer (Quintanilla) alleges that these particular manuscripts arrived too late to be employed (Lyell: 1914, 34, 38).

10 When Christopher Columbus's son Hernando sent one of his assistants from Piedrahita to Alcala to acquire a copy in 1522 to add to his library, he called it "the Cardinal's Bible." In 1568, Juan Páez de Castro referred to it as "the Bible of Cardinal Francisco Jiménez". It was also called the "Trilingual Bible of Alcala" or the "Alcala Bible in six volumes" or the "Bible in four languages." "Complutensian" comes from *Complutum*, the Latin name for Alcala, which in turn was an Arabic word meaning fortification or citadel.

It took time for Greek and Hebrew manuscripts to be procured, but by 1508 work was under way. The actual printing of the Bible, however, did not begin until 1514. By 1517 the six volumes were completed, but the bible was not in circulation yet, awaiting the sanction of Pope Leo X, which was obtained on March 22, 1520. It took still another two years before Cisneros's polyglot Bible was finally put in circulation. Once the sanction of Pope Leo X was obtained, copies had to be sent off for the pope's examination, but the ship carrying the copies suffered shipwreck en route to Italy. This meant that new copies had to be sent, which took time. The volumes for the pope finally entered the Vatican Library on December 5, 1521, and the Bible was officially put on the market early the following year. Moreover, the *Comunero* uprising (1520–1521) had also put a halt to both commercial and academic activity and this may also have been incidental to the delay.

The New Testament and a Greek glossary, with Latin equivalents, were printed first. The appendix, containing a Hebrew lexicon and an elementary Hebrew grammar came next and was followed by the four volumes of the Old Testament, which contained the Hebrew text, the Latin Vulgate, and the Greek Septuagint in three columns side by side, with the Aramaic Targum of Onkelos for the Pentateuch, accompanied by a Latin translation, at the foot of the page. The Greek type used in the New Testament volume was modeled after the style of the handwriting in manuscripts of about the eleventh or twelfth century.[11] The printing was done by Arnao Guillen de Brocar, one of the most prestigious printers at the time, who had set up a shop first in Pamplona, then Logroño, and in 1511 was invited by Cisneros to come to Alcala to print his polyglot bible.[12] Of the 600 printed six-volume sets, only 123 are known to have survived.

As chief editor of the project, Cisneros had recruited the eminent biblical scholar and orientalist, Diego Lopez de Zuñiga [also known by his Latin name, Jacobus Stunica]. When Erasmus's New Testament reached Alcala in 1516, Diego Lopez de Zuñiga collated it carefully with the Complutensian text and found several errors. Cisneros discouraged him from publishing his findings and suggested he communicate them privately with Erasmus, but Zuñiga disagreed. After Cisneros death, which occurred the following year, Zuñiga gave vent to his anger and published his criticisms in *Annotationes contra Erasmum Roterodamum* (Annotations against Erasmus) (Alcala: Brocar, 1520). Contention between the two scholars went on for several years (Preston /Jenkins: 2007, 59–65). The German orientalist Johann Albrecht Widmannstetter, editor of the 1555 *Peshitta*, had correspondence with Diego Lopez de Zuñiga before the Spanish

---

11 For a full description of the Complutensian Polyglot, see Metzger (2005, 138–146); Gonzalo Sanchez-Molero (2014); Luttikhuizen (2016).
12 See Rodríguez Pelaz (1998); Martin Abad (1991).

scholar's death in 1531. Lopez de Zuñiga may have already had a special interest in updating the Complutensian with older manuscripts if for no other reason than to triumph over Erasmus.

The Antwerp Polyglot, or Biblia Regia

The eight-volume Antwerp Polyglot, or *Biblia Regia* (1572), appeared fifty years later. It was printed in Antwerp by Christopher Plantin under the auspices of Philip II.[13] One of the great contributions of the Antwerp Polyglot was the inclusion of the Syriac text along with the Latin, Greek, Hebrew and Chaldean (Aramaic) texts. In the fifty years that spanned between the two polyglots, philological studies had advanced greatly. One step forward was the printing of the Syriac New Testament, or *Peshitta,* in Vienna in 1555.[14] Soon copies of the *Peshitta* were circulating in Antwerp and reached the hands of Christopher Plantin, who requested license and financing from Philip II to print a new polyglot Bible. Permission was granted on the condition that the project be put under the supervision of the Spanish theologian Benito Arias Montano (1527–1598), who had begun his studies in Seville and in 1548 transferred to Alcala to study classical languages and Semitics. Besides supervising the printing, Arias Montano was responsible for the dictionaries (Hebrew-Latin, Greek-Latin, Syriac-Aramaic), grammar rules, etc. Once completed, he took the work to Rome for Pope Gregory XIII's approval, which he received in 1572. Meanwhile, Leon de Castro, professor of Oriental languages at Salamanca, denounced him to the Inquisition for having altered the biblical text and for having made too liberal use of the rabbinical writings, in disregard of the decree of the Council of Trent concerning the authenticity of the Vulgate. As Henry Kamen (2014, 140) points out,

> Some of the bitterest intellectual conflicts of the period originated not in the Inquisition but among university professors. Personal malice and partisan interest were, then as now, potent forces. Perhaps the most notorious conflict in which university men made use of the Inquisition for their own purposes originated in the malicious denunciations of some of his colleagues made by a professor at the University of Salamanca, Leon de Castro.

Arias Montano's innovations—clarifications regarding Jewish architecture, dress, names, history, etc., commentaries on the minor prophets, on Judges, on Isaiah, etc.—were looked upon with suspicion. Montano was aware of these

---

13 For a well-documented history of the printing of the Antwerp Polyglot, see Brekka (2012).
14 For an account of the arrival of the Syriac version of the Bible in Europe, see Luttikhuizen (2006).

intrigues, but was able to remain in favor with the king and even became his head librarian at Escorial in 1576. By 1579, however, the Supreme Council was beginning to suspect Montano of heresy.[15] In May, a brief note was sent to the inquisitors at Seville and Cordoba asking them to look through all their records to see if there was anything testified against him.[16] Towards the end of July a reply was sent from Seville informing the Council that nothing had been found. After Montano's death, however, persecution would come to a head with the posthumous ban of his works in the Spanish Index of Prohibited Books of 1607 (Brekka: 2012, 17, note 20).

Erasmian Influence at Alcala

While the Supreme Council was busy trying to stop Lutheran literature from entering Spain, Erasmian views were having a heyday not only at Alcala but throughout the entire country. Cardinal Cisneros's emphasis in biblical studies and ancient languages, together with the departure from staunch scholasticism and return to the Church Fathers at his newly established University of Alcala, brought with it an interest in Christian Humanism, and as a result enthusiasm among the faculty and students for Erasmus and his writings. The University of Alcala was not only a center of biblical studies, but also the most important focal point for Erasmian studies in Europe.[17] According to Thomas M'Crie (1829, 128), the Spanish monks were diverted for a time from searching after the writings of Luther, by their anxiety to suppress those of Erasmus, from which they dreaded more immediate danger. Erasmus had many enthusiastic followers among the intellectuals for his attacks on clerical abuse and lay ignorance. His most enthusiastic followers were among the most prestigious humanists of the day: Francisco and Juan de Vergara, Bernardino Tovar, Mateo Pascual, Pedro de Lerma, Miguel Carrasco, Hernan Vazquez, the printer Miguel de Eguia, son-in-law to Arnao de Brocar the printer of the Polyglot Bible, just to mention a few. Other prestigious educators and admirers of Erasmus included Bernabe del

---

15 The Supreme Council of the Inquisition (or *Suprema*) was a combination of civil and ecclesiastical powers, established by the Catholic monarchs to which all the local tribunals were subject. Some historians, such as Ames (2005, 12–13) question the Councils motivations. It must be remembered that at the time there was no division between secular and religious, hence doctrinal control took for granted civic control, and vice versa.

16 AHN, Inquisición, lib. 579, fol. 208r; AHN, Inquisición, leg. 2946, in: Lopez Muñoz (2011, 445, doc. 251).

17 There was, for example, the circle that gathered around Miguel Mai, Martin Ivarra, and Bishop Pere de Cardona in Barcelona in the early 1530s. When Mai was called to Rome as ambassador in 1533, the circle broke up. See Bellsolell (2010).

Busto, Lucio Marineo Siculo, Francisco de Bobadilla, Diego Gracian de Alderete, Bernardo Perez de Chinchon, etc.[18]

Francisco de Vergara, a professor at the University of Alcala and a long time friend of Erasmus, was a figure of major importance in the Erasmian movement of Spain. When the Inquisition of Toledo seized the *alumbrada* Francisca Hernandez in 1529 and she began to denounce her former acquaintances, the first names on her list were Juan de Vergara, who had been secretary to cardinal Cisneros and to Alfonso Fonseca, and Bernardino Tovar. She accused them of having Lutheran books and holding Lutheran doctrines. Their long drawn out trials (Longhurst: 1969, 140–294) constituted an important event in the eradication of Erasmianism. Juan de Vergara had left Alcala already in 1520 for Flanders where he became secretary to William de Croy, whom he accompanied to Worms the following year and returned to Spain in 1522. Bernardino de Tovar was incarcerated in 1530; Juan de Vergara in 1533. On December 11, 1534, voting began on Vergara's case. It was finally decided that he abjure *de vehement* at the next *auto-da-fe*, be confined in a monastery for one year, and pay a fine of 1500 ducats. The case dragged on for still another year before the sentence was applied (Longhurst: 1969, 292–294). Vergara's trial records offer valuable information regarding the theological atmosphere of the university and the inquisitorial reaction to the publication of Valdés's *Dialog on Christian Doctrine* (1529).

The period of greatest popularity for Erasmus in Spain was the decade 1520–1530. The first of his works to be printed in Spain was *Enchiridion militis christiani* (Handbook of a Christian Knight), translated by Alfonso Fernandez, archdeacon of Alcor, and printed by Miguel de Eguia in Alcala in 1524. The *Enchiridion* was an appeal to Christians to act in accordance with their faith rather than merely performing the rites of it. Reprints appeared almost immediately in Valencia, Toledo, Lisbon, etc. In a letter to Erasmus written two years later, Alfonso Fernandez, the translator, states, "At court, in the cities, in the churches, in the monasteries, even in the inns and the byways, there is hardly a soul who does not have a copy of *Enchiridion* in Spanish." (Coroleu/Taylor: 2010, 3). The book was a curious amalgam of Christian pietism, stoic principles, and gentle touches of Pauline doctrine in a context of a mild Johanine attitude. According to Jose Nieto (1970, 182), the *Enchiridion* became a double-edged sword that could be employed to lead people to greater Catholic piety or to engender heretical ideas, or, at least, heterodox views. In this sense, it was considered both good and bad, depending on the oscillation of the religious movements that swept over Europe. According to Marcel Bataillon (1966, 339), Erasmianism was much more than a simple movement of protest against the abuses of the unworthy clergy and some ignorant friars. It was a positive

---

18 See Gonzalo Sánchez-Molero (2003); Bataillon (1966, 343, 363, 418, 446, 475–478).

movement of spiritual renovation, an endeavor of intellectual culture dominated by an idea of piety. Erasmus never embraced the Reformation, nor did he pride himself on being a faithful son of the Catholic Church; he advocated a return to primitive Christianity within a unified church. Despite his friendship with popes Julius II and Clement VII, during the papacy of Paul IV (1555–1559) his writings were consigned to the Index of Prohibited Books.

The characteristic note of Spanish humanism was the comparative smoothness with which the transition from medievalism to full recognition of the new learning was effected, and further, the enthusiasm with which the claims of the mother tongue were conceded. Despite this enthusiasm, there were those who opposed Erasmus and accused him of heresy (Coroleu: 2008, 73–92). In the summer of 1527, Inquisitor General Manrique summoned scholars from Salamanca, Alcala, and Valladolid, together with leading theologians of several monastic orders, to the city of Valladolid in order to judge certain suspicious passages (Homza: 1997, 82–83). All the delegates from Salamanca and Valladolid except one pronounced themselves anti-Erasmian.[19] In contrast, all those from Alcala, with the exception of Pedro Sanchez Ciruelo, were pro-Erasmian. It basically boiled down to a debate between scholastics and biblical humanists. No agreement was reached and Manrique dissolved the conference, leaving things as they were. The general opinion among historians is that an episode of plague broke out, which motivated Manrique to dissolve the conference. Prosecutor Diego Ortiz de Angulo, who in 1533 officially accused Juan de Vergara of being "a heretic and apostate against our holy Catholic faith, following, holding, and believing and teaching the errors and perverse, damnable doctrine of the wicked heresiarch Martin Luther," (Longhurst: 1969, 230) gives another version— though later refuted by Vergara:

> Toledo, April 21, 1534
> I, Diego Ortiz de Angulo, hereby make presentation against Vergara … of all the books and writings found in Vergara's possession and of those which Doctor Vergara sent to the Council of the General Inquisition … including both the books of Luther and his followers, as well as those of Erasmus and other persons suspected of being opposed to our holy Catholic faith.… [I likewise ask your graces to direct] that a copy be obtained of the propositions of Erasmus which the University of Paris condemned as heretical, scandalous, erroneous, suspect and offensive to pious ears … because Doctor Vergara has been and is an intimate friend and defender of Erasmus and all his writings and errors. They regularly corresponded with each other as friends, and Doctor Vergara had the archbishop of Toledo send a stipend to Erasmus. Vergara also favored Erasmus in the conference which was held in Valladolid [in 1527] .., and Vergara had such influence and favor with the archbishop of Toledo and other ecclesiastical and secular

---

19 Alonso Enriquez, abbot of Valladolid, author of *Defensiones pro Erasmo Roterodamo*, a work placed on the Papal Index. (Rose: 1971, 159, note 11).

persons that he had the conference dissolved without condemning ... the said propositions [of Erasmus], and against the wishes of the whole assemblage of friars and learned ecclesiastical persons who wanted to condemn [Erasmus] as heretical, erroneous and suspect. (Longhurst: 1969, 287)

The inquisitors were not so content to leave things as they were. Juan de Vergara, who was in prison at the time, was again brought before the inquisitors; Fray Alonso de Virues, the emperor's preacher, was condemned for belittling the monastic state and was imprisoned. For having expressed doubts regarding purgatory in public, Mateo Pascual was imprisoned and his goods were confiscated. Pascual spent four years in the Inquisition prison of Toledo, 1533 to 1537. He spent the rest of his life in Rome, where he died in 1553. Another leading personality who fell under suspicion was the great scholar, and chancellor of the University of Alcala, Pedro de Lerma. In 1537, he was called upon to abjure eleven Erasmian propositions. To avoid further trouble, he left for Paris later that year, where he became dean of the faculty of theology at the Sorbonne.

By the early 1540s, Erasmianism was no longer an articulate force in Spanish intellectual life, nevertheless, it had planted the seed of critical observation. During the decade of the 1550s anti-clericalism escalated. One of its consequences was a move towards greater inner spirituality; the other was open criticism. In 1554, one of the harshest criticisms of the Catholic Church came off the press in the form of a satirical novel: *La vida de Lazarillo de Tormes* (1554). It was printed simultaneously in Alcala, Burgos, Medina del Campo, and Antwerp. Given the subversive nature of *Lazarillo* and its open criticism of the church, the author chose to remain anonymous out of fear of religious persecution. Although he attacked the hypocrisy of the church and the purchase of indulgences, he did not criticize its essential beliefs, nevertheless, the novel was banned and put on the Index of Prohibited Books in 1559. It was the Antwerp version that escaped confiscation and that circulated throughout Europe, and was translated into French (1560?), English (1576), German (1614), and Italian (1622).

Another type of satirical literature was found in the final section of the *Cancionero General* (1511), an anthology of popular songs and verses collected by Hernando del Castillo between 1490 and 1511. The *Cancionero* was arranged into nine sections: works of devotion and morality; love poems; songs; ballads; inventions and fantasies; glosses; Christmas songs; questions and answers; and satirical and burlesque poems. The work enjoyed many reprints with new incorporations and rearrangements of the verses from one section to another. The final section, a series of satirical and burlesque poems, was gradually expurgated until the entire section was eliminated altogether. In 1840, the Spanish philanthropist Luis Usoz y Rio found an extremely rare 1519 edition of the *Cancionero General* in the British Library exclusively dedicated to the last section. In the

1514 edition some verses had been eliminated from this section, but in this 1519 edition the printer-editor Joan Viñao had restored the suppressed compositions and had added a few new ones. As a staunch proponent of the freedom of press, Usoz thought it his patriotic duty to reprint this extremely rare *Cancionero* to show his fellow countrymen that the sixteenth century was not a time of orthodoxy and profound devotion. He saw in these irreverent verses the reverse side of the coin of early modern Spanish spirituality and the hypocrisy of turning a blind eye to literature that not only severely criticized ecclesiastical practices but also did so in a mocking, sacrilegious way. He found in these verses an authentic example of Fray Luis de Leon's description of the times: "In the name of Christianity man has reached such shamelessness and wantonness that he makes music of his vices, and not willing to cover them up, he sings aloud in a merry voice his sins." (Concha: 1981, 27, note 4).

Among the compositions in this *Cancionero*, there was a mock version of the Lord's Prayer for women, a paraphrased version (*a lo profane*) of Psalm 113, lamentations by nuns who found themselves deprived of the sensual joys of life, a satire denouncing the papal nuncio and his attendances's immoral behavior in procuring lodging during a visit they made to Spain around 1490; a dialogued parody carried out between a male and a female sexual organ on legal practices and procedures; and the *Carajicomedia* (Comedy of the Penis), which chronicled the life and martyrdom of Diego Fajardo's genitals, with many side-stories of famous whores, many of them nuns —"the great consolation of friars"—, and narrates how his testicles were finally taken to Rome as relics after his death. Usoz commented extensively on some of the compositions but when he reached the final one, the *Carajicomedia*, his comments were brief:

> The Spaniards who wrote, printed and read these things were anything but devout men, in this they resembled our contemporaries who imitate them. What does this say in favor of the respected elite that for the past centuries guarded the morals and the religion of our enslaved and little evangelized country? Is this an expression of the virtue and glory that distinguished those who burned men and women for reading the Scriptures, making so many noble and noteworthy Spaniards objects of their intolerance, of bloodshed and desolation? (Jauralde Pou/Bellón Cazabán: 1974, 24).

Usoz saw no hidden intention on behalf of the authors, only a simple straightforward example of the general depravity of the time. His opinion was corroborated by the Spanish philologist and historian Ramon Menendez Pidal, who also considered it a product of a demoralized epoch (Alborg: 1978, I, 229), or as a modern critic Antonio Perez-Romero (2005, 91) put it, "The language could not be more irreverent, impious and iconoclastic. Striking even today is the casual discussion of sex and sexual adventures, and above all, the complete lack of guilt." Usoz concluded his *Advertencia al Lector* with the following thought:

This *Cancionero* indirectly alludes to the lack of individual freedom and its consequences. In Spain much is said about freedom, but there is neither freedom of press,
free from political and religious censorship, nor is there freedom of conscience, nor is
there freedom of commerce. All these are the results of individual freedom. (Usoz y Rio,
1841).

Usoz was not only appalled at the content of the compositions, but he was totally
outraged at the socio-political implications of such a publication. How was it
possible that these obscenities were allowed to circulate in print at the very same
time that the works of Luther were confiscated and burned! The prohibition to
read Lutheran literature began in 1521; these burlesque poems were not officially
prohibited until 1559.

Chapter 3:
The Alumbrados-Deixados

We, Lord Alonso Manrique, by divine providence Archbishop of Seville, make it known
that after our very Holy Father entrusted us with the Holy Office of the General Inquisition, we were informed by various people (who were fearful of God and zealous for
our Catholic faith) that in certain places in this archbishopric of Toledo, many people
spoke and proclaimed certain words that appeared to deviate from our Holy Catholic
Faith, and from the common observance of faithful Christians and our Holy Mother
Church. [Such people] gather together, secretly and publicly, in special secret assemblies, and some call them *alumbrados* [the illuminated], *dejados* [the abandoned], and
perfectos [the perfect].

Edict against the Alumbrados (Toledo, 1525)[1]

As the number of books written in Spanish promoting affective spirituality grew,
they inspired people who had spiritual aspirations—but lacked linguistic
training in Latin—to seek God in silent prayer, using their capacity of love rather
than their intellect (Carrera: 2005, 27). One of such publications was Alonso de
Cartagena's *Oracional de Fernán Pérez* (1487), the first systematic treatise on
prayer written in Spanish. In it, Cartagena used the writings of the Church
Fathers to expound the way to know God and to connect with God. He presented
prayer as an internal act of religious virtue (Pérez García: 2014, 88–90). The
growing trend towards disseminating religious and spiritual instruction in the
vernacular is also seen in Hernando de Talavera, the bishop imprisoned because
of his Jewish ancestry. When Talavera was Bishop of Avila, before going to
Granada, he recommended a list of books "written in Spanish"—portions of the
Gospels, Esther, Tobias, Judith, St. Gregory's *Book of Morales* and *Dialogues*,
etc.—for collective reading for the Cistercian nuns "so that they could be easily
understood by all the nuns and all could in consequence profit from their
teachings." (Pérez García: 2014, 91). In his *Dialog on Christian Doctrine* (1529),
Juan de Valdes (2008, 199. Translation and italics mine) encourages the young
priest to read "Jean Gerson's Contemptus mundi, St. Jerome's letters and St.
Gregory's Morals, *which have now been printed in Spanish*, as well as a few things
by St. Augustine." These vernacular translations—many commissioned by
Cardinal Cisneros—had the additional effect of facilitating major developments
in lay spirituality and allowing women increased access to the mystical tradition
(Ahlgren: 1998, 10). As Alison Weber (1999, 147–48) puts it, Cisneros had, in
effect, opened up the church to women and the laity.

---

1 Translation by Lu Ann Homza. (Homza: 2006, 81–82).

The Alumbrado-Deixado Movement

The religious movement of the *alumbrados,* quite independent of any other movement in sixteenth century Europe, manifested itself in popular sectors that had felt the impact of certain mystic literature—John Climacus, St. Bernardo, St. Bonaventure, Angela of Foligno, Santa Catalina of Sienna—and the vernacular translation of the *Gospels and the Epistles,* and other portions of the Bible. The movement arose at a time when people were asking themselves questions such as, how should God be worshipped. The ultimate goal of the followers of this movement was to achieve direct and personal communication with God, or, as Antonio Marquez (1972, 175) puts it, "a mystical return to God." Three groups can be distinguished: the *recogidos,* or mystics; the *visionarios,* of apocalyptic tendencies; and the *deixados,* which for the Inquisition were the "most dangerous heretics," mainly because they not only advocated an interiorized approach to Christianity but also practiced the principles of the "priesthood of the believer," replacing the authority of the Church and its hierarchy for that of the Holy Spirit. According to the Edict of Toledo against the *alumbrados,* issued by the General Inquisitor Alonso Manrique in September of 1525, it was the personal and direct reading of the Scriptures that led the *alumbrados* to religious views very much in accord with those held by the Lutherans. In fact, several times in this document the *deixados* are called "readers of the Bible."

Dating the beginnings of the *alumbrado* movement is open to question. It appears that the term "alumbrado" was first used in 1512 by Friar Antonio de Pastrana, who in a letter to Cardinal Cisneros described a fellow Franciscan from Ocaña he had imprisoned as a "religioso contemplativo *alumbrado* con las tinieblas de Satanas" (a contemplative religious, *illuminated* by the darknesses of Satan) (Longhurst: 1969, 347. Italics mine).[2] Charles F. Fraker Jr. associates the *alumbrados* with the fifteenth-century *Cancionero de Baena* (Songbook of Baena) poets.[3] Fraker's views are useful, particularly his insights into *deixamiento* and the acknowledgment of the multiplicity of doctrinal ideas and opinions within *alumbradismo* (Fraker: 1965, 117). Alonso Burgos (1983, 66–67) reproduces a report sent to Pope Paul IV (September 9, 1558)[4] by Inquisitor General Fernando de Valdes in which Valdes attributes the roots of the "heresies" held by the *alumbrados* and *deixados* in Guadajalara, "that eventually led to the Lutheran heresies," to Juan de Oria, a professor of nominalist philosophy at the

---

2 By the early 1520s we find this same Antonio de Pastrana, along with another Franciscan, Diego de Barreda, active among the *alumbrados* of New Castile and "imbibing the teachings of Isabel de la Cruz" (Longhurst: 1969, 347).

3 These were mainly poets of Jewish descent, whose works were collected by Juan Alfonso de Baena—a Castilian troubadour also of Jewish descent—between around 1426 to 1430.

4 AHN, Inquisición, lib. 245, f. 230r, in: Lopez Muñoz (2011, 132, doc. 49).

University of Salamanca at the turn of the sixteenth century.[5] Angela Selke (1980, 617) contends, however, that "it is most likely that *alumbradismo* had diverse roots." Or, as Javier Montoya (2010, 31) puts it, "*alumbrado* origins are likely a combination of factors: social, historical, religious, cultural and political that cannot simply find attribution in one cause, person or thing."

Another more remote source is Marguerite Porete's *The Mirror of Simple Souls* (McGinn: 1998, 244–265). The book, originally written in Old French, was translated into Latin during her lifetime and fifty years later into Italian and Middle English—*The chastisinge of Goddis children* (1350?) (Saranyana: 2007, 267). Some five years after it appeared in manuscript form, the Bishop of Cambrai condemned the book to be publicly burned in her presence. She was ordered not to circulate her ideas or copies of her book again. Nevertheless, she continued to do so and in 1308 was arrested by the local inquisitor on grounds of heresy. In 1310, a commission of twenty-one theologians investigated a series of fifteen propositions drawn from the book and judged them heretical. Marguerite was burned at the stake for heresy in Paris in 1310 after refusing to recant. For Marguerite, when the soul is truly full of God's love it is united with God and thus in a state of union which causes it to transcend the contradictions of this world. Where she ran into trouble with some authorities was in her description of the soul in a state above the teachings and control of the earthly church. She argued that the soul in such a sublime state is above the demands of ordinary virtue, not because virtue is not needed but because in its state of union with God virtue becomes automatic. The text survived in thirteen manuscripts in four languages, making it among the most widely disseminated vernacular mystical text of the Middle Ages. In this respect, Marguerite's concept of a mystical union with God—and her rejection of all institutional mediation—has strong parallels with the teachings of the *deixados*. Moreover, whereas Andres Martin (1975) points out a parallel between certain of Marguerite Porete's propositions and the mystic principles of the *recogidos*, Saranyana (2007, 271) points out parallels with the *alumbrados-deixados*.

Professor Jose C. Nieto (1997, 95) maintains that it was in Escalona (Toledo), around 1509, that the first seeds of heresy were expressed and crystallized in Spain, long before Luther nailed his thesis on the Wittenberg castle church in 1517. Nieto (1997, 65–82) also suggests that Pedro de Osma, a Spanish theologian and professor at the University of Salamanca, may have been influential in the development of *alumbrado* views. Like Lorenzo Valla in Italy, Osma employed much of his time correcting the Latin text of the New Testament by collating different Greek manuscripts with the text of an ancient Bible preserved in the

---

5 Bataillon (1950, 21–22) saw a deep correspondence between the favorable recepeion of nominalism at Alcalá and the study of original languages applied to biblical studies.

university library. Furthermore, in 1478, Osma published a work on confession in which he maintained, among other things, that confession was not a divine precept and that auricular confession was not necessary. His conclusions provoked so much controversy that the archbishop of Toledo, Alfonso Carrillo, convoked a committee of 52 theologians to examine Osma's book. On May 24, 1479, the committee declared nine of Osma's propositions to be false, heretical, scandalous, and erroneous. He was forced to abjure those propositions relating to the power of the pope, the sacrament of penance, indulgences, and confession that resembled those of John Wycliffe and Jan Hus. He also questioned the clergy's power to grant absolution of sins, and challenged papal infallibility (Rozbicki: 2012, 23). For this, he earned the malediction of Marcelino Menendez y Pelayo as the first Spanish Protestant, and the benediction of Elisabeth Christ as the Spanish Huss (Longhurst: 1969, 345). Copies of his book—*De confessione*—were publicly burned after High Mass on June 15, 1479. Osma died the following year, but his ideas did not die with him. Not only would the students at the University of Salamanca have been familiar with Osma's opinions—or able to procure a copy of Osma's book before all the copies were ordered to be burned—, but also would certainly have found references in Osma to Jean Gerson. An innovating professor of theology from Salamanca like Osma could hardly have ignored the writings of Jean Gerson, especially if the two shared the same critical view of established religious practices. According to Richard Kagan (1991, 110),

> Gerson's *De Probatione Spirituum* and its companion treatise, *De Distinctione Verarum Visionum a Falsis*, became a vademecum no confessor could afford to be without. In Spain, Gerson's influence can first be detected in Sánchez de Vercial's *Libro de los Ejemplos*, written circa 1420.

Jean Charlier de Gerson (1363–1429), often referred to as *Doctor Christianissimus* and *Doctor Consolatorius,* was a French educator and reformer, and Chancellor of the University of Paris. Gerson wished to banish scholastic subtleties from the studies of the university, and at the same time to put evangelical warmth into them, giving them a more spiritual and practical focus. He believed that the study of the Bible and of the Church Fathers was to supersede the idle questions of the school. The French church historian, Louis Salembier (1909), synthesizes Gerson's approach thus:

> Gerson's mystical theology had its own peculiar character. He distinguishes it from scientific theology, which he considered abstract and discursive. His mysticism in its essence is an experimental knowledge of God, which, by love, one perceives in himself. If the inferior powers remain in darkness, the superior faculties, the intellect, and especially pure love, have the freer play, and therefore constitute a sublime state of transport, which surpasses all theoretical learning. Moreover, through close union with

God, it gives us perfect contentment of soul with the entire and definitive appeasement of our desires. Gerson further distinguished a practical part in his mystical theology and laid down the following conditions and means (*industriæ*) preparatory to contemplation: (1) to await the call of God; (2) to know well one's own temperament; (3) to be heedful of one's vocation and one's state; (4) to aim constantly towards greater perfection; (5) to avoid as much as possible a multiplicity of occupations and, in any event, not to become absorbed in them; (6) to set aside all vain desire for learning, i. e. all idle curiosity; (7) to remain calm and practice patience; (8) to know the origin of the affections and passions; (9) to choose the necessary time and place; (10) to avoid extremes, either of abstinence or excess, in sleeping and eating; (11) to indulge in thoughts that excite pious affections; (12) to banish from one's mind all images.[6]

The large number of Gerson's works translated into Spanish—and often reprinted—clearly evidences his popularity in Spain at the end of the fifteenth century.[7] His readers would have ranged from the reformed Franciscan *recogidos* to the *alumbrados-deixados,* and even to Cardinal Cisneros himself. Cisneros especially encouraged the reading of Gerson's *Contemptu Mundi* and he even used it as a textbook (Albert: 2003, 72). Juan de Valdes mentions Gerson twice in his *Dialog on Christian Doctrine* (1529), suggesting a reasonable familiarity with the author and his works. Miguel Perez dedicated his translation of Gerson's *Contemptu Mundi* into Catalan to Isabel de Villena, abbess of the Monestir de la Santa Trinitat in Valencia, in 1482. Ten years later he translated Gerson's *Menosprecio de este mundo* and dedicated it to the same abbess.

The question remains whether the *alumbrados-deixados* received greater influence from Osma or from Gerson or whether their views were simply reinforced through their writings. On the other hand, although the *deixado* leader Pedro de Alcaraz taught that one need not be literate to know the love of God and the time devoted to the pursuit of human knowledge was time stolen from God, he himself was fairly well read. At his trial in 1527, Alcaraz admitted that he was acquainted with the works of Gerson, Pseudo-Dionysius, St. Jerome, St. Augustine, John Climacus, St. Bernardo, St. Bonaventure, Angela of Foligno, and Santa Catalina of Sienna—all translated into Spanish by then. Works translated later by Juan de Molina include Jerome's *Epistolas* (1520), Erasmus's *Enchiridion* (1528), and Gerson's *Tripartito siquiere confesional* (1525). Due to certain expressions found in his translation of Erasmus's *Enchiridion,* Molina was tried by the Inquisition in 1536 and spent time doing penitence in the Monasterio de la Trinidad in Valencia.

---

6 Summary mine. Also see Brian Patrick McGuire (1998), Nieto (1997, 65–82), Elliott (2002).
7 Between 1490 and 1516, a dozen of his works were printed in places that range from Zaragoza, Seville, Burgos, Toledo, Logroño, Montserrat, to Palma de Mallorca.

Guadalajara

Many of these books filled the shelves of the large Mendoza library in their magnificent Renaissance palace at Guadalajara, some forty miles northeast of Madrid. Diego Hurtado de Mendoza de Luna's father had married Maria de Luna y Pimentel and through this marriage had greatly expanded the wealth and possessions of the Mendoza family. Though the family already had a large palace at Manzanares el Real, at the foot of the Guadarrama mountain range, Iñigo Lopez de Mendoza y Luna decided to build another more spectacular palace at Guadalajara "to increase the prestige of his forefathers and his own." Little could he guess that his palace would not only be remembered for its unique architecture, but also as the cradle of the *alumbrado-deixado* movement.

The Mendoza palace—the residence of the dukes of Infantado—is of major importance in our study of the outreach of the Reformation in Spain. In all likelihood, several of the leaders of the *alumbrado-deixado* movement perceived their calling in the parlors of the Mendoza palace at Guadalajara. By the turn of the century, one of the family members, Antonio de Mendoza y Luna (d. 1510), had built himself a smaller palace in the neighborhood, which he bequeathed to his niece, Brianda de Mendoza y Luna (1470–1534), the daughter of his brother Iñigo Lopez de Mendoza y Luna.[8] This second palace also played a major role in the propagation of dissident ideas when Brianda turned it into a *beaterio*, or beguinage.

Beaterios were voluntary religious associations of devout women (*beatas*) who did not take vows. They offered an alternative, and a shelter, to women who felt they had a religious calling but did not wish to enter a convent. Known for her piety, Brianda de Mendoza may have opened her *beaterio* for the purpose of instructing young women or she may have seen the need to offer an already existing group of *beatas* a place for withdrawal and support.[9] The growth of secular tertiary orders—lay monastic communities—was heartily welcomed by devout women. It gave them the opportunity to actively participate in a new-found spirituality without having to take formal vows of chastity, poverty, obedience, or enclosure. It also gave them a status, that of *beatas*, semi-autonomous, popular religious figures in the communities. Beguinages were centers of

---

8 Some historians contend that Antonio de Mendoza y Luna's palace was alive with philo-Lutherans and Erasmians (Castro Sánchez: 2012, 588–589). This is somewhat misleading. Antonio had died already in 1510. This totally discards philo-Lutheran activity. A house full of Erasmian enthusiasts is also debatable. Even Cardinal Cisneros's knowledge of Erasmus was still limited in 1510. The confusion is in the name. It was not Antonio de Mendoza's patronage of Lutherans and Erasmians, but his brother Diego Hurtado de Mendoza de Luna's patronage.

9 Brianda's meticulous accounts reveal that she educated at least four female members of the Mendoza family (Coolidge: 2010, 58–59).

intellectual life, where women could learn Latin, compose music, write poetry, translate sacred works, etc. In 1524, when Brianda's *beaterio* "Nuestra Señora de la Piedad" received official status as a community of Third Order Franciscan nuns, via a bull from Pope Clement VII, she added a wing to the palace, which included a chapel and a school for young girls. There was a strong tradition of women educating other women in early modern Spain,[10] and there is reason to believe that the *beata* Isabel de la Cruz, one of the pioneer leaders of the *alumbrados-deixados*, would have been among the *beatas* that gathered at Brianda's palace. Members of open communities of this type had great social impact as they went from place to place, nursing the sick, instructing young girls, etc.

Though several Inquisition trial records of the *alumbrados* remain to us today, unfortunately records of Isabel de la Cruz's trial do not. Enough remains, however, from the trials of others to reconstruct her career as one of the leaders of the movement. John Longhurst (1969, 91–102) relates that,

> Because [Isabel] considered herself to be a true servant of God, and was annoyingly aware of her mother's human imperfections, as well as those of her brothers and sister, she moved out of the house into a place of her own where she could better devote herself to mystical reflection and the indoctrination of others in the ways of spiritual perfection. It was probably about this time that Isabel ascended to the title of *beata* as a tertiary sister of the Franciscan order.[11]

This would coincide chronologically with the opening of Brianda's beguinage. It is worth noting here that by mid-sixteenth century female communities with loose ties to the church were beginning to arouse ecclesiastical anxieties. Finally the Council of Trent imposed the rule of enclosure for nuns, eliminating the status of secular or lay nuns.[12] It was considered a breach of conduct for women to publicly intervene in theological matters.

---

10 Most women in early modern Spain did not learn Latin, but the daughters of the nobility were an exception. Queen Isabel had included it in the curriculum of her daughters. Beatriz Galíndez, who was probably their tutor, was known as "la latina" for her linguistic skills.

11 Prof. Longhurst took his biographical data from the trial of Isabel's disciple Pedro Ruiz de Alcaraz. AHN, Inquisicion de Toledo, Legajo 106, no. 28, Proceso contra Pedro Ruiz de Alcaraz. See particularly ff. 39r, 106v, 211r.

12 The Twenty-Fifth Session. Ch. V. Provision is made for the enclosure and safety of Nuns, especially those that live without cities. "The holy Synod, renewing the constitution of Boniface VIII, which begins Periculoso, enjoins on all bishops, by the judgment of God to which It appeals, and under pain of eternal malediction, that, by their ordinary authority, in all monasteries subject to them, and in others, by the authority of the Apostolic See, they make it their especial care, that the enclosure of nuns be carefully restored, wheresoever it has been violated, and that it be preserved, wheresoever it has not been violated; repressing, by ecclesiastical censures and other penalties, without regarding any appeal whatsoever, the disobedient and gainsayers, and calling in for this end, if need be, the aid of the Secular arm. The holy Synod exhorts Christian princes to furnish this aid, and enjoins, under pain of

By 1512, Isabel de la Cruz was preaching the principles of mystical abandonment and perfection under the name of *deixamiento,* that is, surrender of
one's will to God and submission of the individual to divine direction in all
things. As a logical corollary to this, she urged her listeners to reject all exterior
forms of devotion such as kneeling in church, making the sign of the cross,
bowing the head and praying aloud. Her clerical followers, mostly Franciscan
friars, were advised to give up disciplines, vigils, fasting and recited prayers,
because these were not to be found as a viable solution on the road to perfection
(Moreno: 2010, 251–272). Within a few years Isabel de la Cruz had achieved
considerable success and prominence in Guadalajara. She had made successful
inroads into the convents of both the Franciscans and the Poor Clares in Alcala.[13]
In addition, her *deixamiento* position had been warmly received by numerous
members of the household of Guadalajara's leading citizen, Diego Hurtado de
Mendoza de Luna, especially by his accountant Pedro Ruiz de Alcaraz.

The fact that several leaders of the *alumbrado-deixado* movement were
closely linked with palace activities is significant. The Mendoza family of Guadalajara was one of the most aristocratic and influential in Spain; many of its
members held high posts in both church and state. While Brianda de Mendoza
was occupied with her beguinage, her uncle, Diego Hurtado de Mendoza y Luna,
who now lived in the large family palace built by his father, was generously
lending his home, and the prestige of his name, to the *deixamiento* movement in
and around Guadalajara. Not only the duke, but also virtually all the members of
his household were involved in the movement. Among the members of the
Mendoza household that warmly received Isabel de la Cruz's *deixamiento* position were the duke's chaplain Alonso del Castillo, the chaplain's assistant Juan
Lopez de Celain, who we will encounter again in Medina de Rioseco, the duke's
flageolet player Diego de Espinosa, Rodrigo de Bivar who was one of his singers,
Garcia de Buytrago his treasurer, Pedro de Albadan a stable boy, Alcocer his hen
keeper, Vega his butler, etc. (Longhurst: 1969, 137). Diego Hurtado de Mendoza
had even redesigned the famous "Salon de los Linajes" into a chapel and employed singers, musicians, minstrels, etc. Bataillon (1966, 183, note 35) contends

---

excommunication, to be ipso facto incurred, that it be rendered by all civil magistrates. But
for no nun, after her profession, shall it be lawful to go out of her convent, even for a brief
period, under any pretext whatever, except for some lawful cause, which is to be approved of
by the bishop; any indults and privileges whatsoever notwithstanding." Theodore Alois
Buckley (trans.), The Canons and Decrees of the Council of Trent, (London: George Routledge and Co., 1851).

13 The convent of the Poor Clares in Alcala de Henares, which was later turned into a community of Second Order Franciscan nuns, was also initially a beguinage founded by Maria de
Toledo, a contemplataive mystic of noble origin. The abbess, Donna Aldonza, received letters
from Juan del Castillo, an *alumbrado* burned at the stake in 1535. (Longhurst: 1969, 89)

that the duke himself, who was known to be a very devout man, may very well have been saved the humiliation of a trial for heresy for having died in 1531.

Pedro Ruiz de Alcaraz, the other *deixado* leader, was an accountant. He was first employed by Pedro Hurtado de Mendoza y Figueroa, Diego Hurtado de Mendoza y Luna's uncle. After Pedro Hurtado's death in 1506, he went to work for his son-in-law, Diego Carrillo de Mendoza, and then for Diego Carrillo's son, Luis Hurtado de Mendoza. Shortly after the death of Luis Hurtado in 1522, Alcaraz entered the Diego Hurtado de Mendoza y Luna household in Guadalajara. From Alcaraz's confession at his trial in Toledo in 1527, we learn that his conversion to the way of thinking of Isabel de la Cruz had already taken place around 1509 (Alcala: 1999, 100). He also confessed that Erasmus's *Enchiridion* supported his views regarding intentionality in external acts (Ahlgren: 1998, 11, note 16). As professor Longhurst (1969, 136) put it,

> More than any other work of Erasmus, the *Enchiridion* emphasized the inner significance of Christianity, with a heavily Pauline mystical approach. In the *Enchiridion* of Erasmus, which bore the official approval of Inquisitor General Manrique, they found expressed essentially the same quasi-mystical approach that they had been emphasizing for some years.

Alcaraz had no university training, but his passion for Holy Writ was such that he was able to quote portions of Scripture at length, which amazed even the most learned theologians at his trial. There was no Spanish translation of the entire Bible at that time; hence, he would have memorized portions found in either the *Vita Cristi* or the *Gospels and Epistles*, or the other religious literature popular with the *alumbrados*. Alcaraz preached the principles of *deixamiento* (submission, surrender, abandonment) with his every-day life. During mass, for example, "instead of kneeling and crossing himself at the proper moments, he would remain rigid as a statue, his arms straight at his sides, his lips unmoving, his eyes unseeing, all the while frozen in deep meditation." (Longhurst: 1969, 99). He maintained that there was no need for external practices such as fasting, kneeling, and the rest (Hamilton: 2010, 103–124). To be saved one needed only to be in the condition of *deixamiento*, in which he/she surrendered his/her will to God. This act of surrender released one from ties to the material world—mainly the church and the priesthood—and allowed a person to fully live within God's grace.

Escalona

In 1523, Pedro Ruiz de Alcaraz left the Mendoza palace at Guadalajara for Escalona, in the valley of the Alberche River near Toledo, to join the household of

Diego Lopez Pacheco, Marquis of Villena and Duke of Escalona. There was not only a spiritual affinity between Mendoza and Pacheco, but there also existed family ties. Diego Hurtado de Mendoza y Luna's nephew, the diplomat, historian and man of letter, Diego Hurtado de Mendoza y Pacheco,[14] was the son of Francisca Pacheco, sister to Diego Lopez Pacheco. In addition, Diego Hurtado de Mendoza y Luna's first wife, Maria Pacheco Portacarerro (d. 1499), was Diego Lopez Pacheco's niece.

At Escalona, Alcaraz became the spiritual director of a group of *deixados* that at that time congregated in the Marquis of Villena's palace. The marquis was a man of deep humanistic and religious concerns and his palace became the center of an important nucleus of religious spirituality. Both Juan de Valdes, of *deixado* (abandonment) tendencies, and Fray Francisco de Osuna, of *recogimiento* (withdrawal) leanings—the sort of mystic withdrawal recommended by Cisneros—, dedicated their first works to the Marquis of Villena. This is noteworthy since these two works—in focus as well as content—reflect very different religious viewpoints. Whereas Osuna's *Tercer abecedario espiritual* (1527), in which he formulated maxims for mystic meditation arranged alphabetically, marked the transition from asceticism to mysticism and had a great impact on Teresa of Avila among others, Valdes's *Diálogo de doctrina christiana* (1529) marked the transition from Erasmianism to Protestantism (Estrada: 2008b, 23).

In the village of Pastrana, on his way from Guadalajara to Escalona, Alcaraz had had discussions with Francisco de Osuna, the spiritual leader of the *recogidos*, that ended in a split between the *recogidos* and the *deixados*, each group going its separate way. Though the two groups shared many principles, they differed in that while *recogimiento* concerned itself with "active seclusion in order to achieve union with God," *deixamiento* called for "passive submission to God's will." Furthermore, whereas *recogimiento* functioned alongside traditional Catholic practices, *deixamiento* rejected these practices (Montoya: 2010, 19) and, most importantly, the Catholic interpretation of justification (Nieto: 1979, 143–145). In 1525, Geronimo de Olivares, an *alumbrado-deixado* from Pastrana, defined the two approaches as follows:

---

14 On leaving the University of Salamanca, Diego Hurtado de Mendoza y Pacheco (1503–1575) abandoned his intention of taking orders. He served under Charles V in Italy, attended lectures at the universities of Bologna, Padua and Rome, and in 1539 was appointed ambassador at Venice. During his years in Venice he built up his library, buying books printed by the Aldine Press and employing scribes to copy Greek manuscripts. The first printed Greek edition of the works of Flavius Josephus (1544) was edited by the Flemish humanist Arnoldus Arlenius, who worked in the Mendoza library. Diego Hurtado represented Spain diplomatically at the Council of Trent. He was never a favourite of Philip II, and a quarrel with a courtier resulted in his banishment from court in June 1568. The remaining years of his life, which were spent at Granada, he devoted to the study of Arabic (which he had learned at home when growing up) and to his history of the Moorish insurrection of 1568–1570.

Recogimiento is a state of mental prayer in which the senses are inactive, one drives out all thoughts from his mind and puts his soul in repose, so that the soul might reach such a state that one will remember nothing about himself nor about God. For, although he will not remember God with his mind, in this state of repose his soul will be united with God. And in order to induce this state, we used to kneel down for a while, and then sit in a corner for a long time with our eyes closed. *Deixamiento* is to make no effort at mental prayer, but to subject oneself to whatever God wills, to let thoughts pass through the mind without heed, for Our Lord so permits it that our spirit may be purged, on condition that our will not give in to our thoughts. (Longhurst: 1969, 102).

In 1524, around the time Alcaraz arrived, the Franciscan church in Escalona witnessed some bizarre scenes. Two Franciscan friars, Juan de Olmillos and Francisco de Ocaña, representing the "apocalyptic" *recogidos*, were busy making proselytes (Nieto: 1977, 3–16). Fray Olmillos, for example, moved the altar to the middle of the church so that more people could witness his ecstasies; Fray Ocaña revealed his millennial program for the reform of the church. Preaching on the text, "Behold we go up to Jerusalem, and all things that are written by the prophets concerning the Son of man shall be accomplished" (Luke 18:31), he told his audience that the people of Escalona were the most blessed in the world for having him there. In another sermon he called for those in power in the church to be "thrown out like pigs." The messianic program revealed to him and Fray Olmillos stipulated that Charles V would defeat the king of France and take over his kingdom, the pope would be deposed by the Marquis of Villena, Ocaña himself would be installed as the new reforming pope, and the illiterate visionary Francisca Hernandez would reform and revise the Holy Scriptures.[15] Here surely was an open challenge to established authority within the church that could hardly be ignored. Yet the Inquisition never moved against Ocaña or the friars that practiced *recogimiento*, but concentrated instead on the *deixados*, who practiced spiritual abandonment to God and who considered the visions, ecstatic fits, and convulsions to be delusions induced by the devil (McKendrick/ MacKay: 1991, 94). On the other hand, there was reason for the Inquisition to consider the *deixados* the most threatening for the church. The leading role that Alcaraz gave to the illumination of the Holy Spirit radically undermined the Catholic principle of hierarchical authority. Instead of the authority of Rome they advocated the authority of the Bible and full salvation as a result of the work of Christ, hence the term *deixado*, meaning literally to abandon oneself to Christ, to partake of his love, and to experience it. Although the element of experience was also shared by the *recogidos*, the *deixados* stressed the importance of the Scriptures.

At Escalona, Ruiz de Alcaraz met young Juan de Valdes. He may have met him

---

15 On Francisca Hernandez see note 19.

earlier at the Mendoza palace in Guadalajara, or at Tendilla or Pastrana. In any case, it is evident that young Juan de Valdes identified closely with the teachings of the *deixados*. In the course of Pedro Ruiz de Alcaraz's trial, Maria de Casalla, Alcaraz's wife, urged the members of the tribunal to listen to the testimony of Juan de Valdes, but the petition was ignored. Jose Nieto (1981, 173) points out their doctrinal affinity:

> We will never really know how deeply Valdes understood the teaching of Alcaraz or his 'intentions', but we have sufficient proof of it in his first publication, *Dialog on Christian Doctrine*, which points in this direction. What is surprising is that absolutely no one of those familiar with the documents of the Inquisition (including Bataillon) has ever made the slightest insinuation in this direction.

Why Juan de Valdes was in Escalona in the early 1520s is uncertain. He was born in Cuenca, a city some 150 miles to the northeast of Escalona. The area was known for its wool production and both the Mendoza and the Pacheco families became extremely wealthy thanks to their sheep and sheep pastures in and around Cuenca (Nalle: 1992, 4). Escalona was a good stopping point on the way from Cuenca up to the trade fairs at Medina del Campo, north of Escalona. Indeed, young Valdes could even have been sent initially to Antonio de Baeza's household and not necessarily to the Pacheco palace.

Antonio de Baeza, governor of the fortress of Escalona,[16] and his wife Francisca de Zuñiga took an active part in the *alumbrado-deixado* movement at Escalona. Baeza's title—*licenciado* (licentiate)[17]—implies that he had a formal university education. He may have graduated in civil law from the nearby University of Salamanca. Not only was Baeza governor of Escalona, but he was also one of the marquis's legal advisers (Ávila Seoane: 2013, 1–23). It is also interesting to note that, as a young man, Antonio de Baeza translated into Spanish Jean Gerson's *De probatione spirituum* (On Proving the Spirits), printed in Antwerp in 1492.[18] Having studied at Salamanca, he may have been among those who became familiar with Gerson through Osma's work. Guillaume Le Talleur had just recently printed the work in Latin in Rouen, an important commercial and manufacturing center, known for its cloth industry, especially its silks. Baeza may have been sent to Rouen to buy silk—or to deliver a con-

---

16 Escalona was a walled fortresss in the 15th century. As a partican of doña Juana la Beltraneja, daughter of Enrique IV, over against Isabel, Diego López Pacheco held out in his fortress until he was defeated in 1480 and obliged to swear allegiance to Isabel. Antonio Baeza's father, Pedro Baeza, was governor of the fortress at that time.

17 Lettered men were often referred to by the degree they held: *bachiller* (B.A.), *licenciado* (M.A.), *doctor* (Ph.D).

18 This information appears in Manuel Serrano y Sanz (1903), and has been repeated by many historians. Unfortunately, I have been unable to find any bibliographical reference to this translation or any copy published in Antwerp in 1492. See also Hamilton (1977).

signment of highly valued Spanish merino wool—and there came across Gerson's *Tractatulus perutilis de probatione spirituum* (Rouen: Guillaum Le Talleur, 1485) (Reid: 2004, 1011–1020).

Besides Alcaraz and the Baeza family, other members of the Pacheco household that held *deixado* views were the marquis's chaplain, Sebastian Gutierrez, and one of his pages, Pedro de Marquina. Marquina entered the service of the marquis as a young boy. He had always impressed the members of the household with his religious fervor and his desire to become a friar. When Alcaraz came to Escalona in 1523, Marquina came under his influence and became an enthusiastic practitioner of *deixamiento*; at mass he would remain rigid in his place, without praying, kneeling, or crossing himself, in imitation of his mentor. During Alcaraz's trial, Marquina's presence in Escalona came to the attention of the Toledo inquisitors. In February of 1529 he was questioned closely about his religious views and apparently managed to convince the inquisitors that if he had erred in the past it was through ignorance, and that he had long since returned to orthodox ways (Longhurst: 1969, 337).

The Baeza family also had close links with the Cazallas in Valladolid. Antonio's wife, Francisca, spent much of her time in Valladolid with her cousin Leonor de Vivero, mother of the Cazallas and a devoted follower of the *alumbrado* leader Francisca Hernandez in the early 1520s.[19] It seems that when Pedro Ruiz de Alcaraz entered the services of the Marquis of Villena he broke fellowship with Francisca Hernandez—who may have been a frequent visitor in Escalona—and encouraged Baeza's wife to do the same. Francisca remembered this and when called before the inquisitors a few years later, revealed the names of many of her ex-companions:

> In its roundup of the Illuminists in the late 1520s, the Inquisition had seized, among others, one Francisca Hernandez, erotic genie of the Illuminists of Valladolid, and (no relation) Diego Hernandez, a libidinous peripatetic who raised a ruckus wherever he went. Francisca Hernandez, at periodic intervals in the 1530s, denounced as Lutherans and Illuminists all the leading Erasmists in Spain. Diego Hernandez was equally fertile: in May of 1532 he named twenty-eight persons—both Erasmists and Illuminists— whom he described as bedfellows in heresy. One year later his memory had improved greatly; this time he listed some seventy persons as Lutherans, which included all the leading humanists at the imperial court and at the University of Alcala. (Longhurst: 1969, 137).

---

19 Francisca Hernandez was leader of the *alumbados* at Valladolid in the 1520s. She later defected and denounced all the leading *alumbrados* and Erasmians in Spain. Francisca was arrested in Valladolid in 1529 and taken to Toledo for trial. Her intimate collaborator, Antonio de Medrano, was tried in 1532. He abjured *de vehementi* and was sentenced to life imprisonment. See Pérez Escohotado (2003).

Once the circle at Escalona was dissolved with the arrest of Pedro Ruiz de Alcaraz in 1524, members of the Baeza family began gravitating around the Cazallas in Valladolid. Antonio de Baeza's daughter, the *beata* Francisca Zuñiga de Baeza, would later be sentenced at the Valladolid *auto-da-fe* of October 8, 1559, together with several of her Cazalla cousins who were burned at the stake, she herself being sentenced to life imprisonment (Longhurst: 1969, 302). We must also mention Antonio de Baeza's sister Juana, married to Jeronimo de Reinosa—nephew of the Bishop of Cordoba, by the same name. Their two daughters, who would both become nuns in the Belen convent in Valladolid, were also among those that gathered at the Pacheco castle to hear Pedro Ruiz de Alcaraz. Jeronimo de Reinosa and Juana de Baeza had eleven children, among which were the two nuns: Catalina, burned at the stake at the *auto-da-fe* of 1559, and Francisca, sentenced to life in prison. It seems that even Antonio de Baeza himself spent some time in prison. This is taken from declarations made in Valladolid on October 12, 1558, before Inquisitor Valtodano, when Dr. Cazalla alleged that Francisca de Zuñiga, daughter of Antonio de Baeza, had a grudge against him because in 1553, just before he left for Germany, his father had wanted his brother Gonzalo Perez de Vivero to marry her, and when everyone had agreed to the terms, Cazalla refused to give his consent "because her father had spent time in the prisons of the Inquisition." (Schäfer: 2014, IV, 1071).

Meanwhile, in Guadalajara, Isabel de la Cruz had continued to carry on her *alumbrado-deixado* activities undisturbed until Maria Nuñez denounced her to the Toledo Inquisition as a heretic in May of 1519. In June, Maria Nuñez told the inquisitors that she remembered more things: Isabel and her disciple Pedro Ruiz de Alcaraz used to mock those who did penance for their sins. At that time, the Toledo inquisitors did not bother to take any action against Isabel. By 1523, the movement was gathering momentum and the inquisitors were persuaded that a menace to orthodoxy existed. On February 26, 1524, Isabel and Pedro Ruiz de Alcaraz were arrested and their long (five-year) trials for heresy began. They were mainly accused of rejecting priestly intermediaries and external rituals such as meditation on Christ's passion, bowing before the Eucharist, praying to saints, etc. In 1525, Inquisitor General Alonso Manrique called a conference of theologians to examine the teachings of the *alumbrados-deixados*. The conference resulted in a formal condemnation consisting of 48 propositions against the *alumbrados*, known as the Edict of Toledo, dated September 23, 1525.[20] These 48 propositions, together with Inquisitorial testimonies and documents, are the primary sources of *alumbrado-deixado* history. The Edict was written up in simple language in a statement-response format. Each statement was followed by a qualification: "heretical," "erroneous," "false," "Lutheran," "scandalous,"

---

20 For an English translation of the full Edict, see Homza (2006, 80–92).

"madness," etc. The Edict was to be read aloud publicly at mass (Márquez: 1972, 282) and functioned,

> As a source of information and as a motivator, in this case to inspire a sense of fear in those that read or listened to it. By publishing information on the practices that were deemed unorthodox the Church was in essence also publishing a checklist from which individuals could verify that the practices that they maintained were correct. (Montoya: 2010, 59).

Between May 1524 and February of 1526 at least a dozen witnesses from Guadalajara, Pastrana, and Toledo were questioned about their activities. The trial dragged on. Finally, in 1527 the judges voted six to three in favor of burning Isabel at the stake (the others favoring life imprisonment). Pedro de Alcaraz was sentenced to life imprisonment along with her and was given one hundred lashes in a public flogging besides.

Medina de Rioseco

Alumbrado-deixado influence was not limited to Guadalajara and Escalona. It also reached Medina de Rioseco, some 150 miles (250 km) north of Escalona. The *alumbrado-deixado* activity at Medina de Rioseco is closely associated with Fadrique Enriquez de Ribera (1476–1539), Marquis of Tarifa. Fadrique Enriquez inherited the castle of Medina de Rioseco in 1489. He was a cousin of king Ferdinand and in 1490 was appointed 4th Admiral of Castile by the Catholic Monarchs. In 1496, he accompanied their daughter princess Joanna to Flanders to marry Philip the Handsome. Fadrique Enriquez was a typical Renaissance man, a lover of books and travel. In 1518 he took a journey to the Holy Land. On his way, he stopped off at the Royal College of Spain in Bologna[21] and commissioned three young scholars there—Juan Genes de Sepulveda, Jaime de Castillo de Villasanta, and Jaime Ponce—to make a translation of the entire Bible from Latin into Spanish for the price of 200 ducats. He also asked them to translate Vincent of Beauvais's *Speculum Historical* into Spanish.[22] When he returned the following year, the work was not yet finished, so he gave them six more months to finish it and forty more ducats.

---

21 The "Real Colegio Mayor de San Clemente de los Españoles" in Bologna was founded by Cardinal Gil de Albornoz in 1364 and has been under the Royal patronage of the Spanish Crown since 1488.

22 This was part of Beauvais's *Speculum Maius* (*The Great Mirror*) (1260), a compendium of all of the knowledge of the Middle Ages. *Speculum Historiale* had been translated into French in 1480.

Over the years Fadrique Enriquez de Ribera continued to purchase book. An inventory of his library of some 250 volumes in 1532 shows his wide spectrum of interests. He may have inherited some of them from his mother, Catalina de Ribera, who had received a well-rounded education in the humanities, like her aunt Queen Isabel. Carmen Alvarez Marquez (1986, 1–40), professor from the University of Seville, has studied the Fadrique Enriquez de Ribera library in detail. Of special interest, and what concerns us here, are Fadrique Enriquez's books of devotion. The list included a copy of *Vita Christi*, four Bibles—two in Spanish, one in Italian,[23] and one in Latin—, several editions of *Gospels and Epistles*, Psalters, etc. The list of Church Fathers included St. Augustine, Jerome, Chrysostom, Isidoro of Seville, Boecio, Gregory the Great, etc. Among the mystics there were Bernard of Clairvaux, Bonaventure, Albertus Magnus, Raymond Llull, Jean Gerson, Catalina of Sienna, Angela of Foligno, Alfonso de Madrigal, Antonius of Florence, Erasmus, Savonarola, etc.[24] The two Bibles in Spanish were very likely manuscript copies of the translation he commissioned. Translations of the Psalms circulated and many passages of the Bible could be found in Montesino's *Gospels and Epistles*, but this would have been the first translation of the entire Bible into Spanish. Bonifacio Ferrer (d. 1417) translated the entire Bible into Catalan at the beginning of the fifteenth century. It was printed in Valencia in 1478, but soon after it came off the press the entire edition was destroyed. In 1645 the last four leaves of a copy of Ferrer's Bible were discovered in a library belonging to the monastery of Portaceli, near Burjassot (Valencia). One of the leaves contained the imprint, indicating the names of the translator and printer, together with the place and year of the impression. According to some authors, Ferrer's Bible underwent, about the year 1515, a second impression, which shared the same fate. (M'Crie: 1829, 192).

Fadrique Enriquez's devotional reading included Pedro Jimenez de Prejano's *Lucero de la vida Cristiana* (Light of the Christian Life), commissioned by the Catholic Monarchs for the instruction of *conversos*, and *Los doce triunfos de los doce Apóstoles* (The Twelve Victories of the Twelve Apostles) by the Carthusian monk Juan de Padilla. These two works, which he purchased in Seville after his return from the Holy Land, may have inspired him to organize a mission point to evangelize his feudal territory of Medina de Rioseco. For this, he first consulted

---

23 This may have been the Bible described by Thomas M'Crie (1827, 73–74): "An Italian version of the Scriptures, by Nicolo Malermi or Malerbi, a Camaldolese monk, was printed at Venice so early as the year 1471 and is said to have gone through no fewer than nine editions in the fifteenth and twelve editions in the sixteenth century. Another version of the Bible was printed in the month of October of the same year, without notice of the translator, printer, or place of printing."

24 Professor Alvarez Marquez (1986, 6) points out that among the books there are no works by Thomas Aquinas or Anselm of Canterbury.

with abovementioned Diego Hurtado de Mendoza y Luna, in Guadalajara, who may have suggested the name Juan Lopez de Celain. In 1523, Celain was in the service of the duke's chaplain, Alonso del Castillo. It was in Guadalajara where Celain made his first contacts with Pedro Ruiz de Alcaraz and the *alumbrados*. He may have studied at Alcala and from there gone to Guadalajara. Celain may even have accompanied Alcaraz to Escalona in 1524 and there met Antonio de Baeza, with whom he later professed a close friendship. The duke of Infantado, at Guadalajara, as well as the marquis of Villena, at Escalona, and his brother-in-law, Fadrique Enriquez, at Medina de Rioseco, showed great interest in the new spirituality of the day. Nevertheless, of the three, Fadrique Enriquez was the only one who attempted to evangelize his estates with the new teaching.

In the summer of 1525, Fadrique Enriquez summoned Celain to his palace and together they laid the groundwork for a project to evangelize the area, which they called "The Twelve Apostles of Medina de Rioseco." Celain's job was to recruit twelve men willing to participate in the project. Fadrique Enriquez promised them lodging and a salary. Celain went first to his circle of Erasmian friends at Alcala and his *alumbrado* friends at Toledo, but he was unable to find twelve "willing apostles" and the project eventually fell through. On the other hand, it was also around this time that trials against the *alumbrados* were under way, and this may have induced Fadrique Enriquez to see things in a different light and he may not have wanted complications with the Holy Office. Once the project was called off, Juan Lopez de Celain left Medina de Rioseco and went to Granada as chaplain of the Royal Chapel there. In 1528, he was denounced before the inquisitors for teaching and spreading *alumbrado*, Erasmian, and Lutheran propositions. He was imprisoned and his goods were seized. A year later, he managed to escape thanks to bribes (Longhurst: 1969, 220) but was captured, brought back to Granada and burned at the stake on July 24, 1530.[25]

---

25 For full details regarding the activities of Juan Lopez de Celain, see Selke (1960, 136–162).

Chapter 4:
Juan de Valdes

Wisdom, which is sweet science, serves to know, to taste, and to experience God. The
more the soul possess of this wisdom, the more it knows, tastes, and experiences. God
can bestow it on a little old lady and on someone who cannot read or write; He can
withhold it from a learned scholar to the point that if you talk to him about it, he
thinks you are speaking to him in a foreign tongue. It is true that one is often confused
with the other, that is to say, wisdom for science, and science for wisdom, just make
sure that by this name of science you do not infer that science which is acquired by
human endeavor, which is the science that puffs up and makes men arrogant.

Juan de Valdes, *Dialog on Christian Doctrine* (1529)

Juan de Valdes (1500?–1541) was born in Cuenca, where his father, Hernando de
Valdes (1460–1530), a man of means and prestige, held the office of alderman.[1]
His mother, Maria de la Barreda (*ca.* 1464–1532), and also very likely his father,
was of *converso* Jewish origin. One of Juan's uncles, the priest Fernando de la
Barreda, was burned at the stake by the Inquisition in 1491 accused of being a
relapsed Jew. We have no information regarding Juan's infancy and early
schooling. On the other hand, we cannot rule out the possibility that young
Valdes was sent to Guadalajara or Tendilla for his basic schooling. It was custom
in those days for the nobility to take in the sons and daughters of prominent
citizens for the purpose of educating them under the tutorage of some renowned
maestro (Bataillon: 1966, 104–105, 111). For example, the Italian historian-
chronicler Peter Martyr d'Angleria came to Spain in 1488, hired by the Spanish
ambassador, Iñigo Lopez de Mendoza y Quiñones (*El Gran Tendilla*), to tutor his
children. Through Cardinal Pedro Gonzalez de Mendoza, Iñigo Lopez's uncle,
Martyr d'Angleria was introduced to the Catholic Monarchs, who sent him on
various diplomatic missions and appointed him royal historian. After 1492,
Martyr d'Angleria's chief task was the education of young nobles with the view
in mind of uprooting the common opinion that learning was incompatible with a
military career. Some historians suggest that Juan de Valdes's brother Alfonso
was one of Martyr d'Angleria's students. Whether or not this was the case, there
did exist a close relationship between the two men. Alfonso de Valdes would
regularly inform Peter Martyr d'Angleria of the events he was eyewitness to,
such as the meeting of the emperor with Martin Luther at Worms (M'Crie: 1829,
124–125). Two of these letters have been preserved, one dated September 1520
from Brussels and a second dated May 1521 from Worms.

---

1 See Jiménez Monteserín (1995).

Dialog on Christian Doctrine (Alcala, 1529)

Very possibly, after Pedro Ruiz de Alcaraz's arrest in February of 1524, young
Juan de Valdes left Escalona and returned to his home in Cuenca. In 1527 we find
him at Alcala studying Greek, Hebrew, Latin, rhetoric, and grammar. Only two
years later his *Dialog on Christian Doctrine* was off the press. References in the
Dialog to authors such as Gerson, St. Jerome, St. Gregory, St. Augustine, and
Erasmus—authors read and held in high regard by his mentor Pedro Ruiz de
Alcaraz at Escalona—, evidence Valdes's theological orientation. One author he
especially recommended was Erasmus:

> ARCHBISHOP: You must certainly have heard of an excellent doctor, a true theologian
> who is still alive, whose name is Erasmus of Rotterdam.
> EUSEBIO: Yes, I have heard of him.
> ARCHBISHOP: Have you read any of his works?
> EUSEBIO: No I haven't because people have warned me not to read them.
> ARCHBISHOP: Well, take my advice. Cast them aside for their ignorance and read and
> study the works of Erasmus and you will see what great benefit you will reap. I want you
> to know that among the works of this Erasmus there is a booklet of *Familiar Colloquies*,
> which he says he wrote so that children would learn Latin and Christianity at the same
> time. In it, he deals with many topics related to Christianity. Among them, he explains
> the Creed almost the same way I have explained it here to you. You needn't wonder that I
> have it so fresh in my memory for I have read it again and again, and with great fruition.
> (Valdes: 2008, 105–106. Translation and note mine)

At Alcala, Valdes would have become further acquainted with the works of
Erasmus, which at that time Miguel de Eguia was busy producing at his shops in
Alcala, Toledo, and Logroño. Titles printed by Miguel de Eguia include: *En-
quiridión o manual del caballero cristiano* (Alcala, 1526, 1527, 1529); *La oración
del Señor que llamamos Pater Noster* (Logroño, 1528); *Sermón de la grandeza y
muchedumbre de las misericorias de Dios* (Logroño, 1528); *Tratado o sermón del
niño Jesus* (Toledo, 1526); *Paraclesis* (Alcala, 1529); *Tractado de las querellas de
la pax* (Alcala, 1529). In the above dialog, the archbishop could have been
referring to *Tres Coloquios* (Valladolid, 1528), which contained three dialogs
translated into Spanish by Luis Mexía that circulated in *pliego suelto* (broad-
sheet) and was enlarged the following year with eleven other colloquia translated
by Alonso Ruiz de Virues, Bishop of the Canary Islands (*Coloquios de Erasmo*,
Seville: Juan Cromberger, 1529). Reprints rapidly appeared.[2] Elsewhere, the
archbishop—Valdes's literary persona—recommends "Erasmus's Enquir-
idión and some other little booklet by him *in Spanish*, like his explanation of

---

2 *Coloquios de Erasmo*, trans. Alonso Ruiz de Virues (Toledo: Cosme Damián, 1530; Zaragoza:
   Jorge Coci, 1530; Toledo: Juan de Ayala, 1532).

the Lord's Prayer and a short sermon on the child Jesus and some coloquies."
(Valdes: 2008, 199. Translation and italics mine)

Indeed, *Dialog on Christian Doctrine* was Valdes's manifesto—his mission
statement—regarding his theological position. Marcel Bataillon considered
Valdes's *Dialog* a "moderate Erasmian catechism," but both Jose Nieto and
David Estrada find Valdes's comments on the Creed, the Decalogue and the
Lord's Prayer closer to Protestant views. This is corroborated by Carlos Gilly
(1982, 95), who finds strong Lutheran influences in the text, and by Marcelino
Menéndez y Pelayo (1881, I, 930), who viewed Valdes's religious position in total
opposition to Catholic doctrinal orthodoxy, labeling him "a staunch Lutheran, a
defender of the horrible doctrine of justification by faith in the sole merits of
Christ." That the main source of Valdes's theology did not come from Alcala is
supported by Juan de Vergara declaration at his trial where he stated that when
Valdes published his *Dialog on Christian Doctrine* he had rebuked him "for not
having studied theology in the university."[3] We must also bear in mind that only
third and fourth-year students were obliged to study theology (Amadó: 1907),
and that the work was already off the press in January of his third year at Alcala.

Very likely Valdes's main interest in matriculating at Alcala resided in the
school's reputation for solid philological training, which would enable him to
read the Bible in the original Greek and Hebrew. He may have acquired a reasonable level of fluency with the help of a tutor and a copy of Erasmus's New
Testament before entering the university, and once there, would also have had
the opportunity to resort to other texts including the Complutensian Polyglot.
This is validated at the end of the *Dialog* where Valdes inserted, as an appendix,
his own translation "from the Greek" of chapters 5, 6, and 7 of the Gospel of St.
Matthew. Because it was prohibited to translate the Bible into the vernacular, he
justified this liberty with a postscript that reads:

> And because the three chapters of the gospel written by St. Matthew, which that
> archbishop of glorious memory spoke so highly of, are often praised in the *Dialog*, I
> decided to translate them into Spanish and add them here so that, having had them
> referred to in the *Dialog*, and wanting to consult them later, you [Illustrious Marquis]
> could do so. (Valdes: 2008, 206. Translation and bracket mine)

Dialog on Christian Doctrine is a commentary on the established items found in
the official Catholic catechism: The Apostles Creed, The Ten Commandments,
The Seven Mortal Sins, The Four Cardinal Virtues, The Three Theological Virtues, The Seven Gifts of the Holy Spirit, The Five Commandments of the Church,
The Lord's Prayer. To these "official" doctrines, Valdes added a brief summary of
the history of salvation, beginning with the Old Testament up to the birth of

---

3 AHN, Inquisicion de Toledo, Proceso contra Juan de Vergara, leg. 223, no. 42, fol. 45v.

Christ. In contrast to earlier explanations of the fundamental doctrines of the church, Valdes's exegesis was not meant for memorization, but for instruction and meditation. The work is presented in the form of a pleasant three-way dialog between an archbishop, a well-intentioned rural priest and an educated monk concerned about the good will—but profuse ignorance—of the parish priest as he attempts to catechize a group of children. The tender care with which the archbishop expounds the fundamental doctrines of the church as they appear in the official catechism, emphasizing the inner spiritual aspect of each article and minimizing outward observance—and often sidetracking the priest's observations—was totally innovating at that time.

The book, which unfolds in a very realistic scenario, is dedicated to Diego Lopez Pacheco, marquis of Villena and duke of Escalona. In all likelihood, the marquis had put into effect the requirement of the Synod of Badajoz (1501) that instructed parents to send "all the children in their household under the age of twelve" to be catechized and each church to assign someone to teach them. As a young man in Escalona, Valdes may have witnessed some of these sessions. The dedication begins thus:

> Most Illustrious Lord Marquis,
> One day, as I was passing through one of your villages, and being told that by command of the lord of these regions, and at his expense, in the churches the priests instructed the children in the principles and rudiments of Christian Doctrine—a practice I had desired to see for a long time—, I entered the church and sat among the children to see if I could learn something profitable that I could introduce into my monastery and also to see if I, with my learning and experience, could help to improve that good work and godly practice. Although the priest that taught the children was uneducated, and was not so well indoctrinated in the things he was teaching as he should have been, for being what he was, I consoled myself and listened pleasantly for a good while. (Valdes: 2008, 84. Translation mine).

In January 1529, Valdes's *Dialog* came off Miguel de Eguia's press at Alcala. Before taking the manuscript to the printer, Dr. Hernan Vazquez, canon of the collegiate church of Los Santos Justo y Pastor in Alcala, read the work and expurgated a few "too daring" passages. Despite this revision, the work was immediately denounced before the Holy Office and Inquisitor General Alonso Manrique ordered a commission of theologians of Alcala to examine the doctrinal content of the work. The report sent back by the commission was favorable, though they recommended that Valdes revise several passages susceptible to misinterpretation. Ecclesiastical authorities in other districts did not share the favorable verdict of the theologians of Alcala and in August of the same year, the Supreme Council prohibited people from reading the book due to the "many errors and ill-sounding things" it contained. As a result, *Dialog on Christian Doctrine* was immediately put on the Index of Prohibited Books, which meant confiscation of all the copies in the hands of book dealers and printers.[4] Despite these severe measures, a few copies had already slipped out of the Inquisitors' reach. For example, Maria de Cazalla, one of the *alumbrado* leaders, had a copy, as her trial records reveal:

> Asked if she knew who wrote the book called *Doctrina Cristiana*, she said she heard it was by one Valdes who was studying at the University of Alcala. [But] she remembered that *bachiller* Tovar reprehended Valdes for having published the book in such a hurry, without further correction and emendation. This defendant [Maria de Cazalla] had a copy of the said *Doctrina Cristiana*, and one day she heard Pedro de Vitoria, of the Order of St. Francis, preach and he said wicked things about the book. This defendant consequently threw it into the bottom of a chest until she would see that the book was cleared [of suspicion]; she ordered her daughters not to read any more of it. She did not remember who sent her the book, except that they sent it from Alcala. (Homza: 2006, 127).

In 1925, the French historian Marcel Bataillon discovered a copy of Valdes's *Dialog on Christian Doctrine* in the Real Monasterio de San Vicente de Forca, in Portugal. It is considered the only extant copy salvaged from Inquisitorial persecution. Today it is kept in the Bibliotheca of the University of Lisbon.

Empathy with the Deixados

The religious syncretism between Juan de Valdes and the *deixados* can be summarized in two basic doctrines: the doctrine of Christian love and the doctrine of illumination by the Holy Spirit (Estrada: 2008b, 34–38). The first key concept contains a radical distinction between the two concepts of love—*eros* and *agape*—and makes any identification of Christian love (*agape*) with Neoplatonism love (*eros*) incompatible. Contrary to the thesis advocated by Antonio Marquez (1972), the *deixados* were not Neoplatonic in their views regarding the relationship man can sustain with the divinity. *Deixamiento* does not imply a dissolving of the human soul into the divinity, but a joyful surrender to the love of God, a total yielding to his grace and saving purposes, to the end that the Divine may reach full actualization in man's life. Angela Selke (1980, 634, note 34) defines the concept of *deixamiento* as "a version of the Lutheran doctrine of the justification by faith." Far from placing man in a paralyzing quietism, the love of God compels the believer to fulfill the demands of the Law under a deep sense of urgency and responsibility, assuming also the joyous ministry of proclaiming the gospel of glad tidings to lost sinners. In other words, *deixamiento* is the individual's response to God's descending in *agape* on him/her. The nu-

---

4 ADC, Inquisición. lib. 224, fol. 46r.

merous references regarding the subject of divine love found in the writings of Juan de Valdes show how clear the agapian interpretation of the God-to-man/ man-to-God relationship was for the Spanish reformer.

The second key concept has to do with the idea of illumination. *Deixamiento* implies a double surrender on the part of the believer: total submission to the love of God and total yielding to the work and guidance of the Holy Spirit. For the *deixados,* personal merits—human achievements in obtaining spiritual goals— are totally discarded; the benefits of the Gospel are all of grace. Moreover, the divine blessings are not something longed for, but present possessions. The blessings of salvation are bestowed through the divine agency of the Holy Spirit: the Father gives the Son for the salvation of the world; the Son achieves a perfect salvation for the lost sinners; and the Holy Spirit applies Christ's salvation to fallen man and illuminates him in all the knowledge and apprehension of spiritual matters.

For Valdes, illumination is the descent of the Holy Spirit to mankind and is part of—and fruit of—the salvation wrought by Christ in favor of the sinner. Hence, it is, from beginning to end, a pure gift of God to mankind (Estrada: 2008b, 154). As a Christian, the believer does not search for the spirit, but already *has* the spirit. The understanding of all the mysteries of salvation is the result of the illumination of the spirit. The ministry of the Law in revealing sin and leading the lost to Christ becomes operative in man's conscience thanks to this illumination. For the *deixados*, as well as for Valdes, contemplation has nothing to do with religious trances or mystical visions, but is a spiritual fruition of the benefits of salvation that the spirit reveals to the believer through the pages of Scripture. This biblical wisdom that the spirit imparts to the believer, writes Valdes, is "sweet science; [it] serves to know, to taste and to experience God. The more the soul possess of this wisdom, the more it knows, tastes and experiences." (Valdes: 2008, 154). As Jose Nieto (1970, 142) points out, to Alcaraz we owe the appearance of something totally new in the spiritual life of that time. This newness is none other than the irruption in Spain of the basic doctrines of the Protestant Reformation. In his writings, Valdes focuses on the activity and the work of the three persons of the Trinity: the Father offers his only begotten Son for the salvation of the world; the Son becomes man and achieves a perfect work of redemption in favor of the sinner; and the Holy Spirit applies the work of Christ in the believer and illuminates him/her in everything related to the knowledge and experience of the truth. Illumination does not require ascetic exercises or special preparation; it is part of the general scheme of God's grace for the believer. The illumination of the spirit is needful in all things—in the renovation of the individual to the image of God, in biblical hermeneutics, in the comprehension of biblical doctrines—to the point that a doctrine as important as justification does not become genuine knowledge in the life of the believer if it is not by the illumination of the spirit. In short, *Dialog on Christian Doctrine* is not a quest for a union of mystic love with God. There is no mention of the classical three-step scheme—*Via purgativa, Via iluminativa, Via unitiva*—of gradual control over one's evil inclinations to a state of perfection, so common to the popular pietistic forms that Cisneros's religious reforms gave rise to (Estrada: 2008b, 37).

Juan de Valdes in Naples

Suspicions of heresy against Valdes increased even more when the close relationship he had maintained with the *deixados* in Escalona became known. Little could the group of Erasmians at Alcala do to defend him in the face of these suspicions of heterodox doctrine. Hence, aware of the implications this growing suspicion of heresy could mean for his personal safety, in 1531 Valdes decided to leave Spain for Italy, where there existed a more tolerant atmosphere. Once in Rome, through the good offices of his brother Alfonso, and friends such as the Catalan humanist Miguel Mai, Spanish ambassador at Rome from July 1528 to February 1533, Valdes obtained employment in Naples at the court of the Viceroy, Pedro Alvarez de Toledo, as overseer of legal sentences and of castles. Comfortably installed in a villa in Chiaia, a gardened neighborhood of Naples overlooking the sea, he began to make acquaintance with men of like-minded spirits: Benedetto da Mantova, Bernardino Ochino, Peter Martyr Vermigli, Marcantonio Flaminio, Pietro Carnesecchi, the marquis of Vico, Galeazzo Caraccioli, and other prominent Italians. Known in Italy as Juan de Valdesso, Valdessio o Val d'Esso (Firpo: 1996), he soon became the spiritual leader of a distinguished and influential group of men and women of different social and political walks of life: nobles, priests, preachers and poets. Among the distinguished ladies were Guilia Gonzaga, Isabel Manrique, Constanza d'Avalos, Caterina Cibo, Vittoria Colonna, Isabel Briceño, Isabel Vilamari, Maria d'Aragona, and others. Guilia Gonzaga became the soul of the Valdes circle, to the point that he even regarded her as his spiritual heiress. Many of these women were widows when they joined Valdes's circle, which perhaps gave them more freedom to come and go and choose their religious orientation.

   A brief biographical sketch of some of Valdes's main followers is in order. Benedetto da Mantova (1499–1562), who would later embrace Protestant doctrines by reading the works of Martin Bucer and Ulrich Zwingli, published *The Benefit of Christ's Death* in 1543.[5] The famous Capuchin preacher Bernardino Ochino (1487–1564) was in Naples in 1536. A few years later, in Venice, he was

---

5 See Caponetto (1972).

denounced for showing sympathy with Luther's doctrine of justification by faith and had to flee. In 1545, he became minister of the Italian Protestant congregation at Augsburg. Later he became pastor of the Italian church at Zurich, but after increasing evidence of his alienation from orthodoxy he was banished from Zurich and went to Poland. Peter Martyr Vermigli (1499–1562) became a very influential figure in the early development of Reformed theology. In 1537 he was elected prior of the monastery of St Peter ad Aram in Naples, where he befriended Valdes and embraced Reformed views. To avoid persecution he fled to Strasbourg, and later to England, where he was appointed to a professorship at Oxford. He spent his final days teaching theology in Zurich. Pietro Carnesecchi (1508–1567) met Valdes earlier in the literary circles in Rome. In Naples Carnesecchi became the leading spirit of the group. When persecution arose he fled but later returned to Italy. With the accession of Pope Pius V in 1566 the Inquisition renewed its activities and on October 1, 1567, Carnesecchi was beheaded.

Among the women that formed part of Valdes's circle there were several well-read, influential noblewomen. Guilia Gonzaga (1513–1566), duchess of Fondi, had also met Valdes earlier in Rome in the literary circles there. She moved to Naples in 1536 and was introduced to evangelical preaching during Lent when she attended services in the church of San Giovanni Maggiore, where Bernardino Ochino was preaching. Duchess Caterina Cibo (1501–1557), a niece of future pope Clemente VII, moved to Naples in 1535 where she began to attend the evangelical circle led by Valdes. There she met Pietro Carnesecchi and other reformers with whom she fully identified spiritually. Vittoria Colonna (1492–1547), marchioness of Pescara, had spent most of her life at her husband's court on the island of Ischia near Naples. After 1530, she made her permanent home in Rome, but often returned to Naples. Like Marguerite de Navarre, with whom she corresponded, Vittoria was also a noted poet. Maria d'Aragona (1503–1568) grew up in Naples. She became intensely involved in the *Spirituali* movement in Naples in the 1530s, attending the salons of Guilia Gonzaga in the convent San Francesco delle Monache and the circle of Juan de Valdes at Chiaia.[6] When her husband was appointed governor of Milan in 1538, she tried repeatedly to bring Ochino to Milan, but in vain. Isabella Bresegna, or Briceño (1510–1567), was the daughter of a Spanish nobleman. Like her close friend Giulia Gonzaga, after hearing the preaching of Bernardino Ochino in 1536 she joined the circle of Juan

---

6 The *Spirituali* were members of a reform movement within the Roman Catholic Church. These "evangelical Catholics" proposed to reform the Church through a spiritual renewal, taking the study of Scriptures as means to that end. They took many of their ideas from older Catholic texts, but also found inspiration in the Protestant Reformation. Cardinal Carafa, who would later become Pope Paul IV, suppressed the *Spirituali* and under him many went on trial before the Inquisition, rapidly exterminating the movement.

de Valdes. In 1547, her husband was appointed governor of Piacenza. In 1553, the Inquisition imprisoned Lorenzo Tizzano, a member of her household. As a result of his confession, Isabella was suspected of heresy. In 1557, as the prosecution of heretics intensified, Isabella fled across the Alps, leaving her family behind. Her husband urged her to return, but she replied that she would live only in a place that permitted freedom of conscience. First she went to Vienna, to the home of a daughter, and from there to Tübingen. After visiting Pier Paolo Vergerio in Tübingen, she moved to Zurich, where Bernardino Ochino was pastor and where her son Pietro joined her. She finally settled in Chiavenna, attending the evangelical church pastored by Agostino Mainardi.

Valdes's time at Naples was brief. He died in 1541. His death was deeply lamented by many who owned him as their spiritual father. In a letter to Pietro Carnesecchi, one of his followers, the historian Jacopo Bonfadio, wrote,

> I wish we were again at Naples. But when I consider the matter in another point of view, to what purpose should we go there, now when Valdes is dead? His death truly is a great loss to us and to the world; for Valdes was one of the rarest men in Europe, as the writings left by him on the Epistles of St Paul and the Psalms of David abundantly demonstrate. He was, beyond all doubt, a most accomplished man in all his words, actions, and counsels. Life scarcely supported his infirm and spare body; but his nobler part and pure intellect, as if it had been placed without the body, was wholly occupied with the contemplation of truth and divine things. I condole with Marco Antonio, (Flaminio) for, above all others, he greatly loved and admired him. (M'Crie: 1833, 150).

Beginning January 1541, Cardinal Gian Pietro Carafa, the future Pope Paul IV (1555–1559), began a systematic investigation of all suspected heretics. The following year, he promulgated a bull whereby the Inquisition was reestablished, condemning Juan de Valdes for heresy, together with all his writings. This gave rise to the diaspora of Valdes's followers. Defying the strict censorship of the Inquisition, however, some of his disciples began the dangerous task of preserving his teaching through the publication of his works. In 1545, there appeared *Alfabeto cristiano: Que enseña el verdadero camino de adquirir la luz del Espíritu Santo* (Christian Alphabet, which teaches the way to acquire the Light of the Holy Spirit), translated from Spanish into Italian by Marco Antonio Magno, Giulia Gonzaga's legal advisor, and printed in Venice by Nicolo Bascarini. Next came *Cinque Trattatelli Evangelici* (Five Opuscules), printed in Rome, and his *Catecismo* (Christian Instruction for Children), printed simultaneously in Rome and Venice in 1545. Some years later, encouraged by Celius Segundo Curione, the exiled Spanish reformer Juan Perez de Pineda published Valdes's Commentaries on Romans and on 1 Corinthians in Geneva. Celio Secundo Curione, the son of a Piedmontese nobleman, became acquainted with the writings of Luther, Zwingli, and Melanchthon through Negri of Fossano, an Augustinian monk, while studying law at Turin. Curione, who was part of the teaching staff at the Monastery of San Ferdiano in Lucca, Italy, fled along with the others in 1542 and became a professor at Basel.[7]

Around 1550, a manuscript copy of Valdes's *Hundred and Ten Considerations*—a collection of meditations that covered the most important themes of Reformation thought and practice—was taken out of Italy by Pietro Paulo Vergerio and printed in Basel by J. Oporinus, with a prologue by Celius Secundus Curione, who wrote:

> By suavity of doctrine and holiness of life, [Juan de Valdess] gained over many disciples to Christ, especially amongst gentlemen and cavaliers, and some gentle women, most praiseworthy and exalted in all that could challenge praise. It seemed as if he had been appointed by God as the instructor and pastor of noble and illustrious persons: although his benignity and charity were such that he surrendered his pleasure to every mean, low, and rude person, and made himself all things to all men in order to gain over all to Christ. And not only this, but he has enlightened some of the most renowned Italian preachers. (Curione: 1865, 205).

The work was immediately translated into German (1555), Dutch (1565), French (1565), and later into English (1638). The English rendering was made by Nicholas Ferrar, the founder of the Little Gidding Community.[8] The English publisher Frederic Chapman, who reissued a facsimile of the work in 1905, describes Ferrar's endeavor as follows:

> When the book finally appeared in type [1550] nine years after the author's death, it was in an Italian translation. It was about sixty years later, in 1612–13, that Nicholas Ferrar set out on his Continental travels in the train of Frederick, Count Palatine, and his bride, the Princess Elizabeth, long affectionately referred to as "The Queen of Hearts." He passed through Holland and Germany, and so into Italy, and eventually home across Spain, after an absence of about five years. During his travels he seems to have collected books, particularly plays, assiduously, and also to have accumulated great store of prints, many of which probably afterwards went towards the manufacture of the famous illustrated concordances which were constructed by the members of the Gidding household. From amongst his collections, at some time when he was reflecting on his youthful vanities—for evidently in this he resembled Valdes, that the lust of the eye and the pride of life had had their period of domination in him—he made salvage of what need not be condemned as profane, and amongst the salvage was the little book from Basle. Of this he made a translation, and even as Master George Herbert submitted his 'Temple' to Ferrar, to decide if it should be published or withheld, so Ferrar submitted his 'Valdesso' to Herbert. The form of the name employed by Ferrar, and here adopted, is an Italian version of Valdes. We have seen that Cranmer used a Latinized form,

---

7 For a detailed account of Curione's life, see M'Crie (1833, 129–133).

8 Little Gidding was the home of a religious community established in 1626 by Nicholas Ferrar. This small community was founded around strict adherence to Christian worship in accordance the Book of Common Prayer and the High Church, that is, the Catholic heritage of the Church of England.

Waldesius; and the French translator turned the name into Val D'esso. The principal modern writers upon and translators of Valdes have been the Dr. Edward Boehmer above referred to, two indefatigable Englishmen, Mr. Benjamin B. Wiffen and Mr. John T. Betts, and a Spanish gentleman, Don Luis Usoz y Rio, and these have very naturally adhered to the spelling which Valdes, as a Spaniard, used himself Mr. Betts, in 1865, issued a new translation of the 'Considerations' into English, but the present is the first reprint of Ferrar's translation in its purity since its original appearance at Oxford in 1638, for the Cambridge edition of 1646 is unrecognizable in its distortions. Frederic Chapman. (Valdes: 1905)

Because Mr. Chapman alludes to John Betts and his 1865 translation, it is also fitting to conclude this chapter with Betts's comments regarding the history of a number of renderings of Valdes's *110 Considerations,* as narrated by Benjamin B. Wiffen (1865, 197–205):

> The Italian version of 1550, the *editio princeps,* has been recently republished by Dr. Ed. Boehmer, of Halle; and there is a recent retranslation of it into Spanish, which has appeared in a handsome edition; Professor Schmidt, of Strasbourg, has also retranslated it into French, although not yet printed; whilst there is a German retranslation of it in progress, if it be not already finished. Of the English version, the first edition appeared at Oxford in 1638, in 4to; another was published at Cambridge in 1646, in 12mo. Nicholas Ferrar, the translator, forwarded his MS. to his friend George Herbert, of Bemerton, for his opinion and advice as to its publication.

John Betts then goes on to describe professor Eduard Boehmer's involvement in the project of retranslating Valdes:

> Dr. Boehmer, who has been so variedly and so long engaged upon Valdes' works, and who has recently become his biographer in Herzog's *Real Encyklopaedie,* prompted by veneration for our author, and knowing that the English translation of Valdes' CX Considerations was in progress, wrote to the translator [Betts], and advised him "to make it as simple in mode of expression as it is in the original, unabbreviated and unchanged," and this advice has been studiously carried out; so that, without obtruding his own ideas, the translator has endeavoured to render those of Valdes as faithfully as Valdes did those of St. Paul. My friend Benjamin B. Wiffen, who is well known for his successful researches in connexion with the writings and life of Valdes, and who has assisted to bring to light various of his works supposed by distinguished scholars to have been utterly destroyed and lost—such, for instance, as Valdes' "Alfabeto Christiano"—has now, in the history of "The Life and Writings of Juan de Valdes" which is prefixed to this translation of the 110 Divine Considerations, given extracts from his writings sufficiently copious to enable the general reader to form a conception of the scope and character of works which cannot be easily obtained for perusal, because, though reprinted, this has chiefly been done not for the public at large, but in order to rescue them from total oblivion, by means of private circulation, and preservation in libraries.

These works of Valdesso are, to use Milton's expression, "the precious life-blood of a master-spirit,"—of an apostle, as it were, to the aristocracy of birth and intellect of his day; whom the Inquisition and the Roman Court feared and hated as an heresiarch, but who was acknowledged and honoured of the Holy Spirit to be the Father in Christ (1 Cor. iv. 15) of such personages as Giulia Gonzaga and Vittoria Colonna, of Peter Martyr Vermiglio and of Graleazzo Caraccioli. Peter Martyr Vermiglio, as Dean of Christ Church, Oxford, appointed by Cranmer interpreter of Holy Scripture, began his career at the University by expounding the First Epistle to the Corinthians—a book upon which Juan de Valdes had written a commentary. At the death of Edward VI, Peter Martyr Vermiglio, to escape the persecution of Mary, had to fly England, and filled Protestant chairs both at Strasbourg and Zurich. His friend and pupil, Bishop Jewel, sought safety in exile likewise, and during many years was received as a member in Peter Martyr's household, living at his table. The Zurich letters witness with what reverence both Archbishop Cranmer and Bishop Jewel held Peter Martyr as the master-spirit in Israel; and can it be otherwise than deeply interesting to the English reader to study the sentiments of Juan de Valdes, who moulded the mind of Peter Martyr, the arch-counsellor of the recognised founders of the English Church?

Chapter 5:
Charles V and the Protestant Revolt

> In Spain the venom of heresy began to take root, some who had communicated with
> those infected kingdoms, bringing the pestilence with them. And if it had not been for
> the most vigilant care of the Fathers the Inquisitors that with suitable cauterisings with
> fire, cut down the cancer, the body of the Spanish republic would have been infected, it
> having commenced with some of the principal members.
> Francisco Nuñez de Velasco, *Diálogos de contencion entre la milicia y la ciencia* (1614).

When Queen Isabel died in 1504, her son-in-law Philip the Handsome succeeded
to the crown in Castile as the husband of her daughter Juana. When Philip died
suddenly in 1506, although Juana was declared mentally ill and unable to reign,
she remained the legal queen of Castile until her death. Juana's father Ferdinand,
who was in Naples at the time of his son-in-law's death, assumed the regency of
Castile until his death in 1516, at which time Juana inherited her father's kingdom—Aragon—as well. After the celebration of Ferdinand's obsequies in
March of 1516, Juana's eldest son, sixteen-year-old Charles, was proclaimed king
of both Castile and Aragon jointly with his mother. Charles, who was living in
Ghent at the time, arrived in Spain eighteen months later, in September of 1517.

Charles V meets Luther

In 1517, Pope Leo X had launched a fund-raising campaign to raise money for
the construction of the grand basilica of St. Peter's in Rome. In response to the
pope's campaign, Luther prepared a placard consisting of ninety-five theses for
debate, which, in accordance with the custom of the time, was nailed on the door
of the Wittenberg Castle church. In response to his arguments, a debate was
proposed. Luther was to come to Leipzig to defend his views before the Catholic
theologian John Eck. The debate lasted eighteen days. Two years later, on June 15,
1520, Pope Leo X, in the papal bull *Exsurge Domine*, warned Luther that he would
be excommunicated unless he recanted 41 of his 95 theses within the next sixty
days. Luther immediately drafted an appeal of his case and sent it to the emperor
of the Holy Roman Empire, Charles V.[1] It took the young king nearly a year to

---

1 After the death of his paternal grandfather Maximilian, in 1519, Charles became the natural
 candidate of the electors to succeed him as Holy Roman Emperor. He defeated the candidacies
 of Frederick III, Elector of Saxony, Francis I of France, and Henry VIII of England. Finally, in
 1530 he was crowned Holy Roman Emperor by Pope Clement VII in Bologna. He was the last
 emperor to receive a papal coronation and at the age of twenty Charles V ruled the largest
 collection of lands since Charlemagne.

reply. Finally, on March 11, 1521, Charles sent Luther an invitation to come to the Diet at Worms with a safe-conduct if he arrived within twenty-one days.

Luther and a small band of supporters entered Worms on the evening of April 16. We are all familiar with Luther's heroic stand before the emperor and the ecclesiastical dignities. On May 6, a final draft of the Edict of Worms, prepared by papal nuncio Girolamo Aleandro (Jerome Aleander), was submitted to the Diet. It called for the burning of Luther's books and the confiscation of his property.[2] It cut him off from the church, called for his arrest, and forbid anyone from harboring or sustaining him. Finally, it warned that anyone who dared to directly or indirectly oppose this decree would be guilty of the crime of *lèse-majesté* (violating majesty). It took Charles V twenty days to sign the edict. Could this suggest internal debates regarding the same? William de Croy, his former tutor and advisor, opposed the violent persecution of Martin Luther, but Charles turned a deaf ear to de Croy's advice and took that of his other advisor, Adrian Florensz, who had been his tutor since he was seven years old. In 1515, Charles had sent Adrian Florensz to Spain to convince his grandfather Ferdinand that all the Spanish lands should come under his rule, and not that of his Spanish-born younger brother Ferdinand—a task Adrian carried out successfully. In recompense, Charles had made him bishop of Tortosa and inquisitor general. In 1517, Pope Leo X made Adrian a cardinal and on January 9, 1522, he became Pope Adrian VI. His papacy lasted only one year, for he died the following year.

Charles V's Entourage

Luther's excommunication produced sympathetic curiosity rather than total rejection. The young Spaniards that formed Charles V's imperial entourage and accompanied the young emperor to Worms in 1521 were intrigued by what they heard and saw. Juan de Vergara, a scholar from Alcala present at the Diet of Worms as secretary to cardinal William de Croy, described the scene thus: "Everyone flocked to see Luther, especially the Spaniards." At his trial in Toledo, twelve years later, Vergara recalled that in Germany the court of his majesty was full of Luther's books (Longhurst: 1969, 235; Bataillon: 1966, 110). Juan de Valdes's older brother Alfonso, who was Charles V's Latin secretary and who accompanied him on his journey from Spain to his coronation as king of Germany at Aachen in October 1520, was also present at the Diet of Worms. At Aachen, Alfonso met both Erasmus and Luis Vives, who were serving in the entourage of Charles V at that time. Erasmus was imperial chancellor and Vives

---

2 By then Luther had published *The Sermon on Good Works*, *The Papacy in Rome*, *The Babylonian Captivity*, and *The Freedom of the Christian Man*.

was companion to Cardinal William de Croy, first chamberlain to Charles V (Schulte Herbrüggen: 1998, 34, note 87). At Worms, Alfonso would also have meet the papal nuncio Pietro Paulo Vergerio,[3] who thirty years later would turn Protestant and would be accredited with having taken out of Italy a manuscript copy of Alfonso's brother Juan's *Divine Considerations.*

As one of the emperor's personal secretaries, Alfonso de Valdes was also present at the Diet of Augsburg in 1530, where he took the part of moderator between Catholics and Protestants. It was there that he met Philip Melanchthon. Thomas M'Crie (1829, 132–133) provides some details of this encounter that he gleaned from trustworthy sources:

> In one of the conversations between these two learned men, held in the presence of Cornelius Scepper, an agent of the king of Denmark, Melanchthon lamented the strong prejudices which the natives of Spain had conceived against the reformers, and said that he had frequently endeavoured, both by word of mouth and by letters, to convince them of the misconceptions under which they labored, but with very little success. Valdes acknowledged that is was a common opinion among his countrymen, that Luther and his followers believed neither in God nor the Trinity, in Christ nor the Virgin; and that in Spain it was thought as meritorious an action to strangle a Lutheran as to shoot a Turk.

While in Augsburg, one of Alfonso de Valdes's duties was to translate the Confession of Augsburg into Spanish for the emperor. Unfortunately, this translation has been lost. In all his activities, whether political or religious, Alfonso displayed a refined irenic spirit. He was a staunch defender of the celebration of a council to put an end to the disputes between Catholics and Protestants. His two dialogs, *Dialogo de Mercurio y de Caron* (1529?) and *Dialogo de las cosas ocurridas en Roma* (1530?) (Dialog of Mercury and Caron, and Dialog of the Things that Happened in Rome), are of great historical and literary value. The doctrinal commentaries of Caron—Alfonso's literary persona—remind us of opinions very similar to those of his brother Juan. Alfonso de Valdes was harsh in his criticism of the Catholic hierarchy for their corrupt morals and earthly ambitions. He was convinced that the sack of Rome by the imperial troops in 1527 complied with a just punishment from God for the ungodly conduct of the papal powers and for their "abominable pagan practices" and the superstitions fostered by the clergy. Regarding the scandal of a warring pope, he comments:

> Where do you find that Jesus Christ commanded his followers to make war? Read all of the gospels, read all the canonical letters, and you only find peace, harmony, unity, love

---

3 Pietro Paulo Vergerio, legate from the pope to the German princes, was the person employed by the German nobleman Burchard Schenk in 1516 to collect relics for the elector of Saxony for the collegiate church of Wittenberg.

and charity. When Jesus was born no bells rang, only the angels sang, *Gloria in excelsis Deo, et in térra pax hominibus bonae voluntatis!* Regarding the Pope, I am amazed. He ought to be the mirror of all Christian virtues and the model we should all admire, who, instead of keeping us all in peace and harmony, even if his life were at danger, wants to make war to obtain and hold that which Jesus Christ told us to despise, and that he should find, among Christians, men who support him in such an enterprise so wickedly, so appalling and so detrimental to the honor of Christ. What blindness is this? We call ourselves Christians and we live worse than the Turks and brute beasts. (Valdes: 1952).

The mercantile interests of Rome did not escape Alfonso's harsh criticism. In *Dialogo de Mercurio y de Caron,* he refers to the spiritual corruption in which Roman Catholicism had fallen as "pestilential." His description of the relics constitutes one of the most graphic and eloquent historical documents of this spiritual darkness. When Mercurio visits the papal seat, he remarks: "for three days I had to cover my nose because of the unbearable stench that issued from Rome." (Valdes: 1952). Without a doubt, the literary gifts of the two Valdes brothers make them important figures in the cultural and religious scenario of the early sixteenth century. Alfonso died of the plague in Vienna in October 1532, about the time his brother Juan was getting ready to leave Rome for Naples. With his passing, says Bataillon (1966, 429), the emperor lost an irreplaceable steward and Erasmianism lost its most zealous advocate.

A Hebrew chronicle narrating the arrival of the Spanish troops in Vienna describes their arrival and the sudden retreat, makes no mention of a plague. According to the chronicle,

On the eighth day of October, Emperor Charles came with his brother Ferdinand to the city of Vienna with a great multitude approximately three times one hundred and forty-three thousand, and there was great fear because the Turks were approaching with 3000 ships. They were there nearly ten days when the Emperor sent his men home without a battle. There was great bewilderment everywhere as to why he mustered them and then sent them home. (David: 2006, 42).

Charles's sudden retreat was obviously due to the impending plague. A dispatch written from Bologna by Dr. Augustine de Augustinis, the Venetian physician resident in London employed on several diplomatic missions by Henry VIII, dated October 14, 1532, states: "One reason for [the Emperor's] leaving Vienna for Italy was the plague, by which the secretary Valdes lost his life." (Letters and Papers, 1880).

Charles V's Attitude towards Dissidence

Charles V had barely assumed his role as emperor when he found himself involved in several conflicts both at home and abroad. Charles had arrived in the Peninsula in 1517 with a large entourage of Flemish attendants to whom he assigned the main public posts. Villages and cities in Castile united in a common cause—known as the *Comunero* Uprising (1520–1521)—to rebel against the absolutist and centralizing pretensions of the monarch in defense of their traditional liberties and privileges. The emperor, who was in Worms at the time, ordered Cardinal Adrian Florensz, whom he had sent to Spain as acting regent, to declare war on the rebels. In April 1521, after intense battles, the royal troops entered the city of Mora in the province of Toledo and massacred the population. Finally, the *comuneros* were defeated near the village of Villalar, in the province of Valladolid, and the rebel leaders were condemned to death.[4] The victory of the coalition in favor of the imperial crown of Castle, says Jose Nieto (1997, 97), made it impossible for a political situation similar to that of Germany with its powerful and independent nobility, or that of Switzerland, to exist in Spain. Although the nobility could—and did—sympathize with spiritual movements that were more or less heterodox, they had neither the power nor the autonomy to defend the civil rights and conscience of their dissident subjects. The little autonomy they enjoyed was irreparably lost with the defeat of the *comuneros*. In Villalar two fundamental liberties died for the whole country: political liberty and religious liberty. As Thomas M'Crie (1829, 119) puts it,

> Formerly the victims of persecution had often found shelter within the independent domains of the nobles, or the privileged walls of great cities. Cardinal Ximenes, by flattering the commons without adding to their real consequence, had succeeded in breaking the power of the nobility. Charles pursued the line of policy, which his minster had begun, by invading the rights of the people. Irritated by the assistance which the latter had given to the attack on their immunities, the nobles stood aloof from the contest which ensued, or sided with the crown. The consequence was, that the commons, after an enthusiastic resistance, were subdued; the cortes and the chartered towns were stripped of their privileges; and the authority of the sovereign became absolute and despotical throughout the united kingdom.

In May of 1521, a week after the *comunero* revolt was crushed and the political dissidents eliminated, the Supreme Council, in the name of the emperor, turned against Spain's religious dissidents and issued instructions that "no person sell nor have nor read nor preach about the books of this heretic [Luther] nor speak of his errors and heresies either in public or in secret." (Longhurst: 1969, 15). In July, when the papal nuncio Aleandro discovered that Spanish editions of Lu-

---

4 Shortly after that massacre, Adrian was elected pope thanks to the support of Charles V.

ther's writings were being printed in Antwerp, he rounded up all the copies he could find and consigned them to the flames of a great public bonfire (Bataillon: 1966, 132). Moreover, it must be remembered that the Protestant revolt had ushered in "a major religious change in the Holy Roman Empire. Charles's northern territories were threatened by the spread of Lutheranism and the Spaniards were taking precautions not to be affected by it." (Hamilton: 1992, 55; Firpo: 2007, 457–480).

In 1538, Charles V found himself involuntarily involved in the Erasmian controversy. Nowhere had Erasmus's writings rouse such sympathetic feelings as in Spain, but gradually two hostile camps formed: the Erasmistas and anti-Erasmistas. In 1526, archdeacon Alfonso Fernandes, the translator of the *Enchiridion*, wrote Inquisitor General Alonso Manrique that certain friars were preaching against Erasmus, and were demanding that certain of Erasmus's writings should be condemned. To examine his writings, Inquisitor General Manrique called together a body of theologians at Valladolid in 1527, but no agreement was reached. Fray Alonso de Virues, who had been the emperor's preacher from 1524 to 1526, and had spoken in favor of Erasmus at the Valladolid conference, was arrested in 1533 and confined to prison in Seville for four years. Finally, in 1537, he was made to abjure his errors, sentenced to confinement in a monastery for another two years, and banned from preaching. In order to save Virues, in May of 1538 Charles obtained from Pope Paul III a bull annulling the sentence. He was restored to favor and appointed bishop of the Canary Island, where he died in 1545 (Kamen: 2014, 98). Alonso de Virues was the first of several of the emperor's preachers to be accused of heresy. More would follow.

The emperor was kept informed of dissident activity in his northern territories, but he also had other matters to deal with in the Mediterranean. The Ottoman admiral Hayreddin Barbarossa had been conducting raids along the coast of Italy and finally conquered Tunis on August 16, 1534.[5] Charles rapidly assembled a large army of some 30,000 soldiers, 74 galleys, and 300 sailing ships and a year later destroyed Barbarossa's fleet and recaptured Tunis. On his way back to Europe, he stopped off at Naples. The city had been hit by pestilence in 1529 and 1530 and was suffering from political disorder. Protestantism had also spread throughout the Neapolitan territories, especially in the capital. It is thought that German soldiers, who, after the sack of Rome in 1527 garrisoned the city for some time, had first introduced Protestant ideas there. M'Crie (1833, 134) adds another detail:

> The Germans were succeeded by a person who, according to the account of a contemporary popish historian, 'caused a far greater slaughter of souls than all the

---

5 Barbarossa's naval victories secured Ottoman dominance over the Mediterranean for more than thirty years, from 1538 until the Battle of Lepanto in 1571.

thousands of heretical soldiery.' This was Juan Valdes, or as he is sometimes called, Valdesso, a Spanish gentleman.

Charles V remained in the city from November 25, 1535, to March 22, 1536, and was entertained royally at the Castel dell'Ovo, a palace located on the island of Megaride, in the Gulf of Naples. His entourage was accommodated at the magnificent palace of the Princes of Salerno, Ferrante de Sanseverino and his Spanish wife Isabel de Vilamari, located just outside the western boundary of the historic center of the city.[6] The emperor's stay in Naples would have coincided with the year the famous Capuchin Bernardino Ochino was guest preacher during Lent in Naples. As a popular preacher he was in great demand during Lent, and everywhere—Siena, Naples, Rome, Florence, Venice—he attracted crowds of people. That year he preached in the church of San Giovanni Maggiore. Among those who went to hear him were Guilia Gonzaga, Vittoria Colonna, Pier Paolo Vergerio, and others who would later join Juan de Valdes's circle. It appears that even the emperor went to hear him and was known to have said that Ochino "preached with such spirit, and so much devotion, that he made the very stones weep." (Eamon: 1996, 153).

For the next several years Charles V was occupied with the Italian Wars. Early on, he had tried to win the German princes to his side by showing lenience in religious matters at the Diet of Speyer in 1526. After his second war with France, in 1529, Charles directed his energies to countering the further spread of the Reformation. That year, at another diet held at Speyer, a decree was issued to annul the concessions granted in 1526, but certain princes and cities protested. It was at the Diet of Speyer of 1529 that the term "Protestant" was used for the first time to designate the German princes who protested against the edict issued that year that overruled concessions made earlier. The Diet of Augsburg (1530) attempted to calm rising tensions, especially due to fears of the rising Ottoman threat and Charles V's desire for Christianity to unite against the Turks. Elector John of Saxony asked Martin Luther, Justus Jones, Johannes Bugenhagen, and Philip Melanchthon to write up a summary of the Lutheran doctrines to be laid before the emperor at the diet.[7] A final form was adopted with the help of

---

6 This property was confiscated by the Inquisition in 1552 and eventually sold in the 1580s to the Jesuits and converted into the Church of Gesù Nuovo. The new church retained the facade with its rustic ashlar diamond projections originally built for the palace.

7 Justus Jonas's great admiration for Erasmus had led him to the study of Greek and Hebrew, but after the Leipzig debate with John Eck in 1519 Martin Luther won his allegiance. Jonas accompanied Luther to the Diet of Worms in 1521 and also played a prominent role in the conferences at Marburg (1529) and Augsburg (1530). Considered today one of the forgotten Reformers, Justus Jonas was in his day a popular Protestant authors in Spain. In the list of confiscated books published by the Inquisition in 1563, many of Jonas's works appear. See Appendix A.

Christian Beyer, bishop of Augsburg, and the imperial secretary Alfonso de Valdes.

In 1544, when Charles V returned to Germany from the Italian War after he had signed the Treaty of Crépy, he had to contend with the demands of the Schmalkaldic League, a defensive alliance of Lutheran princes within the Holy Roman Empire. For fifteen years the League was able to exist without opposition, mainly because Charles was busy fighting wars with France and the Turks. After Charles made peace with France, he focused again on suppressing Protestant resistance within his empire. From 1546 to 1547, he and his allies fought the Schmalkaldic League. Although the League's military forces may have been superior, on April 24, 1547, the imperial forces defeated them at the Battle of Mühlberg. Despite this defeat, by the 1550s Protestantism had established itself too firmly within Central Europe to be ended by brute force.

Following his victory at Mühlberg, Charles V became more ruthless. In 1549, he promulgated The Pragmatic Sanction, which reorganized the Dutch provinces, created new bishoprics, and put into effect new laws against heresy. Indeed, in April 1550, Charles gave orders that the Inquisition in the Netherlands could arrest any heretic, including foreigners. In Germany, his authority was limited by the German princes and he was determined not to let this happen in the Netherlands. Things came to a head in September of 1550 when he published his "Edicto Perpetuo de Augsburgo" against heretics, threatening,

> Anyone, whatsoever his rank or condition, who shall print, transcribe, copy, or knowingly receive, carry, keep, conceal, have in his possession, sell, buy, give, distribute, scatter, or let fall in churches, or on the street, or in other places, any books or writings composed by Martin Luther, John Oecolampadius, Ulrich Zwingli, Martin Bucer, John Calvin, or other heretics or promoters of their sects. (Martínez Peñas: 2012, 51).

The English chronicler and geographer Richard Hakluyt (1584) adds another dimension to Charles's plan of action and relates how it was also the emperor's intention to establish the Inquisition in Antwerp, but that economic factors restrained him:

> Anno 1550. Charles the Fifth, then Emperour, would have had the Spanish Inquisition brought into Antwerp and into the Netherlands; whereabout there was much ado, and that neither the suite of the town of Antwerp, nor the request of their friends, could persuade the Emperour from it, till at the last they told him plainly, that if the Inquisition came into Antwerp and the Netherlands that the English merchants would depart out of the town and out of his countries; and upon declaration of this suggestion, search was made what profile there came and comoditie grew by the haunt of the English merchants. Then was it found by search and enquiry, that within the town of Antwerp alone, there were fourteen thousand persons fed and maintained only by the working of English commodities, besides the gains that merchants and shippers with

others in the said town did get, which was the greatest parte of their living, which were thought to be in number half as many more; and in all other places of his Netherlands by the indrapping of English wool into cloth, and by the working of other English commodities, there were thirty thousand persons more maintained and fed; which in all amount to sixty thousand persons. And this was the report that was given to this mighty Emperour, whereby the town of Antwerp and the Netherlands were saved from the Inquisition.

On the Spanish scene, matters also tightened up that year. Recently appointed archbishop of Toledo, Cardinal Juan Martínez Siliceo, long-time friend of the emperor and tutor of crown prince Philip, strictly imposed the statute of *limpieza de sangre* (cleanliness of blood), which excluded all descendants of *conversos*, heretics, or anyone sentenced by the Holy Office from holding ecclesiastical offices in his archbishopric. Five years later, Philip II—then regent not yet king—extended the regulation and passed a statute requiring a certificate of purity of blood prior to entry into any office in all of Spain. Prior to this, new Christians had only been banned admission to individual religious orders, cathedral chapters, guilds, military orders, or colleges. Sicileo's resolution was emphatic:

> We ordain and order that from now on and forever more all the persons that in this our church are to be incumbents and to have entry as dignitaries, canons, or prebendary chaplains, whether they be famous persons, nobles, sons of nobles, or lawyers graduated from famous universities, must be old Christians, and that none of the above be of Jewish, or Moorish, or heretical descent, and that no one be received or admitted without proof of his old Christian ancestry. (De Espona: 2005, 49)

Having been duly informed by Siliceo before the statute was enacted, the emperor may have considered the "Judaizing" threat resolved. His—and the Inquisition's—next battle was the Protestant threat. Unwilling to allow the wars of religion to come into his other domains, Charles V pushed for the convocation of the Council of Trent (Kamen: 1988, 3–23). By 1555, forced to recognize the failure of his religious policy, and in poor health, Charles decided to abdicate. He announced his intention from Brussels in the presence of his son prince Philip and his sister Mary, queen of Hungary and regent of the Netherlands. In a speech pronounced before the nobles on October 25, 1555, Charles summarized his reign thus:

> Some of you will remember that on the 5th of January of this year, exactly forty years had passed since the day when, in this same hall, at the age of fifteen, I received the rule over the Belgian provinces from my paternal grandfather, Emperor Maximilian. Soon thereafter, the death of my maternal grandfather, King Ferdinand the Catholic, brought to me the rule over an inheritance that my mother was too ill to administer. Thus, at the age of seventeen, I sailed over the sea to take possession of the Kingdom of Spain. When I was nineteen, upon the emperor's death, I undertook to be a candidate for the

Imperial crown, not to increase my possessions but rather to engage myself more vigorously in working for the welfare of Germany and my other provinces, namely the Belgian provinces, and in the hopes of thereby bringing peace among the Christian peoples and uniting their fighting forces for the defense of the Catholic faith against the Ottomans. It was partly the German heresy and partly the envoy of rival powers that prevented me from fully achieving the goal of my efforts. With God's help, I have nonetheless never ceased resisting my foes or striving to fulfill my mission. The campaigns I undertook, some to begin wars, some to make peace, took me nine times to Germany, six times to Spain, seven times to Italy, four times to France, twice to England, and twice to Africa in a total of four great journeys, not to mention the less important visits I paid over the years to my individual realms.

I have crossed the Mediterranean Sea eight times and sailed the Atlantic Ocean twice, not to speak of the journey I made from Spain to the Netherlands for the very serious reasons about which you know. Although involved in many wars, I have never gone happily to battle, and as I take leave of you, nothing is more painful than my inability to leave you in a firm, secure state of peace. Already before my last campaign in Germany, my pitiful state of health prompted me to consider the idea of divesting myself of the burdens of state, but the troubles, which then beset Christendom forced me to give up this plan in the hopes that peace could be restored. Because I felt stronger then than I do now, I held it for my duty to sacrifice my remaining strength and my life for my peoples' welfare. I had almost reached my goal, when the attack by the French king and some German princes called me once more to arms. Against my enemies I accomplished what I could, but success in war lies in the hands of God, who gives victory or takes it away, as He pleases. Above all, avoid those new sects that plague our neighboring lands, and when heresy seeps over your boundaries, do not delay in wiping it out, or it will go badly for you. I must for my part confess that I have often misled myself, either from youthful inexperience, from the pride of mature years, or from some other weakness of human nature. I nonetheless declare to you that I never knowingly or willingly acted unjustly or with unjust force, nor did I ever command or empower another to do so. If actions of this kind are nevertheless justly laid to my account, I formally assure you now that I did them unknowingly and against my own intention. I therefore beg those present today, whom I have offended in this respect, together with those who are absent, to forgive me. (Brady: 1990).

At that point, the emperor turned to crown prince Philip, his son and heir, and pronounced the following words:

Other kings account themselves happy when, at the hour of death, they can set their crowns on their children's heads, but I wished to experience this joy while yet alive, and to see you rule. What I am doing will hardly be imitated in future, as it has rarely been done in the past, but I will be praised for it, if you justify my trust by ruling with the wisdom you have heretofore displayed, and if you continue to be a zealous defender of the Catholic faith, of the law, and of justice, which are the bulwarks of rulership. (Brady: 1990).

Charles V abdicated in January of 1556. The Austrian branch of the Holy Roman Empire passed on to his younger brother Ferdinand and the Spanish branch—the combined inheritances of his parents, Isabel and Ferdinand, together with the kingdoms of Sicily, Naples, and Milan, and the recently discovered territories in the New World—was inherited by his son Philip, who had just become king of England through his marriage to Mary Tudor.

According to the Spanish historian Prudencio de Sandoval, in his *Historia de la vida y hechos del Emperador Carlos V* (1604), shortly before his death, Charles V expressed deep regret that he had not executed Luther at Worms, in spite of his pledged safe-conduct, for he ought to have "forfeited his word in order to avenge the offence to God." In his will, executed in 1554 at Brussels, he charged Philip in the most earnest manner to favor in all ways the Inquisition, "because of the many and great offences to God which it prevents or punishes." (Lea: 1906–07, 499).[8] Philip lost no time in putting into practice his father's admonition to be a "zealous defender of the Catholic faith." In June he sent Bartolome de Carranza, who was still with him in Flanders, back to Spain to take up the duties of his recent appointment as archbishop of Toledo and to deliver letters to his sister, princess Juana, acting governess at that time, and to the Supreme Council, in which he strongly warned them of the danger the advance of Lutheranism posed for the empire (Azpilcueta: 2011, 465). From his retirement in Yuste, Charles V wrote his daughter Juana two very moving letter—dated May 3 and May 25, 1558—in which he expressed his deep concern for the advance of Lutheranism in Spain, insisting again and again in the need for capital punishment regardless who the offenders be (Fernández Álvarez: 1979, 75). These letters were written just after the group of evangelicals had been discovered and incarcerated in Valladolid. Among the "offenders" was his court preacher, Agustin de Cazalla, who would be sent to the stake one year later.

In a letter to his sister, dated October 16, 1558, Philip, who was still in Flanders, informed her that he had received news from friends saying that in Seville Constantino—the preacher who had accompanied him on his European tour only a few years earlier—and Maestro Blanco—prior of the San Isidoro Monastery in Santiponce—had been imprisoned for heresy. Philip added, "It appears that this heresy [Lutheranism] is becoming widespread, hence a remedy must be found before it is too late." Two months later, he wrote her again showing his greatest astonishment, and displeasure, that in all the official correspondence that had arrived from Spain in the past months not a word was mentioned about

---

8 Lea found this information in the 1625 Barcelona edition of Sandoval's work, Vol. II, 740, 777, 792.

this matter, and he again insisted that the most severe punishment be imposed on the offenders.[9]

Aware of this reality, and in the absence of her brother, princess-regent Juana had already issued a proclamation earlier that year that established a severe system of censorship, prohibiting the import of books written in Spanish printed abroad. Adolfo de Castro (1851, 16–17), in his *The Spanish Protestants and their persecution by Philip II*, quotes several early modern Catholic authors corroborating this danger:

> Gonzalo de Illescas, a Catholic author, says in his *Historia Pontifical* (Salamanca, 1569–1573), "In past years, Lutheran heretics in greater or less numbers, were wont to be taken and burnt in Spain; but all those that were so punished were foreigners, viz. Germans, Flemings, or Englishmen. At other times people poor and of mean birth, used to be sent to the scaffold, and to have San Benitos in the churches; but in these later years, we have seen the prisons, the scaffolds, and even the burning pile crowded with illustrious people, and (what is even more to be deplored) persons who in the opinion of the world were greatly superior to others in letters and in virtue. I withhold their names in order not to tarnish with their injured reputation, the fair fame of their descendants, or even of some illustrious houses to whom this poison attaches. They are such and so many that it was believed if two or three months more had been suffered to elapse before applying a remedy to this mischief the conflagration would have spread itself all over Spain, and brought upon her the most dire misfortunes she has ever seen."

> Francisco Nunez de Velasco says, in his *Diálogos de contencion entre la milicia y la ciencia* (Valladolid, 1614), "in Spain it began to take root, (the venom of heresy), some who had communicated with those infected kingdoms, bringing the pestilence with them. And if it had not been for the most vigilant care of the Fathers the Inquisitors that with suitable cauterisings with fire, cut down the cancer, the body of the Spanish republic would have been infected, it having commenced with some of the principal members."

> The chronicler Antonio de Herrera, in *La Historia General del Mundo* (Madrid, 1601), says, "With the good diligence brought to bear by the Holy Office, the evil was marvelously cut short, which if neglected would have greatly increased."

The hopes the Erasmian scholars had set on crown prince Philip during his 1548 European tour were shattered when Philip's entourage returned to Flanders in 1555. By then, the religious and political landscape had changed and Philip was about to embark in his anti-Protestant crackdown (Pérez Fernández: 2012, 299–318). Even the Catholic Encyclopedia describes Philip II as "merciless in the suppression of the Lutheran heresy." One of the characteristics of his reign was its Spanishness. After his return from Flanders in 1559, Philip never again left the Peninsula. He never even seems to have travelled as far as to Seville. His con-

---

9 AHN, Inquisición, lib. 1267, fol. 19r, in: Lopez Muñoz (2011, 122, doc. 45). Brackets mine.

temporaries saw him as a spider sitting motionless in the center of his web (Braudel: 1995, 676).

In September 1559 Philip returned to Spain. His first public appearance was to preside over the second great *auto-da-fe* in Valladolid. Two months later, on November 22, 1559, he gave the final blow to Spanish humanism by promulgating a royal *Pragmatica* that ordered all Spanish youth studying abroad to return home within four months. This proclamation forbade all Spanish subjects to study at foreign universities, with the exception of Bologna, Rome, Naples, and Coimbra, under penalty of confiscation and perpetual exile. Philip based this action on three main reasons: the Spanish universities were losing too many students; too much money was flowing out of the country to maintain students studying abroad; and—last but not least—these students, apart from the hardships, expenses, and dangers they were exposed to, "by communicating with foreigners, are led astray, and abandon the right way." The American historian, William Gilbert (1998), describes the era thus:

> In the reign of Ferdinand and Isabella and in the early sixteenth century, Spain was still open to the rest of the world and receptive to new ideas and experiences. Several universities were founded, and printing was introduced into the country. Before 1500 there were presses in twenty-five Spanish towns, and a law of 1480 permitted the importation of books duty-free. All this was quickly changed by the fear of Protestantism, and in the reign of Philip II this intensified. In 1559, he ordered all Spaniards teaching or studying abroad to return home. The prosecution of leading intellectuals continued and their example was enough to frighten a great many others into silence. Censorship was a constant concern of the Inquisition and of the government as well.

Not only were the students called back and the borders closed, but foreign trade was also affected. English merchants had enjoyed special trade agreements from the time of Henry VIII and the Merchant Venturers of Bristol had had factors at Cadiz and San Lucar de Barrameda since 1526, but religious and political changes in England after 1558 brought them increasingly under the scrutiny of the Inquisition. Instructions sent to the inquisitors at Seville from the Supreme Council in January of 1560 urged them to dispense with the commercial agreements and immunity granted to English merchants trading in Spain and to condemn anyone found guilty of having, or introducing, heretical books, "for in matters of religion it is not fitting to grant concessions, but rather to deal uncompromisingly with them."[10] Nicholas Burton, an English factor living in Cadiz, was one of the first to suffer. He was burned at the stake in Seville on December 22, 1560, for simply having an English Bible among his belongings.

---

10 AHN, Inquisición, lib. 575, fol. 91v, in: Lopez Muñoz (2011, 181, doc. 87)

Clandestine Protestant Literature enters Spain

A recurrent theme in the study of underground Protestantism in sixteenth century Spain is the discovery and confiscation of Bibles and prohibited literature. As the century moved on, many of those who at the University of Alcala had declared themselves Erasmians now turned to the German reformers. Likewise, many of those who travelled abroad as part of the emperor's entourage or participants in the discussions at Trent, or students or professors at the Sorbonne, or simply merchants or book dealers trading at the northern fairs, returned with broader outlooks and more eclectic world views that gave way to inquiring minds in search of more satisfying spirituality.[11] In 1519, even before Luther appeared before the emperor at the Diet of Worms, his books were being sent to Spain. This is evidenced from a letter dated February 14, 1519, written from Basel by Johannes Froben to Luther in which he informed him that:

> Blasius Salmonius, a bookseller of Leipzig, presented me, at the last Frankfort fair, with certain treatises composed by you, which being approved by learned men, I immediately put to press, and sent six hundred copies to France and Spain. My friends assure me, that they are sold at Paris, and read and approved of even by the Sorbonists. Several learned men there have said, that they have long wished to see divine things treated with such becoming freedom. [Francesco] Calvus, a bookseller of Pavia, himself a scholar and addicted to the muses, has carried a great part of the impression into Italy. (M'Crie: 1833, 51).[12]

In March of 1521, Pope Leo X addressed a brief to the Spanish authorities warning them against the introduction of Luther's books. On April 7, even before the Diet of Worms had concluded, Inquisitor General Adrian, who had remained behind in Spain to put down the revolt of the *comuneros*, published the first directive against the writings of Martin Luther:

> We have been informed that some persons, with evil intent and in order to sow cockles in the Church of God and to rend the seamless tunic of Christ our Redeemer, have extended their efforts to bring into Spain the works recently written by Martin Luther,

---

11 "In Italy also," says the Venetian historian, Pietro Paolo Sarpi, speaking of this period, "as there had neither been pope nor papal court at Rome for nearly two years, and as most men looked on the calamities which had fallen on both as the execution of a divine judgment, on account of the corruptions of its government, many listened with avidity to the Reformation; in several cities, and particularly at Faenza, which was situated within the territories of the pope, sermons were delivered in private houses against the church of Rome; and the number of those named Lutherans, or, as they called themselves, Evangelicals, increased every day." Fra Paolo Sarpi (1686), Histoire du Concile de Trente, Amsterdam: G.P. & J. Blaeu, Vol. I, 87, cf. M'Crie: 1833, 84.

12 According to M'Crie (1829, 124), in the course of the following year, Luther's commentary on the Galatians was translated into Spanish, followed by his treatise on Christian liberty and his reply to Erasmus on free-will.

of the order of Saint Augustine, which works are said to be printed in Spanish for publication and sale in this kingdom. It is eminently proper for the honor and service of God and the exalting of our holy Catholic faith that such works not be published or sold, nor appear anywhere in this kingdom, because they contain heretical errors and many other suspect things about the faith. We therefore direct you to order, under pain of grave censures, as well as civil and criminal punishment, that nobody dare to own, sell, or permit to be sold in public or in private, any such books or any parts of them, and that within three days of the publication of your order such books, in both Latin and Spanish, be brought and presented before you. When this is done you will then burn them all in public, directing the notary of your Holy Office to record the names of all persons who possess, sell, publish and bring before you such books, and the records of their burning, including the number of books burned. (Longhurst: 1969, 14)

Two years later, on May 7, 1523, the inquisitors in Navarre received a letter from the Supreme Council denouncing the distribution of Lutheran books and ordered them to publish an edict to the effect that, under pain of excommunication and other heavy censures and civil and criminal punishments, any doctor, licentiate, *bachiller*, cleric or other person, of whatsoever estate, grade or condition he be, who has in his possession any such books—in either Latin or Spanish—must turn them in within fifteen days. Six months later, they received another note:

We are informed that in that province of Guipuzcoa there are some of the said books [in circulation], from which it appears that you did not take the proper action to carry out our directive [of May 7] or to do what we charged you to do. We are very surprised at this. (Longhurst: 1969, 17)

Inquisitor General Alonso Manrique's warnings continued in the same vain. He complained that,

Some persons, showing little fear of God and of the Inquisition, have brought into Spain and have in their possession many books of the accursed heretic Luther and his followers. All persons were ordered to bring to the Inquisition whatsoever books and writings of any and all works written by the said perverse heretic and his followers, and to denounce any persons whom they knew or suspected of having such accursed books of that perverse heretic. (Longhurst: 1969, 18)

An incident regarding the sale of Bibles in 1524 in Murcia is reported by the English historian Rawdon Brown, editor of the Calendar of State Papers in the Archives of Venice. Commenting on the items transported by the Flanders galleys, a small fleet of Venetian trading vessels, Brown remarks:

Of an unexpected article of Venetian trade there is mention on at least one occasion. In December 1524, at the port of Almazarron,[13] some officers belonging to the Venetian

---

13 The Port of Mazarron, located some 50 miles to the south of Murcia, became one of the most important Spanish ports after 1479, when deposits of alum (used for dyeing and tanning)

galleys were arrested by the Holy Office for selling Bibles, with commentaries by the
Rabbi Solomon Raschi, a writer of the twelfth century.[14] The prisoners were conveyed to
Murcia; nor could the ambassador, Gasparo Contarini,[15] obtain any immediate redress
from the Emperor, who assured him he would do everything to preserve the friendship
of the Republic, but the Inquisitors had told him the delinquents had been arrested for
selling books against the faith. (Calendar: 1864, Preface. Notes mine).

It would appear that this "illicit trade" continued because in a report sent to Pope
Paul IV on September 9, 1558, Inquisitor General Fernando de Valdes states that
the number of persons accused of Judaizing had decreased considerably until
recently when a groups of them had been discovered in Murcia.[16] Some were
brought to trial:

> Between 1535 and 1555 we can find barely one recorded in two years. We read of a
> Synagogue where Jews seem to have been able to worship almost openly and the
> officiating Rabbi of which escaped punishment until 1562, when he figured at the Auto
> de Fe in Murcia (Adler: 1908, 27).

Edicts continued to be published—1521, 1525, 1530—requiring all persons
possessing books and other works of Luther and his "perverse followers" to
produce and present such books to the Holy Office. This is gleaned from a
dispatch sent by Diego Ortiz de Angulo, prosecutor in the case of Bernardino de
Tovar, to the inquisitors at Toledo:

> Toledo, December 1, 1530
> I (Diego Ortiz de Angulo) petition your graces to direct one of the notaries of the secreta
> of the said Holy Office to make a certified copy of the publication, reading and contents
> of the edicts which have been read and published by the said Holy Office in this city and
> archbishopric of Toledo, against Luther and his books, works and adherents, since the
> year 1521 to the present, especially the edict which his most reverend lordship,
> Archbishop at Seville and Inquisitor General (Alonso Manrique) issued in Madrid on
> April 12, 1525, and which was read and published on that date in the churches of San
> Gines, Santo Domingo, San Nicolas, San Martin and San Miguel in the city of Madrid,
> when the Emperor's court was there, along with the Archbishop of Toledo (Alonso
> Fonseca) and Doctor Vergara. I ask you to direct that this certified copy be placed in the
> trial records against Vergara's brother Tovar, that it may be clearly shown by the
> certified copy of the publication and reading of the said edicts that although Doctor

---

were discovered in the area. Genovese merchants, who had just recently managed to take over
the mines of Tolfa, were particularly interested in exploiting the Mazarron mines, which gave
them a European monopoly on the sulfate. Montojo Montojo: 1993, 272.

14 These were very likely copies of the Second Rabbinic Bible (1524–25) with commentaries by
Rabbi Solomon Raschi printed by Daniel Bomberg, active in Venice between 1516 and 1549:
Biblia Hebraica Bombergii (Venice: Daniel Bomberg, 1521). Bomberg found a ready audience among the Jews of Italy, whose numbers had grown by exiles from Spain and Portugal,
but there must still have been a market in Spain for these Bibles also.

15 Ambassador to the court of Charles V from April 1521 to August 1525.

16 AHN, Inquisición, lib. 245, f. 230r, in: Lopez Muñoz (2011, 134, doc. 49).

Vergara and his brother Tovar knew they could not keep books or works of Luther and his followers, such having been reprobated by the Catholic Church, and knowing further that they were obligated to produce and present in the said Holy Office the books and works of the said Luther and his adherents which they had in their possession, under pain of major excommunication and other punishments, they (nevertheless) allowed themselves to remain under such pain (of excommunication) for a long period after the prohibition and the reading of the said edicts, (thereby demonstrating clearly) their disregard for the censures and spiritual authority of the holy mother Church and their adhesion to Lutheran errors, their heretical beliefs and their disbelief in the binding power and force of excommunication.

The books dealing with Luther and his followers, which Doctor Vergara sent to his lordship, the bishop of Orense, at the end of August, 1530 did not include all of Vergara's books on the said subject, nor did they include the books which contained the most errors and which could have damaged him the most. Nor did he (send these books) to comply with the edict read and published in Madrid in August of this year (1530), nor through fear of the censures contained therein. If he had been impelled by such considerations, he would have surrendered the books long before, at the time of publication of all the previous edicts. (Instead, he finally surrendered them) only after he learned that his brother was seized in Alcala or that they were planning to do so, in the same month of August and he was afraid his brother might reveal the existence of the said books. (Longhurst: 1969, 185–186)

By 1530, tactics for introducing Reformed literature changed. In order to mislead border or port controls, false names and false title pages were used. On June 13, 1530, the Supreme Council wrote, "there is reason to suspect that the writings of such heretics are being brought to Spain and sold as approved works." All tribunals were therefore directed to obtain from booksellers a list of all books in their shops so that the books by authors whose names were unfamiliar might be examined for theological error. Two months later the Council sent around another letter:

A few days ago we were informed that Martin Luther and others among the followers and adherents of his false opinions, and inventors of other new errors, realizing that they are unable to spread their books and poisonous doctrine in these lands as freely as they would like, have introduced many of their harmful opinions under the names of Catholic authors, giving false titles to their books, and in other instances inserting glosses and additions of false expositions and errors to well-known books of approved and good doctrine. All bookstores are to be diligently searched, and because such books might already be in the hands of private parties, the inquisitors are to include in future edicts against Lutheran books a provision requiring the faithful to come forward and inform them of any Lutheran literature in such Catholic disguise.[17]

---

17 AHN, Inquisición, lib. 320, fols. 321v–322r and 343r–v, in: Longhurst (1969, 19).

This same tactic was used to introduce Reformed literature into Italy, where Martin Bucer's *Commentary on the Psalms* was sold as the work of Aretius Fehnus, Philip Melanchthon's *Common Places* as the work of Messer Ippofilo da Terra Negra.[18] According to Thomas M'Crie (1833, 53–55),

> In spite of the terror of pontifical bulls, and the activity of those who watched over their execution, the writings of Luther and Melanchthon, Zwingli and Bucer, continued to be circulated and read with avidity and delight in various parts of Italy. Some of them were translated into the Italian language, and, to elude the vigilance of the inquisitors, were published under disguised and fictitious names, by which means they made their way into Rome and even into the palace of the Vatican; so that bishops and cardinals unwittingly read and praised works, which, on discovering their real authors, they were obliged to pronounce dangerous and heretical.

In 1530, a great public burning of Lutheran books was staged in Toledo. A similar public burning in Salamanca at about the same time did not stop the illicit trade in forbidden literature.[19] During the decade of the 1530s strong links had been established between book dealers from Lyons (France) and Medina del Campo, just north of Valladolid, famous for its bi-annual fairs. Books had been arriving in reams from Lyons, Paris, Antwerp, Cologne, Genoa, Rome, Turin, and Venice since 1529. But the great innovation in the Medina book trade occurred with the establishment of the *Grande Compagnie Lyonnaise*, formed exclusively to export books—mainly Latin Bibles—from Lyons to Medina del Campo and from there to distribute them in the Spanish market, especially to Salamanca. The books left Lyons for Nantes and from there, through the Bay of Biscay, reached Bilbao and were transported by land to Medina. All of the Latin Bibles printed in 1549 had come off the Giacomo Giunta press in Lyons. Giacomo's brother Giovani, who in Spain changed his name to Juan de Junta, had established himself in Medina del Campo in the 1520s and had created a firm with branches in Salamanca, Burgos, and Valladolid. Exporting Latin Bibles to Spain may have looked like good business, but the Spanish authorities would soon react. The exact number of Latin Bibles imported is hard to calculate, but in Seville alone, in 1552, over 300 Latin Bibles and some 30 commentaries, printed in Lyons between 1531 and 1549, were confiscated.[20]

On March 28, 1534, the Supreme Council sent out another circular to the various courts of the Inquisition regarding Lutheran books:

---

18 Aretius (Martin in Greek) Felinus (Bucer in Latin). Philip Melanchton's real name was Schwartzerdt, which in Greek translates into Melanchton and in Italian Terra Negra [black earth].

19 AHN, Inquisición de Toledo, Proceso contra fray Bernardo, leg. 190, no. 4, in: Longhurst (1969, 20).

20 AHN, Inquisición, leg. 4426, doc. 32, in: Lopez Muñoz (2011, 55, doc. 15).

As you know, some time ago we wrote you telling you to find a way that those that have books or writings or treaties of that evil heretic Marin Luther or of any of his followers or adherents should hand them over to you; and those that know of others who have them should tell you. We believe this measure has been very successful. But because we know that many people from this country have gone to Germany in service of the Emperor, our Lord, where those evil heresies, for our sins, are very widespread and observed, it could have happened that they brought back some book, or books, containing that perverse doctrine and errors, it would be a good thing to publish the edicts anew and to add to the list more books and other authors that contain new errors and doctrines contrary to our holy Catholic faith and against the Holy Apostolic See.[21]

The regulations regarding printing that appeared in the *Recopilacion* (Laws of the Kingdom), decreed by the Catholic monarchs in 1480 and enlarged by a bull issued by Pope Alexander VI in 1501, were expanded in 1539 by Pope Paul III at the request of Charles V. The law imposed three basic stipulations, that is, all publications should include: an ecclesiastic license, or censored approval of both the printed page and the illustrations; a privilege, or entitlement; and a "*tasa*," or price, which was calculated in relation to the paper employed, which at that time was a state monopoly.

Index of Prohibited Books

The arrival, in 1550, of a large trunk of "Lutheran" books sent from Brussels by Gaspar Zapata, smuggled in along with the belongings of a nobleman returning to Seville, may have prompted Inquisitor General Fernando de Valdes to publish his first Index of Prohibited Books in 1551, which resulted in the confiscation of over 300 Latin Bibles in Seville alone. Although the list of confiscated Latin Bibles—together with the names of the owners—appeared in 1552, it seems that the Bibles were seized in a raid carried out late 1549 or early 1550 because, of the 45 Bibles printed in 1549, 34 were still in the hands of book dealers.[22] The first Index of Prohibited Books published in Spain (1551) was a reprint of the Index published by the University of Louvain the previous year, with an appendix dedicated to Spanish texts. Subsequent Indexes were published in 1559, 1583, 1612, 1632, 1640, 1667, 1707, 1747, and 1790. On January 2, 1558, the Supreme Council burned some thirty books that had been confiscated in Valladolid.[23] The

---

21 AHN, Inquisición, lib. 573, fol. 14, in: Lopez Muñoz (2011, 43, doc. 1).
22 In 1544, Inquisitor General Valdes had issued an Index of censured Bibles prohibiting all Latin Bible printed abroad. See Tellechea Idígoras (1962, 236–247); Pinta Llorente (1970, 138).
23 AHN, Inquisición, lib. 323, f. 146, in: Schäfer (2014, III, 137–139, doc. 394).

majority were theological books,[24] but the list also included *Flavius Josephus*,[25] two legal scholars,[26] a mathematician,[27] several historians,[28] a botanist,[29] the story of Gamaliel,[30] and even a tale of knight-errantry.[31] Some of the books were in Latin, others in Spanish. Three books by Constantino Ponce de la Fuente— *Exposición del Primer Psalmo* (1546), *Catecismo Christiano* (1547), and *Confesión de un pecador* (1547)—were ordered to be collected, not burned. This may have been simply a cautionary measure because Constantino had not yet been incarcerated.

That year, Inquisitor General Fernando de Valdes sent a letter to the pope in which he stated that everything possible was being done to stop the selling and the entrance into Spain of prohibited literature, which "is the main cause of this disaster, nevertheless, heretics in Germany and other places, who have correspondence with persons here, keep finding new ways to introduce them."[32] In June, the Supreme Council was obliged to clarify certain information sent out earlier:

> We sent you some days ago edicts to be published in your district, prohibiting anyone to read or have in his possession books on Christian Doctrine or theology printed outside Spain from the year 1550 to the present. Because there seems to be some confusion

---

24 Juan Pérez de Pineda's Nuevo Testamento (Venice, 1556); Sumario breue de la doctrina christiana (Venice,1556); Carta enbiada a nuestro augustisimo principe don Felipe rey de España (Geneva, 1557); Los Psalmos de David: con sus sumarios en que se declara con breuedad lo contenido en cada (Venice, 1557); Jubileo de plenissima remision de pecados concedido antiguamente (n.d.); Juan de Valdes's Comentario o declaración breue sobre la epistola de St. Pablo ad Romanos (Venice, 1556); Epistola 1a de s. Pablo a los Corintios (Venice, 1557); Bernardino Ochino's Ymagen del Antechristo, traducido de italiano por Alonso de Peñafuerte (1545); Bartholomaeus Westhemerus's Phrases seu modi loquendi Divinae Scripturae ex sanctis et orthodoxis scriptoribus (Antwerp, 1539); Andrea Osiander's Armonia evangelica cum suis anotationibus, libri IIII Graece et Latine (Basel, 1537); Erasmus's Ecclesiastes siue de ratione contionandi (Basel, 1543); Sebastian Castellio's Dialogi de sacris literis excerpti (Basel, 1542).
25 Flavius Josephus, Los veynte libros de Flauio Iosepho, de las antiguedades Iudaycas (Antwerp, 1554).
26 Melchior Kling, In quatuor institutionum iuris principis Iustiniani libros enarrationes (Lyon, 1554); Conrad Lagus, Methodica iuris utriusque traditio (Lyon, 1546).
27 Hieronymus Cardanus. Liber de immortalitate animorum (Lyon, 1545).
28 Polydoro Vergilio, La invencion y principio de todas las cosas, traducido por Francisco Thomara (Antwerp, 1550); De rerum inventoribus lib. VIII (1499); Otto Frisingensis, Chronicon siue historia Carrionis (1515?).
29 Leonhart Fuchs, Paradoxorum medicinae libri tres (Paris, 1555).
30 Gamaliel, nuevamente traduzido en lengua castellana, hystoriado y con mucha diligencia reconocido y enmendado (Valencia, 1525; Toledo, 1527).
31 Libro de Caualleria Celestial del pie de la Rosa Fragante (Antwerp, 1554).
32 AHN, Inquisición, lib. 245, f. 230r, in: Lopez Muñoz (2011, 129, doc. 49).

whether this prohibition refers to books in Latin or in Spanish, or both, may it be known that the edict refers to books written in Spanish, not those written in Latin.[33]

Despite all these warning clandestine literature continued to arrive. According to Werner Thomas (2001a, 24), in 1560, 1563 and again in 1564 numerous bales of books coming from Lyons and en route to Valladolid and Medina del Campo were intercepted at the French border.

In January of 1562, the inquisitors at Seville gathered all the books they had confiscated, and classified them. Of all the heretical authors they saved one copy of each "in case they might need them in the future" and burned the rest, "which were many." They saved several Bibles and New Testaments in different languages, and deposited the rest in the Hospital del Cardenal. It occurred to them that since these Bibles no longer had owners it would be more useful if, instead of burning them, "with the permission of the Supreme Council," they were expurgated and sold at public auction for the expenses of the Holy Office. Many other books that still required examination and censuring were also taken to the Hospital del Cardenal for Dr. Gonzalo Millan, chaplain and administrator of the hospital, to inspect.[34]

Not only were prohibited books collected in Seville and Valladolid, but also in other cities throughout Spain. In April of 1558, Francisco Sancho, chair professor at the University of Salamanca who for many years he had been in charge of examining prohibited literature in that city, wrote the Supreme Council a detailed letter regarding the books he had in his keeping and asking how closely the edicts were to be followed.[35] For example, he wanted to know if books that had nothing to do with the Catholic faith, such as books on cosmology or astrology, or Latin or Greek or Hebrew grammars, were to be prohibited. Regarding the prohibition of Bibles and New Testaments in Spanish, he asks if the *Gospels and Epistles* and the Psalms read in Spanish during mass must also be prohibited. The answer he received was to strictly comply with the edict that prohibited all the works by Protestant authors. As for the others, the Council was slightly more accommodating.

Whereas most of the books confiscated up until then were in Latin and were read mainly by the clergy, about this time, the inquisitors were caught unawares by an unprecedented event: anti-Catholic literature—written in Spanish by Spaniards for fellow Spaniards—was being distributed clandestinely in all the major cities. Leaflets favoring Luther were being slipped under the doors or

---

33 AHN, Inquisición, lib. 575, f. LXVv–LXVIr, in: Lopez Muñoz (2011, 123, doc. 46). This refers to the proclamation issued by princess Juana.
34 AHN, Inquisición, leg. 2942, doc. 56, in: Lopez Muñoz (2011, 140, doc. 56).
35 AHN, Inquisición, lib. 575, f. LXv. Francisco Sancho is remembered for his involvement in his colleague Fray Luis de Leon's trial.

tossed over the walls of private homes at night in Avila and Toledo.[36] Diego Ramirez, bishop of Toledo, reported "subversive activity" in Toledo on the evening of October 14, 1559, when leaflets against the Catholic church in rhymed verses (*coplas*) were found in six of the chapels of the cathedral and in the doorways of thirty house throughout the city, all copied in the same handwriting.[37] A dispatch sent home by the Venetian ambassador stationed in Toledo, Paulo Tiepolo, on November 14, 1559, describes another event:

> A few days ago some disturbance took place in the Cathedral here, certain scandalous writings having been disseminated there by some heretic, when the church had a full congregation; which being communicated to the Inquisition, the church doors were instantly closed, free egress being granted to all the inhabitants of Toledo; but all foreigners were searched, which operation lasted more than four hours, the individuals arrested being subjected to personal examination to see if they had any of the documents upon them, they being also compelled to give specimens of their handwriting to be compared with the originals; but ultimately the persons arrested were all released, it having been impossible to detect the culprit. (Calendar: 1890, 132–134).

In January of the following year copies continued to surface here and there, but the author(s) had still not been identified.[38] In Seville, the grammarian Juan de Malara (Mal Lara) was arrested as a suspect, and imprisoned.[39] He was later released. New compositions appeared, some in the same handwriting as the former, others in printed form. One that appeared in print in Seville in February of 1561 and that greatly perplexed the inquisitors began thus: "*Cucaracha Martin, cuan pulidica andáis*" (Cockroach Martin, how masterly you carry yourself).[40] *Cucaracha* (cockroach/black beetle) was a slang term used to refer to monks and priests in allusion to their black robes, hence "Cucaracha Martin" was a direct reference to Martin Luther. Two students—Bartolome Ortiz and Jeronimo de Burgos—, who had several copies of these verses found on them, were arrested. In March, copies were found in the cathedral and duly sent to the Supreme Council. It was not until a year later—February 6, 1562—that Inquisitor Juan Gonzalez de Munebrega informed the Supreme Council that in Seville they had just incarcerated a person (no name) who admitted having distributed the verses in Toledo.[41] This person turned out to be Sebastian

---

36 AHN, Inquisición, leg. 3067, doc. 137, in: Lopez Muñoz (2011, 157, doc. 79); AHN, Inquisición, leg. 3067, doc. 132, in: Lopez Muñoz (2011, 174, doc. 84).
37 AHN, Inquisición, leg. 3067, doc. 133, in: Lopez Muñoz (2011, 174–180, doc. 85). The document reproduces the 60 rhymed verses.
38 AHN, Inquisición, lib. 575, f. 91v, in: Lopez Muñoz (2011, 181, doc. 87).
39 AHN, Inquisición, leg. 2943, doc. 9, in: Lopez Muñoz (2011, 231, doc. 105). Malara was arrested simply because he was a poet and in the past, when Constantino Ponce de la Fuente became canon preacher, he had written verses praising Constantino.
40 AHN, Inquisición, leg. 2943, doc. 10, in: Lopez Muñoz (2011, 232, doc. 106).
41 AHN, Inquisición, leg. 2943, doc. 49–1, in: Lopez Muñoz (2011, 253, doc. 119).

Martinez, a priest from Alcala de Henares who owned a small printing press. He was arrested on February 1 and burned at the stake three months later, on April 26.[42]

Much to the surprise of many, in 1566, Pope Pius V issued a jubilee that absolved all those who owned or had read prohibited literature. The notification perplexed the members of the Spanish Supreme Council who immediately alerted all the tribunals throughout Spain not to make the document public until they had consulted with Philip II, who in turn was to confer first with the pope.[43] Ten years later, in the summer of 1576, the Supreme Council was alarmed again by information obtained from a Lutheran, captive *"en tierra de moros"* (in the land of the Moors), that more than twelve thousand Lutheran books had arrived in the city and four thousand had already been distributed. This may have been an exaggeration, however, the letter continues:

> Because this can cause great harm to the Catholic faith, especially here, where the Lutherans with such diabolic diligence and endless manners endeavor to sow the seed of their sect, a remedy must be found… With all caution, you must find out in whose hands these books are, who brought them here, in what port they arrived, how they entered, who distributed them and to whom, where they were deposited once in the city, and just what books they are.[44]

What had begun at the turn of the sixteenth century as an initial step towards religious reform, with portions of the Scriptures accessible in the vernacular and biblical studies sowing the seed of inquiry, had turned into a nightmare. The Counter-Reformation had won the day. In Spain, freedom of conscience and freedom of press would have to wait another 300 years!

---

42 AHN, Inquisición, leg. 2075, doc. 2, in: Lopez Muñoz (2011, 258, doc. 122).
43 AHN, Inquisición, lib. 497, f. 96v, in: Lopez Muñoz (2011, 362, doc. 173).
44 AHN, Inquisición, lib. 579, f. 4v, in: Lopez Muñoz (2011, 439, doc. 244).

Chapter 6:
The Evangelical Circle at Valladolid

> In past years, Lutheran heretics in greater or less numbers were wont to be taken and
> burnt in Spain; but all those that were so punished were foreigners. At other times
> people poor and of mean birth, used to be sent to the scaffold, and to have San Benitos
> in the churches; but in these later years, we have seen the prisons, the scaffolds, and
> even the burning pile crowded with illustrious people, and (what is even more to be
> deplored) persons who in the opinion of the world were greatly superior to others in
> letters and in virtue. They are such and so many that it was believed if two or three
> months more had been suffered to elapse before applying a remedy to this mischief the
> conflagration would have spread itself all over Spain, and brought upon her the most
> dire misfortunes she has ever seen.
> Gonzalo de Illescas, *Historia Pontifical* (Salamanca, 1569).

During the reign of Charles V Spain had two capitals: Brussels, from where he
conducted diplomacy, and Valladolid, where his daughter princess Juana, as
regent, presided over the councils. All decisions made at Valladolid had to be
ratified by the emperor, which often caused delays in their implementation. The
prolonged absence of Charles led to a gradual slackening of the governmental
machine. Hence, when the emperor abdicated and Philip II returned to his
native Valladolid, the situation in Spain was serious. Socially, economically and
politically, the country was plunged into chaos, racked by deep discontent
aggravated even further by a religious crisis. Despite all the precautions taken
by the Supreme Council to steer the country clear of Lutheran heresy, several
Protestant communities had been discovered in Seville and Valladolid. The
news was received by Charles V, as it was by his son, with consternation, so
much so that it has been suggested that Philip's return to the Peninsula in 1559
was connected with this outbreak of Protestantism. The Danish historian Carl
Bratli (1927, 93) writes that Philip II, having received the bad news about
Seville and Valladolid, "longed only for the moment when he could set foot in
Spain once more."

Carlo de Sesso (1520?–1559)

In the mid 1550s, an Italian nobleman, often referred to as "the mysterious
Italian Carlo de Sesso," was slowly introducing Protestant ideas and literature in
the area around Valladolid. Because he was to become one of the leaders of the
evangelical circle in Valladolid, and because much of the information historians
have passed on regarding him is misleading, we will take time here to unravel
some of the mysteries that enshroud him. Carlo was not the son of the bishop of

Piacenza (Schäfer: 2014, III, 89, note 168), nor was he related to the powerful Milanese family of Trivulzio (Santarelli: 2012, 49–58), nor did he serve in the armies of emperor Charles V as Thomas M'Crie (1829, 233) affirms, though he did meet the emperor personally as a young man when his mother entertained him at her villa in 1532.

Carlo was the son of Countess Cassandra degli Arnaldi and Count Bernadino Sesso. His full name was Carlo Giovanni Lodovico Sesso. He grew up in the Sesso Villa, a country home built by Count Sesso, feudal lord of the area, in Sandrigo, near Vicenza, slightly north of Verona. Because these were small villages, Carlo often referred to himself as being from Verona. Little is known about his family except that he had a cousin, Oliviero Sesso, who was butler of Cardinal Alessandro Farnese and adviser to Pope Paul IV.[1] In 1532, the widowed Countess Cassandra, anxious about the future of her young son Carlo, took advantage of the fact that the emperor was in the area and invited him and his court to a banquet on December 2 at her villa in Sandrigo.[2] Tradition has it that the meal was memorable because that day the emperor ate too many figs and had severe indigestion afterwards.

In the emperor's entourage was Alonso de Castilla y Zuñiga, bishop of Calahorra.[3] An agreement was made that young Carlo would accompany the bishop back to Spain. Under the influence of both the bishop and the bishop's brother, Francisco de Castilla y Zuñiga, Carlo received a well-rounded humanist education. Later, Carlo would marry Francisco's daughter, Isabel de Castilla, and in so doing he would become part of an important aristocratic family. Isabel's father was a great-grandson of Pedro I de Castilla, king of Castile and Leon (1350–1369). An uncle had been Queen Isabel's master of ceremonies and her brother Sancho royal chaplain to Charles V. After their marriage, Carlo and Isabel made their home in Villamediana, near Logroño, where Isabel inherited a large estate from her uncle the bishop, with the condition that her first child be named Alfonso de Castilla.

It was not Carlo de Sesso's imperial duties that brought him in contact with evangelicals, as some authors claim, but members of the Calvinist circles in Vicenza who converted him to their thinking (Amelang: 2007, 433–456; Olivieri:

---

1 Oliviero Sesso was sent to Philip II's court at Toledo in January 1560 by Cardinal Carafa to remind Philip of the great services Carafa had rendered to the Spanish cause during the papal election. During this visit, Oliviero must have learned of the tragic execution of his cousin Carlo only a few months earlier.

2 Hence the saying: "That day there were in Vicenza more counts and knights than gondoliers in Venice."

3 The diocese of Calahorra fell within the jurisdiction of the inquisitorial court that included Santander, Burgos, Navarra, La Rioja, Soria, and the Basque Country. (Ibáñez Rodríguez: 1998, 149).

1992). Sesso returned to Italy in 1550 to collect an inheritance and there came in contact with the heterodox group begun by the ex-Benedictine monk Francesco Negri in Vicenza in the 1530s. Influenced by Lutheran writings, Negri left the monastery in 1525 and went to Strasbourg, where he met Wolfgang Capito and Martin Bucer. He returned to Italy in the 1530s and founded the group at Vicenza. In 1538, Negri moved to Chiavenna where he taught classical languages and helped found the evangelical community there. During that time he wrote a catechism and in 1546 published a book entitled *The Free Will* in which he bitterly attacked the Catholic Church. In the 1550s, Alessandro Trissino and Niccolò Pellizzari were leading figures of the Calvinist movement in Vicenza (Olivieri: 1967, 54–117).[4] During his time in Vicenza, Carlo de Sesso would have become aware that the leading houses of the city— the Trissino, the Thiene, the Pellizzari, and the Pigafetta—were giving their support to Calvinist doctrine (Martin: 2007, 309–329). He may also have met the distinguished Italian humanists Vincenzo Maggi and Lucio Paolo Rosello, who by the mid 1550s also formed part of the evangelical group in Vicenza. It appears that during his stay in Italy Sesso also stopped off at Trent—either out of curiosity or commissioned to do so—where he would have met Donato Rullo and the bishop de Padua, Niccolo Ormanetto.[5]

Sesso returned from his trip to Italy a changed man, but every process of conversion has its period of incubation and here Carlo de Sesso's father-in-law, Francisco de Castilla y Zuñiga, also deserves mention. As a young man, in the court of Isabel and Ferdinand, where he lived "a disordered and riotous life, full of confusion" (García Hernán: 2002, 257), as he confessed later, Francisco experienced a religious conversion. Encouraged by several good friends, "conscious that marriage was the best remedy for his soul and his social condition," Francisco de Castilla left the court and married. He built up an impressive library and spent the rest of his life studying and writing.[6] Strong Erasmian tendencies

---

4 Alessandro Trissino (1523–1609) studied law at Padua and there made his first contacts with a group of Lutherans. With a friend he undertook a clandestine trade in Bibles, discovered in 1563. Trissino was arrested and tortured, but managed to escape. In 1564 he was sentenced in absentia and his effigy burned at the stake in Vicenza. He had emigrated to Chiavenna, where he became a leader of the local Protestant congregation.
5 Donato Rullo had studied in Padua in the early 1530s, coming into contact with Reginald Pole and was part of his entourage at Trent in 1545–46. From Trent Rullo went to Venice, where in 1546 he edited Vittoria Colonna's *Rime spiritual*. He followed Cardinal Pole to England in 1554, and remained in England until after the death of Pole in 1558, when he returned to Italy. Pope Pius V decreed his arrested in the summer of 1566 and he was taken to the prisons of the Inquisition in Rome, where he died on December 10, 1566. Niccolo Ormanetto was among Cardinal Pole's assistants in Brussels, and later in England. In 1566, Pope Pius V summoned him back to Rome and in 1570 appointed him bishop of Padua. From 1572 to his death in 1577, Ormanetto was nuncio in Spain. (Tellechea: 1996, 189–210).
6 Among other things, Francisco de Castilla published a versified version of the book of Pro-

can be seen in his writings (Valladares de Sotomayor: 1787–1791, XXIX, 32). The religious atmosphere in the Castilla household would have encouraged piety and devoutness, which in turn would have stimulated interest in a return to the principles of early Christianity and the companionship of others who shared these views. This is corroborated by the fact that when Carlo de Sesso left for Italy in 1550, one of the inquisitors at Calahorra gave him a list of books to bring back. The list included Calvin's Institutes,[7] Wolfgang Musculus's Commentaries on Matthew and John,[8] Joannes Brenz on John and Luke,[9] Calvin on several Epistles by St. Paul,[10] and Luther's *Canticum graduum,* or comment on Psalm 130, traditionally called *"De profundis."* The inquisitor would hardly have asked Sesso to bring back these volumes if he hadn't had the reassurance that he empathized with the undertaking. This would also explain why Sesso brought back several others, namely, sermons in Italian by "el Capuchino,"[11] two copies of Valdes's *110 Considerations* in Italian,[12] etc.

Carlo de Sesso enjoyed political inroads thanks to his father-in-law and his brother-in-law, Sancho de Castilla, who from 1535 to 1556 was royal chaplain to Charles V and later to Philip II. His father-in-law, Francisco de Castilla (some-times referred to as "Licenciado Castilla"), was a graduate from the University of Valladolid (Espinosa: 2009, 123) and had been *corregidor* (chief magistrate) in Burgos, Murcia, Galicia and Valladolid. These institutionalized posts were royal appointments, and did not imply permanent residence in the city. Most *corre-gidores* were aristocrats with a degree in law. Competent service resulted in promotion. The main task was to administer justice. Carlo de Sesso's own ap-pointment as *corregidor* of Toro implies that he also was a graduate in law.[13] His appointment, which came in 1554 after his return from Italy, suggests that this appointment could have been a recompense of some diplomatic mission he had performed there. If it is correct that Sesso was in Trent and there met with

---

verbs which he included in his *Theorica de virtudes en coplas y con comento* (Zaragoza: Agostin Millan, 1552).

7 Jean Calvin, *Institvtio Totivs Christianae Religionis, Nvnc Ex Postrema Avthoris Recognitione Qvibusdam Locis Avctior, Infinitis Verò Castigatior* (Geneva: J. Gerardus, 1550).

8 Wolfgang Musculus, *Commentariorvm in evangelistam Ioannem* (Basel: J. Herwagen, 1545); *In Evangelistam Matthaeum Commentarii* (Basel: J. Herwagen, 1544).

9 Joannes Brentius, *Evangelion qvod inscribitvr, secvndvm Ioannem* (Frankfurt: P. Brubacchii, 1551); *In Evangelii quod inscribitur secundum Lucam* (Frankfurt: P. Brubacchii, 1551).

10 Jean Calvin, *Commentarii in Epistolam Pauli ad Romanos* (Strasbourg: W. Rihelium, 1540); *Commentarii in priorem Epistolam Pauli ad Corinthios* (Strasbourg: W. Rihelium, 1546); *Commentarii in 4 epistolas ad Gal., Ephes., Philip., Coloss.* (Geneva: J. Girardus, 1548).

11 Bernardino Ochino, *La quarta parte de le prediche en toscano* (Geneva, 1550).

12 Juan de Valdés, *Le cento et dieci divine considerationi del S. Giovanni Valdesso: nelle quali si ragiona delle cose piu utili, piu necessarie, e piu perfette, della christiana professione,* ed. C.S. Curione (Basel: J. Oporinus, 1550).

13 To be a licensed lawyer required eight years of study—a four-year bachelor's degree and four years of professional practice—; to be appointed *corregidor* a total of ten years was required.

Cardinal Pole, the emperor may have commissioned him with a message for Pole, which is what would have taken him to Trent. It must be remembered that Pole was the emperor's choice candidate for the papacy, which had just been lost in favor of Giovanni Del Monte (Pope Julius III). Another personality Sesso may have encountered at Trent was Juan Bernal Diaz de Luco, bishop of Calahorra, who attended the meetings from May 1546 to 1552. Sesso had met him earlier in Spain through his wife's uncle and who Tellechea (1978) believes Sesso may have acted as interpreter for at Trent.

When Sesso returned to Logroño with the books he had purchased in Italy, he found that the Inquisitor that had requested them had died so he kept them for himself and soon began sharing them with others.[14] His post at Toro, which he held from 1554 to 1559, put him in contact with the surrounding villages and the neighboring nobility. His acquaintances ranged from village priests to lawyers to local noble families: the marquises of Poza, of Mota, of Alcañices, of Ulloa, etc. His first converts were the Dominican monk Domingo de Rojas, son of the Marquis de Poza, the lawyer Bachiller Herrzuelo from Toro, and Pedro de Cazalla, a priest in the village of Pedrosa del Rey some ten miles from Toro (Tellechea: 1962, XIX, 44). It appears that Sesso began "proselytizing" around 1554. Isabel de Estrada, a *beata* from Pedrosa, declared on July 11, 1558, "The first time I heard these Lutheran errors, of which I heretofore have confessed, was when the king [Philip] went to England [for his marriage to Mary Tudor]." (Schäfer: 2014, III, 380. Brackets mine).

Sesso seems to have been socially active everywhere. We find his name among the organizers of the *cofradía* (brotherhood) of the Holy Sacrament of Logroño in 1557 with an expressive "*Ojo*" (careful!) written next to it (Labarga García: 2003, II, 1061). Sesso's participation in one of these brotherhoods should not come as a surprise. *Cofradías* were public spaces for socializing, where people of all walks of life—nobles, priests, *beatas*, artisans—mingled and it was expected of influential citizens to belong to these local brotherhoods. They were spaces where laypersons could discreetly interact and discuss and develop forms of spirituality free from the strict tutelage of the ecclesiastic authorities.

When Archbishop Bartolome de Carranza was arrested on the morning of August 22, 1559, in an inn in Torrelaguna and his mailbag seized, certain compromising letters, which the Inquisition reserved for later use, showed that he had had contact with Carlo de Sesso (Homza: 2006, 203). In 1554, just before leaving for England, the two men had met.[15] The circumstances were as follows.

---

14 Ernst Schäfer (2014, I, 472) thought that the story of the Inquisitor and his commission was not true and that Sesso used it as an excuse.

15 The marriage between Prince Philip and Mary Tudor required the presence of competent theologians to facilitate the return of the Anglican Church to papal obedience and Carranza was chosen for this task.

When Sesso stopped at the village of Pedrosa to see Pedro de Cazalla on his way back from Zamora where he had gone to discuss his up-coming appointment in Toro with Antonio de Fonseca, president of the Royal Council of Castle, he had a heated discussion with Cazalla regarding purgatory. Cazalla was outraged. He had never heard Sesso speak in that way and was unsure what to do, whether to denounce Sesso or to consult with Bartolome de Carranza, who had recently returned from Trent and was now rector of St. Gregorio College at Valladolid. Cazalla's duty was to denounce Sesso, yet—according to his confession later— their long-standing friendship impeded that sort of action so he decided to consult with Carranza. After listening carefully to Pedro de Cazalla's dilemma, Carranza thought it would be best if the three men first talked the matter over together. Without further ado, Carranza sent Sesso—who by now was back in Logroño—a letter requesting his presence. Though the letter did not state why he was being summoned, Sesso suspected the reason. When he arrived, he found Carranza relaxed and there was no mention of being denounced. Indeed, as Pedro de Cazalla declared later, the conversation turned into a friendly discussion regarding several German theologians and to his great surprise ended in a cordial embrace.[16]

On his return to Spain in August of 1558, Bartolome de Carranza, now Archbishop of Toledo, learned that both Pedro de Cazalla and Carlo de Sesso had been imprisoned. Not sure what Sesso might confess regarding that meeting, Carranza informed his friend and close collaborator, Juan de Villagarcia, of the conversation. Villagarcia, a Dominican friar from Valladolid, had been a pupil of Bartolome de Carranza and had gone to England with him (Moreno: 2013, 30). On his return to Spain, Villagarcia found that Carranza was in trouble with the Inquisition for alleged Lutheranism, and his own name was linked to the charges. In an attempt to protect Carlo de Sesso, Villagarcia testified that members of Cardinal Pole's household, especially Donato Rullo and Niccolo Ormanetto, knew Sesso and could vouch for him.

Pedro de Cazalla, parish priest of Pedrosa and brother of Dr. Augustin Cazalla, was arrested on April 25, 1558. In his declarations at his trial in May, he said that he had known Sesso for fourteen years, which takes us back to 1545. That year Sesso may have travelled from Logroño to Valladolid with members of the de Castilla family to attend the funerals of future king Philip's first wife, Maria of Portugal, who had died of childbirth four days after the birth of prince Charles.[17]

---

16 AHN, Inquisición, leg. 5353, no.1, fol. 84–85, in: Schäfer (2014, III, 479–480).
17 Maria Manuela, princess of Portugal, (1527–1545) was the daughter of King John III of Portugal. On November 14, 1543, at the age of 16, she married Philip and a year and a half later, on 8 July, 1545, Don Carlos was born. The delivery was difficult. Maria Manela survived her son only four days. She died on August 21, 1545. Philip's third wife, Elisabeth of Valois, would also die of childbirth.

This may have coincided with the time when Sesso's father-in-law was *corregidor* in Valladolid, which, on the other hand, would have given him the opportunity to meet members of the local nobility, as well as members of the court and the clergy. Be that as it may, it was after his return from Italy that Sesso became active in promulgating his convictions of *sola gracia*, justification by faith, and other Reformed doctrines. When the Inquisitors asked Sesso where he had learned those doctrines, he said he had heard them preached publicly in all the churches in Italy some eight years earlier (Tellechea: 1962, 59). The influence of Carlo de Sesso on the evangelical circles in and around Valladolid was significant. Pedro de Cazalla, for example, confessed to the inquisitors that he had read—in Latin—Calvin's Institutes, Musculus's Commentary on Matthew, Brenz's commentaries on John and Luke, Calvin's Commentary on Romans, Luther's books on the Psalms and on Christian Liberty, besides a few books in Italian, such as Juan de Valdes's *Considerations*, etc.[18] These were the very titles Carlo de Sesso had brought back from Italy in the early 1550s!

Dr. Augustin de Cazalla (1510–1559)

Augustin de Cazalla was born in Valladolid. He studied at the College of St. Gregorio in Valladolid under Bartolome de Carranza and at the University of Alcala de Henares under his uncle, Bishop Juan de Cazalla, former chaplain of Cardinal Cisneros, who held a reputation of renowned humanist and Erasmian. From his youth, Cazalla and his siblings had been exposed to heterodox opinions. According to certain declarations made by the *ex-alumbrada* Francisca Hernandez back in 1530 (Longhurst: 1969, 147–149, 154), Dr. Cazalla's father, Pedro de Cazalla, was a close friend of the Vergara brothers at Alcala and shared their sympathies for Luther. Dr. Cazalla's mother, Leonor de Vivero, had had close links with the *alumbrados*, first through Francisca Hernandez, who actually lived in her house for a number of years, and later through her cousin, Francisca Zuñiga, wife of Antonio de Baeza of Escalona.

Cazalla entered the service of Charles V in 1543 as court preacher and personal chaplain, which allowed him to travel throughout Europe with the emperor. The historian Gonzalo de Illescas, in his *Historia Pontifical* (1568), described him as "the most eloquent preacher in Spain at the time."[19] Cazalla

---

18 AHN, Inquisición, leg. 5353, no.1, f. 100, in: Schäfer (2014, III, 533).
19 A very different statement found in the first edition of Illescas's *History of the Popes* nearly caused a diplomatic conflict. When the English ambassador Dr. John Man arrived in Madrid in 1566, he began gathering information regarding the activities of the Inquisition. When Philip II authorized the publication of Gonzalo de Illescas's *History of the Popes* in which the author questioned Elizabeth's virginity and stated that Luther "and his friend Henry VIII"

remained in the emperor's entourage for nearly ten years during which time he had contacts with some of the most prominent Protestant leaders in Europe. He would have been present when Francisco de Enzinas presented his translation of the New Testament to the emperor in Brussels in November of 1543 and would have witnessed how Pedro de Soto, the emperor's confessor, had Enzinas arrested and all his New Testaments collected and burned. Cazalla would also have accompanied the emperor to Worms in May of 1545 and would have witnessed how Charles silenced the Protestant preachers in the city and allowed an Italian monk to inveigh against the Lutherans from the pulpit and to ask God to "exterminate that pestilent heresy." (Robertson: 1822, III, 44). Cazalla would also have accompanied the emperor to Ratisbon in 1546, as he had to Worms the previous year, and would have been present at the theological debates that centered on the Augsburg Confession, the main doctrinal statement of the Lutherans, and heard or read the defense of the confession written up by Philip Melanchthon (Arand: 1998, 461–484). The discussion ended with Charles commissioning the "Augsburg Interim," a list of doctrines and practices to be carried out until a free general council should meet. Several theologians were involved in the final draft of this decree. On the Catholic side were Michael Helding, Eberhard Billick, Pedro de Soto, and Pedro de Malvenda; on the Protestant side, John Agricola, court preacher of Joachim II Hector, Elector of Brandenburg. Pedro de Soto (1493–1563) later served as senior chair of theology at the University of Dillingen, in southern Germany, where he worked with the Bishop of Augsburg to establish a Catholic academic stronghold. In May 1555 he was sent to London to take part in the late stages of the persecutions that led to the executions of the Anglican bishops Hugh Latimer, Nicholas Ridley and Thomas Cranmer, and would have coincided with Bartolome de Carranza. In 1560, de Soto was accused by the Inquisition in Valladolid of being influenced by Lutheranism, largely on the basis of having approved of Bartolome Carranza's *Catechism*. He died in Trent in 1563 while the trial was still in its early stages.

The Protestants were dissatisfied with the Augsburg Interim. In Northern Germany, the cities of Bremen and Magdeburg took up arms. These were turbulent times and Augustin de Cazalla could not have remained indifferent. Charles V's "Proclamation Against Heretics" of April 1550, that allowed the Inquisition in the Netherlands to arrest any heretic, may have been an eye-opener for Cazalla. Had he witnessed Maurice of Saxony's march upon Innsbruck that year, where the emperor lay sick? Was Cazalla present when a Protestant victory forced Charles to sign the Peace of Passau on August 2, 1552, which

---

had both gone to hell within eight days of one another, Dr. Man sent excerpts to Wm. Cecil, who went straight to the Spanish ambassador demanding an explanation. In the second edition, this information does not appear.

granted some freedoms to Protestants and ended all of Charles's hopes at religious unity within his empire? In any case, by the end of 1552, Cazalla was back in Salamanca.

Back in Spain, Dr. Cazalla was elected canon of the cathedral of Salamanca to fill the vacancy left by Pedro Castro Lemos, who had recently accepted a canonry in Cuenca. While in Salamanca, Cazalla was a member of the Royal Council presided over by Antonio Fonseca. Very likely it was there that Cazalla first met Carlo de Sesso (Nieto: 1997, 417). What Cazalla's duties were when he returned to Valladolid in 1556 is unsure; he may have become chaplain to some noble family, which would have put him in touch with Fray Domingo de Rojas and again with Carlo de Sesso. He may also have been one of the spiritual directors of the Cistercian nuns at the Monastery of Belen. Cazalla's sermons have been lost and only the accounts of the *auto-da-fe* in which he was sentenced to the stake give us some information regarding his activities. Unfortunately it is beyond the scope of this survey to include the declarations made by the Cazalla brothers— Augustin, Pedro, and Francisco—at their trials but these declarations shed much light on the social networks in which they moved and their theological discussions, which centered around the doctrine of justification by faith.[20]

The Underground Church Discovered

Around Easter of 1558 the inquisitors pounced on the group and incarcerated them all.[21] Several versions exit as to how the inquisitors learned about the activities of the Valladolid group. One, reported by Thomas M'Crie (1829, 243) and repeated by the majority of authors (Castro: 1851, 10; Wilkens: 1897, 168), states that,

> Juan Garcia, a goldsmith, had been in the habit of summoning the Protestants to sermon; and aware of the influence which superstition exerted over the mind of his wife, he concealed from her the place and times of their assembling. Being gained by her confessor, this demon in woman's shape dogged her husband one night, and having ascertained the place of meeting, communicated the fact to the Inquisition.

This version, which appears in the original report by the inquisitors, begins with *"se dice"* (it is said), a phrase that strongly suggests hearsay.[22] Henry Ch. Lea

---

20 See Schäfer (2014, III, 11, 12, 13, 16, 35, 36, 38, 79, 160, 165, 166, 195, 196, 199, 202, 204, 215, 216, 217, 227, 229, 234, 256, 257, 364, 366, 372, 379, 383, 386, 390, 392, 404, 407, 420, 421, 436, 437, 439, 440, 444, 448, 449, 450, 452, 453, 465, 469, 471, 481, 485, 505, 514, 513, 515, 516, 517, 518, 519, 521, 522, 531, 532, 537, 542, 546, 549, 553, 554, 561, 562, 566, 572, 564, 581, 603, 608, 615, 620, 622).
21 For a summary of this event, see Schäfer (2014, I, 475–514).
22 BNE, Ms. 9175, no. 54, fol. 213–219v, in: Schäfer (2014, III, 46).

(1906–1907, 431) mentions another denouncer, namely, Juana de Fonseca, but gives no supporting evidence. He may have found this information in Schäfer (2014, III, 443, note 518), who mentions it in passing in a note.

Another more historically tenable version is reported by Menendez y Pelayo (1881, IV, 405), who took it from Adolfo de Castro, who found it in Francisco de Santa María's *Reforma de los descalzos de Nuestra Señora del Carmen* (1644, 583). The story involves Isabel de Vilamari de Cardona-Bellpuig, princess of Salerno, and her aunt Catalina de Cardona, who denounced Dr. Augustin de Cazalla to the Inquisition for coming often to the princess's residence while in Valladolid and teaching heretical doctrine. In 1557, Catalina de Cardona, whose father was stationed in Naples, returned to Spain with her niece, Isabel de Vilamari. The princess, known in Italy as Isabella Villamarino, had had all her possessions confiscated when her husband, Ferrante di Sanseverino, prince of Salerno, nephew (twice removed) of Charles V, defied the Spanish viceroy Alvarez de Toledo. In 1542 the Inquisition had been instituted in Rome and its operations were slowly spreading throughout Italy. By 1547 it had been established in the kingdom of Naples, which at that time comprised the entire southern part of Italy. When Ferrante returned to Naples in the fall of 1544, after serving Charles V in his war against Francis I, which concluded with the Peace of Crépy, he had a falling out with the Spanish viceroy Alvarez de Toledo over the implantation of Inquisition tribunals in the Kingdom of Naples. Ferrante tried to convince the emperor to dismiss Toledo, but to no avail. Ferrante's refusal to accept the Inquisition within the Principality of Salerno created a break between him and the Spanish viceroy. As a result, Ferrante fled to France, where he became a Calvinist and embraced the Huguenot cause (Segarra Añón: 2001, 126). In 1552, Sanseverino was declared a rebel by Charles V, who ordered all his possessions confiscated. Earlier, in the 1530s, at the Sanseverino court in Naples an intense intellectual climate had developed, where humanists met, many of which shared the Reformed ideas promulgated by Ochino and Valdes. Their writings gradually produced in Isabel a leaning towards reformed evangelical thought. As a result, her relationship with other same-minded intellectual women such as Giulia Gonzaga, Vittoria Colonna, Catalina Cybo, Isabel Briceño, and others became more intense, participating with them in promoting Christian humanism, based on a rereading of the Bible.[23] Isabel, who shared her husband's staunch opposition to the Inquisition and considered the confiscation of their possessions unfair, wrote Charles V asking for clemency, but received no reply. She then decided that the best way to better her situation was to have a personal interview with the emperor. For this, she offered her services as lady-in-

---

23 For a survey of the spread of Reformed teaching in Naples, see Pasquale Lopez (1976); Massimo Firpo (2007); Peter A. Mazur (2013).

waiting to his widowed sister Eleonor of Austria, queen dowager of Portugal. Finally, in July of 1555, the emperor's secretary, Bernardino Mendoza, informed Isabel that she had permission to travel to Spain. When she arrived in Barcelona, in August, she learned that Eleonor of Austria was still in Brussels with her brother and she had to wait nearly a full year for them to return to Spain. Isabel spent most of this time in Valladolid, where she often attended the sermons of Dr. Augustin de Cazalla. For Isabel, Cazalla's preaching was reminiscent of that of Juan de Valdes and she certainly encouraged his visits, but her aunt Catalina de Cardona, who suspected he was teaching heresy, denounced Cazalla to the Inquisition.

Isabel never did get to speak with Charles V, who on his arrival in Spain in 1558 had retired directly to the monastery of Yuste in Extremadura, where he died in September. In February Eleonor had also died and Isabel requested permission to return to Naples.[24] On October 14, 1559, just as she was about to begin her journey back to Naples, Isabel had a stroke and also died. Could the impact of the *auto-da-fe* celebrated only a few days earlier—October 8—have been the cause? The *auto* was presided by Philip II. As a member of Philip's aunt Eleonor's household, the princess of Salerno would necessarily have been seated in a special reserved area.

> Just below His Majesty's seating area, there was another platform, very elegantly decorated, where Maria de Mendoza, VII countess of Ribadabia [Maria Sarmiento de Mendoza, lady-in-waiting of Empress Isabel de Portugal and widow of Charles V's secretary [Francisco de los Cobos], and her daughter, and Maria de Mendoza's sister sat. Behind them, there was another platform where the wife of the governor of Castile sat. There were also many other platforms, richly decorated, for distinguished ladies.[25]

From her privileged seat, Isabel de Vilamari would have seen her fellow countryman Carlo de Sesso carried to his place on the scaffold. A handwritten ex-

---

24 Eleonor de Austria (1498–1558) married her uncle by marriage, King Manuel I of Portugal on 16 July 1518. Her brother Charles arranged the marriage to avoid the possibility of Portuguese assistance for any rebellion in Castile. Manuel had been married to two of Eleonor's maternal aunts. She became a widow on 13 December 1521, when Manuel died of the plague. As Queen Dowager of Portugal, Eleonor returned to the court of Charles in Spain. In 1526, she was engaged to King Francis I of France during his captivity in Spain. They married on 4 July 1530. They had no children. Eleonor left Spain in the company of her future stepsons, who were now to be released having been held hostage by her brother Charles. Eleonor was crowned queen of France in Saint-Denis on 31 May 1531. As the French queen, Eleonor was used as a contact between France and the Holy Roman Empire. As a queen dowager, Eleonor left France for Brussels in 1548. She witnessed the abdication of Charles in October 1555 and left for Spain with him and their sister Mary in September of the following year. She lived with her sister, Mary, exgoverness of the Netherlands, in Jarandilla de la Vera, some six miles from Yuste, where their brother Charles had retired.
25 BNE, Ms. 9175, núm. 74, fol. 222v–225v, in: Schäfer (2014, III, 88, doc. 384).

planatory note found on a manuscript in the Biblioteca Nacional de España in
Madrid, shelf-number Ms. 1104, states that, "because Carlo de Sesso was a pa-
ralytic, he was carried to his place in the arms of two *familiares*." (Schäfer: 2014,
III, 69, note 126). Was his paralysis caused by the tortures he received in prison?
Isabel would also have witnessed the *auto-da-fe* earlier that year where her
favorite preacher, Dr. Augustin Cazalla, whom her cousin had denounced, was
burned at the stake. The impact of these two *autos* could not have left her
indifferent and could very likely have been the cause of her stroke.

Auto-da-fe, Valladolid, May 21, 1559

Philip II was still in the Low Countries when the first *auto-da-fe* against the
Lutherans in Valladolid took place. It was presided over by Philip's youngest
sister, Princess Juana, along with Philip's fourteen-year-old son Carlos. Juana
was only fifteen when she left Spain to marry the crown prince of Portugal and
returned two years later a widow. At sixteen, she assumed the regency for Philip
II while he was out of the country. She was twenty-one when she presided over
the *auto-da-fe* in Valladolid. Juan Antonio Llorente (1826b, 205) narrates an
incident that occurred that day, which he terms "a scandalous transaction."

> When the court and all the other attendants had taken their places, Don Francis Baca,
> Inquisitor of Valladolid, advanced towards the Prince of Asturias, Don Carlos, and his
> aunt, the princess Juana, to demand and receive from them an oath to maintain and
> defend the Inquisition, and to reveal to it all that might have been said against the faith
> by any person within their knowledge. It had been decreed at the establishment of the
> Inquisition, that the magistrate who presided at an auto-da-fe should take a similar
> oath, but sovereigns cannot be considered as magistrates. Don Carlos and his aunt took
> the oath, but subsequent events show how much he was displeased at the boldness of
> this inquisitor: he was then aged fourteen years.

Not all of the trial records of this *auto-da-fe* have been preserved in their entirety,
nevertheless, the heresies the persons sentenced on the May 21 were accused of
can be summarized as follows:

1. To deny the existence of purgatory.
2. To claim that men were justified through the death of Christ.
3. To accept as valid only two sacraments: communion and marriage.
4. That confession was a mental activity and should be made to God alone.
5. After confession, communion was to be taken in the two forms, bread and
   wine.
6. Not to pray to saints or consider them capable of pleading on one's behalf.
7. To say Mass for the dead was pointless since there was no purgatory.
8. They changed the words of the Ave Maria, not to accept Mary as intercessor.

9. They said the pope had not power to excommunicate.
10. They considered the pope the Antichrist.
11. They believed in clerical marriage.
12. To keep the commandments and articles of faith does not save a person.
13. Masses are not a merchandize that can be bought and sold.
14. Indulgences and jubilees are worthless.
15. Processions and litanies are worthless.
16. Fasting should be done away with.
17. That Martin Luther was another St. Paul.
18. That God was not alive in the monstrance and that transubstantiation was not true.
19. That the majority of those sentenced had Lutheran books in their possession.
20. Some believed that if they were to die they would go straight to heaven "with their boots on." (González Novalín: 1968–1971, II, 249–250).

Ernst Schäfer documented up to 2100 cases of persons that appeared before the Inquisition accused of Protestantism.[26] Among the documents reproduced by Schäfer, there are several full accounts of the May 21 *auto-da-fe* in Valladolid. It seems fitting that we should include one of these accounts here.

On Sunday, May 21, 1559, the festivity of the Holy Trinity, 31 heretics and Lutherans were condemned to the stake, as detailed below. The event took place as follows:

At quarter to six in the morning of the said festivity of the Trinity, Prince Don Carlos and the princess governess [Donna Joanna], who is now in Spain, arrived and made their way to their pavilion to watch the *auto-da-fe*. They arrived in this fashion: there came all the guard, both on foot and on horseback, with their arms, and the prince leading the procession accompanied by the Count of Buendía [Juan de Acuña] followed by all the princess's ladies-in-waiting and the wives of the grandees, and all the noblemen that were in Valladolid at that time, such as the governor of Castile, the marquis of Astorga [Álvaro Pérez Osorio?] and many titled gentlemen and knights. They all made their way up to a platform prepared for them in front of the City Hall, looking towards the walkway called Don Rodrigo Niño, which is where the scaffold of the *auto* was located. Once they were seated, there came all the guard, both on foot and on horseback, of the Holy Inquisition. The order of the procession of the heretics and penitents was this:

From the prisons of the Holy Inquisition to the scaffold there was a fenced off area through which they were to come and at six o'clock sharp they began to enter the plaza as follows: each of the penitents was brought in between two *familiares*.[27] They came in one by one. The first ones to arrive were those considered less guilty. They were all

---

26 Of these 2100, some 220 were burned at the stake and 120 burned in effigy. (Schäfer: 2014, I, 343).
27 Lay servants attached to each individual tribunal, who ran errands for the inquisitors.

wearing their *sanbenitos*[28] and those that were not to be burned carried candles and had their heads uncovered. Those that were to be burned carried green crosses in their hands and a rope around their neck. Their *sanbenitos* were also different: those that were to be burned had hell flames painted on them, the others had one or more crosses of St. Andrew painted on them. There was also another difference, that is, the clergy that were to be burned did not have ropes around their necks until they had been defrocked. Those with the lesser sentences were seated in the lower rows of the scaffold and those that were to be burned in the highest rows.

The scaffold looked like this: it was a large square platform with four rows of graded step-like benches, or bleachers. It was the highest in the whole plaza except for that of the prince and the princess. It was located directly in front of the prince and the princess and the judges and council of the Holy Inquisition. This platform had two raised pulpits at each front end from which the sentences were read. On the two back corners of the platform there were six steps, which led from the bottom to the top. All the rows of benches were open in the back so that the offenders could be seen from all sides. On the highest row was seated the worst offender, that is, Dr. Cazalla, who sat in the corner coming in from the right, and after him came, in order, from the greatest to the least offender. In the front, towards the center, there was another raised pulpit that faced the inquisitors and the judges of the Holy Inquisition and could be seen from any place throughout the plaza. All the offenders rose when their sentences were read. In the center of the scaffold, where the judges and council of the Holy Inquisition were seated, there was another pulpit from which the sermon was read. At six thirty sharp everyone was seated in his/her place and the sermon began, which was preached by Bishop Cano [Fray Melchor Cano, bishop elect of the Canary Islands]. At seven thirty the sermon was finished and the sentences were read. The first was that of Dr. Augustin de Cazalla, which was read from that same pulpit. The others were read alternatively from one or the other of the side pulpits. Sitting next to each offender was a friar.

Dr. Cazalla stood up to hear his sentence. This Dr. Cazalla is a descendent of Gonzalo de Cabra,[29] reconciled, and the son of Pedro de Cazalla and Donna Leonor de Biuero. The case against Dr. Augustin de Cazalla was this: The prosecutor of the Holy Inquisition of Valladolid said that when Dr. Augustin de Cazalla was in Germany he had read, and continues to read, the works of Lutheran heretics and had learned their ways and

---

28 A garment of sackcloth worn at an *auto-da-fe* of the Spanish Inquisition by condemned heretics, yellow with red crosses for the penitent and black with painted flames and devils for the impenitent.

29 Gonzalo Fernández de Córdoba (1453–1515), also called "The Great Captain." He fought in the Conquest of Granada. Able to speak Berber (the language of the emirate), he was chosen as one of the officers to arrange the surrender. He was later appointed Viceroy of Naples in 1504. Jealous of him, King Ferdinand accused him of profligately spending the public treasury to reward his captains and soldiers and he was recalled in 1507. That he was declared "reconciled" suggests he had appeared before the Inquisition in the days when crypto-Jews—those that accepts Christian baptism, yet continued to practice Judaism—were still the main target. What the accusations were is unsure, possibly the very fact that he, and his brother Alonso Fernandez de Alguilar, had protected the New Christians during the hostilities in Cordoba in 1473.

customs and, in particular, preached and taught the doctrine of the sect of the heretic Martin Luther, and that for many years he had held these doctrines and taught them. The heresies of which he was accused were these: first, that he and his followers called themselves *alumbrados*; secondly, that if one has a living faith that Jesus Christ our Redeemer had paid for the sins of the human race the day he died on the cross, that believing this he/she was justified and that no other works were necessary for his/her salvation. He also rejected fasting, oral prayers and oral confession and acknowledged only two sacraments, namely, baptism and the Eucharist. And regarding the sacrament of the Eucharist, priests were not necessary to consecrate nor to administer it from the alter, and that it was foolish to believe what we Christians [Catholics] believe, that the priest can convert the bread in flesh and body of our Lord Jesus Christ and the wine in his blood, nor could it be kept in the sacraria.[30] And that every man and woman, before or after partaking, with living faith and confessing mentally his/her sins, can partake of any sort of baked bread and consecrate the wine, and can partake of both elements, both the bread and the wine, as long as the words of Christ be pronounced as he did the day of the last supper, saying, of the bread, "This is my body, eat it", and of the wine, "This is my blood, drink it." And that these were not to be received physically, but spiritually.

He denied all authority of the pope and his general councils and declared that it was impossible for anyone to rescue any souls from purgatory because there was no purgatory. And men and women must have living faith, and they can be sure of their salvation and their justification, otherwise they will go to hell like the Christians [Catholics],[31] and they need not leave off eating meat or pork the days the church prohibits it. He said that the pope and the priests and the friars were antichristian and that there was no need for priests and friars and that it was a sin to take a vow of chastity or any other vow and that they could all marry because what was now practiced was only an imposition. And that any offense they committed, because of their living faith, would be pardoned. Likewise, man's free will did not allow him to do good but only evil. And Cazalla was a teacher and preacher of these false doctrines and other great offenses against the holy Catholic faith. This accusation of which Cazalla was accused also applied to the other offenders.

During the first interrogatory, the said doctor was asked if he knew the reason he had been arrested. He said that he did not know why he had been arrested except that some people had said evil things about him. In the second visit, he admitted that it was true that he had read many books written by heretics and he still had them in his possession. Though it was true that he did not have permission to have them from the Holy Inquisition, he had the pope's spoken permission, though not in writing. He had been a preacher for 14 years, but had never preached false doctrine, or Lutheran doctrine, nor could that be proved except for last St. Luke's day [October 18, 1557] when he had said that some of the doctrines of the sect of Martin Luther were correct. Among these, he confessed that he approved of the doctrine of justification by faith, denying the power

---

30 A place near the altar of a church where materials used in the sacred rites are deposited or poured away.
31 At that time the word "Christian" and "Catholic" were used indistinctly.

of the pope and his councils, and that of these matters he had exhorted and preached and persuaded some. He did not confess all the charges made against him, nevertheless, there were 40 witnesses that testified against him. He was condemned for apostate heretic, both for the heresies he held and for having formed part of many heretical circles and gatherings and for having been a false friend and companion. He was sentenced to the loss of all his goods, to be defrocked and turned over to the secular authorities, who strangled him and burned him. When his sentence had been read, he wished to speak in his defense but he was not allowed to and they returned him to his seat.

The second offender called to hear his sentence was Francisco de Vivero, clergy, brother of the said Dr. Cazalla. The prosecutor accused him of the same things as the doctor. This Francisco de Vivero did not confess anything until the fourth visit. He confessed that he believed in justification by faith, and that there was no purgatory or Apostolic See. Thirteen witnesses testified against him. In this fourth visit he converted. His sentence was the same as that of Dr. Cazalla because he was a priest. He was strangled and burned.

Donna Beatriz de Vivero, sister of the aforesaid Dr. Cazalla, was accused by the prosecutor of believing that with only faith in God the Christians were saved and that there was no purgatory and that the sacrament was to be received spiritually, not physically, and she did not believe that Christ was present in the Eucharist and that in communion one was to partake of both elements, and that oral confession was unnecessary, but must be done mentally, and that the Holy Spirit did not rule the church and that vows should not be made and that unbaptized children were saved. Thirteen witnesses testified against her. She begged for mercy, but was condemned for apostate heresy against the law of Christ. She was handed over to the civil authorities, strangled and burned.

The fourth offender was Juan de Vivero, accused of the same offenses as the above. In the second visit he confessed that there was no purgatory and he believed in justification by faith and all the other matters. Five witnesses testified against him. He was sentenced to the loss of all his goods, to life in prison, to wear a *sanbenito* over his clothes for the rest of his life, to attend mass and hear a sermon every Sunday and feast day of observance in the church assigned him and to confess and take communion at Christmas, Easter and Pentecost.

The fifth offender was Donna Catalina [Costanza] de Vivero, wife of Hernando Ortiz, royal accountant, and sister of Dr. Cazalla. During the first visit she confessed that in her house a friar [Fray Domingo de Rojas?] had administered communion to everyone there and that although he said many things, sometimes she believed him and others not. For the things she believed she was condemned to the confiscation of all her goods, to appear on the scaffold in a *sanbenito* and with a candle in her hand, and, like her brother Juan de Vivero, to life in prison, to wear a *sanbenito* the rest of her life, to attend mass and hear a sermon every Sunday and feast day of observance, and to confess and take communion at Christmas, Easter and Pentecost.

The sixth party sentenced was the statue[32] of Donna Leonor de Vivero, mother of Dr. Cazalla and the wife of Pedro de Cazalla. She was condemned for the same offenses as the others and she confessed before she died the following: a friar [Fray Domingo de Rojas] had taken her confession one Thursday after dinner. She also confessed many other things that she believed and had been told by learned and scholarly people. For this, and for other things she confessed, and because in her house people met and discussed these heresies, her statue was condemned to be burned and her bones to be exhumed from her tomb in the Monastery of St. Benito and to be burned together with her statue, and that her house be torn down and that no other house be built on that spot ever again and that a marble stone be erected there stating the reason the house was torn down.[33]

The seventh party sentenced was Alonso Perez, clergy, of Palencia, schoolmaster. He was accused of the same offenses as the above. He confessed nothing. He was testified against of the same things as Cazalla and the others. He was condemned, the same as Cazalla and his brother, to be defrocked and handed over to the civil authorities. They burned him.

After these six sentences were read, the bishop of Palencia [Don Pedro de la Gasca] stepped down from the Inquisitors' platform by way of some steps at the back that led to the platform where the penitents were seated and brought down Cazalla, his brother Francisco de Vivero, clergy, and master Alonso Perez, and dressed them all in 'massing' robes. The bishop, dressed only in a white robe and stole and amice,[34] cape and staff, defrocked all three of them. And before they were able to deprive him [Dr. Cazalla] of the last order, he turned on his knees to the prince and princess, and raising his hands, said these words: "Queen, I beg your majesty, for the sake of Christ's passion, you give me leave to say a word so all can see in what law I die." And rapidly they made him turn back towards the bishop, and he said no more. After they had been defrocked, they put on them a sort of cuirass, or harness, and the bishop climbed the steps to where the judges were and they all returned to their seats. And Cazalla, before he sat down, with the cross in his hands, in a loud voice said: "What I want to say is that I want all of you to know that I die in the law of Christ and that I am sorry I offended him and that I deserve that the earth swallow me up for the many and great offences I have committed against him. May the world and the people rejoice to know the great mercy God has manifested to me in that I might acknowledge my sin." And having said this, and other similar things, he sat down.

The eighth party, after the others had been defrocked, was Francisca de Zuñiga de Baeza, widow, of Jewish descent. She was a Lutheran and held the same heresies as the others, though not totally. She was sentences to the loss of her goods, to life in prison, to wear a *sanbenito* the rest of her life, to attend mass and hear a sermon every Sunday and

---

32 Effigy. Leonor de Vivero had died before this event took place.
33 This stone was not removed until the French troops removed it in 1809. (Blaquiere: 1822, 368).
34 A liturgical vestment consisting of an oblong piece of white linen worn around the neck and shoulders.

feast day of observance, and to confess and take communion at Christmas, Easter and Pentecost.

The ninth party was Don Pedro Sarmiento. The accusations against him were the same as the others. He confessed early on that people met in his house to carry on these ceremonies and they even said that those who now call themselves Christians would be killed. He said he had given money and horses to a *religioso* [friar], who was a Lutheran, and that he had not said the Ave Maria for a long time. He believed in mental confession and justification by faith and believed there were no more than two sacraments, baptism and the Eucharist. Forty-two witnesses testified against him. He said that for him the pope did not exist, that he had no power, and that he had not confessed for a year and a half, and believed the same things as Cazalla, and that our free will only made us do evil things, not good things, and that the Inquisition was very evil in that it persecuted good people, and whether or not God wanted, he would go to heaven all dressed up and with his boots and spurs on. He was sentenced to the loss of all his goods, to appear on the scaffold in a *sanbenito* and with a candle in his hand, to life in prison, to wear a *sanbenito* the rest of his life, and not to make use of any military privileges of any sort and that the rights and habit of the knights of Alcantara be taken from him, and that he attend mass and hear a sermon every Sunday and feast day of observance, and take communion at Christmas, Easter and Pentecost.

The tenth party was Mencia de Figueroa, the wife of Don Pedro Sarmiento. She was accused of the same offenses and confessed that she did not believe in purgatory and that the pope was the antichrist, and that someone [Donna Beatriz de Vivero] had told her that the Lord had chosen her and her husband to go to heaven. She also said that thanks to a petition to St. Denis she was saved the life of a child, and that she had also put out a fire with a prayer, and that a Lutheran [Francisco de San Roman] that the emperor had ordered to be burned several years ago here in Valladolid had died a martyr and that the emperor was wrong in ordering him to be killed and burned, and that the Christians [Catholics] should be destroyed. Her sentence was the same as her husband's.

The eleventh party was Don Luis de Rojas.[35] He confessed that he believed that there were no more than two sacraments, baptism and the Eucharist, and that the bread was not transformed into the flesh and body and the wine into the blood of our Lord Jesus Christ, and that the help of the saints was not necessary and that the pope and his ministers were to blame for this and for not allowing the friars and priests to marry, which was wrong. He said that he had wanted to go to Germany; that confession was to be made only to God, and that one could eat before taking the sacrament, and he had done so. He also said that the saints that are venerated on earth, on the day of judgment will be seen in hell, and that the sacrament cleansed us of original sin. Thirteen witnesses testified against him. His sentence was that he should appear on the scaffold in a *sanbenito* and should wear it as long as the Inquisition ordered, with the loss of all his goods, all his military privileges should be taken away and he should be banished from

---

35 Luis de Rojas Enríquez, grandson of the marquis of Poza.

Valladolid and from the Court[36] and not be allowed to leave Spain. He was to attend mass and hear a sermon every feast day of observance, and to confess and take communion at Christmas, Easter and Pentecost.

The twelfth party was Donna Ana Enriquez, the wife of Don Juan Alonso Mexia, citizen of Toro. She confessed that she believed one was not to confess to a priest and that she had confessed five times. She did not believe that the sacrament was preserved in the sacraria nor in the blessings of the church, and that Luther was not just a [saintly] man but rather a saint or an angel. She said more things, like the others, and said, "May it be God's will that I die at the stake for this cause." She was sentenced to the loss of her goods and to come on to the scaffold in a *sanbenito* and carrying a candle, and she was returned to the Inquisition prison. Her privileges were taken away, as were the others'.

The thirteenth party was Don Juan de Ulloa Pereyra, citizen of Toro, knight commander of the military order of St. John, who confessed he held the same doctrines as the above. He was sentenced to come on to the scaffold in a *sanbenito* with a candle in his hand, with the loss of his goods, and to return to the Inquisition prison in his *sanbenito*. He was deprived of his privileges and his habit of the order of St. John and ordered not to enter the Court or Valladolid or to leave Spain.

The fourteenth party was Donna Maria [Mencía] de Rojas, a nun of the Convent of St. Catalina in Valladolid. She was condemned for the errors she confessed. She was ordered to appear on the scaffold in a *sanbenito*, which she was to wear as long as she was a nun. She was returned to her monastery and was relegated to the last place in the choir, the chapter and all other activities of the convent. She was the sister of Pedro Sarmiento.[37]

The fifteenth party was donna Juana [Francisca] de Silva, illegitimate daughter of the marquis of Montemayor. She was sentenced, for the offenses she confessed and were proved, to wear a *sanbenito* and spend the rest of her life in prison, the same as her husband [Juan de Vivero].

The sixteenth party was Anton Dominguez [Minges], carpenter, citizen of Pedrosa. He was sentenced for the offenses he confessed and were confirmed. He was to wear a *sanbenito* for the rest of his life and spend his life in prison, and the same punishment as the others.

The seventeenth party was Leonor de Cisneros, the wife of Bachiller[38] Herrezuelo, citizen of Toro. She was to wear a *sanbenito* for the rest of her life, with life in prison and the same punishment as the others for what she confessed and was confirmed.[39]

The eighteenth party was Ana [Marina] de Saavedra, citizen of Zamora, wife of Cisneros [de Soto de Sotelo], de Toledo. She was sentenced, for the things she confessed and were confirmed, to appear on the scaffold in a *sanbenito*, with the loss of her goods.

---

36 This often refers to Madrid, but could be any city where the king held his court.
37 This is a mistake. She was the sister of Domingo de Rojas.
38 A title indicating an undergraduate degree.
39 In 1568 she was burned at the stake for having relapsed.

The nineteenth party was Juan Garcia [Gracia], silversmith, the convener of the heretics, a citizen of Valladolid. He was sentenced for the offenses he confessed and were confirmed. He was handed over to the civil authorities and burned at the stake, with the loss of his goods, like those that were burned at the stake.

The twentieth party was Anton Bagor,[40] an Englishman, sentenced, for the offenses he committed and were confirmed, to wear a *sanbenito* for one year.

The twenty-first party was Christobal de Ocampo, citizen of Zamora. He shared some of the heresies held by Cazalla and was sentenced to the loss of his goods and to be handed over to the civil authorities to be burned at the stake, like the others.

The twenty-second party was Isabel Dominguez,[41] citizen of Montemayor. She was sentenced, for the offenses she committed and confessed and were proven against her, to life imprisonment and to wear a *sanbenito*, together with the same punishments as the others.

The twenty-third party was Daniel [Gabriel] de la Quadra, citizen of Pedrosa. He was sentenced, for the offenses he confessed, to life imprisonment and to wear a *sanbenito*, together with the same punishments as the others.

The twenty-fourth offender was Cristobal de Padilla, citizen of Zamora. He denied the validity of the Apostolic See and, when one of his servants came out of the church after retrieving a soul from purgatory, Padilla told him that his mule could do the same. He was one of the preachers of that perverse sect; like the others, he denied the sacrament of penance. He was handed over to the civil authorities with the loss of all his goods. They strangled him and burned him.

The twenty-fifth party was Bachiller Herrezuelo, citizen of Toro. He did not want to recant and was burned alive with a clamp on his tongue. The heresies he upheld were that there were no sacraments, nor was there a purgatory, etc. He was also condemned to the loss of his goods.

The twenty-sixth party was Catalina Roman, citizen of Pedrosa. For the heresies she confessed, and were confirmed, she was handed over to the civil authorities, with the loss of her goods, to be burned.

The twenty-seventh party was Catalina Ortega, daughter of prosecutor Fernando Diez, member of the royal council. For the heresies she confessed, and were confirmed, she was handed over to the civil authorities, with the loss of her goods, to be burned.

The twenty-eighth party was Licenciate Francisco de Herrera,[42] citizen of Peñaranda, brother of Perez de Herrera. For the many heresies he confessed, and were confirmed, he was handed over to the civil authorities, with the loss of his goods, to be burned.

---

40 His name appears in different documents as Anton Graso, Anton Baxo, Anton Barcor, Anton Begon.
41 Elsewhere listed as Isabel Rodríguez or Isabel Mínguez.
42 He was the chief customs officer at Logroño who helped Carlo de Sesso to escape.

The twenty-ninth party was Isabel de Estrada,[43] citizen of Pedrosa. For some of the same heresies that the others held, which she confessed and were confirmed, she was handed over to the civil authorities, with the loss of her goods, to be burned.[44]

The thirtieth party was Juana [Catalina] Velazquez, citizen of Pedrosa, a young maiden. For some heresies that she confessed, and were confirmed, she was handed over to the civil authorities to be burned. The prince and the princess and all the knights and ladies that saw her felt great compassion for her because she showed great repentance for her sins, weeping bitterly. She died in the Catholic faith and heartily confessed the faith of Christ, with great signs and tokens. She and Cazalla were the ones that showed the greatest remorse for their sins.

At three in the afternoon the *auto* concluded. Fourteen, and the statue, which makes 15, were taken to be burned. For some unknown reason, Pedro Sarmiento, Juan de Ulloa Pereyra, and Don Luis de Rojas were taken to the city prison; the rest were taken back to the Inquisition prison to later be sent to the prison assigned them to comply with their sentence.

When Cazalla got to the bottom of the stairs of the scaffold, in a very loud voice he said some things that not everyone could hear. And having passed the cross at the 'Puerta del Campo' gate, which marks the city limits, the groups stopped for a quarter of an hour and Cazalla preached to Herrezuelo trying to convert him, but in vain. And again, at the stake, when they were about to tie Cazalla to his pole, he went over to Herrezuelo and begged him not to continue any longer in that wicked sect, but he saw it was to no avail. Then Cazalla climbed to his place (the others had already having been strangled) and spoke some words and gave signs that they might know he died in the Catholic faith. Of the fourteen, only Herrezuelo was burned alive because all the others converted and pleaded for mercy. Some say that one of the guards, either one on foot or on horseback, with a lance or a halberd, stabbed him harshly when he saw he refused to convert. All the guard, both those on foot and on horseback, accompanied them. They filled the street from one end to the other, with the offenders in the center. The stakes were set up just outside the 'Puerta del Campo' gate, facing the gate, and there was a distance of twelve or fourteen feet between each stake.

---

43 Some documents refer to her as Ysabel de la Quadra.
44 Despite the confusion in the first names, the appended material found at the end of *A Discovery* (1569) provides a little more information regarding Isabel de Estrada and Catalina Romana: "Katalina de Estrada, and Isabel Romana, both young women and born at Pedrosa. These were condemned only for denying the authority of the pope and his doctrine of purgatory and for affirming that the communion might be celebrated with any common bread. They were, moreover, charged with a certain letter written by them to some of their friends that were of the same religion, the which letter was at the time of their execution openly read upon the scaffold. Besides this, Isabel Romana was charged further that she said that Martin Luther was a prophet and an apostle sent by God and that the state and order of religious men and women (as they term them) was a mere devise of man's invention, forasmuch as all Christians were religious [priests], that is to say, in her understanding and construction, consecrated to God." (Montes: 1569, Appendix).

May our Lord uphold us and keep us from offending him in similar matters, or others, and that we may be worthy of his holy glory «ad quam nos perducat» (may he guide us).[45]

Another contemporary account of the May 21 *auto-da-fe* in Valladolid is found in a dispatch sent from Brussels to the Doge by Paulo Tiepolo, Venetian Ambassador with King Philip. A brief dispatch, dated May 28, 1559, simply reads, "Advices have been received from Spain that at Valladolid, ten of the principal noblemen of that Province (Leon) have been burnt for heresy." A few weeks later, on June 16, Tiepolo sent a list of the individuals condemned at the *auto*, along with some comments regarding each one:

List of individuals tried and condemned by the Inquisition at Valladolid on the 21st May 1559, Trinity Sunday, in the presence of the most Serene Prince of Spain and Princess of Portugal, Governess (of Spain):
- Doctor Augustin de Cazalla, his Majesty's preacher and chaplain, was degraded and burnt, and all his property confiscated.
- Francisco de Buiero,[46] priest, brother of Cazalla, was degraded and burnt, and all his property confiscated.
- Juan Buiero, brother of the aforesaid, sentenced to confiscation of his property, to perpetual imprisonment, to wear the habit of St. Benedict, to be disqualified from holding any office whatever, under penalty of being burnt for any contravention, to hear mass in the church which will be assigned him, and to confess and communicate [take communion] on the three Easters.
- Donna Costanza de Buiero, sister of the aforesaid, sentenced in like manner.
- Donna Leonora de Buiero, mother of all the aforesaid, being already deceased, they drew her statue to the scaffold, sentencing her property to be confiscated, and her bones, which had been buried in the Monastery of St. Benedict at Valladolid, to be burnt with the statue; and as all the heretics assembled in her house, they sentenced it to be leveled with the ground, an inscription on marble indicating the cause why it had been razed, and forbidding its restoration or removal of the marble at any time under penalty of most severe excommunication, and of banishment from all the realms of Spain.
- The priest, Maestro Alfonso Perez, was degraded and burnt, and his property confiscated. He was a man of forbidding appearance.
- Donna Francisca de Zuñiga had the same sentence as was passed on Juan Buiero.
- Don Pedro Sarmiento, son of the Marquis de Ponza, was sentenced in like manner, and deprived of the Commandery of Calatrava, and the site of his perpetual imprisonment will be assigned him.
- Donna Mencia de Figueroa, his wife, is condemned to the same punishment.
- Don Luis de Roxas, the nephew and heir of the Marquis de Ponza, is sentenced never to leave Spain, nor to enter Valladolid, or any place where the Catholic King holds his

---

45 Real Biblioteca de Palacio, II-2403, in: Schäfer (2014, III, 7–23, doc. 377). Brackets and notes mine.

46 This name, as well as several others, is misspelt. It should read Bivero or Vivero.

Court; his property to be confiscated, and he himself is declared ineligible to offices. On the day of the auto-da-fe, he ascended the scaffold in the habit of St. Benedict, and with a wax torch in his hand.

- Donna Anna Henriquez de Roxas, daughter of the Marquis de Alcanizes, who had her property confiscated, went to the scaffold in the habit of St. Benedict, and with a wax torch.
- Juan de Ullea de Toro, a Knight of St. John, was sentenced to the same punishment as Juan Buiero, and deprived of the Order of Knight of St. John.
- Donna Maria de Roxas, a professed nun, daughter of the Marquis de Ponza, was sentenced to confiscation of her property, and to go to the scaffold in the habit of St. Benedict, and with a candle, to be deprived of a vote, either active or passive, and of all the offices of her Order, and to be the last in the choir and refectory.
- Donna Juana de Silva, wife of Juan de Bivero (Buiero), sentenced to confiscation of her property, and to imprisonment, and without exemption to wear always the habit of St. Benedict.
- Antonio Dominiquez de Pedrosa sentenced to three years' imprisonment in a Benedictine monastery, and to confiscation of his property.
- Leonor de Cisneros de Toro condemned to the same punishment.
- Maria Sayavedra de Zamoza sentenced to imprisonment for life, declared ineligible to any office, to hear mass and sermon, and to confess and communicate on the three Easters, under penalty of being burnt.
- Juan Garcia, goldsmith, sentenced to confiscation of his property and to be burnt.
- Anthony Fason (sic), an Englishman, sentenced to carry a wax candle, to wear the habit of St. Benedict in the monastery to be appointed him, without going out of it, and to confess and communicate and (to hear) mass.
- Christoforo de Ocampo de Zamoza, sentenced to confiscation of his property and to be burnt.
- Isabella Dominguez, sentenced to confiscation of her property and to imprisonment for life.
- Daniel della Quadra, ploughman, sentenced to imprisonment for life in a Benedictine monastery.
- Christoforo de Padilla de Zamoza, one of the first authors and head of the Lutheran sect, sentenced to confiscation of his property and to be burnt.
- The Bachelor Herezuelo de Torro, sentenced to confiscation of his property and to be burnt. He was burnt alive, as he persevered in his heresy, remaining gagged the whole time, not having ever chosen to acknowledge the Holy Church of Rome.
- Caterina Roman, sentenced to the confiscation of her property and to the fire.
- The like sentence was passed on Donna Caterina de Ortega, daughter of the Treasurer.
- The like sentence was passed on the Licentiate Francisco de Herrera, of Jewish lineage; and on Isabella de Strada de Pedrosa, and on Juana Velasquez de Pedrosa.
- The property of the Portuguese Gonzalo Vaiz was confiscated to the Treasury, he himself being burnt for Judaism. (*Calendar of State Papers:* 1890, 94–105. Notes mine).

Auto-da-fe, Valladolid, October 8, 1559

If Dr. Augustin Cazalla was the protagonist of the first *auto-da-fe*, Carlo de Sesso and Fray Domingo de Rojas, son of the Marquis de Poza, were the protagonists of the second auto, celebrated a half year later in the presence of Philip II. When Fray Domingo de Rojas and Carlo de Sesso got word that they were being sought for by the Inquisition, they fled first to Logroño, where they procured a safe conduct from the Viceroy of Navarre, Beltrán de la Cueva y Toledo, to enter France and letters of recommendation to Queen Jeanne d'Albret.[47] At Logroño, Perez de Herrera, *alcalde de sacas* (customs officer), was of great assistance to them, but all was in vain. Rojas and Sesso were seized in June of 1558, brought back to Valladolid. They remained in prison until the *auto-da-fe* of October 8, 1559, when they were sentenced to be burned at the stake along with four others.[48] According to a letter from the Supreme Council to Pope Paul IV, dated September 9, 1558, some five or six months earlier they learned that people were,

> Secretly teaching the evil doctrines of Luther in Valladolid, Salamanca, Zaragoza, Toro, Palencia, and Logroño. Although the investigation and inquisition into this was begun with all possible dissimulation and secrecy, it nevertheless came to the attention of some of the guilty, among whom were Friar Domingo de Rojas, monk and preacher of the Order of St. Dominic, son of the Marquis de Poza, and Don Carlo de Sesso. They fled with precautions, with the monk in layman's clothes, but they were seized in Navarre, where they already had secured a safe conduct to go into France. Many of their accomplices have been seized and are imprisoned, people who are also prominent, illustrious and learned. (Homza: 2006, 188).

According to the appended material found at the end of Montes's *A Discovery* (1569), Fray Domingo took advantage of the moment and, like Dr. Cazalla, addressed the king and those present. The appended text reads thus:

> Fray Domingo de Rojas, a Dominican friar, son to the aforesaid Marques de Poza, who being brought upon the stage [scaffold], and having obtained license of the king to speak a few words in the hearing of the people, began to discourse of the points and articles of Christian religion whereupon the king, being in presence, commanded to remove him. Nevertheless, he proceeded till two of the guards took him and perforce set their engine of wood upon his tongue (which in the treatise before is termed a Barnacle) and so carried him from the scaffold, accompanied with a number of monks, above a hundred, flocking about him, railing and making exclamation against him, some of them urging him to recant, but he, notwithstanding, answered them with a bold spirit

---

47 Jeanne d'Albret was queen of Navarre from 1555 to 1572. She was the acknowledged spiritual and political leader of the French Huguenot movement and a key figure in the French Wars of Religion.

48 For a transcription (in English) of his last declaration made the evening before he was sent to the stake, see Homza (2006, 195).

that he would never renounce the doctrine of Christ. And so passed to the place of execution.

Some historians tend to believe that Sesso and Rojas were kept for the second auto-da-fe so that Philip II could be present. Had this been the case, they would also have reserved Dr. Cazalla, who had been his father's chaplain. The reason was another; Sesso and Rojas were key figures in the accusations against Bartolome de Carranza, as we shall presently see. Though Carranza was under surveillance ever since his return to Spain in the fall of 1558, he was not arrested until August 1559. Had the Inquisitors sent Sesso and Rojas to the stake in May, they would have lost two indispensable witnesses.

Bartolome de Carranza (1503–1576)

Bartolome de Miranda, better remembered as Bartolome de Carranza, archbishop of Toledo, began his studies at Alcala, where his uncle Sancho Carranza de Miranda (d. 1531) was professor of philosophy and theology. Sancho Carranza had studied at the University of Paris, where he also earned a doctorate. He was canon of Calahorra, and Inquisitor of Navarra, and in 1513 appointed professor of philosophy at the University of Alcala. In the anti-Erasmian controversy, he initially lined up with Diego Lopez de Zuñiga and the anti-Erasmians. In 1520 he was sent to Rome as a delegate to Leon X, where he spent three years. On his return he had changed his view towards Erasmus and in 1527 took part in the Conferencia de Valladolid favoring Erasmus and his works.

In 1520, Bartolome de Carranza entered the Dominican order and in 1525 he went to study theology at the University of Salamanca. Two years later he began teaching theology at the Colegio de San Gregorio de Valladolid. Like many of his contemporaries, in 1530 he was denounced to the Inquisition for Erasmian leanings, but the process failed. There were many contradictions in Carranza's life, to the point that Reginaldo Gonzalez de Montes (1569, f. 89v) does not even refer to him by his real name, though he leaves no doubt regarding the person he is referring to:

> Bartolome de Zamora, a monk of the order of Saint Domenic, a man very well learned and one that knew the truth, who afterwards, by the emperor's means, was preferred to the archbishopric of Toledo, whence he was shortly after deposed for heresy, or as it is more probably conjectured, upon some privy grudge which the Archbishop of Seville, high commissioner in the Inquisition, bore unto him and, after many conflicts with the Inquisitors, at length died.

In Protestant circles, Carranza was only too well remembered for his "misdeeds" while in England and Flanders. He and Cardinal Pole were the driving force behind the return of the English universities to Catholicism, heavily penetrated by Protestantism during the previous reign.[49] His name was associated with censorship, persecutions, book-burnings, the proceedings against Thomas Cranmer, archbishop of Canterbury, etc. Another of his missions was to recuperate monastic properties and estates that Eduard VI had confiscated. He even seemed to have initiated the exhumation and dishonorable disposal of the remains of Peter Martyr's wife Catherine Dampmartin in 1557 (Tellechea: 1977a, 186). Carranza was also responsible for compiling a list of Spaniards living in Germany and Flanders that were sending books into Spain (Garrido: 1863, 438). His name would necessarily produce bad vibrations in Protestant circles hence Montes's adjustment—"Bartolome de Zamora"—, a simple stratagem to camouflage his identity without altering the text. Henry Ch. Lea states, "Bartholome Carranza, boasted with gross hyperbole that whilst in England he had caused 30,000 heretics to submit, be burnt, or go into exile." (Dickens: 1964, 365).

Carranza had an eventful life; he was well connected and well travelled. In 1539, as representative to the chapter-general of his order he visited Rome, where he was made Master of Theology at the *studium generale* of the Dominican Order at the Convent of Santa Maria sopra Minerva. He declared at his trial in 1562 that on May 23, 1539, he was licensed by Pope Paul III to have in his possession—and to read—Luther's writings, as well as those of other prohibited authors (Tellechea: 1975, XXX, Part I, xxiii). Either while in Rome, or prior to his visit to Rome, he must have had sympathies for—and known the whereabouts of—Juan de Valdes because from Rome he wrote Valdes, who then was in Naples, lamenting the fact that he did not have time to pay him a visit, but begged him to please send him the names of authors that best expounded the Scriptures because on his return to Spain he was to begin lecturing on Holy Scripture at the Colegio de San Gregorio de Valladolid. Thomas M'Crie (1833, 141–142) offers the following details of this correspondence:

> A treatise drawn up by him under the title of Advice on the Interpreters of Sacred Scripture, which was circulated privately among his acquaintance, was originally sent in the form of a letter to his friend Bartolome Carranza, who afterwards became archbishop of Toledo. [...] This tract was found among the papers of the primate when he was subsequently seized by the order of the Inquisition, and formed one of the gravest articles of charge against that distinguished and long-persecuted prelate. The Advice contained the following propositions, among others: first, that in order to understand the sacred scriptures, we must not rely on the interpretations of the fathers;

---

49 "Jewel spoke thus of the present state of the University of Oxford: That whatsoever had been planted there by Peter Martyr was, by the means of one friar [Pedro de] Soto and another Spanish Monk [Carranza] so wholly rooted out, that the Lord's vineyard was turned into a wilderness." (Fittler/Skelton: 1820–1840, I, 195. Brackets mine). Also see Hegarty (2005, 153–172).

second, that we are justified by a lively faith in the passion and death of our Saviour; and third, that we may attain to certainty concerning our justification. The agreement between these and the leading sentiments maintained by Luther renders it highly probable that Valdes had read the writings of that reformer or of some of his adherents. At the same time we are told that the principal things in this tract were taken from the Christian Institutes of Tauler.[50]

Valdes sent him the list of authors, which very likely coincided with the authors he had recommended—and were published in Spanish and available in Spain—in his confiscated *Dialog on Christian Doctrine*, that is, Erasmus, Jean Gerson, St. Jerome, St. Gregory, etc. together with a copy of his *Considerations*.[51] On his return to Spain, Carranza had copies made of Valdes's letter, which he circulated among his students together with copies of the *Considerations*.[52] According to Fray Domingo de Rojas, Carranza began his very first lesson as Prior of the Dominican convent at Palencia reading Valdes's letter to his students so they would know which authors to read and which not to read. According to Domingo de Rojas, no one was scandalized and they all spoke highly of this advice. Years later, Fray Domingo recalled that despite Carranza's enthusiasm, he never disclosed the name of the author of the letter or the *Considerations*, from which he deduced later that Carranza was well aware that the material was heretical (Schäfer: 2014, IV, 1051).

In 1545, Carranza was sent again as imperial representative to the Council of Trent along with another Dominican, Domingo de Soto. There he took a very active part in the discussions regarding the sacraments and the drafting of the eleven articles on the duty of episcopal residence and other disciplinary matters related to the office of bishops (Kirsch: 1908). Carranza defended the view that the duty of residence was a divine law. One event that must have marked him on his return to Spain was his having to preach the sermon at the *auto-da-fe* in 1546 in which San Roman was sentenced to the stake. Francisca de Zuñiga declared later how he had often spoken of this event with the nuns of the Convent of Belen

---

50 Johannes Tauler was a German mystic. Around 1330 he began his preaching career in Strasbourg. The city contained eight convents of Dominican nuns and perhaps seventy smaller beguine communities. Much of his preaching was directed to these devout women. During his exile (c1339–43) in Basel he became acquainted with the circles of devout clergy and laity known as the Friends of God. It was with them that he taught his belief that the state of the soul was affected more by a personal relationship with God than by external practices. Even Martin Luther found his sermons engaging and instructive.

51 This had to be a manuscript copy of the original Spanish version. The first printed edition of Valdes's *Considerations*, edited by C.S. Curione, was in Italian: *Le cento et dieci divine considerationi del S. Giovanni Valdesso: nelle quali si ragiona delle cose piu utili, piu necessarie, e piu perfette, della christiana professione* (Basel: J. Oporinus, 1550).

52 Among his students at that time were fray Luis de la Cruz, fray Alfonso de Castro, fray Domingo de Rojas, who would later become one of the leaders of the evangelical movement, and fray Juan de Villagarcía, who would become Carranza's closest confidant.

and how they were convinced that he secretly sided with San Roman (Schäfer: 2014, IV, 993).[53]

In 1548, Charles V asked Carranza to accompany prince Philip on his tour of Flanders, but he declined the honor. Had he accepted, he would have coincided with Dr. Cazalla and Dr. Constantino Ponce de la Fuente. Meanwhile, back in Valladolid, Carranza had become the confessor of Francisca de Zuñiga, the daughter of Antonio de Baeza of Escalona (Schäfer: 2014, IV, 988). When Carranza left for England in 1554, he recommended she take on Fray Domingo de Rojas as her confessor, which she did. A close relationship between Carranza and Fray Domingo de Rojas, son of the Marquis of Poza, went back to when Fray Domingo accompanied Carranza on his second journey to Trent in 1552. At his trial in 1559, Fray Domingo related an interesting incident that took place during that journey. At the inn where they were staying in Milan, on the way up to Trent, there were also lodging some Hungarian Lutherans belonging to the entourage of Ferdinand I. While the Spaniards were warming themselves around the fire, one of the Hungarians entered the room and began conversing with the Bishop of Segovia, Gaspar de Zuñiga, who was in the company. At that point, Carranza joined in the conversation and a heated dispute ensued. Finally the other man left. Once they were alone, Carranza admitted to Rojas, "I swear no one has embarrassed me so much in all my life as this man. He masters the Scriptures much better than I do, and he can recite them much better than I can being a professor of theology." (Schäfer: 2014, IV, 1038).

Around 1552 Carranza became part of crown prince Philip's staff. In 1554, when the marriage between Philip and Mary Tudor, queen of England, required the presence of competent theologians in both Catholic and Lutheran doctrine to facilitate the return of the Anglican Church to papal obedience, Bartolome de Carranza and Cardinal Pole were chosen for the task. In January of 1556, Charles V called his son Philip to Flanders, but Carranza stayed on in London another year, where he devoted his time to burning Lutheran books and stamping out heresy. The following year he was in Brussels expurgating and censuring Lutheran literature arriving in Flanders from Germany. For his labors, and against all speculations, Philip II appointed him to the much-coveted post of archbishop of Toledo and he was consecrated at Brussels on February 27, 1558. The newly appointed archbishop left Flanders in June and reached Valladolid in August. Less than a year later, on August 22, 1559, he found himself arrested and imprisoned.[54]

Carranza had been clearly warned by a faithful friend already in May that this

---

53 For an account of Francisco San Roman's contact with evangelicals, see M'Crie (1829, 170–175).

54 AHN, Inquisición, leg. 1822, doc. 11, in: Schäfer (2014, III, 152, doc. 400).

would happen. Indeed, on May 30, 1559, Fray Luis de la Cruz sent Carranza, who was still in Brussels at that time, the following letter:

Last week Saturday I visited the Inquisition prison in Valladolid and, regarding that which I wrote to you about, I spoke with all fourteen of those that were burned:[55] doctor Cazalla and his brother Francisco de Vivero and his sister Beatriz and Licenciate Herrera, and Bachiller Herrezuelo from Toro, and Cristobal de Ocampo, uncle of Inquisitor Vaca de Zamora,[56] master Alonso Perez of Zamora, and Padilla, and a Jew, and widow Catalina de Hortega and Juana Velasquez, the young marquess of Alcañices's maid, Isabel d Estrada and Catalina la Romana and Juan Garcia, the silversmith, and the statue and the bones of the mother of the Cazallas. I also spoke with those who were reconciled, sixteen of which included Pedro Sarmiento, his wife, Luis de Rojas and his cousin Ana, Catalina de Saavedra, wife of an aristocrat from Zamora, called Sotelo de Cisneros, Leonor de Cisneros, wife of Bachiller Herrezuelo, Isabel Dominguez, the niece of our prosecutor, Francisca de Zuñiga, daughter of Antonio de Baeza, and Costanza de Vivero and Juan de Vivero, Cazalla's siblings, Juana de Silva, bastard daughter of the marquis of Montemayor, the wife of Juan de Vivero, two farmhands from Pedrosa and a young Englishman, and Juan de Ulloa Pereyda, knight of San Juan, born in Toro, and Maria de Rojas, a nun from Sta. Catalina.

While I comforted them and fortified them, I asked them how they had come to believe those horrible heresies by which they had been deceived. Luis de Rojas told me that fray Domingo [de Rojas] had told him that God had publicly revealed all this to you and to Father Juan de Villagarcia, and the assurance of faith to Fray Ambrosio de Salazar. He had repeated it also to all the others he had deceived and all of them have declared it before the inquisitors. But I know first hand from two inquisitors that to the question of how he could have taught such profound errors and heresies, fray Domingo answered that he had lied to them about you saying that God had manifested it to you. That was misleading and a lie. And even if he had not said it, the truth would have come out just reading the sentences they were given. Beatriz knew—and this was also read aloud— that fray Domingo had deceived her, yet he wanted to denounce her when, by means of a letter she had written him (dated Simancas, July 10, 1557) he realized she was in error. Padilla was tricked by Carlos [Sesso], Beatriz by Juan Sánchez, Juan Sánchez by Pedro de Cazalla, Pedro de Cazalla by Carlos [Sesso], doctor Cazalla by Carlos and his brother Pedro de Cazalla, Juan de Vivero and his wife and Constanza and her mother, the aged Leonor, by doctor Cazalla, Catalina de Hortega by Juan Sanchez, and these two seduced the silversmith Juan Garcia and the nun Maria; fray Domingo deceived his brothers and his nephew, and Padilla deceived those from Zamora. From this list as well as from the time they confessed to hold these errors, it is evident—even to the devils in hell, who are steeped in evil—that fray Domingo lied saying that to his relatives. As a result, when they heard each other's sentence read, they realized that what he had said to two or three was false and wrong. Nevertheless, Valladolid went up in human flames, and it is believed that the four persons they still hold in custody [Carlo de Sesso, fray Domingo

---

55 They were sent to the stake ten days earlier, at the *auto-da-fe* held on May 21.
56 See Moreno (2012, 202–214).

de Rojas, Juan Sanchez, Pedro de Cazalla], together with seven nuns from the Convent of Belen, and others, and those that after Our Lady of August [August 15] will be brought out in *auto*,[57] are all against you.

The same day that the guardian of San Francisco came to speak to Mencia, the wife of Pedro Sarmiento, to convert her, he said that Carlos [Sesso], fray Domingo [de Rojas], Juan Sanchez and Pedro de Cazalla were being kept in custody until they had taken you prisoner. More than seven persons heard him say that and those blessed judges did not report it or punish that gossip. All those that were burned died correctly except for Herrezuelo, who showed no feelings and remained obstinate in his errors. Francisco de Vivero was uneasy and from time to time uttered some blasphemy. All those that were reconciled were sentenced to wear a *sanbenito* and the majority to life in prison, except Ana Enriquez, who Geronimo Mexia, her brother-in-law, took back to his home scot-free, though her goods have been confiscated, as well as those of Luis de Rojas, who will be sent to Coria with the bishop his uncle, and those of Juan Pereyda, who has been dispossessed of his knightship in the Order of San Juan, and the Englishman, who has been sent to a monastery for a year.

Valladolid, May 30, [1559]. Illustrious Lord. Señor, I kiss the hands of your Lordship. Fray Luis de la Cruz.[58]

Little did Fray Luis de la Cruz suspect that he himself would be taken prisoner a week before Carranza and would find himself among the very persons he mentioned in his letter. Fray Luis was arrested on August 16, 1559. Eighty-one witnesses testified at his trial, many of them at Seville, where he had preached during Lent of 1556. Witnesses 62, 72, 73, 74, 75, and 78 declared that when preaching in the Monastery of Nuestra Señora de Gracia in Seville, he had said, "Oh Lord, if you were to return to earth and preach, they would say you are a Lutheran!" They also certified that he was a close friend of Dr. Egidio, Constantino Ponce de la Fuente, Gonzalo Hernandez, fray Geronimo Caro, fray Casiodoro de Reina, Gaspar Baptista, Juan Gonzalez, "condemned by the Inquisition as Lutheran heretics." Another accusation was that Luis de la Cruz had among his papers a copy of the letter Juan de Valdes had sent to Bartolome de Carranza in 1539. Prosecutor Jeronimo Ramirez insisted that Luis de la Cruz be sent to the torture chamber and torture should be repeated until he confessed that what witness 45—Martin Gutierrez—claimed was true that Cruz had told him about what happened one day when he was saying mass with Carranza.[59] While in prison, Luis de la Cruz tried to escape several times, once he even set fire to his cell.

Bartolome de Carranza was imprisoned a week after Fray Luis de la Cruz. Why

---

57 This would take place on October 8.
58 AHN, Inquisición, leg. 1822, doc. 11, in: Schäfer (2014, III, 152, doc. 400). Notes and brackets mine.
59 AHN, Inquisición, leg. 2942, doc. 76, in: Lopez Muñoz (2011, 155, doc. 76).

would Philip II, who had just named him archbishop of Toledo, allow the inquisitors to treat him in such a humiliating way? It must be remembered that the Dominican theologian Melchor Cano, Inquisitor General Valdes's principal advisor, was instrumental in the arrest of Bartolome Carranza. As archbishop of Toledo and Primate of Spain, Carranza immediately appealed to Rome and Martin Azpilcueta, his lawyer, wrote two letters to the king to remind him of the legal impossibility to judge an archbishop in Spain by canon law (Iglesia: 2011, 510). His trial, which began in the summer of 1562 after he had been in prison for nearly three years, dragged on in Spain until 1564, when he was finally sent to Rome and where he died some ten years later.

A year after Carranza's arrest, Paulo Tiepolo, the aforementioned Venetian ambassador with Philip II, wrote to the Doge:

> The Nuncio brought the pope's determination about the case of the Archbishop of Toledo, who, having been charged with heresy more than a year ago, is in such close imprisonment that he has neither seen nor spoken to anyone. The Archbishop of Seville [Fernando de Valdés], as General of the Inquisition, laid claim to judge him, but the Archbishop of Toledo declared the Archbishop of Seville to be also suspected, owing to several disputes between them. The Archbishop of Seville, alleging that prestige was thus withdrawn from the office of the Inquisition, which is so important in Spain, appealed to the pope. His Holiness however made this case known to several persons, and having heard that besides the strife between the Archbishops various irregularities had occurred, amongst which was the deprivation of the Archbishop of Toledo of the administration of the revenues of the archbishopric before cognisance of the cause, the pope has declared that his Majesty is to depute another impartial person to draw up the proceeding against the Archbishop. Last week the Inquisition arrested the Abbot of Valladolid, brother of the Admiral of Castile, one of the chief grandees in Spain. The accusation against him is that he favoured the Archbishop of Toledo by writing to Rome, and to the Nuncio here, about the Archbishop of Seville and some other members of the Inquisition, calling them, "ignorant and full of prejudice." (*Calendar of State*, 1890).

Not knowing what his evangelical contacts had declared during their trials regarding their conversations, Carranza insisted that as part of the accusations, the trial records of Domingo de Rojas, Dr. Augustin Cazalla, Pedro de Cazalla, Ana Enriquez, Francisca de Zuñiga, and Francisco de Herrera be included in his process. These records were filed as part of Carranza's process and were finally rediscovered thanks to the efforts of professor José Ignacio Tellechea Idígoras (1975, XXX, 233).[60]

Whereas most historians tend to emphasis censorship of his *Catechism* and the animosity Inquisitor General Fernando de Valdes felt for him as the main

---

60 For a full transcription of the report presented against Carranza on May 6, 1559, by prosecuting attorney Licenciado Camino, and Carranza's recusal, see Homza (2006, 199–211).

reasons for Carranza's arrest in August of 1559—both of which are well-founded—, nevertheless, the underlying reality is that, contrary to the accepted legalistic attitude towards heresy involving drastic public punishment, Carranza supported a more private, fraternal and pastoral correction of doctrinal error. This is corroborated by Alonso Lopez in his declaration before Dr. Antonio Nieto in Ciudad Rodrigo on August 12, 1559, where he admitted that "it is Carranza's fault that so many of us are in prison." (Schäfer: 2014, IV, 1073). This statement does not infer Carranza's having denouncing them, but rather his falling short of denouncing them. In other words, if Carranza had "nipped the heresy in the bud," it would not have spread and they would not be in prison. On the other hand, Carranza was well aware of Inquisitor General Valdes's animosity and a month after his arrest compiled a list of 25 complaints regarding his behavior towards him (Homza: 2006, 204–208).

Bartolome de Carranza was not the only bishop of Toledo to be examined by the Inquisition. Despite his declared anti-Erasmianism and his staunch defense of "cleanliness of blood,"—a concept strongly repudiated by the Erasmians (De Espona: 2005, 45)—, Carranza's predecessor, Juan Martinez Siliceo, just barely escaped. The discovery in the summer of 1557 of a delivery of Protestant books in Seville put the Supreme Council on guard. No time was lost in informing the tribunals throughout Spain of the arrival of heretical books and the need to publish local edicts prohibiting them. In a letter from the Supreme Council to the Inquisitors at Toledo, dated October 21, 1557, there was attached the following note: "We have information that the cardinal of Toledo, peace be to him, had many prohibited books in his library. These books should be taken to the Holy Office."[61] This referred to Juan Martinez Siliceo, who had been crown prince Philip's tutor. Fortunately he had passed away some five months earlier. There were many more. Juan Antonio Llorente (1843, 357–371) lists "eight venerable prelates and nine doctors of theology sent by Spain to the Council of Trent that were attacked in secret by the Inquisition" and dedicates a whole chapter to them. The majority were accused of being Lutheran sympathizers simply because they did not find errors in Carranza's *Catechism*.

---

61 AHN, Inquisición, lib. 575, f. 53 y ss, in: Lopez Muñoz (2011, 111, doc. 33).

Chapter 7:
Female Voices in Guadalajara and Valladolid

> My coming to Valladolid from Toro, on January 25, 1558, was like the conversion of St.
> Paul. When I got here, Beatriz de Vivero spoke to me and persuaded me that she had
> discovered the truth of the spirit and her salvation and that she was absolutely sure of
> her salvation and of God's pardon through the merits of the death of Jesus Christ alone
> because she had accepted Jesus Christ through faith, which she called "to put on
> Christ," because thus we are made members of Christ and his brethren, and children of
> the Father through his redemption.
>
> Ana Enriquez (Valladolid, 1558)

At the first *auto-da-fe* against the Lutherans in Valladolid, held on May 21, 1559, fourteen women—and sixteen men—received sentences. Six of the women were sent to the stake. At the next *auto-da-fe*, held on October 8, 1559, six more women—and ten men—were sent to the stake. In other words, of a total of 58 persons sentenced for holding Protestant convictions at those two *autos*, more than half were women. Numerically, the proportion is comparable to that of Seville. Their social status was also similar. Four groups can be distinguished: members of the extended Cazalla family; nuns; *beatas* (lay nuns); and a select group of aristocrats. Many of the professed nuns also belonged to noble families and appear in the documents with the title of *donna* [Lady]. Gonzalo de Illescas, in his *Historia Pontifical y Católica,* makes the following comment regarding these nuns: "they were all young and beautiful, and not happy with simply being Lutherans, they turned into dogmatizers of that damned doctrine!" (Menendez y Pelayo: 1881, IV, 427).

Cases detected in and around Guadalajara fell under the jurisdiction of Toledo; those detected in Zamora and Toro were judged by the tribunal in Valladolid. The prisons were often located in the same building as the tribunals. In Valladolid, the tribunal was located next to the bishop's residence, on what is today Fray Luis de Leon Street. When this building became too small, the inquisitors began contemplating the idea of buying the adjoining houses, but the Supreme Council advised against it because "the walls are very thin, which enables the prisoners to communicate with each other, which is very inconvenient and detrimental to our business." (Bustamante Garcia: 1995, 459–460). The prison was finally moved to a building near the Church of San Pedro. There were different types of prison terms. "Perpetual prison" (*carcel perpetua*) referred to anything from permanent house arrest to confinement in one of the prison houses or some monastery. All prisoners were obliged to wear *sanbenitos*. Within the prison no one took notice, but on the street as they went to mass each Sunday—another requisite imposed on them—their *sanbenitos* were noticeable from far, making them objects of insult and scorn.

The Cazalla Family

The female members of the Cazalla family sentenced by the Inquisition for their Protestant views included Dr. Augustin's mother Leonor Vivero, his sisters Beatriz and Constanza, his sister-in-law Juana de Silva, and Beatriz's maid Isabel Dominguez. At the *auto-da-fe* held in May, Beatriz de Vivero, who was a *beata*, was sentenced to the stake. Beatriz pleaded guilty under torture and begged for reconciliation. Two inquisitors voted in favor and ten against her. Discrepancy in the vote was a factor that hindered her from lawfully being condemned to the stake. As a result, the local inquisitors referred her case to the Supreme Council. The Council showed no clemency, but declared that she be handed over to the civil authorities and be burned (*relajada*). She was accused of taking communion of the two forms, of eating meat on Fridays, disdaining fastings, religious vows and celibacy, believing that unbaptized children of believing parents went straight to heaven if they died, and that Martin Luther was a holy man (Schäfer: 2014, III, 32).

Beatriz Vivero's maid, Isabel Dominguez, was the niece of the choir director of the cathedral. While awaiting trial she shared a cell with Juana Sanchez, who would later commit suicide. Isabel was sentenced to "perpetual prison." When on March 7, 1562, Dr. Simancas, a member of the Supreme Council paid a visit to the prisoners, Isabel declared that she had no complaints, except for the fireplace and the leaky roof, which he ordered to be repaired immediately. The next we hear of Isabel is five years later, on October 11, 1567, when Fernando de Vega de Fonseca visited the prisoners. His report stated: "Isabel Dominguez, maid to Vivero, born in Cuellar, near Montemayor. She says that she is 28 years old and that she was 19 when she was arrested. On May 21, eight years ago, she was reconciled and has spent all this time here. She begs us to have mercy on her." In January of the following year she was allowed to remove her *sanbenito* (Schäfer: 2014, III, 155, doc. 402). She must also have been allowed to leave because on September 7, 1569, she was arrested again and then condemned, on November 11, 1571, to "irremissible prison" and *sanbenito* for life (Schäfer: 2014, III, 164, doc. 411).

Constanza de Vivero received a lesser sentence. She was the widowed wife of Hernando Ortiz, one of the royal accountants, who had been one of Philip II's trustworthy servants. In 1551, he was commissioned to purchase the necessary things for Philip's sister princess Juana's journey to Portugal for her marriage with her cousin the crown prince of Portugal, Juan Manuel de Portugal. Ortiz died in 1556, leaving a debt of 11,000 ducats and thirteen young children (Schäfer: 2014, III, 24, doc. 378). When Dr. Cazalla saw his sister walk up to the scaffold the day of the *auto*, he turned to princess Juana, who presided the event as acting governess, and said, "Princess, I entreat your highness to have compassion on that unfortunate woman, who leaves thirteen orphans." (Llorente: 1843, 204). Because the inquisitors considered she had not sheltered heretics as enthusiastically as the others, Constanza was not sent to the stake, but sentenced to the confiscation of all her goods, life in prison without remission, to wearing a *sanbenito* over her clothes for the rest of her life, and for her offspring to be considered unworthy to hold any public office (Schäfer: 2014, III, 24, doc. 378).

Leonor de Vivero, Dr. Cazalla's mother, had had close links with the controversial *alumbrada* Francisca Hernandez in the early 1520s. Leonor died before the first *auto-da-fe*, but that did not exempt her from enduring the wrath of the inquisitors.[1] Although she had confessed certain "errors" while still alive, they considered that she had died as a Lutheran hence they exhumed her bones, which had been buried in the Monastery of San Benito, put them in a box, and carried them to the scaffold that day.

> It was ruled that she had died as a heretic, that her memory was worthy of defamation and that her estate should be confiscated and her bones were ordered exhumed and burnt publicly along with a likeness of her. Furthermore that her house be leveled, that salt be scattered over the lot and that right there be erected a pillar bearing an inscription explaining the reason for the demolition: "Presiding the Roman Church Paul IV and reigning in Spain Philip II, The Holy Office of the Inquisition condemned to tear down and destroy these houses of Pedro de Cazalla, one of the royal accountants, and Doña Leonor de Vibero his wife because the Lutheran heretics gathered and counseled against our holy Catholic faith and church of Rome. May 21, 1559." (Cristler/ Hall: 2004, 48).

Llorente (1843, 199) confirms this testimony, but with the reservation that he thought the monument had been removed:

> Her memory and her posterity were condemned to infamy, her property confiscated, her body disinterred and burnt with her effigy, and her house razed to the ground, and prohibited from being rebuilt; a monument with an inscription relating to this event was placed on the spot. I have seen the column and the inscription; I have heard that it was destroyed in 1809.

Napoleon abolished the Inquisition as an institution in 1809, but the spirit of the Inquisition lived on. It is uncertain when the inscription was finally removed.

---

1 Leonor de Vivero may have died shortly before the group was arrested in the spring of 1558 because in his confession, made before Inquisitor Guijelmo on October 8, 1558, her son Francisco de Vivero declared that the previous winter his sister Beatriz had written their mother a letter from Palencia. (Schäfer: 2014, III, 436–437).

The Beatas

The belief in women's "natural" predilection toward piety made *beatas*—lay nuns—popular in Spain in the first half of the sixteenth century. However, because *beatas* were women of the *via media* (the middle path), neither strictly lay nor religious, the boundaries of their avocation were fraught with ambiguity (Van Deusen: 2002, 24). Indeed, in general, *beatas* were viewed as neither sacred nor worldly thus reinforcing the ambiguous middle ground upon which most of them trod. The *alumbradas-deixadas* Isabel de la Cruz and Maria de Cazalla exemplify these women. Their rejection of external forms of worship and their call for Holy Scriptures as the basis for direct knowledge of God came dangerously close to Lutheranism and placed them under the scrutinizing eye of the Inquisition.

Isabel de la Cruz carried on her *alumbrado-deixado* activities undisturbed in the Guadalajara area until Maria Nuñez denounced her to the Toledo Inquisition as a heretic in May of 1519. In her first accusation, Maria said that on one of her visits to see Isabel early in 1518, she was reading in St. Bonaventure about how the Lord punished the souls of the wicked for all eternity.[2] Maria said that she cried out in commiseration, "Oh Lord, to think that they must be denied your presence forever and must be tormented," and that Isabel had scolded her. In June, Maria Nuñez told the inquisitors that she remembered more things: Isabel and her disciple, Pedro Ruiz de Alcaraz, used to mock those who did penance for their sins. At that time, the Toledo inquisitors did not bother to take any action against Isabel on the basis of these accusations. By 1523, Isabel had become the recognized leader of the movement, which was gathering momentum throughout New Castile. But by then, the Toledo inquisitors were sufficiently persuaded that a menace to orthodoxy existed. The first hint of real trouble came in late 1523 or early 1524, when the Franciscan provincial, Andres de Ecija, after making a personal investigation of Isabel's teachings, deprived her of her status as lay tertiary sister of the Franciscan order. Very soon after that—on February 26, 1524—the Toledo Inquisition arrested her and her long (five-year) trial for heresy began. She was mainly accused of rejecting priestly intermediaries and external rituals such as meditation on Christ's passion, bowing before the Eucharist, praying to saints, etc. Between May 1524 and February of 1526 at least a dozen witnesses from Guadalajara, Pastrana, and Toledo were questioned about her activities. These interrogations confirmed Inquisitorial suspicions that Isabel had "converted" a good number of persons to the principles of *deixamiento*. In March 1526, Maria Nuñez was again called before the Toledo inquisitors to verify the accusations she had made seven years before and was

---

2 Very possibly this was Bonaventure's *Estímulo de amor divino* (Toledo: Hagenbach, 1505).

asked if she had more to add, and indeed she did. She said that Isabel was always ridiculing sermons she had heard. Two days later Maria Nunez was back with more: Isabel claimed that God was to be found more perfectly in one's spirit than he was in the sacrament of the Eucharist, and that people should not give such reverence to the said sacrament. Finally, in 1527 the inquisitors voted six to three in favor of burning Isabel at the stake; the others favoring life imprisonment. A delay of almost two years followed until April 21, 1529, when Isabel de la Cruz was officially sentenced to life imprisonment as an "inventor of scandalous errors and novelties in the church of God."

Maria de Cazalla, born in Palma del Rio (Cordoba), was of *converso* stock. She was brought to trial in Toledo in 1532 and sentenced in December 1534 to perform public penance in her parish church and to pay fines totaling one hundred ducats. Maria was the mother of six children and had spent most of her life working as a lace-maker in Guadalajara. Her brother, Juan de Cazalla, was a Franciscan friar who had been Cardinal Cisneros's chaplain in Toledo, and later bishop of Avila. Like many intellectuals of his day, he was a declared Erasmian. Maria was first influenced by the *recogidos*, mainly Fray Francisco Osuna, from the "observant" convent of La Salceda. Through them and Brianda de Mendoza, whose *beaterio* was under their ecclesiastical supervision, Maria had access to the parlors of highly educated noblewomen such as Isabel de Aragon and Mencia de Mendoza and their humanist tutor, Juan Maldonado (Smith/Colahan: 2009, 1–9). Likewise, through her brother Juan de Cazalla, she became acquainted with the writings of Erasmus, as well as St. Augustine and St. Bonaventure. When arrested in 1532 and put on trial in Toledo, and accused of being an *alumbrada*, Maria de Cazalla protested strongly. In her defense, she insinuated that she was an Erasmian (Yovel: 2009, 254). Inquisitor Mejia then questioned her regarding her opinion of Luther, Erasmus, Duns Scotus, etc. She admitted that she had read Erasmus's *Paternoster* (in Spanish), as well as the *Enchiridion* and the *Colloquis*, which she considered good works. She was more explicit when asked about Juan de Valdes's *Dialog on Christian Doctrine* (Homza: 2006, 127).[3] Judging from her declarations before Inquisitor Mejia on June 10, 1532, she was a prolific letter writer. Her area of influence included Guadalajara, Alcala, La Salceda, Tendilla, and Pastrana. John Longhurst (1969, 300) offers information regarding one of Maria de Cazalla's devotees in Guadalajara, namely, Maria Catalina Gomez de Ciudad-Real, known as Maria Arias, daughter of Pero Gomez de Ciudad Real:[4]

In the trial of Maria de Cazalla, Diego Hernandez further testified that Maria Arias had written a book in collaboration with Bishop Juan de Cazalla. Bataillon relates how

3 See page 73. For excerpts from the trial of Maria de Cazalla, see Homza (2006, 112–152).
4 For a history of the Gomez de Ciudad Real family and their relationship with Maria de Cazalla, see Gómez de Ciudad Real (2003, xxi–xlix).

Melanchthon, in the Diet of Augsburg in 1530, expressed his admiration for a book written by a Spanish lady zealous for the Gospel. By abbreviating and combining two consecutive passages in the trial of Maria de Cazalla —the first passage treating of Maria Arias, and the second passage treating of the Duchess of Infantado— Bataillon identifies the Duchess as the author of the book in question. However, the trial record clearly identifies Maria Arias as author of the book, and a marginal notation in the manuscript specifically reaffirms the point. Serrano y Sanz tells us that the book was written between 1520 and 1530, and consisted of commentaries on various passages of the Bible. The Lutheran Andrew Osiander, who was present at the Diet of Augsburg in 1530, in a letter dated July of that year, wrote that the book had been translated into Latin by a bishop, who could have been Bishop Juan de Cazalla.

Information regarding the *beatas* sentenced at Valladolid for their Lutheran leanings— Dr. Cazalla's sister Beatriz de Vivero, whom we have already seen, her cousin Francisca de Zuñiga, Juana Sanchez, Ana de Castro, and Isabel de Estrada—is taken from trial records found in Schäfer (2014, III) unless indicated. Unlike the records kept by the inquisitors in Seville, these records are fragmented and repetitive, and even contradictory at times. In order to offer the reader a more flowing narrative, page references are limited.

Beata Francisca de Zuñiga was the daughter of Antonio de Baeza of Escalona and first cousin to the nun, Francisca de Zuñiga de Reinosa.[5] Francisca was admitted to reconciliation, but the price for having "harbored Lutheran errors" was life in prison and the obligation to wear a *sanbenito* for the rest of her life. As a young girl in Escalona, Francisca would very likely have heard Pedro Ruiz de Alcaraz preach. She does not, however, mention him at her trial. On the other hand, Francisca may have been born after 1525 and may not have known Alcaraz (or Juan de Valdes) personally, nevertheless, she would have known about him through her mother and of how he was arrested and put on trial in Toledo.

Isabel de Estrada, a *beata* from the town of Pedrosa del Rey, half way between Valladolid and Zamora, where Dr. Cazalla's brother Pedro de Cazalla had been the parish priest, was burned at the stake at the first *auto*, May 21, 1559. Isabel was among Pedro de Cazalla's converts, along with his sacristan Juan Sanchez, Catalina Roman and Juana Velazquez, all from Pedrosa and all burned at the stake that same day (Santamaria: 2011, 35). Twenty-four-year-old Catalina Roman's declaration before Inquisitor Guijelmo on June 25, 1558, reveals her profound knowledge of the Bible and her theological discernment (Schäfer: 2014, III, 444–446):

---

5 Francisca, her mother (the wife of Antonio Baeza), and her cousin (the daughter of Antonio Baeza's sister Juana) all had the same name. Women did not automatically take their husband's name and it was common practice among aristocrats to take the sir names of their mothers, grandmothers or aunts. This is what makes it difficult to follow family affiliations.

Catalina: Sir, as for justification, I understand, for I have read it in the gospels and in the epistles of St. Paul, that justified through faith, we have peace with God through our Lord Jesus Christ, through whom we have access by faith into this grace wherein we stand, and rejoice in hope of the glory of God. And not only that, but we glory in tribulations also, knowing that tribulation works patience and patience hope, and hope makes not ashamed because the love of God is shed abroad in our hearts by the Holy Ghost which is given unto us.

Inquisitor: Do you believe that this faith alone, by which you say we are justified, is sufficient for our salvation and there is no need for good works?

Catalina: Good works are necessary to show our gratitude for the mercy God bestows on us, to act as his children and show we are Christians and to imitate him as members of his flock.

Inquisitor: Do you believe that being thus justified you can be saved without doing any good works?

Catalina: No, because faith without works is dead and is worthless.

Inquisitor: There seems to be a contradiction here. You say that being justified by faith you have peace with God through his son, implying that by that alone we are saved and that works on our part are unnecessary, at least that is what is inferred from your answer to the previous question when you say that works are an acknowledgment and recognition for an already received benefit.

Catalina: They are needful, as I said, as recognition of the great good [sacrifice] that he performed, and to prove that we are Christians; works are not necessary for our salvation, only as a recognition of that great good.

Inquisitor: Who taught you or told you about or discussed these things with you and whom have you discussed them with?

Catalina: I first heard them from the pulpit preached by Pedro de Cazalla, and later I was reaffirmed in them reading the *Epistles and the Gospels* and in an epistle of St. Paul, but I don't remember which one. And what I have declared, I believe, and I believe it because St. Paul says it in the epistle. I have discussed it with Pedro de Cazalla, the priest from Pedrosa, and with Isabel de Estrada, also from Pedrosa, and with Juan Sánchez, Pedro de Cazalla's servant. And those with whom I have discussed it agree and say it was doctrinally correct.

Juana Sanchez shared a cell with Beatriz Vivero's maid, Isabel Dominguez. Not seeing herself capable of facing death at the stake, Juana cut her veins with a pair of scissors and bled to death in her cell. On the day of the second *auto-da-fe*, on October 8, 1559, her statue, dressed up in a *sanbenito* painted with devils and hell fire, was taken out and she was burned in effigy (Schäfer: 2014, III, 7).

Ana de Castro, a *beata* originally from Palacios de Meneses (Palencia), today called Meneses de Campos, was living in the house of the wealthy international banker Anrriq Bul [Enrique Bull] in Valladolid at the time of her arrest (García Guerra/Luca: 2010, 39).[6] From all indications, she was the eldest of the group of

---

6 Much of the activity of the Enrique Bull-Francisco de Paredes bank was carried out with merchants in Medina del Campo.

women incarcerated. She may have been a widowed sister to Luis de Castro, a banker from Burgos, and like many *beatas*, was probably employed in the Bull household as a duenna, or governess. For believing that there was not purgatory, and other "heresies," she was sentenced to the loss of her goods, life in prison, and obliged to wear a *sanbenito* for the rest of her life. In October of 1567, after Ana had been in prison for eight years, she petitioned to be released. The following year she was allowed to remove her *sanbenito*, but there is no evidence that she was allowed to leave the prison. Her being incarcerated for heresy must have been a great affront for her family. She was a relative of Alonso de Castro (1492–1558), who belonged to the group of jurists known as the School of Salamanca. His works centered on the defense of "true faith" through criminal law. He had accompanied Charles V to the Low Countries for his coronation, at which time he preached to the Spanish merchants there and strongly attacked the Lutherans. His first work, *Adversus haereses* (Paris, 1534), was an encyclopedia of heresies. This work became one of the guidelines for the persecution of heretics in the sixteenth and seventeenth centuries. It was translated into French in 1712. His second work, *De iusta hereticorum punitione libri III* (Salamanca, 1547), made him known as the "scourge of heretics." In Spain he is called the "father and founder of criminal law," but outside of Spain, Castro remains virtually unknown.

The Nuns

The first person to appear on the scaffold at the second *auto-da-fe*— October 8, 1559—was Eufransina de Mendoza, also referred to as donna Frusina, or donna Eufrosina Rios, a lay nun who had taken the habit in the St. Clare Convent in Palermo, Sicily. She had left the convent and returned to Valladolid and had spent most of her time at the home of Maria de Mendoza, countess of Rivadavia, widow of Francisco de los Cobos (1480–1547), who had been Charles V's secretary. Judging by the name, they may even have been relatives. According to Inquisition documents, Eufransina had taken the habit in Palermo. She declared that the very day she took it they declared her a "professed nun," which was against the rules. When a woman entered a convent or abbey, she generally first underwent a period of six months to a year called a "postulancy." If she and the order determine that she had a true vocation, she received the habit and began her novitiate, which lasted one to two years. Upon completion of this period, she could take her temporary vows. Finally, after another few years, she could petition to make permanent vows and then would be considered a professed nun. Eufransina left the convent before the first year was over, claiming she was not a professed nun and therefore was free to leave. From Palermo she went to Naples where she found that the "heresies" she believed were also held there. From Naples she returned to Spain uncommitted and on her own. She was accused of saying that she had a right to renounce her faith and her baptism if she liked and that there were three religious groups. For her, the best one was where people claimed Christ's death as their own and put their salvation and their redemption only in his death. These she considered "true Christians." Eufransina would sometimes meet with the nuns at the Convent of Belen in Valladolid and bring them letters, which she called spiritual letters. She maintained that the death and wounds of Christ were the true purgatory and that they—the Lutherans—were the true church, and that a person could be fully assured that he/she was filled with the grace of God. She said it was wicked to offer bread and wine—that is, to say mass—for the dead. She also insisted that no one could be forced to believe. Eufransina admitted having Lutheran books and having read them. Though most people thought highly of her, twenty-two witnesses testified against her and she was sent to the stake on October 8, 1559. (Schäfer: 2014, III, 76–77).

Marina de Guevara was a professed nun at the Convent of Belen in Valladolid.[7] She was the daughter of Juan de Guevara, 3rd Lord of Treceño, and the grand daughter of Elvira de Rojas, relative of the Marquis of Poza. Her uncle, Alonso Tellez Giron, Lord of Puebla de Montalban, was married to Marina Velez de Guevara, which made her a cousin of the famous cardinal and viceroy of Naples, Pedro Pacheco de Villena.[8] She also belonged to the Velez de Guevara (counts of Oñate) family. On February 11, 1558, Marina was taken from her convent to the prison of the Inquisition. She was called before the inquisitors on February 21 and 27, and again on March 2, for questioning. On May 8, and again on June 12, she requested an audience to add more information to her confession. On July 14 she submitted a written request asking to be acquitted. Finally, on July 29 her case was voted on; one of the judges voted that she be sent to the torture chamber, the rest that she be handed over to the civil authorities to be burned. The Inquisition records say she showed greater contrition than any of the others, but to the very end she insisted that she was dying in the faith if the holy Roman Church. Llorente (1843, 209–211. Notes and brackets mine) fills in some of the details of Marina's case:

> Marina confessed the facts, but could not avoid her condemnation, though she demanded to be reconciled. This was the more surprising, as the inquisitor-general made great efforts to save her life; he was the intimate friend of several of her relations, and

---

7 For an in-depth study of Marina de Guevara's process, see Tellechea (2004).
8 Cardinal Pedro Pacheco de Villena, also known as Pedro Pacheco Ladrón de Guevara, was made a cardinal by Pope Paul III on December 16, 1545, and viceroy of Naples by Charles V from 1553 to 1556. He took part in various conclaves and was made inquisitor of the tribunal of the Holy Office in Rome by Pius IV.

being informed that the inquisitors of Valladolid intended to condemn her, he authorized Don Alphonso Tellez Giron, Lord of Montalban[9] and cousin to Marina, and the
Duke of Osuna [Pedro Tellez Giron], to visit the accused, and press her to confess what
she denied, and the witnesses affirmed, but Marina said that she could not add anything
to what she had already declared. She was condemned to be relaxed, but the sentence
was not immediately published, as it was the custom to do so only on the day before the
auto-da-fe; and as the rules of 1541 allow the sentence of death to be revoked if the
criminals repent before they are given up to secular justice, the inquisitor-general sent
Don Alphonso Giron a second time to his cousin, to exhort her to confess all, and avoid
death. This conduct of Inquisitor General Valdes displeased the inquisitors of Valladolid, who spoke of it as a singular and scandalous preference. Valdes applied to the
Supreme Council, which commanded that the visit should be made in the presence of
one or two inquisitors. This last attempt did not succeed better than the first; Marina
persisted in her declaration, and was burnt.

Catalina de Reynosa was also a professed nun of the Convent of Belen. According
to her confession, she was only 21 years old. One of the documents listing the
persons sentenced at the second auto, states: "Donna Catalina de Reynosa says
she should be called fray Martin because she likes that name very much; she is of
Jewish origin on her mother's side." (Schäfer: 2014, III, 90). Catalina was the
daughter of Jeronimo de Reinosa, 7th Lord of Autillo. Her mother, Juana de
Baeza, was a sister of Antonio de Baeza of Escalona. Of their eleven children, two
were nuns—Catalina and Francisca—, and three were priests: Fray Juan de
Reinosa, Manuel de Reinosa, canon of the cathedral at Palencia, and Francisco de
Reinosa, who had studied at Salamanca and in 1566 went to Rome and entered
the service of Pope Pius V.[10] When her brother returned to Spain in 1572 he was
named archdean of Sepulveda, then abbot of Husillos, and finally bishop of
Cordoba. Catalina also had two brothers who had military careers: Miguel, who
served in Italy, and Luis, who served in Flanders as captain under the Duke of
Alba. Catalina's sister Ines was married to Dr. Cazalla's brother Gonzalo Perez
Vivero. About the time the other nuns were being called before the Holy Office
for questioning, Catalina, of her own accord, sent a written confession to the
inquisitors. Later, when she was questioned regarding her written confession,
she admitted many more "heresies," but she never quite admitted all the heresies
she was accused of by the fifteen witnesses that testified against her. These
witnesses accused her of being their instructor and said that the others called her
"Faith of Martin Luther" and that when they were all singing in the choir she

9 Alphonso Tellez Giron, Lord of Puebla de Montalban, knight of the Order of Calatrava, etc.,
   was the grandson of Juan Pacheco, I Marquis of Villena.
10 Pope Pius V is remembered for being very austere and banishing luxury from his court. He
   also labored to reform the clergy, obliging his bishops to reside in their dioceses, and the
   cardinals to lead lives of simplicity and piety. He diminished public scandals by relegating
   prostitutes to distant quarters, and he forbade bull fights.

would shout, "Sing, sing loud to your Baal, we'll see if he hears you!" and things of that sort. She admitted that she had been catechized by Juan Sanchez, who had introduced into the convent a manuscript copy of his translation of Valdes's *Considerations*. To avoid suspicion, knowing that Valdes was considered a heretic, he had given the book a new title: *Cómo se ha de entender que el hombre fue creado a la imagen y semejanza de Dios* (How we are to understand that man was made in the likeness of God).[11] Jose Ignacio Tellechea (1975) is of the opinion that Juan Sanchez—Pedro de Cazalla'a sacristan in Pedrosa del Rey—had been Juan de Valdes's secretary in Naples and had brought back from Italy two manuscript copies of Valdes's *Considerations* in Italian to translate into Spanish. I am inclined to believe that Juan Sanchez made his translation from one of the copies that Carlo Sesso brought with him when he returned from Italy in the early 1550s.

Francisca de Zuñiga de Reynosa, Catalina's older sister, was also a professed nun at the Convent of Belen. Like the other condemned nuns, she confessed that she believed in justification by faith alone, as well as other Lutheran doctrines. Catalina was burned at the stake and Francisca was condemned to take the lowest place in the convent and to be deprived of all voting rights and not allowed to speak to any layperson without the express permission of the Inquisition.

Felipa de Heredia and Catalina de Alcaraz, two more nuns of noble families, were accused of the same heresies and received the same sentence as Francisca de Zuñiga. Felipa was the daughter of Alonso de Heredia, a steward of Luis Enriquez, 6th Admiral of Castile, which means she was probably born in Medina de Rioseco. She was only twenty-four years old when she was imprisoned. In one of her declarations, made on February 18, 1559, before Inquisitor Vaca, she told him that Pedro de Cazalla and Juan Sanchez would often come to the gate of the convent and talk with her and Margarita de Santesteban, Maria de Miranda, Catalina de Reinosa, Francisca de Zuñiga, Catalina de Alcaraz, and Marina de Guevara about the doctrine of justification by faith, and other doctrines (Schäfer: 2014, III, 228, doc. 416). Catalina de Alcaraz was accused of having given a certain "heretic" money (*dinero en doblones*) to flee the country. After nearly twenty years in prison—in May of 1577—Inquisitors Guijano, Alava, and Quiroga sent a report to the Supreme Council regarding Francisca de Zuñiga, Catalina de Alcaraz, and Felipa de Heredia, and their petitions for release. Francisca de Zuñiga and Catalina de Alcaraz were allowed to remove their *sanbenitos*, and Francisca, in virtue of her age, was restituted to her former monastic category. In the same letter, the inquisitors asked the Supreme Council if Felipa de Heredia could return to her old convent "considering the long time—

---

11 The manuscript was sent to Rome as part of Archbishop Carranza's process and was discovered in the Vatican Library by J. I. Tellechea Idígoras, who reprinted it in 1975.

18 years—she has been in prison." (Schäfer: 2014, III, 162–164). According to
Schäfer, she had been shut up in the insalubrious Monastery of Santa Colomba.

Maria de Miranda, another professed nun from the Convent of Belen, was
twenty-two years old when she was arrested. In the documents, she is referred to
as "the daughter of Miranda, of Valladolid," which could have made her the
grand daughter of Francisco de Zuñiga Avellaneda y Velasco, 3rd Count of
Miranda, or a niece of Bishop Gaspar Zuñiga y Avellaneda (1507–1571) and
great-niece of Cardinal Iñigo Lopez de Mendoza (1489–1535). Or was she the
daughter of Francisco de Zuñiga y Avellaneda, 4th Count of Miranda del Cas-
tañar?[12] As was customary in all these cases, Maria de Miranda's goods were
confiscated, but because she was under age—younger than 25—she was given an
executor for this purpose. In a declaration made before the inquisitors on May
15, 1558, she related an experience she had had some three or four years earlier.
As a result of having been reprimanded by one of the older nuns, she and some of
the other young nuns decided to do certain acts of extreme penitence. They were
severely criticized and scolded for that and unburdened their consciences with a
priest by the name of Antonio de Astudillo, who told them not to single themselves out like that. Also, about the same time, Beatriz de Vivero began coming to
the convent to see her sister's sisters-in-law, Francisca de Zuñiga and Catalina de
Reynosa.[13] Maria de Miranda knew these sisters well "for having been brought
up together and lived in the same house for two years," (Schäfer: 2014, III, 177)
and she delighted to join them and listen to Beatriz speak of God's mercy.
Sometimes Catalina de Ortega would accompany her and would tell Maria that
true penitence was to confess our sins before God, not to do acts of extreme
penitence. From that time on, Maria gave up doing acts of outward penitence.
She became more cheerful, and her conversation was always centered on God's
love and mercy. A year later, around Holy Week, a certain friend of Juan Sanchez,
Juan Garcia, who was employed by Catalina de Ortega as her administrator, came
to walk the Stations of the Cross with them. The next day he came with Juan
Sanchez. The few times she saw Garcia after that, he would talk about sermons he
had heard and about "a certain Sossa." Once Garcia came with one of Maria's
cousins, which she took as a sign that her cousin had also accepted Reformed
teachings. She remembered that every time Juan Sanchez came to the gate of the
convent, he came chanting "Justified by faith we have peace with God through
Jesus Christ our Lord," and that one time he brought a little book that he gave
Marina de Guevara through a ruota, a sort of small revolving door, and that night

---

12 In 1520, the year of his coronation as Holy Roman Emperor, Charles V created 25 grandees,
    known as *Inmemorial Grandees*. The House of Zúñiga received two grandees, one for the
    duke of Béjar and another for the count of Miranda del Castañar.
13 Their sister Ines de Reinoso had married one of Beatriz de Vivero's brothers.

Marina read them the first chapter. Maria was so excited that she wanted to memorize the whole book—which was none other than Valdes's *Considerations*. One of the other nuns, Catalina de Alcaraz, started copying it, but Maria thought it would take her too long so she asked Francisco de Coca to do it for them. (Schäfer: 2014, III, 177–180, doc. 416). Whether or not he accomplished this task is uncertain, but that could be the reason Francisco de Coca was sentenced to prison for three years at the second *auto* (Schäfer: 2014, III, 81).

On May 15, 1558, Margarita de Sanesteban [San Estevan], another nun from the Convent of Belen, sent Inquisitor Guijelmo the following written confession:

Some two years ago, more or less, I became more withdrawn and ceased having the sort of conversation I had before and going to the grille and I began to enjoy conversing with good persons who encouraged me with their company. Among the persons from outside the convent I recall having met Beatriz de Vivero and Catalina de Hortega around Ascension Day of 1557 [May 27], though I do not recall Beatriz de Vivero saying anything special, except that I should love God and confide in him. Once when I was in the choir, in front of other nuns (and I don't remember who they were), Catalina de Hortega said I should admit my guilt and abhor myself and not to practice the results of Adam's wrongdoing, which was sin, and that I should always acknowledge the sin in me and weep for it, for that is true penitence. By doing this I should be aware that the penalty was paid by Jesus Christ and that I should confide in his death and present it to God in payment for my sins and that I should immerse myself in the blood of Jesus Christ that made satisfaction for all, and believe that he was my forgiveness and my head. She said this to me often and I believed it and I exercised in it constantly. I also heard Juan Garcia and Juan Sanchez say the same things speaking between themselves at the grille. And I understood that and it put me at ease and I spoke about it with Marina de Guevara and certain other nuns and we had these conversations often.

To talk about these and other things, and to read Constantino [Ponce de la Fuente][14] and the *Gospels*,[15] sometimes all of us, sometimes only four or five, met together. I could not attend always because I had to fulfill my convent duties, which I regretted. When we were together and a nun appeared that was not one of our group, we were quiet and stopped talking. With these conversations I was content and I would call these nuns, and [the women] that came to see us "sisters." Catalina de Hortega told me that God did not work imperfections, and that if she said there was no purgatory, I should believe it. Just to see what she would say, I said I believed her. But I had many doubts for some days whether that was true or something invented by the church until I asked a priest by the

---

14 On January 2, 1558, the Supreme Council burned some thirty books that had been confiscated in Valladolid. The list included three books by Constantino Ponce de la Fuente: *Exposición del Primer Psalmo* (1546), *Catecismo Christiano* (1547), and *Confesión de un pecador* (1547).

15 This does not refer to the Gospels as they appear today in the context of the New Testament, but to Ambrosio de Montesino's *Epistles and Gospels for the Liturgical Year*, put on the Index of Prohibited Books in 1559 as a result of the decree that prohibited the printing of Scripture in the vulgar tongue.

name of Astudillo. He scolded me in front of Francisca de Zuñiga and Catalina de Reinosa, and he scolded us all for even questioning it. He also told us what other things not to believe regarding the church and the saints. Fifteen days before Easter of this year 1558, when Marina and I were near the front gate of the convent, Juan Sanchez arrived and gave us the book that the Inquisition took away from Marina. I took the book from him and I went to the infirmary and hid it. That night I read a chapter or more, which dealt with the subject of the image of God, to Casilda, Maria Sanchez, Catalina Perez and Maria de Castro, who were in the infirmary. That night I read that same chapter to Marina de Guevara. (Schäfer: 2014, III, 183–185, doc. 416. Notes and brackets mine).

The coincidence in time and content between Maria de Miranda's oral confession and Margarita de Sanesteban's written confession, strongly suggests close collaboration and mutual support between the two nuns. When brought in for questioning, Margarita admitted sending letters of encouragement to the church in Pedrosa del Rey, and saying that she was not afraid to die for having believed Martin Luther's doctrine. Sixteen witnesses testified against her. Margarita de Sanesteban was defrocked, handed over to the civil authorities, and burned.

Maria de Rojas, another nun accused of holding heretic views, was the daughter of the Marquis of Poza and the sister of Pedro Sarmiento de Rojas. The only information the official records give of her is that she was a nun from the Santa Catalina de Sienna Monastery, not like the others who were from the convent of Belen. Among her declarations, she confessed that she would very much have liked to have one of Martin Luther's bones as a relic. She had her goods confiscated and was ordered to wear a *sanbenito*, and for some inexplicable reason, instead of being sent to prison she was simply returned to her nunnery, where she was relegated to the lowest position, and deprived of her right to vote (Llorente: 1843, 203).

The Aristocrats

Besides the nuns that came from noble families, there were other aristocratic women sentenced by the Inquisition for their Lutheran beliefs: Ana Enriquez, Mencia de Figueroa, Isabel de Castilla, Catalina de Ortega, Marina de Saavedra, etc. Some were sentenced to the stake, others to "perpetual imprisonment," the confiscation of their property, the obligation to wear a *sanbenito* over their clothes for the rest of their lives, and never again to wear silver, gold, pearls, or other precious stones.

Mencia de Figueroa was the wife of Pedro Sarmiento de Rojas, son of the Marquis of Poza and knight of the Order of Santiago, which made her sister-in-law to Maria de Rojas, the nun from the Santa Catalina de Sienna Monastery who wanted one of Martin Luther's bones as a relic. Mencia had been a lady-in-waiting for Philip II's younger sisters since 1548. Pedro Sarmiento, her husband, seems to also have belonged to princess Juana's staff (Martinez Millan: 2000, II, 90). They lived in Palencia, some twenty-five miles to the north of Valladolid, where Carlo de Sesso, Fray Domingo de Rojas, Pedro de Cazalla, and Beatriz de Vivero were frequent guests. Both Mencia and her husband were sentenced to life in prison for their Lutheran ideas and to wear a *sanbenito* the rest of their lives (Schäfer: 2014, III, 58, doc. 382). On March 7, 1562, Mencia and her husband, who had now been living in prison for nearly two years, received the visit of Dr. Diego de Simancas, member of the Supreme Council, who was sent to check on the prisoners. He reported that neither Mencia nor her husband had any complaints. In a letter addressed to Inquisitor General Diego Espinosa, six years later, dated March 8, 1568, in which Pedro Sarmiento petitioned to be discharged, it appears that Mencia had passed away the previous year (Schäfer: 2014, III, 156, doc. 403). She may have been around forty years old at the time. According to Antonio Valladares de Sotomayor, Mencia de Figueroa left many children (Valladares de Sotomayor: 1787, 43).

Catalina de Ortega, also spelled Hortega, was the daughter of licentiate Hernando Diaz [Diez], treasurer-fiscal of the Royal Council of Castile (Cooper: 1847, 65). Catalina was among those burned at the stake at the first *auto*, on May 1, 1559. She was a young widow, and it seems that she had just recently widowed. Her husband's name appears twice: once in an official description of the *auto-da-fe*, which included a brief comment on each of those condemned, and again in the placard written in German reproduced by Schäfer. In the first documents she is referred to as the "wife of Captain Loaysa" (Schäfer: 2014, III, 40, doc. 378); in the second document as "*Catharina Ortega, que había quedado viuda del capitán Loysi*" [Catarina Ortega, who had been left a widow by Captain Loysi] (Schäfer: 2014, III, 61, doc. 382). Who this Captain Loaysa was remains a mystery. Did he belong to the illustrious Loaysa-Giron family, or the Loaysa-Mendoza family? Or was he the illegitimate son of Alvaro de Loaysa, who served Charles V's as captain in Milan? (Gómez-Menor Fuentes: 2014). Another possible candidate would be Gabriel Paniagua de Loaysa, 2nd Lord of Santa Cruz de Paniagua, who in 1557 left on a military missions to Peru to subdue an indigenous uprising (Fernandez: 2008). Be that as it may, Catalina's father was Hernando Diaz, sometime referred to as a lawyer, others as royal treasurer.[16] Catalina de Ortega was accused of holding Lutheran doctrines. One of the witnesses that testified against Beatriz de Vivero declared that Beatriz had told him/

---

16 Together with two other lawyers from the University of Valladolid, Hernando Diaz published a compendium of all the laws and decrees promulgated in Spain up to the year 1547. This was an enlarged edition of a work published previously in Alcala in 1540.

her that Carlo de Sesso had taught "heretical doctrines" to Juan Sanchez and Sanchez had taught Catalina de Ortega (Schäfer: 2014, III, 353). Because she confessed under torture, she should not have lawfully been condemned to the stake, but she was. Another record transcribed by Schäfer refers to Catalina as being "very very young and beautiful, perhaps only twenty or twenty-two years of age. She begged the executioner not to hurt her too much, but the poor fellow was not as swift as he was with the others." (Schäfer: 2014, III, 52).

Ana Enriquez de Almansa de Rojas was born around 1535. She was the daughter of Juan Enriquez de Almansa, 2nd Marquis of Alcañices (d.1544) and Elvira de Rojas, and niece by marriage of Mencia de Figueroa. Ana Enriquez had married Juan Alonso de Fonseca y Toledo, Lord of Villasbuenas and Abedillo,[17] and had a son, Alfonso de Fonseca Enriquez, born around 1555. On April 23, 1558, Inquisitor Guijelmo questioned her in her mother's gardens instead of summoning her to his office, and after May 1558, Ana was put under house arrest. On that occasion, Ana Enriquez made the following confession:

My coming to Valladolid from Toro, on January 25, 1558, was like the conversion of St. Paul. When I got here, Beatriz de Vivero spoke to me and persuaded me that she had discovered the truth of the Holy Spirit and her salvation and that she was absolutely sure of her salvation and of God's pardon through the merits of the death of Jesus Christ alone because she had accepted Jesus Christ through faith, which she called "to put on Christ", because thus we are made members of Christ and his brethren, and children of the Father through his redemption. She also told me of many former errors that her whole past life was worthless, together with the devout acts and things that up until then we considered holy, but that the only thing that was worthwhile were the merits of Christ and his death and that in him we had justification enough for our salvation. And when she saw that I was scandalized to hear that our good works were worthless, she said that after receiving Jesus Christ in the spirit our works were good and were a means to thank God for the mercy he had bestowed on us, though they were not sufficient in themselves, and that in all things we were to show that we were the children of such a father and we were to do the things his Spirit showed us and lead us to do. At that point I think I said to her, "What is all this talk about heretics?" and she responded that those were the church and the saints. Then I said, "What about the pope?" and she said to me, "The Spirit of God [the Holy Spirit], he is the pope." She meant this for those who are illuminated.

She told me that what I was to do was to confess my whole life to God and to hold the most saintly deeds of the past as nothingness, and that I was not to confess my sins to men, who have no power to absolve sins and that I was to believe this teaching and receive it by faith and then I would see things clearly. Then I asked her, "What about purgatory and acts of penitence?" To this she responded, "There is no purgatory, nor

---

17 Gonzalo was the eldest son, hence he inherited his father's title and estate; Juan Alonso, the youngest, inherited his mother's title—"Señora de Villasbuenas, Torralva, y Avedillo"—and estates.

any other kind of restitution, only receiving Jesus Christ by faith, and as a result, we receive the pardon of our sins and all his justice." I tried to do what she said regarding confession and receiving Christ and to be at peace with this, but I wasn't totally convinced and I confessed with a priest like before, not due to conviction but for the sake of outward obedience, but I did not mention any of these things to the priest. Likewise, Beatriz de Vivero told me that communion was not celebrated properly and that we were given only half, that is, the body [bread] but not the blood [wine], and that to put the Sacrament in the church was sacrilegious. And because I was not totally convinced and harbored many doubts, I decided to wait until I could speak with Father Domingo de Rojas and for him to explain it to me.

When he came, which was last Easter, and explained to me and confirmed all the things Beatriz had told me, I put my mind at ease and believed it all. He told me he greatly admired Luther and that he was a saintly man and had done all he could to proclaim the truth. And Fray Domingo told me that there were only two sacraments—baptism and communion—and that Christ was not present in communion in the way they would have us believe, because God cannot be bound and after being consecrated leave. And that they make him an idol worshiping him like that, because they only adore a piece of bread. He told me that to worship the crucifix was also idolatry. One night he read to me from a book by Luther regarding the good works required of a Christian. He also told me that once Christ had come and accomplished our redemption, he had freed of all servitude, fastings, vows of chastity, etc., and that in monasteries and convents a thousand profanities were committed and that the worst one was to say mass because there they sacrificed Christ for money, and that only to avoid offence, he wore the habit. (Schäfer: 2014, IV, 979–981, doc. 419)[18]

Ana Enriquez was not the only member of the Rojas family to appear on the scaffold and to hear her sentence read publicly that day. There were also present her mother's brother Pedro Sarmiento and his wife Mencia de Figueroa, her aunt Maria de Rojas the nun, her cousin Luis Enriquez, and her uncle Fray Domingo de Rojas. Fray Domingo was the only member of the family sentenced to the stake. As protocol required, each "culprit" was escorted to his/her place by a priest. It was Ana Enriquez's lot that a relative of hers, the Jesuit Francisco de Borja, 4th Duke of Gandia, should be her attendant.[19] Several documents describe how embarrassed she was to appear in public in those circumstances. Francisco de Borja later described the event as follows:

Among other assignments I received from the Inquisitors was that of communicating to Ana Enriquez her sentence as well as to give her strength and encouragement to face it with patience and a persevering spirit. And with the help of God (which I needed badly) I comforted her to the point that, though she would have preferred to die a lonely

---

18 Also see Menendez y Pelayo (1881, IV, 401).
19 One of Ana's brothers, Juan Enríquez de Almansa y Rojas, was married to Francisco de Borja's daughter Juana. For details regarding Francisco de Borja's participation in the *autos-da-fe* in Valladolid, and the consequences, see Moreno (2010, 364–366).

death rather than endure public ignominy, and though she walked along with the others looking more dead than alive, nevertheless, always showing a Christian attitude and accepting divine justice, this was her only comfort: to think that in exchange for the honor, dignity and distinction lost in that public ignominy, she had received the knowledge of the truth and the pardon of her sins. (Perez Gonzalez, 2013).

This conciliatory attitude of Francisco de Borja towards a person sentenced for heresy greatly contrasts with the harsh words used by other friars on other occasions when referring to "heretics." According to Juan Antonio Llorente (1843, 203), "Anna Henriquez de Rojas was afterwards shut up in a monastery. She was twenty-four years of age, perfectly acquainted with the Latin tongue, and had read the works of Calvin, and those of Constantine Ponce de la Fuente." Schäfer remarks that despite being clearly declared a "Lutheran heretic," neither were her goods confiscated nor was she obliged to wear a sanbenito. These statements are confirmed—and enlarged—in a letter written to Archbishop Bartolome de Carranza by Fray Luis de la Cruz, dated May 30, 1559, only a month after the *auto-da-fe:*

> All those that were reconciled were sentenced to wear a *sanbenito* and the majority to life in prison, except Ana Enriquez, who Geronimo Mexia, her brother-in-law, took back to his home scot-free, though her goods have been confiscated, as well as those of Luis de Rojas, who will be sent to Coria [in the province of Caceres] with the bishop his uncle [Diego Deza Tello], and those of Juan Pereyda, who has been dispossessed of his knightship in the Order of San Juan, and the Englishman who has been sent to a monastery for a year. (Schäfer: 2014, III, 154. Brackets mine)

Juana de Silva de Ribera, and her husband Juan de Vivero—Dr. Cazalla's brother—, were sentenced to prison for life and the confiscation of all their goods. Juana was one of several illegitimate children of Juan de Silva y Rivera, Marquis of Montemayor.[20] Juan de Silva had two illegitimate daughters: Juana and Guiomar de Silva, a nun in the Madre de Dios convent in Toledo. How Juana came to Valladolid and became part of the Cazalla family is unknown. Her father may have sent her there as a lady-in-waiting to one of the princesses as an act of gratitude towards Charles V for having created the title of Marquis of Montemayor for him, which may have had to do with Silva's being in charge of all the festivities when Charles V celebrated his marriage to the Portuguese princess Isabel in Seville in 1526. In any case, as a young girl at court in Valladolid, Juana de Silva may have met Dr. Cazalla's father, Pedro de Cazalla, who was employed

---

20 Juan de Silva y Rivera (1461–1538) had been one of Charles V's staunch supporters in the war of the *Comuneros.* This had cost him the razing to the ground of many of his possessions by the *comunero* rebels. After the war he rebuilt his palace in Villaseca de la Sagra, ten miles to the northeast of Toledo, with materials belonging to the houses of Juan de Padilla —one of the executed leaders of the *comuneros*—in Toledo.

there as an accountant, and through him his son Juan. Juana and her husband began their long life in prison in May of 1559. A year later, in May of 1560, Dr. Morales, a lawyer of the Holy Office, visited the prisoners. Two years later, Dr. Simancas, a member of the Supreme Council, visited them and reported that Juana de Silva and her husband had no complaints regarding the treatment they were receiving. Five years later, on October 11, 1567, they were interrogated separately by Fernando de Vega de Fonseca in compliance with a questionnaire the Supreme Council had compiled (Schäfer: 2014, III, 171, doc. 415). The questions were these:

1. How long have you been imprisoned and how many days elapsed between your arrest and the formal accusation against you?
2. Are you well treated? Have you seen anyone commit any sort of irregularity in the prison?
3. Are you given enough to eat? Do you have enough clothes? Are you given medication when you are sick? Can you see a doctor?
4. Do the inquisitors come to see you and how often and do they respond to your needs?
5. Do the inquisitors give you an audience when you request it?
6. Do the inquisitors provide you with a defense lawyer if you request one?
7. Have you seen any prisoner communicate with another in another cell and in what way?
8. What do you ordinarily eat and how much do you pay the steward for it and does he give you a receipt for it? Does he owe you anything and if he does, since when?
9. Can you think of anything that needs to be improved or repaired in the prison?

After 1567, both Juana de Silva and Isabel Dominguez were allowed to remove their *sanbenitos,* nevertheless, they were to remain in prison.

Leonor de Cisneros, the wife of the lawyer from Toro, Antonio Herrezuelo, was also sentenced to life in prison at the *auto-da-fe* held on May 21, 1559. Eight years later, in the fall of 1567, she was asked to answer the above mentioned questions. Her response to question 8 sheds some light on her day-to-day life in prison:

> To the eighth question, she replied that she was generally given half a pound of beef and all the fruit she wanted and bread and wine. She did not know how much she paid the steward every day for this, or how much she paid the butler, nor did she know if he owed her anything. (Schäfer: 2014, III, 172).

Before she left the hall, the inquisitors warned her to look out for her soul and that, in order not to be condemned to hell, she should unburden her conscience to them and give up the errors she so obstinately held. To this she replied that she did not want to condemn her soul, but to die for Jesus Christ, and that she had nothing else to add. The inquisitor then told her that to die for Jesus Christ meant not to trust in Luther's errors. To this she responded that she knew that through the mediation of Jesus Christ, her sins were pardoned and she did not consider that to be one of Luther's errors, but rather a doctrine found in the gospel. From the answers she gave the inquisitor, it was evident that she was also unyielding regarding the doctrine of confession. When she was asked if confession was necessary, she replied, "Yes it is, to God." (Schäfer: 2014, III, 173). It did not take the inquisitors long to reconsider her case and the following year, at the *auto-da-fe* held in September of 1568, Leonor de Cisneros was sentenced to the stake as a "relapsed heretic" (Illescas: 1568, II, 688). She had been in prison nine years. Henry C. Lea (1906–07, III, 440–441) describes her thus:

> Perhaps the most pitiful case of all was that of his young wife, Leonor de Cisneros. But twenty-three years old, with life opening before her, she had yielded so promptly to the methods of the Inquisition that she escaped with perpetual prison. In the weary years of the *casa de la penitencia*, the burden on her soul grew more and more unendurable and the example of her martyred husband stood before her in stronger light. At last she could bear the secret torture no longer; with clear knowledge of her fate, she confessed her heresy and, in 1567, she was put on trial again. As a relapsed there could be no mercy for her, but recantation might at least preserve her from death by fire, and earnest efforts were made to save her soul. They were unavailing; she declared that the Holy Spirit had enlightened her and that she would die as her husband had died, for Christ. Nothing could overcome her resolution and, on September 28, 1568, she atoned for her weakness of ten years before and was burnt alive as an obstinate impenitent.

Marina de Saavedra, whose name appears as Catalina de Sayabedra, Maria de Sayavedra, Ana de Sayavedra, and Marina de Saabedra throughout the records, was from Zamora.[21] She was the wife of Pablo Cisneros de Sotelo, whose brother, Antonio de Sotelo y Cisneros, was famous for having accompanied Hernan Cortes in the conquest of Mexico. Another distinguished member in the extended Cisneros de Sotelo family was Inquisitor General Diego de Deza. Marina de Saavedra confessed that she came in contact with Protestant teachings through Cristobal de Padilla, tutor to the children of the widowed marchioness of Alcañices, Elvira de Rojas. On May 4, 1558, Padilla confessed before Inquisitors Vaca and Guijelmo that some four or five months earlier, in Zamora, he had gone to speak with the prioress of the Convent of Santa Paula and several of the nuns there. Also present were Marina de Saavedra and her daughter Maria, married to Pedro de Mera, two of Marina's maids, and a widowed neighbor by the name of Leonor de Toro, also referred to as Leonor de Toledo (Schäfer: 2014, III, 403, doc. 417). The Convent of Santa Paula was a sort of beguinage that housed third order Franciscan nuns. There were several of these houses in

---

21 In the documents of the Vatican Library, there is also a certain "Maria de Saavedra, the wife of Francisco Sentero, citizen of Toro, sentenced to loss of goods and prison." (Leon de la Vega: 2012, II, 352).

Zamora and they served as meeting points for women with spiritual concerns. Though Marina, her daughter, her maids, and Leonor de Toro all gathered to hear Cristobal de Padilla, only Marina de Saavedra and Leonor de Toro were later accused of holding Lutheran doctrines. Marina was sentenced at the first *auto-da-fe*, on May 21, 1559, to life in prison. It appears, however, that by 1567 Marina was allowed to return to her home (Moreno: 2015b, 29).

Isabel de Castilla, the wife of Carlo de Sesso, and her niece Catalina de Castilla were also incarcerated and sentenced at the *auto-da-fe* held in Valladolid on October 8, 1559. Isabel was the daughter of Francisco de Castilla, who descended from king Pedro the Cruel.[22] She confessed that her husband had taught her some Lutheran doctrines, but she had given them up. She had wanted to denounce this to the inquisitors for some time, but because she had been ill she hadn't done it sooner. Likewise, she confessed her husband had ordered her to burn certain letters and books when he fled. She begged for mercy and reconciliation and was only condemned to the loss of her goods, to wear a *sanbenito* for the rest of her life, and to be sent to prison. She was also forbidden to wear gold or silver or silk or fine wool, and the loss of all her goods should she relapse. Severe limitations imposed on her descendants were removed in 1630, at the special request of Philip IV, when Pope Urban VIII, "granted to Caterina de Castilla, grand daughter of Isabel de Castilla, wife of Carlo de Sesso, a dispensation to hold honors and dignities, secular and spiritual." (Lea: 1906–1907, II, 442).

Isabel's niece Catalina, the daughter of Diego de Castilla and Catalina de Avalos, confessed that she had believed many of the teachings of Martin Luther and that she had had a book that taught these things. In prison, Catalina shared her aunt's cell. On May 24, 1560, Dr. Morales, a lawyer of the Holy Office, reported that when he visited the prisons the previous day he found that Isabel and her niece were sleeping on rented beds. Whether this was prohibited or simply a comment is uncertain. In May of 1564 Catalina petitioned to have her *sanbenito* removed and for permission to enter the Monastery of Santo Domingo in Caleruega (Burgos) as a nun. The petition was granted (Schäfer: 2014, III, 154, doc. 401). Several years later—on October 22, 1572—the inquisitors at Valladolid wrote the Supreme Council regarding another petition in which Catalina de Castilla asked for permission to be transferred to Murcia to which they also gave their consent.[23] She may have found the winters too cold in Burgos.

Teresa de Oypa (d'Oipa) was the widow of Antonio Torres and was originally from Madrid. She held the same beliefs as the others and received the same

---

22 Peter the Cruel, king of Castile and Leon from 1350 to 1369, married Joan, daughter of Edward III of England. On her way to Castile, Joan travelled through cities infested with the Black Death, contracted the disease and died.
23 For a transcription of Catalina de Castilla's declarations made on April 8 and May 5, 1559, see Homza (2006, 198–199).

punishment: loss of all her goods, life in prison, and the obligation to wear a *sanbenito*. On March 7, 1562, when Dr. Simancas visited the prisoners, Teresa complained that there were big leaks in the roof of her cell and that the custodian had promised he would put new tiles on the roof but had not taken care of it. Teresa de Oypa had been a close friend of the young widow, Catalina de Ortega, burned at the stake at the first *auto*. On November 5, 1569, Teresa de Oypa's daughter Leonor was summoned for questioning in Valladolid and confessed that Fray Rodrigo Guerrero had instructed her and her mother in Lutheran doctrines. Six months later, the inquisitors were still debating whether Teresa should appear again in the next *auto-da-fe*. In fact, information gleaned from several dispatches between the inquisitors and the Supreme Council indicates that in 1570 several members of the Protestant community of Valladolid who had earlier been reconciled—Teresa de Oypa, her daughter Leonor, Fray Rodrigo Guerrero, Pedro Sarmiento, Isabel Dominguez, Francisco de Coca, Juana de Silva—were accused of backsliding, which meant capital punishment. It appears that Leonor de Oypa was reconciled, but her mother was sent to the stake on November 11, 1571, along with Fray Rodrigo Guerrero (Schäfer: 2014, III, 161, doc. 407; Fulgosio: 2002, 67). Teresa de Oypa seems to have been the last female victim of the long list of women sentenced to the stake in Spain for holding evangelical beliefs. Women continued to be summoned before the inquisitors after that, but mainly for witchcraft (Sarrión Mora: 2003).

Beyond the physical—and mental—tribulations of the women involved in the evangelical movements in Seville and Valladolid in sixteenth century Spain, two fundamental aspects stand out: their high level of literacy and their spiritual discernment. Whether one was a consequence of the other, or which came first, is uncertain. On the other hand, these two features were not unique of Spain, but reflect a widespread phenomenon that was taking place throughout Europe as a result of the spiritual awakening produced by the Reformation.

Chapter 8:
Reginaldo Gonzalez de Montes

> To write histories, or books of any kind, there is need of great judgment and a ripe
> understanding.
> *Don Quijote*, Book II, Ch. 3.

Reginaldo Gonzalez de Montes's *Artes de la Inquisición* is a firsthand report of the activities of the Spanish Inquisition to eliminate the evangelical circles that had sprung up in Seville in the latter part of the 1550s. The book, published originally in Latin shortly after the severe persecution of the emerging Protestant community, has three parts: an introduction to the implementation of the Inquisition; a systematic description of its modus operandi; and a brief biographical sketch of a dozen noteworthy Spaniards whose testimony the author defends "in the face of false accusations of their wavering in the faith." Many historians tend to belittle the work and to consider it a piece of exaggerated pro-Protestant propaganda, but I have taken the time to collate the information it contains with contemporary Inquisition records and have found it to be surprisingly accurate and thorough. Consequently, both the author and the work need to be revisited.

The Original Manuscript

The growing deterioration of diplomatic relations between Spain and England makes one suspect that perhaps the original Latin edition of *Artes* was not printed in Heidelberg after all, but in London.[1] Luis de Usoz y Rio (1847–1865, V, viii–ix) points out a curious discovery, made by his collaborator Benjamin B. Wiffen, that there may have been two printings of the 1567 Latin edition. Wiffen had consulted a Latin edition of *Artes* owned by the Anglican clergyman and historian, Joseph Mendham,[2] and observed a difference in the formatting of the

---

1 The printer of the Heidelberg edition, Michael Schirat, was known to have connections with English Protestants, namely, Thomas Cartwright and his circle of friends. See Johnson (1971, 253–268).
2 Rev. Joseph Mendham (1769–1856) was vicar of Hill Chapel, Arden, Warwickshire. His works include *Memoirs of the Council of Trent* (1834), *An Account of the Indexes, both Prohibitory and Expurgatory, of the Church of Rome* (1826), and *The life and pontificate of Saint Pius the fifth* (1832).

title page. A minute collation of the Mendham text and the two editions owned by Usoz revealed only one variant reading, which made Usoz suspect that perhaps instead of two printings of the entire work, only the title page had been reprinted. On the other hand, there could have been two Latin editions, one printed in Germany and the other in London (or in Norwich).

Exiled Spanish Protestants, Dutch Calvinists, and English Puritans were known to have used false imprints profusely. Indeed, John Daye, the printer of Skinner's English version of *Artes* (1568; 1569) and one of the 1569 Dutch renderings, had printed clandestinely during the reign of Mary Tudor under the false imprint of "Roane: Michael Wood." (Evenden: 2002). Persecution and censorship encouraged false attributions on the part of authors, printers, and publishers alike. Crediting a work to an authorized printer, active at an earlier date, was another stratagem. By pinning the job on a deceased printer, someone incapable of defending himself, works appeared that would otherwise have been risky to publish. One example is the 1633 Amsterdam edition of the Geneva Bible. The false imprint claims that the Bible was published by Christopher Barker in 1599. Furthermore, falsifying the name of the printer and the place of publication was also a means to avoid the restraints imposed on English printers by the Stationers Company, the guild that oversaw the printing trade. Moreover, the printing of books in a language other than English was very regulated. At the time *Artes* was printed, only Reginald (Reyner) Wolfe held a royal license, granted him in 1547 by Edward VI, to print books in Latin, Greek, and Hebrew (Plomer: 1915, 86).[3] All precautions were few. By first printing *Artes* in Latin with a misleading imprint, John Daye could outwit any undercover agents sent to search out the author.

Granted the matter of a false imprint may be mere speculation, certain internal evidence raises another issue. Was the original manuscript written in Latin? To present *Artes* as originally written in Latin could have been another stratagem. Even Luis de Usoz y Rio (1847–1865, XIII, 10–11), in an appendix to his reprint of the Latin text, suggests the involvement of two people: a writer and a translator. There is certain textual evidence—variant readings—that not only suggests that the original was written in Spanish, but that the Spanish-to-Latin translator was an Englishman. Several of these variant readings have the appearance of misspelled place names. One misspelling has to do with Inquisitor Juan Gonzalez de Munebrega's bishopric, Tarazona—written Taraçona at that time. The "assumed Latin author" may never have heard of Taraçona, which in the Latin should have appeared as *Turiaso*, and, confusing the 'ç' for a 'g', proceeded to refer to the inquisitor as *Episcopum Tarraconensem, Episcopus*

---

3 Not to be confused with John Wolfe (1548–1601), known for pirating works whose printing rights belonged to others.

Tarraconensis (Bishop of Tarragona). Luis de Usoz y Rio (1847–1865, XIII, 176, 190), who reprinted *Artes* in 1857, tried to justify the error by saying that the inquisitor, who Montes never mentions by name, may have been linked in some way to the diocese of Tarragona. In my opinion, this is simply another proof that the original text was written in Spanish and that the Spanish-to-Latin translator had a limited knowledge of Spanish geography, as did Vincent Skinner when he rendered Barchinon for *Barchinoniae,* instead of Barcelona.

Whoever was responsible for the Latin text—the printer, the assumed author, the translator—must also have had a limited knowledge of scholastic philosophy. To transcribe "Gregorio *Arithmetico*" instead of "Gregorio *Authenticus*"—the name by which this Italian scholastic philosopher Gregory of Rimini (d.1358) was known—is much more than a simple slip of the pen, or as Vermaseren (1985, 71, note 67) suggests, "a faulty reading of his copy by the typesetter in 1567." Another misspelled place name has to do with the bishopric Charles V gave Dr. Egidio in 1550, namely, the bishopric of Tortosa. The original Latin name for Tortosa is *Dertosia.* For some unknown reason, very likely due to linguistic transfer—note the 'o' for the 'e'—, the Latin text reads *Dortossensem* where it should read *Dertossensem.* Another case of linguistic interference, detected by Professor Ruiz de Pablos (2008, 28), is *cruelitatis* for *crudelitatis.*

Another interesting case of what could be considered negative transfer, or cross-linguistic interference, has to do with the color of the tormentor's garments. The Latin text reads: *Is totus est coopertus nigra veste ex lino ad pedes longa astricta* (wholly arrayed from the top of his head to the sole of his foot in a suit of *black* canvas) (Montes: 1569, f. 23r. Italics mine). That the tormentor should be dressed from head to toe in a black garment seems totally logical. In contrast, John Frampton, in his account of the torments received at Triana, describes his tormentors as "two men covered with *white* canvas coats, from their heads to their feet." (Fittler/Skelton: 1820–1840, I, 357–367. Italics mine). Although the room was "lit by only two candles", Frampton would hardly have confused black for white. Raw linen, or canvas, was very difficult—and expensive—to dye. In all probability, they were dressed in cheap, raw cream-color linen garments. If the original (Spanish) manuscript read "un traje *blanco* de lino," negative linguistic transfer would have prompted the (English) translator to render "black" for *blanco,* corroborating my theory that the original text was written in Spanish and translated into Latin by an Englishman.

One unsolved enigma that cannot simply be explained away by linguistic transfer has to do with the archbishop of Toledo Bartolome de Carranza's name. As pointed out earlier, Carranza was sometimes referred to as Bartolome de Miranda, in reference to his hometown Miranda de Arga (Navarra), but never as Bartolome de Zamora, as it appears in the Latin text: *Bartholomeum Zamorensem.* Carranza was a well-known figure. The author of *Artes* is very explicit in his description of him: "A monk of the order of St Domenic, a man very well learned and one that knew the truth, who afterwards, by the Emperor's means, was preferred to the archbishopric of Toledo." Why would he want to distort his name? Was it a distraction or a lapse of memory? This seeming error can only have an explanation if we start with the supposition that the Latin version was a translation from an original Spanish manuscript, and that the "supposed English translator" deliberately altered it. Carranza was not well esteemed by Protestants in England; his name was not associated with "one that knew the truth." In fact, he was still a *persona non grata* in the minds of many Englishmen in 1567. Charles V had sent Carranza to England in 1554 with his son Philip on the occasion of Philip's marriage with Mary Tudor as Philip's personal chaplain and confessor. Carranza's name was associated with censorship, persecutions, book-burnings, etc. He even seemed to have responsible for the exhumation and dishonorable disposal of the remains of Peter Martyr's wife in 1557 (Tellechea: 1977a, 186). This had taken place only a decade earlier. The name "Carranza" would necessarily produce bad vibrations, hence the adjustment—a simple stratagem to camouflage his identity without altering the context.

I am not the first to suggest the work was originally written in Spanish. In the prologue of his German translation of *Artes* (1611), Joachim Beringer states that the little book was first written in Spanish. Unfortunately he gives no justification for the statement. Nicolas Castrillo (1991, 119) also entertains the idea of an earlier Spanish version, but does not substantiate his theory any further than to say he read it in Beringer. In contrast, Ruiz de Pablos (1997) doubts very seriously that the Latin text was a translation from a Spanish manuscript, though, as aforementioned, he did find several instances of Spanish influence on the Latin. He contends that no Spanish version appears on the lists of Prohibited Books hence it is highly unlikely that such a version ever existed. I maintain that it would not have been possible for a printed Spanish version to be listed because it would only have existed in the form of a single hand-written manuscript.

Let us take the assumption one step further. Supposing the original manuscript was written in Spanish, who would have been responsible for translating it into Latin and who would have commissioned it? The timing of the publication was probably coordinated politically with Elizabeth I's chief advisor, William Cecil, whose efforts had a great impact on the English perception of Spain. Based on intelligence received from Sir Henry Norris, the English ambassador stationed in Paris, Cecil warned his fellow countrymen that Spain was uniting with France—in obedience to papal command—in preparation for an attack on England. This threat is repeated in Skinner's Preface to the Reader. Cecil employed a Spanish-literate secretariat to circulate manuscript letters and pamphleteers to create Spanish threats, which were then answered with English propaganda. Professor Hannah Crummé (2011, 7–27) reports an interesting example, namely, the printing of "A Packe of Spanish Lyes: first printed in Spaine in the Spanish tongue, and translated out of the original, (1588),"[4] The pamphlet was printed in two columns, one claiming to be an English translation of intercepted letters and the other "an answer from England." The "lies" are claimed to be direct quotations from letters by Bernardino de Mendoza, Spanish ambassador in Paris, and Diego Perez, head postman in Logroño. This genre of imaginative forms of "rediscovered" letters, bulls, catechisms, etc., was not exclusive to England. It also had its heyday in the Netherlands at that time (Harline: 1987, 52).

Who could have been William Cecil's Spanish-Latin translator? Although no one at either Oxford or Cambridge officially studied Spanish, the two universities produced a number of scholars, statesmen, translators, and tutors who were well versed in the language. Whereas Robert Dudley (Earl of Leicester) got his Spanish-speaking secretaries from Oxford, Cecil got his from Cambridge: Michael Hicks, George Blythe, and Henry Maynard, who specialized in foreign affairs. Skinner, Hickes, Blythe, and Maynard shared the same religious views and by the early 1580s had all become Cecil's full-fledged secretaries. Many young men, who would later enter political circles, attached themselves to some embassy, as was the case of Arthur Atye, who, after receiving an M.A. from Merton College (University of Oxford) in 1562, joined Dr. John Man, when he was sent as ambassador to Madrid. In short, there was no lack of qualified, trustworthy translators to whom this job could have been commissioned.

Who Wrote *Artes*?

Reginaldo Gonzalez de Montes was a pseudonym. While minutely describing the crafty workings of the Holy Office in Seville, the author of *Artes* unfortunately left very few clues regarding himself and his real identity. In effect, the true identity of Reginaldo Gonzales de Montes still eludes us. Nevertheless, a run-through of several proposals regarding his identity is in order. One classic study is that of the Dutch historian Bernard A. Vermaseren, "Who was Reginaldus Gonsalvus Montanus?" (1985). Since Vermaseren's publication, other theories have also appeared, based almost exclusively on extra-textual sources. For example, Dr. Robert Kolb (2005, 299, note 10), Emeritus professor at Concordia Seminary, St. Louis, claims that "Gonsalvio was executed as a Protestant in Naples under the Hapsburg government's policy of suppression of heresy." Dr. Kolb seems to have found this information in the preface of the 1569 German

---

4 Christopher Barker, the printer, is the same name that appears on the false imprint of the 1633 Amsterdam edition of the Geneva Bible.

rendering of *Artes*, but that is not clear. Some scholars credit the authorship of *Artes* to Antonio del Corro simply because he was in England in 1567, the year *Artes* was first published. Others ascribe it to Casiodoro de Reina, author of the first complete translation of the Bible into Spanish. Still others argue for their— Corro-Reina—co-authorship. It is highly unlikely that either Corro or Reina had anything to do with the drafting or publication of *Artes* because both had fled Seville already in 1557 before the Inquisition began clamped down on evangelical dissidents. According to Juan Antonio Llorente (1843, 165), "Raymond Gonzales de Montes was Doctor Egidius's companion in prison, but succeeded in escaping, and was burnt in effigy." The French bibliographer Antoine-Alexandre Barbier (1823, II, 94), in his *Dictionary of Pseudonyms*, describes the 1568 French rendering of *Artes* as, "Traduite du latin de Reginaldus Gonzalvius Montanus. Montanus, moine Dominicain d'Espagne, embrassa la réformation, et souffrit pour elle" (Translated from Latin by Reginaldus Gonzalvius Montanus, a Spanish Dominican monk who embraced the Reformation and suffered for it). Whether this was a guess in the dark, or whether he had some evidence that the author was a Dominican monk is unclear. Barbier may have found the information in Gerdes's *Florilegium Historico-Criticum Librorum Rariorum* (1747). Francisco Ruiz de Pablos (2008, 17–46) uncovers some of the fallacies of these conjectures, but also admits that unfortunately he does not have the solution either. He insists, nevertheless, on the linguistic uniformity of the text, which contradicts the theory of co-authorship.

Most hypotheses focus on the physical location of the author of *Artes* in 1567 (Germany?, Holland?, England?) and his profound Protestant convictions. I suggest that instead of looking for the author among declared Lutheran heretics who had the good fortune to escape the clutches of the Inquisition and were living abroad, we look among the suspected heretics that remained behind. There were passionate defenders of religious freedom, with deep Protestant convictions, who, confined to some monastery, would have had the opportunity to reflect on their experiences at Triana and to put them in writing. In any case, we must look for someone who was still alive and well—and in Seville—in 1563/ 64.

After the *autos-da-fe* of 1562 and 1563, there still remained at Triana some twenty clergy awaiting either their sentence or their destination. Half a dozen come close to filling the profile of the author of *Artes*. There was, for example, Fray Benito, proposed by Ernst Schäfer (2014, I, 218). Fray Benito was a Jeronimite monk from San Isidoro, one that had not fled with the others. He was held prisoner at Triana from 1557 to 1559, and put under house arrest until his escape in 1565.[5] Another candidate is Hernan Ruiz de Hojeda, canon of the

---

5 AHN, Inquisición, leg. 2943, doc. 149–2, in: Lopez Muñoz (2011, 344, doc. 164).

Cathedral, belonging to the circle of Constantino and Egidio, arrested for heresy in 1559, and sentenced to ten years confinement in the House of the Jesuits, deprived of his office, forbidden to teach for the rest of his life and fined 3000 ducats. Or Diego de Mairena, who served seven years of his ten-year sentence in the Dominican Monastery of Regina Angelorum in Seville before transferring to the town of Bornos, near Arcos de la Frontera. Reports came back to the inquisitors that in Bornos Mairena spoke out against the pope, the Holy Office, and the inquisitors, and publicly praised doctor Constantino and Erasmus.[6] There was also Jeronimo de Herrera, administrator of the Hospital de Bubas, among whose belongings the inquisitors found books in Hebrew and in Greek and many hand-written copies of sermons of Egidio and Constantino, and was still in Triana prison in the fall of 1562.[7] Most probable candidates, however, are Fray Domingo de Baltanas and Fray Domingo de Guzman. Baltanas was sentenced privately on February 27, 1563, and sent to a remote monastery in Alcala de los Gazules, where he died in 1567. Guzman was confined for life to the Monastery of San Pablo in Seville.

In the Prologue to the Reader, which is a brief history of the implantation of the Inquisition, the author of *Artes* infers that he began to write his "history" in or before 1557. This section may even have been initially intended as a separate publication. The author's in-depth knowledge of details regarding the activities and designs of the Inquisition lends itself to the supposition that at one time he was closely involved with the Holy Office. He might have been an inquisitor himself—a repented, crypto-Lutheran inquisitor—, but there is no evidence of this sort. He could also have been a consultant, or notary, or prosecutor, or chaplain, or some minor officer, which would have allowed him to become acquainted with the prisoners in the prison at Triana as well as to have access to trial records. Consultants (*calificadores*) were generally more qualified in theology than in law and were called in to examine literature and testimonies to determine orthodoxy; prosecuting attorneys (*fiscales*) presented the accusations; treasurers (*receptores*) were in charge of itemizing the confiscations and doing the bookkeeping; notaries and secretaries wrote up the documents attesting the case; *alguaciles* were in charge of custody; and *familiares* were in charge of spying and informing. If the author of *Artes* had had some relation with the Holy Office, of all the ranks within this complex hierarchy, he would probably have been a secretary, a notary, or a consultant, which would also have given him access to the confiscated literature.

Did the author of *Artes* hold a degree from some institutions of higher

---

6 AHN, Inquisición, leg. 2946, in: Lopez Muñoz (2011, 444, doc. 250).
7 AHN, Inquisición, leg. 2075, doc. 2; leg. 2943, doc. 83, in: Lopez Muñoz (2011, 270, doc. 129; 281, doc. 132). Also see Manuel de Leon (2012, II, 565).

learning in Seville? There were several of such institutions. One was the Colegio de la Doctrina. Juan Perez de Pineda, who fled to Geneva and was burned in effigy in 1560, and Gaspar Baptista, who died in prison and whose bones were burned in 1562, had been teachers at the Colegio de la Doctrina. Another school was the Colegio de Santo Tomas, a university-college founded in 1517 by the Dominican friar and archbishop of Seville, Diego de Deza, as a bulwark of scholastic theology in reaction to the humanist orientation of the University of Alcala. There was also the Estudio General de Latin y del Arabe, founded by Alfonso X the Wise around 1250, and the Colegio de San Miguel, which opened around 1530 under the auspices of the Cathedral Chapter. And there was the Colegio de Santa Maria de Jesus, founded in 1505 by Maestro Rodrigo, which would eventually become the University of Seville. Montes's broad knowledge of both canon and civil law, as well as of history and the classics, is notorious and suggests a scholar, or perhaps a lawyer. He advised his readers to be cautious in their responses and whenever possible to quote Catholic theologians, mainly the scholastics, to confound them:

> I hold him wise who can, upon a little study, make a brief and resolute Christian-like answer, so as he neither hurt his conscience by suppressing or shadowing the truth, nor by his long process give his adversary anything to take hold upon, or have any advantage against him, which (doubtless) is the only mark they shoot at in having him answer it by writing. It is also very good for him that, so often as he can, he support his position making mention of some of their experts in canon law and scholastic theologians (as they call them) for thus shall neither the truth be obscured nor they so easily make a quarrel to his answer, being ratified and confirmed with his adversary's arguments. (Montes: 1569, f. 10v).

The mystery that shrouds the true identity of the author of *Artes* may never be solved, nevertheless, certain facts, based on internal evidence, can serve as clues:
1) He was very knowledgeable regarding the implantation of the Spanish Inquisition and its modus operandi.
2) He was well versed in both civil and canon law, and the classics.
3) He was personally acquainted with the Ponce de Leon family, Rodrigo de Valer, Constantino, and Dr. Egidio.
4) He was well acquainted with prison activities at Triana.
5) He had strong Protestant convictions.
6) He was still alive and probably still in Seville in 1564/65.

Domingo de Baltanas

Fray Domingo de Baltanas was among the first generation of recruits at the Colegio de Santo Tomas. As a young boy, Baltanas (also spelled Valtanas) was sent to the Dominican Convent of San Esteban in Salamanca. In 1508, at the age of twenty, he took the habit there and very likely began teaching in the same institution. In his early 30s he left the Convent of San Esteban for the newly founded Colegio de Santo Tomas in Seville, a sort of finishing school for theologians (Góngora: 1890, Vol. II). Nevertheless, after only a year, he left the hardcore conservative college of Santo Tomas for the Dominican Convent of San Pablo el Real, a center of higher learning to train preachers and missionary priests to evangelize the New World. Baltanas's brief stay at Santo Tomas is a puzzle to historians. Being of *converso* origin (Ortiz: 1971, 87), he must have felt a profound aversion to the laws of cleanliness of blood that Diego de Deza imposed on the incoming faculty and student body. Baltanas had humanist tendencies. In Spain there remained considerable support for humanism even after the debate in 1527 (Homza: 1997, 78–118), but by the time Fernando de Valdes became inquisitor general in 1547 the tide had turned.

Among the early victims in Seville, imprisoned late 1557 and burned at the stake September 21, 1559, was Juan Ponce de Leon.[8] Baltanas had enjoyed a long relationship with the extended Ponce de Leon family that went back to the 1520s when he was Juan's uncle Rodrigo Ponce de Leon's confessor, and the executor of his will. Later Baltanas dedicated his history of Spain—*Compendio de algunas cosas notables de España* (1558)—to Rodrigo as a posthumous tribute. He dedicated another book to Juan Ponce de Leon's cousin, Ana Ponce de Leon, countess of Feria, and another to Ana's daughter, Catalina Fernandez de Cordoba, marchioness of Priego. Baltanas also had connections with the Pacheco family in Escalona. He dedicated *Concordancias de muchos passos difficiles de la divina historia* (1555) (Concordance of many difficult passages in Holy Scriptures) to Isabel Pacheco, daughter of Diego Lopez Pacheco, abbess of the Santa Clara convent in Montilla.

Fray Baltanas was arrested in February of 1561. It seems that the inquisitors had been lying in wait for him for some time—as had been the case with Constantino and Bartolome de Carranza—but weren't quite sure how to go about apprehending him. Finally, they put their arts into practice and sent for the prior of San Pablo with the request that Domingo de Baltanas accompany him. Once within their physical reach, it was simply a matter of not allowing him to leave.[9] Despite all the proposed secrecy, however, Baltanas's arrest did not go unnoticed.

---

8 Juan Ponce de Leon was the son of Rodrigo Ponce de Leon y Guzman, 2nd Count of Bailen, great nephew of Rodrigo Ponce de Leon y Ponce de Leon, 1st Duke of Arcos. He was second cousin to Ana Ponce de Leon y Tellez-Giron, who became a nun in 1554 after the death of her husband Pedro Fernandez de Cordoba y Figueroa, 4th Count of Feria, and to Luis Cristobal Ponce de Leon y Tellez-Giron, 2nd Duke of Arcos.

9 AHN, Inquisición, leg. 2943, doc. 13, in: Lopez Muñoz (2011, 234, doc. 109).

A month later, a dispatch sent to Venice by Paulo Tiepolo, ambassador to Philip II, reported his arrest:

> In Seville the Inquisition has arrested Friar Domenego de Valtanas, of the Order of St. Dominick, in the Province of Andalusia, a man eighty years of age, and of greater authority and reputation for sanctity than any one else in Spain, so that he had a very great concourse of almost all the nobility of the country who went to him to confess. He has been convicted of opinions contrary to those held by the Church. (*Calendar,* 1890, 297).

Two years later, on February 27, 1563, Baltanas's case was finally resolved, but not without dissension among the judges. Inquisitor Gasco was of the opinion that he should be sent straight to the stake; the Bishop of Tarazona pleaded clemency; Carpio and Soto voted that he abjure publicly at the next *auto-da-fe.* Eventually, a midway solution was reached: Baltanas would be defrocked in a private ceremony in the chapel of the prison and sent to a remote monastery for the rest of his life.[10] In effect, two days later he was whisked off to the monastery of Santo Domingo de las Cinco Llagas, in Alcala de los Gazules, 110 km (70 miles) from Seville, where he died in the summer of 1567 at the age of 79.

Domingo de Baltanas was charged of being "*vehementemente sospechoso de herejía*" (strongly suspected of heresy). His crime was not Lutheran heresy, but "*sollicitatio ad turpia*," that is, soliciting and sexually harassing nuns in the convents of which he was prior.[11] At the time he was sentenced this was an unprecedented charge and lacked legislation. It was the Lutheran alarm of 1558 that had led the archbishop of Granada, Pedro Guerrero Logroño, to call the attention of the Holy See to the frequency of the offence and the need of energetic repression. His appeal was heard, and Pope Paul IV, in a brief of February 18, 1559, granted him jurisdiction to punish the offence in his district. On April 14, 1561, Inquisitor General Fernando de Valdes obtained from Pope Pius IV a similar bull granting him the same faculties throughout Spain, but the inquisitors were too busy with the Lutherans at the time to put it into practice. Furthermore, to render it effective, it had to be announced publicly with the Edict of Faith—a list of offenses condemned by the church—which was read once a year. The inquisitors hesitated to include "solicitation" among the offences, fearing the ever-present prospect of scandal. Finally, on July 17, 1562, jurisdiction regarding the offence was confirmed by the Supreme Council,[12] with the reservation that the arrest should be made with the utmost circumspection, and when the case be concluded,

---

10 AHN, Inquisición, leg. 2943, doc. 93, in: Lopez Muñoz (2011, 295, doc. 139).
11 See Beltrán de Heredia (1957, 649–659); Huerga (1958, 93–142); Alejandre (1994); Civale (2007, 197–241); Nieva Ocampo (2007).
12 Antonio Llorente (1843, 356) mistakenly dates the publication of this edict in 1564.

If the accused be a friar he is to be confined in his convent with orders not to preach or hear confessions and if he is a secular priest, he is to be confined somewhere else than where the offence was committed. Above all, the punishment should be secret, so that the people, seeing no results, might be led to believe that there were no wicked men administering the sacrament. (Lea: 1906–1907, II, Ch. 6).

The edict was finally made public in Seville in April of 1563, when the inquisitors read it during Easter services in the cathedral. As a result, in October of 1563, *sollicitatio ad turpia* became officially punishable by the Holy Office. It naturally produced a sensation (Lea: 1867, 501). The author of *Artes* describes the scene in detail:

In the year of our Lord God 1563, it happened that the Holy House was advised and fully bent to lay their baits and spread their nets in certain quarters there, but if they had not, upon better advice, wound them up again, they themselves unawares had given Rome such a blow as I believe all the Lutherans hitherto have not given it a greater. And thus it happened that there were certain persons, more busy a great deal than I believe they should have been, who found great fault with a foul company of monks and other religious men, for abusing their auricular confession, and under the cover thereof misbehaving with honest matrons and maidens that resorted unto them, making it a means to break their vows and to accomplish their purposes. The Holy House thought this indeed worthy of consideration and redress.

Now forasmuch as it was a hard matter to know who these wooers and seducers were, since none was accused particularly and by name (as it happens in a matter wherein a multitude offend), they caused proclamation to be made throughout all the churches within the province of Seville very solemnly, that whosoever knew, of their own personal knowledge or had heard by report of others, of any monks or other religious or spiritual persons (as they call them), that had abused their holy sacrament of confession, to any such abominable acts or enterprises, or that any other spiritual father had dealt in any such like sort with any of his shrift children, that every such person and persons knowledgeable of any such matter should come in within thirty days and denounce it to the Holy House of the Inquisition, prescribing, moreover, very great penalties for such as should refuse or disdain to come in accordingly and to make declaration.

The proclamation was no sooner made and published but there came such a number of women, only inhabitants within the city of Seville, to complain of their spiritual fathers that twenty notaries, and as many inquisitors, would not have sufficed to take the names of such as came in and entered their complaints.[13] Wherefore, the inquisitors having more to do than they could dispatch, gave them another thirty days to come in and do the same. But because so little time would not serve (they came in so thick), they

---

13 Nine days were allowed to present accusations, but "because so many people have appeared to denounce priests who have incurred in this offense, and we are overwhelmed with so much work," the term was extended four months. AHN, *Inquisición*, leg. 2942, doc. 101, cf. Civale: 2007, 223.

gave them so much more respite again the third time, and after that the fourth, and there they were forced to lay a straw for very many honest matrons, and of good calling, partly of a foolish fear and superstition lest they should be excommunicated, and partly in respect of their husbands whom they were loath to offend and bring into a jealousy or suspicion of their honesty, kept themselves at home, thinking to spy out some better opportunity to speak with the inquisitors apart. Whereupon, they attired themselves with veils or mufflers, after the manner of their country, and went to the Holy House as secretly as they could. Notwithstanding, their husbands did so narrowly watch them during all this time that they could not possibly pass so secretly but divers of them were spied, whereby they occasioned their husbands vehemently to suspect their honesties.

On the other side, it was a jolly sport to see the monks and friars and priests go up and down, hanging down their heads all in a dump and a melancholy by means of their guilty consciences, quaking and trembling and looking every hour lest some of the *familiars* should take them by the sleeve and call them *Coram*[14] for these matters. A number even feared lest as great a plague were come among them as the persecution that was so hot about that time against the Lutherans. But the inquisitors, perceiving that these matters thus purposed would redound not only to the great hindrance of themselves but also turn to the decay of the whole Church of Rome, and that this enterprise of theirs, if it should go on and take effect, would be enough to bring all their spirituality into utter hatred and obloquy, but especially tend to the discredit of their auricular confession, which began already to be of very small esteem (although it was a matter that otherwise deserved both straightly to be examined and severely to be punished), suspended it, contrary to all men's expectations, winding up all these matters whereof the court was now orderly and lawfully seized. The report was that the monks and priests had made a common purse and with a good round sum greased the Pope's hand so that he was content to grant a general pardon to all the whole company of confessors of his fatherly love and affection towards them, remitting all offences done or committed by them and commanding the inquisitors to cease from proceeding any further, but wholly to suppress such things as were passed already, not suffering them in any case to come to light.[15] However those that know of the inquisitors' dealings say it is an unlikely matter, affirming that if the pope should grant any such pardon, yet is the Holy Inquisition of such preeminence that, if they take in hand any matter of weight, they will not cease upon the pope's inhibition or counter command, and that it is oftener seen that their authority prevails against the pope's than his against them, as by the following example may more plainly appear. (Montes: 1569, ff. 62v–63v. Notes mine).

The author of these words certainly seems to have been an eyewitness of the event, which would automatically discard all those who had left Seville prior to

14 This is a play on the Latin phrase *Coram Deo*, meaning "into the presence of God."
15 On November 30, 1563, Pope Paul IV published a jubilee and a plenary indulgence for all. In the case of Seville, there were three requisites. These prayers were to be made on two specific holidays, that of Assumption of the Virgin Mary into Heaven (August 15) and San Hermenegildo (April 13), and they were to be made in the church belonging the Hospital del Cardenal.

that date. How must this burlesque tone of an authentic, historical incident be interpreted?

Baltanas was banished from Seville for having molested nuns. Inquisitor Gasco, who was well acquainted with the laws, could hardly have insisted on capital punishment for a crime that lacked regulation. Was the charge of solicitation a facade? Was it Baltanas himself who purposely put them on the wrong track? When asked why he thought he had been summoned—which was the first question the inquisitors asked—, Baltanas answer was that he really had no idea except that it might have to do with some "shameful behavior" he had had with some nuns (Civale: 2007, 237–238). Were there also doctrinal charges? Where exactly did Baltanas stand doctrinally? Based on the content of his published works—mainly his *Doctrina Cristiana* (1555)—, Marcel Bataillon (1966, 544) classifies him as being just a stone's throw away from the Lutherans. Jose Nieto (1997, 284–287), on the other hand, sees him more as an Erasmian than a convinced Protestant. Nieto, who compared Baltanas's position regarding doctrines such as merits, works, grace, etc., with those of Constantino Ponce de la Fuente, finds his terminology much closer to neo-Scholasticism than to Constantino's neo-Testamentarism and concludes that it was his *Apología sobre ciertas materias morales en que hay opinión* (1556) (In defense of certain moral issues that are being questioned), where he condemned bishops who did not reside in their bishoprics, favored silent prayer, defended persons of *converso* origin, etc., that alerted the inquisitors. That same year the inquisitors were questioning the orthodoxy of his *Concordancias de muchos passos difficiles* (1556), not so much for its theological content but because he dared to cite biblical texts in the vernacular. On the other hand, in an earlier publication, Baltanas (1555b, f. 20) bitterly attacked Luther. Could his regard for Luther have changed in the eight years that spanned between 1555 and his release in 1563?

Domingo de Guzman

One of Domingo de Baltanas's colleagues at the Monastery of San Pablo el Real was Fray Domingo de Guzman. Among the 300 Latin Bibles confiscated in 1552, the names of a dozen of friars at the Monastery of San Pablo el Real appeared. Domingo de Guzman was one of them, but Baltanas's name was not on the list. Being Dominicans, both were well acquainted with the role of the Dominicans in the implantation of the Spanish Inquisition and its *modus operandi,* and were well instructed in both canon and civil law. Domingo de Guzman was called before the inquisitors in January of 1558 and questioned regarding heretical books that he had brought with him from Flanders—or having had brought for him—and having shared them with others.[16] Domingo de Guzman was among the recipients of the books smuggled in by Julian Hernandez in the summer of 1557. When the inquisitors got word that Guzman was one of the recipients of these heretical books, orders were given to confine him to his rooms while his books and papers were taken to Triana for examination.[17] It took the inquisitors over a month to examine Guzman's large library—1000 volumes according to the appended information in the 1569 English reprint of *Artes*. Because Inquisitor General Valdes had not yet published his *Index of Prohibited Books* in order to legally support this action, the inquisitors had to resort to Philip II's *Pragmatic Sancion,* published in February of 1558:

> No bookseller or book dealer or any other person of whatever profession he be is allowed to bring in or smuggle [into the country] or sell any book or work printed, or in manuscript form, of those prohibited by the Holy Office of the Inquisition, in any language, be the work or book of any sort, under penalty of death, and the loss of all his goods, and all such books should be burned publically.

Finally, on March 3, 1558, Guzman himself was taken to Triana and put in solitary confinement.[18] His books, already confiscated, were put in secret keeping. Instructions were sent from the Supreme Council that no one should have access to them. A year later, on November 2, 1559, the Council asked the inquisitors at Seville to search among them for a commentary by Luther on Isaiah or on the Prophets, and also one on the Epistle of Saint Paul to the Galatians. The commentaries were found and duly sent to Toledo.

Domingo de Guzman's sentence was finally read at the *auto-da-fe* of July 11, 1563.[19] He had spent more than five years in prison. Earlier that year, in May, he had complained to the inquisitors of bad health, due to his age, and of open sores on his legs. He also complained that his fellow cellmate, Guillermo Gilmerme-son—whom he called a "frog," a term applied to the Flemish in the 17th century—was a terrible cook and that he wanted his servant Juan Guzman back.[20] Initially the inquisitors had wanted to sentence Guzman at the *auto-da-fe* in 1560 to make more room in Triana because the prison was getting too crowded, but for some reason he was not brought out then, or at the next *auto* on October 28, 1562. This was in all probability due to disaccord among the inquisitors regarding the sentence. On May 22, 1563, they finally cast their votes: three voted

---

16 AHN, Inquisición, leg. 2075, doc. 3, in: Lopez Muñoz (2011, 307, doc. 148).
17 AHN, Inquisición, lib. 575, ff. 57r–57v, in: Lopez Muñoz (2011, 117, doc. 39).
18 AHN, Inquisición, lib. 575, f. 59r, in: Lopez Muñoz (2011, 119, doc. 41).
19 AHN, Inquisición, leg. 2943, doc. 100–2; leg. 2943, doc. 100–1, in: Lopez Muñoz (2011, 303, doc. 144).
20 AHN, Inquisición, leg. 2943, doc. 105–2, in: Lopez Muñoz (2011, 305, doc. 145). The inquisitors must have complied with his wishes because Juan Guzman was returned to his service. AHN, Inquisición, leg. 2943, doc. 89–2, in: Lopez Muñoz (2011, 317, doc. 154).

that he should be handed over to the civil authorities and be burned at the stake; the others opted for a more lenient sentence.[21] The majority won and he was sentenced to abjure *de vehementi*, to be defrocked verbally, and to be confined for life to his old monastery, forbidden to read or write, or to have visitors other than those allowed by the inquisitors, and all of his books publically burned in the Plaza de San Francisco.[22] Montes (1569, f. 58r) defines what was meant by abjuring *de vehementi*: "They call it *Abjuration de vehenmenti* when, in hearing and debating a man's cause, it is not clear what is to be determined due to lack of sufficient proof, and because the party himself confessed nothing that deserved any manner of punishment."

It took until the *auto* of July 11, 1563, for Domingo de Guzman to hear his sentence of perpetual confinement read. His old cellmate Guillermo Gilmermeson was burned at the stake that day.[23] A month later, on August 14, 1563, the inquisitors informed the Supreme Council that Guzman was doing penance as ordered in San Pablo el Real.[24] Information appended to the English edition of *Artes* (1569, Appendix) adds a few more details regarding Guzman:

> In the same Act there was brought onto the scaffold one called Fray Domingo de Guzman, a Dominican Friar and a preacher, one of the cloister of St. Paula[25] in Seville, who, having brought divers Lutheran books (as they commonly term them in Spain), lent the same to divers in Seville, and began to profess the gospel and to preach it to others, whereupon, he was apprehended and committed to prison. But, for as much as he was bastard brother to the Duke of Medina Sidonia, and in hope of preferment to some archbishopric, he openly recanted. Howbeit, the inquisitors, fearing to allow any that had been at any time inclined towards like heresy to be preferred to any such place of authority and countenance, first commanded that all his books, which were about 1000 volumes, should be burnt before his face, despite his recantation, and awarded him to perpetual prison.

Indeed, Domingo de Guzman was of noble birth. He was an illegitimate son of Juan Alonso Perez de Guzman, 3rd Duke of Medina Sidonia, and half brother of Juan Alfonso Pérez de Guzman, 6th Duke of Medina Sidonia.[26] He was a relative by marriage to Juan Ponce de Leon, whose father's third wife, Maria Tellez-Giron, widow of the 4th Duke of Medina Sidonia, was the mother of Ana Ponce de

---

21 AHN, Inquisición, leg. 2943, doc. 100–2, in: Lopez Muñoz (2011, 303, doc. 144).
22 AHN, Inquisición, leg. 2075, doc. 3, in: Lopez Muñoz (2011, 307, doc. 148).
23 The document describes Guillermo Guillermeson as "alias Guillermo de Utreque, tailor, citizen of Utrecht, near Holland, galley slave rowing in the ship called "San Pablo", burned alive for Anabaptist and Lutheran heretic, with the confiscation of his goods." AHN, *Inquisición*, leg. 2075, doc. 3, in: Lopez Muñoz (2011, 308, doc. 148).
24 AHN, Inquisición, leg. 2943, doc. 116–1, in: Lopez Muñoz (2011, 312, doc. 150).
25 This should read "St. Paul." Santa Paula was a convent for nuns.
26 Juan Alonso Pérez de Guzmán (1464–1507) married twice and was the father of the 4th, 5th, and 6th Duke of Medina Sidonia.

Leon y Tellez-Giron and Luis Cristobal Ponce de Leon, which made Domingo de Guzman their uncle and Juan Ponce de Leon a distant cousin. This poses another dilemma. Who knew Juan Ponce de Leon better, Baltanas or Guzman? Who knew Egidio better, Baltanas or Guzman? Who knew Constantino better, Baltanas or Guzman? And what about Rodrigo de Valer? Montes's passionate defense of Valer suggests more than a passing, indirect acquaintance.

Guzman could very well have been one of the external consultants called in to examine Rodrigo de Valer in 1541. The author of *Artes* goes into great detail regarding Valer's declarations, all of which are corroborated by Inquisition records. According to the records, Dr. Egidio and Dr. Vargas and "*otras personas*" (others) sanctioned Valer's behavior.[27] It appears that Dr. Egidio was present as a consultant, not merely a friend. When referring to the person that changed Dr. Egidio's life, Montes very specifically states: "His name was Rodrigo de Valer, a man 26 years ago condemned at Seville by the inquisitors." This precision of dates—1538, the date of Valer's first arrest,[28] plus the 26 years that had gone by—corroborates the date Montes repeatedly uses as the year he concluded his history: 1564. The author of *Artes* also relates that Valer spent his last years in a monastery in Sanlucar de Barrameda and that he died at the age of fifty. Was the repeated reference to the year 1564 as the date of completion of the work a stratagem to sidetrack any suspicions regarding the identity of the author? On the other hand, considering that Guzman was sent back to his old monastery San Pablo el Real in the summer of 1563, shortly after his sentence was read, he could have witnessed "the monks and friars and priests go up and down, hanging down their heads all in a dump and a melancholy by means of their guilty consciences, quaking and trembling and looking every hour lest some of the *familiares* should take them by the sleeve and call them *Coram* for these matters." (Montes: 1569, ff. 62v–63v).

Domingo de Azpeitia

One even more likely candidate to consider as the author of *Artes* is the notary Domingo de Azpeitia. We began by saying that the author of *Artes* could have been a repented, crypto-Lutheran inquisitor, but there is no evidence of this sort. We then went on to suggest that he could have been a consultant, a scholar, or a lawyer. The office of notary would have fulfilled all the requirements—and advantages—of those offices and more. As Juan Antonio Llorente (1843, xiii.

---

27 AHN, Inquisición, lib. 574, ff. 96v–97r, in: Lopez Muñoz (2011, 47, doc. 7).
28 Valer was arrested twice: first in 1538 and again in March of 1540. See Boeglin (2007, 113–134).

Brackets mine), who, writing from experience, two hundred years later would compile his own history of the Inquisition, points out, "No one could write a complete and authentic history of the Inquisition, who was not either an inquisitor or a secretary [notary] of the holy office."

Of the dozen or so notaries that signed the various documents issued by the tribunal in Seville between 1550 and 1564, one name that stands out is that of Domingo de Azpeitia. His name first appears in a document dated July 29, 1550, when Dr. Egidio was in prison. The document—a dispatch from the Supreme Council to Charles V—is an acknowledgement of a former letter from the emperor regarding Dr. Egidio's case to which is added a request for information regarding certain individuals that had left Seville very suddenly after Dr. Egidio's arrest. The Council had been notified by the inquisitors at Seville that Diego de la Cruz and Luis del Castillo, friends of Dr. Egidio, had left the city for fear of being arrested, and had gone to Paris. They were particularly interested in finding Luis del Castillo in relation to a booklet he had left with Francisca de Chaves, namely, *Dialogo consolatorio entre la Iglesia Chiquita que está en Sevilla y Jesucristo* (Consolatory Dialog between the Little Church in Seville and Jesus Christ), and to know whether he was the author. Along with the instructions sent to France, went a copy of the booklet, "copied on nine pages of paper, and signed by Domingo de Azpeitia, notary of the secret of the Inquisition at Seville."[29] This brief reference evidences several facts: firstly, that Azpeitia was the notary in charge of documenting Egidio's trial; and secondly, that already in 1550 Azpeitia was aware of the evangelical movement in Seville and knew some of the persons involved, such as Rodrigo de Valer, Dr. Egidio, Constantino, Francisca de Chaves, and Ana de Deza. Unfortunately the booklet has been lost, but as Azpeitia copied the content he would have gotten a better insight into the movement, and sympathized with it and its members, otherwise it is highly unlikely that he would have allowed Ana de Deza to communicate with Dr. Egidio the information she received from, and forwarded to, Diego de la Cruz, Egidio's friend and her former chaplain, through a window in his own apartment (Carceles, 2014).

Domingo de Azpeitia and his wife, Ana Sanchez de Garfias, lived in a private apartment in Triana castle. An incident involving Elvira Nuñez, one of the prisoners, reveals another facet of Azpeitia's personality. Elvira gave birth while she was in prison. At ten o'clock in the morning of March 8, 1560, the jail keeper Pedro de la Haya and the midwife Maria Diez came to Azpeitia's apartment with the newborn child. The midwife did not know the name of the mother, but the jail keeper did and told Azpeitia—secretly—that it was Elvira Nuñez. Azpeitia took the child and gave her to a wet nurse who was breast-feeding his own

---

29 AHN, Inquisición, lib. 574, f. 216r, in: Lopez Muñoz (2011, 52, doc. 12).

daughter. The next day the midwife took the child to another woman, who nursed her for a month, "until the woman's husband came back from the Indies," and then she took her to still another wet nurse, where the child still was a year later, when the inquisitors summoned the midwife to explain what happened. Among other things, the midwife declared that "until he died" Domingo de Azpeitia paid the wet nurse fourteen *reales* every month for the child's maintenance and he gave orders that the next receptor, Pedro de Morga, should continue to pay her the same, which he did.[30] Also, when the child was eight day old, the midwife took her to the Church of St. Ann and had her baptized. Azpeitia asked her to give him the baptismal certificate, which he must have kept.[31] Without this certificate, the child would have been deprived of a name and a status in society. Such concern for the child of a convicted Lutheran was exceptional, especially in 1560 when persecution was at its height. Montes dedicates several pages to the case of the Gomez-Nuñez family, and especially elaborates on the private interviews that Inquisitor Carpio had with Elvira Nuñez, without mentioning any of them by name, or that Elvira gave birth while in prison. On the other hand, since only three persons—the midwife, the jail keeper, and Azpeitia—had knowledge of this incident, by exposing it he would have given away his identity, which he was not about to do.

The number of references found in *Artes* to the presence of a notary documenting conversations, confessions, confiscations, etc., is remarkable:

> Immediately after every arrest done by the *alguazil*, or complaint made to the court of any person by any of the *familiars*, they straightway take from him all the keys of his chests or locks, if he have any, and forthwith send a notary and a certain catchpole with the *alquazil* to take an inventory of all such goods as are in his house, whatever they be. (Montes: 1569, f. 4v)

> As soon as the prisoner is entered within the first gate of the prison, the keeper, having with him a notary, asks him if he has any knife on him, or money, or rings or any other jewels. (f. 5v)

> The advocate and his client may not so much as have a word together secretly on any matter but in presence and hearing of the Inquisitors or of some notary. (f. 5v)

> If the party begins to confess anything, then is he surely caught. For when he has poured out all and said what he can say in these cases (though he do it through the

---

30 Pedro de Morga, who had been one of Charles V's bankers in 1553, became treasurer (*receptor*) of the Holy Office in Seville after Domingo de Azpeitia left in 1561. His banking operations failed in 1575, during the second bankruptcy of Philip II and all his properties were sold at public auction (Bertoméu Fernández: 2014, 107–109).

31 This information appeared in a copy of Elvira Nuñez proceedings (fol. 81) made on February 27, 1561, by notary Eusebio de Arrieta at the request of Inquisitors Gasco, Carpio, and Francisco de Soto. AHN, Inquisición, leg. 2943, doc. 12, in: Lopez Muñoz (2011, 236, doc. 110).

earnest and wicked persuasions of the priest), then he charges him further to confess the same before a notary, otherwise he tells him that his absolution avails nothing. (f. 30v)

But if he refuse, either mistrusting him altogether, or else half in doubt to credit him, yet is he no less endangered by disclosing it to the priest than if he had confessed it before a notary, for this kind of confession is not rightly auricular. (f. 30v)

As soon as they hear any of the prisoners sing or say anything aloud, by and by is there a limer, or two, of the devil, that is to say, one notary or another, with the keeper of the prison, to command them silence and to charge them in the Inquisitor's name to show no mirth upon pain of excommunication. (f. 40v)

The visitation of prisons is commonly once or twice every month kept by the Inquisitors, a notary and the keeper, and for the most part upon a Sunday or some other festival day. (f. 43r)

As official notary of the Holy Office, Domingo de Azpeitia would have been present at the arrest and cross-examination of nearly all the persons mentioned in *Artes:* Juan Ponce de Leon, Juan Gonzalez and his two sisters, Maria de Bohorquez, Maria de Virues, Maria de Cornejo, Isabel de Baena, Francisca de Chaves, Cristobal Losada, Garcia Arias, Dr. Egidio, Dr. Constantino de la Fuente, etc. Curiously, the author of *Artes* makes no mention at all of either Domingo de Guzman or Domingo de Baltanas, which made me suspect it might have been one of them. As notary, Domingo de Azpeitia would also have been present at the declarations made by Julian Hernandez. Among the particulars the inquisitors managed to wring out of Julian was the story of Juan de Leon, the monk who was caught as he was about to board a ship for England and sent back to Seville.[32] The details narrated in *Artes* regarding Juan de Leon's plight can only have come from one who either heard the story directly from Juan de Leon himself or indirectly through Julian's testimony. This occurred shortly before Azpeitia was promoted, hence it would still have been his duty to act as amanuensis.

In August of 1558, Azpeitia was promoted and appointed *receptor* (treasurer).[33] As official treasurer, he was in charge of the finances and the bookkeeping of the Holy Office, hence his unquestioned license to assign a stipend to the wet nurse. In February of 1560, he submitted a detailed report of the ordinary expenses of the Holy Office—salaries, etc.—and the extraordinary expenses, such as those incurred in by the inquisitors in their search for fugitive Julian

---

32 In a letter to the Supreme Council, dated October 25, 1558, the inquisitors at Seville wrote, "Here attached is what Julian Hernandez, imprisoned in the Castle of Triana, has declared concerning Fray Julian [Juan Sastre] when he was in Flanders." AHN, Inquisición, leg. 2942, doc. 51-1, in: Lopez Muñoz (2011, 135, doc. 51). In some documents his name appears as Juan and in others as Julian.

33 AHN, Inquisición, lib. 575, f. LXVIII°v.

Hernandez, what was spent in travelling to Cordoba to arrest Juan Ponce de Leon, and to Murcia to arrest Luis de Sosa and his wife, and to Gibraltar to arrest Juan Gomez de Ribera, etc.[34] Furthermore, the detailed description of the provisions made for the prisoners' maintenance could only have been penned by someone closely involved with the bookkeeping and the day-to-day comings and goings within the prison:

> The order of their diet is answerable to their lodging. The rich pay very large fees to the Holy House and every prisoner is rated at the discretion of the Inquisitor. Out of these fees there is deducted an allowance for his daily charges: 30 *dipondia*, commonly called *maravedis*, whereof 17 make a Dutch batte, 8 and a half a French sol, 10 a Flemish stuiver, which amounts in our reckoning, after the English rate, to 6 pence more or less. However, if any of them be disposed to exceed this amount and have other dainties, he may at his pleasure, so long as he pay for it from his own purse. Yet they deal not so favorably with every sort of prisoners, but only with such from whom they look not for any booty, being confined but for trifling matters. But if they are prisoners that they know, by the information given against them are likely to lose all that ever they have, they will not suffer them to exceed this amount, but let them feed only on a little brown bread and a curtsy of cold water, not suffering them in any case to have any special choice foods besides their ordinary diet, be they ever so rich, because they argue thus: that the more that is spent in that way the less will be their part when it comes to reckoning and riffling. Notwithstanding, if any be so poor that they are not able to live of their own in prison, the king allows them a certain allowance for their daily diet of half a *real* of silver, which is as much as a Dutch batz, and is worth two French sols, that is, three pence sterling.[35]

> Out of this meager allowance is to be defrayed their steward's and launderer's wages. And whatever other necessary charges grow besides must be also deducted. Moreover, of this allowance given them by the king, not half comes to their use for whom it was specially appointed, for it passes through two or three men's hands that will be ready to caress some of it. First through the office of receipt (for so I think they term the treasury), who is accountable for all the revenues that come into the exchequer, and pays for this and other similar uses. And this is the sweetest office in all the Holy House, and therefore only granted to special men, specially favored. Next to him, the steward, or caterer, will have another piece, who will commonly for one penny bestowed demand two. Then the cook that prepares their food and, last of all, the tithe, which is the jailer's fee, who many time gives it to the poor prisoners of his own benevolence. This I have described the more detailed because all these officers have their certain fees out of this small allowance of the king, which, passing through such limed fingers, is so fleeced that it comes not to the prisoner except that every one of these officers will take not only toll, but tithe, before it pass his hands, for in this House, both master and man, from

---

34 AHN, Inquisición, leg. 2942, doc. 82, in: Lopez Muñoz (2011, 182, doc. 88).
35 Vermaseren (1985, 63) sees the detailed rates of exchange quoted by the author as evidence that *Artes* was written out side of Spain, very likely in Antwerp.

head to foot, are all covetous and given to the spoil. (Montes: 1569, ff. 36v–37v. Note mine).

According to the midwife's testimony, it would appear that Azpeitia died some time in 1561. She used phrases such as "all the while he lived" and "after he died." Did he die or was he removed from office? Or, being the treasurer and no longer a notary, whose presence was required on short notice, was he asked to give up his apartments in Triana to make space for the many prisoners that were arriving? On the other hand, he may have stepped down for health reasons or due to his age. In the quiet of his own home, undisturbed and away from the vigilant eye of his colleagues, he could have begun to write his account of the dealings of the Inquisition in Seville. The author of *Artes* does insinuate a sort of retirement at one point. Referring to the works of Constantino Ponce de la Fuente, he states:

> All [Constantino's] works are extant to this day in hand written form, gathered very painfully by one of his listeners named Bab as it shall appear hereafter, *as I can have leisure to publish them*, how excellently well learned he was. (Montes: 1569, f. 94v. Italics mine).[36]

Living in the city of Seville, and not on the other side of the river in Triana, would also have given him the opportunity to see the monks going up and down "hanging down their heads all in a dump and a melancholy by means of their guilty consciences, quaking and trembling and looking every hour lest some of the *familiares* should take them by the sleeve."

One last explanation regarding Domingo de Azpeitia's absence from active involvement with the Holy Office in Seville after 1561 is that he may have left for the West Indies. He may not have gone immediately—authorization could require up to several years—, but we know that a son of his settled in Santiago de Chile. It is uncertain when the son arrived or whether he was born there. No records were kept at that time because there was no stable Spanish court in Chile until around 1583. According to the Chilean historian Thomas Thayer Ojeda (1939–1943, 658), Domingo Azpeitia's son Antonio held the post of chief bailiff in Santiago (Chile) and around 1585 married Elvira de Cervantes Pantoja, a daughter of Pedro Pantoja, mayor of Concepcion (Chile) from 1569–1575. Once a widower, shortly after 1600, Antonio Azpeitia was ordained a priest and later became secretary of the Holy Office (Genealogía Chilena, 2015).

---

36 In May of 1555 Azpeitia recorded the declarations made by eight witnesses against a certain Fray Pedro de Bertadillo for certain irreligious-sounding phrases pronounced in sermons he preached in Medina-Sedonia that year. Was this Bertadillo the "Bab", who so faithfully took down in short-hand Constantino's sermons? Or Jeronimo de Herrera, administrator of the Hospital de Bubas, among whose belongings were found hand-written copies of Constantino's sermons and who was still in Triana prison in the fall of 1562.

Getting the Manuscript Out

Whoever the incognito author of *Artes* was, he would have needed an accomplice to get the manuscript out of the country. There were only two ways to do that, by land or by sea. One intriguing character in this drama was Francisco de Tesa, a French glassmaker (Boeglin: 2006, 118–132). At the *auto-da-fe* of April 26, 1562, Tesa was sentenced to row in the king's galley ships for five years. While serving as a rower, he was overheard to say things in favor of Luther. Denounced to the Inquisition, he was rearrested, taken back to Triana, and put in chains awaiting execution. On the night of May 17, 1563, he broke his chains and escaped through the roof.[37] If Francisco de Tesa escaped with the manuscript under his arm, why did it take so long—from 1563 to 1567—for him to get the manuscript to Heidelberg? Were there other actors involved in the drama? Could Tesa have contacted Antonio del Corro, who was in southwestern France at that time?[38] Corro arrived in England in 1567 with at least one manuscript under his arm, namely, his open letter to Philip II, which he had written that spring while still in Antwerp. Corro must have gone immediately to a printer with his own manuscript considering that his work was printed in French, English, and Latin that very year. Two years later, Corro had another work printed—*Tableau de l'oeuure de Dieu*—by Anthony de Solempne in Norwich, the same year Solempne printed one of the Dutch renderings of *Artes*. Of course, this is pure speculation, but somehow the manuscript *did* leave the country and *did* reach a printer, whether in Heidelberg, or London, or Norwich.

Another actor in this tragedy—to use Vincent Skinner's metaphor—was the English merchant John Frampton. In Lisbon, Frampton had received bills of exchange on Seville, where he was taken prisoner and spent time in Triana. Frampton was back to England sometime in 1567, bankrupt and disheartened. According to his biographers, to solve his financial problems Frampton became a translator, but for some unexplainable reason it took ten years for his first translation—Nicolas Monardes's *Ioyfull newes out of the newe founde worlde* (1577)—to appear.[39] Today Frampton is remembered for his translations, but could he have had a part in smuggling the manuscript out of Spain? Frampton's

---

37 He was burned in effigy at Seville on May 13, 1565. AHN, *Inquisición*, leg. 2943, doc. 149–2, in Lopez Muñoz (2011, 344, doc. 164).
38 There seems to be no evidence Corro was ever in Tonneins. See McFadden (1953).
39 John Frampton's other translations include: Martín Fernández de Enciso, A Briefe Description of the Portes of the West India (1578); Marco Polo, Most noble and famous travels of Marcus Paulus (1579); Bernardino de Escalante, Discourse of the Navigation which the Portugales do Make (1579); Francisco Thamara, A Discovery of the countries of Tartaria, Scithia and Cataya, by the North East (1580); Pedro de Medina, The Arte of Navigation (1581).

contacts before and after his imprisonment were with the English consul in Seville, Hugh Tipton. During the months prior to Frampton's arrest, Tipton— referred to in the Inquisition documents as "Upfiton"—, had been the intermediary between John Ashe, the Bristol merchant whose merchandise had been seized and for which Frampton was responsible,[40] and the treasurer of the Inquisition, Domingo Azpeitia. The detailed account of Frampton's desperate attempt to recover the goods could only have come from someone equally involved in the case (Montes: 1569, ff. 59v–60v).

Moreover, in February 1562, when Frampton was still in Triana, the English ambassador in Madrid, Sir Thomas Chamberlain, advised him, "not to tarry in Spain or Portugal once at liberty, for if he is accused hereafter of anything, though false, he is but a dead man." (Calendar: 1866, IV, 515). Was Frampton's escape a diplomatic accord between Azpeitia, Tipton, Chamberlain, and Madrid? If Frampton enjoyed diplomatic immunity, he would have been allowed to take out as many Spanish books as he wished with the excuse that he was going to translate them. Could he have hid the handwritten sheets between the leaves of the books he carried out of the country? One indication that John Frampton could have been the incognito courier is insinuated in the text itself. At the very end of his story, as a sort of addendum, we discover his name: "His name was John Frampton, a citizen of Bristol" (*Nomen illi erat Johanni Phrontomo civi Bristolensi*). The author of *Artes* could only have known this if he had been present at the interrogatories or had had access to the trial records. The Inquisition documents referred to him as Fronton;[41] the 1568 French translator refers to him as Phrontom. In contrast, Vincent Skinner transcribed his name correctly, Frampton. How did Skinner know his real name?

The coincidence of Frampton's arrival in England in 1567 with the first printing (in Latin) of *Artes* is also intriguing. News regarding the activities of the Inquisition against Englishmen suspected of Protestant leanings reached secretary of state William Cecil via his ambassadors. There seems to be no direct link between John Frampton and William Cecil. Nevertheless, there is an interesting connection between Cecil's gardener, John Gerard, the author of *The Herbal* (1597), and Frampton. Was it Gerard who encouraged Frampton to translate Monardes's work? Historians have often wondered why Frampton chose this work for his first translation. Could the specimens in Cecil's garden— medicinal herbs, sassafras, tobacco, etc.—have come to Gerard's attention thanks to Frampton?

---

40 AHN, Inquisición, leg. 4683 (3), in: Lopez Muñoz (2011, 130–131, doc. 158).
41 AHN, Inquisición, leg. 2075, doc. 1 (2); AGS, Estado, leg. 137, doc. 3, in: Lopez Muñoz (2011, 226, doc. 101).

The Pseudonym

One final observation has to do with the author's pseudonym. The author of
Artes could hardly have devised a more appropriate alias: Reginaldo Gonzalez de
Montes. These three names epitomized the three main bones of contention for
any sixteenth century open-minded Spaniard. The author's choice of pseudonym went beyond a simple reference to individuals he admired. It epitomized the
socio-political realities these men represented: Reginaldo (after Casiodoro de
Reina) represents the right to translate and to possess the Bible in the vernacular;[42] Gonzalez (after the *morisco* preacher Juan Gonzalez) represents the
freedom of conscience; Montes (after the printer Martin Montesdoca) represents
the freedom of press. A more fitting pseudonym could hardly have been possible.

---

42 Though Casiodoro de Reina would not have completed his translation until 1569, nevertheless, the author of *Artes* could have known about the project. It was no secret. Already in
1563, the Spanish ambassador in London, Alvaro de la Quadra, in a dispatch to Philip II
mentioned that Casiodoro de Reina was in London translating the Bible into Spanish. AGS,
Estado, leg. 816, f. 166r, in: Lopez Muñoz (2011, 307, doc. 147).

Chapter 9:
The Evangelical Circle at Seville

> No bookseller or bookdealer or any other person of whatever profession he be is allowed to bring in or smuggle into the country or sell any book or work printed, or in manuscript form, of those prohibited by the Holy Office of the Inquisition, in any language, be the work or book of any sort, under penalty of death, and the loss of all his goods, and all such books should be burned publicly.
>
> Philip II, *Pragmatica* (1558)

In the 1550s, Seville was a bustling maritime crossroads. As money poured into the city, so did people. Seville had a flourishing colony of foreign bankers and merchants involved in transatlantic commerce, which turned the city into one of the most beautiful cities in Europe. Cipriano de Valera (Usoz: 1847–1865, VI, 241–242), an exiled monk and the translator-editor of Calvin's *Institutes* into Spanish, described the Seville of his day thus:

> The city of Seville is one of the most populous, rich, ancient, and fruitful, with the most extravagant buildings in all of Spain. All the treasures of the West Indies come to her. Her fruitfulness is seen in the fertile plains of Ajarafe, where there are olive trees upon olive trees, and from which is extracted such a copious abundance of oil, and in the fertile plains of Carmona and Jerez, so abundant with wheat, and the fields so full of grape vines, orange groves, fig trees, pomegranate trees, and infinite varieties of fruits. The Father of all mercy has not only enriched this city by making her so civil, populous, rich, ancient and with sumptuous architecture, but he has even enriched and blessed her with all spiritual blessings—heavenly blessings in Christ, choosing her from before the foundation of the world (the Apostle Paul says this of the city of Ephesus), so that she would be the first city in Spain that in our time might know the abuses, super-stitions, and idolatries of the Roman Catholic Church, by whom Spain has been for so long deceived.

The Religious Scenario

A distinctive note of the religious scenario of early mid-sixteenth century Seville was the return to biblical sources of Christianity. Luis Hernandez del Castillo wrote from Paris: "Happy are you, Seville, where the truth is preached publicly!" (Bataillon: 1966, 527). This movement was initially encouraged by the writings of Erasmus and later came to full maturity in the degree that the New Testament message of *grace alone* was discovered. In the words of Bataillon (1966, 706), it was a movement of returning to the gospel, which would also have important focal points in Valladolid, Salamanca, Zamora, Toro, Palencia, and Logroño, and which the inquisitors never faltered in qualifying as centers of Lutheran propaganda. The movement's most fervent advocates pertained to the aristocracy and the monastic orders.

The first dispatch from the Supreme Council to the inquisitors in Seville regarding the entrance of prohibited literature is dated September 15, 1540. It states:

> Reverend Lords: Because of the great harm prohibited books coming into these kingdoms has caused to our holy Catholic faith, the Holy Office has made great efforts to point out these dangers, but experience has shown us that is not enough. On the contrary, every day more books arrive and the merchants and book dealers have no fear of being censured or of imposing stricter punishments for transgressors. We hereby send you instructions written up by the Reverend Cardinal Archbishop of Toledo, Inquisitor General Juan Pardo de Tavera, signed by the secretary of this Council. Put them into effect with the diligence and care that the situation requires, as a very important matter concerning you. Keep us always informed of what is done because we know that in Germany and other parts, great diligence is being made to bring into Spain prohibited books in order to spread their errors here, therefore, we must be all the more careful to resist it. We include a list of prohibited and suspicious books that we have learned of here [in Madrid]. Besides these, you may have found others. Send us the list of suspicious books so we can forward it to the other courts so they can be warned which books to seize.[1]

A few years later, the Supreme Council sent specific instruction to Charles's court regarding the activities of one Gaspar Zapata, "who lives in His Majesty's court." Zapata presumably had delivered a trunk of Lutheran books to a knight from Seville, when he left Brussels. These books were seized by the inquisitors at Seville and Zapata was to declare who the books were for, if he sent them in his own name or in the name of another, who wrote to him asking him to send them and who bought them, and anything else related to this business, etc.[2] It is almost impossible to know who was reading these prohibited books in those days, though Reginaldo Gonzalez de Montes (1569, ff. 79v–80v. Notes and brackets mine) gives us some clues:

> In the days of Garcia Arias[3] that there were two sorts of preachers in Seville, and either of them had a great number of auditors disposed to hear each part, as they best fancied the one or the other. The one sort, concerning doctrine and precepts, came nearer to the discipline of Epictetus the Stoic[4] than to the rule of Holy Scripture. But they were

---

1 AHN, Inquisición, lib. 574, f. 21v, in: Lopez Muñoz (2011, 243, doc. 114).
2 AHN, Inquisición, lib. 574, f. 216r, in: Lopez Muñoz (2011, 52, doc. 12).
3 Garcia Arias, better known as Maestro Blanco, prior of the San Isidoro Monastery in Santi-ponce, was arrested October 12, 1558. After four years in prison, he was finally sent to the stake on October 28, 1562. The excuse was that his case was complex and required time. AHN, Inquisición, leg. 2943, doc. 11, in: Lopez Muñoz (2011, 233, doc. 107).
4 According to Epictetus (55 AD–135), we should accept whatever happens calmly and dispassionately. Suffering occurs from trying to control what is uncontrollable. We have no

inferior to Epictetus in that all his sayings and doings were one, but these preachers never ceased calling and crying upon the people to move them to fast often, to mortification, to denying of themselves, to continue in prayer at all times, to think lowly of themselves (which they called humility), and to show the same as well in apparel, countenance, behavior, and speech, as in all the rest of their life. In sum, all their religion, both top and tail (as they say), rested in works and outward exercises of the body, quiet contrary to the other sect, and therefore they would seem to be 'doers' in any case. They left the true exercise of a Christian man, I mean, justice, mercy and faith, the only means to attain true righteousness, and ran in throngs to masses, to hallowed places, to shrift (as they call it) and many other such like trifles, which the Scripture calls spider's webs that will never prove good cloth, hoping, that by these and such like means to be purged and cleansed from their sins. Moreover, they urged poverty with sole and single life, even unto such as were already coupled in matrimony, but especially the vow of obedience, as do the foolish friars, to the end to get them auditors. And this (say they) is the true denying of ourselves, and therefore extolled it as much as the obedience that is due to God himself. Furthermore, in order to keep the people in blindness and ignorance, they dissuaded men from the reading of books written on divinity, especially from Erasmus's works, by which (they said) they would learn nothing but a little pride in their own knowledge. Instead, they referred them to [mystics such as] Henricus Herpio[5] and Bonaventure's works[6] and the A.B.C.[7] and the Scaling of Mount Zion,[8] and such others wherein they should learn humility and obedience towards all, but especially towards their elders and superiors. Among others they also cited to them Manso,[9] Ceballos,[10] Guerra,[11] Pedro de Cordoba,[12] and many more than I can call to mind.

The other sort of preachers dealt more sincerely with the Holy Scriptures, declaring out of them true justice and perfect godliness, and by their means the city, for the space of a dozen full years, with much fruit, fruitfully and effectually heard the gospel of Christ preached concerning true and perfect justification and hereupon came all that plentiful harvest that has been gleaning these eight or ten years, of those good seeds of the gospel, which then were by them so painfully sown. The brightness whereof, as cor-

---

power over external things, and the good that ought to be the object of our earnest pursuit is only found within ourselves.

5 Henricus Herpius, *Espejo de perfeccion, o Teología Mística* (Alcala: Brocar, 1551).

6 Bonaventure, *Estímulo de amor divino* (Toledo: Hagenbach, 1505)

7 Francisco de Osuna, *Tercera parte del libro llamado Abecedario espiritual* (Toledo: Petras, 1527).

8 Bernardino de Laredo, *Subida al Monte Sión* (Seville: Cromberger, 1535).

9 Bartholomeo de Manso, *Confessionale ad utilitatem et directionem ministrorum, rectorum, vicariorumque curatum et ecclesiarum civitatis diocesis Albiensis* (Lyons, 1499).

10 Jeronimo de Zeballos, *Arte real para el buen govierno de los Reyes, y principes, y de sus vasallos* (Toledo, 1523).

11 Unidentified. According to Luis Usoz y Rio, these were such secondary authors that they do not even appear in Nicolas Antonio's bibliographical dictionary, *Biblioteca Hispana nova* (Rome, 1672).

12 Pedro de Cordoba, *Doctrina cristiana para instruccion é informacion de los Indios* (Mexico, 1544).

responds to the nature of light, did so plainly discover all that counterfeit holiness and pharisaical devotion that it could not be otherwise but that there must ensue thereafter, first hatred and then persecution. The chief laborers in this harvest were Constantino, Egidio, and Vargas, doctors all, and men both sober, wise and learned, whose travails in setting forward the gospel in so great mists of ignorance, and the worthy ends which they made at their departures out of this life, since they are worthy of eternal memory so will we defend them that they may not be forgotten.

Montes's account covers the years of maximum persecution against Lutherans in Seville, but according to what he states above, evangelical teaching began earlier. If Constantino entered crown prince Philip's court as chaplain in 1548 and did not return to Seville until 1553, this would take us back to the mid 1540s, which coincides historically with the activities of Rodrigo de Valer, one of the first evangelicals put on trial by the Inquisition in Seville.

Rodrigo de Valer (1505?–1549)

In the late 1530s, Rodrigo de Valer, a young nobleman, citizen of Lebrija, south of Seville on the Guadalquivir River, experienced a religious conversion. Together with a Latin Bible—perhaps one printed in Lyon in 1535, 1536, or 1537 by Jacob Giunti—and a copy of Montesino's *Epistolas y euangelios,* which he could have had easy access to since it was reprinted in Seville in 1526, 1536, 1537, 1540, 1543, and 1549, Valer managed to memorize large portions of Scripture both in Spanish and Latin. Montes (1569, ff. 87r–88r. Notes mine) describes him as follows:

He bent himself wholly, both body and soul, to the exercise of virtue and godliness, to the extreme that a man would scarcely judge him to be a man of this world. Moreover, the wonderful change that appeared to be in him, as well in his speech and behavior as in his apparel, which was fine and suitable before, as gorgeous as might be, became now quite altered into simple stuff and the plainest fashion. This was well liked by some, but on the other side a great number thought it mere madness or stark folly. In his youth time, he had gotten a little smack in the Latin by the help whereof he was conversant in the Holy Scriptures both day and night, so that by continual study thereof, he knew a great part of them by heart and could make application thereof to his purpose sensibly and marvelously readily. He had also daily conflicts with the spiritual men, as they call them, the priests and monks, who were the causes, said he, that not only the state of the clergy, but also all Christendom was so foully corrupted that they were almost hopeless of remedy, for which causes he also divers and sundry times sharply rebuked them. Whereat, this pharisaical generation, greatly astonished at what he said, inquired of him how he attained so suddenly to all this skill in Holy Scriptures, how he durst presume so arrogantly to inveigh against the very supporters and lights of the church. For indeed he spared none, but would tell the proudest of them his mind, being but a layman void of all good university learning and one that had spent the greater part of his time in vain and unprofitable studies.

Likewise, they examined him of what commission he did it, who sent him, how he was called, and by what tokens he declared the same. Rodrigo de Valer answered them truly and with a bold courage that he had not fished for that wisdom and caught it in their most filthy puddles and muddy ditches, but had it by the only goodness of the Holy Ghost, who pours whole floods of grace into the hearts of true believers most abundantly. Finally, he was called to his defense before the Inquisitors, where he disputed very earnestly of the true church of Christ and what were the marks to know it by, how man was justified in the sight of God, and of such other points of religion, the knowledge whereof he confessed that he had attained unto by no means or help of man but the only handiwork of God and his wonderful revelation. Although his madness and frenzy, wherewith the Inquisitors supposed him to be troubled, excused him for that time, so that he might the sooner come to himself again, they condemned him in the loss of all his substance and sent him packing as poor as Job. But he never repented thereof, or became another man, insomuch that within a year or two later, he was sent for again about the same matters and then driven to make recantation.[13] In consideration that they took him to be a lunatic still, they spared him his life, sentencing him nevertheless to wear the *sanbenito* and to suffer perpetual imprisonment during life. At that time, it so chanced that the inquisitors were not half so bad as others that had been before them,[14] so that his process was wound up quietly and executed by madness and folly. And forasmuch as those matters whereof he was most unjustly condemned were strange and not heard of in Seville in those days, he had a *sanbenito* appointed to wear, which to this day is to be seen for a special monument of a notable heretic in the vestry of the chief church in Seville, in a place where every man may easily see it, with this inscription written in capital letters: Rodrigo de Valer, citizen of Lebrija, an apostate, and a false apostle of Seville, that said he was sent from God.

Valer's life was spared when he was declared insane. Nevertheless, the Holy Office saw fit to confiscate his property, "a peculiar way to cure a madman, taking his properties away from him," as Cipriano de Valera (1851, 246) puts it. After his second arrest, on March 3, 1540, Valer was condemned to house arrest in one of the auxiliary prisons belonging to the Inquisition and obliged to hear mass every week at the Church of San Salvador. Four months earlier they had sent a dispatch to the Council apologizing for the delay, which they blamed on the fact that external theologians had to be called in to judge Valer's case and that

---

13 Valer was arrested twice: once some time in 1538 and again on March 3, 1540. On October 8, 1541, the Council sent another letter asking the Inquisitor to examine Valer to see whether he was sane or not. AHN, Inquisición, lib. 574, f. 85r.

14 Here Montes very likely refers to Alonso Manrique, inquisitor general from September 1523 to September 1538, who championed the Erasmian ideal of tolerance and peace. He was more tolerant than his predecessor, Adrian of Utrecht, remembered for his merciless treatment of the rebels in the Comunero Revolt, or Diego Rodriguez de Lucero, remembered for his oppressive and abusive treatment of conversos.

had taken time.[15] But because he continued to publicly contradict the preachers during mass, he was finally sent to a convent in San Lucar de Barrameda, where he died around 1549. Valer's name was closely linked with that of Cipriano de Valera, Francisco de Vargas, and Dr. Egidio. Evidence of this close relationship is found in a dispatch from the Supreme Council, dated December 7, 1541:

> During the process against Rodrigo Valer, we became aware of the fact that doctor Egidio and doctor Vargas and others approved of and validated the things Valer said and the shameful and slanderous things he said against the Holy Office, which encouraged him to say what he said against the Holy Office. Hence, it is right that legal actions be taken against the persons that encouraged this behaviour and that they be punished in accordance to their status. Have the public prosecutor register everything that is done and proceed legally and in accord with instructions from the Holy Office.[16]

Dr. Egidio (1495?–1555)

Dr. Juan Gil, better known by his Latinized name of Egidio, was educated at the University of Alcala, where he studied Sacred Scriptures. When the professor of theology died, he was chosen to replace him. Between 1525 and 1530, Erasmian thought began to penetrate deeply in that institution but when the inquisitors became suspicious of the main promoters, they dispersed: Juan de Valdes had already left for Italy, Constantino returned to Cuenca, Cazalla to Valladolid, and Egidio left for Siguenza. In 1533, Pedro Alexander, who had been rector during the academic year 1531–32 and responsible for furthering biblical studies, was offered the post of canon of the Cathedral of Seville. Unable to occupy the post in Seville because he was sent to the Netherlands as chaplain of Charles V's sister Mary of Austria, governess of the Netherlands, he invited Egidio to take his place.[17] Gonzalez de Montes (1569, ff. 86r–89r) gives us the following account of Egidio's spiritual transformation:

> After being public reader of divinity at Sigüenza, he was sent for to Seville by one Alexander that was his predecessor there, to the end he might be their preacher in the cathedral church in Seville, where he was so highly commended, both for his virtue and learning, that he was made subdean of the church, contrary to their orders, having never been examined by the doctors as the custom is. As for scholastic theology, as was generally and universally received all Christendom over, he was very famous and of great credit, yet he never had attempted to preach openly nor once opened the Bible to read or study the Scriptures. And, therefore, the very first time that he came into the

---

15 AHN, Inquisición, lib. 574, f. 71r, in: Lopez Muñoz (2011, 44, doc. 4).
16 AHN, Inquisición, lib. 574, ff. 96v–97r, in: Lopez Muñoz (2011, 47, doc. 7).
17 According to Francisco de Enzinas (1992, 387), while in the Netherlands, Alexander embraced the Protestant faith, was imprisoned but escaped.

pulpit, contrary to all men's expectations, he was found altogether so unfit for such a function that he began to be extremely discontent with himself and to grow in contempt of others, and by the daily increase thereof, on both parts, they fell so to repent—the one for admitting him so unadvisedly, the other for taking upon himself that office so arrogantly—being unable to discharge it, that they determined to remove him and he himself determined to forsake them. But in the process of time, after he had thus been there for a year or two, it was his chance to meet with one that gave him such instructions (or rather it was the ordinance of God, and provided so well, both for him and for the whole city) that within a few hour's conversation, he learned by that party's means the right way for a preacher to proceed, and what the office and duty of a preacher was, and that to the obtaining whereof, it was told him that he must use other means, other books, and other masters than hitherto he had done. This astonished Dr. Egidio somewhat at the first, hearing this man make such a sermon unto him, but especially marveled to see his boldness, that being but a plain fellow and, as a man would say—a very bumpkin besides that—, one taken not to be very well in his wits, would presume so boldly to teach such a doctor as he was, being neither familiarly acquainted with him nor knowing him to his thinking. Yet, Dr. Egidio, being of a gentle disposition by nature, and hearing him discourse so thoroughly of the duty of a preacher, wherein he acknowledged his own infirmity, did the more easily bridle himself and gave him the hearing quietly. The force of whose persuasions (being a man endued with God's spirit) was so great that, from that day forward, Dr. Egidio was quite altered and became a new man, thinking all his former life and labor evil spent and, therefore, began to tread another path, one that would lead him unto perfect wisdom and learning whereof as then he knew not one step. Furthermore, perceiving his counselor to stand so long upon that point concerned the duty of a good preacher, he took it to be a sufficient calling for him to that vocation, whereof he knew he should neither reap commodity nor estimation in this world. Perhaps many will marvel to hear the party named that was the occasion of so sudden a change and alteration of such a man in so short space, taking upon him to teach him the true way to perfect wisdom.

At length, he began to preach as learnedly, godly and zealously as he had before time done coldly, foolishly and unskillfully. Even the hearers began to feel the marvelous force of that doctrine which these three men of great credit and estimation—Egidio, Constantino, and *el gran* Vargas—taught with one consent, insomuch that the more they grew in knowledge, from their old ignorance and blindness, the more were these men had in reputation among them, and the old hypocrites despised the fact that they had taught them another doctrine to the great peril of their souls. Whereupon, there were daily complaints brought to the Inquisitors' ears of these men, but especially of Dr. Egidio, who of mere simplicity, and by reason that he was in some more authority than the rest, more openly attacked the adversaries of the truth. And they began chiefly to envy him when the emperor, in respect of his exceptional learning and integrity of life, elected him to the bishopric of Tortosa. For then, those hypocrites began to bestir them without reservations and to lay all their heads together to remove him, thinking that if he were once consecrated bishop there, he would cause great confusion in their kingdom. Therefore, they cited him to come before the Holy House where complaint was entered against him by such as were their crafts masters, able to work him mischief.

And to bring it about secretly, they managed to cast him into prison and there be examined.

In July of 1549, Dr. Egidio was proposed by Charles V to the bishopric of Tortosa, but his appointment was cut short by allegations that surfaced regarding his preaching in which some clerics saw elements of Lutheran doctrine. Already in April of 1542, the inquisitors at Seville had sent the Supreme Council information regarding Dr. Egidio.[18] Exactly what the information was is uncertain, we only have the Council's bare acknowledgement of having received the information and that they would look into the matter after Holy Week. It appears that the Council filed it and forgot it. The inquisitors at Seville, nevertheless, kept insisting. A dispatch from the Supreme Council to Charles V, dated July 29, 1550, asked the emperor for advice, mainly because many of Egidio's followers were leaving the county for fear they would be arrested.[19] Meanwhile, Prince Maximilian, who was regent in the absence of Charles, wrote the Spanish ambassador in Rome urging him to stop legal proceedings involved in the papal edicts necessary for Egidio's appointment (Gonzalez Novalín: 1971, I, 178). Two years later the emperor had still not given an answer and Inquisitor General Fernando de Valdes wrote him again concerning the case. The emperor seemed to be playing for time. Meanwhile, Dr. Egidio had already spent nearly two years in the Inquisition prison in Triana. In July, the archbishop of Toledo, on behalf of the Supreme Council, sent instructions to Seville urging the inquisitors to conclude the case as quickly as possible, "considering the long time the doctor has been imprisoned."[20] Finally, in 1552, the emperor suggested the Dominican Domingo de Soto as arbitrator in the case against Dr. Egidio.

Egidio had initially requested that Bartolome de Carranza be his lawyer, but Carranza was abroad attending the sessions at Trent. Domingo de Soto was a scholar of great renown in several fields. He had studied at the University of Alcala and the University of Paris. In 1520, he was appointed professor of philosophy at Alcala and from 1532 on he held the chair of theology at Salamanca. He intervened at the Council of Trent (1545–1547) and was Charles V's chaplain from 1547 to 1550. Despite being a Thomist and sharing Tridentine views on matters of faith, Domingo de Soto is remembered, along with Francisco de Vitoria and other professors of natural law, for his economic theories that reconciled scholasticism and the new political-economic order brought in by Humanism, the Protestant Reformation, and new geographical discoveries.[21] De

---

18 AHN, Inquisición, lib. 574, f. 104v, in: Lopez Muñoz (2011, 48, doc. 9).
19 AHN, Inquisición, lib. 574, f. 216r, in: Lopez Muñoz (2011, 52, doc. 12).
20 AHN, Inquisición, lib. 574, f. 282r, in: Lopez Muñoz (2011, 86, doc. 17).
21 Charles V was unable to keep the royal treasury from going bankrupt, which, as could be expected, had very negative effects on the Spanish economy and on the bankers who had

Soto was known for being moderate in his judgments; nevertheless, Montes (1569, f. 90r) had a very different opinion of him:

> Fray Domingo de Soto, a sophist of great fame in the University of Salamanca and a friar of the order of Saint Dominic, who after great expectation of his coming, at last came from Salamanca to Seville, and there entered disputation, more craftily and subtlety than others had dealt before him, with Dr. Egidio, who was but a plain dealing man and of small foresight. First, pretending much good will towards him, and perceiving that by dealing with him openly he could in no case remove him from his opinion, he fained himself to be of the same opinion with him. He advised him that forasmuch as those articles that presently were called into question were somewhat odious in most men's ears, to the end to moderate them, he would make and publish some apt declaration and exposition thereof, the which he offered to write up for him in the best sort that he could that he might use if it liked him, or else they two could confer about it and set it forth to the better discharge of their consciences, furtherance of the truth, and contentment of the hearers. Whereupon, de Soto wrote up the declaration, they conferred about it and in the end agreed without any controversy.

According to Montes's account (1569, f. 90v), the agreement was not carried out faithfully by de Soto, who proceeded as follows:

> There was a solemn day of hearing appointed by the Inquisitors for that purpose, and two pulpits set in the Cathedral church, the one for Dr. Egidio, the other for de Soto, and all the people were assembled thither. De Soto began his sermon and proceeded accordingly. Immediately after the end thereof, he drew forth of his bosom a declaration quite contrary to that whereupon they were agreed. For in the original document there was nothing but that which conformed to the truth and his own conscience; in this one no such matter but only a plain recantation of all those things whereof he was accused and had been a maintainer of before, for two whole years, and lately also during the time of his imprisonment. But the pulpits were such a distance asunder that by means thereof partly, and partly with the murmur of the common people while every man gave his verdict thereof, there was such a noise that Dr. Egidio could not well understand what de Soto said, but yet, for the good opinion which he had of him, gave him such credit that at the end of every article, when de Soto craftily asked his consent thereto, telling him to speak aloud that the people might hear him or else to signify so much by some countenance or gesture, he did so, confessing that he agreed to all those things which de Soto had read unto him.

Contrary to this view, Professor Nieto (1997, 200), who has carefully analyzed each of the twenty-five propositions, is of the opinion that de Soto actually wanted to favor Egidio:

> From our perspective we want to believe Egidio—we sympathize with his suffering. But conscience prevails and I believe that the balance tips in favor of Soto. Following this

---

financed his projects. All of these events motivated the most brilliant minds of the time, the scholars of the School of Salamanca, to reflect on the financial and banking activities they witnessed. See "Banking during the Reign of Charles V." Accessed November 6, 2014.

interpretation, the events proceeded in this way: Soto read the very declaration that the two had agreed upon by means of a *compromise* that had as its main objective a lighter sentence. Soto accomplished his goal. I believe that all this helps us to fill in and clarify some of the vague details in Reinaldo's account; at the same time Soto's character and intervention emerge with greater clarity, and with greater humanity and integrity than what Reinaldo describes from the standpoint of Gil's account and his own reflection as a refugee and escapee of the Inquisition of Seville.

Inasmuch as the accusations were very serious and being burned at the stake hung by a thread, de Soto had to resort to subtle theological argumentation in order to mitigate the seriousness of the charges, and in this he was a consummate master. Dr. Egidio was sentenced to only three years imprisonment—two of which he had already fulfilled—and ten years removal from his clerical duties. He was absolved of heresy and got away with the minimum penalty. The sentence could not have been lighter. He did not have to spend the entire third year in prison but was transferred to the Monastery of la Cartuja in Jerez de la Frontera.[22] In September of 1553, the cathedral chapter in Seville even decided to resume the payment of his salary. Although he was prohibited to preach or impart religious teaching, nevertheless, he was free to exercise other administrative duties in the cathedral. In this capacity, he served in matters related to abandoned children.

In the summer of 1555, Dr. Egidio made a trip to Valladolid to negotiate a special donation requested by the cathedral of Seville. While he was in the Valladolid area, he met with Carlo de Sesso, Bachiller Herrezuelo, and Pedro de Cazalla several times and at various places. They met at Pedrosa del Rey, at Toro, and at the Rinconada Inn in Valladolid, where Egidio was staying. According to Pedro de Cazalla, they discussed matters such as justification by faith, on which they all agreed.[23] Egidio explained to them why he had been imprisoned, and, among other things, told them that he, Constantino, and Vargas read prohibited literature and when they spoke about Luther or the other reformers in front of other people, they would refer to them by nicknames: Luther was "*el doctor,*" Philip Melanchthon was "*el negro,*" etc.[24]

The long journey to Valladolid was too much for Dr. Egidio and he died shortly after his return. This, however, was not the end of his story. In 1558, Inquisitor General Valdes informed Pope Paul IV that the persons most to blame for the spread of heresy in Seville were the followers of Dr. Egidio, "who in 1552 abjured of his errors, but we now suspect that his recantation was false and insincere and that he tricked the inquisitors, who became seriously infected with

---

22 AHN, Inquisición, lib. 574, f. 296r; lib. 574, f. 305r, in: Lopez Muñoz (2011, 98, doc. 22; 99, doc. 23).

23 AHN, Inquisición, leg. 5353, n. 1, in: Schäfer (2014, III, 532).

24 AHN, Inquisición, leg. 5353, n. 1, in: Schäfer (2014, III, 546).

his poison."[25] Montes (1569, ff. 89r–91v) corroborates Inquisitor General Valdes's statement regarding the attitude of the inquisitors and recounts how the "new inquisitors" changed their minds:

> But at that time, the Inquisitors were not grown so bold as since then they have been, nor indeed dare not burn such a man as he was for these causes, though they were urged and called upon on every side very earnestly so to do. Therefore, seeing that they could in no way make him change or alter his mind, they began to devise how they might save his life because the Emperor, who recently had elected him to so great a bishopric [that of Tortosa], as also the whole chapter of the Cathedral Church in Seville were become very earnest suitors in his behalf. There was also one of the Inquisitors named El licenciado Antonio del Corro, a good and a fatherly old man, who, for that assurance which he had by his own knowledge of the good conversation of Dr. Egidio, and despite the contrary position of his accusers, remained loyal to his very good friend. [...] But within two or three years after his death, the new Inquisitors, thinking that the others, who had examined him, had dealt a great deal more easily with him than became Inquisitors, seeing that they could not summon his spirit to appear before them, which was in quietness and rest, therefore they determined to show their spite towards his carcass and dry bones. Whereupon, they digged him out of his grave, and buried in his place, and under his name, a puppet of straw, brought his corpse upon the scaffold and used it in such sort as they would have done himself that sits in heaven with Christ on the right hand of his Father, if they could have caught him here in earth. But God, that dwells on high, laughs at these their follies.

Several years after Dr. Egidio had passed away, five nuns from the Monastery of Santa Paula in Seville were questioned regarding Dr. Egidio's preaching. They had been enthusiastic devotees of his in the 1540s, but twenty years later, with the persecution that was being launched against anyone with ideas dissenting from official Catholic dogma, they decided to clear their consciences by revealing what they had harbored in their hearts for the past twenty years. Whether by common accord, or individually, they sent letters to their confessors— Fray Diego de Vadillo and Fray Pablo de Santa Ana, both monks of the Monastery of San Geronimo—who, in turn, took these letters to the inquisitors. Their testimony alerted the inquisitors regarding heresies being introduced into the convents through their preachers and spiritual directors. A year later, on September 2, 1560, Inquisitor Gonzalez de Munebrega, bishop of Tarazona, sent the letters to Inquisitor General Valdes, with an apology that he had not seen them until then otherwise he would have sent them earlier. Inquisitors Andres Gasco and Miguel del Carpio were put in charge of investigating the matter. A translation of the original documents follows:

---

25 AHN, Inquisición, lib. 245, f. 230r, in: Lopez Muñoz (2011, 129, doc. 49).

Letter 1

On September 11, 1559, Fray Diego de Vadillo appeared before Inquisitor Carpio and showed him a letter that Leonor de San Cristobal, a nun of the Convent of Santa Paula in Seville had given him, and which, among other things, said the following:

I, Leonor de San Cristobal, declare that some twenty or more years ago, in a sermon preached by Dr. Egidio, I heard him speak against images, calling them idols and that if we venerated them we unawares committed idolatry for we were only to look to heaven. Likewise, that saints could not help us in any way and that our good works, as well as our prayers and our singing, were worth nothing. And that religious orders and ceremonies were all inventions of men and had no value. The reason for this was that Jesus Christ our Lord had paid the price for all of us. He seemed always to have a special concern for our feelings because he insisted that we do all things according to what our will dictated because that was what pleased Jesus Christ, and that was what we had to aim for, for example, if in prayer our will told us to remain seated, we should remains seated. He belittled the ceremonies of putting on the habit as madness, things invented by men, and he gave this example: if St Jerome and St Domingo, and the rest, came back to earth today, they would say "that is not the order I established." By this, we understood that he said it because we were not as observant as we should be and so we applied ourselves even more, thinking he was warning us not to pay so much attention to external matters. I confess my fault if in this I offended our Lord, and at times, while I was listening to these new teachings I wished that our founding mothers were alive, who worked so hard to uphold the order, so they could understand how all that was of little use, as well as other futile acts and devotions, like walking the stations and lighting candles to the saints. All this he considered superfluous. And that is what I also believed until they arrested him the first time. From that time on, I blocked his words out of my mind and detested them, and I now hold them as loathsome and heretical. After that, I listened to Juan Gonzalez, but his preaching was so obscure that I couldn't understand it, only that he condemned good works, belittled ceremonies and false holiness, and that only the works of Christ were of any value. By making this so plain, we were unaware of the harm it did us, and because this is what happened I reveal it to you.

On August 3, 1560, Inquisitor Gasco went to the Monastery of Santa Paula and summoned Leonor de San Cristobal to appear before him. She took the oath and swore to tell the truth and among other things said what follows. She was shown the letter and recognized it to be hers and said that everything in it was true.

When asked what it was that she heard said to the nuns, and other persons that heard Dr. Egidio, and the comment they made regarding the things he said in his sermons, she said that when he was preaching, since he preached in public and was considered such an excellent scholar that everyone flocked after him, everything he said seemed to her like such pleasant instruction and such a gratifying life that she thought that to devote oneself to obligations and to disciplines was excessive. And on certain occasions, speaking with her fellow nuns, she would say, "If only the nuns that proceeded us were alive, who worked so hard to keep the rules and ceremonies of the order and so little good it did them for their salvation; if only they could hear these sermons and enjoy this doctrine with rejoicing and not weary themself so much with things such as singing in the choir or saying prayers or other rules of the order, for they were of no avail for their salvation."

Likewise, she said that she grew cold and noticed that the other nuns also became somewhat apathetic because in the cloister there were three images of Our Lady of different names and on Saturdays they used to walk the stations with each one of them, saying the Hail Mary at each station. But after hearing what Dr. Egidio had to say about this, she became somewhat indifferent to all that and thought it was enough to say the Hail Mary just once and not to walk all the stations. And she thought that although the nuns did not give up completely walking the stations, they didn't do it with the same enthusiasm as before. And they also only half-heartedly put candles to Saint Cosme and Saint Damian and Saint Mark and the others.

I hereby certify that this corresponds with the original document.

Signed: Eusebio de Arrieta, notary of the secret.

Letter 2

On September 11, 1559, Fray Pablo de Santa Ana appeared before Inquisitor Carpio and showed him a letter that Juana de los Reyes, a nun of the Convent of Santa Paula in Seville had given him, and which said the following:

What I have to say about Dr. Egidio's sermons is this: He said so many things that I can't remember them except for one sermon where he talked about external endeavors and said that it was useless to tire the body sweeping and doing self-abasing deeds. I did not want to hear that because in this convent we are very fond of external devotion and I heard his followers defend him on this and in this they were excusing his offense, and I could see that he thought little of the ceremonies and the stations of the order. Juana de los Reyes.

I hereby certify that this corresponds with the original document.

Signed: Eusebio de Arrieta, notary of the secret.

Letter 3

On September 11, 1559, Fray Pablo de Santa Ana appeared before Inquisitor Carpio and showed him a letter that Catalina de San Geronimo, a nun of the Convent of Santa Paula in Seville, had given him, and which said the following:

The words I heard Dr. Egidio pronounce were these: that his sermons gave great uneasiness and after he had dealings with some of the nuns of this convent I saw that devotion became very lax and that the ceremonies of the order were not regarded as highly as before and I heard the nuns utter things in favor of these changes.

Signed: Catalina de San Geronimo.

On August 3, 1560, Inquisitor Gasco, exercising his office at the Monastery of Santa Paula, summoned Catalina de San Geronimo to appear before him. When she appeared, she took the oath and swore to tell the truth.

When she was shown the letter, she recognized it to be her handwriting and to have sent it to the Holy Office. And among other things, when asked in what sense she had noticed that the devotion in the convent had become lax, declared that on Holy Fridays in the morning they would walk the seven stations located in the cloister, in remembrance of the nine places our Lord was carried to, and on Easter, Resurrection Sunday, they would walk other stations in the same cloister, but after Dr. Egidio had been preaching in this convent hardly anyone walked these stations anymore. Likewise, as far as other matters concerning devotion and discipline, she was convinced that after Dr. Egidio had had dealings with the convent, enthusiasm for them had grown cold.

I hereby certify that this corresponds with the original document.

Signed: Eusebio de Arrieta, notary of the secret.

Letter 4

On October 5, 1559, Fray Pablo de Santa Ana appeared before Inquisitor Carpio and showed him a letter that Ana de los Angeles, a nun of the Monastery of Santa Paula, had given him and which said the following:

I, Ana de los Angeles, nun in this Monastery of Santa Paula of Seville, declare that some seventeen years ago, more or less, I once heard Dr. Egidio preach in one of the parlors of this convent, and he was speaking about the people who walk the stations in the churches and said they would come and go to the cross, and that was to adore a stick, and for that they could adore the Lord at home. And that those who went to venerate Our Lady of Rocamador,[26] only venerated a stick dressed up, which scandalized me terribly. I thought it was terrible what he said and I never went to hear him again. I have kept this quiet until now because I am the youngest in this convent and the other nuns considered me out of my mind because I saw that after that sermon some of them were saying, "We have not been true Christians until now." But now that I see how much damage has been done, I denounce this before your lordship.

Signed: Ana de Los Angeles.

Inquisitor Gasco went to the Monastery of Santa Paula and summoned Ana de Los Angeles before him. She took the oath and swore to tell the truth. When she was shown the letter, she recognized it to be hers and that she had sent it and that what it contained was the truth.

When she was asked which nuns had the most dealings with Dr. Egidio, she said the one who was prioress at that time, and the whole convent, and all outsiders, and that the place was filled with people. When asked who were some of the outsiders that came to hear him, she said there were many of his followers, and that she had heard that both

---

26 Our Lady of Rocamador in the church of San Lorenzo in Seville.

[Maria de] Bohorquez[27] and [Maria de] Virues, who they burned at the stake, were there and many other men and women who were his followers.

This corresponds with the original document.

Signed: Eusebio de Arrieta, notary.

Letter 5

On September 11, 1559, Fray Diego de Vadillo appeared in the Castle of Triana before Inquisitor Carpio and showed him two letters that a nun of the Convent of Santa Paula in Seville called Eusebia de San Juan had given him, and which said the following:

Your Reverend Lordship, speaking one day with Francisca de los Reyes about the things Egidio was saying, I said I considered him a true servant of God and that he was convinced of the things he said. And I believed he had died in a state of grace, and she told me that when she found herself in a difficult situation she would commend herself to him and to a nun that was dead, as saints. And when Constantino was arrested, she told me that she had once asked Egidio why he often went to Constantino's house but that Constantino did not go to his, and he said he did that so that everyone would see that they both held the same doctrine.

Signed: Eusebia de San Juan.

Your Reverend Lordship: With reference to your telling me to examine my conscience regarding the things I heard from Dr. Egidio, I must say that since I considered his doctrine so sound and so Catholic, as becomes a servant of God, I never suspected anything but now that it has all been shown to be false, I see how gullible I was. I don't remember anything special, but I do remember one thing: preaching in the parlor of the convent, that we should pray the way our mind led us, either sitting or laying down. That never seemed right to me but I didn't think much of it. I realize that he had removed much of the enthusiasm we had had for external devotions, such as venerating the saints, walking the stations, and other ceremonies of our order, saying that they were inventions of men, which satisfied the desires of the human heart. I beg your lordship to tell me if some of these things affect my conscience, for I am under your charge by the power given you by the Holy Mother Church, to whom I submit myself as a faithful Christian. May our Lord keep your lordship many years in his holy service. I hereby kiss your lordship's hands.

Signed: Eusebia de San Juan.

On August 2, 1560, Inquisitor Gasco summoned Eusebia de San Juan to appear before him in the parlor the Monastery of Santa Paula. When she appeared, she took the oath and swore to tell the truth. When she was shown the two letters, she recognized them to be hers and in her handwriting and that she had given them to the monk to give to the Holy Office.

---

27 If this is correct, Maria de Bohorquez was only ten years old at the time.

When asked to truthfully say what she felt about the things she heard Dr. Egidio say, she said that since Dr. Egidio based so much of what he said in our Lord's words and that only in Him were we to occupy our efforts, that only He had power, and that Jesus Christ had influence over God, suggesting that we were only to serve Jesus Christ and that in Him we were to put our trust. And he implied that the intercession of the saint was of no use, though he did not come right out and say it in so many words, as it appeared later, but I don't remember exactly how he expressed it then. She confessed that she and the majority of the nuns of the convent had lost their enthusiasm regarding the ceremonies of the order, in particular all that of the order which did not conform to God's commandments, which they said were inventions of men, and they were not very committed to the devotion of the saints and walking the stations at Easter, due to what Dr. Egidio had said. And she especially remembered one day, when Dr. Egidio was preaching in the chapel of the convent, before he was taken prisoner, that he spoke about the stations that people would walk on Resurrection Easter morning. She didn't remember exactly what he had said, but she remembered that after that she and some other nuns became more lax in their observances of walking those stations. She hadn't really thought much about it until Juana de los Reyes, another nun in the convent, told her that the observance of walking the stations was so neglected that only two or three nuns did it anymore. Asked what made her give up, or alter, or change her mind about her devotion to the saints, after what Dr. Egidio had said, she declared that by praying to the saints she was diminishing her devotion for Jesus Christ and after that she was less apt to pray to them as intercessors.

I declare that this corresponds with the original document.

Signed: Eusebio de Arrieta, notary of the secret.[28]

The letters seem to have been written some time in 1559 but did not come to the attention of Inquisitor Gonzalez de Munebrega until a year later. Dr. Egidio died in 1556 and was given an honorable burial fit for a canon. Four years later, when it was determined that he had been a heretic, and his bones were dug up and burned, the inquisitors realized that his goods had never been confiscated. The first measure they took was to sell his tombstone, *después de quitadas las letras* (after taking his name off it). This brought fourteen ducats. Next they urged their treasurer, Pedro de Morga, to find Egidio's heirs in order to collect his goods. This turned out to be a mission impossible because Dr. Egidio was from Aragon, too far away to spend time or resources on an amount they were not even sure of.[29]

---

28 AHN, Inquisición, leg. 2942, doc. 78. Notes mine.
29 AHN, Inquisición, leg. 4683 (3), in: Lopez Muñoz (2011, 324, doc. 158).

Dr. Francisco Vargas (1490?–1546?)

We know little about Dr. Vargas. He had been a fellow student with Egidio and Constantino at Alcala, where he earned a doctor's degree in theology in 1525 and after 1529 held the chair of Duns Scotus. According to Klaus Wagner (1976, 314–15), he began his teaching career around 1517 as a professor of liberal arts and was among the professors that examined Juan de Valdes's *Dialog on Christian Doctrine* in 1529. It seems that Vargas, like many others, left Alcala during the academic year of 1532–33. As pointed out earlier, these were troublesome times for critical thinkers and nonconformists. Beltran de Heredia (1971, IV, 120–121) points out that their departure also coincided with the agreement of the faculty to apply the edict of "*limpieza de sangre*" (cleanliness of blood), which excluded children, grandchildren and even great grandchildren from receiving a degree at Alcala.

According to Montes (1569, f. 93v), Vargas held a teaching position in the Cathedral of Seville, where he lectured on the Gospel of Matthew and afterwards expounded the Psalms. In the inventory of books belonging to Dr. Francisco de Vargas, sent in 1546 to his brother Jeronimo de Vargas, vicar in Medinaceli—seventy-three in all and mainly acquired after 1530—, there were several Bibles, one of which was a copy of the Complutensian Polyglot: a *Biblia de ebrayco y griego y latín del Cardenal Fray Francisco Ximénes* (Bible in Hebrew and Greek and Latin by Cardinal Fray Francisco Ximenes) (Wagner: 1976, 318). Montes refers to him as "*el gran* Vargas", an expression the English translator Vincent Skinner retained. Klaus Wagner (1976, 316) thinks that Vargas died sometime in 1546, which would be some six years prior to Egidio's trial and fourteen prior to Constantino's. According to Cipriano de Valera (Usoz: 1847–1865, VI, 251), his bones were later dug up and burned. This may have been decided in August of 1560 after the inquisitors in Seville received a dispatch from the Supreme Council urging them to conclude quickly with the cases of Egidio, Vargas, Constantino, and Domingo de Guzman and to organize the next *auto-da-fe* without delay because the prisons were filling up and more space was needed.[30] At the next auto, held on December 22, both Egidio and Constantino were burned in effigy, but there is no mention of Vargas. As late as 1571, however, his case had not been forgotten. In a brief dispatch, the Supreme Council thanked the inquisitors of Seville for sending the papers and folders related to Vargas's trial records—which they duly return—and they acknowledged the good work of the inquisitors for "utterly annihilating the memory and fame of Dr. Francisco de Vargas, professor of theology."[31]

---

30 AHN, Inquisición, leg. 2942, doc. 86, in: Lopez Muñoz (2011, 189, doc. 94).
31 AHN, Inquisición, lib. 577, f. 209r, in: Lopez Muñoz (2011, 403, doc. 209).

Dr. Constantino Ponce de la Fuente (1502–1560)

Constantino [Ponce] de la Fuente was born in San Clemente, near Cuenca. Although his name does not appears in the university register at Alcala— omitted possibly on account of his Jewish roots—, we know he studied liberal arts at the University of Alcala under Lorenzo Balbo because one of his earliest literary endeavors was a laudatory poem in honor of Balbo which appeared in Lorenzo Balbo's edition of Valerio Flaco's *Argonautica* printed in Alcala by Miguel de Eguia in 1524 (Gonzalo Sánchez-Molero: 2003, 368). Constantino would hardly have composed those verses in his first year, hence, we can suppose that he entered Alcala around 1522, at the age of twenty, which was a bit late considering that most young men entered the university around sixteen. His time at Alcala would have coincided with the years the Erasmian scholar Pedro de Lerma, uncle of the Enzinas brothers, was chancellor of the university.

During his first years at Alcala, Constantino would have studied grammar, literature, rhetoric, and logic. He would then have gone on to the next course of studies known as the *quadrivium*, which included some science, and Hebrew, and Greek philosophy and history. The study of the "seven liberal arts"— grammar, rhetoric, dialectic (logic), arithmetic, geometry, astronomy, and music—, together with the three philosophies—moral, natural, and meta-physical—, covered a basic university education. They were considered neces-sary for the development of intellectual and moral excellence (Cox: 2010). Constantino would have studied the three literary disciplines, or *trivium*, but just how long he was at Alcala remains a mystery. In any case, he did not finish his degree there. Years later, accrediting his eligibility to sit for the public exams for the post of canon at Seville, he declared that he had a licentiate degree in theology from the Colegio de Santa Maria de Jesus in Seville.[32] He never revealed, however, where he obtained his Ph.D.

According to Montes (1569, ff. 92v–93v), before going to Seville, Constantino was offered a post at Toledo and another at Cuenca, which he refused. What he did or where he was between 1525 and 1533 is another mystery. Nevertheless, some years later, Dr. Miguel Majuelo, canon of Saint Just and Pastor at Alcala and professor of theology at the University of Alcala, accused him of "youthful follies, namely marriage, which was before he entered into orders." (Montes: 1569, 95r–95v). Majuelo's accusation did not fall on deaf ears. Once the inquisitors began to suspect Constantino of Protestant leanings, they not only began investigating his writings, but also his past life. In a letter from the Supreme Council to the inquisitors at Seville, dated May 19, 1558, they included a copy of a letter sent to the inquisitors at Granada urging them to make inquiries regarding Con-

---

32 This institution would later become the University of Seville.

stantino's marriage.[33] A year later, the Supreme Council sent another report in which they urged the inquisitors at Granada to interrogate Maria Gonzalez, wife of Joan de Segovia, living in Malaga, regarding this marriage. They also enclosed a copy of Constantino's genealogy and the declarations made by the nun, Elvira de Payares, to Maria Gonzalez regarding Constantino's marriage.[34] There is no record of the results of these inquiries.

Constantino seems to have arrived in Seville in the spring of 1533. On June 13 of that same year the cathedral chapter asked him to become one of their preachers. He was allowed to combine his preaching duties with theological studies and was shortly afterwards ordained. According to Montes, he did not preach as often as Egidio, but his sermons were equally as fruitful and edifying. For more than ten years, Vargas, Egidio, and Constantino preached undisturbed. The general level of religious knowledge—even among broad sections of the clergy—was so low at that time that the detection of heterodoxy came to be a mission impossible for the high ecclesiastical hierarchy. Indeed, it appears that the multitudes that gathered at the Cathedral in Seville to hear the preaching of Dr. Egidio and Constantino Ponce de la Fuente did not have sufficient religious knowledge to discern that the message that they preached differed substantially from traditional Catholic doctrine (Estrada: 2008a, 25). Or as Henry Kamen (1985, 209) points out:

> Over much of Spain, Christianity was still only a veneer. The religion of the people remained backward. The people combined formal religion with folk superstition. In rural areas the world of magic even entered the Church, with many clergy incorporating folk practices—rites, prayers, offerings, dances—into the normal liturgy.

Constantino shared the pulpit at the cathedral with Dr. Hernan Rodrigues, from whom the Inquisition had confiscated four Bibles in 1552[35] and who, according to John Strype (1709), Julianillo had had "great disputations during the time of his imprisonment." Meanwhile, he continued to gain fame as a preacher. On May 18, 1539, Constantino preached the funeral sermon for the empress, Isabel de Portugal.[36] One of the persons present at the cathedral that day was Fadrique Enriquez de Ribera, Marquis of Tarifa, whom we saw earlier in Medina de Rioseco and whose niece, Maria Enriquez de Ribera, would later be questioned regarding her involvement in the evangelical movement in Seville. For the next

---

33 AHN, Inquisición, leg. 714, doc. 49–3, in: Lopez Muñoz (2011, 121, doc. 44).
34 ADC, Inquisición, Miscelánea de Breves, L-224, f. 183r, in: Lopez Muñoz (2011, 137, doc. 53).
35 AHN, Inquisición, leg. 4426, doc. 32, in: Lopez Muñoz (2011, 55, doc. 15).
36 Isabel de Portugal (1503–1539) died after the birth of her sixth child. The emperor was away at the time and her death affected him deeply. He never remarried. In 1580, her son Philip II succeeded the Portuguese throne, claiming his mother's successory rights uniting the Iberian peninsula under one crown.

ten years or so, Constantino was busy writing and publishing a series of religious works, all of which were widely read and reprinted several times until they were put on the Index of Prohibited Books in 1559.[37] Alfonso de Ulloa, a Spanish man of letters and historian working in Venice in the 1540s and 50s, highly praised Constantino's writings in his *Vita dell'inuittissimo e sacratissimo imperator Carlo V* (1575), particularly his *Doctrina Christiana*, which he states was translated into Italian (Llorente: 1827, 221). Ulloa's is the only reference to this translation. On the other hand, once Constantino's works were put on the Index, the Inquisition may have ordered all the copies—and translations—destroyed, which would explain why no copies are extant.

In the summer of 1548 Constantino was appointed crown prince Philip's chaplain and preacher. The contracts were signed in September and in November Constantino left Spain in company of Philip and his large entourage.[38] Eduard Boehmer (2007, II, 10–11. Notes mine) describes Constantino's time abroad thus:

> In November 1548 Constantino embarked with the prince Philip, having inaugurated the voyage by a sermon on All Saints day; Augustine Cazalla also was in the suite. They accompanied the prince through Italy and Germany to the Netherlands, where they arrived, the next spring, at the court of the Emperor. Charles appointed Constantino his confessor and chaplain.[39] When he stayed at Augsburg with Charles and Philip in the time of the diet, in the year 1550,[40] he received Gaspar a Nidbruck[41] in the most friendly manner, who presented himself with a letter of introduction from Francisco de Enzinas. Constantino earnestly pressed Enzinas to return to his family in Spain, or, at least, to settle at Antwerp, proof that the doctor still cherished very illusory hopes for the safety

---

37 See Appendix B.
38 On September 1, the prince signed an order whereby Constantino was to receive 15,000 *maravedís* per year; four days later he increased the amount: "in addition to the 11,000 *maravedís* of his regular yearly salary as chaplain, pay him another 25,000 *maravedís* a year besides." (AGS, C. y S. Reales, leg. 107, ff. 490–491). At that time, the Spanish monetary system consisted basically of *escudos, ducados,* and *maravedis.* In 1537, the *escudo* became the standard gold coin, replacing the *ducado,* which then became a unit of account. In other words, prices were quoted in *ducados* and paid in *escudos.* In 1566 Philip II declared the *maravedí* the official unit of account—not the name of a coin—and it remained so until 1847. In the sixteenth century, one *escudo* = 400 *maravedis.* Prince Philip assigned Constantino a yearly salary of 37.5 *escudos,* which was not exceptional because an ordinary chaplain of a convent earned 50 *escudos,* and a university professor earned 100. Perhaps that is why he added the extra 62.5 *escudos.*
39 This statement is slightly misleading. Constantino was prince Philip's preacher during his European tour; Augustine Cazalla was Charles V's chaplain from 1543 to 1553. Boehmer may have copied this information from M'Crie.
40 Charles V convened the Diet of Augsburg in 1547/48, where the Augsburg Interim was proclaimed. A number of sessions followed. This particular session was that of July 8, 1550.
41 In 1550 Kaspar von Niedbruck, a diplomat in the service of Archduke Maximilian II, was present at the diet in Augsburg. Although he had Protestant leanings, he remained in the service of the Habsburgs.

of persons of such convictions. He seems to have remained at Philip's court during the next three years. He was in England with Philip.[42] About the end of the year 1555 he had returned to Seville from which he had been absent for seven years.

Boehmer took much of his information from Juan Cristobal Calvete de Estrella's *El felicissimo viaje* (1552). Calvete, who had entered the court of Charles V as prince Philip's tutor of pages and later Philip's Latin tutor, took it upon himself to record the prince's journey, which took them from Barcelona to Genoa, Milan, Trent, Germany, and ended in the Low Countries. In April of 1549, they were in Brussels. From there to Louvain, Ghent, Lille, Tournai and Rotterdam, where they were received by an actor dressed up like Erasmus with a pen in one hand and a poem in the other addressed to Philip, and from Rotterdam on to Amsterdam and back to Brussels a year later, where they were received by Charles V and his sister Maria. Among the celebrities in Philip's court, Calvete (1552, f. 7v) writes: "There was also Dr. Constantino, a great philosopher and profound theologian, and one of the most notorious and eloquent men in the pulpit."

Details gleaned from Calvete (1552, f. 7v) tell us that the mass held at the cathedral church of Castello d'Empurias, north of Barcelona near the French border, that prince Philip attended on All Saint's Day [November 1, 1548] was "a very solemn high mass and Dr. Constantino preached a remarkable sermon, as usual." The following day Constantino and the rest of Philip's entourage embarked in a galley in nearby Rosas manned by Andrea Doria that had been waiting there since August and sailed off for Genoa. Doria had brought the emperor's nephew, Archduke Maximilian, to Spain as deputy governor while crown prince Philip was abroad. Easter of 1550 was spent in Brussels, "where the three great preachers of the court preached: Doctor Constantino, Fray Bernardo de Fresneda,[43] and Doctor Augustin de Cazalla, an excellent theologian, a man of sound doctrine and eloquence." (Calvete: 1552, f. 7v).[44]

Calvete's account of the tour ends in May 1550 and was published in 1552. Ten years later, after the *autos-da-fe* in Seville and Valladolid that condemned both Constantino and Cazalla, Calvete's text was expurgated. All mention of these two

---

42 On July 25, 1554, 27-year-old Philip married 38-year-old Queen Mary I of England in London. Constantino would have met Bartolome de Carranza on that occasion.

43 Bernardo Alvarado de Fresneda (1509–1577) was a Franciscan friar. He was also Philip's confessor.

44 Constantino, Fresneda, and Cazalla were contracted as preachers, not chaplains. According to Jose Martínez Millán (2000, 213), the chaplains and priests that accompanied prince Philip were Pedro de Castro (Bishop of Salamanca), Antón Bravo, Francisco de Portugalete, Francisco López de Ávila, Pero Núñez, Francisco de Barrio, Diego Suárez, Rodríguez de Orozco, Pedro de Olivera, Fernán Sánchez, Pedro de Reinoso, Francisco Osorio, Ahumada, Francisco de Barrionuevo and Gallizia.

"famous preachers" was erased. Instructions given in the Index of Prohibited Books, read:

> Calvete de Estrella (Juan Christov.). In his book, *Viage del Principe* [The Prince's Travels], Book 1, sec. "Embarkation," fol. 5, page 2, and fol. 7, page 2, remove all that is in praise of Constantino de la Fuente. In Book 4, fol. 325, remove all that is in praise of Constantino and Agustin de Cazalla.[45]

A century later, another historian, who narrated the important events that took place in Seville from 1246 to 1671, reluctantly restored their names, but with the following reservations:

> The prince set sail from Rosas on November 2, accompanied by many grandees, noblemen and knights, in whose company also went Doctor Constantino de la Fuente, applauded then for being a great theologian and preacher, condemned later for being a perverse heretic, whose pride and presumption were a restraint on him, but being so far from being suspected, he preached for the prince in Barcelona on All Saints' Day. (Ortiz de Zuñiga: 1677, III, 402).

One would expect to find information regarding such an illustrious preacher as Constantino in Fermin Arana de Variflora's 400-page *Hijos de Sevilla ilustres en santidad, letras, armas, artes, ò dignidad* (1791) (Sons of Seville, Famous for their Holiness, Learning, Arms, Arts, and Dignity), but there is no mention of Constantino among the distinguished sons of Seville. The Inquisition had won the day! It would take another fifty years, and the efforts of Luis Usoz y Rio and the English historians Thomas M'Crie and John Stoughton to rescue Constantino's name from oblivion. John Stoughton (2013, 140–141) lists some of the acquaintances Constantino made during his travels throughout Europe:

> James Schopper, of Biberach in Suabia, is mentioned as one who met with him, and his conversation was useful in opening up Protestant truths. Further, he was acquainted with one of whom much has been said in a former chapter, Francisco de Enzinas. Their acquaintanceship is shown in a correspondence between Caspar Nidbruck and Enzinas, the former asking the latter to write to Constantino on his behalf. "You need not mention," he says, "the topic of religion, and without your engaging me too much by your promises, you may affirm this, that what he shall communicate to me will be entrusted to a confidential person" one attached to men of faith and piety. Were you disposed to confer with him upon your own affairs, that would be best done by your informing him of them when I shall be at Augsburg, for I shall easily ascertain how he is affected towards pure Evangelical doctrine, and how he is affected towards you, as also what others think of you." What exactly was the object of this communication does not appear, but it indicates how cautious persons of a certain class were of committing themselves on the subject of religion, and how well known it was to the writer that Constantino and Enzinas were acquainted with one another. Nidbruck wrote again to

---

45 Indice ultimo (1790). Translation mine.

Enzinas, in October 1550, saying: "The venerable man, Dr. Constantino, has received me with great friendliness, and, what with his wisdom and learning, I doubt not that he will be able, assisted by your counsel, to promote what I have proposed, which he promised that he will do, and I do not mistrust his good will." In his letter to Enzinas, Nidbruck adds, "Dr. Constantino most earnestly desires thee to return to thy family, or at least to settle in the Netherlands at Antwerp."

Prince Philip returned to Spain in the summer of 1551. He made several stops on way back to Toledo and finally arrived early in 1552 (Garraín Villa: 1988). At this point, Constantino may have requested a short leave of absence to return to Seville before the whole entourage left for England for Philip's wedding. A dispatch from the Supreme Council to the inquisitors in Seville, dated March 23, 1553, mentions a manuscript by Constantino that they had received from Seville. The parcel also contained a copy of Constantino's *Sermones sobre el primero salmo de David* (Six Sermons on Psalm 1) and his *Catecismo*, as well as comments by Gonzalo de Arciniega and Dr. Melendez regarding suspicious passages in these volumes. The Supreme Council asked the inquisitors in Seville to "very astutely call on Constantino—if he is in the city or when he comes—to see how he reacts to the criticisms."[46] Judging from the dates, it appears that Constantino was requesting permission to reprint the two above-mentioned works and was submitting a new manuscript for approval. From the correspondence that followed, it seems that the Supreme Council had simply sent the books off to Alcala for opinions and returned them and the manuscript to Seville, without pronouncing itself regarding the new manuscript. This surprised the inquisitors at Seville, who sent the manuscript back to Madrid by return of post, and which prompted the following answer from the Council:

> We have received your letter of 21 April with the manuscript that Dr. Constantino says he deposited to be examined for a license for publication. To this effect, could you please send us again the other two books and all the document regarding suspicious passages that we returned to you so we can see how we must proceed in this business.[47]

In September of 1553, the Council wrote again acknowledging receipt of the manuscript by Dr. Constantino entitled *Espejo del estado del hombre en esta presente vida* (A Reflection on Man's State in this Present Life) and said they had sent if off to Alcala where the same theologians that had censored his *Six sermons* had seen it. They were returning the three items, together with the censors' comments, with the recommendation that all the places where Constantino refers to the "faith of the sinners as false" in *El espejo del estado del hombre*

---

46 AHN, Inquisición, lib. 574, f. 374v, in: Lopez Muñoz (2011, 99, doc. 24).
47 AHN, Inquisición, lib. 574, f. 323r, in: Lopez Muñoz (2011, 100, doc. 25).

should be emended.[48] By that time, Constantino had again left for England and the Low Countries and would not be back for another several years.

One of his first commitments on his final return to Seville was to preach the Lent sermons, but he was so weak from a recent illness that he could only preach every other day and had to be carried into the church. His illness obliged him to take "at intervals during the sermon a little wine, a freedom which in the case of a man so highly respected and so much beloved caused no scandal." (Boehmer: 2007, 12). Once he recovered, Dr. Alonso de Escobar,[49] headmaster of the Casa de los Niños de la Doctrina,[50] asked him, and Hernan Ruiz de Hojeda, to become readers at the school (Ollero Pina: 2007, 179). According to Montes (1569, f. 94r), Constantino went through Proverbs, Ecclesiastes, the Song of Solomon, and got half way through the book of Job.

Meanwhile, the cathedral chapter was determined to give Constantino the canonry that Dr. Egidio had left vacant, but it was against the rules of their house to admit him without a public examination, or what they called *oposicion*, which had been their error in choosing Dr. Egidio.[51] The exam was announced on February 15, 1556. Seven candidates registered: Francisco Sanchez, Pedro Zumel, Miguel Majuelo, Miguel de Palacios, Francisco Moratilla, Francisco Melendez, and Constantino de la Fuente (Ollero Pina: 2007, 151–152). The oral exercises were to begin at the end of April, but they had to be postponed a few weeks because on May 11, Constantino's lawyer brought the chapter a certificate, signed by Dr. Nicolas Monardes, Dr. Cabra, and Licenciado Olivares, stating that Constantino was too ill to lecture, preach or speak in public to the point that it would be detrimental to his life (Olmedilla y Puig: 1897, 26). He may have

---

48 AHN, Inquisición, lib. 574, f. 392r, in: Lopez Muñoz (2011, 101, doc. 26).

49 Dr. Alonso de Escobar was the first to occupy the lectureship of Sacred Scripture at the Casa de los Niños de la Doctrina in Seville. In 1552, his uncle, Gil de Fuentes, had left an endowment for this purpose. Bartolomé de Olmedo, a priest who officiated in the Royal Chapel of the Cathedral, and Constantino Ponce de la Fuente were the executors of Gil de Fuente's will in 1552. See Wagner: 1975, 239–247.

50 The Colegio de Niños de la Doctrina, also called the Casa de la Doctrina, took in orphans, foundlings, and abandoned boys between 6 and 20 years of age. The boys were taught Christian doctrine [i. e. the items of the catechism], reading, good manners, elementary notions of Latin, geometry, drawing, as well as certain skills, such as tailoring, carpentry, carding, weaving, knitting, etc. There was also a school for orphan girls: la Casa de la Doctrina de las Niñas. Catalina de San Esteban, daughter of the headmistress was condemned in the *auto-da-fe* of 28 October 1562 to house arrest and prohibited to enter the school again or to teach. AHN, Inquisición, leg. 2075, doc. (2); AGS, Estado, leg. 137, doc. 3, in: Lopez Muñoz (2011, 226, doc. 101).

51 *Oposiciones* are exams that applicants for tenured public-sector jobs must pass in order to occupy the post. The candidates (*opositores*) sit for a series of written and oral exams. All public-sector appointments open to competition must be given ample publicity in order to ensure impartiality. In the case of Egidio, the chapter had been so anxious to have him that they had waived this requisite.

suffered a sort of relapse of his former ailment; nevertheless, he was soon well enough to sit for the exam. Montes (1569, ff. 95r–95v) describes the event as follows:

A day was appointed for the "opposition" and published in the most famous cities in Spain, so that divers came flocking, as if it had been like crows on a carcass. But the wiser sort kept themselves away from encountering with him for the great favor and estimation that he was in, so that there were but only two that abided the brunt: the one called Majuelo, a canon of Alcala de Henares,[52] the other a canon of Malaga, hoping to get some great booty thereby. The first, upon better advice, returned home again shortly after to Alcala; the other canon of Malaga, bolstered by the archbishop [Fernando de Valdes] to spite Constantino, willfully continued the skirmish.[53] Finally, Constantino, being overcome through the great entreaty and persuasion of the Chapter, but especially moved by the importunate suite of a friend of his, to whom I wish he had not yielded so much in this (for then perhaps he had been alive at this time) resolved to sit for the canonship and to dispute after the accustomed order, and thus, by fulfilling that ceremony, he of Malaga would be sent to shake his ears, and the Chapter would prevail against the bishop. There was also at the same time a little zeal which blinded Constantino, lest perhaps some prater or foolish talker should have stepped into the place who would always be barking against good and godly doctrine, whereas, by his accepting the place there was a certain likelihood and hope that the doctrine thereby should have the more free passage. This made him the more willing, rather than for any greedy or covetous desire of attaining any wealth thereby, a vice he always condemned with manly courage. Whereupon, his adversary that stood against him perceiving himself unable to measure up with him, either for learning, countenance or favor, which he found at the Chapter's hand, bent himself wholly to take exceptions to his person and to disable him that way. First, he began to object against all his youthly follies, namely marriage, the which was before he entered into orders, charging him that neither he was rightly ordained, nor came by his degree of Doctorship correctly.

As inferred, Constantino may have been dearly loved by some, but he was also deeply hated by others. He continued to preach at the cathedral, but his adversaries were constantly watching both his conduct and his preaching. Constantino's sermons had a great impact in Seville, particularly among the social elite of the city. Meanwhile, Juan Perez de Pineda, who had fled to Geneva some years earlier and had kept up correspondence with many eminent citizens, was busy promoting the evangelical cause in Seville from a distance. On November 17, 1557, the Supreme Council sent Philip II, who was in Flanders, the following dispatch:

The inquisitors at Seville have written saying that in that city they have seized many books containing heresy. These books have been found in the hands of eminent citi-

---

52 Dr. Miguel Majuelo was canon of Saint Just and Pastor at Alcala, professor of theology at the University of Alcala, and consultant for the Holy Office.
53 Pedro Zumel was Inquisitor General Valdes's candidate.

zens, and have to do with a certain Dr. Juan Pérez, who is living in Frankfort. He was a great friend of Dr. Egidio, and fled Seville when Egidio was arrested. Perez wrote the books and sent them to Seville through a Spanish Lutheran who they have imprisoned. Along with these books, he sent letters to the aforementioned persons. The man is being examined as well as the persons who received the books. Your Majesty will be duly informed of the outcome. They have also written saying that this Dr. Juan Perez has sent many of these books here to Valladolid, but we do no know to whom. We beg Your Majesty to decree that these books to be seized and the persons who have them to be punished because the impudence and craftiness of those heretics is so great that the ministers of the Holy Office cannot cope with it on their own. And it is paramount that in this matter Your Majesty decree with all severity your displeasure so that these heretics refrain from committing such unlawful acts with such boldness.[54]

These books were brought to Seville by Julian Hernandez. His arrest in the summer of 1557 had serious consequences for the evangelicals in Seville. Constantino's name was immediately put on the list of suspects, though he was not arrested at the time. Indeed, instructions from the Supreme Council, dated October 22, 1557, urged the inquisitors to deal carefully with him. Constantino knew that the monks from San Isidoro had fled and if the inquisitors acted too rashly, Constantino might also escape. Hence, orders were that he was not to be questioned regarding any oral statements he had made or any contacts he might have had with any dissidents, but rather regarding certain statements that appeared in his writings. The inquisitors realized that they had to act fast. Orders were that "he should respond to your objections immediately because if you give him time to answer that will give him the opportunity to communicate the matter with others and this would be against our interests."[55]

In view of the development of the evangelical movement in Seville and the increasing number of proselytes, Inquisitor General Fernando de Valdes—"the most inflexible of the inquisitors" (Bataillon: 1966, 701)—with the full power of attorney granted by Pope Paul IV, set in motion what Bataillon (1966, 709) describes as "the new method of repression, based on the terror of example." On August 1, 1558, Constantino preached his last sermon in the cathedral of Seville; fifteen days later, Valdes ordered his imprisonment. For some time Constantino was able to evade the accusations made against him, or as Montes (1569, f. 95v) puts it, "he evaded all the quarrels picked against him by his quick and ready answers (after his accustomed manner) so easily that they could in no way get him to make any open protestation of his faith, by which they hoped to encompass and overcome him."

The final proof of Constantino's unorthodoxy came, however, in a most unexpected way. Constantino kept a clandestine library in the house of Isabel

---

54 AGS, Estado, leg.121, doc. 165, in: Lopez Muñoz (2011, 113, doc. 35).
55 AHN, Inquisición, lib. 575, ff. 57r y ss, in: Lopez Muñoz (2011, 112, doc. 34).

Martinez de Alvo. When Isabel was arrested, her son Beltran suspected his mother, who had been taken to Triana for questioning, had told the inquisitors about the library and when the *alguacil* came to the house, Beltran was sure they were coming for Constantino's books so he took them straight to the part of the house where they were. Montes (1569, ff. 95v–97r. Notes and brackets mine) describes the event thus:

> It happened that about the same time, a very honest and wealthy widow named Isabel Martinez was apprehended in whose house Constantino had hid certain special books for fear of the inquisitors which he might not admit the keeping of in Spain without present peril, whose goods, being confiscated according to the custom of the Inquisition, her son, one Francisco Beltran, had carried away divers chests of the best stuff that his mother had, because he wanted to save some so that these Cormoravants[56] should not devour all. This, coming to the inquisitor's ears by means of his untrusty servant who disclosed it, was the occasion that they sent immediately one Don Luis Sotelo, their *alguazil*, to demand those chests. Sotelo resorted unto him accordingly and as he began to say his message soberly, Beltran, forgetting the chests and supposing that the cause of his coming had been for Constantino's books, took the tale out of his mouth and said: "Don Luis, I know what you come for and therefore if you will promise me on your honesty quietly to depart upon the receipt thereof, I will show you them." The *alguazil*, meaning the chests (as for the books he neither came for them, nor knew of any such), promised him so to do. Whereupon, Beltran carried him forthwith into a secret place far within the house, and plucking forth a stone or two in the wall, showed him Constantino's jewels of paper, indeed far more precious than gold or pearls, whereat the *alguazil*, being somewhat astonished to find what he looked not for, told him that he came to demand no such thing but certain chests of his mother's goods, which he had held from the Sequester.
>
> As for his promise made unto him for his quiet departure, he said he was not bound thereby in this new circumstance, but that be must needs carry both him and his books to the inquisitors. Thus, by these means came all Constantino's writings out of corners to light and to the inquisitors' hands, contrary both to his own expectation and his adversaries, which would have given a great piece of money to have come by them before. And among others of his writings, there was one great volume found, written all in his own hand, wherein (as the inquisitors themselves reported in their sentence which they gave him afterwards upon the scaffold) he openly and plainly, as it were for his own satisfaction, handled these special points, that is to say: the state of the church, the true church and the pope's church, whom he called very Antichrist; the sacrament of the Lord's supper; the invention of the mass, wherein he said that the whole world was deceived and abused through ignorance of the Holy Scriptures; the justification of a Christian man; purgatory, which he termed the wolves' mouth, saying that it was a devise of the monks to feed their own bellies; also Bulls and popish pardons, man's merits, shrift, and other articles of Christian religion. This book, as soon as it came to

---

56 Large diving birds with a long neck, long hooked bill, short legs, and dark plumage, noted for their voracious appetite. This simile is not in the original.

the inquisitors' hands, they demanded of him if he knew his own handwriting. He shifted them off from their purpose a good while, and drove them off from day to day till at last, understanding the will of God, who had now taken away all evasions from him, he acknowledged his own hand and confessed it to be his own writing, maintaining openly that all things therein contained were full of truth and sincerity. "Therefore, (said he) take no further pains in seeking witnesses to testify against me, seeing you have so plain and perfect a confession of my opinion and belief, but do and deal with me as it shall please you."

After this examination and answer, he remained in prison by the space of two whole years, where, partly by occasion of his corrupt and unwholesome diet (though he were not a man greatly curious or dainty therein before time), but chiefly, of very sorrow consuming him to see so much labor both of his own and others his fellows spent in vain upon that good church which now was so miserably sacked, he fell first to be a little crazed, and afterwards, being unable to bear the exceeding heat of the sun which made his prison like a hothouse unto him, was fain to strip himself into his bare shirt and so to continue thus both day and night. By occasion thereof, he fell sick of the bloody flux [dysentery] and within fifteen days died amidst the filth and soil of the prison, rendering up his sweet soul to Christ for the promotion of whose glory he had oftentimes before adventured it most manfully.

Constantino died in prison. His bones were brought out at the *auto-da-fe* held on December 22, 1560, and were burned.[57] His goods had been confiscated when he entered prison and were carefully registered, as was the custom. According to treasurer Pedro de Morga, Constantino had received an annual salary from Philip II since 1548 that came up to some 100,000 maravedis yearly.[58] Likewise, among his possessions there was a small printing press and *aparejos* (riggings), valued at 30,000 maravedis,[59] as well as 367 books that were sold at public auction in September 1562. This, according to Morga, adequately covered the expenses incurred in during Constantino's imprisonment, which came up to 30,672 maravedis. The printing material produced a good price but Morga complained that many of the smaller books were either lost or stolen, but that in general they brought in little money because "there was little interest in that type of book." These would have been books he had in his private library, not those he had in his "clandestine" library. In all probability his collection of "prohibited" books was put in secret keeping at Triana and may have been among those inventoried in 1563.[60] Morga's statement is surprising because one of the books brought out at the public auction was a copy of the Complutenian Polyglot Bible. It was purchased by Fray Lucas de la Sal, who later sold it to fray Martin de Abrego, who

57 AHN, Inquisición, leg. 2075, doc. 1 (2); AGS, Estado, leg. 137, doc. 3, in: Lopez Muñoz (2011, 214, doc. 101).
58 AHN, Inquisición, leg. 4683 (3), in: Lopez Muñoz (2011, 324, doc. 158).
59 AHN, Inquisición, leg. 4683 (3), in: Lopez Muñoz, (2011, 330, doc. 158).
60 For a complete list of authors and titles confiscated up to 1563, see Appendix A.

in turn bequeathed it to the St. Augustine monastery in Jerez de la Frontera.[61] Many years later, in 1575, the Supreme Council asked the inquisitors at Seville to recover it.[62] Whether this was possible or not is unsure.

Among Constantino's papers, was also found a receipt, dated September 17, 1558, signed by the printer Martin Montesdoca for 400 gold escudos.[63] This was a large sum to deposit with a printer. Was it advance payment for the book that was never printed? In 1554, at the height of his printing career, a change seems to have occurred in Martin Montesdoca's life. From then on, he left off printing profane literature and only printed religious material: first two books by the Franciscan mystic Francisco de Osuna, followed by *Luz del Alma* by the Dominican friar Felipe de Meneses.[64] After that, Montesdoca limited his production almost exclusively to works by Fray Domingo de Baltanas. By 1557 Montesdoca was having serious financial problems. The following year, Constantino deposited the 400 gold *escudos* with him (Wagner: 1982, 26). Was this to keep Montesdoca afloat or to print *El espejo del estado del hombre*, or Part Two of his *Doctrina Christina*, or something else? Did Constantino buy out Montesdoca? In November of 1559, Montesdoca, now a widower, sold his shop in Seville and his possessions in Utrera and bought passages for four persons—his two young children, his sister Marina and himself—on the ship "Nuestra Señora de la Antigua" and on January 22, 1561, sailed for Honduras. No doubt events such as Constantino's arrest shortly after he had deposited the money, hastened Montesdoca's departure.

---

61 Lucas de la Sal is also listed as the owner of three confiscated Bibles in 1552. AHN, Inquisición, leg. 4426, doc. 32, in: Lopez Muñoz (2011, 55–80, doc. 15)

62 AHN, Inquisición, leg. 2946, in: Lopez Muñoz (2011, 422, doc. 228).

63 AHN, Inquisición, leg. 4683 (3), in: Lopez Muñoz, (2011, 335, doc. 158). In 1566 Philip II established the value of the *escudo* at 400 *maravedís*, and the ducat at 340 *maravedís*. There were 270 *maravedís* to a peso, and 2 pesos to an *escudo*. Two golden escudos were equivalent to the thaler and thus it was easy to convert other values. See Francis Turner, "Money and exchange rates in 1632," accessed November 10, 2014, macrocoin.net/profiles/blogs/money-and-exchange-rates-in-1632-by-francis-turner.

64 Despite Felipe de Meneses's Erasmian leanings, his work continued to be printed. Even Cervantes praises it. "Thus it came to pass that going along one of the streets Don Quixote lifted up his eyes and saw written in very large letters over a door, "Books printed here," at which he was vastly pleased, for until then he had never seen a printing office, and he was curious to know what it was like. He entered with all his following, and saw them drawing sheets in one place, correcting in another, setting up type here, revising there; in short all the work that is to be seen in great printing offices. He went up to one case and asked what they were about there, …and he moved on to another case, where he saw them correcting a sheet of a book with the title of "Light of the Soul." Noticing it he observed, "Books like this, though there are many of the kind, are the ones that deserve to be printed, for many are the sinners in these days, and lights unnumbered are needed for all that are in darkness." (Cervantes, DQ II, 62).

Julian Hernandez, the Colporteur

Julian Hernandez, known as "Julianillo" (petit Julian) for his size, was born in Valverde del Campo, a village south of Medina de Rioseco. Around 1551 or 1552 he left his native village and went to Paris. From there he went to Scotland and then to Germany, where he was chosen elder in the Lutheran congregation of the Walloons in Frankfurt. Next we find him in Geneva collaborating with Juan Perez de Pineda, who was busy translating, writing, and editing Protestant literature to be sent to Spain. Julian Hernandez rapidly understood his mission to be that of colporteur. He made several journeys from Geneva to Spain. In the fall of 1556 he set off again for Seville with literature and letters from Juan Perez de Pineda for friends and acquaintances in Seville, together with instructions for those who wanted to escape and go to Germany "to live like the Lutherans," but soon after his arrival he was seized. An anonymous report sent to the Supreme Council towards the end of September of 1557 tells how Julian Hernandez was caught:

> In the year 1557, in July, a man came to this city of Seville from Germany. He was a Spaniard, born in Medina de Rioseco, a fool but a staunch Lutheran. His name was Julian. He brought letters and very pernicious prohibited books for many citizens of this city sent by persons who had left our country and gone to Germany to be Lutherans at greater liberty. They sent them because they felt people here were very eager to follow that false idea and evil doctrine. Julian was not able to openly bring these books into Seville due to the safety measures employed by the inquisitors, but with the help and assistance of the people of Seville he got them over the wall by night. He distributed the letters and the books to whom they were addressed. Among the letters there was one for a priest. By mistake he gave it to one by the same name, who, when he saw the poison in the letter —a language totally new for him—, he was shocked. Likewise, when he saw the book, which had a drawing of the pope kneeling at the feet of the devil on the cover page,[65] stating it was printed in Seville with the license of the inquisitors, and that the first proposition declared we were not to trust in our works, he got very upset and went straight to show it to the inquisitors.[66]

Julian Hernandez's arrest led to the arrest of many other members of the underground church in Seville. Montes (1569, f. 73v. Brackets mine) relates the event:

---

65 This drawing was probably inspired by a similar drawing by Lucas Cranach—"The Pope demands his feet to be kissed"—that appeared in Martin Luther's *Passional of Christ and Antichrist* (1521). Or it could be an interpretation of one of Hans Holbein's "Great Dance of Death" emblems (1522) showing the emperor kissing the feet of the pope, surrounded by corpses and devils with letters of indulgence.

66 BNE, ms. 6176, f. 48v, in: Lopez Muñoz (2011, 115, doc. 38). Gonzalez de Montes's account, though more exhaustive, is basically the same. See Montes (1569, ff. 73r–75r).

> But at last, this matter [the arrival of the books] broke out and came to the inquisitors' knowledge, first, by means of a foolish fellow more fearful a great deal than needs be, and afterwards by an unfaithful brother, pretending to profess the Gospel wherein he seemed to have profited reasonably well but shortly after showed himself to be a Judas and a champion for the Inquisition, cloaking and covering his malicious purpose with that counterfeit pretense of religion, and by that means betrayed the whole congregation. Then the inquisitors, well nosed [having a good sense of smell] like the devil, finding a little way in, followed on so far till at length they sprang the whole cove, found the nest, took both young and old, and so made havoc of all.

The testimony of several witnesses at the trial of Gaspar Ortiz in 1559, the blind man living at the Colegio de Doctrina, sentenced on October 28, 1562, to ten years of house arrest and the loss of half his goods, suggests that Julian made more than one trip to Seville.[67] The preacher Juan Gonzalez's sister Catalina, for example, stated that when Juan Perez went to Paris to study (which was around 1550) he wrote her a letter and that Julian had brought letters from Juan Perez for her and for others when he had come to Seville and she had answered the letters, and that when Julian returned to Seville, "two years ago," he brought letters for her and for Gaspar Ortiz in which Perez reproached them for not treating Julian well the other time. Perez de Pineda's reproach clearly suggests at least one previous visit. Catalina's sister also mentions an earlier visit by Julian: "The first time Julian Hernandez came from Germany to Seville he stayed with Gaspar Ortiz." Julian himself corroborated this visit: "When I came from Germany to this city the first time with letters from Juan Perez for Gaspar Ortiz and others, I slept in Ortiz's house one night." In his defense, Gaspar Ortiz's statement suggests an even earlier visit by Julian: "Some three and a half years ago, a young man, who I think is the same who is in prison now, is the same one who brought the books and had brought him a letter from Juan Perez."[68] This "young man" had stayed at his house six or seven days and Ortiz had fed him and given him money for his [return] journey and a letter for Perez. Furthermore, Julian Hernandez testified that on his previous visit, he had had instructions to contact Dr. Egidio and canon Ruiz de Hojeda and to leave the letters with the persons they were addressed to but that Ortiz did not want him to do that on his own, and had his "*negrillo*" (little black servant boy) do it for him, and that the next time he came he also had letters from Perez de Pineda for Ortiz.[69] This suggests that Julian's journey to Seville in 1557 may even have been his third trip.

Julian Hernandez was kept in prison for over three years during which time he was interrogated—and submitted to torture—several times. He was finally sentenced to the stake on December 22, 1560, the same *auto* where Dr. Egidio,

---

67 AHN, Inquisición, leg. 2075 (1), doc. 2, in: Lopez Muñoz (2011, 226, doc. 102).
68 Ortiz was blind hence he could not be sure it was the same person.
69 AHN, Inquisición, leg. 4514 (2), doc. 15.

Constantino de la Fuente, and Juan Perez de Pineda were burned in effigy.[70] The pronouncement was written up in the following terms:

> We hereby declare Julian Hernandez, citizen of Campos, in Valverde, deacon in the Lutheran congregation of the Flemish in Frankfurt, to be an obstinate Lutheran apostate heretic, one who had come to Spain with prohibited and illegal books with the intention of dogmatizing and perverting good and Catholic Christians in the errors and pestilent sect of that evil heretic Martin Luther and his followers. He had remained hardened and unyielding in his ideas and hence had incurred in excommunion and all the punishment such heretics deserve, that is, in confiscation of the goods he had in this country, which are handed over to the authorities and to the royal treasure. First and foremost he must be defrocked in a solemn ceremony as required of those who have taken their first vows, as he says he has. He was turned over to the civil authorities to be burned and because his offense was so great that it cannot be sufficiently punished in his person, the penalty extends to his heirs, that is to his male children and grand-children who are hereby pronounced disqualified to hold any ecclesiastical or public or honorary office or make use of them by common law, by royal pragmatics and in-structions of this Holy Office.[71]

A Network of Dissidents

Correspondence between the inquisitors at Seville and the Supreme Council increased rapidly during the fall of 1557, especially after the capture of Julianillo. They were particularly concerned about finding the most effective ways to proceed against those "wealthy, influential" citizens who had received the lit-erature brought in by Julianillo: Juan Ponce de Leon, Cristobal de Losada, Maria Enriquez de Ribera, Ana de Deza, Domingo de Guzman, etc. In 1556, Andres Gasco had joined the inquisitors in Seville. His uncle Dr. Martin Gasco, who had been canon since 1525, was behind this appointment. As the workload began to pile up for only two—Andres Gasco and Miguel del Carpio—, in September of 1558, Inquisitor General Fernando de Valdes sent for the Bishop of Tarazona, Juan Gonzalez de Munebrega, to join them.[72] Gasco and Carpio often came in conflict with the old bishop. Gonzalez de Munebrega had been an inquisitor for several years elsewhere and was known for his impulsive temperament and lack of scruples. In contrast, Gasco was slightly more cautious and often tried to play for time when deciding on final sentences. They all agreed, however, that the capture of Julian Hernandez was,

---

70 BNE, ms. 9175, f. 258r.
71 AHN, Inquisición, leg. 2942, doc. 117, in: Lopez Muñoz (2011, 197–199, doc. 96).
72 Juan Gonzalez de Munebrega had been inquisitor in Sardenya, Sicily, Cuenca, Valencia, Valladolid, and visiting inquisitor in Catalonia. He was Inquisitor Extraordinary and vice Inquisitor General under Inquisitor General Fernando de Valdes from 1558 to 1562.

The thread that led them to a great ball of wool. They seized five monks from San Isidoro, one of which was the prior of the monastery in Ecija. Eleven monks of the order had fled to Germany, but in all, between those captured and those escaped, they made up sixteen. They also seized a priest, one Juan Gonzalez, who preached in Seville and confessed many people. Besides him, they seized his mother and three sisters, who when they learned he had been taken prisoner ate the letters and buried the books. They took them all prisoners together with all the printed material they found in their house. They have also seized Cantillana, head sacristan of the Cathedral, together with his whole household and his son-in-law the famous physician, Licenciado Losada. Many more are in prison and every day more are being seized. The city would have been totally lost and full of Lutherans if God had not remedied this evil.[73]

Juan Ponce de Leon was the first to be arrested in connection with the literature brought in by Julian Hernandez in 1557. He was the son of Rodrigo Ponce de Leon (1493–1530), Count of Bailen and Duke of Arcos, and a cousin of Luis Ponce de Leon, 2nd Duke of Arcos. Juan Ponce de Leon was one of Julian Hernandez's accomplices in introducing Protestant literature into Seville. He was imprisoned in the fall of 1557 and later released, possibly thanks to the intervention of his cousin.[74] He was rearrested and imprisoned the following year, but there was disagreement among the inquisitors regarding his sentence. The bishop of Tarazona wanted to send him to the stake immediately, but Gasco kept stalling and making excuses. The Council sided with Gasco.[75] Nevertheless, Ponce de Leon was sent to the stake on September 24, 1559, at the first *auto-da-fe* against the evangelicals in Seville.[76] The inquisitors were not content with punishing only him, but extended the dishonor of being burned at the stake for heresy to his male descendants: "His sons and grandsons are not allowed to hold public office or ecclesiastical benefit, etc."[77] An anonymous account of the September 24 *auto-da-fe* reads as follows:

In San Francisco square two large platforms were erected: one for the inquisitors and the Cathedral authorities and for the Franciscan friars; the other for the offenders, together with all the priests and friars of the other orders, and where there was an altar to defrock Juan Gonzalez. And on one side of the square there was another large platform for the city authorities and next to the platform where the inquisitors were seated there was one for the duchess of Bejar and other marquises and knights. Next to the platform of the offenders, there was one for the other nobles and grandees, and placed around the entire square were many scaffolds where multitudes of people were seated. It is said that people started coming to Seville to see the *auto* three days before it

73 BNE, ms. 6176, f. 48v, in: Lopez Muñoz (2011, 116, doc. 38).
74 AHN, Inquisición, leg. 2942, doc. 82, in: Lopez Muñoz (2011, 182, doc. 88); AHN, Inquisición, lib. 575, f. 55v, in: Lopez Muñoz (2011, 115, doc. 37).
75 AHN, Inquisición, leg. 2942, doc. 57, in: Lopez Muñoz (2011, 139, doc. 55).
76 AGS, Estado, leg. 137, doc. 2, in: Lopez Muñoz (2011, 160, doc. 81).
77 BNE, ms. 721, f. 93r. y ss, in: Lopez Muñoz (2011, 456, doc. 262).

was held. So many people came that there was no room in the inns and many had to find
lodging in the country. All the way from the Castle of Triana to the river scaffolds were
put up to accommodate the people. Gates were placed on the Triana bridge so that the
people would not obstruct the view of those in the ships and boats in the river because
there were so many people who wanted to see the event.

The two or three hundred men, well groomed and with their swords, who accompanied
the offenders on foot were a wonder to be seen. They all marched in order with their
drummers and banners before them up to Triana Castle, where they waited at the gate
for the offenders and from there accompanied them to San Francisco square. Around
four in the morning, fifty priests carrying the cross of Saint Ann had gone to the castle
where they met up with forty friars of different orders and they all marched together in
procession with the offenders. For this auto, and to accompany the inquisitors all the
clerics of the cathedral and the various churches of the city were invited and were seated
according to their order and antiquity. First came those of the Cross of Saint Ann with
their abbots and friars, followed by twenty alguaciles with their chief alguacil, don
Sancho. Next to him came the head alguacil of the Holy Office, don Luis Sotelo. Next
came eighty offenders in the habits [sanbenitos] and carrying candles, followed by
twenty-one who were to be burned together with a statue of Francisco de Zafra, who
escaped from the castle. Next came the town council with their sergeant-at-arms before
them followed by the cathedral chapter with their two vergers[78] before them. At the end
came the inquisitors with their crimson banner decorated on one side with the arms of
Saint Peter and the arms of his majesty, which had been newly made for the occasion.
There were three bishops present: one from Lugo, one from Tarazona and one from
Sanabria. This is the order of escort and seniority that was observed in the procession
from Triana to San Francisco square.

It now remains to be told how the orders were assigned to the offenders and what the
offenders did and said the night they were told they were to die. First they summoned
eight Jesuit priests, twelve Dominicans and four of the Trinitarian order, six of the
Victorian order, four of the St. Agustin order and several others of the order of Carmen,
San Francisco and Merced. They all met together from four in the afternoon on Saturday until eight in the evening. Then at nine, the inquisitors called the rector of the
Company of Jesus—the order they put in first place—and his assistant, and that night
they delivered Juan Ponce de Leon to them so they might bring him back to the faith,
because he was a hopeless Lutheran. And although he had been in prison two years
already, he had not given up his Lutheran errors. But after the rector had spoken with
him and confessed him, he did not object to die in the faith as a true Christian
[Catholic]. [Ponce] had held very serious errors and heresies, among which was that he
did not believe in purgatory, that the inquisitors were antichrists, that the pope as not to
be believed or obeyed, nor his bulls to be admitted or obeyed, that confession of sin was
not to be made to priests or abbots but only to God and from the heart, and that the
Eucharist was not to be adored. Once, when he as in the courtyard of the cathedral, he
saw them carry in the Eucharist and he had hidden behind a column to avoid it, and he

78 Officers who carry a rod before a bishop or dean as a symbol of office.

advised others to do the same and he persuaded them not to worship it. He was the first to receive Lutheran books from Germany. He confessed that, after he received the letters from Germany, he asked the person [Julianillo] who brought them where the books were. He [Julianillo] told him that they were hidden in the countryside because he could not bring them into the city without putting himself in danger. Juan Ponce de Leon told him that he wanted to see them and he went alone with his mule and some saddlebags which he filled with book and he brought them back to his house and the following day he began to distribute them among the people he knew would keep the secret. He gave the person who brought the books [Julianillo] twenty ducats to help him with his expenses. A few days later, Juan Ponce de Leon met again with the others on a fish day, and after discussing matters concerning that accursed, satanic sect [Lutherans], they killed some pigeons and ate them. A few days later, they met again to discuss the convenience of having a meeting place in order to read and teach matters concerning that accursed sect. Ponce de Leon offered to buy some land and build a sort of mosque, so there they could learn more about that accursed sect. And Ponce assigned there a certain person, a priest, to be their leader, whose name the sentence does not declare. After that, he would often go to the "quemadero"[79] and would say in a loud voice with his arms raised, "May our Lord grant that for my beliefs I may some day be burned and brought to ashes. Then I will know I am saved. And may my wife and children also suffer with me in this place for the same." On another occasion, he said he wished he had twenty thousand ducats to spend to spread his opinions throughout Spain and thereby teach people to be Christians and to see how misleading their faith was. He also said that to conform he pretended that he confessed, and when it was time for mass [in his private chapel] he would send his servants out on errands so that when they returned they took for granted he had taken communion. And he would hide away in his private chapel and that way he complied with those around him. These characteristics were also present in the others that were burned that day, the same Lutheran errors...

Next they called Father Gonzalez of the Company and his assistant, and they delivered to him licentiate Juan Gonzalez, a priest and preacher, a man who was well known in Seville. He immediately became very upset and began to ask why he hadn't been told [he was to die] six days earlier. Father Gonzalez told him there was no need for that because there was enough time to confess his sins between nine in the evening on Saturday and six in the afternoon on Sunday, when he was to die, and that the person who did not convert in that time would not have converted in the six days either, and that way he calmed him down the best he could. As for his errors, he never came to admit being a Lutheran, only that he had held certain Lutheran propositions. He held the same errors as Ponce de Leon, to which were added certain Islamic errors for which he was convicted in Cordoba when he was twelve years old. This Juan Gonzalez was brought up a Muslim and they could never make him admit that he had offended our Lord while in that accursed sect. He kept reciting many of the psalms of David— Lutheran style—, psalms that had to do with confidence, not with justice or penitence

---

79 A place where people were taken to be burned at the stake, until then mainly Judaizers.

or the fear of God. And to see all of them call on God Lutheran style and language was enough to drive people crazy, but on the other hand they were all confirmed Lutherans.

Juan Gonzalez had aroused some suspicions, but our Lord had had mercy on him. He was formally defrocked on the platform together with a friar from the San Isidro monastery.[80] And standing on the platform with his two sisters, with no shame of fear of God, he spoke to them "in Lutheran language" [Bible verses?], which they understood, and they answered him in the same. At that point the Jesuit father stood up and reprehended him and they gagged him, which greatly upset him. Many Lutheran books were found among the belongings of this Juan Gonzalez. The worst thing was that he never would admit whom he shared his errors with, implying that he did not sin. Thus, though he received punishment for his errors, he did not want others to be punished for his sake. But they all held the same errors as Juan [Ponce de Leon]. Juan Gonzalez was sent to the stake together with two of his sisters who held his same errors.

Next they called in two Dominican friars, and delivered to them a young girl by the name of Maria de Bohorquez...[This part of the narrative is continued in chapter X, p. 234.]

Next, and all at the same time, the inquisitors delivered the other offenders to the other aforementioned priests. Among the offenders was a friar from San Isidro. They tried to make him recant from his errors, which were the same as those of Juan Ponce de Leon, though some were even worse: for example, that the bulls issued by the pope were to be ignored because they were nothing more than pieces of paper, consequently he did not consider himself excommunicated even though the pope excommunicated all those that had Lutheran books, and he had them and read them from before they had been prohibited and he admitted that he and his fellow friars would go into the choir and recite the hours and sing them Lutheran style. While he was a prisoner, he tried to convince some of his fellow prisoners to believe Lutheran doctrines—for which he was willing to die—, but once they realized what he was trying to do they separated him. He was very circumspect in his confession and until he saw that the inquisitors understood him, he did not want to make any declarations. He was upset while on the platform and showed few signs of contrition. He was sent to the stake. He was from Seville and the son of a silversmith.

All those that were sent to the stake, which were twenty-one in all, coincided in Lutheran errors. They also took out, together with these twenty one, a statue of Francisco de Zafra, an incumbent parish priest of the church of San Vicente of this city, who was married to a beata, who was among those they sent to the stake, and with whom he lived as man and wife. As for his man, until now we do not know if he is dead or alive. Of all those sent to the stake that day there is nothing special to report except that Zafra, while a prisoner, escaped from the castle, and as already stated, nothing is known about him up until now. It is believed that if he had been found many things regarding this wicked sect would have been discovered because there is much evidence that they held him in high regard. We will only single out one of these offenders who was a teacher at the

---

80 Either Fray Miguel Carpintero or Fray Francisco Morcillo.

school of the Niños de la Doctrina Cristiana in this city.[81] He was a staunch Lutheran and refused to convert despite all the things they did to him, but stood with his eyes lifted to heaven, as if he were the "más católico" [best Christian] in the world. He was so hardened that after his sentence was read with all his errors, the inquisitors asked him if he still wished to continue in those errors and he answered that he did, that was his wish and none other. At that point the inquisitors ordered the cross to be taken away from him and a clamp put on his tongue, all of which he accepted respectfully, lifting his eyes to heaven as if to thank God that he could suffer for him and his law, because he believed that to hold those errors was to abide by the law of God. He was then greatly pressed by the priests to abandon those opinions so they would not burn him alive, and he more or less insinuated that he would convert. This man held all the same errors as Juan [Ponce de Leon] except regarding confession. After two audiences with the inquisitors, at the third audience he was warned to tell the truth, for which he requested four sheets of paper. He confessed all the same errors as Juan [Ponce de Leon] except that he never allowed the young boys to recite the articles of faith or the Ten Commandments. He also believed that images were not to be worshiped, the simple fornication was not a sin, and that the pope was the antichrist. He also confessed that he had sinned when he had told the inquisitors that those were Lutheran errors and that he hated them, and that he rectified and instead of errors he considered them holy doctrine and that he hoped to be saved by them. This he said on the four sheets of paper. He was sent to the stake and caused great doubts regarding his salvation because until the last minute he had been very critical of the [catholic] faith and very confirmed in his errors.

[The report then tells the case of a false accusation of a black slave against his master.]

It remains to give the name of the persons sent to the stake. They were four women[82] and seventeen[83] men, and the statue of Zafra, the priest who fled. The only one who was a citizen of Seville was Juan [Ponce de Leon] and the friar from San Isidro and the daughter of Pero Garcia de Jerez. All the others were foreigners [not born in Seville].[84] This is all that can be reported so far. After the sentences were read, they were all taken

---

81 Hernando de San Juan, who is described as one who converted at the last minute in order not to be burned alive.
82 There were actually seven women: María de Bohórquez, María de Virués, Francisca López, María de Cornejo, Isabel de Baena, Catalina González, and María González,
83 According to other documents [AHN, Inquisición, leg. 2075, doc. 1; AGS, Estado, leg. 29, doc. 2; BNE, ms. 9175, f. 226r] eleven men were sentenced to the stake for holding Lutheran opinions (Juan Gonçález, Juan Ponçe de León, Hernando de San Juan, Medel de Espinosa, Luis de Ábrego, Carlos de Brujas, Luis de Sosa, Juan de Zafra, Antonio Bouldre, Fray Miguel Carpintero, Fray Francisco Morcillo). Three *moriscos* (Francisco de la Cámara, Diego Ortiz de Herrera, and Diego de Herrera) were burned that day for practicing Muslim beliefs. In other words, a total of fourteen men, not seventeen.
84 Juan Gonzalez and his sisters Catalina and Maria were from Palma de Micergilio; Medel de Espinosa was from Espinosa de los Monteros, Luis de Ábrego was from Niebla, Luis de Sosa was from Tenerife, Juan de Zafra was from Almendral, and Francisca López was from Manzanilla. There were actually only two foreigners: Carlos de Brujas (Flemish) and Antonio Bouldre (French).

to the "*quemadero*" accompanied by the city authorities and a throng of priests and abbots that comforted them along the way.[85]

Cristobal de Losada was arrested about the same time as those mentioned in the above document but he was not sent to the stake with them. He was a well-known and well-connected physician, the personal physician of Maria Enriquez de Ribera, marchioness of Villanueva del Fresno. According to Montes (1569, f. 78v), Losada first came in contact with evangelical teaching through Juan de Cantillana,[86] whose daughter he had fallen in love with:

> This Losada, being a suitor to Juan de Cantillana's daughter, although he had a good social position, handsomely learned and better seen in his faculty than a great many practioners, yet would he not grant unto him his good will for having his daughter to wife till he were for a while a student to Dr. Egidio and learned of him some godly and virtuous instructions. A very hard condition surely for a learned man and one that thought himself sufficiently catechized to submit himself to another man's instruction, but especially to Dr. Egidio who was commonly suspected of heresy at that time. Nevertheless, at length he condescended thereto, whether for virtue sake as desirous of better instruction or for his wife's, I know not.

How long Losada was instructed by Dr. Egidio is uncertain, probably several years. In any case, Losada, together with the parish priest Francisco de Zafra and the printer Luis de Abrego, were Julianillo's main agents in getting his load of clandestine literature into the city. For several years, from Dr. Egidio's arrest to the time Losada was arrested in October of 1557, he "took it upon himself and very well discharged the office of a preacher among the congregation." (Montes: 1569, f. 78v). According to Inquisition records, it was the head monk of the San Isidoro Monastery in Santiponce, Gabriel de Funes, who alerted the inquisitors of Losada's "subversive" activities and his friendship with the monks that had fled, especially Antonio del Corro and Casiodoro de Reina.[87] At his trial, Losada admitted having translated Calvin's *Catechism* from Latin into Spanish and having written several things himself on the Epistles of St. Paul and the Psalms of David. Because he refused to implicate others, on October 2, 1561, it was voted that he be sent to the torture chamber and finally, on January 23, 1562, the inquisitors voted unanimously to send him to the stake, which occurred on April 26, 1562. In all, Losada spent nearly five years in prison. Among Losada's fellow prisoners were many of the leaders of the underground congregation: Juan Ponce de Leon, the *colporteur* Julian Hernandez, the *morisco* preacher Juan

---

85 BNE, ms. 6176, f. 310r. [1], in: Lopez Muñoz (2011, 166–173, doc. 83). Notes and brackets mine.

86 Juan de Cantillana was sentenced to the stake at the *auto* of October 28, 1562. AHN, In-quisición, leg. 4514 (2), doc. 15, in: Lopez Muñoz (2011, 278, doc. 130).

87 AHN, Inquisición, leg. 4514, doc. 15, in: Lopez Muñoz (2011, 349, doc. 166).

Gonzalez, the Dominican friar Domingo de Guzman, the printer Luis de Abrego, etc. Luis de Abrego was sentenced to the stake on September 24, 1559, together with Francisco de Zafra's father,[88] Juan Gonzalez and his two sisters, Juan Ponce de Leon, Hernando de San Juan, Medel de Espinosa, Luis de Sosa, Maria de Bohorquez, Maria de Virues, Francisca Lopez, Maria Cornejo, and Isabel de Baena.[89] Guzman's sentence was not pronounced until July 11, 1563.[90]

One serious problem that confronted the inquisitors at Seville at that time was the lack of space for so many prisoners. According to Montes (1569, f. 32v),

> While Inquisitor Gonzalez de Munebrega remained in commission at Seville, so many were apprehended for professing the gospel, that he was forced to house some of them in his own lodging because all the prisons in the town were not able to receive them, the number was so great.

Seeing that there were not enough cells in Triana to hold all the prisoners, on June 8, 1559, Inquisitor Gonzalez de Munebrega wrote to the Supreme Council asking for a solution.[91] The answer was forthcoming: "those members of the Holy House living in Triana should either share rooms or move out temporarily, but they [the inquisitors] would soon also receive a letter from the king enabling them to make use of houses nearby."[92] This may not have been a welcome thought for some, especially for Andres Gasco, who occupied two sumptuously furnished flats in the Castle of Triana. On his dying bed, in 1566, he confessed: "I have not been the kind of priest that God and his holy apostles ordered and the holy councils instituted and wanted priest to be, but I have been a profane priest, a friend of this world and its pleasures." (Wagner: 1979, 153). Gasco came from a very wealthy family, yet the inventory of his suite at Triana—tapestries, paintings, objects of silver and gold, cut glass, the huge sums of ready money, the collection of precious stones of emeralds and topaz—suggests other sources (Wagner: 1979, 152).

---

88 During the time of elderly Zafra's imprisonment, their possessions were sold, but the money obtained from the sale was not enough to cover the elderly Zafra's expenses while in Triana and money had to be added from the treasury. AHN, Inquisición, leg. 2943, doc. 144 (2).

89 AGS, Estado, leg. 137, doc. 3; AHN, Inquisición, leg. 2075, doc. 1 (2), in: Lopez Muñoz (2011, 160, doc. 81; 274, doc. 129); AHN, Inquisición, leg. 4514 (2), doc. 15, in: Lopez Muñoz (2011, 349, doc. 166).

90 AHN, Inquisición, leg. 2943, doc. 100–2; leg. 2943, doc. 116–1, in: Lopez Muñoz (2011, 303, doc. 144; 312, doc. 150).

91 AHN, Inquisición, leg. 2942, doc. 69.

92 AHN, Inquisición, leg. 2942, doc. 67, in: Lopez Muñoz (2011, 150, doc. 68).

Certain Escapees

We will conclude this section with the story of several individuals who managed to escape, though some were later recaptured. When Julian Hernandez realized he had delivered some of his books to the wrong person, he fled but was caught. The official report states:

> Julian got word of this and fled. But the inquisitors took great pains and sought for him so diligently in all the towns and roads that they caught him in the mountains of Cordoba near Adamuz. The inquisitor locked him in prison on October 7, 1557, together with a nobleman who had fled and was found in Ecija.[93]

Fray Benito, a lay priest from San Isidoro, sentenced to house arrest, escaped in 1565 from the monastery where he had been confined.[94] The parish priest Francisco de Zafra, taken prisoner on October 9, 1557, escaped three weeks later. He was burned in effigy two years later, on September 24, 1559. Juan Antonio Llorente (1843, 213) relates his story:

> The effigy was that of Francis Zafra, the beneficed priest of the parish of St. Vincent of Seville, who was condemned as a Lutheran, but had made his escape. Gonzalez de Montes gives a long account of this man, which I found to be correct, on examining the papers of the holy office. He says that Francis Zafra was well versed in the Scriptures; for some time he succeeded in concealing his inclination to Lutheranism, and was employed by the inquisitors to qualify denounced propositions, and that he was thus enabled to save many persons from being condemned. He had received into his house one of the women called Beates, who (after obstinately supporting the new doctrines) became so much deranged, that he was obliged to confine and scourge her, to calm her violence. In 1555, this woman escaped, and denounced three hundred persons as Lutherans to the Inquisition: the inquisitors drew up a list of them; Francis Zafra was summoned, and although he was mentioned as one of the principal heretics, they could not receive the evidence of a person whose mind was so much disordered. As the holy office never neglected anything that could assist in discovering heresy, this list caused the conduct of many persons to be strictly observed, and more than eight hundred were arrested; Francis Zafra was one of the prisoners, but he contrived to escape, and was burnt in effigy as contumacious.

An anonymous report sent to the Supreme Council from Granada describes Zafra's escape:

> The next day they arrested a beneficiary of the parish of San Vicente in Seville, who shortly after he was imprisoned escaped from the highest tower of the Castle of Triana where they had put him. They cannot tell if it was his own doing or if it was the devil that

---

93 BNE, ms. 6176, f. 48v, in: Lopez Muñoz (2011, 115, doc. 38). Montes's account, though more exhaustive, is basically the same. See Montes (1569, ff. 73r–75r).

94 AHN, Inquisición, leg. 2943, doc. 149–2.

helped him or if it was with the help of some citizens of the city who were afraid he would betray them. They have not found him anywhere. His name is so-and-so de Zafra. Many more are in prison and every day more are being seized. The city would have been totally lost and full of Lutherans if God had not remedied this evil.[95]

For some unknown reason the inquisitors at Seville did not inform the Supreme Council of Zafra's escape immediately. They may have hoped to recapture him themselves and not have to report it. A month went by before they sent the following report:

On the eve of this past All Saints' Day a priest by the name of Francisco de Zafra, beneficiary of the church of San Vicente here in Seville, escaped from the prisons of the Holy Office. He is a little over thirty years old, average height, has a pale thin face, small sad somewhat sunken eyes, a black beard, a big mouth and a big nose. If needs be, when you look at his legs and arms you will find ligature marks of ropes [used in torture]. He has a high-pitched effeminate voice. We think he has gone to Laredo [on the Atlantic coast between Santander and Bilbao] and from there will take a boat to Flanders or England or Germany. And because this person is very important for the Holy Office, we urge you to send notification to your commissioners or the persons the Holy Office has stationed at Laredo to diligently search the ships that are in that port and the inns and boarding houses in order to find the said Zafra. Once found, have him sent, well chained, to the prisons of the Holy Office [here in Seville]. We will cover all the costs in which you may incur.[96]

Several foreigners also managed to escape. For example, Francisco de Tesa, a Frenchman, who escaped from Triana in May of 1563. Tesa, a maker of glass beads by trade, was first arrested and sent to Triana sometime in 1561. At the *auto* held on April 26, 1562, he abjured *de vehementi* and was sentenced to row in the king's galleys for five years. While serving as a rower, he was overheard to say things against the Catholic religion and in favor of Luther. Denounced to the Inquisition, he was re-arrested and taken back to Triana and put in chains awaiting execution. But on the night of May 17, 1563, he broke his chains and escaped through the roof and let himself down the wall by means of a rope he made with pieces of mattress cloth.[97] It was suspected that he returned to France via Bilbao or Laredo.[98] Two years later, Inquisitors Gasco, Carpio, and Pazos informed the Supreme Council that Francisco de Tesa had been seen in Bayona and was going by the name of Carlos. They advised the inquisitors of Valladolid, Zaragoza, Barcelona, and Calahorra to be on the look out for him.[99] He was burned in effigy at Seville. Likewise, Julian Balton, a cabin boy from Saint-Malo

---

95 BNE, ms. 6176, f. 48v, in: Lopez Muñoz (2011, 115, doc. 38).
96 AHN, Inquisición, leg. 2942, doc. 47, in: Lopez Muñoz (2011, 114, doc. 36). Brackets mine.
97 AHN, Inquisición, leg. 2943, doc. 100–1, in: Lopez Muñoz (2011, 303, doc. 144).
98 AHN, Inquisición, leg. 2943, doc. 100–1.
99 AHN, Inquisición, leg. 2943, 104–1.

(France) working on the ship *Margarita,* sentenced to perpetual prison on May 13, 1565, and Jorge de Leni, trumpeter on the same ship, escaped and were burned in effigy at the *auto* held four years later, on May 8, 1569. (Schäfer: 2014, II 459, doc. 294).

Another foreigner that escaped was the Flemish merchant Alejandre Lopez. It is uncertain when Lopez was arrested, but his name appears in the list of those reconciled at the *auto* of September 24, 1559, and sentenced to life in prison.[100] On November 17, 1561, the inquisitors informed the Supreme Council that Lopez had escaped. They notified the inquisitors in Lisbon, where they thought he would go, but doubted if they could find him because he was very "*ladino y avisado*" (crafty and cautious).[101]

The English factor John Frampton was imprisoned some time in November of 1559. According to his testimony, he was put in a cell with "an old man of the city of Seville, one of the aldermen of the city, called there a *jurado*. There was also a scholar of Salamanca, and a preacher, a priest." (Fittler/Skelton: 1820–1840, I, 357–367). The *jurado* may have been Diego de Virues; the scholar from Salamanca must have been Domingo de Baltanas; the preacher was very likely Fray Domingo de Guzman of the Order of Preachers; the priest was probably Diego Lopez, a monk from the San Isidoro monastery. They were in the same cell together for fourteen months.

According to the records of the High Court of Admiralty in London, where Frampton's case was seen in December 1572, he had sailed from Bristol to Lisbon, where he received bills of exchange on Seville for 2,100 ducats for cloth that he sold there. From Lisbon he sailed to Cadiz, where he left his ship, making his way to Hugh Tipton's house in Seville to deposit the bills, and from there he went overland to Malaga to buy wine. During his absence, officers were sent by the Inquisition to search his ship where they found a book that gave them the pretext to accuse him of heresy. He was arrested in Malaga and taken back to Seville in chains where he was questioned, his goods and those of the other merchants he represented immediately confiscated, and he himself put in prison. He was sentenced at the *auto-da-fe* held on December 22, 1560, to a year's confinement in another prison and the prohibition to leave Spain (Beecher: 2006, 113).[102] After his release, with the help of the English ambassador, he continued to claim his confiscated goods. His appeal before the Spanish court was still pending in 1568 when diplomatic rupture between England and Spain caused suspension of all legal actions. By the time relations were renewed, in

---

100 AHN, Inquisición, leg. 2075, doc. 1 (2); AGS, Estado, leg. 137, doc. 2, in: Lopez Muñoz (2011, 212, doc. 101).

101 AHN, Inquisición, leg. 2943, doc. 43, in: Lopez Muñoz (2011, 249, doc. 117).

102 Also see AHN, Inquisición, leg. 2075, doc. 1 (2); AGS, Estado, leg. 137, doc. 3; BNE, ms. 9175, f. 258r, in: Lopez Muñoz (2011, 212, doc. 101; 218, doc. 102).

1573, Frampton had escaped to England and had begun proceedings before the English court.[103] He had made his escape sometime in 1567. Back in England, he wrote an account of his treatment while in Triana and years later the historian John Strype, who had access to official papers, reproduced part of Frampton's story in his *Annals of the Reformation* (1709).

Another case, reported by the inquisitors at Seville in February 1574, was the escape of Catalina de Medina, widow of alderman Juan Alonso de Medina. It appears that Catalina had been imprisoned at one time but absolved. She was re-arrested and sentenced to house arrest for ten years. After only a year the sentence was commuted to fastings, prayers, and hearing mass every Saturday at Our Lady of La Antigua, a chapel within the cathedral. Catalina took advantage of one of these "outings" to the cathedral and escaped along with Cristobal de Escalante, a silversmith, "with whom she was cohabiting."[104] The inquisitors not only lamented the fact that they were heading for Germany to reunite with others "of the Lutheran sect" but that they were taking great quantities of valuables with them. A minute description of the party, how they were traveling, and where they were seen last was sent out. Five days later, Inquisitors Carpio and Salazar offered more information, that is, that a year or so earlier Cristobal de Escalante had made an agreement with a French sea captain to take him, Catalina de Medina, her sister Isabel de Avila, Maria de la Fuente and her sister Leonor de las Casas, together with some of their children and servants to France "in order to practice his profession [silversmith] there."[105] Because these women were on the list of persons suspected of Lutheran leanings, the inquisitors suspected that they were going for other reasons. Consequently, all the seaports within a month's journey from Seville were warned to be on the look out for them:

> Catalina de Medina is around fifty years old, of a fair complexion, and chubby. Her sister Isabel is around thirty-five, good looking, thin, fair complexion. Escalante has dark hair and a thick black beard. He is rather fat with a yellowish complexion and he stutters. It is supposed they have with them a daughter of Catalina's, a girl around fifteen or sixteen years old with a pretty face and good-natured, and a well-built son of nine or ten. It is also supposed they have with them a fourteen-year-old daughter of Escalante's but we do not know what she looks like. They are travelling together, the women in carts owned by Joan Garcia, of Seville, and Escalante on a mule. Fifteen days ago they were seen three leagues (nine miles) beyond Cordoba.[106]

---

103 The Treaty of Bristol (August 1574) was designed to balance shipping loss claims on both sides and inhibit further Inquisition actions against English merchants for religious activities (Beecher: 2006, 320–339).
104 AHN, Inquisición, leg. 2946, doc. 33, in: Lopez Muñoz (2011, 418, doc. 225).
105 AHN, Inquisición, leg. 2946, doc. 175, in: Lopez Muñoz (2011, 420, doc. 226). Brackets mine. Both Calatina and her sister Isabel are referred to with the title "donna" which suggests they belonged to the upper class or the nobility.
106 AHN, Inquisición, leg. 2946, doc. 33, in: Lopez Muñoz (2011, 418, doc. 225).

The group was caught in Valdestillas, just south of Valladolid, and confined to the "secret prisons" (*carceles secretas*) for at least a year. In a letter to the inquisitors at Seville, dated February 20, 1576, the Supreme Council suggested the following sentence for the group:

> The two female slaves—Luisa and Cecilia—, together with Maria de la Fuente's servant girl Isabel, and Catalina, the daughter of Cristobal de Escalante, and Beatriz, the daughter of Catalina de Medina, should be separated from their mistresses and mothers and put in separate cells so they cannot communicate one with the other. Against Cristobal de Escalante is to be added the charge of concubinage, and against Catalina de Medina were to be added the three previous charges for which she had been arrested in the first place. Above all, these four women are to explain the close friendship they had had—under torture if necessary—with Juan Gonzalez y Diego de Figueroa, *relajados*, and with Ana de Deza, Catalina Nuñez, and others strongly suspected of heresy. And at all these interrogatories Pablo García, secretary of the Supreme Council must be present.[107]

Finally, in July of 1576 they were all sentenced to house arrest, but in places far enough apart from each other that there was no way they could communicate.[108]

The Captives in Barbary

Those who saw their lives and families in danger of being taken into custody by the Inquisition, and had the means, sought for ways to escape. One way of escape was by sea, but sixteenth century Mediterranean sea travel had its inherent dangers: disease, shipwreck, storms, pirate attacks, etc. Indeed, Barbary pirates, operating primarily from the ports of Algeria, Tunisia, and Tripoli in Libya— known as the Barbary Coast—controlled the Mediterranean sea lanes. In addition to seizing and plundering ships, captured Christians were sold into slavery. According to the American historian Robert Davis (2004), from the sixteenth to the nineteenth century, the Barbary pirates captured an estimated 800,000 to one million people as slaves. Evidence that there were Spanish evangelicals among the captives held prisoners in Northern Africa is gleaned from a treatise—written in Spanish—by Cipriano de Valera and published in

---

107 AHN, Inquisición, lib. 578, in: Lopez Muñoz (2011, 428, doc. 238). Juan Gonzalez, the morisco preacher, was relajado (burned at the stake) on September 24, 1559; Diego [Suarez] de Figueroa, related to the dukes of Feria, on April 26, 1562. Catalina Nuñez was probably Catalina de Villalobos, wife of the silversmith Pedro de Sosa and aunt of Nuñez sisters hence the error. Catalina was sentenced on December 22, 1560, to life in prison (AHN, Inquisición, leg. 2075, doc. 1 (2)). Her husband was burned in effigy on April 26, 1562.
108 AHN, Inquisición, leg. 2946, in: Lopez Muñoz (2011, 438, doc. 243).

England in 1594.[109] Who these captives were, how many there were, where they were from, and how long they had been there is impossible to know. Some must have been there already in the early 1570s because in 1576 the Supreme Council wrote the inquisitors at Seville that they had learned from "a Lutheran, who *en tierra de moros* (in the land of the Moors) had renounced his faith," that hundreds of Lutheran books had been introduced into Seville that summer.[110]

Valera addresses these captives "as pitiful and oppressed captives submitted day and night to great afflictions and physical labor." We can also deduce from Valera's words that they were recent adherents to evangelical teaching: "I have learned of the great compassion and mercies the Father of all mercies and compassion has bestowed on you in the recent past, who not being brought up and trained in the reading of the Holy Scriptures, and who, of his great mercy, clemency and goodness, according to his eternal council and decree, has desired to remove you from the ignorance in which you were brought up." (Usoz: 1854, VIII, 1. Translation mine). The treatise was essentially a manual of instruction to confirm these recent converts in their faith and to uphold them in reformed doctrine. This, the author states, was necessary because "on account of the profession you make as Reformed Christians you will necessarily have conflicts while you live in Barbary with three different kinds of people: Catholics, Jews and Muslims, but mainly with the devil, who will tempt you with all sorts of temptations" (Usoz: 1854, VIII, 47). It was a very real temptation to convert because converting made them eligible for ransom.

How large and how disperse the community of evangelical captives was in uncertain. It would have included a whole range of individuals from galley slaves serving out their sentences on Spanish ships to families fleeing the Inquisition by ship, captured by Barbary corsairs and carried to Algiers, Tunis, or Tripoli.[111]

---

109 Cipriano de Valera, Tratado para confirmar los pobres cautivos de Berbería, en la católica i antigua fe i religión cristiana i para los consolar con la palabra de Dios en las aflicciones que padezen por el Evangelio de Jesucristo (London: Peter Short, 1594).

110 In 1576, the Supreme Council wrote the inquisitors at Seville that they had learned that Lutheran books had been introduced into Seville from a Lutheran, who "*en tierra de moros*" (in the land of the Moors) had renounced his faith. AHN, Inquisición, lib. 579, f. 4v, in: Lopez Muñoz (2011, 439, doc. 244).

111 All of those sent to the galleys, accused of being "Lutherans" in the *autos-da-fe* between 1562 and 1565, were foreigners. See, for example, AHN, Inquisición, leg. 2075, doc. 3; leg. 2943, doc. 149-2, in: Lopez Muñoz (2011, 307, doc. 148; 344, doc. 164). Inquisition documents are scarce regarding Spaniards sent to row in Philip II's galleys. In a dispatch dated February 4, 1574, the inquisitors at Seville reply to the Supreme Council's inquiry if they had had any cases of laypersons performing mass. No cases had been detect as yet, however, if they did, the person(s) involved would be accused of "practicing the Lutheran teachings of the priesthood of the believer as found in his *De Abroganda Missa* (On the Abuse of the Mass, 1522)." The suggested punishment—following severe torment—was either im-

Though travel by sea to Genoa or some other port entailed dangers, it was preferable to land travel, especially in mountainous Spain. As we have seen above, Cristobal de Escalante, a silversmith from Seville, had first made arrangements with a French sea captain to take him and others to France. What the corsairs ignored was that these particular captives—regardless how wealthy they may have been—had no one to ransom them.

Cipriano de Valera states that he learned about the captives' plight from a most trustworthy source, both in writing and personal communication. Considering that Valera was living in England, it seems logical that his "trustworthy source" should be an Englishman—and a fellow Protestant—who had known these Spanish captives personally and possibly had himself recently been ransomed and returned to London. One likely candidate is Richard Hasleton, captured in 1582 near Almeria, Spain, and returned to London in 1593. Valera's treatise, printed in 1594, and Hasleton's narrative, printed one year later,[112] have two things in common, that is, the "Catholic versus Protestant" theological debate and the ever-present pressure—by inquisitors, masters, or peers—to convert. Hasleton's account shows his steadfastness in his Protestant convictions when brought before the inquisitors in Majorca; Valera's treatise seeks to inform—and confirm—these recent converts in their new faith, should they be called to answer for it.

As for the number of copies printed, who defrayed the cost and the distribution of Valera's publication, it is worth noting that the printer, Peter Short, was a well-established, well-connected printer-publisher. Any of the big trading companies—the Levant Company, the Barbary Company, the Spanish Company—operating between England and the Mediterranean would have been a suitable channel for distribution (Wright: 1943). In the same way that these companies employed ministers and provided edifying books—the Bible, the Book of Common Prayer, John Foxe's Book of Martyrs (printed by Short), Perkin's works (translated into Spanish by Valera)—for the mariners, they would certainly identify with Valera's endeavor and be willing to transport crates of books to be distributed among the Spanish Protestant captives.

From this we can conclude that the arrival of Lutheran literature in the 1570s, the inventories of confiscated and prohibited books in the 1580s, together with the existence of Spanish evangelical captives in Barbary in the 1590s is evidence that the severe measures taken by the Inquisition in the 1560s were not sufficient to eradicate underground Protestantism in sixteenth century Spain.

---

prisonment or galleys. AHN, Inquisición, leg. 2946, doc. 173, in: Lopez Muñoz (2011, 416, doc. 224).

112 Richard Hasleton, Strange and wonderfull things. Happened to Richard Hasleton, borne at Braintree in Essex, in his ten yeares trauailes in many forraine countries. Penned as he deliuered it from his owne mouth (London, 1595), in: Vitkus/Matar (2001, 73–98).

Chapter 10:
Female Voices in Seville

In the Castle of Triana, December, 1561, the lord Inquisitor Francisco de Soto, and I, Eusebio de Arrieta, notary of the secret, took an inventory of the goods and things that the prisoners, that Juan Perez de Alegria was in charge of, had in their cells. In Ana de Deza's cell, we found a *Gospels and Epistles* by fray Antonio Montesino, in Spanish, 280 pages, with a paper binding, and an Hours of Our Lady in Latin, which Ana confessed she had brought with her with the inquisitors' permission the day she entered the prison. When the inquisitor [Francisco de Soto] was about to take the books with him, she begged him not to take the *Gospels and Epistles* because it was her only comfort and she couldn't live an hour without it.

AHN, *Inquisición*, leg. 2943, doc. 46 (December 2, 1561)

A surprisingly large number of women were imprisoned and condemned to the stake in the sixteenth century in Seville accused of spreading Lutheran doctrine. As was the case with the women accused of heresy in Valladolid, what also characterized the majority of the women in Seville was their high degree of literacy. Considering that no organized evangelical congregations existed for them to be under systematic teaching, it is remarkable how well informed theologically they were, a fact not always duly recognized among women. When commenting on the reception of Erasmian thought in Spain in the 1520s, Thomas M'Crie (1829, 129) inserts the following illustrative excerpt:

> John Maldonat, counselor to Charles V, in a letter, dated Burgos, 3 Dec. 1527, after mentioning a certain Dominican who had been active in inflaming the minds of his brethren against Erasmus, adds, "He has acted in the same way with certain intermeddling nuns, and with some noble women, who in this country have great influence over their husbands in what relates to religion."

In a day and age when female education was private and domestic, one possible explanation for their high degree of literacy could be their elevated social position, which allowed them to have private chaplains and private tutors who instructed them and put them in touch with other like-minded women. These religious leaders would also encourage them to read. Barbara Weissberger (1997, 177) puts it this way: "at issue is women's greater freedom to interpret texts, a freedom fostered by increased literacy and private reading, which were enhanced by the introduction of the printing press." Likewise, as the vernacular became the language of works of theology and devotion, more women had access to them. Alison Weber (1999, 147–48) very rightly observes that, by commissioning translations of medieval mystical texts, Cisneros had opened up new spiritual dimensions for women. The first women who seem to have benefited from Cisneros's undertaking were the *beatas* around Guadalajara. For example, the *alumbrado-deixado* leader Isabel de la Cruz read St. Bonaventure's *Estímulo de amor divino.* Her colleague Maria de Cazalla and her daughters read Juan de Valdes's *Dialog on Christian Doctrine.* Several of the women brought to trial in Seville confessed having read Calvin, without specifying which of his books they had read, though it is to be assumed that the work referred to was his Catechism, translated into Spanish from French by Juan Perez de Pineda and very likely among the volumes smuggled in by Julianillo. The inventories of libraries of women in Seville reveal that, among other books, Constantino's *Doctrina Cristiana* was very popular (Alvarez Márquez: 2004). In addition, a copy of *Gospels and Epistles* graced the shelves of all these libraries.

Another interesting feature, which appears in the Inquisition records, is that many of these women were accused of dogmatizing, that is, teaching "heretical" doctrines. This implies that not only were they pious women anxious to expand their knowledge and increase their own personal spirituality, but women who considered themselves sufficiently well instructed in the new doctrines to edify others. Reginaldo Gonzalez de Montes provides us with the example of Leonor Gomez, who was her niece's "schoolmistress and taught her her catechism and belief (for the profession whereof she should presently be executed)." (Montes: 1569, f. 29v). There is no evidence that Leonor Gomez was a *beata* but simply a well-read lay person.

It is beyond the scope of this survey to analyze the rise of literacy among women in early modern Spain, however, one example that illustrates to what degree the printed word had become of vital importance for some women is found in a dispatch sent by the Venetian ambassador Paulo Tiepolo to the Doge and Senate on March 13, 1561. Though the main subject of the dispatch is the disconcerting arrest of Fray Domingo de Baltanas, the reason for his arrest and the consequence are equally disconcerting:

> In Seville the Inquisition has arrested Friar Domenego de Valtanas, of the Order of St. Dominick, in the Province of Andalusia, a man eighty years of age, and of greater authority and reputation for sanctity than any one else in Spain, so that he had a very great concourse of almost all the nobility of the country who went to him to confess. He has been convicted of opinions contrary to those held by the church, as follows: that he had given to a young lady of noble birth a little book, containing all that he meant her to believe, with which book the young lady shut herself up in her room every day, and remained there a long while, which her father having remarked several times, he asked her what she was doing, and not receiving a satisfactory answer he had her watched, and discovering that she read a book, he asked her what book it was, to which she replied that it was a book about things for which she would not refuse to die; so her father then knew that it must be an heretical book. As this affair did not pass so secretly as not to be heard by some of the household, he, fearing that someone might accuse him to the Inquisition, the penalty being as great for those who do not accuse of what is known to them, as for the person who offends, in order to guarantee himself against confiscation of property to the utter ruin of his family and all his children, determined

to accuse his own daughter, who, being put in prison, confessed that she had received the book from the friar [Valtanas]. It is therefore greatly feared that the friar must have distributed many of these books amongst his penitents, and that this mischief may have spread amongst many nobles and chief personages. (Brown/Bentinck: 1890, 297–306).

The woman's family name is not given, neither have I found any reference to the case in Montes or in the Inquisition records consulted. Was the book one Domingo de Baltanas himself had written? Was it a Latin Bible? Was it a copy of *Gospels and Epistles*, which, as Ana de Deza declared, was her only comfort? Recent studies of reader-response theory focus on the appeal of works of fiction to the female reader, hopefully some day further studies will explore the appeal of works of theology to sixteenth century female readers.

The Bohorquez Sisters

The Bohorquez sisters, Maria and Juana, were the daughters of the prominent judge and wealthy nobleman, Pedro Garcia de Jerez y Bohorquez. Maria, the younger of the two, was born around 1533 and was an illegitimate daughter. She was well educated; she knew Latin and some Greek (Montes: 1569, f. 71r) and had a prodigious memory. On the other hand, assuming that Dr. Egidio was the spiritual director of the Bohorquez family, it would not have been unusual for him to have taught her Latin and Greek. According to the testimony of those that knew Maria, she memorized the *Gospels and Epistles* "to be able to give sound answers of her faith in case some day she was called before the inquisitors." She also had "many Lutheran books, which she memorized so that when the time came that they would be taken away from her, she would know the content well enough to defend herself, and to persuade others, with authority."[1]

Maria de Bohorquez lived in the parish of San Roman, the same parish where the convent of Santa Paula was located.[2] Maria de Virues may have been her duenna, or governess.[3] As such, it was her duty to educate Maria and this would include her spiritual supervision as well as her secular education. As a young girl Maria frequented the convent of Santa Paula, along with Maria de Virues, to hear Dr. Egidio.[4] They must have gone often to hear Dr. Egidio over the ten years— approximately 1540 to 1550—that he preached for the nuns at Santa Paula. Very

---

1 BNE, ms. 6176, f. 310r, in: Lopez Muñoz (2011, 166, doc. 83).
2 Seville was divided into 24 parishes after the reconquest in 1248 by king Fernando III. Since that time, aldermen were called "veinticuatros" (24 s).
3 It would be interesting to be able to establish a relationship between Maria de Virues and Jeronima Agustina Benita de Virues, daughter of Dr. Alonso de Virues, known for her mastery of Latin.
4 AHN, Inquisición, leg. 2942, doc. 78, in: Lopez Muñoz (2011, 191, doc. 95).

likely it was through Dr. Egidio that these two women met other female members of the underground evangelical circle in Seville, in particular Maria de Cornejo and Isabel de Baena. Inquisition records describe Maria de Cornejo as "alias *beata*, a Lutheran heretic, false teacher and false friend, impenitent, in whose house secret meetings were held where Lutheran doctrine was approved of and taught." Isabel de Baena is described in similar terms: "a Lutheran heretic, teacher and false friend, impenitent, who took in and sheltered heretics and in whose house secret meetings were held where Lutheran doctrine was approved of and taught."[5] After Cornejo and Baena were sentenced to the stake on September 24, 1559, orders were given to tear down both of their houses, to spread salt on the lots, and to place a marble slate there explaining what their offense was and why this was done.[6] Maria de Bohorquez was sent to the stake at the same *auto* as Maria de Cornejo and Isabel de Baena, accused of being an "obstinate heretic." An anonymous report of the September 24 *auto* states that only four women were sent to the stake that day: "those that were sent to the stake, which were twenty-one in all, four women and seventeen men" is misleading.[7] Although the total number—collated with three other documents—is correct, the correlation is wrong. There were actually seven women and fourteen men.[8] Did the anonymous reporter purposely downplay the involvement of women in the underground evangelical movement?

Maria Bohorquez's married sister Juana was imprisoned about the time Maria was sent to the stake. She was the second wife of Francisco de Vargas y Silva, Lord of Higuera de Vargas. Juana and Francisco had two sons: Garci Perez de Vargas, who would later inherit his father's title, and Diego de Vargas. Juana was pregnant again when she entered Triana prison. She was initially treated well, but died of internal injuries caused by the rack, shortly after giving birth. The Inquisition records simply state: "Lady Juana de Bohorquez, wife of Francisco de Vargas, citizen of Seville, imprisoned for adhering to the teachings of the Lutheran sect, died in the prisons of the Holy Office. Acquitted."[9] Reginaldo de Montes (1569, ff. 61r–62v), on the other hand, offers more details regarding Juana's story:

> About the same time more or less, the house of the Inquisition at Seville apprehended a certain noblewoman whose name was Doña Juana de Bohorques, the lady and wife of one don Francisco de Vargas, a noble gentleman and Baron of Higuera, daughter of one

---

5 BNE, ms. 9175, f. 226r, in: Lopez Muñoz (2011, 163, doc. 82).
6 AGS, Estado, leg. 137, doc. 2; BNE, ms. 9175, f. 226r, in: Lopez Muñoz (2011, 161, doc. 81; 164, doc. 82).
7 BNE, ms. 6176, f. 310r. [1], in: Lopez Muñoz (2011, 166, doc. 83).
8 See Chapter VII, notes 83 and 84.
9 AHN, Inquisición, leg. 2075, doc. 1 (2); AGS, *Estado*, leg. 137, doc. 3, in: Lopez Muñoz (2011, 212, doc. 101).

Pedro Garcia Xeresio, a very rich citizen of Seville. The cause of her trouble was that a sister of hers, called Maria de Bohorques, a virtuous virgin and one that afterwards was burned for her profession and faith, had confessed in the extremity of her torments that she had conversation with her sister in these matters of religion several times.

This lady, when she was first committed to prison, was with child well nigh half a year, in respect whereof, neither did they shut her up so closely nor dealt with her so harshly as they used to deal with others, for the regard of that which was within her. Notwithstanding, within four days after her deliverance, they took the child away from her and the seventh day after they shut her up in a small cell, treating her in all things as they did the other prisoners, and with as much cruelty as they used with any, insomuch that in all her miseries the only comfort that she had was that of the good company of a certain virtuous maiden that was her fellow prisoner for a time, but afterwards sent to the stake. Indeed, she bore this young girl such good will, that, being at one time carried forth to the rack and recarried to prison, very strained there on, and so shaken in pieces that having a bed of reeds which served them both to lie on, more painful a great deal than easeful, whereon she tumbled as well as she could, though hardly God knows and to her great pain and grief, the good Lady being unable to alleviate her, yet showed exceptional tokens of love and compassion towards her. The same maid was scarce recovered, or her joints well knit again, but the said Lady was likewise carried out to be served in the same sort, and was so terribly tormented in the 'burrie and trough' that by reason of the exceeding tight straining of the strings piercing to the very bones of her arms, her thighs and shins, she was carried to her cell half dead and more, the blood gushing out of her mouth in so great abundance that it could not be otherwise but that something was broken within her body. But after eight days God delivered her from these ravening lions and set her with Himself in everlasting rest and peace.

The reports of this the inquisitors labored earnestly to suppress, lest it should be noised abroad among the common people that they had so villainously torn in pieces this tender lady upon the rack. But the person responsible of this their tyranny could not hold it in. Now surely, if she had been a witch, or a traitor to her husband, or a murderer of her own children, and the temporal magistrate had dealt so with her to make her confess these horrible facts, if of him had been told the story, he would have paid for it full dearly, if so be that he had thus cruelly, and without all reason, treated anyone. Yet the Holy House does not take into account such matters, but may rack to death even those whom they themselves after more precise and exact proof acquit for innocent, and escape scot free, as it came to pass in the example of this virtuous lady. For being one of such social status and of so good name and fame that they must necessarily yield some account of her case unto the common people, they were destitute of proofs sufficient (though they had left no device or policy unpracticed that they could imagine), but seeing the matter so apparent to all the world by no means it could be dissembled. Therefore, the very first day of their next *auto* they caused their sentence which they had given upon her to be openly read there unto the people on this wise: "Forasmuch as this lady died in prison (without showing how or by what means, I guarantee you), and upon diligent hearing and consideration of her cause is found innocent, therefore, the Holy House wholly acquits and discharges her of all suites and quarrels commenced against her by the fiscal, and restores her to her former estate of estimation and honor, absolving her clearly from all guilt and crime, and thereupon commands that restitution be made of all such goods as were seized into the treasury into the hands of such persons as have right and title thereunto, &c." Thus, after that they had most beastly murdered her on the rack, they made her this goodly amends to denounce her not guilty. God will one day (no doubt) ask an account of this their beastly and barbarous tyranny, inasmuch as they maintain it by the same power and authority in earth, which He has ordained for the revenge of these and such like injuries.

Montes's detailed accounts suggests that he must have either known both of the Bohorquez sisters well or he must have been a very direct witness of their experiences at the hands of the inquisitors. He may have known them already before they were committed to prison, or he may have been the notary present during their interrogatories, whose duty it was to be present when witnesses— and offenders—were examined and to transcribe everything that was said. Montes (1569, ff. 70v–72r) is also very thorough in his account of Maria Bohorquez:

The first thing that occasioned [Maria] Bohorques to such earnest study of the Scriptures was a little skill which she had in the Latin tongue, wherein it was lawful to read the Scriptures as often and as long as she wanted, being restrained and forbidden that in no case the common people should read them in their own tongue. Yea, her schoolmaster, Dr. Egidio, a man who she specially chose for his singular integrity of life, as well as for his excellent learning, was wont to give this testimony of her: that he never came into her company but he learned something, and hence departed always better learned than he came.

During the time of her imprisonment, the monks and Dominicans had great disputations with her, marveling as much at the passing excellency of her wit in answering all their subtle and sophistical objections, and (as it were) cutting them so quickly with the sword of God's word, as also at the wonderful memory which she had in citing the Holy Scriptures so readily, in so much that after they had done disputing and reasoning with her, they gave very good testimonies of her constancy and sober behavior, though they termed it stubbornness and obstinacy. After they had kept her for a long time in that dark dungeon, and there caused her to endure all the cruel and extreme torments that might be (by means thereof they forced her to confess of her own sister that she was also one of the same religion, which was the occasion first of her sister's imprisonment, and so consequently of her death, being murdered most cruelly among those villains by extreme torments), they brought her forth upon the scaffold with several other godly men and women, whereof I made mention before, however, she came out with a look of joy and mirth and conquest over the Holy Inquisition, rather than the contrary; this strange countenance of mirth, for as much as it was rare to see in her, expressed by her singing psalms to God, the inquisitors of spite and malice, sought to alter into another tune by setting a clamp on her tongue along the way as she went, which, notwithstanding, before they came to the scaffold, they undid again.

When they had read their sentence upon her openly, and given judgment of death, the inquisitors asked her whether she would recant or not, acknowledging her heresies which heretofore she had most willfully maintained. Whereupon she answered them roundly that neither she would, nor truly could, confess so much. And so from there she passed with her other companions to the place of execution, accompanied with these hypocrites still calling upon her and her fellows along the way to add "the Church of Rome" to their creed. But she, among the rest, most stoutly withstood them. Notwithstanding, the abominable villains, to the intent to blemish their good name and renown by their most villainous treacheries, strangled them with halters as though they had at their last hours returned to the Romish church, in consideration whereof, the inquisitors, taking pity on them, would not suffer them (say they) to be burned alive.

The inquisitors were also very impressed with Maria Bohorquez's erudition as well as her character. A lengthy report of how they tried to make her recant is of interest because it also describes Maria's doctrinal position:

Next they called in two Dominican friars and they delivered to them a young girl by the name of Maria de Bohorques, the daughter of a foremost citizen of this city called Pero Garcia de Jerez, father-in-law of the Lord of Higuera. The young woman was the illegitimate daughter of the aforesaid and of the age of twenty-six. The friars entered her room and she received them cheerfully. She asked what they wanted. They told her what they came for and that she was to die, and that she should accept the will of Our Lord. She answered that she knew she would have to die and be a martyr for what she believed, so what did these fathers want from her? If they came to tell her to believe in God, she already did. The aforesaid fathers said that was what they came for and to comfort her and strengthen her and also to undo the errors and heresies she was persuaded to die for. Because, although she held them as a remedy for her salvation, actually they were the means of her condemnation and with that she would go to hell. And since she had the remedy in her hands, she ought to take advantage and apply it, for afterwards she would no longer have it.

The friars pressed her trying to make her understand what she had to do for her remedy and her salvation and to all this she gave no answer until the friars gave up trying to persuade her. Then she spoke, saying that they should not worry about her because if she was content to condemn herself in the beliefs she held, and not to save her soul, she would certainly drop them. But because she considered them to be her remedy, there was no need to try to persuade her to give them up because she was fully persuaded of the truth of these beliefs and she was determined to die for them. Moreover, as she had earlier maintained and insisted on with the other Jesuit friars, they should stop troubling her again thinking their words might move her. And if they wanted to convert her via debate, the debate should be centered on contrasting her doctrines over against theirs.

The friars that had spoken to her earlier had debated with her and she had responded with her arguments, and those of other authorities, and now she again earnestly began to put forth her own views. And for each error they mentioned she brought in many reasons, and evidence that she took from the Old and New Testament that confirmed her errors, saying that that was the true meaning, in order to defend her Lutheran errors. In short, in the sentence pronounced against this young woman, none of the other offenders accused of Lutheran opinions had put forth arguments in defense of the sect like Maria de Bohorquez had.

From the hour they told her she was to die, friars of nearly all the orders took turns trying to convert her, but to no avail because she was so hardened and so convinced of her damned opinions. Finally, the friars, tired of arguing with her, seeing they could not convince her to return to the Holy Roman Church, left, cursing her, some in tears seeing her hard heart and blindness. And this went on until the time they took her out [to the scaffold]. This young women knew Latin well and some Greek and that knowledge was part of her madness and blindness, because she showed that all the friars, and even the inquisitors, were ignorant and that she understood the language as well as they did and she understood the literal meaning of the Holy Scriptures and what she said about all this was correct and she did not have to believe any different. The amount of Scripture she knew from memory astonished the friars and she gave it all a Lutheran interpretation even though these authorities in their writings seemed to say something different from what she interpreted. She also said she had books that interpreted the Scripture in that sense.

Her errors were similar to those of Juan [Ponce de Leon], except that some were even worse, such as, that there was only one sacrament—baptism—and not seven. She laughed at and made fun of the sacrament of Extreme Unction, saying why must those that die be anointed with oil. As for the sacrament of the Eucharist, she could not believe that our Lord who was in heaven by magic entered into that bread, nor could the wine become the blood of our Lord Jesus Christ. Neither were images to be venerated or the saints invoked. This young woman had many Lutheran books, which Juan Ponce de Leon said she had memorized and that she studied them continuously in case she was arrested she would have arguments and authority to defend herself and to persuade others with her Lutheran errors.

It so happened that on the scaffold there was an argument between Juan and this woman which shows how hardened she was. Juan tried to persuade her to convert to the Catholic faith and to return to the obedience of the Holy Roman Church and to forget the sermons of Fray Casiodoro [de Reina], friar of the Monastery of San Isidro, she had heard in certain places and in certain meetings, and that she should forget those views she had of the Old Testament. She let him talk and when he was finished retorted in a few words calling him an idiot and a windbag, and that that was not the time to talk but for each one to meditate on Christ in silence. He refused to be silent. Then he turned to the friars that accompanied her and said that she was a very good Christian and trusted in God and that she believed she would be saved, and she was cheerful all the while as one who is in deep thought, giving the impression that in her heart she accepted what Juan had told her. She told the friars they annoyed her because they insisted that she give up her errors.

This young woman, for as much as they said and preached to her refused to convert until three in the afternoon by the persuasions and entreaties of friars and abbots. Although later she still continued to amuse herself contrasting her views with those of our holy Catholic faith, she was burned and would to God that he may have pardoned her and not taken into account her offences and sins. They say she died in our holy faith, though this is questionable, and that she left her sister, the wife of Francisco de Vargas, Lord of Higuera, behind in prison, because she was jealous because their father had given her a large dowry. The sister remains in prison. God will reveal the truth.[10]

Juan Antonio Llorente also relates the story of the Bohorquez sisters, which he very likely found in Montes.[11] He then goes on to point out how their story became part of a nineteenth century epistolary novel: *Cornelia Bohorquia. Historia verdadera de la Judith española* (Cornelia Bohorquia. The True Story of the Spanish Judith). The story, written in Spanish, was first printed anonymously in Paris in 1801 (Mackenzie: 1997, 235–252). It was then translated into French and went through several editions. Later it appeared in Portuguese and German. In Spain, the Inquisition prohibited the novel and only after 1820 was it allowed into the country. Llorente (1843, 216), who would have seen it in Paris, makes the following comment regarding its publication:

> The history of [Donna Maria Bohorques] ought to be made known, on account of some circumstances in her trial, and because a Spaniard has composed a novel under the title of "Cornelia Bororquia," which he affirms to be rather a history than a romance, although it is neither the one nor the other, but a collection of scenes and events badly conceived, in which he has not even given the actors their true names, from not having understood the History of the Inquisition by Limborch. This historian has mentioned two of the ladies by the names of Cornelia and Bohorquia, which means Donna Maria Camel, and Donna Maria Bohorquia. The Spanish author has united these names, to designate Cornelia Bohorquia an imaginary person. He has supposed a love-intrigue between her and the inquisitor-general, which is absurd, since he was at Madrid. He has also introduced examinations, which never took place in the tribunal. In short, the intention of the author was to criticize and ridicule the Inquisition, and the fear of being punished for it induced him to fly to Bayonne. A good cause becomes bad when falsehood is employed in its defense: the true history of the Inquisition is sufficient to show how much it merits the detestation of the human race, and it is therefore useless to employ fictions or satire. The same may be said of the "Gusmanade," a French poem, containing assertions false and injurious to the memory of St. Dominic de Guzman, whose personal conduct was very pure, though he may be blamed for his conduct to the Albigenses.

Stories of this type proliferated in the nineteenth century (Muñoz: 2010, 71–81). *Les Mystères de l'Inquisition* (The Mysteries of the Inquisition), written in 1845 by V. de Féréal, was a similar tale, that is, the love-intrigues of an inquisitor and his victim. It appeared first in French and shortly afterwards was translated into English. To give the story credibility, it contains historical notes by Manuel de Cuendias, who claimed he took his information from Llorente. The novel was an

---

10 BNE, ms. 6176, f. 310r, in Lopez Muñoz (2011, 166, doc. 83). Brackets mine.
11 I base this supposition on the fact that Llorente gives Maria's age as 21—the same as Montes—whereas the Inquisition records say she was 26.

instant success and remained in print for decades.[12] Antonio Gavin's story of a young lady who, along with 50 others, was forced to become part of a seraglio kept by the inquisitors, also became very popular in the nineteenth century and was also reprinted over and over.[13]

Francisca de Chaves

Francisca de Chaves, referred to initially as *beata,* was born in Gibraleon, some 60 miles southwest of Seville. Documents written ten years later refer to her as a *monja profesa* (habited nun) from the monastery of Santa Isabel.[14] This change in status may not have been her own choice, but in the interval of these ten years, the Council of Trent had done away with the status of secular nuns and female tertiary orders and imposed enclosure: "for no nun, after her profession, shall it be lawful to go out of her convent, even for a brief period, under any pretext whatever, except for some lawful cause, which is to be approved of by the bishop."[15] As a *beata*, or secular nun, she had had the freedom to come and go. Her relationship with the evangelical leaders went back to the time she was still a *beata,* hence, Montes (1569, f. 77r), who may have met her later during her imprisonment in Triana, is mistaken when he states: "A wonderful thing to consider how the perfect knowledge of Christ could come to her through such iron doors and grates," and that "in all her life time she had had no great conversation with men." According to information gleaned from Inquisition records, Francisca had had contact with Luis Hernandez del Castillo and Juan Perez de Pineda before they fled. Already in 1550 her name appeared in a dispatch sent by the Supreme Council to Emperor Charles V as the owner of a copy of the pamphlet entitled *Diálogo consolatorio entre la Iglesia que está en*

---

12 Within a decade the novel had been translated and published in several languages: *The Mysteries of the Inquisition* (Philadelphia: Lippincott, 1845, 1846); *The Mysteries of the Inquisition* (London: G. Peirce, 1845); *Misteri dell'Inquisizione* (Paris, 1847); *Misterios de la Inquisicion* (Mexico: V. García Torres, 1850); *Gli orrori della Inquisizione* (Torino: Perrin, 1850); *The Young Dominican Or, Life in the Inquisition* (Philadelphia: Lippincott, Grambo, & Co, 1853); etc.

13 Antonio Gavin, *A Master-key to Popery* (Dublin, 1724; Cincinnati, Ohio, 1832, 1833, 1834; Hartford, Connecticut, 1845, 1846, 1848; Boston, 1854, 1855, 1856; New York, 1854, 1855, 1856, 1860; Philadelphia 1855).

14 AHN, Inquisición, leg. 2075, doc. 1 (2); leg. 4514 (2), doc. 15; AGS, Estado, leg. 137, doc. 3, in: Lopez Muñoz (2011, 212, doc. 101; 349, doc. 166). This convent was founded in 1490 by Isabel de Leon Farfan, widow of Gonzalo Farfan de los Godos. After the disentailment of the church's landed property (*desamortización*) in 1837, it was used as a prison for women and a "Casa de Arrepentidas" [home for repentant prostitutes]. Today it is occupied by the Hijas de María Dolorosa, an order of Filipino nuns.

15 For the full text of the decree, see Chapter III, note 12.

Sevilla y Jesucristo (Consolatory Dialog between the Little Church in Seville and Jesus Christ). In the same dispatch, she was also accused of having correspondence with "Luis Hernandez del Castillo, who has fled to Paris." As witness at the trial of Gaspar Ortiz—held prisoner at Triana from November 1558 to October 1562—she declared, among other things, that Ortiz had in his possession four sermons by Luis Hernandez del Castillo, whom she considered her mentor. She also declared that when women asked Ortiz for copies of sermons, he would say they had enough with Dr. Constantino's *Catechism*.[16]

Francisca de Chaves was related to several women connected with the evangelical circle in Seville.[17] She was a relative of Isabel Martinez de Alvo, the woman in whose house Dr. Constantino de la Fuente kept his secret library. She was also related to the daughters of Alonso de Illescas, Leonor, Isabel, and Ana, who were all imprisoned in Triana suspected of heresy and who we will see later. Early on, Francisca de Chaves may also have been active in her hometown of Gibraleon. The execution of five women from Gibraleon—Leonor Gomez, her two daughters Elvira and Teresa, her niece Lucia Gomez, and her sister Leonor Gomez—accused of being "unyielding Lutheran heretics" and sentenced to the stake in the same *auto* as Francisca—, can hardly be dismissed as pure coincidence. They all appeared at the *auto-da-fe* held in St. Francisco Square in Seville on December 22, 1560. Francisca de Chaves had a wooden bit in her mouth, a rope around her neck, and a *sanbenito* with devils painted on it over her habit.[18] Among the Inquisition documents that have been preserved, there is the following document, written up by Inquisitor Juan Gonzalez de Munebrega, bishop of Tarazona, describing Francisca de Chaves's doctrinal position, which justified their having condemned her to the stake:

> This cause was seen by me, Juan Gonzalez, by the grace of God and the Holy Roman Church Bishop of Tarazona, member of his majesty's council, and at present attending and presiding over the affairs and causes of this Holy Office, together with the inquisitors against the heretical wickedness and apostasy in the city and archbishopric of Seville and Cadiz, by apostolic and ordinary authority, a process of criminal litigation pending between the reverend licentiate Diego Muñoz, prosecutor of the Holy Office, the accuser, and offender, the accused, Francisca de Chaves, confirmed nun of the Monastery of Santa Isabel of Seville, here present.
>
> Based on the accusation against Francisca de Chaves presented to us by the prosecutor [Diego Muñoz] in which he states that, with no fear of God, the aforesaid, as a godless Christian, departing from the Holy Mother Apostolic and Catholic Roman Church, and following after new doctrines and Lutheran errors condemned by the church, that she

---

16 AHN, Inquisición, leg. 4514 (2), doc. 15, in: Lopez Muñoz (2011, 349, doc. 166).
17 AHN, Inquisición, leg. 2075 (2), doc. 46, in: Lopez Muñoz (2011, 199, doc. 97).
18 AHN, Inquisición, leg. 2075, doc. 1 (2); AGS, Estado, leg. 137, doc. 3, in: Lopez Muñoz (2011, 226, doc. 101).

is a heretic. And considering that she unyieldingly states and affirms many things contrary to our holy Catholic faith and Christian religion, speaking evil things of the pope and censuring the church, she declared that men cannot excommunicate, which she could prove from a book she had that showed that the pope could not excommunicate, she made fun of people who were absolved of excommunication. And wanting to know more than her status allowed, she had often met with other people to talk about matters concerning the faith and had taught them the doctrine and errors she held, insinuating that this was contrary to what the church preached. Likewise, she showed compassion for those who followed Catholic doctrine and not hers, saying, "Heed your ways! Don't you see you are going to hell!" She admitted she had many prohibited books that contain many blasphemes and heresies, and one in particular that contained an abominable dialog in which it was suggested that there were two churches: one small (underground) of true Christians here in the city of Seville, which had a pastor and whose sheep were the true Christians of that flock and were righteous, and the other church which was large, widespread and inflexible, and governed by evil Christians and dominated by, and in the hands of, Pharisees.

Francisca de Chaves confessed, and wrote in her own hand, that good works were of no avail because Christ paid for our sin with his death. She admitted that she had favored and protected many persons who shared her opinions and had not declared them to this Holy Office so that they could not be punished, and hence they continued in their errors. This and many other things appear in the accusation against her. With this her confession, the prosecutor asked us to pronounce a definitive sentence declaring Francisca de Chaves an apostate heretic of our Holy Catholic faith and an instigator, teacher and protector of heretics, and to condemn her to the most severe penalties that the law establishes, by handing her over to the civil justice, and declaring that all her goods be confiscated. This he implored the Holy Office to comply with, and that the full hand of justice fall on her.

Taking into consideration what Francisca de Chaves replied to these accusations, together with the words and evidence of thirteen witnesses, and the confession she made to us in which she declared openly that in the sacrament of the alter, the blood and body of our master and redeemer Jesus Christ was not actually present, as is taught and practiced in Germany, and which she believed to be correct, especially as it was taught by Martin Luther and others, such as Philip Melanchthon and others, who understood it fully. Furthermore, taking into consideration that she confessed that there was no purgatory for anyone, because justification is by faith, neither did she find it reasonable to confide in one's merits or that merits had any value, but that the achievements of Christ were sufficient and that works were not only unnecessary and worthless, but did not pay for our sins, nor were worthwhile practicing. Considering that she also confessed openly and clearly that the children of God were those that experienced justification in their conscience and that only Christ's justice was valid, which he gave us through faith solely in the merits of Jesus Christ, not by works, which are worth nothing before God. And that for her, good works meant believing and having true faith and a true knowledge of Jesus Christ and that those who were going to heaven were going there because of God's promise and mercy, not because of their good deeds. And that she did not consider it a sin to break the commandments of the pope or of the inquisitors or of the priests. And although the pope banned the reading of prohibited books, and even if she read them and had in her possession writing against the Catholic Church, she did not think that the excommunication that resulted from this could affect her. And that she thought nothing of eating things prohibited by the Church of Rome on Fridays or Esther or Ember days,[19] except that she abstained from eating them in front of people she might scandalize, but for herself it was not a sin, because the gospel prohibited nothing. These, she claimed, were practices introduced by men to make people mortify themselves and do penance.

Likewise, she said that she believed that God had given only one commandment: to believe. And there was only one sin: unbelief. She believed that original sin has never been pardoned; it remains forever, even in the righteous.[20] She also believed there was no other catholic church than the Lutheran church, whose members held the Lutheran faith, and that was the faith she believed and held. She hoped that the Lutheran doctrine would spread throughout the world and that all those who held that doctrine had the power to examine and to absolve sins, and that these were the pastors and sheep of Jesus Christ. She considered Dr. Egidio to be one of these pastors and she herself one of his sheep. She believed that the Catholic Christians, who owed obedience to the Holy Apostolic See, were wolves and false ministers and dumb dogs that did not preach the truth of the gospel. For her, the true gospel was the doctrine she declared, which contradicted the Catholic Church. She believed the pope was the Antichrist and all his ministers those that ruled the Church of Rome, but she had overcome all the things held by the Church of Rome and lived unaffected by them. She considered those that ruled and governed the church, and those that considered the doctrine she believed evil, to be the princes of this world and their holiness to be worldly. And now she is sure and firmly believes everything she read in the books and tracts that had come into her hands, especially one titled *Diálogo consolatorio entre la iglesia chiquita que está en Sevilla, perseguida de los fariseos grandemente, y el propio Jesucristo* (Consolatory Dialog between Jesus Christ himself and the little church in Seville, greatly persecuted by the Pharisees). For her, the pastor of that little church was Dr. Egidio. She would very much like to hear the teaching and doctrine of a man like Egidio again because the women[21] were all fickle and light-headed. What she meant was that she would like to see a man that preached the gospel and was willing to die for it. And what she meant about the women was that the man who preached that gospel should be consistent and not look back, like those that had fled,[22] but should be like Dr. Egidio, who had recanted.[23]

---

19 Four calendar events—after Pentecost, after the first Sunday of Lent, after the feast of St Lucy (December 13), and after the feast of the Holy Cross (September 14)—of three days (Wednesday, Friday, and Saturday) of prayer and fasting.

20 If the statement given here by Inquisitor Gonzalez is correct, it totally contradicts her previous doctrinal position, which was in clear accordance with Lutheran teaching. Reformed doctrine, in accordance with the Scriptures, affirms that Christ's work of redemption covers original sin, from which all other sins derive. Was this a false charge?

21 The nuns in her convent?

22 She probably meant the monks from the Monastery of San Isidoro, Cipriano de Valera, Casiodoro de Reina, Antonio del Corro, etc.

23 Throughout the Inquisition records, words such as "heretic," "burned," etc., tagged on to the

Considering her resoluteness and determination, we told her that it caused us much sorrow to see such an intelligent woman persist in such pernicious doctrine and we begged her, for the sake of God our Lord, that she renounce it and return to the bosom of the Holy Roman Catholic Church, who as a loving mother always has her arms open to receive those that have gone astray, and that if she did so out of a pure heart, not falsely, we offered her all the mercy we could. Besides this, we told her that in order for her to fully understand how manifestly heretical and erroneous was the doctrine she professed, we would call in learned men, not in law, but well-read in the Holy Scripture and in the words of our master and redeemer Jesus Christ. To this she answered that she would like to obey us, but the testimony of her conscience did not allow her to do so because, if she did, it would not be of a pure heart, but falsely, for her conscience would not allow her to do anything else but what she so often declared, and not from what she had read or the words of modern men, but by experience. And seeing her delusion so great, we told her that the testimony of her conscience proceeded from a false spirit and that she had no reason not to listen to persons that could teach her the true doctrine and who could show it to her through the living and truthful words of the Holy Gospel and the Sacred Scripture. And she should not close the door to this because not wanting to be illuminated by the Holy Spirit was to manifestly resist the Spirit.

We told her that the experience [of conversion] she said she had, or could have had, was a fantasy, not a revelation, because one can only have that experience if it is accompanied by the testimony of miracles or the Sacred Scripture. To this, she answered with great liberty that it was not in order to resist the Holy Spirit that she did not want to hear what the scholars had to say, but because even if the very teachers who had taught her the doctrine she believed—doctors Egidio and Constantino, of whose teaching she was perfectly satisfied, and especially doctor Constantino's—told her something different from what they had preached, she would not believe them because the testimony of her conscience was greater than their words, because she was convinced that she had this truth written in her heart with the finger of God. And though what she said might sound presumptuous, she was convinced that the Word of God gave those that believe it boldness to be able to say this and certify it through faith alone. That is why she thought there was no need for any of the things we offered her, for that was sufficient and she held it more certain than the testimony of all the scholars in the world because she believed that all of them together did not have the zeal we had. Despite all this, and her stubbornness and tenacity, we agreed to bring in learned theologians to persuade her of the manifest delusion in which she was.

For several days, these men spoke with her and reasoned with her with the authority of the Holy Scripture and the Holy Gospel. In the end, stubborn like Pharaoh, she continued in the false and abominable doctrine she confessed. Considering all this, having seen and examined the case as required, and with unanimous accord and deliberation with knowledgeable and conscientious persons, in the name of Christ we pass judgment on the accused in accordance with the charges and recognition of the process that the prosecutor amply proved in his accusation and suit. We hereby declare his case well

---

name of persons condemned, are common. Here Inquisitor Gonzalez de Munebrega adds, "who had retracted," in case the reader harbored any doubts.

proven and that the aforesaid Francisca de Chaves proved nothing that could exonerate her. Therefore, we must declare, and do declare, that Francisca de Chaves has been, and is, an unyielding heretic, an apostate Lutheran, dogmatizer and teacher of the sect of Luther and his followers, greatly offending God our Lord and his Holy Catholic faith and the gospel, and hence has fallen and is guilty of the sentence of major excommunication and subject to it and to all the penalties that such obstinate heretics bring upon themselves, who in the name of Christians commit such offences. Likewise, we hand over the aforesaid Francisca de Chaves to the civil justice, in particular to the mayor of the city and to his deputies, whom we most affectionately beg and urge to deal kindly and mercifully with her. This is our final and definitive resolution and, as such, we conclude and declare it in this document.[24]

The Gonzalez Sisters

Catalina and Maria were the sisters of the preacher Juan Gonzalez, of New Christian *converso* stock, of *morisco* origin "de los mudéjares."[25] They were from Palma de Miçergilio (Palma del Rio), where there had been a large Moorish community (*morería*) at the end of the fifteenth century (Boeglin: 2010, 22–23). The two sisters were sent to the stake in Seville at the *auto-da-fe* held on September 24, 1559. They had been active members of the little underground evangelical church and had maintained an epistolary relationship with Francisco de Cardenas, who had left Seville with his wife and was living in Geneva.[26] In the fall of 1557 they carried a letter—very likely one Julian Hernandez had brought with him from Geneva—sent by Francisco to his brother Antonio de Cadenas, which the latter denounced to the Holy Office and which led to the arrest of the sisters.[27] Several documents state that they were "relapsed", that is, that they were reoffenders.[28] Their brother Juan (the preacher), also burned at the stake that day, was accused of never having abjured of his Muslim faith;[29] their brother Jeronimo was burned at the stake on April 26, 1562, and at the next *auto*, held on October 28 that same year, their brother Francisco was sentenced to 200 lashes and to serve in the royal galleys for three years. Their mother, Isabel Gonzalez, was also imprisoned and was still awaiting sentence in October of

24 AHN, Inquisición, leg. 2075 (2), doc. 46, in: Lopez Muñoz (2011, 199, doc. 97). Notes mine.
25 The "mudéjares" were Muslims who remained in Spain after the Christian Reconquista, but had not converted to Christianity, unlike *moriscos* who had converted.
26 At the third *auto-da-fe*, held April 26, 1562, Francisco de Cardenas, his wife Ana de Mairena, and her sister Maria de Trigueros, the wife of Costantin Espada, a Venecian, were burned in effigy.
27 AHN, Inquisición, leg. 4519, doc. 10 (b), in: Lopez Muñoz (2011, 290, doc. 137).
28 BNE, ms. 9175, f. 226r; AHN, Inquisición, leg. 2075, doc. 1, in: Lopez Muñoz (2011, 159, doc. 80; 164, doc. 82).
29 BNE, ms. 6176, f. 310r. [1], in: Lopez Muñoz (2011, 166, doc. 83).

1562.[30] Juan Gonzalez, the preacher, was imprisoned for teaching Lutheran doctrine, but refused to confess that he held heretical doctrines, affirming that his opinions were founded on the Holy Scriptures, and consequently he could not be a heretic. This example was imitated by his sisters. The evening before the *auto*, however, Catalina admitted that her spiritual director had been Fray Luis de la Cruz, who taught her that we are justified by faith and not by good works.[31]

Francisca Lopez

There was also a *beata* by the name of Francisca Lopez sentenced to the stake the same day as the Gonzalez sisters. She was a weaver— very likely a silk weaver— from Manzanilla, some twenty-five miles to the west of Seville, but living in Seville. Women in the sixteenth century had a choice between—or more often forced into—marriage or the convent. Poor women, who did not dispose of the required dowry to enter a convent, became *beatas*. Weaving and embroidering were professions many *beatas* practiced. Since these were domestic activities, it allowed them into people's homes and gave them the opportunity to instruct the female members of the family in spiritual matters. According to the Appendix inserted in the 1569 English edition of *Artes*, Francisca was the wife of the parish priest Francisco de Zafra, who escaped from Triana. This is corroborated by an Inquisition document,[32] and may have been revealed by Francisca Lopez herself. Being a parish priest of the church of St. Vicente Martir, and Francisca a *beata* employed by one of his wealthy parishioners, it was not difficult for them to meet. At the *auto-da-fe* held on September 24, 1559, Francisco de Zafra was burned in effigy and Francisca Lopez was burned in person.

The Gomez-Nuñez Family

Elvira Nuñez and her sisters, Teresa and Lucia Gomez, were from Gibraleon, the city where Francisca de Chaves was from. The documents regarding the relationship between Elvira, Teresa, and Lucia are somewhat contradictory. Some describe them as sisters, others as cousins; still other documents refer to Elvira and Teresa as sisters and Leonor Gomez as their cousin. The confusion arises because they carry different surnames. Their mother married twice, which would explain the names and would make them stepsisters. What confuses the

---

30 AHN, Inquisición, leg. 2075 (1), doc. 2, in: Lopez Muñoz (2011, 270, doc. 129).
31 AHN, Inquisición, leg. 1822, doc. 11, in: Lopez Muñoz (2011, 526, doc. 290).
32 BNE, ms. 6176, f. 310r, in: Lopez Muñoz (2011, 166, doc. 83).

relationship even further is that the mother and the aunt also had the same name (Leonor Gomez) and were married to men with the same name, one to Hernan Nuñez, a physician from Gibraleon, and the other to Hernan Nuñez, an apothecary from Lepe.[33] The sisters, together with their mother and aunt, were imprisoned in August of 1559 and sent to the stake in December the following year. Their grandmother, Elvira Diaz, was imprisoned along with them but must have died while in prison. She was burned in effigy at a later *auto*.[34]

On August 8, 1560, Inquisitor Juan Gonzalez de Munebrega, bishop of Tarazona, called Lucia Gomez to be brought before him from her cell to continue her confession. She had been in prison a year and had been questioned several times before. The inquisitor admonished her to tell the truth, "for this is what exempts people from punishment." He was particularly suspicious of these women because they persisted in declaring exactly the same thing(s) and he suspected they had devised some way to communicate with each other despite the fact that they were in separate cells. The document narrates the interview as follows:

> She was asked if she had told her mother or her sisters, or anyone else in the prisons of the Holy Office, any of the things she had confessed after she was put to the rack, and if she did, how. She told him that in the time that Pedro de Herrera was jailer, when she and her mother and her sister Teresa talked to each other, she and Teresa agreed that Teresa should tell her sister Elvira that whenever she went out to make a bowel movement [in the common toilet in the patio] she should leave some sort of sign somewhere and a paper under it. And this they continued to do. At first the sign was a brick with a little mark on top of it. After the brick was taken away, they used the rim of an old pan. Then they put a little heap of dirt on top of the paper and they left it there. That was how she communicated with her sister Elvira things like "Don't forget about the pack of letters we sent to Diego Juarez", or things like, "Tell me what's going on, for God's sake, for they are killing me." And in the same way her sister informed her of many things that she had confessed, things Lucia had forgotten, but she did remember about the matter regarding the letters of the Mairena women[35] that they had shown licentiate Diego Juarez. And in another note her sister had said, "Certainly, my dear, for I have declared everything I have heard from the day I met that devil, and everything that Diego said to me and I to him." By this Lucia understood the devil to be Catalina de Villalobos,[36] her aunt, and Diego to be licentiate Diego Juarez. Elvira and Lucia passed on other information but Lucia could no longer remember the details, for as soon as she

---

33 Hernan Nuñez escaped and on May 13, 1565, he was burned in effigy. AHN, *Inquisición*, leg. 2943, doc. 149–2, in: Lopez Muñoz (2011, 345, doc. 164).

34 AHN, Inquisición, leg. 4683 (3), in: Lopez Muñoz (2011, 324, doc. 158).

35 One of these could have been Ana de Mairena, absent, burned in effigy.

36 Catalina de Villalobos, the wife of the silversmith Pedro de Sosa, was sentenced at the same *auto* as her nieces, the Gomez sisters. Because she recanted, she was only sentenced to life in prison and the loss of her goods. AHN, Inquisición, leg. 2075, doc. 1 (2); AGS, Estado, leg. 137, doc. 3, in: Lopez Muñoz (2011, 226, doc. 101). Her husband, Pedro de Sosa, had fled and was burned in effigy at the *auto-da-fe* held on April 26, 1562.

had written it down she forgot it. At the beginning they would put the signs in the corner, in front of the public toilet, but now in the wall itself near the ground in a little heap of dirt. Lucia did not communicate directly with her mother, because by telling Elvira, she would tell her mother. And she again begged, in tears, for us to have mercy on her for the love of God.[37]

Five days later, on August 13, 1560, Lucia Gomez was again called before Inquisitor Gonzalez de Munebrega.

He warned [Lucia] not to tell anyone, by word of mouth or in writing, about her imprisonment, or that of her sisters; they should say nothing that is not true, or what they confessed or what was said against anyone, because that generates too much curiosity. If she did, she would be punished accordingly and they would show no mercy. She was then asked how her sister Elvira informed her mother, Leonor Gomez, in order for her to confess the same things that the two sisters confessed. Lucia wasn't sure but she supposed Elvira communicated with her the same way the two sisters did, by putting notes under a little heap of dirt. The inquisitor then asked her who gave her the paper and pen to write these notes. To this Lucia answered that for paper she had torn off a sheet of the publication of witnesses they had given Catalina Jimenez,[38] her cellmate, that she kept in her chest, and at other times she used the paper spices were wrapped in and that the ink was the juice of a lemon or orange or some other citrus fruit and the pen was a little reed. Asked how she was able to read what was written, she said that by heating it the letters could be seen.

When asked what sign she and her sister had to be able to distinguish which heap of dirt was hers or her sister's because it could be someone else's, she said the sign was the rim of a white pan and they would keep moving it until it came next to the heap of the other. It was also true that for a long time they had no news from each other until [Gaspar de] Benavides's housekeeper and his children helped them to communicate with each other again.[39] And later, when [Pedro de] Herrera[40] brought them together, they decided

---

37 AHN, Inquisición, leg. 2942, doc. 85, in: Lopez Muñoz (2011, 186, doc. 93). Notes mine.
38 Catalina Jimenez was the wife of Luis de Abrego, the printer. She was sentenced at the same *auto* as the Gomez women to life in prison and released eight years later, on May 25, 1568. AHN, Inquisición, lib. 575, f. 324v, in: Lopez Muñoz (2011, 374, doc. 181).
39 Montes (1569, ff. 38v–39v.) describes the relationship between Benavides and the prisoners thus: "Gasper de Benavides, (for covetousness and cruel dealing, a monster rather than a man) had grown so greedy that he would defraud the poor prisoners of part of their small allowance, meager already in itself for lack of good food, but worse a great deal by means of his plundering victuals stolen from them that he would sell in Triana. For instance, such money as should have been paid to a laundress for washing the prisoner's clothes, he put wholly into his own purse, not regarding how sluttishly the prisoners went for a good while, without any changes. And thus he deceived both the inquisitors and the treasurer, who assigned the keeper in his accounts for such and such money paid and assigned to the prisoners' benefit, for whose weekly expenses it was appointed. And herein mark, I beseech you, the notable negligence and slippery dealing of both parties. First the winking of the inquisitor at the keeper's behavior, and secondly the keeper's unjust oppression of the poor prisoners. But indeed, it is not a very hard matter to deceive them that will never take pains to sift out a truth. For if any of the prisoners received some injury at the keeper's hand, or had

to use the pan. When asked if she had put a note there again in order to inform the others after she had told the Inquisitors, she responded that she had and in the same

---

complained at any time or grudged about anything at all, the cruel tyrant would find the means to get even with them, for he would remove him from the place that he was in before and thrust him into some deep dungeons, which they call *mazmorra*, and there would keep him alone for two or three days, giving him not so much as a little straw to lie upon, and as for his diet, neither should it be wholesome nor yet sufficient to hold life and soul together, but likely to kill him, or at least to breed some extreme sickness. All the which would be done without commission or warrant from the inquisitors and yet would he very craftily and maliciously make the prisoner believe that he did it wholly by the inquisitor's special commandment. Now if any that had been so injuriously dealt with, intending to complain thereof to the inquisitors, should desire him to request a day of hearing (as none may solicit that matter save only the keeper), the crafty knave, suspecting that hereby he should make a rod for his own tail, would make the prisoner believe that he had so done, and would tell him that it could not be granted at that time. And thus, with such forged answers he would keep the poor prisoner in that deep dungeon twelve or fifteen days till he thought his anger were somewhat mitigated and his courage thoroughly cooled. And then at length he would move him back to his old cell again, making the poor man believe that he had cause to thank him for the compassion and pity that he took upon him. But this travelled to the inquisitors, and became an earnest suitor to them to get him released. In sum, such filtching was used and such extremity showed towards the prisoners that divers men of very good credit and estimation with the inquisitors complained thereof, whereupon, he was committed to prison, and found guilty of divers kinds of treacheries. Yet, notwithstanding, in giving sentence upon him, he found the inquisitors his very good lords and masters, who knew full well that he had been a full sure stake to their Holy House and a trusty servitor, so that his sentence was easy enough, nothing like what was given to the other man, his successor, who only suffered the mother and her daughters to meet and talk together for the space of but one half hour, though for his misdeeds, well known and probed by him, he deserved to be dealt with in as evil a way as the other was for his pity and mercifulness."

40 Montes (1569, ff. 37v–38v) describes Herrera as a totally different sort of person: "The keeper [Pedro de Herrera], being of a good nature, consented and allowed them to be together by the space of half an hour. And after they had a little shown their affections, and done their duty each to the other, the daughters to their mother and she to them again, he brought each one to her own cell where she was before. Within a few days after, the keeper seeing the same persons in most terrible torments, and fearing lest the very extremity thereof would drive them to confess that small courtesy and favor which he showed them in allowing them to meet and talk together but only for half an hour, went to the Holy House, confessed his act and prayed pardon, supposing, like a fool, by his own confession to have escaped the penalty thereof. But the inquisitors (to whom it is second nature to abhor all kind of humanity) deemed it so heinous an offence that they commanded him forthwith to be ordered into prison. Wherein, partly due to the great extremity that was shown to him and partly the very thought of it and a certain fancy that took him, (becoming somewhat melancholic) he went insane. And yet, despite his infirmity and madness, they pardoned him not one jot of his punishment. After he had been kept a whole year in a vile cell, they brought him upon their triumphing stage, having a *sanbenito* on his back and a rope about his neck like a felon, and there gave sentence upon him: first to be whipped about the city in the high streets and to have 200 lashes bestowed on him, and afterwards to serve in a galley ship as a slave for five years." Pedro de Herrera's sentence is confirmed in AHN, Inquisición, leg. 2075, doc. 1 (2), in: Lopez Muñoz (2011, 212, doc. 101).

way she had described, and that she had told Elvira that if she were asked, she should tell the truth.[41]

A week later, on August 16, 1560, Lucia Gomez was again called before Inquisitor Gonzalez de Munebrega. Among other things she was asked if she had told Catalina Jimenez, her cellmate, about the paper notes and if she had given Catalina Jimenez one to put under the heap of dirt or if Catalina had brought her one. She said that Catalina Jimenez had seen her write them and had put them there and picked them up for her the days she did not go out to the public toilet or when she was menstruating and couldn't leave her cell.[42]

The Nuñez sisters, their mother, and their aunt were sent to the stake on December 22, 1560.[43] Two months later, a letter was received from the Supreme Council demanding certain details regarding Elvira. Inquisitors Gasco, Carpio, and Francisco de Soto called in the notary, Eusebio de Arrieta, to bring them the records showing the exact date when a search warrant went out authorizing Elvira's capture and the date she was imprisoned because this information did not appear on her trial records. The notary certified that the warrant was sent out on August 17, 1559, and that on August 23 orders were given that Cristobal Perez and Cristobal de Tordesillas, *familiares* of the Holy Office, proceed to arrest Elvira Nuñez, her mother Leonor Gomez, her sister Teresa Gomez, and her cousin Leonor Gomez, and to confiscate their goods. Likewise, the notary certified that Inquisitor Carpio had had his first interview with Elvira on September 2 of that year.[44]

The Supreme Council had a special interest in knowing the exact date Elvira Nuñez entered Triana prison because she gave birth there on March 8, 1560, and they wanted to know if she was already pregnant when she entered.[45] Not satisfied with the testimony of the midwife, Maria Diez, regarding the day and the hour of Elvira delivery, the inquisitors called in Elvira Nuñez's cellmate, Elvira de Alvo, to know exactly when they had put the two women in the same cell and if Elvira had given birth while they were together.[46] Alvo responded that they had brought her in around January and that, in effect, while they were together she had given birth to a daughter. They wanted to know if Alvo had asked whose

---

41 AHN, Inquisición, leg. 2942, doc. 85, in: Lopez Muñoz (2011, 186, doc. 93). Notes mine.
42 AHN, Inquisición, leg. 2942, doc. 85, in: Lopez Muñoz (2011, 186, doc. 93).
43 AHN, Inquisición, leg. 2943, doc. 162, in: Lopez Muñoz (2011, 218, doc. 102).
44 AHN, Inquisición, leg. 2943, doc. 12, in: Lopez Muñoz (2011, 236, doc. 110).
45 BNE, ms. 9175, f. 258r; AHN, Inquisición, leg. 2943, doc. 12; leg. 2943, doc. 13, in: Lopez Muñoz (2011, 218, doc. 102; 236, doc. 110; 234, doc. 109).
46 Elvira de Alvo was the daughter of Isabel Martinez de Alvo in whose house Dr. Constantino had his clandestine library. She was married to the merchant Pedro Ramirez. She was very likely put in Elvira Gomez's cell with her the last months of her pregnancy because she was also a mother and had experience.

daughter the child was or if Elvira had told her. She couldn't remember, but since it wasn't her business she hadn't asked either. They asked if the child was premature to which she responded that when she had come to her cell she had asked her when the child was due and she had said in March. They asked her if the child was healthy to which she responded that it was a healthy, full term child, that the birth had been easy and that Elvira was only laid up four or five days and was then sent back to her own cell. After that they called in the midwife again to certify that the child was truly a full term child and how she could know that, to this she gave a lengthy response regarding the easy delivery, the child's healthy color, etc.[47] With this information, on February 27, 1561, Inquisitors Gasco, Carpio, and Soto sent Elvira Nuñez's trial records off to the Supreme Council, duly complemented, together with the testimony of Elvira de Alvo and the midwife, certifying that she was six months and six days pregnant when she entered Triana.[48] On March 18, the Council acknowledged receipt of the letter with a note that simply said: "we are pleased to learn that Nuñez was already pregnant when she entered prison."[49] This was a very delicate matter. Had she got pregnant while in prison, the paternity of the child could be tagged onto someone in charge, such as the jail keeper, or even one of the inquisitors, or it could also imply negligence on the part of the jail keeper, who would have allowed the inmates to mix. The results of the treatment received by Juana de Bohorquez in the fall of 1559 may have caused the local inquisitors to slightly change their tactics. Instead of sending women directly to the torture chamber, they "counterfeited compassion towards them" as Montes puts it.

Inquisitor Carpio had his first interview with Elvira Nuñez on September 2, 1559, shortly after she had been imprisoned.[50] Montes (1569, ff. 28r–30r) narrates this and subsequent meetings:

> The maiden, being but simply witted, was soon induced to credit the fair promises and allurements of this flattering Father, and thereupon began to open unto him certain points of religion whereof they often conferred among themselves, in a way almost as if one would give holy things to a dog or cast pearls before a swine. The Inquisitor, having gotten this thread by the end, labored to unwind the whole ball, and calling in the maiden many times before him to the end that her depositions might be entered by order of law, made her believe that he would take it up and end it so reasonably that she should receive no manner of harm thereby. And in the last day of hearing, he made a repetition unto her of all his former promises as to set her at liberty again, and such like, but when the time came that she looked for the performance thereof, there was no such matter, but to the contrary. My lord the Inquisitor and his adherents, perceiving how

---

47 AHN, Inquisición, leg. 2943, doc. 12, in: Lopez Muñoz (2011, 236, doc. 110).
48 AHN, Inquisición, leg. 2943, doc. 13, in: Lopez Muñoz (2011, 234, doc. 109).
49 AHN, Inquisición, lib. 575, f. CXIIv, in: Lopez Muñoz (2011, 184, doc. 91).
50 AHN, Inquisición, leg. 2943, doc. 12, in: Lopez Muñoz (2011, 236, doc. 110).

this devise had brought things to light which all their extremities could in no case do, to the end to make her confess the rest, determined once again to have her upon the rack, wherein she endured most intolerable pains both upon the pulley and the trough, until they had, as it were in a press, wrung out of her as well her belief, also forced her to accuse those persons whom they had hunted after so long. For the damsel, through very extremity of pangs and torments, was driven to betray her own natural mother, and sisters, and divers others that were immediately apprehended and afterwards put to the torments and in the end sent to the fire.

Moreover, the self same maiden later played a notable part in testimony of her belief, for when she was brought up onto the solemn scaffold with other of her companions, there to be seen of all the people and every one to hear sentence of death pronounced upon them, as she returned to her place again, having heard her judgment, which was 'to be burned', she came to her aunt, who had been her schoolmistress and taught her the catechism and the beliefs, the profession whereof she should presently be executed, and with a bold courage without change of countenance, bending her head downward maidenly, gave her most hearty thanks for that exceeding great benefit in taking the pains to instruct her, and prayed pardon at her hands if at any time she had offended her, for that she was now at the point of taking her death and departing this life. Her aunt, on the other hand, comforted her as stoutly, willing her to be of good cheer and to let nothing disquiet her, for she hoped in God that she would be with Christ ere it were long. And this she did in the presence and hearing of all the people, but especially of all those of the Holy House and their adherents. This aunt of hers was the self same woman, which a year or two before, being mad, had exposed the whole congregation to the Inquisitors, whereof I made mention before, who being restored to her former wits again, by the goodness of God, as well as the relics of her disease would let her, now both confessed His truth and, for the same, endured most horrible and loathsome imprisonment and torments, was openly whipped, and remained in prison during the rest of her life.

Juana de Mazuelos

Together with the Nuñez sisters, their mother and their aunt, Juana de Mazuelos was also sentenced to the stake at the *auto-da-fe* that took place in Seville on December 22, 1560.[51] Her mother, Maria de Mazuelos, and her sister Costanza de Herrera were sentenced to life in prison and loss of all their goods. A year and a half later, Juana's father, Aparicio de Contreras, and her husband, Juan Bautista, were also sentenced to life in prison. Two of her brothers, Francisco and Juan, had fled to Geneva earlier.[52] Francisco joined the Italian church and established

51 AHN, Inquisición, leg. 2075, doc. 1(2); AGS, Estado, leg. 137, doc. 3, in: Lopez Muñoz (2011, 226, doc. 101).

52 AHN, Inquisición, leg. 2943, doc. 162, in: Lopez Muñoz (2011, 376, doc. 185). In 1565, the inquisitors intercepted a letter sent by Francisco Mazuelos to Diego Martinez, "a friend of his

himself as a lace merchant in Geneva, where he died in 1596 at the age of sixty (Boehmer: 2007, III, 158). Curiously, Montes makes no mention of the Mazuelos, but among the Inquisition documents there is a lengthy legal document, written up by Inquisitor Gonzalez de Munebrega, describing, as he did in the case of Francisca de Chaves, the accusations against Juana de Mazuelos. The document reads thus:

> Based on, and according to, the accusation against Juana de Maçuelos presented to us by the prosecutor in which he states that, being the aforesaid a baptized Christian, with no fear of God our Lord or the Holy Catholic faith, or evangelical norms, or what the Holy Mother Apostolic Roman Catholic Church teaches, has become a follower of the false and reprobate sect of Martin Luther and his henchmen, and obstinately holds and believes his errors and heresies, and believing she is saved in that sect, says that the pope is the antichrist, that bulls and pardons and indulgences are worthless because we have them in Jesus Christ. Likewise, she says that the Holy Sacrament of the altar is in memory of what Jesus Christ our Lord did for us; it is in remembrance of His passion and is a token of love that manifests His mercy and that, after it is consecrated, His body and blood are not there, but in the hearts of some good faithful Christians, and not in others, and that with anything a Christian eats, whether bread or fruit, as long as he/she acknowledged it came from God, he/she received the body of our Lord Jesus Christ. And that man is saved through faith in Him and keeping the Ten Commandments and doing works of faith and charity, not through works such as confessing, taking communion, or receiving any other sacraments of the church, that there is no purgatory or any other merits but those of Christ. Nor is it necessary to comply with fastings, for He fasted for all of us. Likewise, priests, monks and friars should marry. And as accomplice and cover up of heretics, knowing who these persons were, the aforesaid, in approval of their doctrine, had contact with and communicated with these persons and showed them favor and kept silent and did not denounce them to the Holy Office as is required.

> Hence, based on her confession, and as far as he was concerned, and nothing else, he urged us, that for her definitive sentence, we declare Juana de Mazuelos a Lutheran heretic, one who favored and harbored heretics, and as a result has incurred in a sentence of major excommunication and consequently she should be condemned to the most severe penalty under law and she should be delivered to the secular authorities to be burned and all her goods be confiscated and be handed over to the royal treasury, and that our Holy Office implore that in all this full justice be made.

> Taking into account how Juana de Mazuelos responded to the above accusation and to the depositions of six witnesses, and how she confessed before us that she had been instructed that for God neither the mediation of the saints nor of Our Lady were necessary, and for which she used a Bible verse that said, "Come unto me all you that are tired and afflicted and I will give you rest," [Matt. 11,28] and that Christ said these words in the gospel and that it was not necessary to go to anyone else but Him, implying that those who did not believe those words would go to hell, and she was persuaded of

and a heretic," persuading him to come to Geneva. AHN, Inquisición, leg. 2943, doc. 156, in: Lopez Muñoz (2011, 355, doc. 167).

that, and also she had been taught that the person that trusted in God and believed that Jesus Christ had come to pay the penalty for sin should not fear purgatory, because it did not exist, and that is what she believed. Likewise, a person was not obliged to make a true confession to the priest but only to confess a few sins out of duty, and that she believed that bulls, jubilees, fastings, prayers, and other things required by the Catholic Church were not enough to pardon sins, only the blood of Christ could do that, and that these things had not value of their own, and that we were not obliged to fast.

Furthermore, she said that the pope had no authority to oblige us to do things here on earth because he was only a man; and that we were only to adore God and not images. She confessed that if she hadn't said these things before she thought she didn't sin by not saying them, but that, on the contrary, she sinned by discovering them because she had been told that even though she was taken prisoner by the Holy Office, she should keep silent because if she said them and did harm to her neighbor, she would go to hell, and that she should be mindful that God required that we love our neighbor. She also said that when a certain person said Mass, she and others said, "today we have a faithful minister." She also said other things that we will not repeat here in order not to add to the confusion and to offend the sensitive ears of good Catholic Christians, for which she asked God to forgive her for, since they were matters pertaining to Jesus Christ, she did not think they were sinful. With tears in her eyes, she also begged us to have mercy.

Having seen and examined the case, and reached an agreement after having deliberated with learned and knowledgeable persons, we decree, *Cristi nomine invocato,* that, in accord with the indictment and charges in the case that fully verify the procurator's accusation, and backed by a number of witnesses and by the confession made by Juana de Mazuelos herself in our presence, we rule the case closed and consequently declare the said Juana de Mazuelos to be an apostate Lutheran heretic to the great offence of God our Lord and the holy Catholic faith and gospel, and as such has fallen and incurred in major excommunication and all the other penalties and censorships that similar heretics bring upon themselves, who under the name of Christians commit such offences, and in the confiscation of all her goods from the day she entered this place, which the receptor of this Holy Office will put into the royal treasury. And because we were not convinced of her conversion, but on the contrary we believe that she only confessed in order to save her life and not because she had given up the heresies and errors she had admitted earlier, and so not to infect others, being a wolf in sheep's clothing, we rule she be burned and turned over to the civil justice, to the mayor of this city and his officers, whom we affectionately beg to deal benign and kindly with the aforesaid Juana de Mazuelos. We also rule that her children, if she has any, be declared unworthy, unable to obtain ecclesiastic benefits, or public office, or honors, nor wear gold, silver or silk, or any of the things that our common laws and decrees and the Holy Office prohibits unworthy persons to wear. This is our final and definitive resolution, and as such, we conclude and declare it in this document.[53]

The above document, drawn up by Juan Gonzalez de Munebrega, is another example of how unwittingly the inquisitors themselves revealed—and preserved

---

53 AHN, Inquisición, leg. 2075 (2), doc. 46, in: Lopez Muñoz (2011, 199, doc. 97).

for us today—doctrinal positions held by dissenters that would otherwise be nearly impossible to discover.

Mariana (or Maria) Enriquez de Ribera

Mariana Enriquez de Ribera was born in Seville around 1522. She married Pedro Portocarrero, marquis of Villanueva del Fresno, but had no children. Her husband died in 1557, and she inherited his title, hence the documents often refer to her as "la marquesa." We have already encountered several members of Mariana's family in previous chapters. She was the niece of Fadrique Enriquez de Ribera, who in 1525 invited Juan Lopez de Celain to organize a mission point called "The Twelve Apostles of Medina de Rioseco." She came from a very cultured family, whose members had magnificent libraries. Her uncle Fadrique Enriquez had a library of some 250 books. It is uncertain where his books went after his death in 1539. Mariana's brother Per Afan de Ribera, duke of Alcala de los Gazules and marquis of Tarifa, and viceroy of Naples from 1559 to 1571, inherited his uncle's titles and Mariana may have inherited the library.[54] On the other hand, Per Afan de Ribera had his own large library, which he had sent to his palace in Bornos when he returned from Italy. Another brother, Fadrique Enriquez de Ribera, had spent much of his time in Flanders as part of Charles V's court. A third brother, Fernando Enriquez de Ribera, 3rd Marquis of Tarifa, 2nd Duke of Alcala de los Gazules, married Juana Cortes, the daughter of the conquistador Hernan Cortes. Juana also had a large library, as well as Mariana's niece by marriage, Ana Tellez-Giron, the daughter of Pedro Giron, who had married Mariana's nephew Fernando Enriquez de Ribera y Cortes (Álvarez Márquez: 2004, 19–40).[55]

For years, Mariana Enriquez de Ribera sat under the preaching of Dr. Egidio and Constantino, which implies that her contacts with the evangelicals of Seville may have gone back to the early 1550s. In any case, she was one of the recipients of the books and letters smuggled into Seville by Julianillo. On January 22, 1558, the Council sent instructions to the inquisitors at Seville to examine her privately in her palace-residence, the "Casa de Pilates,"[56] and if needs be to also question

---

54 As viceroy, Per Afan [Perafan] Enriquez de Ribera prevented the promulgation of the decrees of the Council of Trent and also Philip II's wish to introduce the Spanish Inquisition into the Kingdom of Naples.

55 The Tellez-Giron were cousins of Marina de Guevara, a nun from the Convent of Belen in Valladolid sentenced to the stake.

56 The construction of this palace was begun by Pedro Enriquez de Quiñones and completed by Pedro's son Fadrique Enriquez de Rivera (I Marquis of Tarifa). On October 20, 1520, Fadrique returned from a trip through Europe and the Holy Land. During Lent in 1521, he

her brothers, Per Afan and Fadrique, "but not before questioning the march-ioness."[57] Nevertheless, Fadrique Enriquez de Ribera, who spent much of his time in Flanders as part of Charles V's court, was later questioned in relation to Diego de la Cruz, who had been Ana de Deza's chaplain and had fled.[58]

Mariana's spiritual development may have been strongly influenced through her physician Christobal de Losada, who had become the leader of evangelical movement. The marchioness was questioned in June of 1558, but her case seems to have been dismissed at the time. In November of 1561 she was reported seen going to the Triana prison to bring "alms" to someone. Prisoners had to provide for their own maintenance, which was taken out of the goods confiscated, but this was often not enough and outside support was appreciated. This incident, together with the information they already had concerning her, alerted the in-quisitors once again.[59] In February of 1562, the Supreme Council asked the inquisitors at Seville to send them a copy of the marchioness's process, which suggests she had again been questioned.[60] In January of 1574, the inquisitors at Seville were again reviewing her declarations to find evidence against her brother Fadrique.[61]

Ana de Deza

The inquisitors had both Mariana Enriquez and Ana de Deza watched carefully. Ana de Deza also came from a very distinguished family. From her mother's side, she was a great niece of Inquisitor General Diego de Deza. She was well read and of all the learned women in Seville at that time, she had one of the largest private libraries (Álvarez Márquez: 2004, 23). In the same dispatch that instructed the inquisitors to visit Mariana Enriquez in her palace, in March of 1558, there were also instructions that Ana de Deza be summoned "with the greatest dissim-ulation" to the Castle of Saint George in Triana and that while she was being questioned someone should be sent to her house to confiscate all her books and papers, a procedure practiced also in the case of Domingo de Guzman and

inaugurated the observance in Seville of the *Via Crucis* (Stations of the Cross). The route began in the *Chapel of the Flagellations* of his palace and ended at a pillar located not far from the *Templete*, or *Cruz del Campo* (The Cross of the Field) located outside the city walls. This route ran the same distance of 1321 paces supposed to have separated the praetorium of Pontius Pilate from Calvary. The palace became known as the *Casa de Pilatos*. It was declared a National Monument in 1931.

57 AHN, Inquisición, lib. 575, ff. 57r–57v, in: Lopez Muñoz (2011, 111, doc. 34).
58 AHN, Inquisición, leg. 2943, doc. 71, in: Lopez Muñoz (2011, 268, doc. 71).
59 AHN, Inquisición, leg. 2943, doc. 41–2, in: Lopez Muñoz (2011, 245, doc. 116).
60 AHN, Inquisición, lib. 575, f. 126r, in: Lopez Muñoz (2011, 254, doc. 120).
61 AHN, Inquisición, leg. 2946, in: Lopez Muñoz (2011, 415, doc. 223).

Constantino. Ana de Deza's relatives, Aldonça de Puertocarrero and Isabel de Guzman, "if they were still alive," were also to be summoned in order to ratify what they had testified against Ana, and to send a copy of the process against Egidio in order to group together all the information against her.[62] Ana de Deza's contacts with the evangelical movement went back to the days of Dr. Egidio. She was questioned several times during Dr. Egidio's trial,[63] and later again regarding Diego de la Cruz, who had been her private chaplain.[64] She was not at all intimidated by the inquisitors. Indeed, it appears that when Dr. Egidio was imprisoned in Triana, Ana bribed the wife of the notary Domingo de Azpeitia to allow her to speak with him through a small window that communicated with his cell (Cárceles, 2014). Later, when Dr. Constantino was imprisoned, she and Isabel Martinez de Alvo communicated with him by letter thanks to little gifts they gave the jail keeper, Pedro de la Haya.

During the time Ana de Deza was in prison, and Juan Perez de Alegria was the jail keeper, he would often allow his wife to spend time with Ana in her cell. Sometimes, Alegria's assistant, Juan de Salamanca, would either take Alegre's wife to Ana's cell or fetch her from there—as he declared later—, which was totally prohibited. Ana also suborned Juan de Salamanca to carry messages in and out of the prison to her brother Garcia Tello.[65] She was sent to the torture chamber in November of 1561 and again in February of 1562, and was almost at the point of death at one time,[66] nevertheless, it appears that during her imprisonment, she had more liberty than others. This was probably due in part to the fact that her cousin, Juan Gutierrez Tello, was an important judge in the city and the inquisitors were careful to have him on their side in case they needed his favors, as is implied in a letter written in 1569, when one of them needed a certificate issued by the Casa de la Contratacion [House of Trade] for his servants so they could accompany him to the West Indies.[67]

At one point, suspecting that some of the prisoners could have secretly brought some books into their cells, the inquisitors had all the cells checked. In Ana de Deza's cell they found a copy of Ambrosio Montesino's *Gospels and Epistles* and a *Book of Hours* in Latin. Ana refused to allow them to take the *Gospels and Epistles* away from her, because "it was the only comfort she had."[68]

---

62 AHN, Inquisición, lib. 575, ff. 57r–57v, in: Lopez Muñoz (2011, 111, doc. 34).
63 AHN, Inquisición, lib. 575, ff. 57r y ss, in: Lopez Muñoz (2011, 111, doc. 34).
64 AHN, Inquisición, leg. 2943, doc. 144–2; AHN, Inquisición, leg. 2942, doc. 49–1, in: Lopez Muñoz (2011, 340, doc. 163; 120, doc. 43).
65 AHN, Inquisición, leg. 2943, doc. 41–3, in: Lopez Muñoz (2011, 245, doc. 116).
66 AHN, Inquisición, leg. 2943, doc. 41–3, in: Lopez Muñoz (2011, 245, doc. 116); AHN, Inquisición, leg. 2943, doc. 49–2, in: Lopez Muñoz (2011, 253, doc. 119).
67 AHN, Inquisición, leg. 2944, doc. 130.
68 AHN, Inquisición, leg. 2943, doc. 46.

Ana's response here is similar to that reported by the Venetian ambassador. Was she the young noble woman to whom Fray Baltanas gave the little book? Was it her father, alderman Dr. Nicolas Tello, member of the royal council, who denounced her? In one of the interrogatories, the inquisitors stated that they "regretted things had gone so far; it wasn't their fault but they were only acting in conformity with the law because *when a father chastised a son he does so not because he lacks mercy but he is forced to do so because the son has transgressed.*"[69] Whether this was simply a metaphor or referred to her father's denouncing her is unclear. In any case, the *Gospels and Epistles* had been put on the Index of Prohibited Books in 1559 as a result of the decree that prohibited the printing of the Scripture in the vulgar tongue. Ana was exposing herself to further punishment by keeping it with her. The inquisitors also suspected that she had spoken with the jail keepers. To this she responded that if they could come up with witnesses, she would tell them the truth, if not, she would not answer this accusation.[70]

Ana de Deza was sentenced at the *auto-da-fe* of April 26, 1562, to six years house arrest, and the confiscation of her library and a third of all her goods.[71] Her reputation for finding ways to communicate with the outside world even determined the place the Inquisitors chose for her house arrest. They selected the house of two "very honest" women in Triana, "across the river from Seville in order to avoid the coming and going of visitors she might have if they confined her to a house in Seville." They did, nevertheless, give her strict orders not to have any visitors without their permission. After two years she became seriously ill with problems of the liver and the spleen and requested permission to leave the house in order to take walks because she felt she urgently needed to have some physical exercise. A physician verified the ailment, and the inquisitors consulted their superiors. The Supreme Council not only granted her permission to take walks but, due to the seriousness of the ailment, reduced her sentence from six years to four and gave their consent for her going to live in Seville with her brother Garcia Tello de Deza.

Ana de Illescas

Ana de Illescas was of New Christian stock of *morisco* origin, like the Gonzalez sisters (Fernandez Chaves/Perez Garcia: 2011, 53). She was brought before the inquisitors on August 10, 1560. At the first interrogatory, which took place on

---

69 AHN, Inquisición, leg. 2943, doc. 41–3, in: Lopez Muñoz (2011, 245, doc. 116). Italics mine.
70 AHN, Inquisición, leg. 2943, doc. 41–3, in: Lopez Muñoz (2011, 245, doc. 116).
71 AHN, Inquisición, leg. 2943, doc. 46.

August 12, she said she was twenty five years old and the daughter Alonso de Illescas and one of his slaves. Her mother could have been Juliana Daça, of *morisca* origin, who had been a slave of Alonso de Illescas, and was sentenced at the same *auto* as Ana de Illescas.[72] Ana was married to Alonso Álvarez, a wealthy wine merchant. She was the half sister of alderman Juan Nuñez de Illescas, Leonor de Illescas, and Isabel de Illescas, married to alderman Guillen de Cassaos. All three sisters spent time in the Inquisition prison in Triana. When Ana was questioned on August 10, 1560, she admitted that she shared Francisca de Chaves's beliefs and had often accompanied her to hear Dr. Egidio, Constantino, Luis Hernandez del Castillo, Juan Gonzalez, and Bartolome de Olmedo preach. She confessed that Francisca had taught her not to believe in purgatory, or in the merits of the saints, or in fastings, or good works, or bulls, etc., and that she had not practiced these things for the last six years.[73] Ana de Illescas was well read. She had read Dr. Constantino's *Summa Pequeña de Doctrina* (1543) as well as Erasmus's *Declaración*.[74] She also mentioned a book written by Francisca de Chaves that she had read in manuscript form.

In April of 1561, after being put to the torment to confess in *caput alienum* (knowledge of the crimes of others) and having nothing else to add, Ana de Illescas was admitted to reconciliation, but she had to wait another year in prison, until the *auto-da-fe* of April 26, 1562, to hear her sentence read: confiscation of all her goods and *carcel perpetua* (life in prison). Offenders sentenced to *carcel perpetua* were sent to a special prison. In Seville, this prison was located in the district of Salvador in a building the Holy Office rented at that time from Alonso Fernandez de Santillan. In 1562 he raised the rent and the inquisitors considered moving the prison to a sugar warehouse in the district of la Magdalena, but they finally came to terms with Fernandez de Santillan. Due to the increase in prisoners after 1562, the Holy Office found it necessary, nevertheless, to rent an adjoining house belonging to Antonio de Hervas in order to accommodate the women (Cárceles: 2014).

A later, undated anonymous report sent to the Supreme Council by inquisitors Miguel del Carpio and Dr. Francisco Pazos informed the Council of Ana's good behavior while in prison and that it might be a good idea to commute her sentence. An interesting paragraph reads:

---

72 AHN, Inquisición, leg. 2075, doc. 2, in: Lopez Muñoz (2011, 257, doc. 122).
73 AHN, Inquisición, leg. 4519, doc. 10 (d), in: Lopez Muñoz (2011, 282, doc. 133).
74 AHN, Inquisición, leg. 4519, doc. 10 (d), in: Lopez Muñoz (2011, 282, doc. 133). This could refer to *Declaracion del Pater noster* (Antwerp: Juan Gravius, 1549), or *De morte declamatio D. Erasmi in genere consolatorio* (Lugduni, 1529), translated into Spanish and printed in Antwerp as *Preparación y aparejo para bien morir* (Antwerp: Martin Nuncio, 1555).

We have been informed that in all the time Ana de Illescas has been sitting out her sentence of perpetual imprisonment, her husband has not once got in touch with her or visited her or favored her in any way. That being the case, it seemed to us that if she were willing to give a substantial amount for some good pious cause her *sanbenito* and her prison sentence could be commuted. We think she could easily give this amount because she is a highly regarded daughter of Alonso de Illescas and the sister of Juan Nuñez de Illescas, who, together with their relatives, are among the wealthiest citizens of Seville. We inform you of this because you may not be aware of it.[75]

Isabel Martinez de Alvo

At the *auto-da-fe* that took place in Seville on October 28, 1562, nine individuals were condemned to the stake and eighteen sentenced to various degrees of imprisonment. This time no women were among those condemned to the stake. Among those receiving various degrees of imprisonment was Isabel Martinez de Alvo,[76] the widow in whose house Constantino had hidden certain books for fear of the inquisitors. She is first mentioned in the declarations made by Ortiz, when he named the three main recipients of the books brought in by Julian Hernandez: Juan Gonzalez, Isabel Martinez and Canon Hojeda. The books (and letters) were very likely not meant for her, but for Constantino. However, when Isabel was arrested in relation to the books, the inquisitors immediately stepped in to confiscate her goods.[77] Because this confiscation was considered penance money, which meant that the goods confiscated went to the Holy Office and not to the king's treasury, the inquisitors were only too anxious to put their hands on them.[78] Taking into consideration that not only Isabel, but also her children knew about the books—otherwise her son would not have been able to take the *alguaciles* straight to them—, and had not denounced Constantino, the whole family was punished. Isabel Martinez de Alvo was sentenced to ten years of house arrest and the confiscation of half her goods. She was sent to the house of a widow who lived near the monastery of Nuestra Señora de la Victoria, in Triana, so she could go to mass every Sunday. Her daughters, Elvira and Leonor, and her son Francisco received lesser sentences.[79] Her son, Francisco Beltran, was sen-

---

75 AHN, Inquisición, leg. 4519, doc. 10 (d), in: Lopez Muñoz (2011, 282, doc. 133).
76 AHN, Inquisición, leg. 2075 (1), doc. 2, in: Lopez Muñoz (2011, 222, doc. 103).
77 AHN, Inquisición, leg. 2075 (1), doc. 2, in: Lopez Muñoz (2011, 274, doc. 129).
78 Pedro de Morga estimated all of Isabel Martinez de Alvo's possessions in some 313,900,000 *maravedis*. Because she did not have money in ready cash, and if her lands were sold they would probably not bring that amount, it was decided that she would pay the amount required by the Holy Office in three payments. AHN, Inquisición, leg. 2943, doc. 49–2; leg. 2943, doc. 94–1, in: Lopez Muñoz (2011, 300, doc.141; 298–299, doc. 140).
79 AHN, Inquisición, leg. 2075 (1), doc. 2, in: Lopez Muñoz (2011, 222, doc. 103).

tenced to public whipping and was prohibited to leave the city without permission, under penalty of being sent to the galley ships for life. He was obliged to go daily to the House of the Jesuits for instruction and to pay 500 ducats for expenses incurred in by the Holy Office. Isabel Martinez's daughter Elvira was sentenced to two years of house arrest and 200 ducats for expenses incurred in by the Holy Office. She and Catalina de Cassaus, a widow sentenced at the same *auto*, were sent to the house of two different widows who lived near the church of Saint Ann in Triana. Isabel's daughter Leonor did not have to appear at the public *auto-da-fe*, but heard her sentence in the chapel of the Triana prison where she abjured *de levi*— that is, she admitted a minor error. She was also sentenced to pay 200 ducats for expenses incurred in by the Holy Office. Ten years later, in March of 1573, Isabel Martinez de Alvo's reclusion was commuted to simply fastings, pilgrimages, etc.

Catalina de San Esteban

On October 28, 1562, Catalina de San Esteban, daughter of the governess of the Casa de la Doctrina de las Niñas, an orphanage for girls, appeared on the scaffold to hear her sentence. She had spent nearly two years in Triana awaiting her sentence.[80] Having abjured *de vehementi*, she received a sentence of reclusion and the prohibition of ever again entering the Casa de Doctrina, or any institution where Christian Doctrine—the articles of faith—was taught or where she could either teach it or receive it. This suggests that Catalina had previously been an instructor at the Casa de la Doctrina de las Niñas. In 1544, her mother, Ines Mendez de Sotomayor, had founded the Casa de las Niñas for poor orphan girls. There the girls were taught the rudiments of Christian Doctrine together with a craft or a skill that would facilitate their later being placed with a family dedicated to that particular craft. In 1560, Ines Mendez appointed her son Juan Mendez de Sotomayor patron of the institution and her granddaughter Ines Mendez lifelong governess (*comendadora perpetua*). These appointments produced long and involved legal proceedings that nearly caused the institution to close (Montoto: 1991, 133–136). Catalina must have been a nun, because in a dispatch sent to the Supreme Council, the inquisitors reported that Catalina de San Esteban was sent to the strictest monastery of her order which is in Jerez de la Frontera, because it is the most "observant" of her order.[81]

---

80 AHN, Inquisición, leg. 2075 (1), doc. 2, in: Lopez Muñoz (2011, 222, doc. 103).
81 AHN, *Inquisición*, leg. 2943, doc. 83, in: Lopez Muñoz (2011, 281, doc. 132).

Chapter 11:
The Exiles

Freedom, Sancho, is one of the most precious gifts that heaven has bestowed upon men;
no treasures that the earth holds buried or the sea conceals can compare with it; for
freedom, as for honour, life may and should be ventured.
Don Quijote, Book II, Ch. 58.

Besides the men and women, members of the evangelical circles in Seville and
Valladolid who gave up their lives for their faith, the names and achievements of
the exiled Spaniards scattered throughout Europe must also be included in this
survey. Some of them are remembered for their translations of the Scriptures
into Spanish, others for their translations of the works of the northern reformers, and others for attaining prominent positions in foreign universities.
There were also those who contributed economically to the cause of the Reformation, as was the case of the Spanish merchant Marcos Perez living in
Flanders. One recurrent theme in this chapter is that of intrepid individuals who
not only fled for their lives in the face of severe persecution, but who faced all
sorts of vicissitudes in order to further the cause of the Reformation among their
fellow countrymen back in Spain (Moreno: 2009).

Geneva, City of Refuge

The majority of the Spanish exiles first sought refuge in Geneva. Indeed, Geneva
became the asylum for persecuted Protestants from all countries. If the population of Geneva in 1550 was around 13,000, it reached a peak of 21,400 in 1560.
Among the 279 fugitives who received the rights of citizenship in that city on one
single day in 1558, there were 200 Frenchmen, 50 Englishmen, 25 Italians, and 4
Spaniards (Schaff: 1882–1910, VIII, 375). From Juan de Valdes's circle in Naples,
came many Italian refugees in the early 1540s fleeing the Inquisition. It is worth
noting that it was in the Valdesian circle in Naples that Peter Martyr Vermigli,
who would become an influential figure in the development of Reformed theology both on the continent and in England, first read the works of the Protestant
reformers and embraced the pivotal doctrine of justification by faith alone.
Numerous religious exiles from Florence and Pisa first took refuge in Lucca
where Peter Martyr Vermigli was prior of the Basilica of San Frediano, but they
were forced to leave. Among the exiled Luccese Reformers were remembered
eminent scholars such as Emmanuel Tremellius, Girolamo Zanchi, Massimiliano

Celso Martinengo, Niccolo Balbani, etc., and entire families, such as the Burlamachi, the Calandrini, and the Diodati. As early as 1542, there was at Geneva a
congregation of Italian refugees, which had the chapel of d'Ostie assigned to it by
the council and was under the pastoral care of Bernardino de Sesvaz. In 1551,
Galeazzo Carraccioli, the eldest son of Nicol-Antonio Carraccioli, marquis of
Vico, one of the grandees of Naples, became their pastor.

Thousands of religious refugees passed through or took up residence in
Geneva between 1535 and 1575: English, Dutch, Spanish and Italian exiles, men
and women of all walks of life. Geneva became an important printing center
thanks to the wave a refugees of the 1550s that brought master printers such as
Jean Girard, Jean Crespin, Roberts Estienne. Indeed, the influx of craftsmen,
bankers, and merchants, transformed Geneva economically during the sixteenth
century

The earliest Protestant Spaniard we find in Geneva, according to Eduard
Boehmer (2007, II, 43), is the translator of Calvin's catechism from French into
Spanish dated 1550. In the preface, he begs that, "should his Spanish be found
defective, it may be pardoned on account of his absence from Spain, which had
been so long that a man of more lively intelligence than himself might have been
estranged from the native language." Next would follow Juan Perez de Pineda,
who probably arrived around 1552, and the Jeronimite monks who must have
arrived in the fall of 1557. Eduard Boehmer (2007, III, 157) lists Juan Perez, Juan
de Viria, Juan Moreno, Juan de Lion, Cypriano de Valera, Lope Cortes, Juan de
Molino, Juan de Medina, and Juan Alonso Baptista, as persons requesting citizenship on October 10, 1558, and "on the same day the Spaniards were allowed
henceforward to have the gospel preached to them in the temple S. Germain, in
their own language, as there was an aged man of good conduct willing to preach.
This man was Juan Perez [Jehan Purius, or Pierius]. He had stayed there already
for some time."

The Spanish exiles that fled the Spanish Inquisition were given the same
privileges that had been already granted to the Italians and since most of them
understood Italian, they joined the Italian church there, but they did not stay
long. With the death of Mary Tudor in November of 1558, many of the English
exiles in Geneva decided to return to their native country and many of the
Spaniards accompanied them.

Francisco de Enzinas

Francisco de Enzinas (1518–1552), also known as Francis Dryander (from the
Greek *drus*, which can be translated *encina* [ever-green oak tree] in Spanish) or
Françoys du Chesne (in French), or Francisco de Elao—the name that appears

on his translation of Calvin's *Catechism* (1540)—, was a classical scholar, translator, and author.[1] Although he was not among those that fled Spain, nevertheless, he can be considered a religious exile in the sense that he could not have returned to Spain without being imprisoned by the Inquisition. He was both an evangelical and a humanist, terms closely connected in the Reformation era, indicating someone who studied the text of Scripture in its original languages rather than the theology of the schools, who drew his convictions from the Bible rather than from systematic theology.

Enzinas was born in Burgos, an important commercial center in northern Spain. His father was a successful wool merchant, brother to Pedro de Lerma, dean of the faculty of theology at the Sorbonne. Francisco's mother died when he was a child and his father remarried. His stepmother, Beatriz de Santa Cruz, was a relative of the wealthy merchant Jeronimo de Salamanca Santa Cruz.[2] Francisco was sent to the Low Countries around 1536 for commercial training in one of his uncles' firms, but instead of pursuing a promising business career, in 1539, he enrolled at the Collegium Trilingue of Louvain. His brother Diego de Enzinas, who also had been sent to Flanders for commercial training but had enrolled at the Collegium Trilingue the previous year, may have encouraged him to do so. At Louvain, the two brothers fell under the spell of humanist scholarship. Indeed, it was Erasmus's influence that first turned Enzinas from his family's commercial interests to the world of letters and, ultimately, the evangelical faith. From Louvain, Diego Enzinas went to Paris—possibly invited by his uncle Pedro de Lerma, who had just recently become dean of the faculty of theology at the Sorbonne—and Francisco, who must have shown promise as a scholar, was allowed to continue his studies of Greek under Philip Melanchthon at Wittenberg.

Their uncle Pedro de Lerma (1461–1541) had been professor of divinity and one of the first chancellors of the University of Alcala and had represented the pro-Erasmus faction at the conference in Valladolid in 1527 called to investigate Erasmus's writings. Once the tide turned and the anti-Erasmians won the day, Lerma resigned as chancellor of Alcala and returned to Burgos. In 1537, he was denounced to the Inquisition of Toledo as suspected of Lutheran opinions and spreading Erasmian views. To avoid further trouble, Lerma moved to Paris that year, where he became dean of the faculty of theology at the Sorbonne. His nephew and successor at Alcala, Luis de Cadena, soon fell under the same

---

1 See Bergua Cavero (2006); Boehmer (2007, I, 133–184); Nelson (2004).
2 Members of the de Salamanca family—Miguel, Gabriel, Pedro, Jerónimo—were important merchants, manufacturers and bankers from Burgos living in Antwerp with close connections to the court. See Fagel (2002, I, 159–170).

suspicion and followed his example. The young Enzinas brothers—Diego and Francisco—only knew Pedro de Lerma for a short time, for he died in 1541.

In March 1542, Diego was back in Antwerp supervising the printing of a little book titled *Breve y compendiosa institución de la religión Cristiana*, a translation made by his brother Francisco of Calvin's 1538 Latin Catechism, to which he had appended a translation of Martin Luther's *Freedom of the Christian Man*. The work contained a prologue by Francisco expressing the Protestant idea of justification by faith in a language and irenic spirit similar to that of Juan de Valdes. Diego planned to smuggle copies of the book into Spain, but the Spanish Inquisition learned of his plan and his family sent him to Italy for safety. The Roman Inquisition, however, which had just been reinstated that year, soon arrested him. He was tried, and sentenced to the stake in Rome in March 1547.

Meanwhile, while boarding at Philip Melanchthon's house in Wittenberg, Francisco finished his translation of the New Testament into Spanish. He straightway took it to Antwerp to be printed by Steven Mierdman despite a new edict from Charles V prohibiting all books printed without imperial permission.[3] Taking advantage of the fact that the emperor—to whom his New Testament was dedicated—was in Antwerp, Enzinas decided to bypass the law and present the first copy off the press (with the imperial *imprimatur* missing from the title page) to the emperor personally. Sympathy at court for Enzinas, thanks to his uncle Pedro de Lerma's connections, got him an interview with Charles V, but due to the emperor's fear of examining matters of faith, he turned the New Testament and its translator over to his Dominican confessor, Pedro de Soto, for examination. The outcome was Francisco's arrest in December of 1543 and imprisonment in Brussels. Louis van Schore, president of Brabant, destroyed the entire edition. In the Prologue of his New Testament, Enzinas gave three reasons for having published it:

> All the other nations of Europe already enjoy the privilege of having the Bible translated into their language and they call the Spaniards superstitious because they still do not have the Bible in their language. No royal or papal decree prohibits this publication. And although some may deem such translations dangerous in the time of heretics, be assured that heresies do not come from reading the Bible, but from the perverse explanations of evil men who distort the Holy Scriptures for their own perdition. (PROEL, 2014).

After a dramatic escape from prison in February 1545, Enzinas made his way back to Wittenberg and wrote an account of his adventures: *De statu Belgico et religione Hispanica* (Report on the Situation in Flanders and the Religion of

---

3 Steven Mierdman began printing in Antwerp. Some time after 1546, to escape proceedings for having printed heretical books, he went to England. On the accession of Mary Tudor, Mierdman moved to Emden, where he continued printing until his death in 1559.

Spain) (Wittenberg, 1545), better known as his *Memoirs*. The next year in Basel, he published an account of the murder of his friend Juan Diaz, *Historia vera de morte sancti viri Ioannis Diazii Hispani* (The True Story of the Death of the Saintly Spaniard Juan Diaz) (Basel, 1546), which became a best seller. For his *Book of Martyrs* (1557), Ludwig Rabus used material from Francisco de Enzinas, whom he knew from Wittenberg, when Rabus was a student there. Although Rabus abridged Enzinas's stories faithfully, one of Rabus's most dramatic chapters retells Enzinas's story of Juan Diaz, for which Martin Bucer had written a preface.

In 1548, Enzinas was in Strasbourg where he married Margaret d'Elter, a fellow religious exile from Belgium whom he had met the previous year in Basel at the home of the exiled Belgian nobleman, Jacques de Bourgogne, Lord of Falais. The following year, the couple moved to England, where Thomas Cranmer took them into his palace at Lambeth and soon afterward appointed Enzinas to teach Greek at Cambridge. That year Enzinas was on a committee with Bishop Cranmer, Martin Bucer, Peter Martyr Vermigli, Pablo Fagius, and Immanuel Tremellius deliberating on the reform of the Book of Common Prayer, which indicates both his level of scholarship and the high esteem the Reformers had for him. Enzinas's move to Cambridge was also influenced by the wish of Lady Catherine Willoughby, Duchess of Suffolk, that he should tutor one of her sons. By this, the Duchess was able to accomplish two things at the same time: be true to her Protestant convictions and to her Spanish blood, which she traced through her mother, Maria de Salinas, lady-in-waiting to Catherine of Aragon, Henry VIII's first wife.[4]

The plague that hit Strasbourg in the winter of 1552–53 first killed Enzinas and a month later his wife Margaret, leaving their two infant daughters to become wards of the city. The German reformer Philip Melanchthon, who had been a close friend, offered to take one of them into his home in Wittenberg, but the city refused. Enzinas's *Memoirs* were published posthumously in French

---

4 María de Salinas, Lady Willoughby (1490–1539) was a Spanish noblewoman who served as lady-in-waiting to Catherine of Aragon, Queen of England. On June 5, 1516, Maria de Salinas married the English nobleman, William Willoughby, 11th Baron Willoughby de Eresby. They had one child, Catherine, who became 12th Baroness Willoughby de Eresby and Duchess of Suffolk. Grimsthorpe Castle was given to the family by Henry VIII on the occasion of Maria's marriage. In 1526, Lord Willoughby died. Maria then spent several years fighting for control of the Willoughby estates on behalf of her daughter. In August 1532, shortly before Catherine of Aragon's marriage to Henry VIII was annulled, Maria was ordered to leave Catherine's household. Maria's daughter, Catherine Willoughby, Duchess of Suffolk, became a close friend of Henry VIII's sixth wife, Catherine Parr. After Henry's death in 1547, the duchess helped fund the publication of one of Catherine Parr's books, *The Lamentation of a Sinner* (1547). Beginning in 1550, the duchess helped establish Stranger churches for foreign refugees, principally Dutch, who were fleeing religious persecution on the Continent.

translation (Ste. Marie aux Mines, 1558) through the efforts of his wife's relatives in Strasbourg. They have since been translated into modern French,[5] German,[6] and Spanish.[7] His collected letters, which include correspondence with Philip Melanchthon, Heinrich Bullinger, Martin Bucer, John Calvin, and other religious figures, students, rulers, and printers of the period, have recently been translated from the original Latin into Spanish and published by Ignacio J. Garcia Pinilla (1995). Unfortunately, Enzinas's works, which offer an interesting dimension to the history of the Reformation, have not yet been translated into English.

Pedro Alejandro

Pedro Alejandro (c.1498–1563), like Francisco de Enzinas, embraced the Protestant faith while living abroad and never returned to his native Spain. Pedro Alejandro, better known in Europe as Pierre Alexandre or Peter Alexander, had been rector of the Universidad de Alcala (1531–32) and responsible for furthering biblical studies when Egidio, Vargas, and Constantino were there. In 1533, Alexander was offered the post of canon of the Cathedral of Seville. A year later, he was sent to the Netherlands as chaplain of Charles V's sister Mary of Austria, dowager queen of Hungary, then governess of the Netherlands, and Dr. Egidio took his place in Seville. While in the Netherlands, Alexander embraced the Protestant faith. He was brought to trial, but he managed to escape thanks to a friend before the sentence—burning at the stake—was pronounced. Francisco de Enzinas (1992, 388–400) relates Alexander's story in his *Memoirs*. It was Alexander's trial, which lasted an entire year—and his escape on November 25, 1544—that made Enzinas aware of how risky his own situation was. Enzinas learned of Alexander's escape through a mutual friend, which suggests that the two men had met earlier, perhaps in 1543 in Antwerp, where Enzinas had taken his New Testament to be printed, or in Brussels, where Mary of Austria had her court and where Enzinas presented his New Testament to the emperor. They would also have had a mutual friend in Enzinas's uncle, Pedro de Lerma, who had been professor of divinity at Alcala. In any case, Alexander seems to have been very fond of Enzinas, as can be appreciated from the way he addresses him: "*Al muy docto y erudito señor Francisco de Enzinas, amigo y hermano muy*

5 Francisco de Enzinas, *Mémoires de Francisco de Enzinas: texte Latin inédit avec la traduction Française du XVIe siècle en regard 1543–1545* (Brussels: Muquardt, 1862).
6 Francisco de Enzinas, *Denkwuerdigkeiten* (Leipzig: Duerz, 1897).
7 Francisco de Enzinas, *Memorias: historia del estado de los paises, bajos, y el estado de la religión de España* (Buenos Aires: La Aurora 1960); *Memorias*, Francisco Socas (trans.), (Madrid: Ediciones Clásicas, 1992).

querido" (To the extremely learned and scholarly Francisco de Enzinas, a very dear friend and brother). (Enzinas: 1995, 105, 165, 363).

When in 1544 it appeared that Alexander might have been acquitted, Pedro de Soto, Charles V's confessor, convinced the emperor that if a solemn lesson was not learned by giving Alexander the most severe punishment instead of letting him off scot-free, the whole country would be lost. When the emperor learned of his escape, he was very upset, "*incluso juró solemnemente que jamás perdonaría a un traidor o a un luterano*" (he even solemnly swore that he would never forgive a traitor or a Lutheran) (Enzinas: 1992, 390). The following week a notice appeared on all the church doors to the effect that if Alexander did not appear by January 2, he would be declared excommunicated *in absentia*. Alexander, of course, did not appear and Francisco de Zon, a theologian from Louvain who was one of the judges during his trial, publicly proclaimed him a heretic, worthy of being beheaded or burned. According to Enzinas, Zon's words were so disrespectful and offensive that even those who had very little knowledge of reformed doctrine at the time began to show greater sympathy towards it.

Peter Alexander went first to Strasbourg and from there to Heidelberg where he became professor of theology and canon law (1546–48). Next we find him in England, officiating as canon in Canterbury (1548) and rector of All Hallows, Lombard Street, in 1552. On March 7, 1554, he was cited together with seven other rectors to appear in Bow Church, London, before Harvey the Vicar-General of Canterbury, all charged with having married, which was contrary to the laws of the Anglican church. Only two made a personal appearance; Alexander may have already left the country. In 1547, in Germany, he had married Marguerite Vauville, the daughter of Richard Vauville, who would later become pastor of the first French congregation in London in 1550. Peter Alexander was cited again in his capacity of prebendary, along with Bernardino Ochino, who had also married. By not appearing, they were pronounced "contumacious heretics." A sentence of suspension of their functions, deprivation of their prebends, and prohibition to live with their wives was pronounced upon them (Dixon: 2013, 142–147; 1977, 551–560).

From London, Alexander went back to Strasbourg, where he pastored the French-speaking congregation from 1555 to 1560. After that he returned to England again, where it appears he became secretary to Bishop Cranmer and where he died in 1563 (Leon de la Vega: 2012, I, 596). In 1558, while on the continent, he published a two-volume work in Latin under the pseudonym Simon Alexius.[8] His father-in-law, Richard Vauville, who had been called to England to co-pastored the French congregation in London in 1550, along with

---

8 Simon Alexius, *De origine novi Dei missatici, quondam in Anglia mortui, nunc denuò ab inferis excitati* (Geneva: Jean Crespin, 1558).

François de la Riviere, remained in London to serve the French believers until 1555, at which time he and his wife moved to Frankfurt, where they both died of the plague the following year.

Luis del Castillo and Diego de la Cruz

At the time of Dr. Egidio's first arrest in 1550 no specific actions were taken against Protestants in Spain, nevertheless, some men thought it wise to leave the country, among them were Juan Perez de Pineda, whom we shall deal with later, Luis Hernandez del Castillo, and Diego de la Cruz. These three were the first documented religious exiles that resulted from the activities of the Spanish Inquisition against the Protestants in Seville. First they took up residence in Paris and were joined by Dr. Juan Morillo. Morillo was born in Aragon. He had studied in Louvain and Paris in the 1530s (Leon de la Vega: 2012, I, 406). After attending the Council of Trent in 1545, he had joined the household of Cardinal Reginald Pole, where Protestant literature was read and discussed and the influence of Juan de Valdes was strongly felt. At this stage, there seems to have been no suspicion that Morillo held Protestant views, although he is reported saying later that if he was a heretic, Pole and Bartolome Carranza—who at that time also formed part of Cardinal Pole's literary circle at Rome—had made him one (Kinder: 1985, 133). From Rome, Morillo went back to Paris until 1553, where he shared living facilities with Juan Perez de Pineda, Luis Hernandez del Castillo, and Diego de la Cruz. From Paris, Morillo went to Antwerp, where he joined a group of French-speaking Protestants of Calvinist persuasion, whom he co-pastored for a time with François de la Riviere. This congregation eventually moved to Frankfurt, at which time Diego de la Cruz also joined them. It seems that Morillo was poisoned shortly after that, "a victim of the intolerance of his homeland against his beliefs, an intolerance which, extending far beyond Spain's national frontiers, would stop at nothing." (Kinder: 1985, 157).

Luis Hernandez del Castillo, alias Luis Fernandez or Luis del Castillo, was the author of the pamphlet entitled *Diálogo consolatorio entre la Iglesia que está en Sevilla y Jesucristo* (Consolatory Dialog between the Little Church in Seville and Jesus Christ) that the inquisitors found among the personal papers of Francisca de Chaves, a nun at the Convent of Santa Isabel in 1550. Castillo's co-exile, Diego de la Cruz, seems to have organized a letter-carrying service between Spanish exiles in Antwerp, Cologne, Louvain and other places, before being caught and tried before the Inquisition (Kinder: 1985, 133). A dispatch sent from the Supreme Council to Emperor Charles V on July 29, 1550, requested his arrest:

Instructions for His Majesty's court: First, let Gaspar Zapata, servant of Fadrique Enriquez, brother of the Marquis of Tarifa, who lives in His Majesty's court, be examined under oath and tell and declare if he knows where the priest Diego de la Cruz, who lived some years in Seville and is now in Flanders, and was a friend of Dr. Egidio, resides at present. It is highly advisable to know where he resides now and for His Majesty to give command to arrest him and to send him to one of the Inquisitorial courts of Spain so that from there he can be taken to Seville where he has been called to testify by the Holy Office.[9]

Nine years later, Diego de la Cruz had still not been caught. In 1557, in Frankfurt, he had given Julian Hernandez thirty ducats to bind the books that he was taking to Spain.[10] On April 28, 1559, the bishop of Tarazona, inquisitor in Seville, wrote the Supreme Council: "Would to God we could catch Juan Perez and Diego de la Cruz. Believe me, then we would be able to discover great secrets."[11] The search was still on three year later. Inquisitors Carpio, Gasco, and Soto informed the Supreme Council that they now had more concrete information regarding Diego de la Cruz:

He must now be between 50 and 55 years of age, medium height, a little chubby, and with a slight hunchback, fair skin, thick [downcast] eyelids, a long puffy face, a greying beard, and a high-pitched voice. This is what he looked like some thirteen years ago, more or less. A witness who saw him in Flanders some nine years ago says he had a rather thin face. As far as that is concerned, he may have changed since then because the witnesses here do not say he had a thin face, but a long, somewhat puffy face. Either Fadrique Enriquez de Ribera, who now lives in Valladolid and saw Diego de la Cruz in Flanders just after he left Seville, or some of the servants he had there, might be able to give you more details about him and his whereabouts.[12]

Diego de la Cruz must have been captured some time after 1565 because he still appeared as "absent" in the list the inquisitors had compiled that year of clergy who had been condemned and whose goods had been confiscated within the past twelve years. A curious statement in this report reads: "Diego de la Cruz was a poor priest when he was taken prisoner, hence there were no goods to be confiscated because it seems he had none."[13] The account was compiled in February of 1565 by Francisco de Naveda, notary of the secret prisons of the Inquisition, who states that he checked all the books and registers that the inquisitors at Seville had kept for the last twelve years, and that he faithfully recorded everything he found there.

---

9 AHN, Inquisición, lib. 574, f. 216r, in: Lopez Muñoz (2011, 52, doc. 12).
10 AHN, Inquisición, lib. 574, f. 216r, in: Lopez Muñoz (2011, 52, doc. 12).
11 AHN, Inquisición, leg. 2942, doc. 64, in: Lopez Muñoz (2011, 147, doc. 64).
12 AHN, Inquisición, leg. 2943, doc. 71, in: Lopez Muñoz (2011, 268, doc. 127).
13 AHN, Inquisición, leg. 2943, doc. 144 (2), in: Lopez Muñoz (2011, 340, doc. 163).

Gaspar Zapata

Another group of dissident carefully watched by the inquisitors were printers who sympathized with the evangelical movement: Gaspar Zapata, Martin de Montesdoca, Luis de Abrego, etc. Zapata was able to escape; Montesdoca left for the New World before he was put on the wanted list; Abrego was not so fortunate and was burned at the stake at the first *auto* against the Lutherans in Seville. One of the accusations against Zapata was that he had printed certain verses entitled "Against the Papists" that Sebastian Martinez, a priest from Alcala, would leave on the streets and in the churches of Seville and Toledo at night, and for which he was burned at the stake in 1562.

Professor Jaime Moll (1999, 5–10) suggests that Zapata was not actually a printer, but the owner of the print shop, and that he began printing in 1544 but may have entered the service of the marquis of Tarifa, as secretary, soon afterwards. Indeed, Gaspar Zapata was in the service of one of the leading Andalusian noble families, the Ribera-Enriquez family, which allowed him to tour Europe with the court of Charles V. Was that the reason for the abandonment of his profession as a printer? Zapata's connections with the evangelical circle in Seville went back to the early 1550s, to the days of Dr. Egidio. Friction with the Inquisition also began about that time. In a letter dated July 29, 1550, the Supreme Council sent the emperor the following instructions:

> Gaspar Zapata should also be asked if he delivered a trunk of Lutheran books to Antonio de Guzman, a knight from Seville, when he left Brussels. These books have been seized by the Inquisitors at Seville. Have him declare who the books were for and if he sent them in his own name or in the name of another, and who wrote to him asking him to send them and who bought them and anything else related to this business, such as what he did with them before he embarked, etc., that is, anything else that might shed light on the case. This information should then be carefully and secretly sent to the Inquisitor General or to the Supreme Council of this kingdom of Spain in a sealed envelop.[14]

Zapata must have been examined immediately. The results were sent on August 10, from Augsburg, to the Supreme Council.[15] Only an acknowledgement of receipt of the letter remains, not the results.

In 1559, Gaspar Zapata is mentioned as secretary of Fadrique Enriquez de Ribera's brother, Per Afan de Ribera, duke of Alcala de los Gazules, who was about to take up the post of viceroy of Naples that year. Zapata's connections with Zaragoza (his wife was from there) suggest that he may have already been

---

14 AHN, Inquisición, lib. 574, f. 216r, in: Lopez Muñoz (2011, 53, doc. 12). Antonio de Guzman was Charles V's ambassador in Augsburg, Germany.
15 AHN, Inquisición, lib. 323, f. 118r, in: Lopez Muñoz (2011, 55, doc. 13).

employed by Per Afan de Ribera while the duke was viceroy of Catalonia, from 1554 to 1558. Did Fadrique Enriquez find it risky to emply someone "suspected of subversive activity" and so he sent him off to his brother? It appears that Per Afan was counting on taking Zapata with him to Naples. In March of 1559, when Per Afan de Ribera and his household were in Barcelona, ready to embark for Naples, the Inquisition of Barcelona received an order from the Supreme Council to detain Gaspar Zapata, "secretary to the Duke of Alcala, and his wife, Isabel Tristan, and a certain Francisco de Mendoza,[16] ...for it has been reported that they are planning to sail with the duke."[17]

Only a few days later, on April 2, 1559, the inquisitor in Barcelona, Lope Martinez de Lagunilla, bishop of Elna, informed the Supreme Council that Zapata had escaped but that they had taken his wife, Isabel Tristan, prisoner. In this letter, he adds some interesting details:

> His wife [Isabel Tristan] says that he went to present himself to the inquisitors because of what they accused him of [in 1550], that had to do with a few books of the *Doctrine Christiana* that had been entrusted to him in Flanders and that he brought them back to Spain wrapped in his clothes, without knowing they were prohibited. The woman is imprisoned and the Inquisition has put her in the house of Hieronymo Sorribes, treasurer of this tribunal, in company of a married daughter of hers, who is indisposed and weak, and care is being taken that no one communicate with her. Inventory of her goods has been made by the official deputies assigned for that purpose, and they are few from what they tell me. All this has been reported to the inquisitors of Seville. Please send a trustworthy person to fetch this woman and money for the expense, for here we have none, and the *alguazil* is sick with quartan fevers and his son is gone to work his lands. In all this time that she has been imprisoned, nothing has been heard regarding her husband. And, considering what she told us is true, what surprises us is that until now the inquisitors of Seville have not mentioned him in their letter; I will do as you say in your letter and, in order to reduce expenses I will do everything in my power to capture Francisco de Mendoza, so that the two can be sent to Seville together.[18]

Gaspar Zapata must have escaped to Italy because on July 10, 1559, the prosecutor in Barcelona, Pedro Vila, wrote the Inquisitor General saying: "...as for Zapata, servant of the duke of Alcala [Per Afan de Ribera], there is a report that he is in Italy, in Venice."[19] Zapata's wife, Isabel Tristan, who the inquisitors sent someone to fetch for from Barcelona, arrived in Seville at the end of May, at a

---

16 AHN, Inquisición, lib. 575, f. LXXIIIIv; leg. 2942, doc. 63, in: Lopez Muñoz (2011, 146, doc. 63).

17 AHN, Inquisición, lib. 736, f. 374r, in: Lopez Muñoz (2011, 143, doc. 59).

18 AHN, Inquisición, lib. 736, f. 376r, in: Lopez Muñoz (2011, 144, doc. 61). Brackets mine. Is this the same inquisitor that Henry Kamen is referring to when he states, "In 1559 an inquisitor from Barcelona informed that *"por siete o ocho vezes hemos quemado aquí en casa montones de libros"*? (Kamen: 2011, 113).

19 AHN, Inquisición, lib. 736, f. 399r, in: Lopez Muñoz (2011, 154, doc. 74). Brackets mine.

time when, according to the complaints of the bishop of Tarazona, there were so many prisoners in Triana that they hardly knew where to put them.[20] In December of 1560 she was still in prison, but two years later, at the *auto-da-fe* held on October 28, 1562, she was acquitted, probably thanks to the good offices of the duke of Alcala. At that same *auto* her husband was burned in effigy.[21]

The following year the Spanish ambassador in London, Alvaro de la Quadra, informed Philip II in a ciphered letter that a certain Francisco Zapata, a friend of Casiodoro de Reina, and his wife had arrived in London:

> There arrived here from Genoa a few days since a man who calls himself Don Francisco Zapata, and says he is an Andalusian. He is accompanied by his wife [Isabel Tristan], who is from Zaragoza. He is a great heretic and therefore lives in the house of the preacher Casiodoro, who has recently married again. I understand the man comes to reside here [in London] and revise with Casiodoro and others a Bible that he is translating into vulgar Castilian. He is a man of 50, short and thin. He says he was for some time in the household of the prince of Condé. London, June 26, 1563.[22]

In all likelihood, Francisco Zapata was a false name Gaspar Zapata was going by then. What is also of interest here is how all these exiles had knowledge of each other's whereabouts.

Years later, in January 1574, the inquisitors at Seville were still reviewing the trial records of Gaspar Zapata and Isabel Tristan in order to find some evidence against Per Afan de Ribera. The only evidence they found was that Isabel Tristan declared that when she was captured in Barcelona and kept prisoner in the house of the receptor of the Inquisition, Per Afan de Ribera came to speak to her and she begged him to tell her husband to present himself to the Holy Office in Seville and the duke promised he would do that for her.[23] If Per Afan de Ribera actually contacted Isabel's husband for her, or brought her a message from him, is uncertain, but someone must have told her where she could find him, and where he could find Casiodoro de Reina, otherwise Isabel Tristan and Gaspar de Zapata would not have been in London the following year helping Reina with his Bible.

---

20 AHN, Inquisición, leg. 2942, doc. 66, in: Lopez Muñoz (2011, 149, doc. 67). In this document her husband is referred to as Luis Zapata.
21 AHN, Inquisición, leg. 2075 (1), doc. 2, in: Lopez Muñoz (2011, 270, doc. 129).
22 AGS, Estado, leg. 816, f. 166r, in: Lopez Muñoz (2011, 307, doc. 147). Brackets mine. Louis de Bourbon (1530–1569) was the first member of his family to carry the title of Prince of Condé. He was the younger brother of Antoine de Bourbon who married Jeanne d'Albret, Queen of Navarre. After serving as a soldier in the wars against the Habsburgs in the defense of Metz in 1552 and St. Quentin in 1557, in 1558 he declared his conversion to Protestantism and along with his brother in 1559 joined the Huguenots. In 1562, along with Coligny, he directed a Huguenot force that was defeated in Normandy. Condé was imprisoned but released the following year. He died in the battle of Jarnac, in Aquitaine, southwest France, in March 1569. (Mullett: 2010, 107).
23 AHN, Inquisición, leg. 2946, in: Lopez Muñoz (2011, 415, doc. 223).

On the other hand, the reference in the ambassador's letter to the prince of Condé, also suggests the route she may have taken, that is, from Seville to Zaragoza (her home town) and from there to Navarre and up through the French Protestant territory of Jeanne d'Albret to La Rochelle and from there to London.

Gaspar Zapata and his wife were still in London in 1565. Menendez y Pelayo reproduces a letter from ambassador Guzman de Silva to Philip II, dated April 26, 1565, that Adolfo de Castro found in Simancas when he was preparing the second edition of his *Historia de los Protestantes Españoles*. The letter is of interest and sheds a bit more light on Zapata's activities. It reads as follows:

> This circle here of Spanish heretics is dying out. Gaspar Zapata, who I understand was Secretary or servant of the Duke of Alcala [Per Afan de Ribera], a clever man and of good wit, expected from the Holy Office a safe conduct in order to return to [Spain]. To my great satisfaction, I have managed to get him out of here with his household and wife, and he has gone to Flanders, with a safe-conduct from the Duchess of Parma, until instructions come from Spain. His wife insists they hurry. I am informed that no one has been able to stop her from meeting with these heretics. [Zapata] was with the admiral and count [prince of Condé] in the last war,[24] and there he married this native Spaniard from Zaragoza, who was with Madame Vendôme. I understand that it would do Your Majesty, and our nation, a better service if these lost Spaniards were *reducidos*, because here they make a greater fuss over one Spanish heretic, to defend themselves with him, than 10,000 that are not, and [Zapata] is a person for whom they had a high regard and was well treated. I hope that by his example more of them will be *reducidos*, for, in accordance with the evils of these heretics, their fear of being caught is greater than their knowledge of the truth. The duke of Alcala has been most helpful in this by sending me some advice that I have showed him; but the principal means, I understand, has been God, who has helped through his good will. (Menendez y Pelayo: 1881, 630. Note and brackets mine).

The ambassador's letter reveals an interesting detail easily overlooked with respect to the relationship between Philip II and Jeanne d'Albret, Queen of Navarre: "[Zapata's wife] was with Madame Vendôme." Philip II refused to refer to the Navarre monarchs as king or queen; instead, he insisted on addressing them as "Vendôme" and "Mme de Vendôme." At one point he sent his ambassador, Juan Martinez Descurra, to Jeanne in order to convince her that the king of Spain would tolerate no preaching or exercise of the new religion. She was to rest assured that if he gave the signal within a month she will lose all her possessions and the house of Navarre and Foix would disappear. Philip also insinuated that a repentant Jeanne might be considered as a bride for the Spanish heir, prince

---

24 This refers to the first large battle of the French Wars of Religion, which took place at Dreux, in northern France, on December 19, 1562. Condé commanded the Huguenots and was captured at Dreux in 1562. The following year he was set free and negotiated the Peace of Amboise with the Catholic party in 1563, which gave the Huguenots some religious toleration.

Carlos. However, on the margin of one of his ambassador's reports, he noted in
his own hand, "This is quite too much of a woman to have as a daughter-in-law. I
would much prefer to destroy her." The plan was to kidnap Jeanne d'Albert and
deliver her to the Inquisition. He would then take possession of her lands in the
Bearne and elsewhere, thus destroying "the heart of Calvinism in France" and
establishing Spanish power north of the Pyrenees (Scott/Sturm-Maddox: 2007,
30–31). The conspiracy was only defeated by the sudden illness of the officer to
whom its execution had been entrusted (M'Crie: 1829, 334–335).

One problem with the above cited text is the word *reducidos* (put to death,
arrested, controlled, subdued, brought back to the church). The ambassador
wrote, "It would do your majesty a better service if these lost Spaniards were
reducidos." Zapata was burned in effigy in Seville in 1562; the ambassador's
letter was written in 1565. Was Zapata privately executed in Flanders? Was his
being sent to Flanders a way to keep him in check? If the ambassador's report
suggests that Zapata returned to the church, then there seems to be a conflict
with the official version. Many years later, in 1591, a notary was asked to go back
to the files and make a copy of the sentence pronounced against Zapata. The
sentence read at the *auto* in Seville in 1562 said:

> I, Hernando Servicial de Villavicencio, notary of the Holy Office in Seville, truly swear
> that among the documents kept in the vaults of the secret chambers of this Inquisition,
> in book three of those condemned, but missing, there is a process against Gaspar
> Zapata, printer, secretary of the duke of Alcala, citizen of Seville, and at the end of the
> process there is the sentence pronounced against the aforesaid Gaspar Zapata and
> other culprits whose names are omitted here, which reads as follows:

> Seen by us, the inquisitors and the bishop of Cadiz, as ordinary, against the heretical
> wickedness and apostasy in the city and archbishopric of Seville, a process of criminal
> litigation pending between the accuser, the reverend licentiate Diego Muñoz, prose-
> cutor of the Holy Office, and the accused, declare: Gaspar Zapata, printer and publisher
> of books, citizen of Seville, (and others whose name we omit here), on the grounds of
> the crime of heresy and apostasy of which the prosecutor accuses them, reported and
> registered in the accounts of this Holy Office, are accused of the crime of heresy and
> apostasy. And for fear of being caught, and in order to live more freely in those errors
> and heresies, have fled, and though every effort has been made to capture them, they
> have not been found, as appears in this report, [the prosecutor] has entreated us to
> officially summon the aforesaid to appear before us within the time we appointed to
> defend themselves before the prosecutor and to remain here until the final sentence has
> been pronounced.

> For this, he urged that in all things the Holy Office apply full justice. And because we
> considered his request just and reasonable, and based on the information he gave us, we
> summoned them to appear personally before us, for the sake of holy obedience and
> under penalty of major excommunication, and to respond regarding the faith, and why
> they had left the city, and to defend themselves and to settle the matter with the

prosecutor. For this we promised to listen to everything they had to say and allege that we would act in all fairness towards them. If, on the contrary, they failed to appear at the appointed time, we would hear the prosecutor and proceed against each one of them and declare them excommunicated. All this was made public and the prosecutor declared their inaction before us and at his request we declare them disobedient rebels and publicly excommunicated. Because they remained in that state for over a year the prosecutor urged us to declare them heretics and to sentence them (that is their statues) to the stake and all their goods confiscated and handed over to the royal treasury. This has been seen and discussed and approved by knowledgeable and trustworthy persons.

Cristi nomine invocato

On the charges and merits presented, we declare Gaspar Zapata and the others [not mentioned] to be disobedient rebels for not having appeared before us in the time appointed, nor later, in order to respond regarding the faith, thus confirming the crime of heresy of which they are suspected, and for having been excommunicated and persisted in that state for over a year by reason of their crime of heresy, and that Gaspar Zapata (and the others) must be handed over to the civil authorities, and in their name Francisco Chacon, mayor of the city of Seville, to be burned, and their statues in their name. We likewise declare that their goods (and incomes) from the day after the year they were excommunicated be confiscated and given to the royal treasury and that their sons and grandsons be deprived of all ecclesiastic benefits and secular offices, public or honorific, and be declared unworthy to hold them in the future.
Signed: Andrés Gasco, Carpio, Juan de Ovando, Francisco de Soto.[25]

This sentence was read at the public *auto-da-fe* held in Seville on October 28, 1562. Had Zapata returned to the church there would certainly have been a note on the document. The report conceals the names of the others but they could have been the Venetian Costantin Espada and the German banker Adrian Fucar (or Fugger), listed in other documents as condemned in effigy that day with confiscation of goods.[26]

Francisco de Mendoza, who was in Gaspar Zapata and Isabel Tristan's company, and had been Constantino Ponce de la Fuente's servant and had fled when Constantino was arrested, managed to escape at that time. A search had been made earlier, in February of 1559, in Cuenca and Malaga, but to no avail. The main interest of the inquisitors in 1559 was to learn from Mendoza whether or not Constantino had been married.[27] In the spring of 1564, Francisco de Mendoza voluntarily surrendered and offered the inquisitors some incriminating information regarding Ana de Deza and Isabel Martinez de Alvo,

---

25 AHN, Inquisición, leg. 2950, in: Lopez Muñoz (2011, 465, doc. 270).
26 AHN, Inquisición, leg. 2075 (1), doc. 2, in: Lopez Muñoz (2011, 270, doc. 129).
27 ADC, Inquisición, Miscelánea de Breves, L-224, f. 183r, in: Lopez Muñoz (2011, 137, doc. 53).

who he said communicated secretly with Dr. Constantino when he was in prison.[28] A report describing the results of the search in Barcelona in 1559 reads:

> In a letter to the Supreme Council, dated May 15, 1559, prosecutor Pedro Villa reports that "a page of the duke of Alcalá, called Francisco Lasso, has been caught. He has the same description as that given by the inquisitors of Seville for Francisco de Mendoza. I think he is the same person, because he is very well known and because at the Duke's house some call him Mendoça. The capture was made as quietly as possible and in a way that nothing was perceived by the Duke. But the Commissioner treated him very badly and then he went to tell the Duke, and wanted me to go too, but I refused. He was alone in a prison with the jail keeper. Later the commissioner put him in with three others… and today they are playing skittles in the gardens of the jail. I think the same *alguazil* that takes Mrs. Zapata down to Seville will take him with him. I hope to God that few servants of the duke will have to appear in this court because this has been very upsetting for me." Pedro Vila also complained of the laxity Isabel Tristan enjoyed while in prison, writing and receiving letter, receiving visits from the duke of Alcala, who intercedes for her before the inquisitor of Barcelona so that she be sent to Seville with the guarantee that she be treated well.[29]

Juan Perez de Pineda

Juan Perez de Pineda (1500–1567), sometimes referred to as Pieres or Pierius or Perrucellus (Boehmer: 2007, II, 57), was born in Montilla, in the province of Cordoba. Details regarding his activities prior to his escape to Geneva around 1550 are scarce. He was employed as a civil servant under the orders of Charles V in Rome in 1526, that is, as secretary to the Spanish ambassador, the duke of Sesa, and prior of the Church of Osma (Moreno: 2004, 83; Kinder: 1976, 283). He was witness to the sack of Rome by Charles V's troops in 1527. The following year we find him living with the bishop of Gurk, Antonio de Salamanca, whose house had been spared (Boehmer: 2007, 58). From Rome, Perez went to Naples but was back in Rome by 1530, where he could have met Juan de Valdes, and not in Naples as Leon de la Vega (2012, 491) claims. A vice–chancellor at Naples, in a letter dated August 28, 1530, writes: "By a letter from Rome I learn that poor Juan Perez had arrived there and that on his way to Naples, being about 30 miles from Rome, between Velletri and Sermoneta, he had been attacked, and that nothing further had been heard of him." (Boehmer: 2007, 59; Perez de Pineda: 1981, iii–x).

On his return to Spain, around 1547, Perez de Pineda settled in Seville where he became a close friend of Dr. Egidio. Perez de Pineda held a Ph.D. in theology and canon law and soon became headmaster of the Colegio de Doctrina. He left

---

28 AHN, Inquisición, leg. 2943, doc. 127–1, in: Lopez Muñoz (2011, 318, doc. 155).
29 AHN, Inquisición, lib. 736, f. 416r–v. See Moll (1999).

Seville when he got notice of the intention of the inquisitors to arrest him as
suspected of Lutheranism.[30] It seems he went to Paris first, with the pretext of
studying there, and then on to Geneva, where for several years Jean Crespin's
press was busy printing his publications. Perez was held in high esteem by both
Calvin and Beza as he labored among the exiled community there. During this
time in Geneva, Perez de Pineda also had abundant correspondence with Lutheran sympathizers throughout Spain, mainly in Seville, as the letters distributed by Julianillo in 1557 revealed. On November 17, 1557, the Supreme
Council sent Philip II the following dispatch:

> The inquisitors at Seville have written saying that in that city they have seized many
> books containing heresy. These books have been found in the hands of eminent citi-
> zens, and have to do with a certain Dr. Juan Pérez, who is living in Frankfort. He was a
> great friend of Dr. Egidio, and fled Seville when Egidio was arrested. Perez wrote [the
> books] and sent them to Seville through a Spanish Lutheran [Julianillo], who they have
> imprisoned. Along with these books, he sent letters to the aforementioned persons. The
> man is being examined as well as the persons who received the books. Your Majesty will
> be duly informed of the outcome. They say that this Dr. Juan Perez has sent many of
> these books here to Valladolid, but we do no know to whom.[31]

Juan Perez de Pineda was a prolific writer and editor. Between 1556 and 1560 he
published Juan de Valdes's commentaries on Romans and on I Corinthians, a
catechism he compiled himself, a translation of the Psalms, a letter of consolation to the oppressed Christians, etc. A New Testament printed in Geneva by
Crespin in 1556 lacking the name of the translator and carrying a false imprint is
attributed to Juan Perez de Pineda. The similarity between Perez de Pineda's New
Testament and Francisco de Enzinas's suggests that Perez may have owned one
of the few copies that were salvaged. In 1559, Jean Crespin also printed Perez's
translation into Spanish of Calvin's Catechism made from the French: *Catechismo a saber es formulario para instruyr los mochachos en la Christiandad*
(Catechism, that is, a form by which to instruct children in the fundamentals of
Christianity). In 1559, Perez de Pineda also translated the Flemish historian John
Sleidan's Latin oration addressed to the Emperor Charles V. Perez de Pineda
redirected—and adapted—it to Philip II and explained to the king that the
subjection of the kingdom of Spain to the Holy See is the cause of wars and

---

30 Several other men that had been teachers at the Colegio de Doctrina de los Niños were
   burned at the stake: Hernando de San Juan and Luis de Sosa were burned at the stake on
   September 24, 1559. Gaspar Baptista, another teacher, was sentenced at the *auto* of April 26,
   1562, but because he had died before that date, he was burned in effigy. AHN, Inquisición,
   leg. 2075, doc. 2, in: Lopez Muñoz (2011, 258, doc. 122).
31 AGS, Estado, leg.121, doc. 165, in: Lopez Muñoz (2011, 113, doc. 35). Among the books
   burned in Valladolid on January 2, 1558, there was one written in Spanish entitled "Letter
   written to our augusto prince, don Felipe, king of Spain."

suffering of the Spanish people. The following year, he translated and revised the Latin work of the German reformer Urbanus Regius, *Doctrina vetus & nova* (Old and New Doctrine). Though Perez de Pineda's works carry false imprints and fictitious printers—"Venice: Pedro Daniel" and "Venice: Juan Philadelpho"— they were all printed in Geneva. Using false imprints was common practice in order to make it more difficult to trace the author, especially if the author was a Spaniard on the inquisitors' blacklist.

Many of these works were published thanks to the financial aid of Miguel Monterde, rector of the recently established Estudio Mayor, an institution of higher learning at Zaragoza, who acted as intermediary in passing money on to Perez. On August 20, 1558, Inquisitor Gaspar Cervantes at Zaragoza wrote the Supreme Council that they had arrested a wealthy clergyman known as rector Monterde, in whose possession they found several letters from Juan Perez, "who we understand is the same person who wrote certain prohibited books that were taken to Seville." (Kinder: 1985, 131–160). Inquisitor Gaspar Cervantes described Monterde as a close friend of Dr. Morillo, of Cazalla, of Egidio, and of Francisco Mudarra— a declared Erasmian (Fernández Martín: 1993)—, as well as of Dr. Mateo Pascual, "all of which are noted heretics, as you know."[32]

Perez de Pineda's time in Geneva not only coincided with that of the Jeronimite monks from Seville, but also with the English Marian exiles (1555–1560). His contact with them would also explain how two of his works were so soon translated into English: *Breve tratado de la doctrina antigua de Dios* (Jehovah, a Free Pardon) and *Epistola Consolatoria* (An Excellent Comfort to all Christians).[33] They were both done by the same translator and published in London in 1576, who may have found a sympathetic publisher in the bookseller and bibliographer Andrew Maunsell, who later would make a name for himself as the compiler of the first English "Books in Print" catalogue of books listed in alphabetic order, and under general headings.[34] The publications of Juan Perez de Pineda's works would have been some of his earliest undertakings. Though he published many books, his main interest was theology. The translator, John Danyel, was the father or uncle of the poet Samuel Danyel and the songwriter John Danyel and a friend of Michelangelo Florio, who had fled to England during the reign of Edward VI and was pastor of the Italian Protestant congregation in London in 1550. Michelangelo Florio was among the English exiles in Geneva

---

32 AHN, Inquisición, lib. 961, f. 581r, in: Lopez Muñoz (2011, 125, doc. 48).
33 See Appendix B.
34 Andrew Maunsell, The First part of the Catalogue of English printed books which concerneth such matters of divinity as have been either written in our own tongue, or translated out of any other language, and have been published, to the Glory of God, and Edification of the Church of Christ in England. Gathered into alphabet and such method as it is by Andrew Maunsell, bookseller, etc. (London: John Windet, 1595).

and John Daniel may also have been. Where the title-page reads "…and now translated into English by John Danyel, of Clements Inne, with divers additions by him collected and thereunto annexed," one would expect additional paragraphs but instead, throughout the text, the translator interpolates statements of his own, camouflaged behind phrases such as "by report of an Englishman, my friend (this translator)" (f. 136v), or "as my translator tells me, …". (f. 137r).[35]

Shortly after 1560, Perez de Pineda left Geneva. He did not follow the English exiles, as some of the monks did, but after stopping off at Frankfurt and Paris, he settled in Blois, Duchess Renée de Ferrara's hometown, where he had received a call from the pastors to be their minister. He later became Renée's chaplain when she exiled to her castle at Montarges in 1564. A convinced Calvinist for the whole of his eighteen years in exile, Juan Perez de Pineda died in Paris in 1567. He had been burned in effigy in Seville of December 22, 1560, accused of being a "heretical Lutheran dogmatizer and teacher of that sect, as well composer-author-typesetter and distributor of false, prohibited and heretical books."[36]

The Cardenas-Mairena Family

Another group of religious exiles that fled Seville some time around 1555–56 just before the severe persecution set in was a group of laypersons. It included Francisco de Cardenas, his wife Ana de Mairena and her brother Melchor Diaz, Maria de Trigueros and her husband Costantin Espada, and Pedro de Sosa—not to be confused with Charles V's secretary—. Inquisition records describe the group as "the heretic Francisco de Cardenas, his wife and two of her brothers, and others, left some two or three years ago and went to live in Geneva, land of Lutherans, and they were all burned in effigy."[37] From Geneva, they sent letters back to Seville via Julianillo. Francisco de Cadenas sent letters to his brother Antonio, who was later arrested for not having denounced the content of the letters.[38] Likewise, the Mairena sisters sent letters to Teresa Gomez and her

---

35 This practice of the translator considering himself co-author was typical of nineteenth century translators, not of the Elizabethans, who, besides their delight in rhetorical devices so typical of that age—repetition, assonance, alliteration, puns and witty conceits—, were noted for taking special care to explain references to foreign history or culture unfamiliar to their readers.

36 AHN, Inquisición, leg. 2075, doc. 1 (2); AGS, Estado, leg. 137, doc. 3, in: Lopez Muñoz (2011, 212, doc. 101).

37 AHN, Inquisición, leg. 4519, doc. 10 (b), in: Lopez Muñoz (2011, 282, doc. 133). Constantin Espada may have left slightly earlier. He may have been one of the individuals burned in effigy with Gaspar Zapata.

38 AHN, Inquisición, leg. 4519, doc. 10 (b), in: Lopez Muñoz (2011, 282, doc. 133).

daughters.[39] Judging by the date, very likely some of these letters were among those that Julianillo delivered when he arrived in Seville in 1557. Francisco de Cardenas, his wife Ana de Mairena, her brother Melchor Diaz, Maria de Trigueros, and Pedro de Sosa were burned in effigy on April 26, 1562.[40]

The Jeronimite Monks

Already in the early 1550s several of the monks at the monastery of San Isidoro in Santiponce (Seville) had adopted a critical view of the official Catholic Church. They could foresee harsh repression by the Holy Office and, according to Montes (1569, f. 83r), they "determined with themselves to forsake their nest and to flee into Germany, where they might live with a great deal more safety of their lives and freedom of their consciences, a very bold enterprise (doubtless) and, as some thought, both rash and desperate." Twelve of these monks fled Spain in the spring of 1557 with the purpose of meeting again in Geneva within a year. To avoid suspicion, they took different routes: some by way of Genoa and Savoy, others by way of Antwerp. On July 12 of that year the Supreme Council sent a lengthy letter to the inquisitors at Seville in which mention is made in passing of certain monks imprisoned and others that had fled.[41] Julian Hernandez later confessed that he had met up with some of them, without specifying if it was in Geneva before he left for Seville, or along the way somewhere, either in Frankfurt or Antwerp. This is deduced from a statement in a letter written by the Supreme Council on October 22, 1557, instructing the inquisitors of Seville to ask Julian where the escaped friars were and how they were dressed when he saw them (*en qué hábito los vio*).[42] In November, the Supreme Council finally sent a full report with names to Philip II, who had left England in July and was now in Flanders:[43]

> The inquisitors at Seville have written regarding certain information they have of certain monks of the monastery of San Isidoro, near Seville, who are suspected of serious errors and of holding Lutheran opinions. They have taken three monks prisoners, but others have fled, namely, Fray Francisco de Farias, prior of the monastery, Fray Pablo, procurator of the monastery, Fray Antonio del Corro, Fray Pelegrina de Paz, who was prior in Ecija, Fray Casiodoro [de Reina], Fray Juan de Medina, Fray Miguel

---

39 AHN, Inquisición, leg. 2942, doc. 85, in: Lopez Muñoz (2011, 186, doc. 93).
40 AHN, Inquisición, leg. 2075, doc. 2, in: Lopez Muñoz (2011, 209, doc. 100).
41 AHN, Inquisición, lib. 575, ff. 50r–50v, in: Lopez Muñoz (2011, 109, doc. 32).
42 AHN, Inquisición, lib. 575, f. 57r y ss, in: Lopez Muñoz (2011, 111, doc. 34).
43 One of the monks not mentioned by name was Fray Bartolome de Gomez Hernandez, whose nephew requested admission to the Holy Office in 1584 as a familiar, but was rejected on the basis that his uncle was among the monks that fled. AHN, Inquisición, leg. 2948, in: Lopez Muñoz (2011, 452, doc. 259).

Carpintero, Fray Alonso Baptista and Fray Lope Cortes. The inquisitors have information that these monks are in Geneva and that in that city there are many [Spaniards] that hold the same opinions. They have begun legal actions against them.

They also report that in Seville they have seized many books containing heresies. These books have been found in the hands of eminent citizens, and have to do with a certain Dr. Juan Perez, who is living in Frankfort. He was a great friend of Dr. Egidio, and fled Seville when Egidio was arrested. Perez wrote the books and sent them to Seville through a Spanish Lutheran [Julian Hernandez] who they have imprisoned. Along with these books, [Dr. Juan Perez] sent letters to the aforementioned persons. The man [Julian Hernandez] is being examined as well as the persons who received the books. Your Majesty will be duly informed of the outcome.

The inquisitors have also written us saying that this Dr. Juan Perez has sent many of these books here [to the court] in Valladolid, but we do no know to whom. We beg Your Majesty to decree that these books to be seized and the persons who have them to be punished because the impudence and craftiness of those heretics is so great that the ministers of the Holy Office cannot cope with it on their own. And it is paramount that in this matter Your Majesty decree with all severity your displeasure so that these heretics refrain from committing such unlawful acts with such boldness.[44]

In the words of Reginaldo Gonzalez de Montes (1569, f. 75v),

The Inquisitors took the departure of the monks so badly, for forsaking their order as well as for renouncing their religion, that though they were but few in number, yea but a handful (to speak of) in respect of the world, yet they determined to plague them surely if they could come by them, and thereupon sent out their flies to lie in wait for them everywhere that they should pass, especially at Cologne, Frankfurt, Antwerp and all the highways that lay from Geneva that way, and also all the ways on the other side from Geneva to Milan. The costs thereof were allowed out of the king's treasury largely enough, both of the king's own liberality and of the desire the Inquisitors had to catch them.

It remains a mystery exactly when and how these twelve monks managed to flee the country unsuspected. A letter sent by the Supreme Council on July 12, 1557, acknowledging receipt of the information received earlier regarding the fugitive monks, suggests that the monks must have left Seville in the spring of 1557.[45] How they left is more difficult to ascertain. The answer might be found in a careful reading of other documents that suggest the existence of a "false jubilee" circulating in Seville in 1556. Since the days of pope Paul II, the Catholic Church had celebrated a year of jubilee every twenty-five years (1450, 1475, 1500, 1525, etc.). This entailed full pardon of all one's sins if certain conditions were fulfilled

44 AGS, Estado, leg. 121, doc. 165, in: Lopez Muñoz (2011, 113, doc. 35). For Philip II's reply and further correspondence between Inquisitor General Valdes and the king regarding this matter, see Homza (2006, 181–191).
45 AHN, Inquisición, lib. 575, ff. 50r–50v, in: Lopez Muñoz (2011, 109, doc. 32).

such as pilgrimages to certain shrines or churches during that particular year. The year was officially proclaimed by the pope and copies of the proclamation were sent to all the bishops to be read publicly in all the churches. To proclaim 1556 or 1557 a year of jubilee would have been exceptional, an "extraordinary jubilee year." Could the monks from San Isidoro have invented a stratagem whereby they invented an extraordinary jubilee year stipulating that all those who wanted to appropriate the benefits of the jubilee had to make a pilgrimage to Rome? They could have printed up copies and with this document the monks could have left totally unsuspected, dressed in their ordinary habits. This would certainly have been acceptable and would have allowed them to leave the country unmolested.

It seems that the inquisitors knew nothing of this jubilee until several of the monks that had remained behind were arrested a few months later. On October 22, 1557, the authorities at Seville sent a copy of this "false jubilee" to the Supreme Council and received the following response: "We have seen the jubilee you sent. You must inquire if more copies have arrived by other means so they can be collected because it would be terribly inconvenient if such a pernicious thing should be seen or fall into the hands of some Catholic Christian."[46] Further instructions followed in December: "Regarding the books brought in by Julian, make sure it is true what you say that they were burned, and do the same with the jubilee."[47] This done, the inquisitors seem to have dismissed the matter until May of 1562, when they informed the Supreme Council regarding the confirmation of a new director for the San Isidoro monastery and mention is made again of the false jubilee. The circumstances are as follows. After Garcia Arias—known as *Maestro blanco* for his white hair—, prior of the monastery, was arrested and imprisoned, Fray Pedro de Aragon was chosen as prior of the monastery, but Fray Gabriel de Funes disagreed with that choice and requested that the appointment be annulled. The inquisitors admitted that they had been too busy at the time with the *autos-da-fe* to look into the matter, but now were forwarding Fray Funes's appeal, together with another copy of the spurious heretical jubilee (*jubileo heretico contrahecho*) that they had sent earlier. The letter strongly implies that Fray Francisco Farias, former prior of the monastery, and one of the monks that fled, had copies of this false jubilee:

> We are somewhat suspicious of the relationship between Fray Pedro [de Aragon] and Fray Martin de Aragon and the fugitive friars, and the fondness and friendship they professed towards them, and the reason why the fugitives insisted that Fray Pedro be chosen and that they went as far as to send this petition to Fray Francisco Farias's

---

46 AHN, Inquisición, lib. 575, f. 57r-v, in: Lopez Muñoz (2011, 112, doc. 34).
47 AHN, Inquisición, lib. 575, f. 55v, in: Lopez Muñoz (2011, 114, doc. 37).

brother, together [with Fray Gabriel de Funes's letter] we are sending a copy of the spurious jubilee.[48]

Is this what the Supreme Council was looking for among maestro Garcia Arias's papers, in the letter sent to the inquisitors at Seville, dated July 12, 1557?

> We received the reports against the monks and against maestro Arias and we think it advisable that you give instructions that the monks that are denounced, and whose names are mentioned in the reports, be arrested and examined. Call in the consultants of the Holy Office for this. As for those that have left, find out where they are, for if they are where they can be arrested, deal with this matter immediately, if not, we will send you opportune instructions. As for maestro Garcia Arias, he should be summoned before you in the presence of some trustworthy theologians and shown some writings mentioned in the report. If he recognizes the writings to be his, he should explain why he was denounced and you and the consultants must act in consequence. If he denies it, inform us of what you decide to do. It would also be wise if, while you are examining him, you confiscate all his books and papers, because if *that which has been reported* is found among them, that would be clear evidence that the charges against him are true. Beatriz de Farias and her sister, the wife of Martin de Morales, might be able to clarify things in this matter. It would be advisable that these two women be tactfully examined and if they turn out to be guilty, you must likewise act in consequence.[49]

The question remains: Did Garcia Arias, prior of the monastery of San Isidoro at the time the monks fled, have a copy of the false jubilee? Did Fray Farias's sisters also have a copy? What does the phrase "if they turn out to be guilty" imply?[50] It appears that there were a number of copies of this jubilee in circulation. Were the "instructions for those who wanted to escape and go to Germany to live like the Lutherans" that Julianillo brought with him to Seville in 1557 copies of these false jubilees? Professor Garcia Pinilla (2012, 47) suggests that, along with Perez's *Catechism*, the book dealer Pedro Bellero may have brought a copy—or copies— with him from Frankfurt to Antwerp in the spring of 1557. Boehmer (2007, II, 64. Italics mine), found similar information in *Documentos Inéditos para la Historia de España* (1842, V, 529–533), and which reads:

> Concerning the trade in heretical books between Germany and Spain, a bookseller, who was examined by the Inquisition of the Netherlands, gave interesting details, in the beginning of the year 1558. This man, Peter Veller, who was engaged in the extensive business of Stels at Antwerp, testified that some Antwerp booksellers fetched, twice a year from the fairs at Frankfort on the Main, the new works which were published by

---

48 AHN, Inquisición, leg. 2943, doc. 61, in: Lopez Muñoz (2011, 266, doc. 125).
49 AHN, Inquisición, lib. 575, ff. 50r–50v, in: Lopez Muñoz (2011, 109, doc. 32). Italics mine.
50 Five years later, in a letter to the Supreme Council, dated January 8, 1562, the inquisitors at Seville attach the "reports containing information against the two Farias sister, Beatriz and Luisa" because they couldn't agree as to whether or not the sisters should be arrested and they needed the Council's opinion. AHN, Inquisición, leg. 2942, doc. 96.

the heretics in Latin and in Spanish. Veller himself had carried to the Netherlands copies of the Spanish „Letter to our Lord the King" and of *the Bull forged by the heretics.* He had seen great barrels filled with these Bulls and Letters which were destined to be sold in Spain. Veller further said that Peter Vilman, a bookseller at Antwerp, had book-depots at Medina del Campo and at Seville.

This would not have been an isolated case of forged bulls and jubilees. In the last Index of Prohibited Books, printed in Madrid in 1790, three spurious jubilees are listed. The second one was printed in Seville some time before 1611 (Guibovich Perez: 2003, 306); the last one is dated March 3, 1759:

- Jubileo de plenissima remisión de pecados, concedido antiguamente. Acaba: "Dado en la Corte celestial del Paraíso y desde el origen del Mundo, con privilegio eterno, &c."
- Jubileo del Año Santo, con nombre del Padre Luis Sánchez de la Compañía de Jesus, y titulo fingido de ser impreso en Sevilla.
- Jubileo. En ninguno, aunque sea plenísimo, se concede por él facultad á los Confesores para absolver del pecado de la Heregia externa. Edicto de 3 de Marzo de 1759. (Indice ultimo: 1790, 146).

Boehmer (2007, II, 51) concludes that "in all probability, the bull forged by the heretics, which in the beginning of the year 1558 Peter Veller [Pedro Bellero] confessed to have carried to the Netherlands was nothing else but [Juan Perez de Pineda's] Summary of Indulgences." I disagree, but be that as it may, the monks had planned their flight well and had succeeded. Reginaldo Gonzalez de Montes (1569, ff. 75r–76v. Notes mine) relates the plight of a monk who followed them later. His account reveals more details regarding their flight:

Juan de Leon, a monk of San Isidoro cloister. This man at first was a tailor in Mexico, that famous city in the West Indies called Nova Hispania, and at his return back to Seville again, felt in his conscience (as many good men do) a certain fear of God, though blind and not proceeding of knowledge, whereby he was moved to become a monk. His fate was such, by God's good means, who did so provide for his desperate attempt, that he entered into San Isidro's cloister in Seville, where the greater part of the convent at that time was well affected in religion. But after he had been schooled there by the space of two or three years, and conversant among them, he began to be weary of this monkish and solitary kind of life, and sought means to forsake his order, as he did indeed, coloring the matter with his continual disposition to sickness. And yet, being once out, had such a desire to talk with his former schoolmasters that had instructed him in the true and perfect religion that he returned to the monastery again for the sake of fellowship and for their company. But all in vain, for during the time of his absence, all they, for whose sake he entered into that ill-favored order once again, had left their cowls and were fled into Germany. Whereupon, he, perceiving that there was no place for him there, determined to alter his purpose as soon as he could learn for certain what was become of his old companions, and where they were gone.

But here perhaps some evil disposed persons will call him a double apostate, in forsaking his order twice. But the wiser sort will give him double honor therefore, and account him the godlier man two to one. Therefore, trudging after his fellows and (as it were) tracing them, he met with them at length at Frankfurt, with much ado both for the painfulness of his journey and the perils of passage, and from there went with them to Geneva to meet with the rest of his acquaintances that were settled there.

About the same time, by means of Queen Mary's sudden death[51] and that the crown of England descended upon the most gracious lady, Queen Elizabeth, they of the English congregation that by reason of the late tyranny were dispersed here and there in Germany were by God's good grace called home again into their own country. Whereupon, divers Spaniards that sojourned at Geneva, thinking England a fitter place for their congregation, accompanied the Englishmen that returned homewards into England and for their greater safety divided themselves into several companies, for the inquisitors took the departure of the monks so badly, for forsaking their order as well as for renouncing their religion, that though they were but few in number, yea but a handful (to speak of) in respect of the world, yet they determined to plague them surely if they could come by them, and thereupon sent out their flies to lie in wait for them everywhere that they should pass, especially at Cologne, Frankfurt, Antwerp and all the highways that lay from Geneva that way, and also all the ways on the other side from Geneva to Milan. The costs thereof were allowed out of the king's treasury generously enough, both of the king's own liberality and from the desire the inquisitors had to catch them. And, God knows, much ado there was, sparing neither labor nor cost, to find half a dozen dogs to do this feat, and to hunt them out, besides other great privileges and immunities that were promised to anyone that would undertake to bring them again. A strange thing to consider how the inquisitors detest and abhor the light of the Gospel that they persecute it to the very death.

This fellow had gotten himself a companion, one Juan Fernandes of Valladolid, a very godly man, and purposing to pass together to England through Germany, were laid in wait for at Argentine[52] by means whereof they were followed and captured in a certain port in Zealand as they were taking ship to cross over into England. And being apprehended, this Juan de Leon took the arrest with such good courage that he never changed countenance at all, but as soon as the messengers said what their errand was, he answered them straightway: "Well, (quod he) let us go in God's name, for He (no doubt) will be with us." Whereupon, they were both brought back into the town and there racked most pitifully in order to make them denounce their other companions and within a few days after were shipped and carried into Spain. Each of them during the time that they were in the ship, having an iron chain wrought like a net that covered both head and face, within there was a device of iron made like a man's tongue, which, being thrust into their mouths, took away the use of their tongues. And in these continual pains and torments, besides other devices and fetters of iron wherewith they were bound both hand and foot, they were brought into Spain and there delivered into the inquisitors' prisons: Juan de Leon to the inquisitors' prison at Seville, and his fellow

---

51 Mary I (February 18, 1516 –November 17, 1558)
52 Strasbourg = *Argentoratum* (*Argentina* in medieval Latin).

to Valladolid, where he was afterwards, in defense of God's cause, executed by fire and burned alive, as was also one Doctor Cazalla, a companion of his, a little before him, whose brother or sister's daughter this man had married. Juan de Leon remained a great while in prison, where he tasted the inquisitors' tyranny, suffering both hunger and cold and also endured all their torments one after another, and at the last was brought forth in their solemn show, arrayed like the others that had continued and persevered as he had done. It was a pitiful thing to behold and (no doubt) would have made many a man afraid to see so grisly a sight, and such a ghost as he was. His face so overgrown with hair, his body as lean as a rake, having nothing left to cover his bones save only the very skin; and to the increase of his pain, their barnacle was set upon his tongue that it was loathsome to see the long streams of phlegm come out of his stomach and hang dropping from his mouth to the ground as he stood upright. But when the sentence of death was pronounced upon him, having then his tongue released and set at liberty, to the end that he might abjure and recant (as they supposed he would have done), he made such a confession, with such a serene countenance, so quietly, without any apparent emotion or affection, though in few words, yet so effectually as if he had been in his best estate and more liberty that ever he was in.

At the very last hour of his death, there was assigned unto him a certain monk to dispute with him, one of the same cloister that he himself had once been in, and whose novice he was the first year after that he entered that unlucky order, that he might remind him of the principles of his old popery and superstition. However, the more means that they used to assault him with the stronger he grew and the more able to resist them, for Christ (doubtless) like a good captain defended His soldier. In the end, he was executed as cruelly as in his lifetime he had been tormented miserably, but with as quiet and patient a mind as might be. For so it was always to be expected that so good a man as he should make so good an end.

Some historians have belittled this account as another of Montes's inventions; however, Inquisition records prove the story to be authentic. This monk's name appears in the records as "Fray Juan Sastre, lay friar of the San Isidoro Monastery, born in Palencia, whom the king sent prisoner from Flanders."[53] Since many monks took on different names when they entered the monastery, he may have been known by both Sastre [tailor], in reference to his former profession, and Leon referring to his place of birth (Palencia is in the province of Leon). On December 22, 1560, he appeared on the scaffold in a *sanbenito* painted with devils, a rope around his neck and a bit in his mouth, and was burned at the stake.

Montes's statement (1569, f. 75v) that "divers Spaniards that sojourned at Geneva, thinking England a fitter place for their congregation, accompanied the Englishmen that returned homewards into England" could explain why we find some of the Isidoro monks scattered throughout Europe the following year organizing congregations and also suggests that there were many Spaniards living in various places throughout Europe that had embraced the Protestant

---

53 BNE, ms. 9175, f. 258r, in: Lopez Muñoz (2011, 218, doc. 102).

faith. The first congregation of Spanish-speaking Protestant refugees was established at Antwerp and was of Calvinistic persuasion. Antonio del Corro was
pastor there until 1567. By the mid-sixteenth century, Calvinism had found
support among the lesser nobles and town leaders in the Spanish Netherlands.
Religious dissent was strongest in Ghent and Antwerp. There were some Spanish
congregations in Germany, but as M'Crie states, on account of the Calvinistic
leanings of many of the Spaniards on the subject of the Eucharist, they were
coldly welcomed by the German Lutherans (M'Crie: 1829, 349). In France, especially in Lyons and Montauban, the Spanish Calvinists found wholehearted
support from the Huguenots. Nevertheless, of all the European countries, England was the safest place for Spanish refugees.

Two of the monks—Francisco Farias and Nicolas Molino—must have gone
directly from Geneva to London. Eight years later they were denounced by one of
their countrymen, which nearly caused a diplomatic incident (M'Crie: 1829,
371–372). There was a Spanish Reformed congregation in London to which
Casiodoro de Reina was pastor, but when Reina left a number of the members
joined the Italian church, as was the case of Francisco Farias. Others later joined
the Anglican Church, as was the case with Antonio del Corro and Adrian
Saravia,[54] who were disappointed with the controversies of the continental
Calvinist leaders and their constant doubting of the doctrinal position of the
Spanish Reformers. M'Crie (1829, 370–371) inserts an interesting quote from the
Anglican bishop, John Jewel, in which he compares the Spaniards who came to
English in the retinue of Philip II, and stayed throughout the reign of Mary
Tudor, with their Protestant countrymen who arrived in 1559:

> These are few, those were many; these are poor and miserable, those were lofty and
> proud; these are naked, those were armed; these are spoiled by others, those came to
> spoil us; these are driven from their country, those came to drive us from our country;
> these came to save their lives, those came to have our lives. If we were content to bear
> those then, let us not grieve not to bear these.

One distinguishing trait of the Spanish Reformers was their irenic spirit. They
did their utmost to avoid strife. Having fled from the intolerance that dominated
Spain, they expected to find in the Protestant countries an atmosphere of religious liberty and tolerance, but this was not always the case. Indeed, their
spiritual independence was at times the cause of some friction with the northern

---

54 Adrian Saravia (1531–1613) was born in Flanders, in Hesdin (Pas de Calais), of Protestant
    parents. His father, Cristóbal Saravia, was Spanish and his mother, Elisabet Boulanger, was
    Flemish. He emmigrated to England during the reign of Elisabeth, but in 1582 was back on
    the continent teaching Scripture at Leiden. He returned to England in 1587 as director of a
    Latin school in Southampton. As a Hebrew scholar, he was appointed one of the translators of
    the King James Version of the Bible, his part being Genesis to the end of II Kings. He was the
    only translator who was not native English.

Protestant leaders. For example, it was taken amiss that they should express disagreement with the execution of Servetus. They were always under the suspicion of *servetism,* especially by Theodor Beza, who treated them with his unfailing accusation of their being "followers of Servet." (Hauben: 1967, 5, 18). On the other hand, the Spanish Reformers also suffered as a result of the general prejudices and resentments northern Europeans held against anything Spanish at that time. As children of their time, to a certain degree some Protestant leaders shared these prejudices.

Reina, Valera, and Corro

Of the dozen monks that took refuge in Geneva, some became scholars of great renown. For example, Antonio del Corro became a Bible commentator and professor of theology at the University of Oxford as well as an eminent applied linguist; Casiodoro de Reina translated the Bible into Spanish; Cipriano de Valera, who later revised Reina's translation, was the author of several historical and doctrinal works, as well as the translator of John Calvin's *Institutes of the Christian Religion* into Spanish.[55]

Casiodoro de Reina (1520–1594) was born in Montemolin, in the Province of Badajoz. It is not sure when he entered the Jeronimite monastery of San Isidoro in Santiponce, outside Seville. His evangelical preaching goes back to the days of Dr. Egidio, as well as his friendship with members of the evangelical circle, as one witness testified at the trial of Fray Luis de la Cruz in Valladolid in 1559: "*los errores y herejías que fray Casiodoro enseñó y comunicó al dicho don Juan Ponçe son muchos e diversos de la secta luterana*" (the errors and heresies that Fray Casiodoro taught and imparted to Juan Ponce [de Leon] are many and manifold and are those of the Lutheran sect).[56] Casiodoro fled with the dozen other monks when they came under suspicion by the Holy Office for their Protestant tendencies. As did others, and as was their initial plan, Reina first turned to Geneva but soon left for England and in 1559 was serving as pastor to the Spanish Protestant refugees in London, and where he married—or remarried, according to the Spanish ambassador in London: "the preacher Casiodoro, who has recently married again."[57] His second wife, who he married in 1561, was Anna, daughter of a Spanish merchant, Abraham Leon from Nivelles (Belgium), living in Frankfurt, and widow of Dr. Thomas le Feure (Kinder: 1975, 25).

On January 21, 1561, Casiodoro de Reina, still the head of the Spanish Prot-

---

55 See Appendix B.
56 AHN, Inquisición, leg. 1822, doc. 11, in: Lopez Muñoz (2011, 526, doc. 290).
57 AGS, Estado, leg. 816, f. 166r, in: Lopez Muñoz (2011, 307, doc. 147).

estant community in London, presented the French Consistory of the Strangers' Churches a confession of faith (Reina: 1988).[58] His purpose was to have the Spanish church accepted on the same status as the other foreign churches, or Stranger Churches as they were called.[59] The following year the Spanish refugees were granted permission to hold services in Santa Maria de Haras. Reina was also working on his translation of the Bible, which he had begun some years earlier and would take him another five or six years to finish. In the spring of 1564, Casiodoro and his family left England for the continent. The following three years were spent going from one place to another, trying to avoid the spies sent out by the Inquisition: Heidelberg, Strasbourg, Bergerac, Antwerp, etc. They finally settled in Frankfurt, where Reina was granted citizenship. During this time in Frankfurt, he finished his translation of the Old Testament. In 1567, he moved to Basel, where he finished translating the New Testament and had the entire Bible printed in 1569.[60]

In Frankfurt, Casiodoro was active in the French Reformed Church. Years later, in 1862, M. Schroeder, pastor of that church, compiled a dossier with documents concerning Casiodoro de Reina, taken from the church archives.[61] Once his translation of the Bible was finished, Casiodoro continued to write. In 1573, he published commentaries on the Gospel of John and the Gospel of Matthew.[62] That same year he received a small inheritance from Alfonso Baptista, one of the monks from the monastery of San Isidoro that fled Spain, but had remained in Geneva and had established himself as a merchant. Among his heirs, Alfonso Baptista named "Casiodoro de Reina at Frankfort, Francisco Faries, Juan de Molino, and Cipriano [de Valera] schoolmaster, all three resident in London, bequeathing to each of them a fourth part of his estate." (Boehmer: 2007, III, 151). Upon Reina's death in 1594, in Frankfurt, his son Marcos took over his pastoral duties with the French Reformed Church.

Cipriano de Valera (1532–1603) was an accomplished Greek and Hebrew scholar who later revised Casiodoro de Reina's translation of the Bible. He had

---

58 The full title was: "Christian Confession of Faith, compiled by several faithful Spaniards who, fleeing the abuses of the Church of Rome and the cruelties of the Spanish Inquisition, left their homeland to be received in the Church of the Faithful by brethren in Christ." This Confession of Faith was also translated into German, probably for the benefit of the congregation in Frankfurt: *Das ist Bekenntnis des Christlichen Glaubens* (London: Cassel, 1601). See also Reina (2010, 370–401).

59 See Pettegree (1986).

60 Professor Rady Roldan-Figueroa (2006a; 2006b; 2005a; 200b) has published several interesting studies on Reina's early 1569 translation.

61 A manuscript copy of this document, written between 1563 and 1573 in French and Latin, is now part of the Luis Usoz y Rio collection kept in the Biblioteca Nacional de España, shelf number: BNE, U-17-6.

62 See Appendix B.

also been a monk at the monastery of San Isidoro and had fled together with the other monks in 1557. After a year of two in Geneva, where he joined the Italian church, Valera traveled to England where he established his residency. He may have gone first to Dublin, where he tutored young Nicholas Walsh, who in 1578 would become Bishop of Ossory (Boehmer: 2007, III, 151). After that, Valera taught for some years at Cambridge and Oxford before moving to London where he devoted his time to writing and translating. One of his first works was a volume entitled *Dos tratados* (Two Treatises: on the Pope and on the Mass). A few years later this work was translated into English by John Golburne and enjoyed several editions, both in Spanish and in English. His masterful rendering of Calvin's *Institutes of the Christian Religion* was printed in London in 1597. Prior to this, he had published his *Tratado para confirmar en la fe cristiana a los cautivos de Berbería*, a treatise to confirm the believers enslaved by the Moors in North Africa in their Christian faith and Reformed doctrines. To this treatise was attached the history of the false miracles of a nun at Lisbon, Maria de la Visitacion. The story was appended to a second edition of Valera's *Two Treatise* in 1599 and the following year was translated into English and appended to John Golburne's English translation of the *Two Treatise*.[63] The English version described Maria de la Visitacion as the person whom Philip called to bless the standard of his Invincible Armada.

In 1598, Valera published a New Testament, which was part of Casiodoro de Reina's Bible that he was revising and a few years later, in 1602, he had his revision of the entire Bible printed in Amsterdam. Meanwhile, in 1599, under the pseudonym Guillermo Massan, Valera published his translation of William Perkins's *Reformed Catholic*, and in 1600 he published *Aviso a los de la Iglesia Romana, sobre la indiccion del Iubileo*, translated into English that same year. The work was also translated into French, but this rendering has been lost. In 1704 another publication—*A Full View of Popery*—appeared which may have been a new title for one of Valera's previous works or an abridged edition of several.[64]

Cipriano de Valera was from Fregenal de la Sierra (Extremadura), the same town as Arias Montano, the scholar Philip II commissioned to oversee the printing of the *Biblia Regia*. He died in 1603 in the Netherlands shortly after the

---

63 Two Treatises The First, of the Liues of the Popes, and Their Doctrine. The Second, of the Masse: the One and the Other Collected of That, Which the Doctors, and Ancient Councels, and the Sacred Scripture Do Teach. Also, a Swarme of False Miracles, Wherewith Marie De La Visitacion, Prioresse De La Annuntiada of Lisbon, Deceiued Very Many: and How She Was Discouered, and Condemned. The Second Edition in Spanish Augmented by the Author Himselfe, M. Cyprian Valera, and Translated into English by Iohn Golburn (London: Iohn Harison, 1600).

64 For a full list of his publications, see Appendix B.

printing of his revision of Reina's Bible was completed. A recent trip to Fregenal de la Sierra revealed that the town has preserved the memory of Arias Montano with a plaque on the house where he was born, a street that carries his name, and a commemorative bust that adorns a park. In contrast, the memory of Cipriano de Valera has been totally ignored and forgotten.

Antonio del Corro (1527–1591), also known as Corrano, de Corran, or Corranus, was born in Seville. He was the nephew of an inquisitor of the same name, and one of the Jeronimite monks from San Isidoro that left Spain in 1557. A nephew-uncle kinship between the elderly Antonio del Corro (1472–1556), inquisitor and canon, and Antonio del Corro, monk from San Isidoro, is corroborated in the words of the elderly Corro's will (1556), where several times he mentions "*el bachiller Antonio del Corro, mi sobrino, sucesor en mi calongía*" (Antonio del Corro, my nephew, successor in my canonship).[65] Inquisitor Corro was born in northern Spain and was the grandson of Juan Valdes, one of the conquistadors of Panama. During his lifetime he travelled to France, England and the Low Countries, where he acquired a humanist mind-set. He became a canon in Seville in 1531, in which position he may have been responsible for calling some of the men from Alcala to Seville in the early 1530s. Montes (1569, f. 89v) refers to the elderly Corro in these words:

> There was also one of the inquisitors named El licenciado Antonio del Corro, a good and a fatherly old man, who, for that assurance which he had by his own knowledge of the good conversation of Dr. Egidio, and despite the contrary position of his accusers, remained loyal to his very good friend.

It is difficult to know just when and how young Antonio del Corro became acquainted with the writings of the Reformers. In a letter to Heinrich Bullinger dated July 7, 1574, he states that as early as 1554, he had been acquainted with Bullinger's writings. This was prior to the mass confiscations of prohibited "heretical" literature and also prior to the death of Inquisitor Corro, which suggests that young Antonio may have consulted these works—possibly purchased during the elderly Corro's travels throughout Europe—in his uncle's library.

After his departure from Spain, Antonio del Corro spent the next eight years between Lausanne—where he studied for eighteen months at the Academy—, Béarn, Burdeos, Toulouse, Bergerac, and Montargis.[66] On Calvin's recommendation, he became tutor to seven-year-old prince Henri, future king Henry IV, at the d'Albret court.[67] In France, Corro used the name Bellerive, and served

---

65 BMS, Fondos Modernos, ms. 841, doc. 353, in: Lopez Muñoz (2011, 475, doc. 280).
66 See McFadden (1953); Vermaseren (1986, 530–568).
67 Jeanne d'Albret (1528–1572) was the daughter of Henri d'Albret, who between 1517 and 1555 ruled the independent kingdom of Navarre in the Pyrenees and the Duchy of Béarn. Her

as a minister in the dukedom of Béarn. With the Edict of Amboise in 1563, however, and the expulsion of foreigners, many non-native ministers such as Corro, Perez de Pineda, and even Casiodoro de Reina found refuge at Montargis under the protection of Duchess Renée of France.

In September of 1566, Charles de Melle, a minister at Antwerp, invited Antonio del Corro to come to Antwerp, "for we hope your coming will be of incalculable advantage to our poor country, as you could benefit not only the faithful who speak our language [French], but also the Italians and Spaniards both here and in Brussels and Bruges." (Boehmer: 2007, III, 16). Corro remained in Antwerp until 1568. During this time he wrote two open letters. Both of these letters were later translated into English and published. The first, dated January 2, 1567, was addressed to the pastors of the Walloon church, in which he tried to quell the disagreements between Lutherans and Calvinists. He begins his letter thus:

> We call each other Martinists, Calvinists, Osiandrians, Melanchthonians, Brentians etc. and we are right in doing so as long as we do not fix our eyes upon the advancement of the glory of Christ and his church, which is catholic and universal, and upon that alone. Some take their confessions of faith, catechisms, commentaries and traditions for something like a fifth gospel. We have not been baptized in the name of Martin, Zwingli or Calvin, but in the name of the Father and the Son and the Holy Ghost, and therefore we detest and hold in abomination all those names and surnames of sects: Martinists, Zwinglians, Calvinists and the like.[68]

In the other letter, addressed to Philip II, Corro exhorted the king to read and study the Bible and, as the Jewish kings of the Old Testament did, to always keep the Books of the Law handy and to "read and meditate in them continually." He also stated that it wasn't fair that in Constantinople, which was a Muslim city, the Sultan allowed Jews, Christians, and Muslims to live together in peace, and yet, Philip, being an enlightened Christian monarch, was not protecting his own subjects, who were Protestant. (Moreno: 2013, 8–10; 2008, II, 589–602). When Antwerp fell to the duke of Alva in 1585, Corro left for England with his wife Mary and his two sons, where he would reside until his death.

In London, Antonio del Corro and his family first lodged in a house belonging to the duchess of Suffolk and began his labors as pastor of the Spanish church. Shortly after his arrival he began ministering to a group of some 200 Spanish

---

mother was Marguerite d'Angoulême. Jeanne married Antoine de Bourbon in 1548, who reigned as King of Navarre between 1555 and his death in 1562. Jeanne's announcement of her conversion to Protestantism in 1560 led a large-scale move in that direction on the part of some of the highest ranks of French society. In 1566 she set up a Protestant college at Orthez in Béarn. She died of tuberculosis in 1572.

68 Boehmer (2007, III, 22–24) inserts the letter in full (in English), as well as the context in which it was written.

sailors who had been taken prisoner and interned in Bridewell, a sort of correctional for vagrants. These Spanish sailors had survived the wreckages along the western coast of Scotland and Ireland after the defeat of the Spanish Armada in 1588 and were taken prisoner. Cipriano de Valera seems to have ministered to them as well (Boehmer: 2007, III, 151). This greatly annoyed the Spanish ambassador, Guera d'Espes. According to the ambassador, del Corro distributed several books among these men: "*un libro lleno de blasfemias que circula en este país en tres idiomas*" (a book full of blasphemies that circulates in this country in three languages), as well as Perez de Pineda's *Breve tratado de la doctrina antigua de Dios*, which was another title for his *Doctrina Cristiana* (Santoyo: 1973, 312–318). Could the former have been Montes's *Artes*, which by 1569 had been translated into English, French, and Dutch, and printed in London by John Daye? That same year—1569—Corro published his *Tableau d'Oeuvre de Dieu* (Table of God's Works), a summary of Christian Doctrine, in which he moderately questioned the Calvinist doctrine of predestination and which brought no little controversy (Roldan-Figueroa: 2009, 389–425).

By 1571, Corro had made a definitive transition to Anglicanism. That year he was appointed reader of divinity at the Temple and in 1574 he published his lectures—*Dialogus theologicus*—, which appeared in English translation the following year.[69] In 1575, Corro registered at Oxford for a D.D. degree and was admitted as a divinity reader in 1579. Under Robert Dudley, Earl of Leicester, chancellor of the university at that time, he became the center of a circle of Hispanists at Oxford and the most prominent authority on the Spanish language at the university at this time. As an applied linguist, Corro is credited for having written the first Spanish grammar in English. This was actually an English translation made by John Thorie of a grammar written by Corro to teach Spanish to French speakers, and published in Oxford in 1586. Corro's pioneer work would be followed shortly afterwards by grammars, dictionaries, and dialogs compiled by linguists such as Thorie, Percyvall, Minsheu, etc. Thomas M'Crie (1829, 345) does well to remind us that what was lost in Spain bore fruit in other countries.[70]

---

69 The Temple was originally the headquarters of the Knights Templars. In 1346, the Knights Hospitaller leased the buildings to lawyers. When the Knights were dissolved by Henry VIII in the Reformation, the barristers stayed on and it became a sort of political finishing school for young lawyers.

70 See Appendix B for a full list of del Corro's publications.

The Reina-Valera Bible

Three years before the publication of the second Spanish polyglot, the *Biblia Regia* or *Antwerp Polyglot* (1572), and forty years before the King James Version appeared, Casiodoro de Reina's translation of the complete Bible into Spanish appeared in Basel. In his Exhortation to the Reader, Reina states that it took him twelve years all told—between illnesses, travel, and fatigue—to complete the task, nine of which were dedicated exclusively to mastering Hebrew and to translating. For this undertaking, he made use of the oldest and most reliable texts at hand. He admitted that his greatest difficulty was to properly translate Hebrew names and concepts, which he explains at length and for which he states he consulted primarily the Biblia de Ferrara (1553),[71] Daniel Bomberg's Masoretic Text printed in Venice in 1525, and Sanctes Pagninus's Hebrew-Latin Bible (1528),[72] as well as the Septuagint. For the New Testament he used Robert Stephanus's 1551 Greek New Testament,[73] and the Syriac New Testament (*Peshitta*) edited by the German orientalist Johann Albrecht Widmannstetter and printed in Vienna in 1555.[74] Reina regretted that it was too late for him to consult Immanuel Tremellius's edition of the *Peshitta* (1569), which appeared in Geneva the same year his *Biblia del Oso* (Basel: Samuel Apiarius, 1569) was being printed in Basel.[75] He also consulted Juan Perez de Pineda's Spanish New Testament printed in Geneva in 1556.

Reina's translation is popularly known as the *Biblia del Oso* (Bible of the Bear). The name comes from the printer's device: a complex image representing a bear reaching in a tree hollow for honey. On the ground, an open Bible displays

---

71 The Biblia de Ferrara, called a "ladinada" version, was written in Spanish but with Hebrew syntax. It was printed in Ferrara in 1553 by Abraham Usque (Duarte Pinel), a Portuguese Jew originally from Huesca, Spain, and financed by another Spanish Jew, Yom-Tob ben Levi Athias (Jeronimo de Vargas). The Biblia de Ferrara was for the exiled Spanish Jews expelled from the Iberian Peninsula what Septuagint had been for the Jews at Alexandria and the Babilonian Talmut had been for the Jews in Mesopotamia. It enjoyed several reprints in Salonica (1568) and Amsterdam (1611, 1630, 1646, 1661, 1695, etc.).

72 Pagninus's Hebrew-Latin Bible (Lyons, 1528) gave an interlinear and word-for-word translation of the Hebrew with the Hebrew vowel points and with the Latin translation appearing above the Hebrew text. This Bible was long considered the most convenient Hebrew Bible for those beginning to learn Hebrew.

73 Robert Stephanus produced four editions of his *Greek New Testament:* 1546, 1549, 1550, and 1551. The 1551 edition contained Erasmus's Latin translation and introduced verses for the first time. Reina introduced verses in both the Old and New Testament.

74 For a history of how Syriac came to occupy a prominent place among biblical languages and the printing of the *Peshitta*, see Luttikhuizen (2006, 9–37).

75 Johann Albrecht Widmannstetter introduced the *Peshitta* in Catholic circles in 1555; Immanuel Tremellius in Protestant circles in 1569. Tremellius's text was reprinted in Antwerp, 1571, 1573, 1575; Paris, 1584; Nuremberg, 1599, 1600; Köthen, 1621, 1622; Paris, 1645; London, 1653; Gutbir, 1664; Sulzbach, 1684; Leiden, 1709; etc.

the four Hebrew letters of God's sacred name. The image has been identified as the printing device of Samuel Biener or Apiarius ("the bee-keeper"). The bear refers to the heraldic animal of his native city, Bern, and the bees to the printer's name. A deeper meaning of the image is revealed by a quote from Psalm 119,103: "How sweet are thy words onto my taste! Yea, sweeter than honey to my mouth." The quote reinforces the printer's device as an allegorical representation of the thirst for God's word. Whether this full meaning was readily perceptible or not, the image certainly captured the readers' imagination (Bible, 1569).

In the summer of 1567, Reina travelled to Basel to sign the contract and to make an initial deposit of 400 guilders with the printer Oporinus for the printing of 1100 Bibles. A year later, before the printing had begun, Oporinus died. The Spanish banker in Antwerp, Marcos Perez, came to Casiodoro's rescue with 300 more guilders and a new contract was signed with Thomas Guarin for the printing of 2,600 Bibles.[76] The final printing was financed between Marcos Perez and the Lutheran pastor at Basel, Simon Sulzer. The text was slightly revised 33 years later by Cipriano de Valera and reprinted in Amsterdam in 1602.[77] The New Testament was reprinted in Amsterdam in 1625 and again in 1708 by Sebastian de la Enzina, an Anglican minister, pastor of the "Congregation of the honorable merchants of Spain" in Amsterdam. This 1708 edition was reprinted a century later by the British and Foreign Bible Society. The great demand for Spanish New Testaments required continued reprints of cheap Bibles in the years that followed—1813, 1817, etc.—, coinciding with the massive influx of Spanish exiles. Four centuries later, after a dozen or so revisions, the Reina-Valera Bible is still used in Protestant churches throughout Spain and South America.

A year after Valera printed his revision in Amsterdam, the Swiss-born Italian Calvinist theologian and translator Giovanni Diodati published his translation of the Bible into Italian.[78] In a letter to the Synod of Alencon, France, dated May 1, 1637, Diodati wrote the following regarding the Valera revision:

---

76 Thomas Guarin (1529–1592) was born in Tournai. He worked in Lyons as a bookseller, but by 1557 was in Basel, where he married the daughter of a printer and took over his father-in-law's small press at his death. Along with the reprint of classical works, Guarin issued several editions of the Bible in Latin and German, and one in Spanish. His printer's device was a palm tree, but the device the Spanish Bible carried was that of Apiarius. (Kinder: 1975, 52).

77 For an exhaustive critique of Valera's revision, see Roldan-Figueroa (2009, 411–438). Also see Calvin George (2004).

78 An Italian version of the Scriptures by Nicolo Malermi, a Camaldolese monk, was printed at Venice as early as 1471 and is said to have gone through no fewer than twenty editions. Malermi's translation was made from the Vulgate. A version more faithful to the original had long been desired by the learned. This was at last executed by Antonio Brucioli, whose Italian version of the New Testament was printed at Venice in 1530. Another version of the Bible was printed in the month of October of the same year, without notice of the translator, printer, or place of printing. (M'Crie: 1833, 73–74).

> The new Spanish translation of Cyprian de Valera hath produced incredible effects in
> Spain; no less than three thousand copies having penetrated, by secret ways and
> conveyances, into the very bowels of that kingdom. Let others publish the fruit of my
> Italian version, both in Italy and elsewhere (M'Crie: 1829, 374).

Though Casiodoro de Reina's translation would not have been printed until
1569, nevertheless, the Spanish ambassador in London knew about it already in
1563: "[Zapata] has come to revise with Casiodoro and others a Bible which he is
translating into vulgar Castilian."[79] A letter sent from Antonio del Corro to
Casiodoro de Reina in January of 1565, in which he mentioned the translation,
was intercepted and reported to Philip II.[80] This gave rise to the false assumption
that the Bible had already been printed. The inquisitors at Seville reassured the
Council that they would do everything in their power to make sure copies did not
enter the country:

> As for the Bible in Spanish that Fray Casiodoro has printed, we have been, and always
> are, most diligent and watchful that such books do not enter this kingdom, and all the
> commissioners at the ports have been well warned to use all possible care [that they do
> not enter].[81]

In 1571, the Supreme Council ordered the confiscation of all the copies that could
be found. Aware of these impediments, sometimes the cover and title page were
substituted for other authors, as was the case of those that carried the title page of
Ambrosio Calepinus's famous Latin Dictionary. Another stratagem was to
change the date and place of printing on the title page, which explains why some
copies carry false printer's marks such as "Frankfurt 1602," "Frankfurt 1603," or
"Frankfurt 1622."

As a result of the repressive actions of the Inquisition, the Bible became an
unknown book in Spain. As late as the middle of the nineteenth century when
George Borrow, working under the auspices of the British and Foreign Bible
Society, was travelling through Spain and offering the Bible to booksellers and
the public at large, he received the following responses:

> I entered into discourse with several individuals, but found them very ignorant; none
> could read or write, and their ideas respecting religion were anything but sat-
> isfactory,—most professing a perfect indifference. I afterwards went into a bookseller's
> shop and made inquiries respecting the demand for literature, which, he informed me,
> was small. I produced a London edition of the New Testament in Spanish, and asked the
> bookseller whether he thought a book of that description would sell in Cadiz. He said
> that both the type and paper were exceedingly beautiful, but that it was a work not
> sought after, and very little known. I did not pursue my inquiries in other shops, for I

---

79 AGS, Estado, leg. 816, f. 166r, in: Lopez Muñoz (2011, 307, doc. 147).
80 AHN, Inquisición, lib. 575, f. 201v, in: Lopez Muñoz (2011, 338, doc. 161).
81 AHN, Inquisición, leg. 2944, doc. 93, in: Lopez Muñoz (2011, 375, doc. 183).

reflected that I was not likely to receive a very favourable opinion from booksellers respecting a publication in which they had no interest. I had, moreover, but two or three copies of the New Testament with me, and could not have supplied them had they even given me an order. (Borrow: 1842, Chapter XV. Italics mine).

I had a dépôt of five hundred Testaments at Coruña, from which it was my intention to supply the principal towns of Galicia. Immediately on my arrival I published advertisements, according to my usual practice, and the book obtained a tolerable sale— seven or eight copies per day on the average. *Some people, perhaps, on perusing these details, will be tempted to exclaim, "These are small matters, and scarcely worthy of being mentioned." But let such bethink them, that till within a few months previous to the time of which I am speaking, the very existence of the gospel was almost unknown in Spain, and that it must necessarily be a difficult task to induce a people like the Spaniards, who read very little, to purchase* a work like the New Testament, which, though of paramount importance to the soul, affords but slight prospect of amusement to the frivolous and carnally minded. (Borrow: 1842, Chapter XXVI. Italics mine).

Clerical Marriage

When the monks from San Isidoro arrived in Geneva, they were confronted with another reality: clerical marriage put into practice. The sixteenth century Reformation was a revolution in all respects. One of the most visible changes brought about in the early 1520s was clerical marriage. Martin Luther's marriage to a former nun became one of the icons of the Reformation, but he was neither the first monk to enter into marriage, nor the first to marry a nun, nor the first to write in favor of clerical marriage. The Catholic Church did not regard marriage as its most exalted state. Though a sacrament, marriage was not considered to be spiritually edifying; it was a remedy for sin, not a recipe for righteousness (Witte: 2005). Marriage was considered subordinate to celibacy; marital love less wholesome than spiritual love. Clerics, monastics, and other servants of the church unable to forgo marriage were not worthy of the church's holy orders and offices. The Reformers rejected the subordination of marriage to celibacy and the celebration of marriage as a sacrament. Celibate life led too easily to concubinage and too often hindered the activities of the clerical office. Calvinism emphasized that marriage was not a sacramental institution of the church, but a covenantal association of the community. In other words, whereas Catholics emphasized the spiritual (or sacramental) perspective of marriage, Protestants emphasized its social (or public) perspective.

Closely related to clerical marriage is the role women played in this new reality. Much has been written about the early Reformers and their views on clerical marriage, but woefully little is known about the women who stood beside them (Plummer: 2012, 211–243). The Protestant Reformation had left devout women with religious vocations with few choices. Previously, many could consider entering a convent or a beguinary. This, however, was not the ideal state for those who saw their religious calling as something beyond contemplative meditation. The cloistered life of the convent separated them from the world and denied them the opportunity to be a direct influence on their neighbors. For many of these women, the Reformation was a godsend in this sense. It gave them the opportunity to address their calling in a new way. As pastors' wives, they could fill a spiritual and charitable void in the community, they could tend the sick and the dying, and they could educate children and young girls. Katharina Schutz, who married her pastor-priest Mathias Zell in Strasbourg in 1523, is an example. She placed her calling within the doctrine of the "priesthood of believer." (Plummer: 2012, 228; Methuen: 2010, 707–728). The doctrine of the priesthood of believers constituted the starting point of Reformation thought. Luther first brought it to the attention of evangelical-minded Christians in his *To the Christian Nobility of the German Nation* (1520):

> That the pope or bishop anoints, makes tonsures, ordains, consecrates, or dresses differently from the laity, may make a hypocrite or an idolatrous oil-painted icon, but it in no way makes a Christian or spiritual human being. In fact, we are all consecrated priests through Baptism, as St. Peter in 1 Peter 2,9 says, "You are a royal priesthood and a priestly kingdom." (Wengert: 2005).

Whether out of conviction or out of convenience, most of the Jeronimite monks that fled to Geneva married once they got settled. The only case registered of clerical marriage among evangelicals in Spain is that of Francisco de Zafra, the parish priest of San Vicente in Seville who escaped from Triana the eve of All Saints' Day 1557. We only know his wife's name: Francisca Lopez, a *beata* born in Manzanilla (Huelva) and residing in Seville. An Inquisition document states that they were "living together as husband and wife."[82] Francisca had little opportunity to fulfill her new vocation. She was condemned to the stake at the *auto-dafe* in Seville held on September 24, 1559, accused of being a dogmatizer, a traitor, a deceiver, and an impenitent Lutheran heretic.[83]

The names of the wives of the Spaniards living abroad can be gleaned from several sources. Boehmer (2007, III, 33–34) lists a few who were attending the Stranger Church in London:

> A certificate of the Lord Major on the strangers in London in 1568 gives interesting particulars as to their numbers: "Anthony Coran in Cripplegate ward, preacher in the Italian church, born in Spain; tenant to the duchess of Suffolk; Mary his wife; John and James, their children; David de Dieu and Joan Leveresse, their servants, they go to the Italian church." The following Spaniards are mentioned as associating with the Italians:

---

82 BNE, ms. 6176, f. 310r, in: Lopez Muñoz (2011, 166, doc. 83).
83 AHN, Inquisición, leg. 2075, doc. 1, in: Lopez Muñoz (2011, 158, doc. 80).

Francis de Farias, Spaniard, and Jacomina his wife, his children, and Nicolas Duprey, his servants, silk-weavers, go to the Italian church. Fernando Almarez, Spaniard, a buttonmaker, goes to the Italian church... Sanchie [Sanchez], born in Spain, has an English woman to his wife.

It is logical to suppose that several of the exiled monks found wives among the Italian refugee community living in Geneva. Although the first wave of Italian refugee families belonged to the patrician class of merchant-bankers—the Balbani, Burlamachi, Calandrini, Diodati, and Turrettini—who married within their own group, nevertheless, their households would have included eligible marriageable relatives. By 1560, there were around fifty households in Geneva consisting of citizens from Lucca (Grell: 2011, 32; Adorni-Braccesi: 2007, 513–534). Moreover, French Protestant refugees had also begun arriving in Geneva in ever increasing numbers after 1546. That year, more than 4,000 arrived from Provence alone (Grell: 2011, 250). In the same way that Geneva had become a melting pot of Calvinist refugees and where many found partners, the same can be said for Strasbourg. It was at Strasbourg where John Calvin met and married Idelette de Bure, where Peter Martyr Vermigli met and married Catherine Dampmartin, where Immanuel Tremellius met and married Elisabeth Grune-cieux, etc. It was also at Strasbourg where the Spanish scholar Francisco de Enzinas married Margaret d'Autel (d'Elter in Flemish), the epitome of the type of woman many of the Reformers married: an ex-nun, cultured, refined, devout, discerning, etc.

Margaret d'Elter was born in Guelders some time between 1510 and 1515. In 1527 she entered the noble chapter of the Sainte Waudru convent at Mons, for which she had had to produce evidence of eight generations of nobility in order to enter.[84] Margaret left the convent in June of 1547 when the Dutch nobleman Jacques de Bourgogne, Lord of Falais, sent Valerand Poullain to the Netherlands to try to recuperate his confiscated lands and to fetch his sister Antoinette, canoness of the Sainte Waudru convent at Mons, and two others: Isabelle de Hamericourt and Margaret d'Elter. Isabelle stayed in Basel, but Margaret went to Strasbourg to keep company with her cousin Anne t'Serclaes, who would shortly afterwards marry the Englishman, and future bishop, John Hooper.

---

84 Her great great grandfather was the powerful 14th century Flemish knight, Hugon d'Autel, whose grandson Huart II, Lord d'Autel, even coined his own currency in his castle of Laroche. Huart II became the civil and military governor of the Duchy of Luxembourg. By the end of the 16th century the castle of Autel and the title had passed into the hands of several noble families, one of which was Margaret's father, Johann Elter (Jean II d'Autel), Lord of Sterpenich. Margaret's father managed to unite the entire family estate by buying up the rights of his sisters. Margaret's mother, Catherine de Palant (Katharina von Palandt zu Laurenzberg), was also of noble birth. She was the daughter of Jean von Palant, Lord of Nothberg.

Margaret d'Elter and Francisco de Enzinas were married in March 1548 and shortly afterwards moved to England. That year many families left Strasbourg for England, among them Bernardino Ochino, Martin Bucer, Peter Martyr Vermigli, Pablo Fagius, Jan Utenhove, and Immanuel Tremellius as a protest to the agreement arrived at by Catholics and Protestants in 1548, known as the "Augsburg Interim." Once in England, Archbishop Thomas Cranmer housed some of them temporarily at his own home and then secured temporary positions for them. For Enzinas, he found a position as professor of Greek at Cambridge. That year their daughter Margarita was born. When Enzinas returned to Strasbourg in November 1549 in order to print his Spanish translations of Lucian, Livy, and Plutarch, Margaret stayed in England because of the infant's delicate health and the perils of winter travel, but she joined him the following summer, accompanied by her niece Anna d'Elter.[85] A second daughter was born at Strasbourg in 1551. But the following winter both Margaret and her husband were victims of the plague. The orphan daughters, Margarita and Beatriz, became wards of the city. In July 1555, Margaret's niece Anna d'Elter took them in when she married the French humanist Guillaume Rabot de Salene.[86] The couple promoted the interests of the orphans and later arranged for the publication of Enzinas's *Memoirs*, which they translated from Latin into French. Meanwhile, Beatriz de Santa Cruz, Francisco's step mother, tried to gain custody of the girls, which resulted in a legal battle that was still going on in 1566.

Margaret d'Elter was much esteemed by her husband's colleagues. James Haddon, brother of the Greek scholar William Haddon, was very impressed. He wrote Enzinas from Oxford, in September 1548, shortly after their arrival, and closed with these words: "Please most affectionately give my greetings to your wife, that outstanding and exemplary woman." (Enzinas: 1995, 421). In a letter to Enzinas, the Polish Reformer, Jan Laski, who may have met the Enzinas at the newly established Dutch Stranger Church in London on their arrival, of which he would be superintendent after 1550, wrote: "I saw your wife only once, and I'm glad to have had a glimpse of her. Congratulations. May the Lord, who joined you together, bless you both. Fondly greet her in my name." (Enzinas: 1995, 407).

---

85 She was the daughter of Margaret's brother Jean III d'Elter and his first wife, Elizabeth Ansembourg. Considering her father remarried in 1521, she may have been orphaned young and put in the convent with Margaret, and later accompanied her to Strasbourg in 1547 and then to England.

86 Not to be confused with his cousin by the same name who was a cavalry officer. Anne's husband was a scholar employed in the court of count Frederic Count Palatine, "who gave [Guillaume Rabot] in marriage a rich heiress of this country, Anne d'Elter, the daughter of Jean III d'Elter and his [first] wife, Elizabeth Ansembourg." (Carl Wahlund (1889), *La philologie française au temps jadis*, Stockholm: Imprimerie centrale, 9). It appears that Guillaume Rabot had been a professor at Wittenberg before going to Strasbourg (Arnaud: 1890).

Peter Martyr Vermigli, who had married in Strasbourg and was now living in Oxford with his wife, Catherine Dampmartin, answered Enzinas's invitation to come and live with them at Cambridge in these terms: "I want you to know that nothing makes me happier than to see you, and for my wife to be able to chat with your lovely wife. My wife hardly leaves the house and leads a very lonely life because she does not know English." (Enzinas: 1995, 429). A month later Vermigli wrote again in the same terms: "You can't imagine how happy both me and my wife are for your decision to come and see us soon, and that you are coming together with your extraordinary wife, who I cannot express how greatly loved and esteemed she is by my wife." (Enzinas: 1995, 425). Tokens of affection for their colleagues' wives is a common denominator found in the correspondence of all the Reformers, especially those in Strasbourg (Rummel: 2005). They indicate the caliber of these women and their newfound vocation and also the high regard their husbands—and their husband's colleagues—had for them, which contrasted greatly with the opinion the Roman Catholics had of women who married ex-priests.

Chapter 12:
Repression Continues

> Very great is the risk to which he who prints a book exposes himself, for of all impossibilities the greatest is to write one that will satisfy and please all readers.
>
> *Don Quijote*, Book II, Ch. 3.

The aftermath of the *autos-da-fe* in Valladolid and Seville in 1559 and 1560, designed to remove the Lutheran threat from Spanish soil, was not one of ends accomplished but rather of more oppression and more repression. In Seville, many *autos* followed those of 1559 and 1560 in which more Lutherans or Lutheran sympathizers were sentenced: April 26, 1562; October 28, 1562; July 11, 1563; May 13, 1565; May 8, 1569; November 14, 1574; February 10, 1577; May 1, 1583; April 13, 1586; June 14, 1592; March 14, 1599. Though fewer and fewer offenders were sent to the stake, nevertheless, the ceremony and the different parties that attended—nobles, bishops, civil authorities, etc.—and those that marched through the streets ahead of the offenders as they made their way from Triana to the scaffolds set up in San Francisco Square—the boys from the Colegio de Doctrina with their candles, the various religious orders with their banners reciting the litany, the *alguaciles* and *familiares*, the inquisitors, and all the members of the Holy Office according to their rank, etc.—remained the same.[1]

Many records are missing, nevertheless, as late as 1587, the inquisitors at Seville voted to burn the bones of "Mencia Gonzalez, deceased, wife of Francisco Nuñez de Sosa, from Cadiz."[2] The records do not specify if her offense was holding Lutheran views or Judaizing. As Werner Thomas (2001a, 240) points out, it was actually after the *autos* of 1559 that the inquisitorial courts of Spain became aware of the great infiltration of Protestantism in the peninsula. All sorts of measures were taken to stop the "Protestant menace" and the flow of heretical literature into Spain. Processions were organized; false distribution networks were set up as bait in order to trap contacts into disclosing their identity (Thomas: 2001a, 245; Reguera: 1984).

---

1 For a full description of the ceremony held in Seville on October 28, 1562, see Schäfer (2014, II, 439–444, doc. 290).

2 AHN, Inquisición, leg. 2948, in: Lopez Muñoz (2011, 344, doc. 164).

More Oppression, More Repression

The Venetian ambassador, Paulo Tiepolo, reported an *auto-da-fe* in Toledo on March 12, 1561, in which twenty-two persons were accused of being Lutherans; four were sent to the stake and eighteen received a lesser penalty. What may have urged him to report this incident was that one of the individuals sent to the stake was an Italian and among the others who received lesser sentences was a German nobleman (Calendar, 1890). Indeed, a distinctive note in the *autos* of the 1560s was the increasing number of foreigners sentenced. Among the thirty offenders that appeared at the *auto* celebrated in Valladolid on October 28, 1561, all but two of the fourteen offenders were foreigners. Most of them were Frenchmen. In 1561, the inquisitors at Zaragoza informed the Supreme Council of an *auto-da-fe* celebrated a few days earlier, and added,

> It is paramount that the punishment, both of Lutherans and of *conversos*, be exemplary because we are in a part of the country where there are many Béarnesses and Frenchmen and other foreigners that profess Luther's heresies, hence we send them to the galleys.[3]

That same day they wrote Philip II, saying,

> We have taken very strong actions against the Lutherans, as strong as the law permits, in order to make them aware of, and fear, the sort of punishment they will receive if they come into your majesty's kingdom.[4]

Six years later, these same inquisitors sent Philip II another letter in which they informed him that,

> Fifty-six offenders were brought out in the last *auto-da-fe*, nearly all of them Lutherans. They were all foreigners, from France, Gascuña and Bearn, and were all condemned to serve in your majesty's galleys because that is the punishment we feel that most terrifies them and keeps them from entering your kingdom.[5]

Able bodies to supply the king's galleys were welcome, but they posed another problem: did the king want his ships filled with heretics? After the Battle of Lepanto in 1571, in which Spain participated with 14 ships, which necessarily carried many Lutheran rowers, Philip II came up with a plan to

> Create an Inquisition for heretics who might be found on ships. As the authority of the inquisitor-general did not extend beyond the dominions of the King of Spain, it was considered necessary to apply to the Pope, who in 1571 granted the brief, which was demanded, authorizing the inquisitor-general to create the new tribunal, and appoint judges and officers. It was first known by the name of the "Inquisition of the Galleys,"

---

3 AHN, Inquisición, Lib. 988, f. 84.
4 AHN, Inquisición, Lib. 988, f. 87.
5 AHN, Inquisición, Lib. 988, f. 134.

but it was afterwards called the "Inquisition of the Fleets and Armies." It existed but for a short period, as it was found to impede the progress of navigation. (Llorente: 1843, 190–191).

In January of 1563, the inquisitors at Seville informed the Supreme Council that,

> At present there are five ships docked in the Guadalquivir rowed by many Flemings who are forced rowers and many of them are Lutherans. They have just recently arrived from Flanders. We will take legal action against them and do justice, for great harm requires a great remedy.[6]

It is uncertain whether these five ships docked in the Guadalquivir river—the *San Pablo*, the *San Juan*, the *Santa Marcelina*, the *El Angel*, and the *Francesca*—came together or whether the *El Angel* came separately the previous year because at the *auto-da-fe* held on October 28, 1562, three of the men from the *El Angel*—a cook, a carpenter and regular sailor—were sentenced to the stake and seven to perpetual imprisonment.[7] The majority of the victims sentenced at the *auto-da-fe* at Seville, held of July 11, 1563, were foreigners (6 to the stake; 9 to life imprisonment; 10 to lesser punishments). The six foreigners sent to the stake—mainly Flemish and Dutch—were galley slaves serving on the *San Pablo*.[8] Being galley slaves indicates that they were repeated offenders. One of them was Guillermo Guillermeson, "alias Guillermo de Utreque," a tailor, accused of being an Anabaptist and a Lutheran—slightly contradictory ways of thinking but for the inquisitors part and parcel of the same heresy. Persecution against Anabaptists reached its zenith in the Netherlands in the 1550s hence several of the other galley slaves may also have been Anabaptists. An edict issued in 1550 read: "Foreigners suspected of heresy, and in particular the Anabaptists, are not to be admitted here without an attestation from the parish of their last place of residence." (Krahn: 1968, 209).

At the *auto* of May 13, 1565, six persons were burned in effigy (4 foreigners); seven foreigners were sentenced to life in prison and confiscation of goods, and three to the galleys.[9] At the *auto* of May 8, 1569, three galley slaves from the *Bastardilla* and one merchant were burned at the stake (Schäfer: 2014, II, 459, doc. 294). All four men were from Mons (Belgium), where persecution was strong. Although the final list of those sentenced in the *auto-da-fe* of April 24, 1569, has been lost, according to a document describing the preparations for the *auto-da-fe*, all but one of those sentenced to the stake were Frenchmen.[10] At the *auto* of November 14, 1574, seven foreigners were sentenced. Of the four sen-

6 AHN, Inquisición, leg. 2942, 97, in: Lopez Muñoz (2011, 289, doc. 136).
7 AHN, *Inquisición*, leg. 2075 (1), doc. 2, in: Lopez Muñoz (2011, 270, doc. 129).
8 AHN, *Inquisición*, leg. 2075, doc. 3, in: Lopez Muñoz (2011, 308, doc. 148).
9 AHN, Inquisición, leg. 2943, doc. 149–2, in: Lopez Muñoz (2011, 344, doc. 164).
10 AHN, Inquisición, leg. 2944, doc. 135, in: Lopez Muñoz (2011, 383, doc. 192).

tenced to the sake, two escaped and were burned in effigy. At the *auto* of February 10, 1577, of the ten persons sentenced, nine were Englishmen (three to the stake). At this *auto* a Spanish monk, a galley slave on the ship *Ocasion*, who had been tried twice in Valladolid and once in Murcia for some other cause, declared himself a Lutheran hoping that way to be free from rowing. He was sentenced to 400 lashes and back to the galley ship (Schäfer: 2014, II, 463, doc. 296). Schäfer documents more *autos* in Seville in which more foreigners were sentenced to the stake, accused of holding Lutheran doctrines.[11] For example, at the auto held on May 1, 1583, thirty-five—mainly Germans—were sentenced (five to the stake, one of which was a case similar to the above mentioned monk). (Schäfer: 2014, II, 464, doc. 298).

At the *auto-da-fe* celebrated in Valladolid on October 28, 1561, Fray Rodrigo Guerrero, a monk from the convent of La Merced in Seville and teacher of theology, was the first to be sentenced. He had declared himself a Lutheran in 1559, but because he was ill his case was postponed and he was not included in the list of persons to appear at the 1559 *auto*. In 1561, he retracted, nevertheless, he was sentenced to irremissible life in prison (Schäfer: 2014, III, 92, doc. 386). It appears that ten years later, the Supreme Council suspected that he had relapsed and he was sent to the stake on November 11, 1571 (Schäfer: 2014, III, 161, doc. 407). In 1567, the inquisitors at Valladolid reported the number of cases of Lutherans and Lutheran sympathizers that they had sentenced between 1562 and 1567: 15 persons burned at the stake; 7 escapees burned in effigy; 7 deceased burned in effigy; 13 reconciled; 120 prison sentences; 23 absolved; 49 case suspended; 40 awaiting trial; 12 remaining in prison (Schäfer: 2014, III, 174). Despite all this diligence, they informed the Supreme Council in 1570 that Valladolid was still "full of Lutherans" and that in August they had arrested six or seven more.[12] No Spaniards were among those sentenced in the *autos* that followed: October 1, 1570; October 2, 1580; August 3, 1588, which is the period covered by Schäfer (2014, III, 98–100, doc. 387–390).

The Index of Prohibited Books Expanded

The unexpected arrival of still more clandestine literature after the 1559–1560 *autos* in Seville and Valladolid prompted Philip II to expand the list of prohibited books in 1583. Among the 200 books added to the Index that year, were books

---

11 Schäfer documents cases in Barcelona, Logroño, Valencia, Zaragoza, Córdoba, Cuenca, Granada, Llerena, Murcia, Santiago from 1552 to 1600. (Schäfer: 2014, II, 7–113).

12 AHN, Inquisición, leg. 3190, in: Moreno (2012a, 375).

confiscated and inventoried by Dr. Heredia.[13] These included a copy of Calvin's *Commentary on Isaiah*, Wolfgang Musculus's *Commentary on Romans*, Savonarola's *Exposicion del psalmo Inte domine speraui*, a book by Sebastian Munster, another by Justus Jonas, several by Petrus Ramus, Bartolome de Carranza's *Catechism*, Juan Perez de Pineda's *Letter to Philip II*, a half dozen books by Erasmus, including his New Testament, and a "rare copy" of Ambrosio Montesino's *Epistles and Gospels for the Year*, and others.

Another document, written up some time after 1610, lists more books confiscated by the Inquisition at Seville between 1583 and 1609. Among these publications—many by Catholic authors—there were Bibles in Spanish "sent from La Rochelle" that contained *"ciertas cosas del Calepino"* (certain things by Calepinus).[14] This Bible was actually Casiodoro de Reina's *Biblia del Oso*, printed in Basel in 1569. In 1581, the bishop of Basel, Blarer von Wartensee, informed cardinal Charles Borromeo, archbishop of Milan, that 1,600 copies of a Bible in Spanish had been printed in Basel and that 1,400 copies had been sent from Frankfurt to Antwerp. Aware of the strict censorship imposed on books entering Spain, in order to facilitate entry, in Antwerp the title page of these Bibles was substituted with the title page of the Italian lexicographer Ambrosio Calepino's famous Latin Dictionary.[15] This explains the phrase *"con ciertas cosas del Calepino."* Other books were Calvin's *Institutes* "printed in England in Spanish," and two catechisms by Calvin "printed by Ricardo del Campo," one in 1596 and the other in 1600. There was also a New Testament—*Testamento Nuevo y Catecismo, de Teodoro Beça, en lengua española*—and a Catechism "in Spanish" attributed to Theodor Beza. This was another false title page because Beza's works were not translated into Spanish. This publication was actually Casiodoro de Reina's *Testamento Nuevo*, revised by Cipriano de Valera and printed in London by Richard Field. Another work by Cipriano de Valera and printed by Richard Field that appeared on the list was his "Treatise on the Pope and the Mass," and his translation of William Perkins's, *A Reformed Catholike* (1597). Some books were banned straightaway and burned; others were expurgated.[16]

Expurgation became a somewhat liberalizing alternative to total prohibition. It legalized the reading of certain works after objectionable passages were deleted (Bleiberg/Ihrie: 1993, I, 374). The person responsible for introducing a

---

13 AHN, Inquisición, leg. 4426, doc. 31.
14 La Rochelle was an important Huguenot stronghold on the Atlantic coast. With its impregnable walls and its own powerful navies, Rochelle was the Venice of France. It was also the Geneva of France, the city of refuge to which Protestants from all parts of the country fled.
15 This could have been the Basel edition and which would have circulated in Protestant circles: *Ambrosii Calepini Dictionarivm vndecim lingvarvm* (Basel: Sebastian Henricpetri, 1590).
16 AHN, Inquisición, lib. 575, ff. LXv, in: Lopez Muñoz (2011, 120, doc. 42). See also Kamen (1998); Perez (2012).

policy of expurgation was Benito Arias Montano, Philip II's chaplain and librarian. In 1569, Montano began work on an Expurgatory Index, which was published in 1571,[17] though it would appear that the practice of emending banned literature had begun somewhat earlier.[18] Inquisitor General Gaspar Quiroga justified the publication of an enlarged Index in 1584, alleging that "the preceding Catalogues had not sufficed to put a stop to the increasing heresies."[19] More supplements were added in 1707, 1739 and 1747. The last Spanish Index (*Indice ultimo*)—of over 5500 entries—was printed in 1790, conveniently compiled in alphabetical order with curious abbreviations to minimize space. The nineteenth century English clergyman turned historian, Joseph Mendham (1830, 253–254), summarizes the preface of the 1790 Index thus:

> After a due amplification concerning human malice and pestilent novelties and stating the fact that condemned works had been published in the country under plea of ignorance, and that the last Index had become rare, the Inquisitor professes his determination to publish an Abridgment, or alphabetic Compendium, which should comprehend, not only the contents of the Index of 1747, but likewise all the works which had been prohibited, or sentenced to expurgation in fore-cited Edicts [up] to Dec. 13, 1789. This would close the door to the excesses of printers and booksellers, as well as private persons, and prevent the evils consequent upon the introduction of such pernicious commodities into the kingdom. For the credit of this Index, and of the nation to which it belongs, *Regla V* [Rule V] deserves to be particularly notices as a relaxation of former intolerance with respect to vernacular translations of the Scriptures.

Connections Abroad

Once it was assumed that the principle leaders of the evangelical movement in Seville and Valladolid had been eliminated, the inquisitors turned to Spaniards living abroad suspected of heresy.[20] Aware that Julian Hernandez, the colporteur who carried Protestant literature from Geneva to Spain, could be a well of information regarding Spaniards living abroad who either were part of or had

---

17 See Bujanda (1988, 2002); Dávila Pérez (2002). Ironically, several of Montano's own works were expurgated in 1607 (Jones: 1978, 121).

18 AHN, Inquisición, leg. 2944, doc. 117 (dated, December 10, 1568); AHN, Inquisición, leg. 2944, doc. 121 (dated, January 15, 1569).

19 In Quiroga's Index, Erasmus occupies 33 folios, that is, from fol. 81 to 114 (Mendham: 1830, 93).

20 AHN, Inquisición, leg. 2943, doc. 136; AHN, Inquisición, lib. 575, f. 197v; AHN, Inquisición, leg. 2943, doc. 156; AHN, Inquisición, lib. 575, f. 367v; AHN, Inquisición, leg. 2944, doc. 57; AHN, Inquisición, leg. 2944, doc. 62; etc.

frequented Lutheran circles, the inquisitors interrogated him. The document narrating the interrogation states:

> In the Castle of Triana, October 4, 1560, Inquisitors Gasco and Soto, sitting in their conference room in the morning, called for Julian Hernandez, prisoner in the jails of this Holy Office, and having sworn to tell the truth, said that he knew the name of the city in the king's realms where every holy day [Sunday] more than 18 or 20 groups of people met that profess and follow the Christian religion as Lutherans, that is, preach and administer the sacraments of communion and baptism and sometimes also marry people similar to the way the Lutherans do in Germany and other places.

> Asked in what city, in our lord the king's realms these gatherings meet, he said the city was Antwerp, which is in Brabant, and half of those that meet together are foreigners from that city, mainly Walloons, and the other half are Flemish or foreigners.

> Asked how he knew that there were so many groups and who the people were and what nationality they were, he said he was told by the minister and elders of the gatherings, but he didn't know their names, only that the minister was from Provence [in southern France]. There was only one minister, but there were as many elders as gatherings, and they are French and Walloons. On Sundays and holidays these groups met in different places, and because the minister cannot be everywhere at the same time, an elder joined him in turn to pray and preach, and the minister preaches sometimes at one meeting and other times at another. And if he could recall, he would tell them their names.

> Asked in what houses, or places, each of these groups met, he said he would tell them everything they wanted to know if they complied with the orders of the bishop [of Tarazona] to give him a New Testament. He was told to answer the question. He said that sometimes they met in one place, and other times they met in another, and the place he knows, because he was there, was in the house of the merchant Jean le Blond, who lives in the Rue de Tournay under the coat of arms of France, and in the house of the merchant Jacques Sanglier, in the Rue del Eperne, and in the house of the trimmings maker, Nicolás Vuelpin, in a village near Antwerp as you leave through the Red Gate, a married elder; Jean le Blond was also a married elder. He had also been elsewhere but cannot remember. But in the places named, he was present during the assembly and in each place saw a small room full of men and women who had all come to hear the preaching of the Christian religion, Lutheran style, by a minister called master François de la Rivière, who was also a minister in Guesalia [Westphalia], where he is now, and came [to Antwerp] some times, but had been a minister of the Walloon church in Frankfurt.[21] He also said he attended another gathering in Antwerp in the house of the

---

21 François (Pérussel) de la Riviere was the first minister of the Walloon refugees at Canterbury. In 1550, Edward VI appointed him minister of the Walloon Church at London. At the accession of Queen Mary, when many of the foreign Protestants left England, he remained behind for the consolation of those who were unable to leave London. Soon afterwards, however, he left for Antwerp. From there he was called as minister of the French congregations at Wesel (1554) and Frankfurt (1557), after which he returned to London for a short time. Riviere became chaplain to the prince of Condé in 1561. As Condé's chaplain, he had a significant role in the French Reformed churches, attending the provincial synods

merchant Pierre Balduin, but could not remember the street where he lived, but that in his house François de la Rivière had baptized a child Lutheran style. He also heard that they met in the house of another Walloon merchant, friend of Jean le Blond, whose name he cannot recall at present, and also in the house of another French merchant whose name he does not recall either.

Asked what Spaniards, who are now in Spain or have been in Spain recently, or plan to come to Spain, attended these meetings, and which meeting, he said that he only knew of fray Julian, a Dominican friar, from Aragon or Navarra. He also thought that Felipe de la Torre, chaplain to King Felipe, and who he thought was from Aragon or Tarazona, knew about these assemblies and that he was on very friendly terms with the people who attended, especially with fray Julian, but Felipe de la Torre was not as open about it as fray Julian.[22] And the persons that fray Julian was on friendly terms with were the merchant Pierre Balduin, already mentioned; also with Jehan le Blond, Juan Rogier, book dealer, and the innkeeper Jean Botiller, and the Walloon merchant, friend of Jehan le Blond, and other people whose name he could not remember.

Asked what other cities, villages or hamlets belonging to our lord the king, he knew of or had visited where there are other Lutheran gatherings. He had not seen any others, but had heard that there were groups in Tournay, Lila, Armentier, Ghent, Flanders, Mons de Henao, Valençien, and Arrás, but that in these places they did not meet in the city like in Antwerp, where those assembled have professed not to return to Catholicism nor to have anything to do with the Catholic Church either directly or indirectly.

Asked if he knew who some of the people were that gathered in these towns and where, he said he only knew that the people in Antwerp knew the names of the people and the places. As for the places the Flemish met, he knew that from having heard it from them, but did not recall the names of the people nor the places, but that the Walloons knew it.[23]

On December 12, 1563, the inquisitors received information from the Florentine book dealer Andrea Pejioni that from Lyons (France) books were shipped to La Rochelle, where one Peregrino del Baño, "a great Lutheran heretic," shipped them along with other merchandize to his brother Andrea del Baño, who had a shop in Seville.[24] On October 9, 1566, the Supreme Council sent a note to the inquisitors at Seville, accompanying a copy of part of a letter Madame de Parma, governess of Flanders, sent to Philip II, in which they urged them to visit all the bookshops, especially those in Cadiz. In a note to the Council later that month, dated October 26, 1566, the inquisitors informed them regarding their visit to the bookshops:

throughout France. He died some time before 1570. His daughter and her husband were killed during the St Bartholomew's Day massacre.

22 José Antonio Maravall calls him a "belated Erasmian." (Nieto: 1997, 409–411). Also see Truman (1984, 83–93).

23 AHN, Inquisición, leg. 4442, doc. 47. Notes and brackets mine.

24 AHN, Inquisición, leg. 2943, doc. 124, in: Lopez Muñoz (2011, 316, doc. 153).

The visits to the bookshops and the book dealers began yesterday, the 25th. At 9 o'clock in the morning all the shops in Seville were simultaneously occupied by *familiares* of the Holy House so that it was impossible for one to warn another, or to hide or remove a single book. Later, we—licenciado Carpio and licenciado Quintanilla—, the archbishop's deputy (provisor), and the ecclesiastical judge ordered that each one of the shops be secured with new locks. We will visit them one by one.[25]

Likewise, the inquisitors were to appoint a sheriff to search the ships, as well as the personnel aboard.[26] One of the Spaniards active in sending literature to Spain was Marcos Perez, a wealthy spice-merchant living in Antwerp.[27] The inquisitors knew that he sent books to his factor in Lisbon and to his brother-in-law in Seville, Francisco Nuñez Perez, and to Rodrigo de Illescas, who owned a soap factory in Seville.[28] Finally, in July of 1567, the Supreme Council ordered the prosecution of "heretics living in Flanders, with possessions in Spain."[29] There was, however, a legal problem. The inquisitors at Seville regretted that, "although Marcos Perez's parents are Spanish, he was born in Flanders hence we have no jurisdiction over him."[30]

The Supreme Council had received first-hand information regarding Marcos Perez through Andres de la Torre, a Spanish merchant living in Antwerp. The interrogatories produced interesting information regarding the Spaniards in Antwerp that had embraced Lutheran doctrines, as well as the complex network of business partners and players involved in the smuggling of Protestant literature into Spain:

Asked if he [Andres de la Torre] had heard or knew of anything that was against, or seemed to be against, the holy Catholic faith that he should denounce to the Holy Office, he said that in Spain he had heard nothing of that sort, but that he had just come by land from Flanders some thirteen days ago and that there he had heard and seen many things contrary to the holy Catholic faith, which was most regretful. Asked if the things he had heard and seen contrary to the holy Catholic faith in Flanders were said or done

25 AHN, Inquisición, leg. 2944, doc. 29–2, in: Lopez Muñoz (2011, 359, doc. 172). See also Vázquez de Prada (1970, 147–155).
26 AHN, Inquisición, lib. 575, f. 354v.
27 Around 1575, Marcos Perez's son Lodovico joined the exiled Italian Calvinst banker, Cesare Calandrini, in creating a company trading in silk and velvet. Between 1597 and 1603, this company became one of the most prominent businesses importing English cloth via Hamburg. Their fathers had served as elders in the Calvinist church in Antwerp. (Grell: 2011, 114).
28 AHN, Inquisición, lib. 575, f. 367v; 575, f. 374r; lib. 575, f. 374r; leg. 2944, doc. 29–2, in: Lopez Muñoz (2011, 358, doc. 170; 359, doc. 172). Rodrigo de Illescas was an uncle of Ana de Illescas (see Chapter X). He had business connections with the Enriquez de Ribera brothers, and may even have had shares in Pedro de Morga's bank. For details, see Antonio Acosta Rodríguez, *et al*, La Casa de la Contratación y la navegación entre España y las Indias (Seville: Universidad de Sevilla, 2003).
29 AHN, Inquisición, lib. 576, f. 71r, in: Lopez Muñoz (2011, 369, doc. 177).
30 AHN, Inquisición, leg. 2944, doc. 57, in: Lopez Muñoz (2011, 370, doc. 178).

by native Spaniards or by the Flemish, he said that they were all Flemish, except that he had lived in Antwerp for eight years and there he knew of a man by the name of Marcos de la Palma, who is both a merchant and a factor. This man's parents and ancestors were from Galicia, but he didn't know what city. There was also another man by the name of Marcos Perez in Antwerp, whose father was Luis Perez and his mother Luisa de Segura, who were from the county of Niebla, and these two men were Lutherans. And this Marcos Perez is a prominent citizen and very rich, and when madam Margarita, the governess, came to Antwerp, he left the city and they say he went to Germany, and Marcos de la Palma did the same.

Also, in Antwerp, last December or this January, there was a man who had come from France, dressed in ordinary clothes, and people said he was a Spaniard and had been a friar in the Monastery of San Isidoro, and they said he was a nephew or cousin of an inquisitor of this city called Corro. This man came to preach to those of the Lutheran sect. And although Andres de la Torre did not see him himself, he heard it said that he had preached a sermon, both publicly and in private, in the city, but he didn't know how many sermons he preached. The Spaniards that live there went to complain to the governor of the city so he would be punished. The governor asked for information concerning how he preached. The people informed him and he was ordered not to preach anymore. Although he still preached a few times, he left the city when the other Lutherans left on account of the arrival of Margarita, Madame de Parma, governess of Flanders. Asked if the Spaniards in Antwerp that are Lutherans had business contacts in Seville, or in other parts of Spain, and with whom, he said that Marcos de la Palma was poor and he wasn't sure he had business contacts. On the other hand, Marcos Perez and his brother Luis Perez, and a sister by the name of Ines Perez, the wife of Marcos Nuñez Pérez, brother of Francisco Nuñez Perez, citizen of Seville, had a business and carried on trade in Seville and other parts, such as Lisbon, and at the fairs at Medina del Campo and Villalon del Campo. And in Seville, they did business with Francisco Nuñez Perez, but he wasn't sure what the trade was because it was public knowledge that in 1561 Marcos Perez and his siblings had dissolved the joint company and each one had gone his separate way. And last year, it was rumored in Antwerp that Marcos Perez had taken his family and business to Germany. Consequently, Andres de la Torre did not know if he has a house or property in Spain.

He was next asked if in Seville he knew a certain Antonio Anselma, a Flemish factor. Yes, he knew him and he knew that he was an agent for people in Antwerp. Asked who he did business for, he said for Giles Ofeman and Pietro Panuçio, but he wasn't sure if he worked for others also. And this Antonio Anselmo had come to Seville some five years ago as an agent for people in Antwerp. Then he was asked what his opinion was of Giles Ofeman and Pietro Panuçio, and if they were considered Catholics or Lutherans. To this he answered that in Antwerp, the Catholics considered them Lutherans because in Antwerp they openly went to listen to the sermons of the Lutherans. And that Andres de la Torre had heard Petro Panuçio say publicly that he had had one of his children baptized Lutheran style, in other words, as soon as they are born they take them to a place where they have their services and there the person who preaches baptizes the child. But he wasn't sure whether Petro Panuçio had taken the child to that place or if the child was baptized in his house, but what he was sure about was that he had the child baptized the way the heretics do because he did not take the child to any of the Catholic churches. He had also heard, and it was public knowledge, that Giles Ofeman had given money for the maintenance of the Lutheran preachers and that he had treated them very well. This was public knowledge among the Catholics. People say he wants to leave Antwerp, but when [Andres de la Torre] left the city, which was at Easter time, he had not yet left. He thinks that if the king goes to Flanders, he will leave.

Next he was asked if he knew other Flemish citizens known for their Lutheran beliefs and who have business contacts in Spain. To this he answered that among the Lutherans there are 'Martinists', 'Calvinists' and 'Anabaptists' and that at the time of the riots in Antwerp in the month of March this year, when the Catholics took up arms in defense of the city and the king, the Martinists, who are the ones that follow Martin Luther's teachings, attacked the Catholics and Andres de la Torre and other Spaniards saw that among them were the Sanfortes, who are known to be followers of Luther. The Sanfortes have a relative in Seville who does their business for them here, but Andres de la Torre did not know where he lived or what his name was. He also knew of other Flemish businessmen who traded in Seville and in Cadiz, but he did not know who their factors were. This was all he could tell them at that time. He was admonished to keep the secret, which he promised. This passed before me, Andres Carvajal, notary.

On June 28, 1567, Inquisitor Quintanilla summoned to appear before him in the Triana castle Francisco Hernandez de Cabia, a broker and citizen of Seville… When asked if he knew why he had been summoned, he said he supposed it had something to do with certain Flemish merchants. He suspected this because the previous Thursday as he was walking along the banks of the river with Pedro Lopez Martinez, a merchant from Seville, Lopez told him that Andres de la Torre, who had just come from Flanders, told him that Antonio Anselmo's employer was a Lutheran heretic and a leading one in Antwerp, and that was the reason he was in such a hurry to collect the money from the property and he had even ceded some of the debt that was owed to Antonio Anselmo to canon [Juan de] Urbina, canon of the Cathedral. [Francisco Hernandez de Cabia] said that this was a matter that had to be talked over with the Inquisitors, and that is what they did that very day. And Francisco Hernandez de Cabia noticed that Antonio Anselmo was more insistent on collecting payments in the last three months than he had been before. And he knew this because when he urged Rodrigo Alonso, a broker who owed him money, to pay him, he said they were putting pressure on him from Flanders. Likewise, Pedro Lopez Martinez told him that another person whose debt had been ceded to canon Urbina was that of Francisco de Escobar. And knowing all that is what made him suspect he was called before the inquisitor. When asked if he knew the names of the Flemish merchants Antonio Anselmo did business for, he replied that he did business for many men, from Antwerp as well as from other places but that he didn't know their names and even though he had heard them he couldn't remember them because they were foreign names. Who could tell them the names of the merchants Antonio Anselmo represented were Roberto de Acle, a Flemish merchant living in Santa Cruz, and Cristian Arot, who lives in Abades street, next to Jeronimo Manrique and Pedro Ribas, and those who live in the same house as Cristian Arot, who are all Flemish, and Francisco del Río, son-in-law of Lantadilla. When asked if Pedro Lopez Martinez had told him the name of Antonio Anselmo's employer, the one that was a Lutheran and leader of the Lutherans, he said he could not remember. He swore this was the truth, and was admonished to keep the secret, which he did. This passed before me, Andres Carvajal, notary.

On June 30, 1567, Inquisitor Quintanilla summoned the merchant Pedro Lopez Martínez, to appear before him... He suspected he had summoned him regarding certain things he and Francisco Hernández de Cabia had told the inquisitor concerning Antonio Anselmo, a factor employed by some Flemish merchants. Some ten days earlier Pedro Lopez Martinez and been talking to Andrés de la Torre, a merchant who had just come from Flanders, and he had asked him about some people there that traded with others in Seville, in particular he had asked who employed Antonio Anselmo, what their trade was and if they were Catholics or Lutherans, because he had heard they were Lutherans, and he had heard that from many people in Seville, but he could not remember their names. He also asked why Antonio Anselmo was in such a hurry to collect the money people owed him, and it was Andrés de la Torre who told him that Antonio Anselmo's employers were Lutherans, and that one of them was a leader, though he did not say their names... And he knew that Francisco de Escobar had ceded 280,000 *maravedis* to canon Urbina... When asked who else in Seville might know that Antonio Anselmo's employers were Lutherans, he said Andres de la Torre who lives next to Luis Sanchez Dalvo on Abades Street might know, and also Francisco Nuñez Perez, because one of his sons had just recently returned from Flanders and was in Seville now, and Francisco del Rio, merchant. Asked whether the transactions Antonio Anselmo carried out for his employers were of great significant, he replied that they represented the largest volume of commerce between Seville and Flanders. Asked if he knew other factors in Seville who worked for Flemish merchants who were suspected of belonging to the Lutheran sect, he said that Andres de la Torre told him that Juan de Sanforte and partners, who live in Flanders, whose factor in Seville is Pero Pablo Bernegal, were Lutherans, but he know of no others. He swore this was the truth, and was admonished to keep the secret, which he did. This passed before me, Andres Carvajal, notary.[31]

The name Juan de Sanforte was not new for the inquisitors. Sanforte was a wealthy Flemish merchant with property in Seville. In 1557 he was in Seville acting as an interpreter between Dirike Smith and Francisco Nuñez Perez, Marcos Perez's brother-in-law. At that time Smith purchased a large quantity of olive oil to be sent to Antwerp to the heirs of Marcos Perez's brother Luis (Otte: 2008, 143). In March of 1561, the inquisitors had intercepted a letter written by Agustin Boacio to his wife from Bordeaux in which he states: "In ten days I will be returning to Flanders where Juan de Sanforte resides. If you like, you can write me there."[32] They could have summoned him then, but at that time the inquis-

---

31 AHN, Inquisición, leg. 2944, doc. 52, in: Lopez Muñoz (2011, 363, doc. 175). Notes and brackets mine.
32 AHN, Inquisición, leg. 2943, doc. 15, in: Lopez Muñoz (2011, 240, doc. 111).

itors were more interested in capturing Boacio, who had escaped, than investigating Sanforte.

Agustin Boacio was born in Genoa. After spending a few years in Cadiz, where he married, he had gone to Mexico. In 1558, while working at the silver mines in Zacateca he was denounced for things he had said against the pope, purgatory, praying to the saints, oral confession, fastings, walking the Stations of the Cross, etc. He was put in prison and tried several times. He confessed that while in Cadiz he had learned from a man from Mantua, who had been in England, many things about Luther and his teachings. He also read prohibited books, mainly the writings of Savonarola. He was finally sentenced on March 16, 1560, to be sent back to Spain to appear before the inquisitors at Seville and to serve out his sentence. When the ship reached the Azores, there was a terrible storm and Boacio managed to free himself from where he was confined and escape.[33] When the fleet reached Spain, the captain presented the list of prisoners to the authorities (Conway: 1927, 73), but not the trial records (*procesos*), which left the inquisitors perplexed and unable to act at that time.[34] Three years later, on January 8, 1563, captain Bernardo de Nidino appeared before Inquisitor Gasco—"without being summoned"—to tell him that when he was in Flanders in July the previous year, in the Stock Exchange at Antwerp, a certain broker came up to him asking if he would like to buy some brocaded cloaks. In the conversation the broker said that those cloaks would bring a high price if they were sold in the New World, which made captain Nidino ask if he had been there. The man said he had, and had returned in one of Juan Gallego's ships that had docked in the Azores and that in another ship he had sailed to Lisbon and from there to Flanders. This made captain Bernardo de Nidino suspect he was Agustin Boacio, the man who was sent prisoner from Mexico and had escaped. When captain Nidino returned to Seville, he went to see Juan Gallego. The description of the broker coincided with the person Gallego brought back, and they concluded it was Agustin Boacio.

One month later, on February 22, 1563, Inquisitors Gasco and Pazos informed the Supreme Council that they had learned from an intercepted letter that Boacio was trying to persuade his wife, who was in Cadiz, to go up to Antwerp. The letter—from a Jesuit preacher living in Antwerp—, dated January 4, stated:

In this city [Antwerp] there is a fugitive heretic who has been here for a long time and is doing great harm. I have learned from another Spaniard, a Catholic and a friend who acts as a spy for me, that he is going to print a pernicious book in Spanish that explains the heresies of these times. It is a translation he has made and plans to send it to Spain in the near future. It is a dialog between a Catholic and a Lutheran. I have also learned that

33 AHN, Inquisición, leg. 2942, doc. 108. Also see Majad (2008).
34 AHN, Inquisición, leg. 2942, doc. 98, in: Lopez Muñoz (2011, 293, doc. 138).

a Spaniard that was a friar in San Isidoro and who fled is now in London and has translated and printed a Bible in Spanish to send to Spain and that he has a brother in Spain who he plans to bring to London in order to convert him. The other heretic has a wife in Cadiz who is Catholic. He has also sent for her and if she comes he will certainly pervert her too.[35]

The Supreme Council acknowledged receipt of the letter, but suggested prudence in order to avoid scandal.[36] Finally, in November, the Council informed the inquisitors at Seville that, by order of the king, Agustin Boacio had been imprisoned in Antwerp and that he would be sent to Seville.[37]

Foreign Targets

Not only Flemish merchants but also English merchants were under strict surveillance. Since the time of Henry VIII, the Merchant Venturers of Bristol had carried on trade in Cadiz and San Lucar de Barrameda, but religious and political changes in England after 1558 brought them increasingly under the scrutiny of the Inquisition. In 1560, the Supreme Council sent the inquisitors at Seville instructions urged them to dispense with the commercial agreements and immunity granted to English merchants trading in Spain and to condemn anyone found guilty of having, or introducing, heretical books, "for in matters of religion it is not fitting to grant concessions, but rather to deal uncompromisingly with them."[38] As Anglo-Spanish relations deteriorated following the ascent of Elisabeth I to the throne, more and more Englishmen were incarcerated on lesser and lesser charges. Diplomatic dispatches spanning the years 1559 to 1568 show how tension gradually increased between the two countries over the decade. The English ambassadors stationed in Spain were not exempt of the repercussions. As a Protestant, ambassador Sir Thomas Chaloner was not invited to official doings and had to depend on his *chargé d'affaires* William Phayre for information. Dr. John Man, the next ambassador, was prohibited from holding religious services in his home and was even asked to take up residence outside the city "as one not meet to live in this Court" (Bell: 1976, 75–93). An Anglo-Dutch trade embargo was imposed by Philip in 1568. In response, Elizabeth ordered the seizure of forty Spanish ships harbored in England. To retaliate, Philip responded by ordering that all English ships in Spain were to be seized and in the summer of 1571 the English ship the *Peter* was detained in Ayamonte and

35 AHN, Inquisición, leg. 2942, doc. 98, in: Lopez Muñoz (2011, 293, doc. 138).
36 AHH, Inquisición, lib. 575, f. 157v.
37 AHN, Inquisición, leg. 2942, doc. 107, in: Lopez Muñoz (2011, 314, doc. 152).
38 AHN, Inquisición, lib. 575, f. 91v, in: Lopez Muñoz (2011, 181, doc. 87).

one of the sailors, George Huester, was incarcerated.[39] Trading relations were only normalized after 1573. Finally, in 1575, Elisabeth I sent Sir Henry Cobham as ambassador extraordinary to Madrid. Cobham was emphatic: good relations between the two countries depended entirely on Philip's restricting the activities of the Inquisition against English merchants. As a result, the Supreme Council informed the inquisitors at Seville not to take action against the English if their offence was "committed at sea."[40] Nevertheless, the following year, the *Red Leon*, together with its cargo, was seized when it anchored in the port of Santa Maria, near Cadiz. The helmsman, the boatswain, and the owner of the merchandize were arrested and their goods confiscated. One of the sailors on board had denounced certain "suspicious" activities among other sailors, such as prayers and reading of "heretical" literature.[41] The English ambassador did all he could to release these prisoners, but could not stop the inquisitors from sending two of them to the stake.

Relations were again severed in 1584, and all the English citizens resident in Spain, as well as all the merchants, were forced to abandon the country. Many would not return until 1604. The Holy Office took action against those that stayed. That is, 35 crewmembers of the *Manuela* and the entire crew of the *Maria de Gracia* were incarcerated (Thomas: 2001a, 287).[42] Even the English chronicler, Richard Hakluyt, expressed concern for the safety of English sailors. He used the treatment they received at the hands of the inquisitors as another reason to look to the West as a better place for trade:

> English trades are grown beggarly or dangerous, especially dangerous in all the king of Spain's dominions, where our men are driven to fling their Bibles and prayer books into the sea and to forswear and renounce their religion and conscience and consequently their obedience to her Majesty… In all the king of Spain's dominions our men are either enforced with wounded consciences to play the dissembling hypocrites, or be forced to deny the religion maintained at home, or cruelly made away in the Inquisition. Moreover, [the king of Spain] being our mortal enemy, and his empire of late being increased so mightily, and our necessity of oils and colours for our clothing trade being so great, he may arrest almost the one half of our navy, our traffic and recourse being so great to his dominions. In trading with these countries [Newfoundland] we shall not need, for fear of the Spanish bloody Inquisition, to throw our Bibles and prayer books over board into the sea before our arrival at their ports, as these many years we have

---

39 AHN, Inquisición, leg. 2945, in: Lopez Muñoz (2011, 405, doc. 211).
40 As late as 1583, the Inquisitors at Seville were still wondering if the "less restrictive" measures towards Englishman, issued in 1575, were still in effect. AHN, Inquisición, leg. 2947, in: Lopez Muñoz (2011, 450, doc. 256).
41 AHN, Inquisición, leg. 2946, doc. 9, in: Lopez Muñoz (2011, 431, doc. 239).
42 For reports concerning certain of the crew members of these vessels, see AHN, Inquisición, leg. 2946, in: Lopez Muñoz (2011, 450, doc. 256; 461, doc. 266), AHN, Inquisición, leg. 2950, in: Lopez Muñoz (2011, 463, doc. 269); and Schäfer (2014, II).

done and yet do, nor take such horrible oaths as are exacted of our men by the Spanish searchers, to such daily willful and high offence of Almighty God, as we are driven to continually in following our ordinary traffic into the king of Spain's dominions. (Hakluyt: 1584. Modern spelling mine).

French Huguenots were the next target group. By the second half of the sixteenth century, many French Huguenots were crossing the border into Navarre, Aragon, and Catalonia to escape the wars of religion. Many of them were craftsmen and artisans and had no problems finding work for as Robert Kerr (1824, Vol. 18, 379. Italics mine) points out in his massive historical study, *A General History and Collection of Voyages and Travels*,

> The exports [from Antwerp] to Spain consisted chiefly of metals, woolen cloth, linen, wax, madder, wheat, rye, salted meat and fish, furniture, tools, and everything produced by human industry and labour, *to which the lower classes in Spain have an utter aversion.*

Moreover, the progress that Calvinistic doctrines were making in Spain is evident from an ordinance of the Supreme Council reproduced by Juan Antonio Llorente (1843, 271):

> Don Louis de Benegas, the ambassador of Spain at Vienna, informed the Inquisitor-General, on the 14th of April, 1568, that he had learnt from particular reports, that the Calvinists congratulated each other on the peace signed between France and Spain, and that they hoped that their religion would make as much progress in Spain as in England, Flanders, and other countries, because the great number of Spaniards who had secretly adopted it might easily hold communication with the Protestants of Beam, through Aragon.

According the Werner Thomas (2001a, 258–270), between 1558 and 1575, over a thousand five hundred foreigners—mainly Frenchmen—suspected of, or sympathetic towards, Protestantism were arrested in Spain. The years 1563, 1565, and 1570 stand out as the years of greatest activity against foreigners, especially in Catalonia, where dozens of Frenchmen were burned at the stake.[43] It was even prohibited to employ French primary-school teachers for fear they would defile the youth (Thomas: 2001a, 256). After 1570, with the Peace of Saint-Germain that ended the Third War of Religion, the promise of religious freedom predisposed many Huguenots to return to their homeland. Nevertheless, as the century came to a close, the French again became the main target of the Holy Office. 1592 was a dark year for the Huguenots that had remained in Spain; eleven persons were sent to the stake and twenty-five to the galleys (Thomas:

---

43 For reports of foreigners arrested in the 1580s, see AHN, Inquisición, leg. 3681 (2), doc. 27; AHN, Inquisición, leg. 2949; AHN, Inquisición, leg. 2950, in: Lopez Muñoz (2011, 459, doc. 264; 461, doc. 266; 463, doc. 268; 463, doc. 269); AHN, Inquisición, leg. 1592/28 and 2135/22 and lib. 730, 735, 736, 737, 760, in: Schäfer (2014, II, 7–13).

2001a, 293). When war broke out with France three years later, the French were ordered to abandon Spanish territory. On the other hand, after the Edict of Nantes (1598), which turned France into a pluralistic society, fewer dissident citizens found it necessary to immigrate.

With the Edict of Nantes, French Protestants were granted freedom of conscience. They were admitted to all schools without a certificate of Catholicity and could open schools of their own. They were admitted to all employments and functions, and seats were to be reserved for them on the Royal Council. Spain was not about to follow suit. As professor Carroll Johnson (1982, 140) puts it,

> In Spanish terms, the Edict of Nantes would amount to nothing less than the repeal of the *estatutos de limpieza de sangre* and even, perhaps, a return to the old Spain of the three religions, certainly a radical reordering of not only religious, but social and economic life as well.

Hans Avontroot (1559–1633)

As international commerce increased in the Canary Islands thanks to the sugar industry, the presence of Dutch merchants of Calvinist convictions also increased.[44] The arrest of eighty sailors and merchants between January and April 1593 nearly left the islands without supplies and suppliers. Despite all the repression, there still remained a few staunch defender of religious liberty, not afraid to make their voices heard in the wilderness. One example was Hans Avontroot (John Aventrot), a wealthy Dutch sugar merchant living in the Canary Islands. Born in 1559 in Flanders into a Protestant family, Hans Avontroot went to the Canary Islands as a young man to manage Paulus Vandale's sugar mill. Avontroot's first encounter with the Inquisition occurred around 1589 when Alonso Redondo, nuncio of the Holy Office, informed him that Inquisitor Madaleno wanted to visit the islands, but did not have enough money to do so. He asked Avontroot to advance a certain amount, which he did, only to find out later that it was all a lie.

About this time, Vandale, the owner of the sugar mill, died and Avontroot married his widow. Vandale's children objected to the marriage and began to find reasons to denounce Avontroot to the Inquisition: his criticism of fasting and oral confession; eating meat during lent; not going to mass, etc. When the pope issued a jubilee and a priest was sent to the sugar mill to confess the people

---

44 The power vacuum left on the Barbary Coast, once the Portuguese were forced out in 1541, was a strong incentive for the English to begin exploring that market too. The Inquisition records at Seville mention several Englishmen imprisoned in the Canary Islands. One, Nicholas Haler, arrested in 1555 is referred to as a "Scottish Lutheran." Another, Thomas Nichols, was arrested in 1563.

working there, Avontroot sent him away saying that the only purpose of those jubilees was to rob good Christians of their money. In the face of all this, Inquisitor Madaleno decided to arrest him in 1590. He was not imprisoned, which some of the officers of the inquisition did not approve of. Meanwhile Avontroot had also established business contacts in South America, and seems to have spent the next four years there.[45]

He was back in Flanders in 1603 when Felipe III devaluated the Spanish currency. Being a conscientious businessman, this upset Avontroot greatly. He wrote a letter to the king's prime minister, Francisco Gómez de Sandoval, Duke of Lerma, saying that a much better solution would have been to confiscate all the property of the church, to which Lerma replied that it was not in the king's power to do such a thing. In April of 1609, when the Twelve Years' Truce was signed between Spain and Holland, Avontroot was in Madrid again and, as a highly respected businessman, was being consulted by Spanish authorities on commercial and financial matters. On that occasion, he gave Lerma another letter for the king, but it was ignored. In November of that year, Avontroot returned to the Canary Islands, where his wife was dying, and later returned to Holland, via the Peninsula, where he again met with Lerma and handed him another letter for the king. Lerma did not like the content of the letter and refused to forward it to the king. In the face of this, Avontroot decided to give it to the king personally. He arranged an interview with Andres de Prada, secretary of the Council of State, but after hearing Avontroot's reason for requesting the interview, Prada told him to leave the country, which he did. In 1611, Avontroot sent his nephew Jan Coot to the duke of Lerma again with another letter for the king in which he argued that the pope was the cause of the loss of the seventeen provinces of the Netherlands, and of the suffering of the Spanish colonies under their enormous taxes (Good: 1914, 27). He urged Philip III to deliver his lands from the papacy. He had the letter printed in Dutch (1613) and in Spanish (1614) and added an exhortation to the grandees and nobles of Spain in the hope that the king would grant them the privilege of examining the matter for themselves. The 45-page letter was full of quotations, both from the New and Old Testament, in which Avontroot drew a parallel between the Flemish rebellion and the prophesies in the Book of Revelation. In other words, the war between the king and his subjects was a war between the empire of Christ and the pope. The separation of Flanders announced the triumph of Christ hence the king should break with Rome and pass laws in favor of the freedom of conscience and of religion, which would be the only way to pacify his subjects. In order to make sure his message reached the

---

45 According to the bylaws of the Casa de Contratacion (House of Trade), foreigners were not allowed to do business in the West Indies, but they must have made an exception with Avontroot.

king, he sent his nephew to El Escorial with copies. Meanwhile, Avontroot had sent 7,000 copies of his letter to Lisbon to be distributed throughout the peninsula, but the Inquisition confiscated them and burned them. Jan Coot was arrested and sent to the galleys for six years. Avontroot, on hearing what they had done with his pamphlet and his messenger, remarked: "That the Inquisition has sent my innocent servant to the galleys, that I commend to God; but that they have destroyed my seven thousand pamphlets, that concerns me, and I feel obliged again to send the tract." So he had the pamphlet printed a second time in 1615, in Dutch, German, Latin and Italian, and the next year in French (Good: 1914, 27).

In 1627, Avontroot wrote his "Epistle to the Peruvians" in which he appealed to the Peruvians[46] to repudiate the king of Spain because of his oppression, and to open their eyes to the fact that Rome was relying on the wealth of the silver mines to persecute Protestants. He reminded the Peruvians that when Charles, the previous king of Spain, had conquered Peru, he had issued a decree that the Indians who had aided him in the conquest should be freed in the fourth generation. And he reminded them that this came due in 1628, and he therefore called them to rise to their rights and reject the king of Spain. He had this letter printed and had eight thousand copies sent to South America; three thousand, signed by the Holland States-General, were sent to Buenos Aires to promote their uprising (Good: 1914, 29). In 1628 he also published separately his translation into Spanish of the Heidelberg Catechism to which he added the Dutch Reformed liturgy, together with the Nicene and Athanasian Creeds. Earlier, in 1621, he had also translated Montes's *Artes de la Inquisicion* into Dutch.[47]

In 1631, Avontroot again accompanied a group of businessmen to Madrid to seek a remedy for the financial situation. There he again dared to plead for religious liberty. Philip IV's reply was to deliver him to the Inquisition. After seven months in the Inquisition prison in Toledo, he was sentenced to the stake on May 22, 1632, in Zocodover Square.[48] Not only was Avontroot punished, but also his sons-in-law and daughters-in-law: their status and offices were taken away and they were forbidden to wear gold, silver, pearl, precious stones, silk,

---

46 In those days the whole of South America, except Brazil, was referred to as Peru, and its inhabitants as Peruvians.

47 For further details regarding Avontroot's story and his translations see Good (1914); Millares Carlo (1935); Hernández Millares (1935); Cioranescu (1974); Thomas (1992); Fajardo Spínola (1998); Lechner (1992); Resines Llorente (1992; 2003).

48 After his death, an account of his trial was published at Amsterdam in Dutch: Copy van't Proces ende Sententie teghens Joan Avontroot Die gekomen is in Spangien in't Hof an Madrid, om te spreken met den Koningk van liberteyt van Conscientie, maer vande Inquisiti gevangen en na Toledo ghebracht (Amsterdam: Gersit Jansz Arenteyn, 1632).

beads, fine broad cloth, ride on horseback, bear arms, take part in military drill, etc.

The Inquisition Finally Abolished

A brief overview of the continued repression of dissidents up to the final abolition of the Inquisition is in order. Let us retrace our steps slightly. As the American historian Henry Charles Lea (1906–1907, IV, 500) put it,

> It was natural that Philip II, in his will, executed March 7, 1594, should reiterate to his son and successor the injunctions, which he had received from his father. The Inquisition was to be the object of special favor, even greater than in the past, for the times were perilous and full of so many errors in the faith. Philip III had not energy enough to be an active persecutor and if, under the guidance of Lerma, he expelled the Moriscos, under the same tutelage he made peace with England in 1605 and a truce with Holland in 1609, to the disgust of the pious who could not understand any dealings with heretics.

Although the Treaty of London, signed in 1604, that concluded the nineteen-year Anglo-Spanish War obliged the Holy Office to treat English offenders with less severity, it did not grant religious tolerance for Englishmen living in Spain or protect them from being punished by the Inquisition for any outward manifestation against the established religion. If during the twenty years prior to the signing of the Treaty some eighty Englishmen were arrested by the Inquisition, during the twenty years that followed only thirty were brought to trial (Thomas: 2001a, 316). However, during the Thirty Years' War (1618–1648) the agreements regarding religious tolerance established in the Treaty of London were suspended and during the long reign of Philip IV—from 1621 to 1665—the Inquisition again increased its activity against foreigners. Juan Antonio Llorente (1843, 503–505) lists a number of *autos* celebrated during the thirty-four year reign of Philip IV:

> On the 30th of November, 1630, an *auto-da-fe* was held at Seville, when six persons were burnt in effigy, and eight in person; fifty were reconciled, and six absolved *ad cautelam*. On the 21st of December 1627, a general *auto-da-fe* was celebrated at Cordova, composed of eighty-one condemned persons; fifty-eight were reconciled, among whom were three sorcerers. In 1632, a grand general *auto-da-fe* was held at Madrid, at which the king and all the royal family attended. Seven persons were burnt, with four effigies, and forty-two reconciled; they were almost all Portuguese, or of Portuguese parents… On the 22nd of June 1636, another general *auto-da-fe* was held at Valladolid, composed of twenty-eight persons. The punishment inflicted on the Jews seems entirely novel: one hand was nailed to a wooden cross, and in that state they were obliged to hear read the report of their trial, and the sentence which condemned them to perpetual im-

prisonment for having insulted our Saviour and the Virgin by their blasphemies… The cities of Toledo, Cuenca, Granada, and Seville, also celebrated *autos-da-fe* in 1651, 1654, and 1660, when many persons were burnt.

Charles II, whose reign lasted from 1665 to 1700, is remembered for his illnesses and his grave disabilities. Llorente (1843, 513) describes the *auto* held in 1680— commemorated in a famous painting by Francisco Ricci—in these words:

> When Charles II married Maria Louisa de Bourbon in 1680, the taste of the nation was so depraved, that a grand *auto-da-fe*, composed of a hundred and eighteen victims, was considered as a proper and flattering homage to the new queen; nineteen persons were burnt, with thirty-four effigies.

When the next monarch, Philip V, ascended to the throne, the court also decided to celebrate the event with an *auto-da-fe*, but the king did not attend. This, however, was no indication that the Inquisition had lost its influence or that the king had any intention of changing matters. According to Llorente (1843, 519),

> A yearly *auto-da-fe* was celebrated by all the tribunals of the Inquisition, during the reign of this prince; some of them held two, and three were performed at Seville and Granada. Thus, without including those of America, Sardinia and Sicily, seven hundred and eighty-two *autos-da-fe* took place at Madrid, Barcelona, the Canaries, Cordova, Cuenca, Granada, Jaen, Llerena, Logroño, Majorca, Murcia, Santiago, Seville, Toledo, Valencia, Valladolid and Saragossa.

During Philip V's reign, Freemasonry became one of the main targets of the Inquisition. In 1738, the inquisitor general published an edict that called for denunciations within six days under pain of excommunication and a fine of 200 ducats. Two years later, the king published an edict under which Freemasons were sent to the galleys.[49] By mid century Jansenism also occupied the attention of the Holy Office.[50] Father Torrubia, censor of the Inquisition, attempted to carry out a plan to exterminate all Freemasons in Spain. In order to achieve this, he made use of the vast network of spies available to the Inquisition, and, using a false name, joined the Order himself. He was able to draw up a list of 97 lodges, which he handed over to the Inquisition in Madrid and which led to the arrest of thousands of Freemasons throughout Spain (McGregor: 2015).

Matters improved with the reign of Charles III. There was a remarkable decrease in the number of public *autos-da-fe*. In 1767, Spanish Freemasonry de-

---

49 The edict also extended to Portugal. See Coustos (1746).

50 *Jansenism* was a religious movement that entailed an austere form of piety and rigorous morality. Spanish Jansenism did not share the same theological heritage as its French counterpart and was based instead on the humanist and Erasmian traditions of sixteenth century Spain, which promoted personal spirituality and reading of Scriptures. Jansenism was opposed by many in the Catholic hierarchy, especially the Jesuits, who especially opposed the Jansenist view of human nature.

clared itself independent from England and Count d'Aranda, Charles III's Prime Minister, became the first Grand Master. Many members of the high nobility joined the Lodge. The reign of Charles III coincided with the Age of Enlightenment and its socio-political manifestation in the form of a movement within the Catholic Church known as "second" Jansenism. The case of Benito Jeronimo Feijoo is of interest. As a monk, he had a special license from the Inquisition to read foreign works, which "enlightened" him and led to his outspoken criticism of Spain's intellectual climate. Through a series of essays, *Cartas eruditas y curiosas* (Inquiring and Erudite Letters), which he published between 1742 and 1760, he introduced the ideas of foreign writers to his fellow countrymen. As Professor Smidt (2010, 420), in her excellent study of the Spanish Enlightenment, points out,

> Some Spaniards were inspired by European scientists and philosophers, others the classical models of the Greek and Roman world, yet many Spanish *ilustrados* took their cue from authentically Spanish courses of Christian humanism that came out of the Erasmian tradition of 16th-century Spain and the *alumbrado* trait of the individual's study of Scripture as well a co-ed group discussion of it. Gregorio Mayans y Siscar (1699–1781) was one nobleman whose writings championed Christian humanism and internal religiosity in the spirit of Erasmus… Known in the 18th century for his veneration of Erasmus and other great humanists of the Renaissance tradition, Mayans focused on a variety of themes, including ecclesiastical history, religious superstition, intelligible preaching and ecclesiastical relations in society.

The shared interests of the Jansenists and the followers of the Enlightenment (*Ilustrados*) had serious consequences for the Jesuits. Their common interests included a hatred for scholasticism, more internal forms of piety, a reduction in privileges and exemptions for the clergy, and above all the expulsion of the Jesuits (Smidt: 2010, 429).

By the time Charles IV became king in 1788, Spanish Jansenism appears to have carried the church to the threshold of true renovation. The ban on vernacular translations of the Scriptures was lifted by an edict in 1782. The same year the ban was lifted, the Jesuit priest José Miguel Petisco began a translation of the Vulgate into Spanish, but was unable to finish it due to the dissolution of the Company and the expulsion of the Jesuits. The first decree prohibiting the reading of the Scriptures in the vulgar dates back to the Councils of Lateran and Verona in 1229 (Llorente: 1843, 15). As late as 1747, Inquisitor General Perez de Prado, bishop of Teruel, bitterly lamented the misfortunes of the age he lived in, saying, "That some individuals had carried their audacity to the execrable extremity of demanding permission to read the Holy Scriptures in the vulgar tongue, without fear of finding in them deadly poison." (Llorente: 1843, 111).

Inquisitor General Felipe Bertran's decision to approve the publication and reading of Scripture in the vernacular in an edict published in 1782, proved controversial and highlighted the fact that there were two theological camps within the Church: one that advocated an external, formulaic religiosity, and another that advocated an internal, anti-ceremonial religiosity (Smidt: 2010, 440). Meanwhile, king Charles IV had commissioned a priest of the Piarist Order, the eminent biblist and preceptor of his son Ferdinand, Felipe Scio de San Miguel, to do a translation from the Vulgate. Scios's ten-volume, profusely annotated and illustrated Latin-Spanish edition appeared in 1793. Despite the size and the price, in less than a year the first edition was totally sold out. José Miguel Petisco's work was completed in 1823 by Félix Torres Amat and published in six volumes.[51]

The events of the French Revolution brought a renewed trend towards conservative positions. Now Liberalism had become the greatest threat. The vast number of works written on the rights of individuals and the duties of nations to protect the rights of individual citizens alarmed Charles IV. While the Spaniards read these books with avidity, the king and his ministers dreaded the contagion of this political doctrine. The church feared that Liberalism would deprive her of her monopoly on education and her claim to ultimate authority on all matters of conscience. In an attempt to stop it, the inquisitor general was urged to seize all the books, pamphlets, and French newspapers relating to the revolution, as well as the works of modern philosophers—Voltaire, Rousseau, Montesquieu, etc. Under the pretext that they had scanty moral and artistic value, the Council of Castile even decreed that no license be granted for the publication of works of fiction—written or translated from French.[52] This prohibition was not lifted until 1808 (Establier Perez: 2008, 162).

Charles IV's secretary of state, Mariano Luis de Urquijo, suggested suppressing the Inquisition and applying its revenues to the establishment of useful and charitable institutions, but the king was not in favor. Hopes of change dissipated with the fall of Urquijo in 1800. Those in favor of change turned their faces towards France, but that also had a price. Indeed, it was Napoleon Bonaparte who is credited for finally abolishing the Spanish Inquisition. A brief account of the context and the circumstances that brought this about is opportune. After the defeat of the combined Spanish and French fleets by the

---

51 The British and Foreign Bible Society printed several thousand copies of cheap Spanish New Testaments (Scio's translation) to distribute among the exiles in the early 1820s. When the Quaker prison reformer William Allen met Torres Amat in Barcelona during his tour of Spain in 1833 and was given a copy of Amat's translation, he remarked , "[Amat] has translated the whole of the Old and New Testament, including the Apocrypha, into pure Castilian Spanish, which is to be more elegant than the translation of our British and Foreign Bible Society translation." (Allen: 1847, III, 136).

52 This may explain in part why a French translation of Daniel Defoe's Robinson Crusoe—*La vie et les avantures de Robinson Crusoe* (Amsterdam, 1720)—appeared in the Index of 1747 and remained there.

British at the Battle of Trafalgar in 1805, Spain and France agreed to punish England by partitioning Portugal, a long-standing British ally. Napoleon insisted on positioning French troops in Spanish territory to prepare for a French invasion of Portugal, but once this was done, he continued to move additional troops into Spain without any sign of an advance into Portugal. As more troops moved from France into northern Spain to support their colleagues in Portugal, they seized Barcelona and began moving towards Madrid. Charles IV panicked and in an attempt to flee the country he met with an angry patriotic mob at Aranjuez. He escaped with his life, only after agreeing to abdicate in favor of his son Ferdinand. In March of 1808, Ferdinand VII was installed. When riots broke out in Madrid in May, Napoleon forced Ferdinand to abdicate and the crown was transferred to Napoleon's brother Joseph Bonaparte, as Joseph I.[53] A new constitution was drafted by Napoleon and accepted by a group of higher nobility and clergy that he had summoned to Bayonne, just over the French border. Although it recognized the freedom of industry and trade, it did not recognize the freedom of religion. In fact, it recognized the Catholic religion as the official religion of Spain and forbade the exercise of other religions. The presence of foreign troops caused uprisings to continue throughout Spain. In November, Napoleon decided to intervene. He entered Madrid on December 4, 1808, and five days later made the following speech, known as the "Declaration of Chamartin."

> I have preserved the spiritual orders, but with a limitation of the number of monks. There is not a single intelligent person who is not of the opinion that they were too numerous. Those of them who are influenced by a divine call, shall remain in their cloisters... Out of the surplus of the monastic property, I have provided for the maintenance of the pastors, that important and useful class of clergy. I have abolished that court which was a subject of complaint to Europe. Priests may guide the minds of men, but must exercise no temporal or corporeal jurisdiction over the citizens.

Although many intellectuals collaborated with the French regime, believing that collaboration with France would modernize Spain, popular resistance to foreign occupation continued. Finally, the military defeat suffered by the French forced Joseph I to leave Spain in June 1813. Most of Bonaparte's supporters fled into exile along with the retreating troops. Meanwhile, the *Cortes* (Parliament) had moved to Cadiz and was operating as a government in exile. Liberal factions dominated the body and passed the Constitution of 1812, which among other things abolished the Inquisition thanks to the untiring efforts of men such as Antoni Puigblanch (1816), who defended strongly the abolition of the Inquisition with the publication of a series of pamphlets under the pseudonym Nathanael Jomtob entitled *"La Inquisición sin mascara"* (The Inquisition Un-

---

53 The uprising was immortalized by Francisco de Goya in two famous paintings: *Dos de mayo*, also known as *La carga de los mamelucos*, and *Los fusilamientos del 3 de mayo*.

masked). With the return of Ferdinand VII, Puigblanch, like many other liberals, escaped to England, where he published an English edition of his book: *The Inquisition Unmasked* (1816), which was translated into German the following year as *Die entlarvte Inquisition* (Weimar: 1817). Puigblanch returned to Spain in 1820, but was back in England again in 1823, where he remained until his death.

On March 22, 1814, Ferdinand VII returned to Spain and on May 4 he declared that he did not recognize the Constitution of 1812. His next course of action was to reinstate the Inquisition and one year later readmit the Jesuits. A week after Ferdinand's return, arrests of liberals began, marking a new triumph for absolutism in Spain. Llorente (1843, 567–568. Note mine) describes the political milieu:

> On the 22nd of February, in the same year, the Spanish assembly at Cadiz, which styled itself the General Cortes, suppressed the Inquisition, restoring to the bishops and secular judges their jurisdictions, that they might prosecute heretics in the same manner as before the existence of the Inquisition. This measure was the cause of long discussions in the tribune, and many orators pronounced speeches of great eloquence. The liberty of the press, which then existed, allowed many works to be published both for and against the Holy Office. Its partisans neglected nothing in its defense; in short, all that could possibly be advanced in favour of such a tribunal as the Inquisition was published at Cadiz during this celebrated discussion. But reason prevailed; not because the majority of the voters were irreligious persons, or Jacobins,[54] but because the Cortes found an irresistible strength in the reasoning, which condemned a tribunal that had been so fatal to the prosperity of the nation for three centuries... These measures of the Cortes were however useless. Bonaparte restored the crown of Spain to Ferdinand, by a treaty at Valence in 1813, and in March, 1814, the king re-entered Spain; on his arrival at Valencia, he was immediately surrounded by persons imbued with the Gothic prejudices of the age of chivalry, and one of the first measures of his administration was the reestablishment of the Holy Office, on the 21st of July, 1814. In the preamble to the royal decree, Ferdinand informed the people, that the object of the restoration of the Inquisition was to repair the evil caused to the religion of the state by the foreign troops, who were not Catholics; to forestall that which might be caused hereafter by the heretical opinions imbibed by a great number of Spaniards, and to preserve the tranquility of the kingdom; that this measure was desired by learned and virtuous prelates, and by different bodies and corporations, who reminded him that, in the sixteenth century, Spain had preserved herself from the contagion of heresy, and the errors which desolated other countries.

The king's position was tenuous. Soon uprisings broke out and before the situation got out of hand the king agreed to the demands of the revolutionaries.

---

54 The Jacobins were the most radical of the political groups formed in the wake of the French Revolution. Led by Maximilien de Robespierre, they controlled the government from June 1793 to July 1794, known as the Reign of Terror.

Three years of liberal rule followed. During the three-year interlude of 1820–23—known as the *Trienio Liberal*—the Constitution of 1812 was restored and the gates of the Inquisition prisons were opened. Decrees were issued abolishing entailed lands, closing monasteries and nationalizing their lands, reducing the church tithe to half, etc. In the winter of 1821, anti-government riots began. In August of 1822, right-wing extremists took power, repressing the uprisings. The following year, Ferdinand VII returned the second time and again restored his absolutist regime. During the second reign of Ferdinand VII— known as the "Ominous Decade"—, which went from October 1, 1823, to his death on September 29, 1833, the Inquisition returned under the name of Congregation of the Meetings of Faith. On July 26, 1826, the schoolteacher Cayetano Ripoll was executed for holding and teaching deist principles. He was the last person known to be executed by the Inquisition. Although the Spanish Inquisition was formally abolished by a Royal Decree signed on July 15, 1834, by regent Maria Christina, Ferdinand VII's widow, nevertheless, the spirit of the Inquisition lived on in what was known as the Tribunal of the Faith, and more recently as the Supreme Sacred Congregation of the Holy Office, renamed in 1985 the Congregation for the Doctrine of the Faith (CDF) and still active today.

Chapter 13:
The Spanish Reformers Rediscovered

> I grant that the behaviour of books, like that of men, must be watched. Books are not
> absolutely dead things; they have a potency of life in them to be as active as that soul
> was whose progeny they are. But then they are more than living; a good book is the
> precious life-blood of a master-spirit, embalmed and treasured up on purpose to a life
> beyond life. The destruction of a good book ends not in the slaying of an elemental life,
> but strikes at that ethereal and fifth essence, the breath of reason itself.
>
> John Milton, *Areopagitica* (1644)

Even before the archives were open to the general public, fanciful minds were inventing horror stories set in the dungeons of the Inquisition. The French fairy-tale writer Madame d'Aulney was perhaps the first to portray the evils of the Spanish Inquisition in *Relation d'un voyage en Espagne* (1691), followed by Antonio Gavin's *A Master-key to Popery* (Dublin, 1724), which tells the story of a young lady in a seraglio kept by the Inquisitors. Gothic fiction—stories that were half historical mystery and half thriller with elements of romance—thrived on the mysterious and found a well of material in stories related to the Inquisition. To cite a few examples: Matthew Lewis's *The Monk* (1796); Ann Radcliffe's *The Italian* (1797); Mary Martha Sherwood's *The Nun* (1833); Maria Monk's *The Awful Disclosures of Maria Monk* (1836); etc. Despite the fact that the Inquisition's power had dwindled, English writers seized on the image of the Inquisition, like a giant black spider, constantly spinning, trying to keep the fragments together and now and again catching the unwary in its webs.

Access to the Historical Archives

In the mid 1830s the archives of the Spanish Inquisition became part of the National Historical Archives housed at Simancas—where official documents had been kept since the days of Philip II—and were opened to the public for historical research in 1844, though access was limited.[1] Special authorization was required in order to examine the documents yet that could not prevent pilfering of one sort or another, which explains how documents found their way into libraries in northern Europe. As the concept of religious toleration developed, theologians and philosophers, and scholars in general, became more aware of—and interested in—places where religious toleration was not practiced. Likewise, as history developed as an academic discipline, so did the demand for authentic primary documentary sources. Access to the archives of the Spanish Inquisition,

---

1 The archives were transferred from Simancas to Madrid in 1914.

which up to the nineteenth century were basically still in tact, has allowed historical research to become what it is today.[2]

Daniel Gotthilf Moldenhawer (1753–1823)

One of the first laypersons to receive authorization to see Inquisition records was the Danish philologist Daniel Gotthilf Moldenhawer, first director of the Royal Library at Copenhagen. Moldenhawer was not only given permission to examine documents but also to remove them. During the two periods he spent in Spain (1783–84, 1786–87), Moldenhawer collected some 150 documents for a history of the Spanish Inquisition that he proposed to write but never accomplished. In March of 1782, he and Thomas Christian Tyshen, a German orientalist and theologian, arrived in Madrid. They spent two months in El Escorial compiling a catalog of the manuscripts in the library of the monastery and visited many private libraries.[3] In 1786, Moldenhawer returned to Spain on a confidential diplomatic mission. These visits took place during the reign of Charles III whose primer minister, Count d'Aranda, was the Grand Master of the Spanish Free-masons at the time and who may have been all too happy to allow Moldenhawer, who was also a Freemason, to go through the archives. Some ten years later, Juan Antonio Llorente, whom we have quoted often throughout this study, also had full access to the archives.

Juan Antonio Llorente (1756–1823)

Juan Antonio Llorente began his ecclesiastical career as secretary to the bishop of Burgos. From Burgos he went to Logroño as commissioner for the Inquisition, and from there, in 1788, to Madrid as general secretary of the Supreme Council. Shortly afterwards, he entered the service of Charles IV's prime minister, Manuel Godoy, whose political persuasions he shared. In 1793, Enlightenment-minded Inquisitor General Manuel Abad y la Sierra commissioned Llorente to write a history of the origins of the procedures of the Inquisition, which the Inquisitor wanted to use to introduce certain reforms. Although Abad fell in disgrace the following year due to his Jansenist leanings and the project was never termi-nated, Llorente had had the opportunity to submit a written report suggesting

---

2 For a brief overview of the trajectory, see Robin Vose (2010).
3 From the notes Moldenhawer made of his trips, Emil Gigas later wrote a book: *Spanien omkring 1789. Kulturhistoriske Fragmenter efter D.G. Moldenhawers Rejsedagbøger* (Copen-hagen: Gyldendal, 1904). For excerpts, see Emil Gigas, Un voyageur allemand-danois en Espagne sous le règne de Charles III, Revue Hispanique 69 (1927), 341–520.

possible reforms. However, in the eyes of the Holy Office, his relationships with members of the Jansenist movement made him a suspect of having revealed secrets and, as a result, in 1801, he was deprived of his title of secretary of the Inquisition.

From the beginning, Llorente collaborated with the new regime as advisor for ecclesiastical matters and overseer of state properties, which included the national archives (Dufour: 2015). In 1809, he was entrusted with the archives of the Supreme Council and of the Inquisition, which contained all the resolutions of the council, the royal ordinances, the papal bulls and briefs, the papers of the affairs of the tribunal, and all the information concerning the genealogies of the persons employed in the Holy office. With this material Llorente wrote a dissertation entitled "A Memorial in which the opinion of the Spaniards concerning the Inquisition is examined," which he read before the Royal Academy of History in 1811 and which the Academy published separately the following year. Llorente's article was given ample publicity. The government authorities also encouraged him to continue his research into the archives of the Inquisition, the outcome of which was *Anales de la Inquisición de España* (1812–1813), which comprehended all the events that took place in the tribunals from 1477 to 1530 and would become part of his four-volume *Critical History of the Inquisition* (1826) which he compile in exile in France and which first appeared in French (Llorente: 1817–1818).

Andrew Thorndike (1778–1840)

Another person who had access to Inquisition documents—thought unexpectedly—was Andrew Thorndike, an American businessman from Boston. In the spring of 1820, when the doors of the Inquisition prisons were opened in Barcelona, Andrew Thorndike, found himself at the right place at the right time, and with sufficient intuition to value what the mobs were destroying. Andrew Thorndike had been a resident in Barcelona since 1806. He owned part of a shipping firm with his uncle Israel Thorndike and had business interests in Barcelona as well as in Buenos Aires. Thorndike's business activities in Barcelona were closely linked with those of the US consuls at that time, John Leonard and Richard McCall (Hargreaves/Hopkins: 1983). In 1816, Andrew Thorndike was in trouble with the local authorities as deduced from a letter sent on May 21, 1816, by Thomas L.L. Brent, US *chargé d'affaires* to Spain, to President James Monroe regarding "charges against Andrew Thorndike, an American merchant at Barcelona." Five months later, on October 27, George Erving, U.S. Minister to Spain, sent another dispatch to President Monroe demanding "release of Andrew Thorndike, an American who has been imprisoned on charges of having aided the French." (Preston: 2001, II, 668). President Monroe's intervention was repaid generously by Andrew's uncle Israel Thorndike the next summer when he was invited to spend a day at the Thorndike mansion at Beverly, Massachusetts.

Next we hear of Andrew Thorndike on the streets of Barcelona on March 10, 1820, the day the angry mobs stormed the Inquisition prison located in the Plaza del Rei and began throwing everything they found out the windows.[4] With the help of the US consul, Richard McCall, Thorndike gathered up many documents, crated them, and sent them off to Boston. He may have sent them directly to George Ticknor, recently appointed professor of French and Spanish at Harvard University, and friend of the family. The Thorndikes had close links with Harvard. Israel Thorndike, his uncle, had just recently commissioned Edward Everett, another professor from Harvard, to purchase the library of Professor Christoph Daniel Ebeling, of Hamburg, which consisted of 4,000 volumes on American history and antiquities, for the Harvard Library. Be that as it may, in 1828, part of these documents appeared in a publication entitled, *Records of the Spanish Inquisition, translated from the Original Manuscripts.* The translator-editor, Samuel Kettell, explained how the manuscript came into his hands:

> These papers are a part of the Records of the Inquisition of Barcelona, and were obtained during the revolution, which broke out at Cadiz in 1819. The province of Catalonia, of which Barcelona is the capital, was one of the most forward and zealous to embrace the cause of freedom. Its inhabitants have, in all times, been distinguished for their daring and determined spirit, and their ardent love of liberty. The revolution moved with rapid strides from the Isle of Leon to the Ebro. On the 28th of February 1820, the governor of Tarragona received a summons to repair immediately to Madrid, and in a few days the insurrection burst out in the former place. On the 14th of March, two days after this, it exploded at Barcelona... The populace demanded, with loud cries, of the Captain General, that the Inquisitorial Palace should be thrown open. What answer was given by Villacampa to this demand, does not appear. A body of twenty thousand persons rushed to the Inquisition, stormed at the gates, and demanded admittance. Those within told them to wait a few minutes and the gates should be opened. This interval they improved to make their escape, and in a short time the populace, growing impatient, burst the gates and rushed in. Every part of the premises was immediately filled. The dungeons were broken open; the prisoners released, and the papers cast out at the windows. For several days these were thrown in great numbers about the streets of the city, and a small portion of them, after passing through various hands, came into the possession of a gentleman of this city, who at that period was

---

4 The scene was immortized in a print by the French painter Hippolyte *Lecomte:* "Destruction of the Inquisition in Barcelona, 10th March 1820." Whether Lecomte was actually present on that day is debatable. However, his reputation for accuracy is a guarantee that the building that appears in the print is the original palace of the Inquisition in Barcelona, which was located in the Plaza del Rei, demolished in 1823. The print may have been a commission. The Liberals used all possible means to defend the benefits of the new political regime. Images gave large portions of the illiterate population access to political agendas.

travelling in Spain. These papers were forwarded to Boston in 1820. It was thought that a publication of these documents would be received with much interest and satisfaction by the community, as nothing of the kind has ever before seen the light. There are indeed some authentic and well written compilations relating to this subject, as well as a few narratives given by persons who have been imprisoned in the dungeons of the Holy Office; but a copious and minute detail of the forms and proceedings observed in the trials and investigations of the Inquisitorial Tribunal, such as is afforded in the following pages, has never, till this moment, existed in print. Should the Holy Office again rear its head in Spain, perhaps the *fiscal* and *calificadores* might do the publisher and translator of this work the honor to take some notice of their labors. It is to be hoped, however, that these most illustrious and apostolical Señores may not very soon have occasion to obtain for either of us any such notoriety. (Kettell: 1828, Preface).

Whether it was Ticknor or Kettell who selected the cases that appear in the publication is unsure, but the "left over" documents were sent to the Thorndike residence in Boston. Upon Andrew Thorndike's death in 1840, his son George Herbert moved to Philadelphia and donated the papers to the American Philosophical Society. The following year, George Herbert went to Buenos Aires to protest government action in confiscating most, if not all, of his father's large possessions in that country. He succeeded in recovering a large portion of the estate and set sail for the US in route to Spain, where he planned to also claim the confiscation of his father's properties and money in Barcelona. Unfortunately, the ship he was on disappeared in a storm. The documents remained with the Philosophical Society until 1962 when they were transferred to the University of Pennsylvania and can now be consulted in the Henry Charles Lee Library under the title of "Thorndike Collection of Inquisition Manuscripts 1532–1819." The documents include 242 items and have been classified and arranged in 6 series: I. Inquisition documents, 1532–1819 (2 boxes); II. Genealogies, 1573–1769 (1 box); III. Civil records, 1565–1798 (2 boxes); IV. Financial records, 1556–1796 (6 folders); V. Church records, 1771–1785 (4 folders); VI. Historical documents, 1757–1797 (13 folders). These records do not include relevant information regarding the main topic of our survey but are another example of how dispersed documents related to the Spanish Inquisition have become, and reveals how even the data bank Gustav Henningsen compiled in the 1980s of thousands of cases is not complete (Contreras/Henningsen: 1986). Another depository that has yet to be cataloged is the one located in the Joanina Library of the University of Coimbra, Portugal. It appears that most of the trial records—mainly against Portuguese crypto-Jews—kept there belong to the grand *auto-da-fe* held in Madrid in 1680 to celebrate Charles II's betrothals.[5]

Besides the four boxes of original documents, the Lea library also has 66 boxes

---

5 This is a personal observation made when I visited the Joanina Library briefly in May of 2000.

of transcripts from the Inquisition's archives at Alcala, Simancas, the Biblioteca Nacional de Madrid, and from the municipal archives of Seville, which were the chief sources for Lea's *History of the Inquisition of Spain.* Henry Ch. Lea himself consulted some of the Thorndike documents:

> Many documents were gathered in the streets and sent to the United States, which have mostly perished through neglect, but some which were secured by Mr. Andrew Thorndike, then a resident of Barcelona, were presented, in 1840, to the American Philosophical Society, through whose courtesy I have been enabled to use them. Some cases, from a similar source were translated and printed in Boston, in 1828, under the title of "Records of the Spanish Inquisition, translated from the original Manuscripts." After the great riots of March 1820, when Catalan mobs sacked the palace of the Barcelona Inquisition and threw its papers everywhere, an enterprising Yankee visitor named Andrew Thorndike manage to acquire a few of its trial records, which he later had translated into English and published at Boston in 1828. Three trials dated from the 1630s [cases of Pierre Ginistra, 1635; Juan Duran, 1632; and Philippe Léonard, 1637] Two were born in France. The Yankee traveler had stumbled across a reasonably representative sample of Barcelona's inquisitorial activity. Turning the century after 1540: about two-thirds of its prisoners were Frenchmen charged with heresy or some type of heretical propositions, and one third were Catalans charged with non-heretical offenses (i. e. witchcraft). (Lea: 1906–1907, Book 9, Ch. 1, note 110).

The boxes of original documents kept in the Lea Library do not contain all the documents picked up on the streets of Barcelona that day in 1820. Indeed, Professor Ticknor may have kept some of the records for himself. This is deduced from a letter written by the German-American political philosopher, Francis Lieber, to Mrs. Ticknor years later. On November 6, 1870, Lieber had written Ticknor the following note:

> Do you remember that a long time ago, you directed my attention to a book just then (I mean in '29 or '30) published, giving the literal translation of trials of the Inquisition picked up by the American consul, I think, in Barcelona? I remember the book perfectly well, —a thin octavo; the first trial was that of a poor ticker accused of having eaten brawn on a Friday. (Lieber: 1882, 402).

Professor Ticknor may have been ill (he died the following year) and, in his stead, Mrs. Ticknor answered Lieber's note, to which Lieber replied:

> It is very odd that almost at the very moment I received your kind letter I recovered the sought-for book in my library. The title is "Records of the Spanish Inquisition" (1828), translated from original manuscripts, Boston, Samuel G. Goodrich; and on the fly-leaf are these words, written my myself: "Mr George Ticknor tells me that this work was published by Mr. Kettell of Boston from the manuscript processes which the United States Consul, Mr Thorndike, at Barcelona, saved when, during the revolution, the archives of the Inquisition were destroyed. Mr. Thorndike sent a whole boxful to Boston, and Mr. Ticknor owns some of the processes given in this book. Everything

given in this book is authentic. Boston, April 1831. F. Lieber." ...I remember now that Mr. Ticknor told me at the time that the archives were thrown into the street, and some of the trials were picked up. (Lieber: 1882, 403).

Luis de Usoz y Rio (1805–1865)

If Juan Antonio Llorente, Andrew Thorndike, and Gustav Henningsen are credited for rescuing many original Inquisition records, the Spanish Hebrew scholar Luis de Usoz y Rio must be credited for rescuing the writings of many of the forgotten sixteenth century Spanish Reformers. This pioneering intellectual gave up a brilliant academic future to dedicate his life—and family fortune—to a cause that until then had been buried in oblivion, that is, to locate and republish the lost writings of the sixteenth century Spanish Protestant Reformers: Juan de Valdes, Constantino Ponce de la Fuente, Francisco de Enzinas, Perez de Pineda, Antonio del Corro, Cipriano de Valera, and others. Usoz's laudable efforts deserve our greatest respect. His twenty-volume set of *Reformistas Antiguos Españoles*, published clandestinely between 1847 and 1865—a period of constant political changes in Spain—is remarkable. This contribution alone would be enough for him to be remembered as a man of deep convictions, serious scholarship and unprecedented patriotism. Ostracized by his peers, it took great stamina to build a library of thousands of prohibited books and to clandestinely edit and reprint the writings of compatriots condemned by the Inquisition at a time when freedom of press was still more theoretical than real (Vilar: 1994a), or as the eminent Hispanist William Knapp (1899, I, 328) puts it, at a time "when liberty of conscience in Spain still meant ruin to those who embraced it, unless they be too poor to have social bonds or too lowly to attract official persecution."

Luis de Usoz y Rio was born in Chuquiraca, what today is Sucre (Bolivia). He came from a highly cultured family. His mother, Maria Antonio del Rosario del Rio Unquia y Arnedo, had been a translator before her marriage.[6] His father, Jose Agustin de Ussoz y Mozi, originally from Navarre, held a degree in law. Shortly after their marriage in 1798, they left for South America where Jose Agustin de Ussoz had been offered a post as civil magistrate in the Real Audiencia of Charcas, the court that oversaw the silver mines at Potosi. In the popular uprising of May 25, 1809, the Usozs firmly opposed governor Garcia Leon de Pizarro, which led to friction with general Goyeneche and their banishment from Sucre in 1810, and the imprisonment of Jose Agustin. Five years followed of hardships, illnesses, and constant moves from one place to another until the

---

6 For information regarding Maria Antonio del Rosario de Rio y Arnedo, see Establier Perez (2008) and Rípodas Ardanaz (1993).

death of Maria Antonio de Rio in Arequipa (Peru) in June of 1816. Three years later, Jose Agustin Ussoz y Mozi returned to Spain with his five young children: Maria Manuela, Mariano, Luis, Maria Dolores Francisca, and Santiago, who was barely a year old. A year after their arrival Jose Agustin Ussoz passed away and the children were put under the care of their paternal uncle Santiago Ussoz y Muzi, a distinguished diplomat, who in 1823 Ferdinand VII appointed minister of state.

Under his uncle's care, Luis received a well-rounded education. At the University of Alcala he studied law, humanities, and classical and oriental languages. He began studying Hebrew under Luis Francisco Pascual Orchell y Ferrer, at the Reales Estudios de San Isidro in Madrid. His next Hebrew teacher—at the University of Alcala—was Antoni Puigblanch, who had fled to England with the return of Ferdinand VII in 1814 but returned to Spain to his post at the university as professor of Hebrew in 1820. After graduating from the University of Alcala, Usoz went to Italy to do graduate work at the Real Colegio de San Clemente de los Españoles in Bologna. With a doctorate in both civil and canon law under his arm he returned to Spain in 1836 to a country that had just recently thrown off the repressive authoritarian rule of Ferdinand VII and was enjoying for the first time a measure of liberty.

On his return, Usoz resumed friendship with some of his old classmates: the orientalist Pascual de Gayanos, the philologist Juan Calderon,[7] and Agustin Duran, who was compiling his *Romancero General* (1849–51). The following year, Usoz was teaching Hebrew at the recently opened Ateneo de Madrid and Gayangos Arabic. Gayangos was also working at the Biblioteca Nacional cataloging books that had come from the libraries of convents and monasteries expropriated by the ecclesiastical confiscations (*desmortización*) of prime minister Mendizabal. That year George Borrow, *colporteur* for the British and Foreign Bible Society, arrived in Madrid (Knapp: 1899). Borrow was a born linguist and one of his first stops was the Biblioteca Nacional in order to find material in *caló*, the Gypsy dialect. There he met Gayangos, who introduced him to Usoz. Borrow's mission—to print and distribute the Bible—fascinated Usoz, for he had never even seen a Bible until he began studying Hebrew. Shortly afterwards an anonymous article appeared in the local newspaper (*El Español*, March 18, 1836) defending the free distribution of the Bible (Giménez Cruz: 1990). Usoz himself had had serious difficulties in finding a Bible when he began studying Hebrew. His acquaintance with George Borrow changed his world-view in many ways. Borrow set up a small bookstore on Principe Street, which Usoz managed while Borrow was out distributing New Testaments,[8] but soon political

---

7 See Vilar Ramírez (1994, III, 619–626); Moreno Berrocal (2005).
8 In order not to find himself in trouble with the authorities, Borrow distributed the Felipe Scío

changes again brought restrictions and in 1838 the shop was closed and the Bibles impounded. The following year Borrow was imprisoned but Usoz could do nothing to help him, he was in Italy on his honeymoon.

Usoz married the wealthy widow, Maria Sandalia de Acebal Arratia, sister of the politician-banker-merchant, Francisco de Acebal Arratia.[9] He may have met her through Pascual Gayangos, who was a frequent visitor and participant in the social gatherings and literary circle that met at the Acebal Arratia residence in Madrid.[10] The couple spent the first year of their two-year honeymoon in Rome. The following year, their journey took them to Florence, then to Paris, and finally to London (Knapp: 1899, I, 335–336). Usoz had several reasons to visit England. He wanted to make acquaintance with the heads of the Bible Society and he wanted to meet Jeremiah Wiffen, the translator of Garcilaso de la Vega into English, and to learn something about the Society of Friends. His curiosity regarding the Quakers was brought on by two things. Several years earlier, a travelling salesman had sold him a copy, in Spanish, of Robert Barclay's *Apology for the True Christian Divinity, As the Same Is Held Forth, and Preached by the People, Called, in Scorn, Quakers,*[11] which he had read with interest, and Jeremiah Wiffen's epithet, which stated that he was a "member of the Society of Friends."

Usoz and his wife arrived in London in the spring of 1840.[12] That year three important events were taking place in London: the executive meeting of the British and Foreign Bible Society; the yearly assembly of the Quakers; and the first World Anti-Slavery Society Convention. George Borrow, who was also in London, accompanied Usoz to the meeting of the British and Foreign Bible Society and there introduced him to the eminent linguist, Josiah Forster

---

de San Miguel translation of the New Testament, which he had printed without notes. These bibles carried a false imprint. They were actually printed in Barcelona at the "Imprenta Antonio Bergnes y Cia" and sent in reams to Madrid to be bound.

9 Maria Sandalia's first husband, the wealthy businessman Manuel de Angulo Cano, died in March of 1837 and was buried in the family pantheon (#337) in the San Isidro cementary in Madrid on March 15, 1837. In the documents kept in the archives of the Prado Museum Maria Sandalia is referred to as "señora de Angulo" (wife of Angula).

10 Another member of the group was the painter Jose de Madrazo, director of the Prado Museum from 1838 to 1857 and who painted a full-length portrait of Maria Sandalia de Acebal in 1820.

11 Translated into Spanish in 1710 by Felix Antonio de Alvarado, a Spaniard living in London who also translated the Book of Common Prayer in 1707. Copies of Barclay's *Apology* could have been brought to Spain and distributed even before 1833 when the Quaker prison-reformers, Stephen Grellet and Wm. Allen, visited Spain. See Allen (1846, vol. III).

12 There is some discrepancy here. According to Benjamin B. Wiffen, Usoz arrived in London early 1839 (Boehmer: 2007, 10). In contrast, the correspondence between Usoz and Borrow evidences early 1840, that is, in a letter written from Florence, dated January 7, 1840, he says that in February he will be in Paris and from here hopes to cross over to England. The next letter was sent from Paris, dated February 18, 1840, and the next, from London, dated May 7, 1840. (Knapp: 1899, I, 335).

(Boehmer: 2007, 10). Forster, a Quaker and member of the British and Foreign Bible Society, introduced Usoz to George William Alexander and Benjamin B. Wiffen, abolitionists whose doctrines Usoz readily adhered to. Usoz and his wife returned to Spain in the fall of 1841. During their year in London, living at 15 Jermyn Street, Usoz spent most of his time between second-hand bookstores and the British Library.[13] He also met several Spanish exiles among which was his former friend the philologist Juan Calderon, who would become a dear collaborator and would spend hours at the British Library copying old books and manuscripts for Usoz.[14]

The time spent in London was decisive for Usoz. His priorities changed completely. Though he would certainly have been acquainted with the *autos-da-fe* and the persecution of Protestants in sixteenth century Spain through publications such as that of Joseph Lavallée, Juan Antonio Llorente, and Thomas M'Crie, Usoz's interests turned to the works of the Spanish Protestants who fled and he resolved to locate and republish them. The first step in this direction was to make a list of these "prohibited" books. This took him to the archives in Simancas and a page-by-page search through the over 300 hundred pages of tiny print and curious abbreviations of the last Index of Prohibited Books (Usoz: 1847–1865, V, Appendix 12, 79–95). Usoz would have gone through this volume line by line because not always was the author mentioned, as for example the following entries, which today we know belong to Juan and Alfonso Valdes:

- Dialogi de Mercurio et Charonte.
- Dialogo de la Doctrina Christiana, compuesto nuevam. por un cierto Religioso.
- Dialogo dónde hablan Lactancio y un Arcediano, sobre lo que sucedió en Roma el año 1527.
- Dialogo de Mercurio y Caronte. (Indice ultimo: 1790, 75).

Usoz would have found only one brief reference to Juan de Valdes:

- Valdesio, Valdesius or Valdes (Joan.), I. cl. Wrote a *Brief Commentary on the First Epistle to the Corinthians*, which also circulates as 'anonymous'. (Indice ultimo: 1790, 272).

As for Perez de Pineda, Usoz found three works:

---

13 It was during that time that Usoz found, and printed, the rare edition of the *Cancionero General* with the burlesque verses. See Chapter III.

14 Juan Calderon (1791–1854) was an ex-Franciscan monk who had immigrated to southern France for political reasons in 1829. There, through some members of the British Bible Society, he converted to Protestantism. From France, Calderon went to England where he was ordained in the Anglican Church. In 1843, he was back in Spain where he published a Spanish grammar, which years later would become the official textbook for teaching Spanish to foreigners. Calderon returned to England, where for a time held the chair of Spanish at King's College.

- Pérez (Dr. Juan). Su *Catecismo* que falsam. dice fue visto por los Inquisidores. Item, *Psalmos traduc.* Item, *Sumario de la Doctrina Christiana.* (Indice ultimo, 1790, 209).

For Constantino Ponce de la Fuente only one work was listed:

- Fuente (Constantino de la). I. cl. Especialm. Su *Confesión del Pecador.* (Indice ultimo: 1790, 109).

Cipriano de Valera is dismissed simply as:

- Valera (Cypriano de), commonly known as "The Spanish Heretic." (Indice ultimo: 1790, 272).

In contrast, Casiodoro de Reina, the translator of the Spanish Bible is erroneously listed as a German theologian:

- Remius, or Reimius, or Reinus (Cassiodoro de). Germ. Th. I. cl. (Indice ultimo: 1790, 228).

The Spanish Bible in question—the edition revised by Valera and printed in Amsterdam—is listed as:

- *Biblia en lengua española, traducida de la Verdad Hebraica:* which falsely states that it was seen and examined by the Inquisition, printed in Amsterdam. (Indice ultimo: 1790, 29).

Because "Carrascon" was the first book Usoz rediscovered, he decided it would become volume I of what he would call *Reformistas Antiguos Españoles.* It was printed in San Sebastian in 1847 by Ignacio R. Baroja, though the printer's name does not appear on the title page. Juan Perez de Pineda's *Epsitola Consolatoria,* which Usoz had seen when in London but had been unable to convince the owner, Canon Riego, a Spanish refugee, to sell to him at the time, constituted volume II. Usoz and Wiffen continued their search and managed to find copies of old Spanish works in the hands of used-book dealers and private libraries in London, Edinburgh, Paris, Altona, Gotthingen, Madrid, Halle, Brussels, Dublin, etc. Some of these works had to be copied page-by-page, line-by-line; others could be purchased outright. Once the volumes were located they had to be sent to Madrid. For this, Usoz had to find a sympathizing customs agent willing to see that they passed custom controls unmolested. In Madrid he could count on Jose Sanchez Balsa and in San Sebastian on the Basque editor, Fernando de Brunet. But Usoz also used other means, and persons: agents belonging to the British Foreign Bible Society, the British diplomatic service, British railway engineers (many of which were Quakers), the *colporteur* James Thomson, the Methodist minister W.H. Rule, etc. Even the Catalan printer-professor—and Quaker sympathizer—, Antonio Bergnes de las Casas, on his travels to and from London served at times as a courier. By this means, over the years Usoz was able to compile a library of some ten thousand prohibited books. Details of how and where these volumes were acquired, and the difficulties in sending them to Spain are gleaned from the abundant correspondence between Usoz, Wiffen, and Brunet, which is kept in the archives of the library of Wadham College, Oxford (Vilar: 1994a; Rios Sanchez: 1998; Vilar/Vilar: 2010).

Most of the twenty volumes of *Reformistas Antiguos* were printed "anonymously" in Madrid by Jose Martin Alegria in his shop located on Ancha de San Bernardo Street—and after 1860 at Paseo del Obelisco 2, assisted by Jose Cruzado, a prestigious Protestant printer,[15] except for three that were printed by Ignacio Ramon Baroja, uncle of the novelist Pio Baroja, in his shop in San Sebastian. Usoz not only financed the printing of all the volumes he published in his collection of *Reformistas*, but he also added prologues and notes. Professor Knapp (1899, I, 364–5) adds this comment regarding Jose Cruzado: "I was acquainted with Cruzado many years, from 1869 (when his presses were in the Calle de Dos Amigos) to 1877, and I often talked with him of the dangers attending the impression of the Ancient Spanish Reformers; the night visits of the *alguaciles*, and the connivance of the government ministers who were well aware of what Usoz was doing, but did not interfere so long as he kept quiet."

Luis de Usoz was a very scrupulous scholar as his notes, compiled later by Eduard Boehmer, show. In 1850, as Usoz was putting the finishing touches to the introduction to his brother's translation of Reginaldo Gonzalez de Montes's *Artes de la Inquisición*, he received a package from Wiffen containing two books that had just been published in England, one in London and the other in Dublin.[16] The titles and the content were basically the same, but the second editor-author had added some fresh information. He incorporated the story of Giacinto Achilli, a former Dominican monk liberated from the Inquisition prison at Castel Sant'Angelo that very year, a narrative entitled "Deliverance by the French" taken from Antonio Gavin's *Master-key to Popery*,[17] and a story narrated

---

15 Jose Cruzado would later print the hymn book for the Methodist congregations: *Himnos para el uso de las congregaciones españolas de la Iglesia Protestante Metodista* (Madrid, J. Cruzado, 1869), and the first Spanish Anglican bishop Juan B. Cabrera Ivars's liturgy: *Liturgia de la Iglesia Española Reformada* (Madrid: José Cruzado, 1889) and catechism: *Catecismo de doctrina y vida cristiana* (Madrid: José Cruzado, 1887).

16 Charles H. Davies, History of the Inquisition, from its Establishment to the Present Time, with an Account of its Procedure and Narratives of its Victims (London: Ward & Co., 1850); and Philip Dixon Hardy, The Inquisition: Its History, Influences, and Effects, from Its First Establishment to the Present Time: Including Its Recent Proceedings Relative to Dr. Achilli, &c. &c, with Engravings (Dublin: Philip Dixon Hardy and Sons, 1850)

17 Antonio Gavin, *A Master-key to Popery* (Dublin, 1724).

by one of Napoleon's former generals on how he blew up a palace of the Inquisition in Madrid in 1809. Hardy introduced the latter story thus:

> Interesting narrative of the demolition of the Palace of the Inquisition, in the year 1809, by the orders of Marshal Soult—as narrated by the officer commanding the division by which it was destroyed. For the perfect authenticity of the narrative, reference was at the time made to Mons. de Lile, then a pastor of one of the Evangelical Churches of France, who, as Col. of the 117th regiment, under Soult, had taken a prominent part in the transaction.

The story must have puzzled Hardy, who in the same volume included an abstract of the Memoirs of Don Juan Van Halen, imprisoned in 1816, for he added a final note:

> By a reference to the foregoing statement relative to Madrid, it will be seen that this horrible place was shortly afterwards rebuilt—and from the statement of Col. Van Halen, given at page 136, it appears that even before the rebuilding some unfortunate beings were condemned to suffer imprisonment and torture in the old dungeons which had escaped the fury of the soldiers. (Hardy: 1850, 214).

The story was pure invention and when Usoz read it he became extremely upset. Though he was no friend of the Inquisition, he stood up for historical truth and could not condone the invention of a story of the demolition of a palace of the Inquisition located in Chamartin by French soldiers. He did what was in his power at the moment to stop the myth and, in an appendix to his brother's translation of *Artes*, he denounced the author, Johann J. Lehmanowsky, for falsifying facts (Usoz: 1847–1865, V, Apendix V, 20ss). Likewise, in England, Benjamin Wiffen did all he could to stop Lehmanowsky's claims. But it was already too late. Since 1834, Lehmanowsky had been travelling throughout the Middle West lecturing on his participation in heroic battles and how in 1809 he and his regiment blew up the last prison of the Inquisition in Madrid and rescued a hundred men, women, and children half naked, half starved. His audiences loved the story of the Inquisition and it began to appear in newspapers and religious magazines across the United States. It appeared as tract # 460 of the American Tract Society in 1835. Ten years later, it appeared translated into French, as chapter 51 in V. de Féréal's novel *Mystères de l'Inquisition et autres sociétés secrètes d'Espagne* (Paris, 1845), accompanied by an impressive a full-page sketch of an imposing Spanish prison. But when it was inserted in an American edition of Jean P. Perrin's prestigious *History of the Ancient Christians* (Philadelphia, 1847), and various reprints of Foxe's *Book of Martyrs*, it almost became dogma. It is not surprising, therefore, that it should soon appear in publications such as Hardy's *History of the Inquisition*.

Despite Usoz's collaborator Benjamin Wiffen's emphatic protest in "Notes and Queries," the story continued to appear in the US and in the United Kingdom. In 1551 it was inserted in Timpson's *The Inquisition Revealed* (1851, 302–312), the following year in Pike's *The Curse of Christendom* (1852, 261–264). When in 1554 James Bell (1854, 424ss), the author of *The Mystery Unveiled,* justified his having included Lehmanowsky's story because he had found it in the highly regarded Scottish journal *Christian Treasury,* Benjamin Wiffen became very alarmed and published a lengthy article in the prestigious literary journal "Notes and Queries" (August 4, 1854) in which he put forth factual information obtained from persons living in Madrid in 1809—furnished by his friend Luis de Usoz—to refute Lehmanowsky's story. Wiffen's note received empathetic support from the much-travelled Englishman, Lord Monson, who had been in Madrid in 1820 and had seen with his own eyes the old Inquisition palace on Maria Cristina Street.

When issues of "Notes & Queries"—with both Wiffen's and Monson's notes—reached Philadelphia, certain American subscribers began questioning Lehmanowsky's story. At the time, Lehmanowsky, who was still alive and living comfortably in Indiana, decided to ignore the notes; after all, England was far away and very few Americans had even heard of "Notes & Queries." However, a letter from an American subscriber to the editor of the New York newspaper *The Independent* questioning the intervention of the French troops in 1809 brought a passionate refutation from Lehmanowsky. He immediately wrote the New York editor to protest, ending his letter thus:

> And now, Mr. Editor, I think I have done so far my duty in answering this very learned gentleman, who made the criticism in the Notes and Queries. But allow me to remark, that I am astonished that any one should wait twenty years since my first statement, to correct the same. It seems to me that those who were always wishing to have this statement hushed up, waited until they were sure Marshal Soult and Col. De Lisle were dead, and no doubt suspected Col. Lehmanowsky was also numbered among the dead, so that they may have free play; but they are mistaken.

> Colonel Lehmanowsky. Hamburg, Clark co. Indiana, Dec. 15, 1854.

> (Notes and Queries 11, January–June 1855).

Notes & Queries's American agent found the debate interesting and sent a copy of the letters off to headquarters in London. When Luis de Usoz y Rio, also a subscriber to "Notes & Queries," read Lehmanowsky's reply letter in the next issue, he went straightaway to a notary public, together with four witnesses who were living in Madrid in 1809, and had an affidavit drawn up in which they testified—as eye witnesses—that there never existed an Inquisition palace in Chamartin, as Lehmanowsky claimed, and that the whole story was an invention. The case aroused such interest that in 1858 the editors of "Notes and Queries" published a separate monographic volume with all the correspondence—including Lehmanowsky's response and a translation of Usoz's affidavit—dedicated solely to the case. For a time, at least in England, publishers abstained from reprinting the story.

At the turn of the century, however, the case came up again when, in Boston, Charles C. Starbuck—who seemingly was totally ignorant of the earlier polemics—, in his column in the Boston newspaper, The Sacred Heart Review, under the title "The Polish Imposter and the Inquisition Again," insisted on the discredit of such stories to serious historical research.[18] This echoes a statement by Juan Antonio Llorente a century earlier: "A good cause becomes bad when falsehood is employed in its defense: the true history of the Inquisition is sufficient to show how much it merits the detestation of the human race, and it is therefore useless to employ fictions or satire." (Llorente: 1843, 216). It has been suggested that Edgar Allan Poe drew his inspiration for "The Pit and the Pendulum" from Lehmanowsky's story. Others contend that Poe took his information from Llorente. Neither of these suppositions is totally correct. Though the rescue of Poe's victim by French soldiers may have come from Lehmanowsky, information regarding the torture of the pendulum came from an unreferenced note added by the English editor—or translator—of the abridged London 1826 edition of Juan Antonio Llorente's *History of the Inquisition*, which was reprinted in Philadelphia in 1843—the same year Poe published "The Pit and the Pendulum"—and reads as follows:

> When the Inquisition was thrown open, in 1820, by the orders of the Cortes of Madrid, twenty-one prisoners were found in it, not one of whom knew the name of the city in which he was: some had been confined three years, some a longer period, and not one knew perfectly the nature of the crime of which he was accused. One of these prisoners had been condemned, and was to have suffered on the following day. His punishment was to be death by the pendulum. The method of thus destroying the victim is as follows: The condemned is fastened in a groove, upon a table, on his back; suspended above him is a pendulum, the edge of which is sharp, and it is so constructed as to become longer with every movement. The wretch sees this implement of destruction swinging to and fro above him, and every moment the keen edge approaching nearer and nearer: at length it cuts the skin of his nose, and gradually cuts on, until life is extinct. (Llorente: 1843, Preface, Footnote 1).

After 1855, Luis de Usoz y Rio considered the case closed and went back to editing the writings of the Spanish Reformers, which continued for another ten years.[19] He also continued to enlarge his library, among which were many valuable first editions. For example, he owned an *editio princeps* copy of Montesino's four-volume 1502 rendering of *Vita Cristi*. Usoz's widow, Maria Sandalia

---

18 Editorial Note. The Sacred Heart Review 131 (August 13, 1898). Also see his editorial note in The Sacred Heart Review 285 (October 8, 1898).

19 See Appendix C.

del Acebal, donated it, along with his entire library of some 10,000 volumes, to the Biblioteca Nacional at Madrid in October of 1873, only one month before Martinez-Campo's coup d'état. She had waited eight years after her husband's death to make the donation. The political scenario had not been propitious for dissidents until the First Spanish Republic, established in February of 1873. William Knapp, who visited Usoz's widow in Madrid in 1872, may have encouraged her to make the donation then. Knapp (1899, I, 339) was in Madrid again in 1876, shortly after she passed away, and reported:

> I was called upon by the librarian of the Biblioteca National to look over Mr. Usoz's papers and books at the death of Madame, my information is at first hand. The library (10,000 vols.) went to the "National" and the remaining copies of the Reformers were handed to Mr. Corfield to distribute to Spaniards."[20]

At the time of his death, which occurred on September 17, 1865, at the age of 60, Luis de Usoz was about to venture on a new project, that is, the drafting of a history of the Reformation in Spain. Initially this project was to be carried on by Benjamin B. Wiffen, but it was again thwarted by Wiffen's death.

Misunderstood by his contemporaries, belittled by Marcelino Menendez y Pelayo, and dismissed as a religious fanatic by later literary critics, Usoz is finally—after 150 years—receiving the recognition he deserves from his fellow countrymen thanks to a new scholarly approach to religious pluralism that exists currently in Spain.

Benjamin Barron Wiffen (1794–1867)

Benjamin Wiffen had been to Spain in 1839 and had met with prominent members of the government in order to promote the abolition of slavery. On his way to Lisbon in 1843, he stopped off at Seville, where his friend Luis de Usoz was busy book-hunting. Usoz showed him his first find: a rare copy of *El Carrascon,* a work written by Fernando de Tejeda, a monk from Burgos who had fled to England around 1620.[21] He also showed him an old copy of Constantino Ponce de la Fuente's *Suma de Doctrina* (1551) that he had found in Lisbon. Wiffen (Memorial, 2015) then remembered that a Quaker friend of his, Richard Thomas How, had once shown him an "old work by a Spaniard, which represented essentially the principles of George Fox." This happened to be one of Juan de Valdes's works, very likely Nicholas Ferrar's rendering of Valdes's *Ciento y diez consideraciones.* According to Usoz, as a consequence of that meeting, "Benja-

---

20 Richard Corfield was secretary of the British and Foreign Bible Society at Madrid from 1870 to 1883.
21 For details regarding *El Carrascon*, see Roldán-Figueroa (2010; 2013).

min Wiffen was at once made a literary proselyte, an indispensable proselyte" and their joint project to find the works of "those Spanish writers who were persecuted for their attachment to Christian liberty" began (Boehmer: 2007, 29).

Back in England, Wiffen proceeded to search diligently for their writings and to send copies back to Usoz. He was able to obtain—or make—copies of the works of Juan Perez de Pineda, Francisco de Enzinas, Cipriano de Valera, Juan Nicholas y Sacharles, Constantino Ponce de la Fuente, and Juan de Valdes. Twenty years later, Wiffen put his experiences into writing: "Notices and experiences of Benjamin B. Wiffen in relation to the works of the early Spanish Reformers, their discovery and republication in the series called the *Reformistas Antiguos Españoles*." This information was published posthumously by Eduard Boehmer (2007, 27–57) in what he entitled *Bibliotheca Wiffeniana: Spanish Reformers of two centuries from 1520. Their lives and writings according to the late Benjamin B. Wiffen's plan and with the use of his materials.* The outcome of the twenty-five-year Usoz-Wiffen partnership was the republication of twenty works, two of which were printed in England and the rest clandestinely in Madrid and San Sebastian between 1847 and 1865.[22]

William Knapp (1899, I, 334, 363) greatly lamented the fact that the chief merits of compiling and editing the *Reformistas Antiguos Españoles* should later fall on Benjamin Wiffen and not Luis de Usoz:

It does not often happen that a scholar who devotes a life of valuable service to the investigation and illustration of history and religion, has the ill fortune to have the rewards of his toil and the expenditure of his wealth so completely appropriated by others as in the case of him whose name heads this article. ... Foreigners, it appears, through ignorance of the facts, will continue to cite the results that Luis de Usoz has left us, by other names than the true and legitimate one.

This now extraordinarily rare Collection is erroneously and very unjustly attributed to Mr. Wiffen, especially since the appearance of Ticknor's *History of Spanish Literature*, Bonn's Supplement to Lowndes' Catalogue, Brunet's Manuel, 1863 (art. Juan Perez). The simple facts are these: The origin and execution of the series, i. e. the editing, notes (save vols. ii. and xv. done in company with Wiffen), and entire expense of originals and manufacture, are all due to Don Luis de Usoz y Rio.

Knapp's comment regarding Ticknor's *History* is probably based on a statement found in George Ticknor's (1872, II, 494) enlarged 4th edition:

A few tracts and treaties by Spanish Protestants, such as Perez de Pineda, Enzinas etc. were printed. But their number was very small. A list of them, and of nearly all the works of Spanish Protestants, published to spread the faith of their authors, can be found in the interesting notice by B. B. Wiffen, prefixed to his reprint of the "Epistola Consolatoria por Juan Perez," 1848.

---

22 See Appendix C.

Knapp may have based his comment on that and a lengthy—rather ambiguous—note in which Usoz's name is mentioned in passing, and Wiffen's is insinuated as the rediscoverer of Valdes and his work:

> [Alfonso de Valdes's two dialogs] were prepared and published anew in 1850, without date or place, but I suppose in Madrid by the same person who in 1860 prepared and edited the "Dialogo de la Lengua." For what relates to the brothers Valdes, see the editions of the "Ciento y Diez Consideraciones," 1855 and 1863, the edition of the "Alfabeto Christiano," 1861, that of the "Dialogo de la Lengua," 1860,—all I suppose printed in Madrid, though not so designed by their editors, Don Luis de Usoz y Rio and Benjamin B. Wiffen, a Quaker gentleman living near Bedford, and brother of the translator of Garcilaso de la Vega. A Life of Juan de Valdes, containing everything that can probably be known of him, was written by Friend Wiffen and published in London in 1865; but I had not the benefit of it when the preceding remarks were prepared, as that was a year earlier. (Ticknor: 1872, II, 24–25, note 44).

But credit where credit is due. Had it not been for Benjamin Wiffin, Usoz would never have been able to carry out his project. As Wiffen himself put it:

> The learning was [Usoz's], so was the talent and the outlay; mine were the advantages of liberty and free action and residence in a country which furnished the readiest means for the acquisition of this kind of knowledge. We were both favored with leisure, we both had the simple and independent means of livelihood, we wanted no more. (Boehmer: 2007, 54)

Rediscovering the works of Juan de Valdes—mainly his *110 Considerations*—put Wiffen in contact with other like-minded inquiring scholars. Wiffen first found a copy, in Italian, in Trinity Library, Cambridge. Then, through a Dutch antiquarian bookseller, he obtained another copy, one that had belonged to Acronius, a Frisian who occupied the chairs of mathematics and medicine at Basel when the book was printed in 1550. Wiffen showed the book to his friend Frederick Seebohm, who shortly afterwards wrote him offering to finance the printing of the volume—via subscription—if he found someone to edit the Italian. Among the subscribers were John Betts and his wife Mary. Knowing that the Betts had spent many years in Italy and mastered the language, Seebohm suggested they translate Valdes into English and add a brief biography. This Wiffen did with the help of Mary Betts. The result was: *Life and Writings of Juan de Valdés, Otherwise Valdesso, Spanish reformer in the Sixteenth Century, with a translation from the Italian of his Hundred and Ten Considerations by John T. Betts.*[23]

---

23 John T. Betts and his wife Mary also translated other works of the Spanish Reformers: *Juan de Valdés' Minor Works; Commentary upon Our Lord's Sermon on the Mount; Commentary upon the Gospel of St. Matthew; Spiritual Milk, or Christian Instruction for Children; XVII*

That year, 1865, John and Mary Betts travelled to Spain to meet Usoz, who was seriously ill with tuberculosis. During their brief stay, Usoz asked Betts to translate into English some of the works of another of his favorite authors, namely, Constantino Ponce de la Fuente. For this, the couple moved to Seville to more fully immerse themselves in the culture of the city in which Constantino had lived and worked. They never met Usoz again for he died within a few months. On their return to England, the Betts published the translation—*The Confession of a Sinner* (1869)—together with a bibliographical sketch of Constantino by Benjamin Wiffen. When Wiffen died three years later, the Betts first decided to continue the Usoz-Wiffen project on their own, but finding themselves incapable, and unqualified, for such a task, they delegated the project to Eduard Boehmer.

Eduard Boehmer (1827–1906)

The German philologist Eduard Boehmer was professor of Romance Languages, and librarian, at the University of Halle. His interest in the Spanish Reformers took another path. In 1851, he accompanied the elderly German theologian Dr. Friedrich August Tholuck to London to attend a meeting of the Evangelical Alliance, the first in a series of international conferences of evangelical Christians.[24] The two men were guests at the home of Sir Culling Eardley, president of the British branch of the Alliance, known for his campaigns in favor of religious liberty. While they were there, Juan Calderon, an exiled Spanish philologist living in London and friend of Luis de Usoz y Rio, brought Dr. Tholuck a copy of Adolfo de Castro's *The Spanish Protestants and Their Persecution by Philip II, a Historical Work* (London, 1851), which had just come off the press.[25] After reading this work, Boehmer, who was already familiar with some of the works of Juan de Valdes, became deeply interested in Spain and in 1858 travelled to Cadiz to meet Adolfo de Castro. On his return trip he passed through Madrid where he purchased volumes I, III, IX, X, XI, and XII of Usoz's series from a book dealer. In an appendix of one of the volumes he found the following address: "Benjamin B.

Opuscules. Translated from the Spanish and Italian and edited by John T. Betts (London: Trubner & Co. 1882),

24 A second conference was held in Paris in 1855 and a third in Berlin in 1857. At the Berlin conference, Angel Herrera de Mora, an exDominican and former professor of philosophy at the University of Madrid exiled in London, spoke. Mora had just published his autobiography in which he related the precarious state of affairs existing in Spain regarding freedom of conscience in the mid ninenteenth century.

25 This was a translation of Castro's *Historia de los Protestantes Españoles y de su persecución por Felipe II* (Cadiz, 1851). An enlarged edition, in English, appeared three years later: *History of Religious Intolerance in Spain* (1853).

Wiffen, Mount Pleasant, zerca de Woburn, Condado de Bedford, 1°m, 21, 1853."[26] Boehmer wrote to Wiffen asking where he could purchase a copy of volume IV, which was Alfonso de Valdes's *Two Dialogs*. In the letter he told Wiffen that he had found a copy of the original Italian text of Valdés's *Considerations* in a library in Germany. Though the two men never met personally, a strong friendship was established. The first outcome of their labor together was a facsimile edition of the original Italian of Valdés's *Considerations*.

It had been Wiffen's desire, towards the end of his life, to compile a catalog that would include all the information he and Usoz had collected over the years regarding the Spanish Reformers "in order to serve as a manual for scholarly reference and to establish them as a class of writers." (Boehmer: 2007, 5). He began arranging the material, but died shortly afterwards. It was then that John and Mary Betts sent all of Wiffen's papers, notes, letters, and books to Eduard Boehmer for him to undertake the completion of the work, hence the subtitle: "Spanish Reformers of two centuries from 1520. Their lives and writings according to the late Benjamin B. Wiffen's plan and with the use of his materials."[27] To Usoz's twenty-volume collection Boehmer added two more volumes: Juan de Valdes, *El Salterio* (1880); Juan de Valdes, *Trataditos* (1880). These two volumes were printed at the expense of Usoz's friend, Fernando de Brunet. The following year, Boehmer issued a new Spanish edition of Constantino Ponce de la Fuente's sermons on the first Psalm and in 1882 Boehmer prepared for the press Valdes's *Spiritual Milk* (in Italian, Spanish, and German). Besides this, Boehmer contributed to making known the works of the Spanish Reformers in Germany with over twenty articles published in prestigious journals between 1861 and 1902.[28] It was this keen interest on the part of many nineteenth-century German scholars for the persecution of Protestants in sixteenth century Spain that prompted Ernst Schäfer to travel to Simancas to study the archives there and which culminated several years later in his three-volume *Beiträge* (1902).

Eduard Boehmer's efforts were possible thanks to his move from Halle to Strasbourg. In 1879 he was appointed emeritus professor of the University of Strasbourg, which released him of his academic duties and allowed him time to publish the aforementioned works and to spend the last years of his life organizing and compiling what became the three-volume *Bibliotheca Wiffeniana*,

---

26 Note the peculiar way of writing the months: "1°m" = first month, January. Ordinal numbers were also used by the Quakers for the days of the week.

27 Eduard Boehmer was responsible for the edition, but John Betts, who was an excellent translator, "controlled all that presented itself in the different languages, whether English or German, Spanish or Italian or French, Latin or Greek, contributed with his observations." (Boehmer: 2007, II, xi).

28 See Luttikhuizen (2009, 61–62).

a detailed catalog of all the notes and editions found up until then of the writings that appear in Usoz's collection, together with a brief biography of each writer.[29]

Centro de Investigación y Memoria del Protestantismo Español (CIMPE)

Between 1981 and 1984, the Catalan editor-book dealer, Diego Gomez Flores, printed a facsimile edition—a print-run of 300 numbered sets—of the entire *Reformistas Antiguos Españoles* series, including Boehmer's volumes.[30] It is uncertain what motivated Gomez Flores to undertake this project. Being an antiquarian bookseller he may simply have been attracted by the subject. On the other hand, with legal restrictions lifted after the death of Francisco Franco[31] and renewed interest abroad in the Spanish Inquisition in the 1970s, which sent scholars back to the original documents, Gomez Flores may simply have wanted to contribute to the bank of primery sources with a facsimile edition of Usoz's *Reformistas Antiguos Españoles.* At the same time, the production of facsimile editions was encouraged in Catalonia by institutions such as the Societat Catalana de Bibliofils, the Institut d'Estudis Catalans, and the Biblioteca de Catalunya, and Gomez Flores's undertaking may have been a commissioned project. In all likelihood the Biblioteca de Catalunya would have had on hand a set of the original collection from which he could make his copy. It was Usoz's desire that sets be placed in all public libraries. In Catalonia, this task may have fallen to his friend Antonio Bergnes de las Casas, a Greek scholar and rector of the University of Barcelona from 1868 to 1874. Moreover, Bergnes's antipathy for the political, economic, and individual repercussions brought about by four hundred years of oppression, and his sympathy towards the open-minded Quakers, made him responsive to social needs—in particular to the need to educate the populace—and this may have prompted him to make sure sets of Usoz's collection were placed in various institutions.

Today, Usoz's project is being continued in Seville by the Centro de Investigación y Memoria del Protestantismo Español (CIMPE) under the direction of Emilio Monjo Bellido, who has already reprinted ten volumes.[32] Modern-spelling editions, with new introductions, are being made of most of the writings found in the Reformistas Antiguos Españoles series. In addition, translations are being

---

29 A facsimile edition of *Bibliotheca Wiffeniana* was printed in one volume in 2007 by Analecta Ediciones, Pamplona, Spain.
30 See Appendix C.
31 As late as the 1950s, the Barcelona printer Angel Estrada was still subject to fines and confiscations of paper and Bibles. Personal communication.
32 See Appendix C.

made of works that still remained in Latin.[33] Several of these volumes are also currently being translated into English. Until recently these writings have not attracted much attention outside of Spain because of the general neglect of the history of the Spanish Protestant Reformers and also because of linguistics barriers. As they become available in English, they will offer scholars a wider spectrum in their study of the outreach of the sixteenth century Protestant Reformation. In 1899, the prestigious Hispanist, William Knapp (1899, I, 334), wrote:

> The country to which Mr. Usoz belonged, after having ignored his labours for more than thirty years, save to insult his memory, is not likely, even now when liberty of conscience is only nominal, to take up the tardy vindication of one whose works form the chief storehouse of information for the obscure period in Spain of religious controversy, i. e. the sixteenth century.

The main aim of this book has been to vindicate the memory of those men and women who died for their "Lutheran" convictions, of those who were fortunate enough to escape, and of those who rediscovered their stories and their works. Hopefully, these pages will serve as an introduction for persons in the English-speaking world who were unaware of this much ignored side of Spanish history and, at the same time, may encourage further research that will answer the many questions we have left unanswered.

---

33 Volumes newly translated from Latin by Fco. Ruiz de Pablos and published by E. Monjo Bellido as part of *Obras de los reformadores españoles del siglo XVI*, include: Casiodoro de Reina, *Comentario al Evangelio de Juan* (2010); Antonio del Corro, *Comentario Dialogado de la carta a los Romanos* (2010); and Antonio del Corro, *Comentario a Eclesiastés* (2011).

Works Cited and Further Reading

ADLER, ELKAN NATHAN (1908), Auto de fé and Jew, London: H. Frowde.

ADORNI-BRACCESI, SIMONETTA (2007), Le chiese italiane del rifugio e i luoghi del-l'esilio, in: La Réforme en France et en Italie: contacts, comparaisons et contrastes, Philip Benedict/Silvana Seidel Menchi/Alain Tallon (eds.), Rome: École française de Rome, 513–534.

AHLGREN, GILLIAN T.W. (1998), Teresa of Avila and the Politics of Sanctity, Ithaca, NY: Cornell University Press.

ALBERT, CARMEN/MARÍA DEL MAR FERNÁNDEZ VEGA (2003), Un Inventario anó-nimo en Castilla la Nueva: 1494–1506, Madrid: CSIC.

ALBORG, JUAN LUIS (1978), Historia de la literatura española, 4 vols., Madrid: Gredos.

ALCALÁ, ANGEL (1999), The Grievous Price of Victory, in: Women in the Inquisition: Spain and the New World, Mary E. Giles (ed.), Baltimore: Johns Hopkins University Press, 98–118.

ALCALÁ, ANGEL (ed.) (1987), The Spanish Inquisition and the Inquisitorial Mind, Boulder, CO: Columbia University Press.

ALEGRE PAYRÓN, JOSÉ MA. (1990), La censura literaria en España en el siglo XVI, Revue Romane 25, 428–441.

ALEJANDRE, JUAN ANTONIO (1994), El veneno de Dios: la Inquisición de Sevilla ante el delito de solicitación, Madrid: Siglo Veintiuno Editores.

ALLEN, WILLIAM (1847), Life of William Allen: With Selections from His Corre-spondence, 3 vols. London: C. Gilpin.

ALONSO BURGOS, JESUS (1983), El luteranismo en Castilla en el siglo XVI, San Lorenzo de El Escorial: Editorial Swan.

ALVAREZ MÁRQUEZ, CARMEN (1986), La Biblioteca de Don Fadrique Enríquez de Ribera, I Marqués de Tarifa (1532), Historia, Instituciones, Documentos 13, 1–40.

ALVAREZ MÁRQUEZ, CARMEN (2004), Mujeres lectoras en el siglo XVI en Sevilla, HID 31, 19–40.

AMADÓ, R.R. (1907), Article "University of Alcalá", The Catholic Encyclopedia, New York: Robert Appleton Company. http://www.newadvent.org/cathen/01271a.htm. Ac-cessed January 6, 2015.

AMELANG, JAMES S. (2007), Exchanges Between Italy and Spain: Culture and Religion, in: Spain in Italy: Politics, Society, and Religion 1500–1700, Thomas James Dandelet/John A. Marino (eds.), Leiden: Brill, 433–456.

AMES, CHRISTINE CALDWELL (2005), Does Inquisition Belong to Religious History, The American Historical Review 110.1, 12–13.

ANON. (1588), Packe of Spanish Lyes Sent Abroad in the World: first printed in Spaine in the Spanish tongue, and translated out of the originall. Now ripped up, unfolded, and by just examination condemned, as conteyning false, corrupt, and detestable wares, worthy to be damned and burned. London: Christopher Barker.

ARAND, CHARLES P. (1998), The Texts of the Apology of the Augsburg Confession, Lutheran Quarterly 12.4, 461–484.

ARIAS MONTANO, BENITO (1571), Indice Expurgatorio, Antwerp: Plantini.

ARMESTO, FELIPE (1988), Humanist, Inquisitor, Mystic: Cardinal Jimenez de Cisneros, History Today 38.10, 33–40.

ARNAUD, EUGÈNE (1890), Guillaume Rabot de Salène, humaniste ignoré du XVIe siècle, étude historique, Paris: Grassart.

ARRÓNIZ, OTHÓN (1968), Alfonso de Ulloa, servidor de don Juan Hurtado de Mendoza, Bulletin Hispanic 70, 437–457.

ÁVILA SEOANE, NICOLÁS (2013), Diplomática señorial en el tránsito de la Edad Media a la Moderna: los documentos de Diego López Pacheco para el gobierno de Escalona, Revista Escuela de Historia 12.1, 1–23.

ÁVILA SEOANE, NICOLÁS/OSCAR LÓPEZ GÓMEZ (2011), Catálogo del Archivo Histórico Municipal de Escalona: anticipo provisional, Escalona: Ayuntamiento de Escalona.

AVONTROOT, JOHANNES (1614), Carta de Juan Aventrot al poderosísimo Rey de España, Amsterdam: Pablo Ravensteyn.

AVONTROOT, JOHANNES (1632), Copy van't Proces ende Sententie teghens Joan Avontroot Die gekomen is in Spangien in't Hof an Madrid, Amsterdam: Gersit Jansz Arenteyn.

AVONTROOT, JOHANNES (trans.) (1963), El Catecismo de Heidelberg: enseñanza de la doctrina christiana redactado por Zacarías Ursino y Gaspar Oleviano, y publicado en 1563 [1628], Madrid: Librería Nacional y Extranjera, 1885; Rijswijk: Fundación Editorial de Literatura Reformada, 1963.

AZPILCUETA, MARTIN DE (2011), La Inquisición de Felipe II en el proceso contra el Arzobispo Carranza, Anuario Jurídico y Económico Escurialense 44, 491–518.

BALTANÁS, DOMINGO DE (1555), Doctrina christiana: en que se tracta de seys cosas, Seville: Martin de Montesdeoca.

BANKING during the Reign of Charles V and The Doctrine of The School of Salamanca. antique-banks.blogspot.com.es/2012/06/banking-during-reign-of-charles-v-and.html. Accessed November 6, 2014.

BARBIER, ANTOINE-ALEXANDRE (1823), Dictionnaire des ouvrages anonyme et pseudonymes composés, traduits ou publiés en français et en latin, avec les noms des auteurs, accompagné de notes historiques et critiques, 2 vols., Paris: Barrois l'aîné.

BATAILLON, MARCEL (1937), Erasme et l'Espagne, Paris: E. Droz.

BATAILLON, MARCEL (1950, 1966), Erasmo y España: estudios sobre la historia espiritual del siglo XVI, Mexico: Fondo de Cultura Económica.

BEECHER, DONALD (2006a), John Frampton of Bristol, Trader and Translator, in: Travel and Translation in the Early Modern Period, Carmine Di Biase (ed.), Amsterdam: Rodopi, 103–122.

BEECHER, DONALD (2006b), The Legacy of John Frampton: Elizabethan Trader and Translator, Renaissance Studies 20.3, 320–339.

BELL, GARY M. (1976), John Man: The Last Elizabethan Resident Ambassador in Spain, Sixteenth Century Journal 7.2, 75–93.

BELL, JAMES (1854), The Mystery Unveiled, or Popery as its Dogmas and Pretensions Appear in the Light of Reason, the Bible, and History, Edinburgh: Paton and Ritchie.

BELLSOLELL, JOAN (2010), Miguel Mai y Antonio Sebastiano Minturno en la corte de Carlos V, Studia Aurea 4, 139–162.

BELTRAN DE HEREDIA, VICENTE (1957), Nota crítica acerca de Domingo de Baltanás y de su proceso, Ciencia Tomista 84, 649–659.

BELTRAN DE HEREDIA, VICENTE (1971–73), Miscelánea Beltrán de Heredia: colección de artículos sobre historia de la teología española, 4 vols., Salamanca: Editorial OPE.

BENITO RUANO, ELOY (2003), Literatura denigrante y apologética sobre Felipe II, in: La monarquía de Felipe II, F. Ruiz Martin (ed.), Madrid: Real Academia de la Historia, 439–454.

BERGUA CAVERO, JORGE (2006), Francisco de Enzinas: un humanista reformado en la Europa de Carlos V, Madrid: Trotta.

BERNALDEZ, ANDRES (1515), Cronica de los reyes catolicos, ms.

BERTOMÉU FERNÁNDEZ, JUAN ANTONIO (2014), Privilegios y Querellas en la Sevilla Barroca, Seville: Editorial Cultiva.

BETTS, JOHN T. (1869), Constantino Ponce de la Fuente, The Confession of a Sinner, with a biographical sketch by Benjamin B. Wiffen, London: Bell & Daldy.

BETTS, JOHN T./MARY BETTS (1882), Juan de Valdés' Minor Works: Commentary upon Our Lord's Sermon on the Mount; Commentary upon the Gospel of St. Matthew; Spiritual Milk, or Christian Instruction for Children; XVII Opuscules, London: Trubner & Co.

BIBLE in Spanish (1569), rarebiblesatmobia.org/curators-choice-2/bible-portrait-gallery/bible-in-spanish-1569. Accessed January 8, 2015.

BIRCH, WALTER DE GRAY (1903), Catalogue of a Collection of Original Manuscripts Formerly Belonging to the Holy Office of the Inquisition in the Canary Islands: And Now in the Possession of the Marquess of Bute, Edinburgh: William Blackwood and Sons.

BLAQUIERE, EDWARD (1822), An Historical Review of the Spanish Revolution, Including Some Account of Religion, Manners, and Literature, in Spain, London: G. & W.B. Whittaker.

BLEIBERG, GERMÁN/MAUREEN IHRIE (1993), Censorship in Spanish Literature, in: Dictionary of the Literature of the Iberian Peninsula, Westport, CT: Greenwood Press.

BLOCKMANS, WIM PIETER (2002), Emperor Charles V, 1500–1558, Isola van den Hoven-Vardon (trans.), New York: Oxford University Press.

BOEGLIN, MICHEL (2006a), Contribution à l'étude des protestants de Séville (1557–1565): sociabilités et sensibilité religieuses, Hispanic Bulletin 108.2, 343–376.

BOEGLIN, MICHEL (2006b), Luteranos franceses en la España de los Austrias. Aspectos culturales de un conflicto religioso, in: Actas del I Congreso Hispanofrancés, La cultura del otro, Español en Francia, Francés en España, Manuel Bruña Cuevas, et al (eds.), Seville: Universidad de Sevilla, 118–132.

BOEGLIN, MICHEL (2007a), J.A. Llorente: España y la Inquisición: Memoria histórica acerca del tribunal de la Inquisición, seguida de Carta al Señor Clausel de Coussergues sobre la Inquisición española, Seville: Renacimiento.

BOEGLIN, MICHEL (2007b), Valer, Camacho y los 'cautivos de la Inquisición.' Sevilla 1540–1541, Cuadernos de Historia Moderna 32, 113–134.

BOEGLIN, MICHEL (2010), Entre la cruz y el Corán: los moriscos en Sevilla (1570–1613), Seville: Ayuntamiento de Sevilla.

BOEHMER, EDUARD (2007), Bibliotheca Wiffeniana: Spanish Reformers of two centuries from 1520. Their lives and writings according to the late Benjamin B. Wiffen's plan and with the use of his materials, 3 vols., [Straßburg/London, 1874–1904]; Pamplona: Analecta Editorial.

BORROW, GEORGE (1842), The Bible in Spain: Or, the Journeys, Adventures and Imprisonemnts of an Englishman in an Attempt to Circulate the Scriptures in the Peninsula, London: Ward, Lock and Co.

BRADY, THOMAS A. (trans.) (1990), From the Reformation to the Thirty Years War, 1500–1648. The Abdication of Emperor Charles V (1555/56), in: German History in Documents and Images (GHDI). Vol. I, Alfred Kohler (ed.), Quellen zur Geschichte Karls V, Darmstadt: WBG/Washington, DC: German Historical Institute. germanhistorydocs. ghi-dc.org/pdf/eng/Doc.68-ENG-Abdication1556_en.pdf. Accessed October 18, 2014.

BRATLI, CARL (1927), Felipe II, rey de España: estudio sobre su vida y su carácter, Ángel Custodio Vega (trans.), Madrid: B. del Amo.

BRAUDEL, FERNAND (1995), The Mediterranean and the Mediterranean World in the Age of Philip II, 2 vols., Berkeley, CA: University of California Press.

BREKKA, PAMELA MERRILL (2012), The Antwerp Polyglot Bible (1572): Visual Corpus, New World 'Hebrew-Indian' Map, and the Religious Crosscurrents of Imperial Spain, PhD diss., University or Florida.

BUJANDA, J.M. DE (1988), Index d'Anvers, 1569, 1570, 1571, Sherbrooke, Quebec/Geneve: Droz.

BUJANDA, J.M. DE (2002), Index Librorum Prohibitorum. 1600–1966, Montreal/Geneve: Droz.

BÜSCHING, ANTON FRIEDRICH (1755), Commentatio de vestigiis Lvtheranismi in Hispania, Goettingae: Hager.

BUSTAMANTE GARCÍA, AGUSTÍN (1995), El Santo Oficio de Valladolid y los artistas, Boletín del Seminario de Estudios de Arte y Arqueología 61, 455–466.

BUSTOS TÁULER, ALVARO (2010), Ambrosio Montesino y el 'Exercicio de la continua predicación': poesía, mecenazgo y sermón en su Cancionero (Toledo, 1508), Revista de poética medieval 24, 93–126.

CALENDAR of State Papers (1864), Venice, Rawdon Brown (ed.), London: Her Majesty's Stationery Office, Vol. 1, 1202–1509. http://www.british-history.ac.uk/cal-state-papers/venice/vol1/v–cviii. Accessed August 7, 2014.

CALENDAR of State Papers (1866), Elizabeth, 1561–1562, Joseph Stevenson (ed.), London: Her Majesty's Stationery Office, Vol. 4, 515–524. http://www.british-history.ac.uk/cal-state-papers/foreign/vol4/pp515–524. Accessed August 9, 2014.

CALENDAR of State Papers (1890), Venice, 1558–1580, Rawdon Brown/G. Cavendish Bentinck (eds.), London: Her Majesty's Stationery Office, Vol. 7. www.british-history.ac.uk/source.aspx?pubid=999&page=1. Accessed August 28, 2014.

CALENDAR of State Papers, (1894), Spain (Simancas) 1568–1579, Martin A.S. Hume (ed.), London: Her Majesty's Stationery Office, Vol 2, 46–63, http://www.british-history.ac.uk/cal-state-papers/simancas/vol2/pp46–63. Accessed May 29, 2015,

CALVETE DE ESTRELLA, JUAN CRISTOVAL (1552), El felicissimo viaje del muy alto y muy poderoso principe Don Phelippe, hijo del emperador Don Carlos Quinto maximo, desde España á sus tierras de la baxa Alemaña, con la descripcion de todos los estados de Brabante y Flandes, Antwerp: M. Nucio.

CALVIN, JEAN (1597), Institución de la Religion Christiana: compuesta en quatro libros, y dividida en captiulos. Y ahora nuevamente traduzida en Romance Castellano, por Cypriano de Valera, London: Ricardo del Campo.

CANCIONERO de Obras de Burlas Probocantes a Risa (1841), Luis Usoz y Rio (ed.), London: William Pickering.

CANCIONERO GENERAL (1511), Valencia: Cristófal Koffman.

CAPONETTO, SALVATORE (1972), Benedetto da Mantova: Il beneficio di Cristo, Florence: Sansoni.

CAPONETTO, SALVATORE (1999), The Protestant Reformation in Sixteenth-Century Italy, Kirksville, MO: Thomas Jefferson University Press.

CÁRCELES de la Inquisición, in: Historia de Sevilla en el Siglo XVI, Universidad de Sevilla. personal.us.es/alporu/histsevilla/inquisicion_carceles.htm. Accessed October 23, 2014.

CARRANZA, BARTOLOME (1972), Comentarios sobre el catecismo de Doctrina Cristiana, diuididos en quatro partes, [1558], J.I. Tellechea Idigoras (ed.), 2 vols., Madrid: Biblioteca de Autores Cristianos.

CARRERA, ELENA (2005), Teresa of Avila's Autobiography: Authority, Power and the Self in Mid-sixteenth-century Spain, London: Modern Humanities Research Association and Maney Publishing.

CARTAGENA, ALONSO DE (1487), Oracional de Fernán Pérez, Contemplación sobre el Salmo 'Juzgadme, Dios', Murcia: Lope de la Roca y Gabriel Luis de Arinyo.

CASTRILLO BENITO, NICOLÁS (1991), El 'Reginaldo Montano', primer libro polemico contra la Inquisición española, Madrid: CSIC.

CASTRO SÁNCHEZ, ALVARO (2012), Las noches oscuras de María de Cazalla. Poder, fe y deseo en la modernidad española, Anuario de Historia de la Iglesia 21, 588–589.

CASTRO, ADOLFO DE (1851), The Spanish Protestants and their Persecution by Philip II, a Historical Work, Thomas Parker (trans.), London: Charles Gilpin.

CASTRO, ADOLFO DE (1853), History of Religious Intolerance in Spain: or, an Examination of Some of the Causes which Led to that Nation's Decline, London: William and Frederick G. Cash.

CERVANTES, MIGUEL DE (1885), The Ingenious Gentleman Don Quixote of La Mancha, John Ormsby (trans.), New York: Thomas Y. Crowell & Co.

CHAREYRE, PHILIPPE (1998), L'édit de Nantes et les Protestants. Entre commémoration et Histoire, Bulletin de la Société des Amis du Château de Pau 136, 17–28.

CHARLES, ELIZABETH R. (1862), The Martyrs of Spain and the Liberators of Holland: the story of the sisters Dolores and Costanza Cazalla, London: J. Nisbet.

CHARLES, ELIZABETH R. (1871), Los mártires de España. Una historia verdadera, Madrid: A. Duran.

CHRISTMAN, MIRIAM (1967), Strasbourg and the Reform: A Study in the Process of Change, Cambridge: Yale University Press.

CIORANESCU, ALEJANDRO (1974), Un visionario en la hoguera. La vida y las obras de Juan Bartolomé Avontroot, Anuario de estudios atlánticos 20, 543–610.

CIVALE, GIAN CLAUDIO (2007), Domingo de Baltanás, monje solicitante en la encruciada religiosa, Hispania Sacra 119, 197–241.

CONCHA, VICTOR G. DE LA (ed.) (1981), Fray Luis de León, Salamanca: Universidad de Salamanca.

CONTRERAS, JAIME (1987), The impact of Protestantism in Spain 1520–1600, in: Inquisition and Society in early modern Europe, Stephen Haliczer (ed.), London: Croom Helm, 47–63.

CONTRERAS, JAIME/GUSTAV HENNINGSEN (1986), Forty-four Thousand Cases of the Spanish Inquisition (1540–1700): Analysis of a Historical Data Bank, in: The Inquisition in Early Modern Europe: Studies on Sources and Methods, Gustav Henningsen/John Tedeschi/Charles Amiel (eds.), Dekalb, IL: Northern Illinois University Press, 100–129.

CONTRERAS, JAIME/MARIA ANGLES CRISTÓBAL MARTÍN (1994), Logroño y el Santo Oficio del Reino de Navarra: centro de control social, centro de poder, in: Historia de la ciudad de Logroño, José Luis Gómez Urdáñez (ed.), Logroño: Ayuntamiento de Logroño, Vol. III, 71–91.

CONWAY, G.R.G. (1927), An Englishman and the Mexican Inquisition, 1556–1560; being an account of the voyage of Robert Tomson to New Spain, his trial for heresy in the city of Mexico and other contemporary historical documents, Mexico City: G.R.G. Conway.

COOLIDGE, GRACE E. (2010), Guardianship, Gender, and the Nobility in Early Modern Spain, Aldershot: Ashgate.

COROLEU, ALEJANDRO (2004), Humanismo en España: de Nebrija al erasmismo, Insula: revista de letras y ciencias humanas 691/692, 2–3.

COROLEU, ALEJANDRO (2008), Anti-Erasmianism in Spain, in: Biblical Humanism and Scholasticism in the Age of Erasmus, Erika Rummel (ed.), Leiden: Brill, 73–92.

COROLEU, ALEJANDRO/ BARRY TAYLOR (eds.) (2010), Humanism and Christian Letters in Early Modern Iberia (1480–1630), Newcastle: Cambridge Scholars.

CORTIJO OCAÑA, ANTONIO (2003), Vida de la madre Catalina de Cardona por fray Juan de la Miseria. Un texto hagiográfico desconocido del siglo XVI, Dicenda. Cuadernos de Filología Hispánica 21, 21–34.

COUNCIL OF TRENT (1848), The canons and decrees of the sacred and ecumenical Council of Trent. The Twenty-Fifth Session. Chapter V, J. Waterworth (ed./trans.), London: Dolman, 232–289.

COUSTOS, JOHN (1746), The Sufferings of John Coustos For Free-Masonry, and for His Refusing to Turn Roman Catholic, in the Inquisition at Lisbon; Where He Was Sentenc'd, During Four Years to the Galley; and Afterwards Releas'd, London: W. Strahan.

COX, NOEL (2010), History of Medieval Education, Middle Ages European Learning, in: Academical Dress in New Zealand. A study. www.academicapparel.com/caps/History-College-Education.html. Accessed November 6, 2014.

CRESPIN, JEAN (1608), Histoire des martyrs [1570], Geneva: héritiers d'Eustache Vignon.

CRISTLER, CLARENCE C./HARRY H. HALL (eds.) (2004), The Missing Chapter from 'The Great Controversy'. Brushton, NY: Teach Services, Inc.

CRUMMÉ, HANNAH LEAH (2011), The Impact of Lord Burghley and the Earl of Leicester's Spanish-Speaking Secretariats, Sederi 21, 7–27.

CURIONE, CELIO SEGONDO (1865), Letter to the Christian Readers, in: Life and writings of Juan de Valdés, Spanish Reformer in the sixteenth century, B.B. Wiffen (ed.), London: Bernard Quaritch.

DAVID, AVRAHAM (ed.) (2006), A Hebrew Chronicle from Prague, C. 1615, Leon J. Weinberger/Dena Ordan (trans.), Tuscaloosa, AL: University of Alabama Press.

DAVIS, ROBERT C. (2004), *Christian Slaves, Muslim Masters:* White Slavery in the Mediterranean, the Barbary Coast and Italy, 1500–1800, New York: Palgrave Macmillan.

DÁVILA PÉREZ, ANTONIO (ed.) (2002), Correspondencia conservada en el Museo Plantin-Moretus de Amberes, Alcañiz: Instituto de Estudios Humanísticos.

DE ESPONA, JOSE RAFAEL (2005), El Cardenal Silíceo, príncipe español de la contrareforma, Anales de la Fundación Francisco Elías de Tejada 11, 41–61.

DE LA PINTA LLORENTE, MIGUEL (1970), Aspectos de la Inquisición española bajo la administración del Arzobispo don Fernando de Valdes-Salas, Actas del Simposio 'Valdés-Salas': conmemorativo del IV° Centenario de la muerte de su fundador D. Fernando de Valdés (1483–1568): Su personalidad. Su obra. Su tiempo, Oviedo: Universidad de Oviedo, 129–146.

DEFOURNEAUX, MARCELIN (1973), Inquisición y censura de los libros en la España del siglo XVIII, Madrid: Taurus.

DENIS, PHILIPPE (1977), Pierre Alexandre et la discipline ecclesiastique, Bibliothèque d'Humanisme et Renaissance 39.3, 551–560.

DENIS, PHILIPPE (1984), Jacques de Bourgogne, seigneur de Falais, in: Bibliotheca Dissidentium. Répertoire des non-conformistes religieux des 16 et 17 siecles, André Séguenny (ed.), Baden-Baden: V. Koerner, Vol. IV, 9–52.

DEVOUT THIEF (1997), in: Miracles of our Lady, Richard Terry Mount/Annette Grant Cash (trans.), Lexington, KY: University Press of Kentucky.

DICKENS, ARTHUR GEOFFREY (1964), The English Reformation, New York: Schocken Books.

DICKENS, ARTHUR GEOFFREY (1969), The Counter Reformation, New York: Harcourt, Brace & World.

DIXON, RICHARD WATSON (2013), History of the Church of England: From the Abolition of the Roman Jurisdiction [1881], London: Forgotten Books.

DOMINGUEZ ORTIZ, ANTONIO (1971), Los Judeoconversos en Espana y America, Madrid: ISTMOS.

DUFOUR, GERALD, Juan Antonio Llorente, de servidor a crítico de la Inquisición. http://www.vallenajerilla.com/berceo/florilegio/inquisicion/servidorycritico.htm. Accessed May 28, 2015.

DUGDALE, RICHARD (1680), A Narrative of Unheard of Popish Cruelties Towards Protestants Beyond Seas: or, A New Account of the Bloody Spanish Inquisition, London: John Hancock.

DURÁN, AGUSTÍN (1849–1851), Romancero general, 2 vols., Madrid: M. Rivadeneyra.

EAMON, WILLIAM (1996), Science and the Secrets of Nature: Books of Secrets in Medieval and Early Modern Culture, Princeton, N.J.: Princeton University Press.

ELLIOTT, DYLAN (2002), Seeing Double: John Gerson, the Discernment of Spirits, and Joan of Arc, American Historical Review 107.1, 26–54.

ENCINA, FRANCISCO ANTONIO (1954), Historia de Chile desde la prehistoria hasta 1891, 4 vols., Santiago de Chile: Editorial Nascimento.

ENZINAS, FRANCISCO DE (1992), Memorias, Francisco Socas (trans.), Madrid: Clásicas.

ENZINAS, FRANCISCO DE (1995), Epistolario, Ignacio J. García Pinilla (ed./trans.), Geneva: Droz.

EPISTOLAS Y EVANGELIOS por todo el año (1512), con sus doctrinas y sermones segun la reformacion & interpretacion que desta obra hižo fray Ambrosio Montesino, Toledo.

ERASMUS (1524), Enquiridio o manual del cauallero Christiano, Alcala: Miguel de Eguia.

ERASMUS (2005), Coloquios familiars: edición de Alonso Ruiz de Virues (siglo XVI), Andrea Herrán/Modesto Santos (eds.), Barcelona: Anthropos.

ESPINOSA, AURELIO (2009), The Empire of the Cities: Emperor Charles V, the Comunero Revolt, and the Transformation of the Spanish System, Leiden: Brill.

ESTABLIER PEREZ, HELENA (2008), Las 'Luces' de Sara Th***. Maria Antonio de Rio Arnedo y su traducción dieciochesca del Marques de Saint-Lambert, Anales de Literatura Española 20.

ESTEVA DE LLOBET, MARIA DOLORS (1996), Las cárceles interiores de Maria de Cazalla. Analisis de un proceso inquisitorial, Lectora 2, 94–111.

ESTRADA, DAVID (2008a), Introduction to Exposición del Primer Psalmo dividida en seis sermones by Constantino Ponce de la Fuente, Seville: Editorial MAD, 7–133.

ESTRADA, DAVID (2008b), Introduction to Diálogo de Doctrina Cristiana by Juan de Valdes, Seville: Editorial MAD, 7–82.

ESTRADA, DAVID (2012), La Biblia en la litertura castellana de la Edad Media, in: Huellas del Cristianismo en el Arte. La literature, Ricardo Moraleja Ortega/Manuel Garcia Lafuente (eds.), Madrid: Consejo Evangélico de Madrid, 97–157.

EVENDEN, ELIZABETH (2002), Patents and Patronage: The Life and Career of John Day, Tudor Printer, PhD diss., University of York. etheses.whiterose.ac.uk/2455/1/DX223036.pdf. Accessed July 10, 2013.

EYMERIC, NICOLÁS (1821), Manual de Inquisidores, para uso de las Inquisiciones de España y Portugal, Montpellier: Feliz Aviñon.

FAGEL, RAYMOND (2002), Los mercaderes españoles en Flandes y la Corte: poder económico y poder político en dos redes de intermediarios, in: Actas. Congreso Internacional Espacios de poder: Cortes, ciudades y villas (s.XVI–XVIII), Jesús Bravo Lozano (ed.), Madrid: Universidad Autónoma, Vol. I, 159–169.

FAJARDO SPÍNOLA, FRANCISCO (1998), Los Protestantes Extranjeros y la Inquisición Canaria durante el reinado de Felipe II, Revista de Historia Canaria 180, 99–124.

FANTAZZI, CHARLES (2008), A Companion to Juan Luis Vives, Leiden/Boston: Brill.

FÉRÉAL, M.V. DE (1845a), Mystères de l'inquisition et autres sociétés secrètes d'Espagne, Paris: Boizard.

FÉRÉAL, M.V. DE (1845b), The Mysteries of the Inquistion and Other Secret Societies of Spain, Philadelphia: Lippincott/London: G. Peirce.

FERNANDEZ ALVAREZ, MANUEL (1920). Lutero y el luteranismo estudiados en las fuentes versión española, Manila: Tip. Pontificia del Col. de Sto. Tomás.

FERNÁNDEZ ÁLVAREZ, MANUEL (ed.) (1979), Corpus documental de Carlos V, 5 vols., Salamanca: CSIC, Vol. IV (1554–1558).

FERNANDEZ CHAVES, MANUEL F./RAFAEL PEREZ GARCIA (2011), En los márgenes de la ciudad de Dios: Moriscos en Sevilla, Valencia: Univeridad de Valencia.

FERNÁNDEZ MARTÍN, LUIS (1993), Francisco Mudarra difamador y protegido de San Ignacio, Rome: Archivum Ilistoricum Societatis Iesu.

FERNANDEZ, ALFONSO (2008), Historia y anales de la ciudad y obispado de Plasencia [1627], A Coruña: Orbigo.

FIRPO, MASSIMO (1996), The Italian Reformation and Juan de Valdes, Sixteenth Century Journal 27.2, 353–364.

FIRPO, MASSIMO (2007), Reform of the Church and Heresy in the Age of Charles V: Reflections of Spain in Italy, in: Spain in Italy: Politics, Society, and Religion 1500-1700, Thomas James Dandelet/John A. Marino (eds.), Leiden: Brill, 457–480.

FITTLER, JAMES/WILLIAM SKELTON (eds.) (1820–1849), Strype's Works, 5 vols., Oxford: Clarendon Press.

FOXE, JOHN (1563), Acts and Monuments, www.hrionline.ac.uk/johnfoxe

FRAKER Jr., CHARLES F. (1965), The 'Dejados' and the Cancionero de Baena, Hispanic Review 33.2, 97–117.

FRAKER Jr., CHARLES F. (1966), Studies on the Cancionero de Baena, Chapel Hill, NC: University of North Carolina Press.

FULGOSIO, FERNANDO (2002), Crónica de la provincia de Valladolid, Valladolid: Maxtor.

GARCÍA GUERRA, ELENA MARÍA/GIUSEPE DE LUCA (2010), Il mercato del credito in età moderna. Reti e operatori finanziari nello spazio europeo, Milan: Franco Angeli.

GARCÍA HERNÁN, ENRIQUE (2002), Escritores políticos palentinos del Siglo de Oro, PITTM 73, 245–273.

GARCÍA HERNÁN, ENRIQUE (2010), El ambiente alumbrado y sus consecuencias en la Compañía de Jesús según Jerónimo Nadal, Jerónimo Zurita 85, 193–205.

GARCÍA ORO, JOSÉ (1992), La Iglesia de Toledo en tiempo del Cardenal Cisneros: 1495–1517, Toledo: Estudio Teológico de San Ildefonso.

GARCÍA PINILLA, IGNACIO J. (2012), Lectores y lectura clandestina en el grupo protestante sevillano del siglo XVI, in: Lectura y culpa en el siglo XVI, María José Vega Ramos/Iveta Nakládalová (eds.), Barcelona: Universidad Autónoma de Barcelona, 45–62.

GARCÍA PINILLA, IGNACIO J. (ed./trans.) (1995), Francisco de Enzinas, Epistolario, Geneva: Droz.

GARRAÍN VILLA, LUÍS JOSÉ (1988), Pedro de Cieza de León en Llerena, Trujillo: Asociación Cultural Coloquios Históricos de Extremadura. www.chdetrujillo.com/pedro-de-cieza-de-leon-en-llerena/ Accessed June 23, 2014.

GARRIDO, FERNANDO (1863), Historia de las persecuciones políticas y religiosas occuridas en Europa desde la Edad Media hasta nuestros días, Barcelona: Salvador Manero.

GEDDES, MICHAEL (1741), The Spanish Protestant Martyrology, London: J. Churchill.

GENEALOGÍA CHILENA. http://www.genealogiachilenaenred.cl/gcr/IndividualPage.aspx?Id=I15128. Accessed January 4, 2015.

GEORGE, CALVIN (2004), The History of the Reina-Valera 1960 Spanish Bible, Kearney, Neb.: Morris Publishing.

GERDE, DANIEL (1747), Florilegium Historico-Criticum Librorum Rariorum: Cui Multa simul scitu iucunda adsperguntur, Groningen: Spandaw & Rump.

GILBERT, WILLIAM (1998), Spain from Ferdinand and Isabella to Philip, in: The Renaissance and The Reformation, Chapter 18, http://vlib.iue.it/carrie/texts/carrie_books/gilbert/18.htmlvlib.iue.it/carrie/texts/carrie_books/gilbert/18.html. Accesssed March 14, 2014.

GILLY, CARLOS (1982), Juan de Valdés, traductor y adaptador de escritos de Lutero, in: Miscelanea de Estudios Hispánicos. Homenaje de los hispanistas de Suiza a Ramón Sugranyes de Franch, L. López Molina (ed.), Montserrat: Abadia de Montserrat, 85–106.

GIMÉNEZ CRUZ, ANTONIO (1990), George Borrow and the Spanish Press, in: Proceedings of the 1989 George Borrow Conference, Gillian Fenwick (ed.), Toronto: The George Borrow Society, 19–31.

GÓMEZ DE CIUDAD REAL, ÁLVAR (2003), La Orden de Caballeros del Príncipe de Borgoña, Romero Valiente, Jesús (ed.), Madrid: CSIC.

GÓMEZ-MENOR FUENTES, JOSÉ-CARLOS, Los Loaysas de Talavera de La Reina, Señores de Huerta de Valdecarabanos. www.realacademiatoledo.es/files/anales/0027/06.pdf. Accessed December 20, 2014.

GÓNGORA, DIEGO IGNACIO DE (1890), Historia del Colegio Mayor de Santo Tomás de Sevilla, Seville: E. Rasco.

GONZÁLEZ NOVALÍN, JOSÉ LUIS (1971), El Inquisidor General Fernando de Valdés (1483–1568). Su vida y su obra, 2 vols., Oviedo: Universidad de Oviedo.

GONZALO SÁNCHEZ-MOLERO, JOSÉ LUIS (2003), El erasmismo y la educación de Felipe II (1527–1557), Madrid: Universidad Complutense.

GONZALO SÁNCHEZ-MOLERO, JOSÉ LUIS (2014), V Centenario de la Biblia Políglota Complutense. La Universidad del Renacimiento. El Renacimiento de la Universidad/ The Fifth Centennial of the Complutensian Polyglot Bible. The University of the Renaissance. The Rebirth of the University, Madrid: Universidad Complutense.

GOOD, JAMES I. (1914), The Heidelberg Catechism In Its Newest Light, Philadelphia: Publication and Sunday School Board of The Reformed Church in The United States.

GRAÑA CID, MARÍA DEL MAR (1992), Religiosos in via. Franciscanos y caminos en Castilla La Nueva (1215–1550), Actas del I Congreso Internacional de Caminería Hispánica, Guadalajara: Aache Ediciones, Vol. II, 127–148.

GRELL, OLE PETER (2011), Brethren in Christ: A Calvinist Network in Reformation Europe, Cambridge: Cambridge University Press.

GUIBOVICH PÉREZ, PEDRO M. (2003), Censura, libros e inquisición en el Perú colonial, 1570–1754, Seville: CSIC.

HAKLUYT, RICHARD (1584), Discourse of Western Planting, www.gutenberg.org/files/25645/25645-0.txt. Accessed November 26, 2014.

HAKLUYT, RICHARD (1907), The Principal Navigations [1589], New York: E. P. Dutton & Co.

HALICZER, STEPHEN (1995), Sexuality in the Confessional: A Sacrament Profaned, Oxford: Oxford University Press.

HAMILTON, ALASTAIR (1977), A Recent Study in Spanish Mysticism, The Heythrop Journal 18.2, 191–199.

HAMILTON, ALASTAIR (1992), Heresy and Mysticism in Sixteenth-Century Spain. The Alumbrados. Cambridge: James Clarke.

HAMILTON, ALASTAIR (2010), The Alumbrados: Dejamiento and its Practitioners, in: A New Companion to Hispanic Mysticism, Hilaire Kallendorf (ed.), Leiden/Boston: Brill, 103–124.

HARDY, PHILIP DIXON (1850), The Inquisition: Its History, Influences, and Effects, from Its First Establishment to the Present Time: Including Its Recent Proceedings Relative to Dr. Achilli, Dublin: Philip Dixon Hardy and Sons.

HARGREAVES, MARY W.M./JAMES F. HOPKINS (eds.) (1983), The Papers of Henry Clay. Volume 6, Secretary of State, 1827. Lexington: University Press of Kentucky.

HARLINE, CRAIG E. (1987), Pamphlets, Printing and Political Culture in the Early Dutch Republic, Dordrecht: Martinus Nijhoff.

HAUBEN, PAUL J. (1967), Three Spanish Heretics and the Reformation: Antonio del Corro, Cassiodoro de Reina, Cypriano de Valera, Geneva: Droz.

HEGARTY, ANDREW (2005), Carranza and the English Universities, in: Reforming Catholicism in the England of Mary Tudor: the Achievement of Friar Bartolomé Carranza, John Edwards/Ronald W. Truman (eds.), Aldershot: Ashgate, 153–172.

HENNINGSEN, GUSTAV/JOHN A. TEDESCHI/CHARLES AMIEL (1986), The Inquisition in Early Modern Europe. Studies on Sources and Methods, Dekalb: Northern Illinois University Press.

HERNÁNDEZ MILLARES, JORGE (1935), Índice de los papeles de la Inquisición de Canarias del Archivo Histórico Nacional, El Museo Canario 7, 54–66.

HERNANDO DE TALAVERA (1496), Breve e muy provechosa doctrina christiana en romance para enseñar niños a leer, Granada: Meinardus Ungut and Johann Pegnitzer.

HOMZA, LU ANN (1997), Erasmus as Hero, or Heretic? Spanish Humanism and the Valladolid Assembly of 1527, Renaissance Quarterly 50.1, 78–118.

HOMZA, LU ANN (2006), The Spanish Inquisition, 1478–1614: An Anthology of Sources, Indianapolis: Hackett.

HUERGA TERUELO, ALVARO (1958), El proceso de la Inquisición de Sevilla contra el maestro Domingo de Valtanás: 1561–1563, Boletín del Instituto de Estudios Giennenses 17, 93–142.

HUERGA TERUELO, ALVARO (1978–1994), Historia de los alumbrados, 5 vols., Madrid: FUE.

HUERGA TERUELO, ÁLVARO (1984), ¿Luteranismo, erasmismo o alumbradismo sevillano?, Revista Española de Teología 44.2, 465–514.

HUME, MARTIN A.S. (1906), The Great Lord Burghley, London: James Nisbet.

IBÁÑEZ RODRÍGUEZ, SANTIAGO (1998), La diócesis de Calahorra a mediados del siglo XVI según el libro: Libro de visita del Licenciado Martín Gil, Brocar 21, 135–183.

IGLESIA, JESÚS DE LA (2011), La Inquisición de Felipe II en el proceso contra el arzobispo Carranza, Anuario Jurídico y Económico Escurialense 44, 491–518.

ILLESCAS, GONZALO DE (1568), Historia pontifical, y catholica, en la qual se contienen las vidas y hechos notables de todos los Summos Pontifices Romanos, Salamanca: Domingo de Portonarijs.

INDICE ULTIMO (1790) de los Libros Prohibidos y mandados expurgar para todos los reynos y señoríos del católico rey de las Españas, don Carlos IV. Contiene en resumen todos los libros puestos en el Indice Expurgatorio del ano 1747, y en los Edictos posteriores, hasta fin de Diciembre de 1789, Agustin Rubin de Cevallos (ed.), Madrid: Antonio de Sancha.

INSTITUT ARCHÉOLOGIQUE du Luxembourg (1906), Annales, Arlon: F. Bruck.

JAURALDE POU, PABLO/JUAN ALFREDO BELLÓN CAZABÁN (eds.) (1974), Cancionero de obras de burlas provocantes a risa, Madrid: Akal.

JIMÉNEZ MONTESERÍN, MIGUEL (1995), Introduction to Conquenses Ilustres by Fermín Caballero [1875], Cuenca: Ayuntamiento de Cuenca.

JOHNSON, ALFRED FORBES (1971), Books Printed at Heidelberg for Thomas Cartwright, in: Selected Essays on Books and Printing, Percy H. Muir (ed.), Amsterdam/ New York: Van Gendt/Abner Schram, 253–268.

JOHNSON, CARROLL B. (1982), Organic Unity in Unlikely Places: Don Quijote I, 39–41, Bulletin of the Cervantes Society of America 2.2, 133–154.

JONES, JOHN A. (1978), Pedro de Valencia's Defence of Arias Montano: The Expurgatory Indexes of 1607 (Rome) and 1612 (Madrid), Bibliothèque d'Humanisme et Renaissance 40.1, 121–136.

KAGAN, RICHARD L. (1991), Political, Prophecy, and the Inquisition in Late Sixteenth-Century Spain, in: Cultural Encounters: The Impact of the Inquisition in Spain and the New World, Mary Elizabeth Perry/Anne J. Cruz (eds.), Berkeley: University of California Press, 105–120.

KAGAN, RICHARD L. (2010), Clio and the Crown: The Politics of History in Medieval and Early Modern Spain, Baltimore: Johns Hopkins University.

KALLENDORF, HILAIRE (ed.) (2010), A New Companion to Hispanic Mysticism, Leiden/ Boston: Brill.

KAMEN, HENRY (1985), Inquisition and Society in Spain in the Sixteenth and Seventeenth Century, Bloomington: Indiana University Press.

KAMEN, HENRY (1988), Toleration and Dissent in Sixteenth-Century Spain: The Alternative Tradition, The Sixteenth Century Journal 19.1, 3–23.

KAMEN, HENRY (2011), La Inquisición Española. Una revisión histórica, 3rd ed., Barcelona: Crítica.

KAMEN, HENRY (2014), The Spanish Inquisition: A Historical Revision, 4th ed., New Haven: Yale University Press.

KERR, ROBERT (1824), A General History and Collection of Voyages and Travels, 18 vols., London: William Blackwood.

KESS, ALEXANDRA (2008), Johann Sleidan and the Protestant Vision of History, Aldershot: Ashgate.

KETTELL, SAMUEL (ed.) (1828), Records of the Spanish Inquisition, Translated from the Original Manuscripts, Boston: S. Goodrich.

KINDER, ARTHUR GORDON (1975), Casiodoro de Reina: Spanish Reformer of the Sixteenth Century, London: Tamesis Books.

KINDER, ARTHUR GORDON (1976), Juan Pérez de Pineda (Pierius): a Spanish Calvinist Minister of the Gospel in Sixteenth-Century Geneva, Bulletin of Hispanic Studies 53.4, 283–300.

KINDER, ARTHUR GORDON (1985), A Hitherto Unknown Group of Protestants in Sixteenth-Century Aragon, Cuadernos de Historia Jerónimo Zurita 51/52, 131–160.

KINDER, ARTHUR GORDON (1990), Un documento interesante sobre la persecución de herejes españoles en Flandes: los gastos del contador Alonso del Canto entre 1561 y 1564, Diálogo Ecuménico 25, 67–86.

KIRSCH, JOHANN PETER (1908), Article "Bartolomé Carranza", The Catholic Encyclopedia, New York: Robert Appleton Co., http://www.newadvent.org/cathen/03376a.htm. Accessed November 20, 2014.

KNAPP, WILLIAM I. (1899), Life, Writings and Correspondence of George Borrow, 2 vols., New York: G.P. Putnam's Sons/London: John Murray.

KOHLER, ALFRED (ed.) (1990), Quellen zur Geschichte Karls V. Darmstadt: WBG.

KOLB, ROBERT (2005), From Hymn to History of Dogma. Lutheran Martyrology in the Reformation era, in: More Than a Memory: The Discourse of Martyrdom and the Construction of Christian Identity in the History of Christianity, Johan Leemans (ed.), Leuven: Peeters, 301–313.

KRAHN, CORNELIUS (1968), Dutch Anabaptism. Origin, Spread, Life, and Thought (1450–1600), The Hague: Martinus Nijhoff.

LABARGA GARCÍA, FERMÍN (2003), Datos históricos sobre el culto al Santisimo en la ciudad de Logroño en Religiosidad y ceremonias en torno a la eucaristía, in: Actas del Simposium, II, Instituto Escurialense de Investigaciones Históricas y Artísticas, Francisco Xavier Campos (ed.), El Escorial: Ediciones Esurialenses, 1047–1069.

LABAT, JEAN-BAPTISTE (1730), Voyages du P. Labat en Espagne et en Italie, Paris: Rue Saint Jacques.

LAVALLÉE, JOSEPH (1809), Histoire des inquisitions religieuses d'Italie, d'Espagne et de Portugal, Paris: Capelle et Renard.

LAZARILLO DE TORMES (1554), Burgos: Juan de Junta.

LEA, HENRY CHARLES (1867), History of Sacerdotal Celibacy within the Christian Church, Philadelphia: Collins.

LEA, HENRY CHARLES (1967), Chapters from the Religious History of Spain Connected with the Inquisition, Philadelphia: Lea Brothers [1890]. Reprinted, New York: Burt Franklin.

LEA, HENRY CHARLES (1901), The Moriscos of Spain; Their Conversion and Expulsion. Philadelphia: Lea Brothers.

LEA, HENRY CHARLES (1906–1907), A History of the Inquisition of Spain, 3 vols., New York: Macmillan.

LECHNER, JAN (1992), Contactos entre los Países Bajos y el mundo ibérico, Amsterdam: Rodopi.

LEON DE LA VEGA, MANUEL DE (2012), Los protestantes y la espiritualidad evangélica en la España del siglo XVI, 2 vols., Madrid: Fundación Pluralismo y Convivencia.

LETTERS AND PAPERS (1880), Foreign and Domestic, Henry VIII: October 1532, Volume 5: 1531–1532, www.british-history.ac.uk/report.aspx?compid=77495. Accessed May 19, 2014.

LETTERS AND STATE PAPERS (1892–1899), Relating to English Affairs Preserved Principally in the Archives of Simancas. Martin Hume (ed.), 4 vols., London: H.M. Stationery Office.

LIEBER, FRANCIS (1882), Life and Letters of Francis Lieber, Thomas Sergeant Perry (ed.), Boston: James R. Osgood.

LIMBORCH, PHILIPPUS VAN (1816), History of the Inquisition, London: Simpkin and Marshall.

LLORENTE, JUAN ANTONIO (1817–1818), Histoire critique de l'Inquisition d'Espagne, depuis l'epoque de son établissement par Fedinand V, jusqu'au régime de Ferdinand VII, tirée des pièces originales des archives du Conseil de la Suprême, et de celles des tribunaux subalternes du Saint-office, Alexis Pellier (trans.), 4 vols., Paris: Treuttel & Würtz.

LLORENTE, JUAN ANTONIO (1821), Oordeelkundige geschiedenis der Spaansche inquisitie, Amsterdam: Sepp en Ypma.

LLORENTE, JUAN ANTONIO (1823), Geschichte der Inquisition, Léonard Gallois (trans.), Leipzig: Leopold Voss.

LLORENTE, JUAN ANTONIO (1826a), A Critical History of the Inquisition of Spain: From the Period of its Establishment by Ferdinand V to the Reign of Ferdinand VII, Composed from the Original Documents of the Archives of the Supreme Council and from those of Subordinate Tribunals of the Holy Office, London: G.B. Whittaker.

LLORENTE, JUAN ANTONIO (1826b), History of the Spanish Inquisition: abridged from the original work of M. Llorente, late secretary of that institution; by Leonard Gallois; translated by an American, New York: G.C. Morgan, John P. Haven, and Gray and Bunce.

LLORENTE, JUAN ANTONIO (1843), A Critical History of the Inquisition of Spain: From the Period of Its Establishment by Ferdinand V to the Reign of Ferdinand VII, Philadelphia: James M. Campbell.

LONGHURST, JOHN E. (1950), Erasmus and the Spanish Inquisition: the Case of Juan de Valdés, Albuquerque: University of New Mexico Press.

LONGHURST, JOHN E. (1953), Luther and the Spanish Inquisition: the Case of Diego de Uceda, 1528–1529, Albuquerque: University of New Mexico Press.

LONGHURST, JOHN E. (1957), La beata Isabel de la Cruz ante la Inquisición, Cuadernos de Historia de España 25–6, 279–303.

LONGHURST, JOHN E. (1958a), Alumbrados, erasmistas y luteranos en el proceso de Juan de Vergara, Cuadernos de historia de Espana 27, 99–163.

LONGHURST, JOHN E. (1958b), The first English Lutherans in Spain, Humanisme et Renaissance 20, 143–157.

LONGHURST, JOHN E. (1959), Luther in Spain, 1520–1540, American Philosophical Society 103.1, 66–93.

LONGHURST, JOHN E. (1969), Luther's Ghost in Spain (1517–1546), Lawrence, KS: Coronado Press.

LÓPEZ FERNÁNDEZ, AMBROSIO (1996), The Renaissance Environement of the First Spanish Grammar Published in Sixteenth-Century England, Sederi 7, 99–105.

LÓPEZ MUÑOZ, TOMÁS (2011), La Reforma en la Sevilla del siglo XVI, 2 vols., Seville: Editorial MAD.

LOPEZ, PASQUALE (1976), Il Movimiento Valdesiano a Napoli, Naples: Fiorentino.

LOVETT, GABRIEL H. (1967), Introduction to A Critical History of the Inquisition of Spain by Juan Antonio Llorente, Williamstown, Mass: John Lilburne Co.

LUTTIKHUIZEN, FRANCES (2006), El siríaco en la transmisión de documentos bíblicos, Tu Reino 13, 9–37.

LUTTIKHUIZEN, FRANCES (2009), La reforma en España, Italia y Portugal, siglos XVI y XVII, Bibliografía actualizada. Seville: Editorial MAD.

LUTTIKHUIZEN, FRANCES (2016), The Ximenez Polyglot, Unio cum Christo 2.1, 83–98.

LYELL, JAMES P.R. (1914), Cardinal Ximenes, Statesman, Ecclesiastic, Soldier and Man of Letters, with an Account of the Complutensian Polyglot Bible, London: Grafton & Co.

M'CRIE, THOMAS (1828), Geschichte der Fortschritte und Unterdrückung der Reformation in Italien im sechszehnten Jahrhunderte, Leipzig: J.C. Hinrichs.

M'CRIE, THOMAS (1829), History of the Progress and Suppression of the Reformation in Spain in the Sixteenth Century, Edinburgh: W. Blackwood.

M'CRIE, THOMAS (1831), Histoire des progrès et de l'extinction de la Réforme en Italie, au seizième siècle, Paris: Cherbuliez/Geneva: Même Maison.

M'CRIE, THOMAS (1832), Geschiedenis van den voortgang en de onderdrukking der Hervorming in Italië, in de zestiende eeuw, Dordrecht: F. Boekee.

M'CRIE, THOMAS (1833), History of the Progress and Suppression of the Reformation in Italy in the XVIth century [1827], 2nd ed., Edinburgh: Blackwood/London: Cadell.

M'CRIE, THOMAS (1835), Geschichte der Ausbreitung und Unterdrückung der Reformation in Spanien im sechzehnten Jahrhunderte, Stuttgart: Fr. Brodhag.

M'CRIE, THOMAS (1835), Istoria del progresso e dell'estinzione della riforma in Italia nel secolo sedicesimo tradotta dall'Inglese, Paris: Baudry.

M'CRIE, THOMAS (1838), Geschiedenis der uitbreiding en onderdrukking van de hervorming in Spanje in de zestiende eeuw, Amsterdam: W. Brave.

M'CRIE, THOMAS (2008), Historia de la reforma en España en el siglo XVI, Adam F. Sosa (trans.), Buenos Aires: La Aurora/México: Casa Unida de Publicaciones [1950]; Seville: Renacimiento.

MACKENZIE, ANN L. (ed.) (1997), Spain and Its Literature: Essays in Memory of E. Allison Peers, Liverpool: University Press.

MAJAD, MUSA AMMAR (2008), Libros, arte, cultura e inquisición en Nueva España. www.letralia.com/182/ensayo02.htm. Accessed July 26, 2015.

MÁRQUEZ, ANTONIO (1971), Juan de Valdés, teólogo de los alumbrados, La Ciudad de Dios 184, 214–228.

MÁRQUEZ, ANTONIO (1972), Los alumbrados: orígenes y filosofía 1525–1559, Madrid: Taurus.

MARTIN ABAD, JULIÁN (1991), La imprenta en Alcalá de Henares 1502–1600, Madrid: Arco Libros.

MARTIN GOMEZ, MARIA (2013), Crisis en la temprana modernidad. Casiodoro de Reina, in: Crisis de la Modernidad y Filosofías Ibéricas, Jose Luis Mora/Della Manzanero Fernandez/Martin Gonzalez (eds.), Madrid: Fundación Ignacio Larramendi, 187–198.

MARTIN GOMEZ, MARIA (2015), El pensamiento filosófico de María de Bohorquez, in: Filosofías del Sur, Jose Luis Mora García/María del Carmen Lara/Óscar Barroso/Elena Trapanese/Xavier Agenjo (eds.), Madrid: Fundación Ignacio Larramendi, 109–120.

MARTIN, ANDRES (1975), Los recogidos. Una nueva vision de la mísitca española (1500–1700), Madrid: FUE.

MARTIN, JOHN J. (2007), Elites and Reform in Northern Italy, in: La Réforme en France et en Italie: contacts, comparaisons et contrastes, Philip Benedict/Silvana Seidel Menchi/Alain Tallon (eds.), Rome: École française de Rome, 309–329.

MARTÍNEZ MILLÁN, JOSÉ (2000), La corte de Carlos V, 3 vols., Madrid: Sociedad Estatal para la Conmemoración de los Centenarios de Felipe II y Carlos V.

MARTÍNEZ PEÑAS, LEANDRO (2012), La Legislación de Carlos V contra la herejía en Los Paises Bajos, Revista de la Inquisición 16, 27–61.

MATTHIESSEN, FRANCIS OTTO (1931), Translation, an Elizabethan Art, Cambridge, Mass: Harvard University Press.

MAZUR, PETER A. (2013), The New Christians of Spanish Naples 1528–1671, Basingstoke: Palgrave Macmillan.

MCFADDEN, WILLIAM (1953), The Life and Works of Antonio del Corro (1527–1591), PhD diss., Queen's University, Belfast.

MCGINN, BERNARD (1998), The Flowering of Mysticism, Men and Women in the New Mysticism (1200–1350), New York: Crossroad.

MCGREGOR, MARTIN I., The History and the Persecutions of Spanish Freemasonry. www.freemasons-freemasonry.com/history-spanish-freemasonry.html.   Accessed March 8, 2015.

MCGUIRE, BRIAN PATRICK (ed./trans.) (1998), Jean Gerson: Early Works, New York: Paulist Press.

MCKENDRICK, GERALDINE/ANGUS MACKAY (1991), Visionaries and Affective Spirituality during the First Half of the Sixteenth Century, in: Cultural Encounters. The Impact of the Inquisition in Spain and the New World, Mary Elizabeth Perry/Anne J. Cruz (eds.), Berkeley: University of California Press, 93–101.

MENDEZ APARICIO, JULIA (1981), Impresos de Pedro Hagenbach que se conservan en la Biblioteca Pública de Toledo, Toletum: boletín de la Real Academia de Bellas Artes y Ciencias Históricas de Toledo 12, 9–41.

MENDHAM, JOSEPH (1830), The Literary Policy of Rome Exhibited in an Account of her Damnatory Catalogus or Indexes, etc, 2nd ed., London: Duncan.

MENENDEZ Y PELAYO, MARCELINO (1881), Historia de los Heterodoxos españoles, 3 vols., Madrid: Librería Católica de San José.

MENENDEZ Y PELAYO, MARCELINO (1910), Procesos de protestantes españoles en el siglo XVI, Revista de archivos, bibliotecas y museos. Reprinted in Obras Completas, Madrid: V. Suárez, 1911–32, Tomo XLI, 428–640.

MENENDEZ Y PELAYO, MARCELINO (2009), A History of the Spanish Heterodox. Book One, Eladia Gomez-Posthill (trans.), London: Saint Austin Press.

MENESES, FELIPE DE (1554), Tratado de la doctrina. Luz del alma christiana contra la ceguedad y ygnorancia, Valladolid.

METHUEN, CHARLOTTE (2010), Preaching the Gospel through Love of Neighbour: The Ministry of Katharina Schütz Zell, The Journal of Ecclesiastical History 61, 707–728.

METZGER, BRUCE M. (2005), The Text of the New Testament: Its Transmission, Corruption, and Restoration, 4th ed., New York: Oxford University Press.

MILLARES CARLO, AGUSTÍN (1935), Algunas notas y documentos referentes a Juan Bartolome Avontroot, El Museo Canario 6, 1–26.

MOLL, JAIME (1999), Gaspar Zapata, impresor sevillano condenado por la Inquisición en 1562, Pliegos de Bibliofilia 7, 5–10.

MONTER, WILLIAM (1990), Frontiers of Heresy. The Spanish Inquisition from the Basque Lands to Sicily. Cambridge: Cambridge University Press.

MONTES, REGINALDO GONZALEZ DE (1567), Sanctae Inquisitionis hispanicae artes aliquot detectæ, ac palam traductæ, Heidelberg: Michael Schirat.

MONTES, REGINALDO GONZALEZ DE (1568, 1569), A Discovery and playne Declaration of Sundry Subtill Practises of the Holy Inquisition of Spayne. Set forth in Latin by Reginaldus Gonsalvius Montanus and [recently] translated, Vincent Skinner (trans.), London: John Daye.

MONTES, REGINALDO GONZALEZ DE (1625), A full, ample and punctually discovery of the barbarous, bloudy, and inhumane practises of the Spanish Inquisition, against Protestants, London: John Bellamie.

MONTES, REGINALDO GONZALEZ DE (1982), Artes de la Inquisizion española: Primer traduczion castellana de la obra escrita en latin por el español Raimundo Gonzalez de Montes, in: Reformistas Antiguos Españoles, Vol. V, L. Usoz y Río/B.B. Wiffen (eds.) [1851]; Barcelona: Diego Gómez Flores.

MONTES, REGINALDO GONZALEZ DE (1983), Inquisitionis Hispanicae [1567], Reformistas Antiguos Españoles, Vol. XIII, L. Usoz y Río/B.B. Wiffen (eds.) [1856]; Barcelona: Diego Gómez Flores.

MONTES, REGINALDO GONZALEZ DE (2008), Artes de la Santa Inquisición Española, Francisco Ruiz de Pablos (trans./intro.), Seville: Editorial MAD.

MONTES, REGINALDO GONZALEZ DE (2010), Artes de la inquisicion espanola, David Gonzalez Romero (ed.), Cordoba: Almuzara.

MONTESINO, AMBROSIO (1502), Vita Cristi Cartuxano romançado por fray Ambrosio, 4 vols., Alcala de Henares.

MONTESINO, AMBROSIO (1512), Epistolas y evangelios por todo el año con sus doctrinas y sermones segun la reformacion & interpretacion que desta obra hiźo fray Ambrosio Montesino. Por mandado del rey nuestro señor, Toledo.

MONTESINOS, JOSÉ F. (1956), Introduction to Diálogo de las cosas ocurridas en Roma by Alfonso de Valdés, Madrid: Espasa-Calpe.

MONTOJO MONTOJO, VICENTE (1993), El Siglo de Oro en Cartagena (1480–1640): evolución económica y social de una ciudad portuaria del Sureste español y su comarca, Cartagena: Editum.

MONTOTO, SANTIAGO (1991), Esquinas y conventos de Sevilla, Seville: Universidad de Sevilla.

MONTOYA, JAVIER A. (2010), El Sabor de Herejia: the Edict of 1525, the Alumbrados and the Inquisitors' usage of locura, MA Thesis, University of Florida.

MORENO BERROCAL, JOSÉ (2005), La historia evangélica de la comarca de Alcázar de San Juan (siglos XVI–XXI), Alcázar de San Juan: Patronato Municipal de Cultura.

MORENO, DORIS (2001), Carlos V y la Inquisición, in: Carlos V europeísmo y universalidad: Actas del congreso internacional, Granada 2000, Francisco Sánchez-Montes/ Juan Luis Castellano (eds.), Madrid: Sociedad Estatal para la Conmemoración de los Centenarios de Felipe II y Carlos V, Vol. II, 421–436.

MORENO, DORIS (2004), La invención de la Inquisición, Madrid: Marcial Pons.

MORENO, DORIS (2008a), Antonio del Corro y su 'Carta enviada a la Majestad del Rey Felipe' (1597): una propuesta de tolerancia religiosa, in: Homenaje a Antonio Domínguez Ortiz, Juan Luis Castellano (ed.), Granada: Universidad de Granada, Vol. II, 589–602.

MORENO, DORIS (2008b), Introduction to La reforma en España en el siglo XVI by Thomas M'Crie, Seville: Renacimiento.

MORENO, DORIS (2009), Corazones partidos: judíos y protestantes en el exilio, in: Las Españas que (no) pudieron ser: herejías, exilios y otras conciencias (s.XVI–XX), Manuel Peña Díaz (ed.), Huelva: Universidad de Huelva, 39–58.

MORENO, DORIS (2010), De la reforma Católica a la Contrareforma. Algunas reflexiones, in: Franciscanos, mísitcos, herejes y alumbrados, Alvaro Castro Sánchez (ed.), Cordoba: Universidad de Cordoba, 251–272.

MORENO, DORIS (2012a), Francisco de Borja y la Inquisición, in: Actes Symposi Internacional Francesc de Borja (1510–1572), home del Renaixement, sant del Barroc, Santiago La Parra/Maria Toldrà (eds.), Gandia: Institut Internacional d'Estudis Borgians, 364–366.

MORENO, DORIS (2012b), La discrecionalidad de un inquisidor. Francisco Vaca, ¿el primer abogado de las brujas? BIBLID, 202–214.

MORENO, DORIS (2013a), Antonio del Corro, defensor de la tolerancia, Andalucia en la historia 42, 8–10.

MORENO, DORIS (2013b), Cadena de oro para atraer a los herejes. Argumentos de persuasión y estrategias de supervivencia en Fray Juan de Villagarcía, O.P., Discípulo de Fray Bartolomé de Carranza, Hispania Sacra 65, 29–71.

MORENO, DORIS (2015a), Los Jesuitas, la Inquisición y la frontera espiritual de 1559, Bulletin of Spanish Studies: Hispanic Studies and Researches on Spain, Portugal and Latin America 92, 1–23.

MORENO, DORIS (2015b), Marina de Saavedra, una mujer en la frontera confesional (Zamora, 1558–1559), Cuadernos de Historia Moderna 40, 15–30.

MORENO, DORIS (2016), Marina de Saavedra: A Devout Laywoman on a Confessional Frontier (Zamora, 1558–1559), in: Devout Laywomen in the Early Modern World, Alison Weber (ed.), New York: Routledge, 219–234.

MORENO, DORIS (2017), Casiodoro de Reina, Seville: Centro de Estudios Andaluces.

MOSHEIM, JOHANN LORENZ (1765), An Ecclesiastical History, Ancient and Modern, from the Birth of Christ, to the Beginning of the Present Century, Archibald Maclaine (trans.), 2 vols., London: A. Millar.

MULLETT, MICHAEL A. (2010), Historical Dictionary of the Reformation and Counter-Reformation, Lanham, MD: Scarecrow Press.

MUÑOZ, DANIEL (2008), La Inquisición española como tema literario: política, historia y ficción en la crisis del antiguo regimen, Rochester, NY: Tamesis.

MUÑOZ, DANIEL (2010), The Abolition of the Inquisition and the Creation of a Historical Myth, Hispanic Research Journal 11, 71–81.

MUÑOZ, GERARDO (2013), ¿Por qué se suicidó el cónsul holandés? April, 22, 2013. www.diarioinformacion.com/opinion/2013/04/22/suicido-consul-holandes/1365814.html. Accessed May 4, 2015.

NALLE, SARA T. (1992), God in La Mancha: Religious Reform and the People of Cuenca, 1500–1650, Baltimore: Johns Hopkins University Press.

NAPOLEON to the Corregidor of Madrid (1808), Declaration of Chamartin. www.napoleon-series.org/research/government/diplomatic/c_corregidor.html. Accessed February 20, 2015.

NELSON, JONATHAN L. (2004), Article "Francisco de Enzinas", New Oxford DNB, Oxford: University Press, Vol. 18.

NIETO, JOSÉ C. (1970), Juan de Valdés and the origins of the Spanish and Italian Reformations, Geneva: Droz.

NIETO, JOSÉ C. (1974a), Juan de Valdés on catechetical instruction: The 'Dialogue on Christian Doctrine' and the 'Christian Instruction for Children', Bibliothèque d'Humanisme et Renaissance 36, 253–272.

NIETO, JOSÉ C. (1974b), Mystical theology and 'salvation-history' in John of the Cross: Two conflicting methods of Biblical interpretation, Bibliothèque d'Humanisme et Renaissance 36, 17–32.

NIETO, JOSÉ C. (1975), En torno al problema de los alumbrados de Toledo, Revista Española de Teología 35, 77–93.

NIETO, JOSÉ C. (1977), The Franciscan Alumbrados and the Prophetic-Apocalyptic Tradition, Sixteenth-Century Journal 8, 3–16.

NIETO, JOSÉ C. (1978), The Heretical Alumbrado-Dexados: Isabel de la Cruz and Pedro Ruiz de Alcaraz, Revue de Littérature Comparée, Hommage des comparatistes à Marcel Bataillon 52, 293–313.

NIETO, JOSÉ C. (1979), Juan de Valdés y los orígenes de la Reforma en España e Italia, México: Fondo de Cultura Económica.

NIETO, JOSÉ C. (1981), Juan de Valdés' Two Catechisms: The Dialogue on Christian Doctrine and the Christian Instruction for Children, Wm. B. Jones/Carol Jones (trans.), Lawrence, KS: Coronado Press.

NIETO, JOSÉ C. (1984), El carácter no místico de los alumbrados de Toledo 1509(?)–1524, in: Inquisición española y mentalidad inquisitorial, Angel Alcalá (ed.), Barcelona: Ariel, 410–423.

NIETO, JOSÉ C. (1986), L'Hérésie des alumbrados, Revue d'Histoire et de Philosophie Religieuses 66, 403–418.

NIETO, JOSÉ C. (1987a), Juan de Valdés, in: Contemporaries of Erasmus: A biographical register of the Renaissance and Reformation, P.G. Bietenholz/T. Deutscher (eds.), Toronto: University of Toronto Press, Vol. III, 368–370.

NIETO, JOSÉ C. (1987b), The Non-Mystical Nature of the Sixteenth-Century Alumbrados of Toledo, in: The Spanish Inquisition and the Inquisitorial Mind, Angel Alcalá (ed.), Boulder, CO: Social Science Monographs, 431–456.

NIETO, JOSÉ C. (1997), El Renacimiento y la otra España: visión cultural socioespiritual, Geneva: Droz.

NIETO, JOSÉ C. (2001), Herejía en la Capilla Imperial: Constantino Ponce de la Fuente y 'la imagen del Diablo', in: Carlos V y la quiebra del humanismo político en Europa (1530–1558), J. Martínez Millán (ed.), Madrid: Sociedad Estatal para la conmemoración de los Centenarios de Felipe II y Carlos V, Vol. IV, 213–224.

NIETO, JOSÉ C. (2004), In memoriam Luis Usoz y Río, 1805–1865. Constantino Ponce de la Fuente, 'De la Iglesia y sacramentos': Constantino Ponce de la Fuente reformador conquense, Bibliotheque d' humanisme et renaissance: travaux et documents 66, 39–68.

NIEVA OCAMPO, GUILLERMO (2007), «Servir a Dios con Quietud», La Elaboración de un Modelo Regular Femenino para las Dominicas Castellanas a Mediados del Siglo XVI, Hispania Sacra 119, 163–196.

NOTES AND QUERIES (1858), Choice Notes from 'Notes & Quieries': History, London: George Bell.

OLIVIERI, ACHILLE (1967), Alessandro Trissino and Calvinist Movement Vicentino in the Sixteenth Century, Rivista di storia della Chiesa in Italia 21, 54–117.

OLIVIERI, ACHILLE (1992), Riforma ed eresia a Vicenza nel Cinquecento, Rome: Herder.

OLLERO PINA, JOSÉ ANTONIO (2007), Clérigos, universitarios y herejes: La Universidad de Sevilla y la formación académica del cabildo eclesiástico, in: Universidades Hispánicas. Modelos territoriales en la Edad Moderna (I): Santiago, Toledo, Sevilla, Barcelona y Huesca, L.E. Rodríguez-San Pedro Bézares/J.L. Polo Rodríguez (eds.), Salamanca: Universidad de Salamanca, 107–196.

OLMEDILLA Y PUIG, JOAQUÍN (1897), Estudio histórico de la vida y escritos del sabio médico español del siglo XVI, Nicolás Monardes, Madrid: Hernández.

ORTIZ DE ZUÑIGA, DIEGO (1677), Annales ecclesiasticos y seculares de la Ciudad de Sevilla, 3 vols., Madrid: Garcia Infançon.

ORTIZ, ANTONIO DOMINGUEZ (1971), Los Judeoconversos en Espana y America, Madrid: ISTMOS.

OTTE, ENRIQUE (2008), Sevilla, siglo XVI: materiales para su historia económica, Seville: Centro de Estudios Andaluces.

PASTORE, STEFANIA (2010), Una herejía española. Conversos, alumbrados e Inquisición (1449–1559), Madrid: Marcial Pons.

PÉREZ CANO, MARÍA TERESA (1997), Patrimonio y ciudad, el sistema de los conventos de clausura en el centro histórico de Sevilla, Seville: Universidad de Sevilla.

PÉREZ DE PINEDA, JUAN (1981), Epístola Consolatoria, in: Reformistas Antiguos Españoles, Vol. II, L. Usoz y Río/B.B. Wiffen (eds.) [1848]; Barcelona: Diego Gómez Flores.

PÉREZ ESCOHOTADO, JAVIER (2003), Antonio de Medrano, alumbrado epicúreo: proceso inquisitorial (Toledo, 1530), Madrid: Verbum.

PÉREZ FERNÁNDEZ, JOSÉ (2012), Translation and the Early Modern Idea of Europe, Translation and Literature 21.3, 299–318.

PÉREZ GARCÍA, RAFAEL M. (2014), Communitas Christiana: The Sources of Christian Tradition in the Construction of Early Castilian Spiritual Literature, ca. 1400–1540, in: Books in the Catholic World During the Early Modern Period, Natalia M. Alvarez (ed.), Leiden/Boston: Brill, 88–90.

PÉREZ GONZÁLEZ, MARIA, Una amiga de Teresa sentenciada por la Inquisición: Ana Enríquez. delaruecaalapluma.wordpress.com/2013/03/15/la-amiga-de-teresa-sentenciada-por-la-inquisicion-ana-enriquez-i/. Accessed December 16, 2014.

PÉREZ-ROMERO, ANTONIO (2005), The Subversive Tradition in Spanish Renaissance Writing, Lewisburg, PA: Bucknell University Press.

PEREZ, JOSEPH (1962), L'Université d'Alcala en 1520–1521, Bulletin Hispanique 64, 214–222.

PEREZ, JOSEPH (2005), The Spanish Inquisition: A History, Janet Lloyd (trans.), New Haven, CT: Yale University Press.

PEREZ, JOSEPH (2012), Breve Historia de la Inquisición en España, Barcelona: Crítica.

PEREZ, JOSEPH (2014), Cisneros, el cardenal de España, Madrid: Taurus.

PETERS, EDWARD M. (1989), Inquisition, Berkeley: University of California Press.

PETTEGREE, ANDREW (1986), Foreign Protestant Communities in Sixteenth-Century London, Oxford: Clarendon Press.

PIKE, JOHN B. (1852), The Curse of Christendom, or the Spirit of Popery Exhibited and Exposed, London: T. Ward & Co.

PINTO CRESPO, VIRGILIO (1977), El proceso de elaboración y la configuración del Índice y Expurgatorio de 1583-84 en relación con los otros índices del s. XVI, Hispania Sacra 30, 201-254.

PLOMER, HENRY ROBERT (1915), A Short History of English Printing 1476-1900, London: Kegan Paul, Trench, Trübner & Co.

PLUMMER, MARJORIE ELIZABETH (1996), Reforming the Family: Marriage, Gender and the Lutheran Household in Early Modern Germany, 1500-1620, PhD diss., University of Virginia.

PLUMMER, MARJORIE ELIZABETH (2012), From Priest's Whore to Pastor's Wife: Clerical Marriage and the Process of Reform in the Early German Reformation, Farnham, Surrey: Ashgate.

PRAGMÁTICA (November 22, 1559), es.wikipedia.org/wiki/Pragm%C3%A1tica_de_22_de_noviembre_de_1559.

PRESTON, DANIEL (2001), A Comprehensive Catalogue of the Correspondence and Papers of James Monroe, 2 vols., Westport, Conn.: Greenwood Press.

PRESTON, PATRICK/ALLAN K. JENKINS (2007), Biblical Scholarship and the Church: A Sixteenth-Century Crisis of Authority, Aldershot: Ashgate.

PROEL, Grandes traductores de la Biblia. www.proel.org/index.php?pagina=traductores/enzinas. Accessed July 26, 2014.

PUIGBLANCH, ANTONI (1816), The Inquisition Unmasked: Being an Historical and Philosophical Account of That Tremendous Tribunal, Founded on Authentic Documents, and Exhibiting the Necessity of its Suppression as a Means of Reform and Regeneration, William Walton (trans.), 2 vols., London: Baldwin, Cradock, and Joy.

RABUS, LUDWIG (1557), Historien der Heyligen Außerwölten Gottes-Zeügen, Bekennern und Martyrern, 6 vols., Strasbourg: Samuel Emmel.

RAWLINGS, HELEN (2006), The Spanish Inquisition, Malden, MA: Blackwell.

REGUERA, IÑAKI (1984), La Inquisición española en el País Vasco: el tribunal de Calahorra 1513-1570, San Sebastián: Txertoa.

REID, DYLAN (2004), Renaissance Printing and Provincial Culture in Sixteenth-Century Rouen, University of Toronto Quarterly 73.4, 1011-1020.

REINA, CASIODORO DE (1988), Confesión De Fe Christiana = The Spanish Protestant Confession of Faith (London, 1560/61), Arthur G. Kinder (ed.), Exeter: University of Exeter.

REINA, CASIODORO DE (2010), The Confession of the Spanish Congregation of London (1560/61), in: Reformed Confessions of the 16th and 17th Centuries in English Translation: Vol. 3, 1552-1566, James T. Dennison Jr. (ed.)/David H. Vila (trans.), Grand Rapids, MI: Reformation Heritage Books, 370-401.

RESINES LLORENTE, LUIS (2003), La primera edición castellana del Catecismo de Heidelberg (1627), Estudio agustiniano 38.2, 291-329.

RIOS SANCHEZ, PATROCINIO (1998), Bibliofilos protestantes en Baroja. Pedro de Vegas, el librero de los visionarios, Anales de Historia Contemporanea 14, 359-375.

RIPODAS ARDANAZ, DAISY (1993), Una ignorada escritora en la Charcas finicolonial: Maria Antonio del Rio y Arnedo, Investigaciones y ensayos 43, 165–207.

ROBERTSON, WILLIAM (1822), The History of the Reign of the Emperor Charles V, Emperor of Germany; and of All the Kingdoms and States in Europe, During His Age, 3 vols., Albany: E. Hosford.

ROBIN, DIANA (2007), Publishing Women: Salons, the Presses, and the Counter-Reformation in Sixteenth-Century Italy, Chicago: University of Chicago Press.

ROBIN, DIANA/ANNE R. LARSEN/CAROLE LEVIN (eds.) (2007), Encyclopedia of Women in the Renaissance: Italy, France, and England, Santa Barbara, CA: ABC-CLIO, 2007.

RODRÍGUEZ PELAZ, CELIA (1998), La ilustración en los impresos de Guillén de Brocar, Ondare 17, 437–445.

RODRÍGUEZ-SAN PEDRO BEZARES, LUIS ENRIQUE (2013), La Universidad de Salamanca del Medievo al Renacimiento, 1218–1516/29: aspectos históricos, poderes y saberes, Salamanca: Ediciones Universidad de Salamanca.

ROLDAN-FIGUEROA, RADY (2005), Casiodoro de Reina as Biblical Exegete: Studies on the 1569 Spanish Translation of the Bible, Th.D. diss., Boston University School of Theology.

ROLDAN-FIGUEROA, RADY (2006a), 'Filius Perditionis': The Propagandistic Use of a Biblical Motif in Sixteenth-Century Spanish Evangelical Bible Translations, The Sixteenth Century Journal 37.4, 1027–1055.

ROLDAN-FIGUEROA, RADY (2006b), Reina's Vision of a Truly Reformed Ministry: A Reconstruction from the Fringes of the 1569 Spanish Translation of the Bible, in: Lay Bibles in Europe 1450–1800, M. Lamberigts/A. A. den Hollander (eds.), Leuven: Peeters Publishers, 159–181.

ROLDAN-FIGUEROA, RADY (2006c), 'Justified Without the Works of the Law': Casiodoro de Reina on Romans 3,28, in: The Formation of Clerical and Confessional Identities in Early Modern Europe, Wim Janse/Barbara Pitkin (eds.), Leiden: Brill, 205–224.

ROLDAN-FIGUEROA, RADY (2009a), Antonio del Corro and Paul as the Herald of the Gospel of Universal Redemption, in: A Companion to Paul in the Reformation, R. Ward Holder (ed.), Leiden/Boston: Brill, 389–425.

ROLDAN-FIGUEROA, RADY (2009b), Translation, Guided Reading, and Anti-Roman Catholic Propaganda in the Reina-Valera Bible (1602): The Rendering of Deuteronomy 23,17[18], in: Infant Milk or Hardy Nourishment? The Bible for Lay People and Theologians in the Early Modern Period, W. François/A. A. den Hollander (eds.), Louvain: Peeters Publishers, 411–438.

ROLDAN-FIGUEROA, RADY (2010a), The Ascetic Spirituality of Juan de Ávila (1499–1569), Leiden/Boston: Brill.

ROLDAN-FIGUEROA, RADY (2010b), Religious Propaganda and Textual Hybridity in Tomás Carrascón's 1623 Spanish Translation of the Jacobean Book of Common Prayer, The Seventeenth Century 25.1, 49–74.

ROLDAN-FIGUEROA, RADY (2013), Tomás Carrascón, Anti-Roman Catholic Propaganda, and the Circulation of Ideas in Jacobean England, History of European Ideas 39.2, 169–206.

ROSE, CONSTANCE HUBBARD (1971), Alonso Núñez De Reinoso: The Lament of a Sixteenth-Century Exile, Rutherford, NJ: Fairleigh Dickinson University Press.

ROTH, CECIL (1964), The Spanish Inquisition, New York: W.W. Norton & Co.

ROZBICKI, MICHAL JAN/GEORGE O. NDEGE, (eds.) (2012), Cross-Cultural History and the Domestication of Otherness. London/New York: Palgrave Macmillan.

RUIZ DE PABLOS, FRANCISCO (1997), Introduction to Artes de la Santa Inquisición española de González Montes, Madrid: UNED.

RUIZ DE PABLOS, FRANCISCO (2003), Errores antiguos y actuales sobre González Montes, debelador de la Inquisición Española, Hispania sacra 55, 237–252.

RUIZ DE PABLOS, FRANCISCO (2008), Introduction to Artes de la Santa Inquisición Española by Reginaldo Gonzalez de Montes, Fco. Ruiz de Pablos (trans.), Seville: Editorial MAD.

RUIZ DE PABLOS, FRANCISCO (2014), Introduction to Protestantismo Español e Inquisición en el Siglo XVI by Ernest H.J. Schäfer, Francisco Ruiz de Pablos (trans.), 4 vols., Seville: Editorial MAD.

RUMMEL, ERIKA (1999), Jimenez de Cisneros: On the Threshold of Spain's Golden Age, Tempe, AR: Arizona Center for Medieval and Renaissance Studies.

RUMMEL, ERIKA (2008), Biblical Humanism and Scholasticism in the Age of Erasmus, Leiden: Brill.

RUMMEL, ERIKA (ed./trans.) (2005), The Correspondence of Wolfgang Capito, Toronto: University of Toronto Press.

SALEMBIER, LOUIS (1909), Article "Jean de Charlier de Gerson", The Catholic Encyclopedia, New York: Robert Appleton Company. http://www.newadvent.org/cathen/06530c.htm. Accessed May 10, 2015.

SÁNCHEZ HERRERO, JOSÉ (1986), La literatura catequética en la Península Ibérica, 1236–1553, En la España Medieval 5, 1051–1118.

SANTA MARÍA, FRANCISCO DE (1644), Reforma de los descalzos de Nuestra Señora del Carmen de la primitiva observancia, Madrid: Diego Díaz de la Carrera.

SANTAMARIA DEL RIO, DAVID (2011), Los otros creyentes. El hecho religioso no católico en la provincia de Zamora, Zamora: Semuret.

SANTARELLI, DANIELE (2012), Dal conflitto all'«alleanza di ferro». A proposito delle relazioni tra il Papato e la Spagna nella crisi religiosa del Cinquecento, Studi Storici Luigi Simeoni 62, 49–58.

SANTOYO, JULIO-CÉSAR (1973), Antonio del Corro y Pedro de Zubiaur: el episodio de Bridewell, Boletin de Estudios Históricos sobre San Sebastián 7, 312–318.

SARANYANA, JOSEP IGNASI (2007), La noción de «libertad» en el contexto de la mística neoplatónica. A propósito del Speculum animarum simplicium de Margarita Porete (†1310), Anuario de Historia de la Iglesia 16, 265–278.

SARRIÓN MORA, ADELINA (2003), Beatas y endemoniadas. Mujeres heterodoxas ante la inquisición. Siglos XVI a XIX, Madrid: Alianza.

SCHÄFER, ERNST H.J. (1902), Beiträge zur Geschichte des spanischen Protestantismus und der Inquisition im sechzehnten Jahrhundert, 3 vols., Gütersloh: C. Bertelsmann.

SCHÄFER, ERNST H.J. (2014), Protestantismo Español e Inquisición en el Siglo XVI, Francisco Ruiz de Pablos (trans.), 4 vols., Seville: Editorial MAD.

SCHAFF, PHILIP (1882-1910), History of the Christian Church, 8 vols. New York: C. Scribner's sons.

SCHULTE HERBRÜGGEN, HUBERTUS (1998), Morus ad Craneveldium: litterae Balduinianae novae (More to Cranevelt: new Baudouin letters), Leuven: Leuven University Press.

SCIO DE SAN MIGUEL, FELIX (1790-93), La Biblia vulgata Latina traducia en espanōl y anotada conforme al sentido de los santos padres, y expositores cathòlicos, Valencia: Joseph y Thomas de Orga.

SCOTT, VIRGINIA/SARA STURM-MADDOX (2007), Performance, Poetry and Politics on the Queen's Day: Catherine de Médicis and Pierre de Ronsard at Fontainebleau, Aldershot: Ashgate.

SEGARRA AÑÓN, ISABEL (2001), Humanismo y reforma en la corte renacentista de Isabel Villamarí: Escipión Capece y sus lecturas, Quaderns d'Italia 6, 123-135.

SELKE, ANGELA (1953), Algunos aspectos de la vida religiosa en la España del siglo XVI: los alumbrados de Toledo, PhD diss., University of Wisconsin, Madison.

SELKE, ANGELA (1960), Vida y muerte de Juan López de Celaín, alumbrado vizcaíno, Bulletin Hispanique 62, 136-162.

SELKE, ANGELA (1980), El iluminismo de los conversos y la Inquisición. Cristianismo interior de los alumbrados, resentimiento y sublimación, in: La Inquisición Española—Nueva visión, nuevos horizontes, Joaquín Pérez Villanueva (ed.), Madrid: Siglo Veintiuno, 617-636.

SERRANO Y SANZ, MANUEL (1901, 1902), Juan de Vergara y la Inquisicion de Toledo, Revista de archivos, bibliotecas y museos 5, 896-912; 6, 29-42, 466-486.

SERRANO Y SANZ, MANUEL (1903), Pedro Ruiz de Alcaraz, iluminado alcarreno del siglo XVI, Revista de Bibliotecas y Museos 7, 9-10.

SMARR, JANET LEVARIE (2005), Joining the Conversation Dialogues by Renaissance Women, Ann Arbor: University of Michigan Press.

SMIDT, ANDREA J. (2010), Luces de la fe: the Cause of Catholic Enlightenment in 18th-century Spain, in: A Companion to the Catholic Enlightenment in Europe, Ulrich L. Lehner (ed.), Leiden: Brill, 403-452.

SMITH, WARREN S./CLARK COLAHAN (2009), Spanish Humanism on the Verge of the Picaresque: Juan Maldonado's Ludus Chartarum, Pastor Bonus, and Bacchanalia, Leuven: Leuven University Press.

STANFORD, CHARLOTTE A. (2011), Commemorating the Dead in Late Medieval Strasbourg: The Cathedral's Book of Donors and Its Use (1320-1521), Burlington, VT: Ashgate.

STOCKDALE, JOHN JOSEPH (1810), The History of the Inquisitions: Including the Secret Transactions of those Horrific Tribunals, London: Stockdale.

STOUGHTON, JOHN (2013), The Spanish Reformers. Their Memories and Dwelling-Places [1883]; Reprint. London: Forgotten Books.

STRYPE, JOHN (1709), Annals of the Reformation and Establishment of Religion, and Other Various Occurrences in the Church of England, During the First Twelve Years of Queen Elizabeth's Happy Reign. 2 vols. London: J. Wyat.

TELLECHEA IDÍGORAS, JOSÉ IGNACIO (1962), Biblias publicadas fuera de España secuestradas por la Inquisición de Sevilla en 1552, Bulletin Hispanique 64.3, 236-247.

TELLECHEA IDÍGORAS, JOSÉ IGNACIO (1975), Las ciento diez divinas Consideraciones: recensión inédita del manuscrito de Juan Sanchez (1558), Salamanca: Biblioteca de Estudios Ecuménicos.

TELLECHEA IDÍGORAS, JOSÉ IGNACIO (1977a), Fray Bartolomé de Carranza y el Cardenal Pole: un navarro en la restauración católica de Inglaterra (1554–1558), Pamplona: Diputación Floral.

TELLECHEA IDÍGORAS, JOSÉ IGNACIO (1977b), La reacción ante el luteranismo (1520–1559). Tiempos recios. Inquisición y heterodoxias, Salamanca: Sígueme, 23–32.

TELLECHEA IDÍGORAS, JOSÉ IGNACIO (1978), Don Carlos de Seso y el Arzobispo Carranza. Un veronés introductor del protestantismo en España (1559), in: Miscellanea Cardinal Giuseppe Siri, Raffaele Belvederi (ed.), Genoa: Tilgher.

TELLECHEA IDÍGORAS, JOSÉ IGNACIO (1996), De nuevo sobre Don Carlos de Seso. Una carta de Carranza al Inquisidor Guigelm, Diálogo Ecuménico 31, 189–210.

TELLECHEA IDÍGORAS, JOSÉ IGNACIO (ed.) (1962), Archivo Documental Espanol Publicado por la Real Academia de la Historia. Madrid: Real Academia de la Historia.

TELLECHEA IDÍGORAS, JOSÉ IGNACIO (ed.) (1975), Fray Bartolomé Carranza: documentos históricos, Vol. 30, Madrid: Real Academia de la Historia.

TELLECHEA IDÍGORAS, JOSÉ IGNACIO (2004), Doña Marina de Guevara, Monja Cisterciense Luterana?: Edición y Comentario de un Proceso Inquisitorial, Madrid: Fundación Universiatria Española.

THAYER OJEDA, THOMAS (1939–1943), Formación de la sociedad chilena y censos de la población de Chile entre los años 1540 a 156, 3 vols., Santiago: Prensas de la Universidad de Chile.

THOMAS, WERNER (1992), El hombre que intentó convertir al Rey de España: Hans Avontroot (1559–1633), Foro Hispánico 3, 43–64.

THOMAS, WERNER (2001a), La represión del protestantismo en España, 1517–1648, Leuven: Leuven University Press.

THOMAS, WERNER (2001b), Los protestantes y la Inquisición en España en tiempos de Reforma y Contrarreforma, Leuven: Leuven University Press.

THOMSETT, MICHAEL C. (2010), The Inquisition. A History, Jefferson, NC: McFarland & Co.

TICKNOR, GEORGE (1872), History of Spanish Literature, 3 vols., 4th ed., Boston: Osgood.

TIMPSON, THOMAS (1851), The Inquisition Revealed in its Origin, Policy, Cruelties and History, with the Memoirs of its Victims in France, Spain, Portugal, Italy, England, India, and other countries, London: Alylott and Janes.

TORRES AMAT, FELIX (1823), La Sagrada Biblia nuevamente traducida de la Vulgata latina al español, aclarado el sentido de algunos lugares con la luz que dan los textos originales hebreo y griego, e ilustrada con varias notas sacadas de los Santos Padres, Madrid: León Amasita.

TRUMAN, RONALD W. (1984), Felipe de la Torre and his Institución de un rey christiano (Antwerp, 1556): the Protestant Connexions of a Spanish Royal Chaplain, Bibliothéque d'Humanisme et Renaissance 46, 83–93.

TURNER, FRANCIS, Money and exchange rates in 1632. macrocoin.net/profiles/blogs/money-and-exchange-rates-in-1632-by-francis-turner. Accessed June 29, 2014.

TYSACK, DONALD (2013), Glass, Tools and Tyzacks, 4th ed., www.tyzack.net.

ULLOA, ALFONSO DE (1575), Vita dell'inuittissimo e sacratissimo imperator Carlo V, Venice: Bottegha d'Aldo.

USOZ Y RÍO, LUIS (ed.) (1841), Cancionero de Obras de Burlas Probocantes a Risa, London: William Pickering.

USOZ Y RÍO, LUIS/B.B. WIFFEN (eds.) (1847–1865) Reformistas antiguos españoles, 20 vols., San Sebastián: Ignacio R. Baroja/Madrid: J. Alegre.

VALDÉS, ALFONSO DE (1952), Alfonso de Valdés and the sack of Rome Dialogue of Lactancio and an archdeacon, John E. Longhurst (trans./intro./notes), Albuquerque: University of New Mexico Press.

VALDÉS, ALFONSO DE (1965), Diálogo de Mercurio y Carón, José F. Montesinos (ed.), Madrid: Espasa-Calpe.

VALDES, JUAN DE (1638), The hundred and ten considerations of Signior Iohn Valdesso: treating of those things which are most profitable, most necessary, and most perfect in our Christian profession, Oxford: Leonard Lichfield.

VALDES, JUAN DE (1905), Divine Considerations. The English Translation of Nicholas Ferrar. With George Herbert's Prefatory Epistle, Frederic Chapman (ed.), London: John Lane.

VALDES, JUAN DE (1925), Diálogo de doctrina cristiana: reproduction en facsimilé de l'exemplaire de la Bibliothèque Nationale de Lisbonne (edition d'Alcalá de Henares, 1529), Marcel Bataillon (intro./ed.), Coimbra: Imprensa da Universidade.

VALDES, JUAN DE (2008), Diálogo de Doctrina Cristiana [1529], Seville: Editorial MAD.

VALERA, CIPRIANO DE (1982), Tratado para confirmar en la fe cristiana a los cautivos de Berbería, in: Reformistas Antiguos Españoles, Vol. VIII, L. Usoz y Rio y B.B. Wiffen (eds.) [1854], Barcelona: Diego Gómez Flores.

VALLADARES DE SOTOMAYOR, ANTONIO (ed.) (1787–1791), Semanario erudito, que comprehende varias obras inéditas, críticas, morales, instructivas, políticas, históricas, satíricas, y jocosas mejores autores antiguos, y modernos, 34 vols., Madrid: Blas Roman.

VAN 'T SPIJKER, W. (1996), The Ecclesiastical Offices in the Thought of Martin Bucer, John Vriend/Lyle D. Bierma (trans.), Leiden: Brill.

VAN DEN BERG, MACHIEL A. (2009), Friends of Calvin, Grand Rapids, MI: Wm B. Eerdmans.

VAN DER ELST, CONSTANT (1859), Une dernière victime belge du Saint-Office. 1632: J. B. Avontroot, Revue Trimestrielle 6.23, 160–175.

VAN DER GRIJP, KLAUS (2005), Bibliografia de la Historia del Protestantismo Español, Salamanca: Universidad Pontificia de Salamanca.

VAN DER VEKENÉ, EMILE (1982–1992), Bibliotheca bibliographica historiae sanctae inquisitionis: bibliographisches Verzeichnis des gedruckten Schrifttums zur Geschichte und Literatur der Inquisition, 3 vols., Vaduz, Liechtenstein: Topos.

VAN DEUSEN, NANCY (2002), Between the Sacred and the Worldly, Redwood, CA: Standford University Press.

VAN HOVE, BRIAN (1992), Beyond the Myth of The Inquisition: Ours is The Golden Age, Faith and Reason. www.ewtn.com/library/humanity/mythinqu.htm

VAN LENNEP, MAXIMILIAAN F. (1901), De Hervorming in Spanje in de zestiende eeuw, Haarlem: De Erven Loosjes.

VAN LENNEP, MAXIMILIAAN F. (1984), La historia de la reforma en España en el siglo XVI, Jorge Fliedner (trans.), Grand Rapids, MI: Subcomisión Literatura Cristiana.

VÁZQUEZ DE PRADA, VALENTÍN (1970), La Inquisición y los libros sospechosos en la época de Valdés-Salas (1547–1566), Actas del Simposio Valdés-Salas conmemorativo del IV Centenario de la muerte de su fundador. Don Fernando de Valdés (1483–1568). Su personalidad. Su obra. Su tiempo, Oviedo: Universidad de Oviedo, 147–155.

VERMASEREN, BERNARD ANTOON (1985), Who was Reginaldus Gonsalvus Montanus? Bibliothèque d'Humanisme et Renaissance 47, 47–77.

VERMASEREN, BERNARD ANTOON (1986), The Life of Antonio del Corro (1527–1591); Before his stay in England. Part I. In Spain and France, Archives et Bibliothéques de Belgique 57, 530–568.

VERSLUIS, ARTHUR (2006), The New Inquisitions: Heretic-Hunting and the Intellectual Origins of Modern Totalitarianism, Oxford: Oxford University Press.

VILAR, JUAN BAUTISTA (1994a), La formación de una biblioteca de libros prohibidos en la España isabelina: Luis Usoz y Río, importador clandestino de libros protestantes (1841–1850), Bulletin Hispanique 96.2, 397–416.

VILAR, JUAN BAUTISTA (1994b), El filólogo, helenista y reformador religioso Juan Calderón, en la emigración liberal española de 1823–1833, in: Antiguo Regimen y Liberalismo. Homenaje a Miguel Artola, P. Fernandez/M. Ortega (ed.), 3 vols., Madrid: Alianza Editorial, III, 619–626.

VILAR, JUAN BAUTISTA/MAR VILAR (2010), El primer hispanismo británico en la formación y contenidos de la más importante biblioteca española de libros prohibidos. Correspondencia inédita de Luis de Usoz con Benjamín Wiffen (1840–1850), Cuadernos de Historia Contemporánea 33, 349–351, Seville: Editorial MAD.

VITA CHRISTI. Olivro da Vida de Jhesu Christo (1495), Bernardo de Alcobaça (trans.), Lisbon: Valentim Fernandes and Nicolaus de Saxonia.

VITA CRISTI CARTUXANO (1502), Romançado por fray Ambrosio (Montesino), 4 vols., Alcala de Henares.

VITKUS, DANIEL J./NABIL I. MATAR (2001), Piracy, Slavery, and Redemption: Barbary Captivity Narratives from Early Modern England, New York: Columbia University Press.

VOSE, ROBIN (2010), Introduction to Inquisition Polemics and Histories, Hesburgh Libraries of Notre Dame, Department of Rare Books and Special Collections. University of Notre Dame. http://www.library.nd.edu/rarebooks/digital_projects/inquisition/collections/RBSC-INQ:COLLECTION/essays/RBSC-INQ:ESSAY_PolemicsAndHistories. Accessed May 3, 2015.

WAGNER, CHRISTINE (1994), Los luteranos ante la Inquisición de Toledo en el siglo XVI, Hispania Sacra 46, 473–507.

WAGNER, KLAUS (1975), Los maestrso Gil de Fuentes y Alonso de Escobar y el círuclo de 'Luteranos' de Sevilla, Hispania Sacra 28, 239–247.

WAGNER, KLAUS (1976), La biblioteca del Dr Francisco de Vargas, compañero de Egidio y Constantino, Bulletin Hispanique 78, 313–324.

WAGNER, KLAUS (1979), Lecturas y otras aficiones del Inquisidor Andres Gasco (d.1566), Boletín de la Real Academia de la Historia 176, 149–184.

WAGNER, KLAUS (1981), La Reforma protestante en los fondos bibliográficos de la Biblioteca Colombina, Revista española de teología 41, 393–463.

WAGNER, KLAUS (1982), Martin de Montesdoca y su prensa: contribución al estudio de la imprenta y de la bibliografía sevillanas del siglo XVI, Seville: Universidad de Sevilla.

WALTHER, DANIEL (1965), Marguerite D'Angoulême and the French Lutherans. A Study in Pre-Calvin Reformation in France: II, Andrew University Seminary Studies 3, 49–65.

WEBER, ALISON (1999), Little Women: Counter-Reformation Misogyny, in: The Counter-Reformation: The Essential Readings, David M. Luebke (ed.), Oxford: Blackwell, 143–162.

WEBER, ALISON (ed.) (2016), Devout Laywomen in the Early Modern World, New York: Routledge.

WEISSBERGER, BABARA F. (1997), Resisting Readers and Writers in the Sentimental Romances and the Problem of Female Literacy, in: Studies on the Spanish Sentimental Romance, 1440–1550: Redefining a Genre, Joseph J. Gwara/E. Michael Gerli (eds.), London: Tamesis, 173–190.

WENGERT, TIMOTHY (2005), The Priesthood of All Believers and Other Pious Myths, Institute of Liturgical Studies Occasional Papers, Valparaiso, IN: Valparaiso University.

WIFFEN, BENJAMIN B. (1865), Life and Writings of Juan de Valdés, Otherwise Valdesso, Spanish reformer in the Sixteenth Century, with a translation from the Italian of his Hundred and Ten Consideracions by John T. Betts, London: Bernard Quaritch.

WIFFEN, BENJAMIN B., Memorial of Richard Thomas How addressed to those who knew him not. Written by B.B.[Wiffen], ms. reference Z- 813/1, Bedfordshire and Luton Archives and Records Service. http://discovery.nationalarchives.gov.uk/details/rd/afc34891-0ffe-4c22-ad91-87f96d948ac6. Accessed June 1, 2015.

WILKENS, CORNELIUS A. (1888), Geschichte des spanischen Protestantismus im sechzehnten Jahrhundert, Gütersloh: C. Bertelsmann.

WILKENS, CORNELIUS A. (1897), Spanish Protestants in the Sixteenth Century, Rachel Challice (trans.), London: William Heinemann.

WITTE Jr., JOHN (2005), Sex, Marriage, and Family in John Calvin's Geneva: Courtship, Engagement and Marriage, Grand Rapids, MI: Wm. B. Eerdmans.

WRIGHT, LOUIS B. (1943), Religion and Empire: The Alliance between Piety and Commerce in the English Expansion 1558–1625, Chapel Hill: University of North Carolina Press.

XIMÉNEZ, DIEGO (1552), Enchiridion o manual de doctrina christiana (que tambien puede seruir de confessionario) diuidido en cinco partes, Lisbon: Germão Galharde.

YOVEL, YIRMIYAHU (2009), The Other Within: The Marranos: Split Identity and Emerging Modernity, Princeton, NJ: Princeton University Press.

Appendix A — Confiscated Books

Prohibited Book collected by the Inquisition in Seville and kept in the secret vaults of the Inquisition at Seville (Undated, but presumably 1563).[1]

Antonius Corvinus = Anthony Corvinus (1501–1553)
— *Colloquia Theologica, libri 2*[2]
— *Colloquia Theologica, libri 3*[3]
— *Postilla in evangelia et espistolas*[4]
— *Idem de Sanctus*[5]
— *Theologia ex Augustino et Crisóstomo deprompta*[6]
Andrea Osiandro = Andreas Osiander (1498–1552)
— *Armonía evangelica cum annotationes*[7]
Andreas Hyperius = Andreas Gerhard Hyperius (1511–1564)
— *In epistolam ad Romanos exegeta*[8]
— *De causis escecationes multorum*[9]
— *De honorandis magistratibus conmmentarius*[10]
Andreas Althamerus = Andreas Althamer (1500–1539)

---

1 AHN, *Inquisición*, leg. 2073, doc. 5.
2 Antonius Corvinus, *Colloquiorum Theologicorum Libri duo, in cŏmodum Theologiae candidatorum, Iam primum aeditis*t (Strasbourg: W. Köpfel, 1537).
3 Antonius Corvinus, *Colloqvia Theologica, Qvibus Iam Tertivs Liber accessit, antehac non æditus* (Strasbourg: W. Köpfel, 1540).
4 Antonius Corvinus, *Postilla in Euangelia dominicalia, cum additione locorum, in Epistolas & Euangelia, cum de tempore tum de Sanctis, totius anni* (Strasbourg: W. Köpfel, 1540).
5 *Idem.*
6 Antonius Corvinus, *Augustini et Chrysostomi theologia: ex libris eorundem depromta; inque communes locos digesta* (Halle, 1539).
7 Andreas Osiander, *Harmoniae Evangelicae Libri IIII: Graece Et Latine, In quibus Evangelica historia ex quatuor Evangelistis ita in unum est contexta* (Basel: Froben, 1537).
8 Andreas Hyperius, *In Pauli ad Romanis Epistolam Exegema* (Marburg, 1549).
9 Wrongly attributed. Franciscus Lambertus, *De causis excaecationis multorum seculorum commentarius* (Nuremberg: J. Petreius, 1525).
10 Andreas Hyperius, *De honorandis magistratibus commentarius in quo Psalmus 20 enarratur, ej. in Psalmum 12 paraphrasis* (Marburg: C. Egenolph, 1542).

— *Conciliationes locorum*[11]
— *Sylva biblicorum nominum*[12]
Antonii Melisii (unidentified)
— *Liber sententiarum et fatismi dicritionis contra grecos*[13]
Aretius Benedictus = (Martin Bucer's pseudonym)
— *Sacrorum psalmorum libri 5*[14]
Arsacio Schofer = Arsacius Seehofer (1503–1545)
— *Enrratio evangeliorum dominicalium*[15]
Abatís Urspergensis = Burchard of Ursberg (c.1177–c.1231)
— *Chronicon*[16]
Bartholomeus Westhemerus = Bartholomäus Westheimer/Vesthemerus (1504–1550)
— *Farrago concordantium bibliae*[17]
— *Frases sacrae scripturae*[18]
— *Conciliacionum hac consensum sacrosanctae scripturae*[19]
Bernardinus Ochinus Senensis = Bernardino Ochino (1487–1564)
— *La quarta parte de le prediche en toscano*[20]
— *Expositio epistolae Pauli ad Romanos*[21]
Conradus Lagus = Konrad Lagus (1500–1546)
— *Methodica iuris universi*[22]
Constantino de la Fuente = Constantino Ponce de la Fuente (1502–1560)
— *Doctrina Christiana Grande*[23]
— *Suma de la doctrina christiana*[24]

---

11 Andreas Althamerus, *Conciliationes Locorum scripturae, qui specie tenus inter se pugnare uidentur: Centuriae duae* (Nuremberg: Petreius, 1548).
12 Andreas Althamerus. *Sylva biblicorum nominum* (Basel: Thomam Wolphium, 1535).
13 Is this part of Peter Lombard's *Liber Sententiarum* (Paris, 1518)?
14 Benedictus Aretius. *Psalmi: libri quinque* (Strasbourg: Ulricher, 1529).
15 Arsatius Schofer. *Enarrartiones Evangeliorum Dominicalium ad dialecticam Methodum, & Rhetoricam dispositionem accommodatae* (Augsburg, 1539).
16 Burchardus Urspergensis, *Chronicum abbatis Urspergensis, continens historiam rerum memorabilium, a Nino Assyriorum rege ad tempora Friderici II* [1515] (Strasbourg: C. Mylium, 1552).
17 Bartholomeus Westhemerus. *Farrago concordantium insignium totius Bibliae* (Basel: T. Wolff, 1528).
18 Bartholomeus Westhemerus, *Phrases seu modi loquendi divinae scripturae, ex sanctis et orthodoxis scriptoribus* (Antwerp, 1536).
19 Bartholomäus Westheimer, *En damus lector Conciliationem ae consensum sacrosanctae scripturae et patrum orthodoxorum* (Zurich: Gesner et Wyssenbach, 1552).
20 Bernardino Ochino, *Prediche* (Geneva, 1550).
21 Bernhardini Ochini Senensis, *Expositio Epistolæ diui Pauli ad Romanos* (Augsburg: P. Ulhardus, 1550).
22 Conradus Lagus, *Methodica Juris Utriusque Traditio, Omnem Omnium Titulorum, Tam Pontificii, Quam Cæsarei, Juris Materiam Et Genus Complectens, etc.* (Paris, 1545).
23 Constantino [Ponce] de la Fuente, *Doctrina Christiana, en que está comprehendida toda la información que pertenece al hombre que quiere servir a Dios. Parte primera* (Seville: Juan Canalla, 1548, 1549; Antwerp: Juan Steelsio [Latio], 1554, 1555).
24 Constantino [Ponce] de la Fuente, *Summa de doctrina Cristiana compuesta por el muy*

— *Exposición sobre el psalmo "Beatus Vir"*[25]
— *Catecismo Christiano*[26]
— *Confesión de un pecador*[27]
Conradus Gesnerus = Conrad Gessner (1516–1565)
— *Biblioteca universalis, 1 et 2 tomi*[28]
Conradus Clauserus = Konrad Klauser (1515–1567)
— *De oratione liber*[29]
Christophorus Hofman = Christoph Hoffmann (–1553)
— *De penitentia commentariorum, libri 3*[30]
— *Comentaria in epistolam ad Philippenses*[31]
Celii Segundi Curionis = Celio Secundo Curione (1503–1569)
— *Familiar y paterna instrucción de la cristiana religión,* en francés[32]
— *Selectarum espistolarum, libri 2*[33]
— *Quatro lettere christiane, con uno paradoso,* en toscano[34]
Christophorus Hegendorfius = Christophorus Hegendorfius (1500–1540)
— *Annotationes in evangelium Marci*[35]
Conradus Pellicanus = Conradus Pellicanus (1478–1556)
— *Omnia opera,* en 6 tomos[36]
— *Index bibliorum*[37]

---

reverendo señor el Doctor Constantino en que se contiene todo lo principal y necessario que el hombre christiano deue saber y obrar (Seville: Juan Cromberger, 1543, 1544).

25 Constantino [Ponce] de la Fuente, *Exposición del primer psalmo de David: cuyo principio es «Beatus Vir» dividida en seys sermones* (Seville: Juan de León, 1546; Seville: C. Alvarez, 1551; Antwerp: G. Simón, 1556).

26 Constantino [Ponce] de la Fuente, *Cathecismo Christiano, para instruir a los niños* (Seville: Juan de León, 1547; Antwerp: G. Simón, 1556).

27 Constantino [Ponce] de la Fuente, *Confesión de un pecador penitente delante de Jesucristo, redemptor y juez de los hombres* (Seville: Juan de León, 1547; Évora: Andrés de Burgos, 1554; Antwerp: G. Simón, 1556).

28 Conrad Gesner, *Bibliotheca universalis: sive Catalogus omnium scriptorum locupletissimus, in tribus linguis, Latina, Graeca, & Hebraica extantium* (Zurich: C. Frosch, 1555).

29 Conrad Clauserus, *De oratione liber ad illustrissimi principis & ducis Suffolchiae, regis Angliae consilarii, filias* (Zurich: C. Frosch, 1553).

30 Christophorus Hoffman, *De Poenitentia Commentariorvm Libri Tres. Avtore Christophoro Hoffman, Concionatore Ihenensi* (Frankfurt: P. Brubach, 1540).

31 Christophorus Hoffman, *Commentarius in epistolam Pauli ad Philippenses* (Frankfurt: P. Brubach, 1541).

32 Celio Secondo Curione., *Una familiare et paterna institutio della Christiana religione* (Basel: J. Oporinus, 1550).

33 Celio Secondo Curione, *Selectarum epistolarum libri duo* (Basel: J. Oporinus, 1553).

34 Celio Secondo Curione, *Quatro lettere Christiane, con uno paradosso, sopra quel detto Beati quegli che piangono & un sermone, o uer discorso del'orazione* (Bologna: M. Pietro & Paulo Perusini fratelli, 1552).

35 Christoph Hegendorphius, *In omnia Marci capita, adnotationes recognitae* (Haguenau: J. Secerium, 1526).

36 Could this refer to Conrad Pellicanus's *Commentaria Bibliorum* (Zurich: C. Frosch, 1538)?

37 Conrad Pellicanus, *Index Bibliorum* (Zurich: C. Frosch, 1537).

— *In omnes epistolas Pauli et Canonicas*[38]
Erasmus Rotherodamus = Desiderius Erasmus (1469–1536)
— *Moria encomium con comento*[39]
— *Eclesiastés sive modus concionandi*[40]
— *Exmologesis*[41]
— *Colloquios,* en romance[42]
— *Enquiridion del caballero cristiano,* en romance[43]
Erasmus Sarcerius = *Erasmus Sarcerius* (1501–1559)
— *In evangelia dominicalia postilla*[44]
— *In epistolas Pauli ad Philippenses, Colossenses, Thesalonicenses*[45]
— *In epsitolas Pauli ad Corintios*[46]
— *Retorica plena exemplis*[47]
— *Catechismus*[48]
— *In epistolas Pauli ad Galatas et Ephesios*[49]
— *In Matheum et Marcum scholia*[50]
— *In epistolas dominicales*[51]

---

38 Conrad Pellicanus, *In omnes apostolicas epistolas, Pauli, Petri, Jacobi, Joannis et Judae. Commentarij* (Zurich: C. Frosch, 1539).

39 Desiderius Erasmus, *Moriae Encomium* (Lyons: S. Gryphius, 1540; Basel: H. Froben & N. Episcopium, 1540, 1551).

40 Desiderius Erasmus, *Ecclesiastae sive de ratione concionandi. Libri IV* (Basel: Froben, 1544).

41 Desiderius Erasmus, *Exomologesis, sive modus Confitendi per Erasmum Roterodamum* (Basel, 1530).

42 Desiderius Erasmus, *Colloquios de Erasmo traduzidos [del] latin en romance: porque los que no entiēden la lengua latina gozen assi mismo [de] doctrina de tan alto varon* (Seville: J. Cromberger, 1529; Toledo: C. Damián, 1530; Zaragoza: J. Coci, 1530; Toledo: Juan de Ayala, 1532).

43 Desiderius Erasmus, *Enchiridion o Manual del Cauallero Christiano de D. Erasmo Roterodamo en romance* (Alcalá: Miguel de Eguía, 1526, 1527, 1529, 1533; Zaragoza, 1528; Valencia: Jorge Costilla, 1528; Valencia: Juan Joffre, 1528; Seville: Jacobo Cromberger, 1528).

44 Erasmus Sarcerius, *In Euangelia Festivalia Postilla, Ad Methodi Formam expedita* (Frankfurt: C. Egenolff, 1539, 1540, 1544).

45 Erasmus Sarcerius, *In Epistolas ad Philipp., Coloss. et Thessalonic. pia et erudita scholia* (Frankfurt: C. Egenolff, 1542).

46 Erasmus Sarcerius, *In D. Pauli Epistolas ad Corinthios eruditae ac piae meditationes* (Strasbourg: Rihelius, 1544).

47 Erasmus Sarcerius, *Rhetorica Plena ac referta exemplis, quae succinctarum declamationum loco esse possunt* (Marburg: Eucharius, 1537).

48 Erasmus Sarcerius, *Catechismus. plane nouus, per omnes ferè quaestiones & circumstantias, quae in iustam tractationem incidere possunt, in usum scholarum & templorum* (Leipzig: W. Günther, 1550).

49 Erasmus Sarcerius, *In epistolas D. Pauli, ad Galatas et Ephesios, piae atque eruditae annotationes, pro rhetorica dispositione* (Frankfurt: C. Egenolff, 1542).

50 Erasmus Sarcerius, *In Marcum evangelistam iusta scholia* (Basel: Bartholomäus Westheimer, 1541); *In Matthaeum Evangelistam iusta et docta scholia, per omnes rhetoricae artis cirumstantias methodice conscripta et locupletata* (Basel: B. Westhemerum, 1544).

51 Erasmus Sarcerius, *Erasmi Sarverii In evangelia dominicalia postilla* (Marburg: C. Egenolff, 1541).

— *In Iessum Syrach*[52]
— *In Evangelium Ioannis*[53]
— *Loccorum comuni ex consensus divinae scripturae*[54]
— *Exposiciones in evangelia festivalia*[55]
— *Dictionarium ecclesiasticae doctrinae*[56]
— *Dialectica multis exemplis illustrata*[57]
— *Nova methodus in precipuos scripturae divine locos*[58]
Fridericus Furias Coeriolanus = Fadrique Furió Ceriol (1527–1592)
— *Bolonia sive de libris in vernaculam lingua vertendis libri 2*[59]
Franciscus Lambertus = Franz Lambert (1486–1530)
— *In regulam Minoritarum et contra universas perditionis sectas*[60]
— *In Micheam Naum Abacuch*[61]
— *In quatuor ultimis minores profetas*[62]
— *In Amos Abdiam et Ionam profetas*[63]
— *In Evangelium Luca comentarius*[64]
Georgius Aemilius = Georgius Aemilius/Oemmel/Emilius/Öhmler/Oemler (1517–1569)
— *Hystoria seu lectionum evangelicarum explicatio*[65]

52 Erasmus Sarcerius, *In Jesum Sirach integra scholia* (Frankfurt: C. Egenolff, 1543).
53 Erasmus Sarcerius, *In Ioannem Euangelistam Iusta Scholia summa diligentia, ad perpetuae textus cohaerentiae filium* (Basel: B. Westhemerum, 1540).
54 Erasmus Sarcerius, *Locorum communium ex consensu diversae scripturae* (Basel: J. Bebel, 1547).
55 Erasmus Sarcerius, *Expositiones in epistolas dominicales ac festivales, ad methodiformam ferè absolutae* (Frankfurt: C. Egenolff, 1540).
56 Erasmus Sarcerius, *Dictionarium scholasticae doctrinae, in quo et horrendos abusus, et multa alia ad sacram scripturam rectè intelligendam non inutilia, cernere licebit.* (Basel: J. Bebel, 1546).
57 Erasmus Sarcerius, *Dialectica multis ac uariis exemplis illustrata, una cum facilima syllogismorum expositoriorum, enthymematum, exemplorum, inductionum, & soritum dispositione* (Frankfurt: C. Egenolff, 1551).
58 Erasmus Sarcerius, *Nova methodus in praecipuos Scripturae divinae locos, antea ea fide & illo ordine, nec edita, nec visa: quare is tandem credat se integrũ habere Methodi Sarcerianae exemplar, qui postremam hanc editionẽ sibi comparaverit* (Basel: M. Isingrin, 1546).
59 Fadrique Furió Ceriol, *Bolonia sive de libris sacris in vernaculam linguam convertendis, ibri duo* (Basel: J. Oporinus, 1556).
60 Franciscus Lambertus, *In regvlam Minoritarvm, et contra uniuersas perditionis sectas, Francisci Lamberti commentarii vere Evangelici* (Strasbourg: Herwagen, 1525).
61 Franciscus Lambertus, *Commentarii, in Micheam, Naum, et Abacuc* (Strasbourg: Hervagius, 1525).
62 Franciscus Lambertus, *Commentarii in quatuor ultimos Prophetas, nempe Sophoniam, Aggeum, Zachariam et Malachiam* (Strasbourg: Hervagius, 1526).
63 Franciscus Lambertus, *In Amos, Abddiam, et Ionam Prophetas, Commentarij Francisci Lamberti* (Strasbourg: Hervagius, 1525).
64 Franciscus Lambertus, *In divi Lucae Evangelium commentarii* (Strasbourg: Hervagius, 1525).
65 Georgius Aemilius, *Historiarvm Sev Lectionvm Euangelicarum, quæ ueteri more Dominicis atque Festis diebus in Ecclesia tractari solent, Explicatio diligens & noua* (Basel: J. Oporinus, 1551).

Guillermus Postellus = Guillaume Postel (1510–1581)
— *De orbis térrea concordia libri 4*[66]
Gaspar Cruçigero = Caspar Creuziger/Cruciger, (1504–1548)
— *Enarrationes Symboli Niceni libri 2*[67]
— *In Evangelium Ioannis ennarratio*[68]
Gaspar Megandro = Caspar Megander (1495–1545)
— *In Epistolam Pauli ad Ephesios*[69]
— *In Epistolam Pauli ad Thimoteum et Titum*[70]
Henricus Bulingerus = Heinrich Bullinger (1504–1575)
— *In quatuor evangelia, en dos cuerpos*[71]
— *In Epistolas Pauli et Canonicas*[72]
— *De gratia Dei iustificante*[73]
— *De scripturae sancte autoritate*[74]
— *Brevis Antiboaci sive secunda responsio*[75]
— *Sermones decades due tomus primus*[76]
— *De origine herroris*[77]
— *Quo pacto cum aegrotantibus agendum sit*[78]
— *Adversus omnia catabatistarum prava dogmata*[79]

---

66 Guillaume Postel, *De orbis terrae concordia libri quatuor: multiiuga eruditione ac pietate referti, quibus nihil hoc tam perturbato rerum statu uel utilius, uel accommodatius potuisse in publicum edi* (Basel: J. Oporinus, 1544).
67 Caspar Creutziger, *Enarratio Symboli Niceni Complectens ordine doctrinam Ecclesiae Dei fideliter recitatam; Accesserunt priori editioni plures Symboli partes* (1550).
68 Caspar Creutziger, *In Evangelivm Iohannis Apostoli Enarratio Caspari Crucigeri recens edita* (Strasbourg: C. Mylius, 1546).
69 Caspar Megander, *Gasparis Megandri Tigurini, in epistolam Pauli ad Ephesios commentarius: unà cum Ioannis Rhellicani epistola monitoria* (Basel: H. Petrus, 1534).
70 Caspar Megander, *In diui Pauli epistolas tres, ad Timotheum & Titum, Gasparis Megandri, Bernensis ecclesiastae, diligens ac breuis expositio, recens aedita* (Basel: T. Platterum, & B. Lasium, 1535).
71 This seems to be wrongly attributed and could refer to Johannes Oecolampadius, *In quatuor Evangelia enarratione* (Cologne: Quentel, 1536).
72 Heinrich Bullinger, *In epistolas apostolorum canonicas septem commentarii Heinrychi Bullingeri* (Zurich: C. Frosch, 1537).
73 Heinrich Bullinger, *De Gratia Dei iustificante* (Zurich: C. Frosch, 1554).
74 Heinrich Bullinger, *De Scripturæ Sanctæ authoritate: certitudine, firmitate et absoluta perfectione, deque episcoporum institutione & functione, contra superstitionis tyrannidisque Romanæ antistites* (Zurich: C. Frosch, 1538).
75 Heinrich Bullinger, *Brevis anti Bole, sive, Responsio secunda Heinrychi Bullingeri ad maledicam implicatamque Ioannis Cochlei de Scripturae & ecclesiae authoritate replicam unà cum expositione de sancta Christi catholica ecclesia* (Zurich: C. Frosch, 1544).
76 Heinrich Bullinger, *Sermonum decades duae accesserunt ex quarta decade sermones duo, De Evangelio et De poenitentia* (Zurich: C. Frosch, 1549).
77 Heinrich Bullinger, *De origine erroris, in divorum ac simulachrorum cultu* (Basel: T. Wolff, 1529).
78 Heinrich Bullinger, *Quo pacto cum Aegrotantibus...agendu sit* (Zurich: A. Frysius, 1540).
79 Heinrich Bullinger, *Adversus omnia catabaptistarum prava dogmata* (Zurich: C. Frosch, 1535).

Hermanus Bodius = (Martin Bucer's pseudonyms)
— *Unio dessidentium*[80]
Henricus Cornelius Agripa = Heinrich Cornelius Agrippa von Nettesheim (1486-1535)
— *De oculta philosophia*[81]
— *De vanitate scientiarum*[82]
Hermanus Bonnus = Herman Bonnus (1504-1548)
— *Fárrago precipuorum exemplorum de Apostolis et Martiribus*[83]
Hieronimus Vuclerus = Hieronymus (Jerome) Weller (1499-1572)
— *De officio ecclesiastico politico et economico*[84]
— *Ennarratio epistolarum dominicalium*[85]
Huldericus Zwinglius = Ulrich Zwingli (1484-1531)
— *Omnium operum tomus primus tertius et quartus*[86]
Iacobus Fabrus Stapulensis = Jacques Lefèvre d'Étaples (1455-1536)
— *In evangelia*[87]
— *In Epistolas Pauli*[88]
Ioannes Calvinus = John Calvin (1509-1564)
— *Libellus de Cena Domini*[89]
— *In Esaiam Prophetam*[90]
— *In Pulum et canonicas et acta apostolorum*[91]
— *In Genessim*[92]

---

80 Hermanus Bodius, *Unio dissidentium, libellus omnibus unitatis ac pacis amatoribus utilissimus: ex praecipuis Ecclesiae Christiane Doctoribus* (Basel: N. Bryling, 1551).

81 Henricus Cornelius Agrippa, *De occulta Philosophia libri tres* (Cologne: Soter, 1533).

82 Henricus Cornelius Agrippa, *De incertitudine et Vanitate scientiarum declamatio inuectiua, denuo ab autore recognita et marginalibus Annotationibus aucta* (Cologne, 1536).

83 Hermann Bonnus. *Farrago praecipvorvm exemplorum de apostolis, martyribus, episcopis, et sanctis patribus veteris ecclesiae* (Halle: P. Braubach, 1539).

84 Hieronymus Weller [Vuellero], *De officio ecclesiastico, politico, et oeconomico: libellvs pivs et ervditvs* (Nuremberg: J. Montani & U. Neuberi, 1552).

85 Hieronimus Wellerus, *Enarratio epistolarum dominicalium recens Edita, et locupletata* (Nuremberg: Montanus & Neuberus, 1551).

86 Huldrychus Zwingli, *Opera D. Hvldrychi Zvinglii, uigilantissimi Tigurinæ ecclesiæ Antistitis: partim quidem ab ipso Latine conscripta, partim uerò è uernaculo sermone in Latinum translata* (Zürich: C. Frosch, 1545).

87 Jacobus Fabrus Stapulensis, *Commentariee initiatorii in quatuos evangelia* (Meaux: S. Colinaeus, 1522).

88 Jacobus Fabrus Stapulensis, *Iacobi Fabri Stapvlensis, theologi celeberrimi, commentarij in epistolas catholicas. Iacobi I. Petri II. Ioannis III. Ivdae I* (Antwerp: J. Gymnicum, 1540).

89 Jean Calvin, *Consensio mutua in re sacramentaria ministrorum Tigurinae ecclesiae, et D. Joannis Calvini ministri Genevensis ecclesiae, jam nunc ab ipsis authoribus edita* (Zurich: R. Vuissenbachij, 1551).

90 Jean Calvin, *In Esaiam Prophetam* (Geneva: Adam & Jean Riveriz, 1552).

91 Jean Calvin, *Commentarii integri in Acta apostolorum; Commentarii integri in epístolas canonicas* (Geneva: Crispin, 1551).

92 Jean Calvin, *Commentaire de M. Jean Calvin sur le pemier livre de Moyse, dit Genese* (Geneva: J. Gerard, 1554).

— *Interim adulter Germanorum*[93]
— *Brevis instructio contra Anabatistas*[94]
— *Istituio christianae religionis*[95]
— *Harmonia evangelica*[96]
— *In Epistola Prima ad Corinthios,* en francés[97]
— *Provisión hecha sobre las diferencias de la religión,* en francés[98]
— *Prefacio in exemplum memorabile in desperationes cuiusdam*[99]
Ioannes Draconitem = Johannes Draconites (1494–1566)
— *Comentariorum evangeliorum libri 2*[100]
— *In Danielem prophetam*[101]
Ioannes Spangebergo Herdosiani = Johann Spangenberg (1484–1550)
— *Margarita theologica*[102]
— *In acta apostolorum*[103]
— *In epistolas dominicales*[104]
— *In evangelia et epistolas dominacales et de Sanctus*[105]

---

93 Jean Calvin, *Interim adultero—germanum: cui adjecta est, vera christianæ pacicationis, et Ecclesiæ reformandæ ratio* (Geneva: J. Girard, 1549).

94 Jean Calvin, *Brevis instructio muniendis fidelibus adversus errores sectae Anabaptistarum: item adversus fanaticam et furiosam sectam Libertinorum, qui se spirituales vocant* (Strasbourg: W. Ribelius, 1546).

95 Jean Calvin, *Institvtio Totivs Christianae Religionis, Nvnc Ex Postrema Avthoris Recognitione Qvibusdam Locis Avctior, Infinitis Verò Castigatior* (Geneva: J. Gerard, 1550).

96 Jean Calvin, *In evangelium secundum Matthaeum, Marcum et Lucam commentarii: Harmonia Evangelica* (Geneva: R. Stephanus, 1553).

97 Jean Calvin, *Commentaire de M. Iean Calvin, sur La Seconde Epistre aux Corinthiens traduit de Latin en François* (Geneva: J. Girard, 1547).

98 Jean Calvin, *L'Interim, c'est à dire provision faicte sur les differens de la religion en quelques villes & pais d'Allemagne. Avec la vraye façon de réformer l'Eglise chrestienne.* (Geneva: J. Bourgeois, 1549).

99 Francisci Spieræ, *Qui quod susceptam semel Evangelice veritatis professionem abnegasset, damnassetque, in horrendam incidit desperationem, Historia, a' quatuor summis viris, summa fide conscripta: cum clariss. virorum Præfationibus, Cælii S.C.& Io. Calvini, & Petri Pauli Vergerii Apologia* (Basel: J. Herwagen, 1550).

100 Johannes Draconites, *Commentariorum evangelicorum de Jesu Christo filio Dei libri duo: Catechismus praeterea adiectus est* (Basel: Rob. Winter, 1545).

101 Johann Draconites, *Commentarius In Danielem Ex Ebraeo uersum. Cum Oratione & Indice* (Marburg: A. Kolbe, 1544).

102 Johann Spangenberg, *Margarita theologica, continens praecipuos locos doctrinae christianae, per quaestiones breviter et ordine explicatos, omnibus Pastoribus, verbi preconibus et ecclesiae ministris summe utilis et necessaria* (Wittenberg: Ĝeorg Rhau, 1541).

103 Johann Spangenberg, *Acta apostolorum breviter enarrata et in dilucidas quaestiones redacta* (Frankfurt: C. Egenolff, 1546).

104 Johann Spangenberg. *Evangelia Dominicalia in versiculos extemporaliter versa.* Wittenberg, 1539; *Epistolae, per totum annum Dominicis diebus in ecclesia legi solitae, per quaestiones explicatae, & illustratae* (Frankfurt: C. Egenolff, 1545).

105 Johann Spangenberg, *Explicationes Evangeliorvm Et Epistolarvm, Qvae Dominicis Diebvs More Vsitato Proponi In Ecclesia Popvlo Solent: In Tabvlas Svccinctas, Et Ad Memoriam Admodum utiles, redactae: unà cum Tabulis Euangeliorum de Sanctis* [1544].

Ioannes Oecolampadius = Johannes Oecolampadius (1482–1531)
— *In Epistolas Pauli ad Romanos et Hebreos*[106]
— *Annotationes in evangelium Ioannis*[107]
— *In epistolam ad Colosenses conciones*[108]
— *In Iob et Danielem prophetam*[109]
— *In Ezechielem prophetam*[110]
— *In Evangelium Mathei*[111]
— *In Genessim*[112]
— *Annotationes in Osseam, Ioelem, Amos et Abdian prophetas*[113]
Ioannes Bugenhagius Pomeranus = Ioannes Bugenhagen (1485–1558)
— *In quatuor capita priores Epistole ad Corinthios*[114]
— *Idem in epistolas Pauli ad Galatas, Ephesios, Philippenses, Colosenses, Thesalonicenses duas, Thimoteum duas, Titum, Pholomenum et denique Hebreros*[115]
— *Ennarrationes in Ieremiam prophetam*[116]
— *In Deuteronomium et Samuelem hoc est, in 29 libris*[117]
— *In Iob*[118]

---

106 Joannes Oecolampadius, *In epistolam B. Pauli Apost. ad Rhomanos adnotationes a Ioanne Oecolampadio Basileae praelectae, cum indice* (Basel: A. Cratander, 1525).

107 Joannes Oecolampadius, *Annotationes piae ac doctae in Euangeliũ Ioannis, D. Ioanne Oecolampadio autore* (Basel: A. Cratander & J. Bebel, 1533).

108 Joannes Oecolampadius, *In epistolam d. Pauli ad Collossenses. Conciones aliquot piae ac doctae ad tempora nostra valde accomodae, nunc primum in lucem aeditae* (Bern: Apiarius, 1546).

109 Joannes Oecolampadius, *In librum Job exegemata; ejusdem In Danielem prophetam libri duo.* (Geneva: J. Crispin, 1553).

110 Joannes Oecolampadius, *In Prophetam Ezechielem Commentarivs D. Ioan. Oecolampadij, per Vuolfgangum Capitonem ditus* (Strasbourg: Apiarius, 1534).

111 Joannes Oecolampadius, *Enarratio in Euangelium Matthaei D. Io. Oecolampadio autore: & alia nonnulla quae sequens pagella indicabit* (Basel: A. Cratander & J. Bebel, 1536).

112 Joannes Oecolampadius, *Homilias in Genesin LXVI (Ioanne Oecolampadio interprete) et alia quaedam* (Basel: H. Froben, J. Hervagium & N. Episcopium, 1530).

113 Joannes Oecolampadius, *In minores quos vocant, prophetas Joannis Oecolampadii lucubrationes quaecunque ab ipso editae, et post decessum ex ipsius praelectionibus colectae et publicae factae extant; Commentarii omnes in libros Prophetarum* (Geneva: J. Crispin, 1558).

114 Johannes Bugenhagius, *Ioannis Bvgenhagii Pomerani commentarius, In quatuor capita prioris Epistolæ ad Corinthios, de sapientia & iusticia dei quæ Christus est, et de autoritate sacræ scripturæ & doctrinæ Apostolicæ in ecclesia Christi* (Wittenberg: Lufft, 1530).

115 Johannes Bugenhagius, *Annotationes Io. Bugenhagij Pomerani in epistolas Pauli, ad Galatas, Ephesios, Philippenses, Colossenses, Thessalonicenses primam & secundam. Timotheum primam et secundam. Titum. Philemonem, Hebraeos* (Nuremberg: Petreius, 1524).

116 Joannes Bugenhagen, *Psalterium Davidis, et Integri Loci sacre doctrine, ex omnibus Prophetis, cum quibusdam aliis piis canticis* (Wittenberg: P. Seitz, 1544).

117 Johannes Bugenhagius, *Annotationes In Deuteronomium, In Samuëlem prophetam, id est, duos libros Regum. Ab eodem prterea conciliata ex Euangelistis historia passi Christi & glorificati* (Strasbourg: Knobloch, 1524).

118 Johannes Bugenhagius, *In Hiob annotationis* (Altenburg: Gab. Kantz, 1527).

— *In Psalmos*[119]
— *In Evangelia Dominicalia*[120]
Ioachimus Vadianus = Joachim Vadian (1484–1551)
— *Aphorismorum libri 6 de consideratione Eucharistiae*[121]
Ioannes Gastius = Johannes Gast (1505–1552)
— *In orationem dominicam*[122]
— *Protevangelion de natalibus Iesu Christi et ipsius matris*[123]
— *Tomus secundus convivalium sermonum*[124]
Ioannes Yndagine = Joannes Indagine (1467–1537)
— *Chiromantia*[125]
Ioannes Valdesius = Juan de Valdés (1500?–1541)
— *Comentario sobre la Epístola de San Pablo a los Romanos en romance*[126]
Iuan Pérez de Pineda = Juan Pérez de Pineda (1500–1556)
— *Comentario sobre los salmos de David en romance*[127]
Ioannes Sleydanus = Johannes Sleidan (1506–1556)
— *De statu religiones*[128]
Iustus Ionas = Justus Jonas (1493–1555)
— *Cathecismus pro pueris in ecclesiis, etc.*[129]

---

119 Johannes Bugenhagius, *Pomerani Bugenhagii In librum psalmorum interpretatio: Wittembergæ publice lecta* (Nuremberg: Petreius, 1524); *Psalterium Davidis, Et integri loci sacrae doctrinae: ex omnibus Prophetis. Cum quibusdam alijs pijs Canticis* (Wittenberg: P. Seitz, 1544).

120 Johannes Bugenhagius, *Indices quidam Ioannis Bugenhagii Pomerani in Evangelia (ut vocant) Dominicalia, Insuper usui temporum et sanctorum totius anni servientia* (Wittenberg: Lufft, 1523).

121 Joachim Vadianus, *Aphorismorum libri 6 de consideratione eucharistiae* (Zurich: Frosch, 1536).

122 Johann Gast, *In Orationem Dominicam Salvberrimae ac sanctissimæ meditationes ex libris Catholicorum Patrum selectæ* (Basel: R. Winter, 1543).

123 This work is mistakenly attributed. Guillaume Postel et Theodorus Bibliander, *Protevangelion, sive de natalibus Jesu Christi, & ipsius matris Virginis Mariæ, sermo historicus divi Jacobi minoris: Evangelica historia, quam scripsit beatus Marcus. Vita Joannis Marci evangelistæ* (Basel: J. Oporinus, 1552).

124 Johann Gast, *Tomvs. Convivalivm Sermonvm, Vtilibvs Ac Ivcvndis Historijs, & sentenijs, omni ferè de re, quae in sermonem, apud amicos in dulci conuiuiolo, incidere potest, refertus* (Basel: N. Brylinger, 1548).

125 Ioannes Indagine, *Chiromantia* (Strasbourg: Schottus, 1522, 1531, 1534).

126 Juan de Valdés, *Comentario o declarazion breve i compendiosa sobre la epístola de San Pablo apóstol á los Romanos, muy util para todos los amadores de la piedad christiana* (Venice: Iuan Philadelpho [Geneva: Crespin], 1557).

127 Juan Pérez de Pineda, *Los Psalmos de David con sus Sumarios, en que se declara con brevedad la contenido en cada Psalmo, agora nueva y fielmente traducidos en romance Castellano por el doctor Juan Pérez, conforme a la verdad de la lengua Sancta* (Venice: Pedro Daniel [Geneva: Crespin], 1557).

128 Johannes Sleidanus, *De statu religionis & reipublicæ, Carolo Quinto, Caesare, commentarij* (Strasbourg: J. Rihelium, 1556).

129 Justus Jonas, *Catechismus propueris et juventute, in ecclesiis & ditione illustriss. principium, Marchionum Brandeborgensium* (Wittenberg: P. Seitz, 1543).

— *Prefacio methodica scripture totius*[130]
Ioannes Piscatorius = Joannes Piscator (1500?-1555?)
— *Epitome operum Augustini*[131]
Iodovicus Wilichius = Jodocus Willich/Vuillichius (1501-1552)
— *In Ioanem, in Abdian prophetas*[132]
— *In Evangelia dominicalia*[133]
Ioannes Rivius = Joannes Rivius (1500-1553)
— *Quo se pactum iuventus in hisce religiones disidiis severe devere*[134]
— *De conciencia, libri 3*[135]
— *De admirabili dei consilio*[136]
— *De disciplinis quae de sermone agunt ut de gramatica, dialetica de Rethorica*[137]
Ioannes Puperus = Johann Pupper (1400-1475)
— *De libertate christiana*[138]
Iodoco Rimhisio (unidentified)
— *In epistolam Pauli ed Philipensis*
Ioannes Agrícola = *Johannes Agricola* (1494-1566)
— *Annotationes in Evangelium Lucae*[139]
Iosephus Iudeus = Flavius Josephus (c.37-c.100)
— *De antiquitatibus*, en romançe[140]
Ioannes Brentius = Johann Brentius, or Brenz, (1499-1570)
— *In Evangelium Ioannis*, dos tomos[141]
— *In Esaiam Prophetam*[142]

---

130 Justus Jonas, *Praefatio in epistolas divi Pauli apostoli ad Corynthios* (Erphordia, 1520).
131 Johannes Piscatorius [Pessellius], *Omnium operum Divi Avrelii Avgvstini, episcopi hippo-nensis, Epitome* (Augsburg: H. Steiner, 1537).
132 Jodocus Willich, *In Abdiam Commentaria Rhetoricorum More Conscripta* (Frankfurt, 1550).
133 Jodocus Willich, *Dispositio in evangelia dominicalia omnibus declamatoribus, tam ec-clesiasticis quàm scholasticis utilissima* (Basel: Westheimer, 1542).
134 Joannes Rivius, *Quo se pacto juventus in hisce religionis dissidiis gerere debeat ll. II.* (Basel, 1546).
135 Joannes Rivius, *Joannis Rivii de conscientia libri III. Ejusdem de spectris et apparitionibus umbrarum, seu de veteri superstitione, liber I* (Leipzig: N. Wolrab, 1541).
136 Joannes Rivius, *De admirabili Dei consilio, in celando mysterio redemptionis humanae libri tres Ioanne Rivio* (Basel: J. Oporinus, 1545).
137 Joannes Rivius, *De iis Disciplinis, quae de sermone agunt, ut sunt grammatica, dialectica, rhetorica: libri XVIII* (Leipzig: N. Wolrab, 1543).
138 Johann Pupper von Goch, *Dialogus de quatuor erroribus circa evangelicam legem exortis, etc.* (Zwolle: S. Corver, 1521).
139 Joannes Agricola, *In Evangelivm Lvcae Annotationes Ioannis agricolæ Islebij, summa scripturarum fide tractatæ* (Nuremberg: J. Petreius, 1525).
140 Josephus Judeus Flavius, *Josephi Judei historici preclara opera nō parua accuratiōe & dili-gentia recēter ip̄ressa de antiquitatib' libri viginti de Judaico bello libri septem de antiqua Judeorū origine* (Paris, 1519).
141 Joannes Brentius, *Evangelion qvod inscribitvr, secvndvm Ioannem, centvm qvinqva-gintaqvatvor homiliis explicatum* (Frankfurt: P. Brubach, 1551).
142 Joannes Brentius, *Esaias, Propheta: Commentariis explicatus* (Frankfurt: P. Brubach, 1550).

— *In libros Iudicum*[143]
— *In Amos et Iob Prophetam et Acta Apostolorum*[144]
— *In Essodum*[145]
— *In Evangelium Lucae,* dos tomos[146]
— *In Samuelem*
— *Explicatio Epistolae ad Galatas*[147]
— *In Ecclesiastem Salomonis*[148]
— *Cathecismus*[149]
— *In Epistolam Paulii ad Philemonem*[150]
— *Index copiosus omnium homiliarum*[151]
— *In Iosué*
— *Ennarratio in Evagelia Dominicalia*[152]
Luccas Lossius = Lucas Lossius (1508–1582)
— *In Novum Testamentum annotationes*[153]
— *Eiusdem cathecismus*[154]
— *Tomus secundos in Lucas et Iohannem*[155]
— *Cantica Sacra veteris ecclesie Selene*[156]
Leonardo Culmanus = Leonhard Culmann (1497–1562)
— *Thesaurus locorum ex Viteri et Novo Testamento*[157]

---

143 Joannes Brentius, *In Librvm Ivdicvm et Rvth Commentarii* (Halle: P. Brubach, 1544).
144 Joannes Brentius, *In Prophetam Amos. Expositio* (Frankfurt: P. Brubach, 1545).
145 Joannes Brentius, *In Exodvm Mosi Commentarii* (Frankfurt: P. Brubach, 1544).
146 Joannes Brentius, *In Evangelii quod inscribitur secundum Lucam, duodecim priora capita, Lucam, duodecim priora capita, homiliæ centum & decem* (Frankfurt: P. Brubach, 1551).
147 Joannes Brentius, *Explicatio Epistolae Pavli ad Galatas* (Frankfurt: P. Brubach, 1550).
148 Joannes Brentius, *Ecclesiastes Salomonis, cum commentarijs Ioannis Brentij* (Haguenau, 1529).
149 Joannes Brentius, *Catechesis puerilis* (Halle: Brubach, 1540).
150 Joannes Brentius, *In Epistolam Pavli Ad Philemonem, Et In Historiam Esther Commentarioli* (Halle: Brubach, 1543).
151 Joannes Brentius, *Index copiosus omnium homiliarum, centum videlicet, & nonaginta D. Iohannis Brentij in evangelion quod secundum Lucam inscribitur* (Halle: Brubach, 1540).
152 Joannes Brentius, *Enarrationum evangeliorum dominicalium* (Erfurt: W. Stürmer & G. Stürmer, 1550).
153 Lucas Lossius, *Annotationum Lucae Lossii, in Novum Testamentum Jesu Christi Nazareni, ueri promissi & exhibiti Messiae &c. Continens narrationem Actorum apostolicorum, eorumque explicationem* (Frankfurt: C. Egenolff, 1552).
154 Lucas Lossius, *Catechismvs, hoc est, Christianae Doctrinae Methodvs: in qua non solum vera & Catholica Ecclesiae sententia proponitur, sed & argumentorum* (Frankfurt: C. Egenolff, 1554).
155 Lucas Lossius, *In quo continentur duo Euangelistae, Lvcas & Ioannes* (Frankfurt: C. Egenolff, 1562).
156 Lucas Lossius, *Psalmodia, hoc est, Cantica Sacra Veteris Ecclesiae Selecta: Quo ordine, & Melodijs per totius anni curriculum* (Nuremberg: G. Hayn, J. Petreius, 1553).
157 Leonhard Culmann, *Thesaurus Locorum Communium Copiosissimus: Ex Veteri et nouo Testamento, cum fideli ac perspicua interpretation* (Nuremberg: Daubmannus, 1551).

— *Breve formula examinandorum*[158]
— *Quomodo aficti agroti [sic] sunt consolandi*[159]
Marsilius Patavinus = Marsilius of Padua (c.1280–1342)
— *Opus insigne qui Tutulion fecit auctor Deffensoren pacis*[160]
Martinus Bucerus = Martin Bucer (Butzer) (1491–1551)
— *Ennarrato in Evangelium Ioannis*[161]
— *Scripta duo adversaria Bartholomei Latomi et Buceri*[162]
Martinus Lutherus = Martin Luther (1483–1546)
— *Omnium Operum tomus primus, secundus, tertius, quartus et sextus*[163]
Melchioris Kling = Melchior Kling/Clingius (1504–1571)
— *Super Instituta*[164]
Michael Servetius = Miguel Servet (1511–1553)
— *Tractatus contra Trininatem*[165]
Nicolaus Gallus = Nicolaus Gallus/Hahn (1516–1570)
— *Disputatio de diaphoris et mutaciones presentis status*[166]
Othonis Prumfelsii = Otto Brunfels (1488–1534)
— *Annotationes theologis trium linguarum*[167]
— *Pandete scripturarum*[168]
Othone Wermulero = Otto Werdmüller (1511–1552)
— *De dignitate usu et método philosophis morales*[169]
Petrus Viretus = Pierre Viret (1511–1571)

---

158 Leonhard Culmann, *Breues Aliquot Formulae Examinandorum Sacerdotum, Ecclesiasticum munus subire cupientium* (Nuremberg: J. Montanum, & V. Neuberum, 1552).

159 Leonhard Culmann, *Qvomodo Afflicti Ægroti et Moritvri sunt instituendi atque consclandi, quomodo tentationes Satanæ & mors uincenda, breuis instructio ex uerbo Dei collecta* (Nuremberg: V. Neuberum, 1550).

160 Marsilius Patavinus, *Opus insigne cui titulum fecit autor defensorem pacis, quod questionem illam jam olim controversam, de potestate papae et imperatoris excussissime tractet* (1522).

161 Martin Bucer, *Enarratio In Euangelion Iohannis, Praefatio, Summam Disputationis & Reformationis Bern. complectens* (Strasbourg: J. Hervagium, 1528).

162 Martin Bucer, *Scripta duo aduersaria D. Bartholomaei Latomi et Martini Buceri De Dispensatione sacramenti Eucharistiae. Inuocatione diuorum. Coelibatu clericorum* (Strasbourg: W. Rihelij, 1544).

163 Martin Luther. *Tomus primus [—septimus] omnium operum* (Wittenberg: J. Lufft, 1551).

164 Melchior Kling, *Melchioris Kling Ivreconsvlti clarissimi in quatuor Institutionum Iuris Principis Iustiniani libros Enarrationes de integro in gratiam Studiosorum & praxim forensem sectantium* (Lyon: Rovillius, 1546).

165 Michael Servetus, *De Trinitatis Erroribvs Libri Septem. Per Michaelem Serueto, aliâs Reues ab Aragonia Hispanum* (Haguenau: J. Setzer, 1531).

166 Nikolaus Gallus, *Dispvtatio De Adiaphoris & mutatione praesentis status pie constitutarum ecclesiarum: Cvm Praefatione* (Magdeburg: Rhodius, 1550).

167 Otto Brunfels, *Annotationes Othonis Brunfelsii, rei medices doctoris peritissimi, theologiae, trium linguarum, variarumque artium insignite eruditi, in quatuor evangelia et acta apostolorum* (Strasbourg: G. Ulrich, 1535).

168 Otto Brunfels, *Pandectae Scripturarum Veteris & Noui Testamenti* (Strasbourg: J. Schott, 1535).

169 Otho Werdmüller, *De ministro ecclesiae, sermones III in solennibus coetibus ecclesiastarum urbis et agri Tigurini* (Zurich: C. Frosch, 1551).

— *Diálogo de la desorden que está al presente en el mundo,* en francés[170]
— *De la virtud y uso de la palabra de Dios,* en francés[171]
— *Exposición sobre la oración dominical,* en francés[172]
— *Epístola enviada a los fieles que conversan entre los Papistas,* en francés[173]
— *De vero verbi Dei, Sacramentorum et ecclesie ministerio*[174]
— *Admonición y consolación a los fieles que se determinan de salir de entre los papistas*[175]
Petrus Martir Vermilio = Pietro Martire Vermigli (1499–1562)
— *In selectissimam Epistolam Prioris ad Corinthios*[176]
— *Disputatio de eucharistiae sacramento*[177]
Paulus Constantinus Phrigionis = Paulo Fagius/Phrygio (1483–1543)
— *In leviticum explanation*[178]
Paulo Faggio = Paulo Fagius/Phrygio (1483–1543)
— *Comentarium hebraycum Rabi Kimchi in decem psalmos*[179]
— *Targum hoc est paraphrasis, etc.*[180]
— *Exegesis sive exposition dictionum hebraicorum*[181]
Petrus Artopeius = Petrus Artoaeus/Peter Becker (1491–1563)

---

170 Pierre Viret, *Dialogues du desordre qui est a present au monde, et des causes d iceluy, & du moyen pour y remedier: desquelz l'ordre & le tiltre sensuit, 1. Le monde à l'empire. 2. L'homme difformé. 3. La metamorphose. 4. La reformation* (Geneva: J. Gerard, 1545).

171 Pierre Viret, *De la vertu, et usage du ministere de la parolle de Dieu, & des sacremens, dependans d'icelle & des differens qui sont en la chrestienté, à cause d'iceux* (Geneva: J. Girard, 1548).

172 Pierre Viret, *Exposition familière de l'oraison de notre Seigneur Jésus—Christ et des choses dignes de considérer sur icelle* (Geneva: J. Gerard, 1548).

173 Pierre Viret, *Admonition et consolation aux fideles qui deliberent de sortir d'entre les Papistes, pour eviter idolatrie, contre les tentations qui leur peuvent advenir* (Geneva: J. Girard, 1547).

174 Pierre Viret, *De vero verbi Dei, sacramentorum, & ecclesiæ ministerio, lib. II. De adulterinis sacramentis, lib I. De adulterato Baptismi sacramento, & de sanctorum oleorum vsu & consecrationibus, lib. I. De adultera cœna Domini, & de tremendis sacræ missæ mysteriis, lib VI* (Geneva: R. Stephani, 1553).

175 Spanish translation of Pierre Viret: *Admonition et consolation aux fideles qui deliberent de sortir d'entre les Papistes* (Geneva: J. Girard, 1547).

176 Pietro Martire Vermigli, *In selectissimam D. Pavli priorem ad Corinthios epistolam, D. Petri Martyris Vermilii Florentini, ad sereniss. regem Angliae, &c. Edvardvm VI. commentarii doctissimi.* Editio secunda, priori longe emendatior (Zurich: C. Frosch, 1567).

177 Pietro Martire Vermigli, *Defensio Doctrinæ veteris & Apostolicæ de sacrosancto Eucharistiæ Sacramento* (Zurich: C. Frosch, 1559).

178 Paulus Constantinus Phrygio, *In Leviticvm Explanatio Pavli Constantini Phrygionis, Omnia eius operis mysteria, quæ multa pulcherrimaque sunt, ita explicans, ut cuiuis doctori Ecclesiastico ad ædificationem maximopere sint usui futura* (Basel: Petrus, 1543).

179 Paul Fagius, *Commentarium Hebraicum Rabbi D. Kimhi in decem primos Psalmos Davidicos* (1544).

180 Paul Fagius, *Thargum, hoc est, Paraphrasis Onkeli chaldaica in Sacra Biblia: ex chaldaeo in latinum fidelissime versa, additis in singula fere capita succinctis annotationibus* (Strasbourg: G. Machaeropoeum, 1546).

181 Paul Fagius, *Exegesis sive expositio dictionum hebraicorum literalis et simplex in quatuor capita Geneseos* (1542).

— *De prima rerum origine aphorismi*[182]
— *Engeliçe conçiones*[183]
Philypus Melanchton = Philip Melanchthon (1497–1560)
— *Omnium operum tomus primus et tertius*[184]
— *Selectissimarum orationum tomus tertius*[185]
— *In Danielem Prophetam*[186]
— *Erothemata dialectics*[187]
— *Annotationes in Epistolas ad Corinthios*[188]
— *Initia doctrinae physicae*[189]
— *De coniugio comonefaçiones collecti*[190]
— *De penitençia doctrina*
— *Selectarum declamationum, tomus primus*[191]
— *Hystoria de victa et actis Martini Lutheri*[192]
Polydorus Vergilius = Polidoro Virgili/Vergilius/Vergil of Urbino (c.1470–1555)
— *De inventoribus rerum*[193]
Reinaldus Lorichius Adamarus = Reinhard Lorich/Reinhardus Hadamarius (1510–1561)
— *Funebris conçiones quindecim mediçinalium*[194]
Sebastianus Munstherus = Sebastian Münster (1488–1552)
— *Cathalogus omnium preçeptorum legis Mosaicae*[195]
— *In Evangelium Mathei hebraiçe scripto*[196]

---

182 Petrus Atropaeus, *De prima rerum origine, ex libro Geneseos, breves aphorismi* (Basel: H. Petrus, 1546).

183 Petrus Artopaeus, *Postilla Evangeliorum et epistolarum Dominicarum et praecipuorum Testorum totius anni pro sholasticis et novellis Praevicatoribus breves annotateines Petri Artopaei (vulgo Becker)* (Basel: H. Petrus, 1550).

184 Philipp Melanchthon, *Operum tomi quinque* (Basel: Heruagium, 1541).

185 Philipp Melanchthon, *Orationes aliquot lectu dignissimae* (Haguenau: Kobian, 1533).

186 Philipp Melanchthon, *In Danielem Prophetam Commentarius in quo seculi nostri status corruptissimus, & Turcicae crudelitatis finis describitur* (Basel: Westhemerus, 1543).

187 Philipp Melanchthon. *Erotemata Dialectices Continentia ferè integram artem, Ita scripta, ut iuuentuti utiliter proponi poßint* (Wittenberg, 1552).

188 Philipp Melanchthon, *Annotationes in Epistolam Pauli ad Romanos unam, & ad Corinthios duas diligentiß. recognitae* (Nuremberg: Petreius, 1524).

189 Philipp Melanchthon, *Initia doctrinae physicae, dictata in academia Vuitebergensi … iterum edita.* (Wittenberg: J. Lufft, 1550).

190 Philipp Melanchthon, *De coniugio piae commonefactiones* (Wittenberg: J. Crato, 1551).

191 Philipp Melanchthon, *Dialectices Philippi Melanchthonis, Libri quatuor ab autore nuper ipso deintegro in lucem conscripti ac editi* (1529).

192 Philipp Melanchthon, *Historia de vita et actis Martini Lutheri* (Frankfurt: Zöpfel, 1557).

193 Polydorus Vergilius, *De inventoribus rerum libri tres: M. Sabellici de artium inventoribus ad Baffum carmen* (Strasbourg: M. Schurer, 1509).

194 Reinhard Lorich, *Funebres contiones quindecim* (Frankfurt, 1548).

195 Sebastian Münster, *Catalogus omnium praeceptorum legis Mosaicae, quae ab Hebraeis sexcenta et tredecim numerantur: cum succincta Rabbinorum expositione & additione traditionum, quibus irrita fecerunt mandata dei* (Basel: H. Petrus, 1533).

196 Sebastian Münster, *Evangelium secundum Matthaeum in lingua Hebraica: cum versione Latina atque succinctis annotationibus* (Basel: H. Petrus, 1537).

— *In utraque Pauli epistolam ad Corinthios*[197]
— *Mesias Christianorum et Iudeorum etc.*[198]
— *Cosmographia universalis*[199]
Sebastianus Meyer = Sebastian Meyer (1465–1545)
— *In Apocalipsim Ioannis*[200]
— *In utramque divi Pauli Epistolam ad Corinthios*[201]
Sebastianus Castaliom = Sebastian Castellio/Castellión/Castello (1515–1563)
— *Salterium reliquaque sacrarum litterarum carmina*[202]
Theodorus Bibliandrus = Theodore Bibliander (1509–1564)
— *De ratione temporum etc.*[203]
— *De legitima bindicatione christianismi*
— *Protevangelion sive de natalibus Iesu Christi*[204]
— *Oratio ad enarrationem Esaye*[205]
Thomas Venator = Thomas Venatorius (1488–1551)
— *De virtute Christiana*[206]
Vincentius Obsopeius = Vincentius Opsopoeus (-1539)
— *Epigramata greca*[207]
Wolphangus Lacius = Wolfgang Laz (1514–1565)
— *Liber de passione domini nostril Iesu Christi cum aliis*[208]

---

197 Wrongly attributed. Unknown.
198 Sebastian Münster, *Messias christianorum et Judaeorum hebraice & latine* (Basel: H. Petrus, 1539).
199 Sebastian Münster, *Cosmographiæ uniuersalis Lib. VI. in quibus, iuxta certioris fidei scriptorum traditionem describuntur, Omniũ habitabilis orbis partiũ situs, propriæque dotes. Regionum Topographicæ effigies. Terræ ingenia, quibus fit ut tam differentes & uarias specie res, & animatas & inanimatas, ferat* (Basel: H. Petrus, 1552).
200 Sebastian Meyer, *In Apocalypsim Iohannis Apostoli D. Sebastiani Meyer Ecclesiastae Bernen[sis] Commentarius, nostro huic sæculo accommodus, natus, & æditus* (Zurich: Frosch, 1539).
201 Sebastian Meyer, *In Vtranque D. Pavli Epistolam Ad Corinthios, Commentarii D. Sebastiani Meieri, ad expostionem Patrum orthodoxorum D. Chrysostomi, Augustini, Ambrosii* (Frankfurt: Brubach, 1546).
202 Sebastianus Castellio, *Psalterium, reliquaque sacrarum literarum Carmina et Precationes, cum argumentis, et brevi difficiliorum locorum declaratione; Sebast. Gastalione interprete* (Basel: J. Oporinus, 1547).
203 Theodorus Bibliander, *De ratione temporum, Christianis rebus & cognoscendis & explicandis accommodata Liber unus* (Basel: J. Oporinus, 1551).
204 Theodorus Bibliandrus, *Protevangelion: sive de natalibus Iesu Christi, & ipsius matris Virginis Mariae, sermo historicus divi Iacobi minoris, consobrini & fratris Domini Iesu, apostoli primarij, & episcopi Christianorum primi Hierosolymis* (Basel: J. Oporinus, 1552).
205 Theodorus Bibliandrus, *Oratio Theodori Bibliandri ad enarrationem Esaiae prophetarum principis dicta Tiguri III idus ianuarij à natali Christi Domini anno MDXXXII* (Zurich: C. Frosch, 1532).
206 Thomas Venatorius, *Thomae Venatorii de virtute christiana: libri III; praeterea index additus praecipuas sententias complectens* (Nuremberg: Peypus, 1529).
207 Vincentius Opsopeus, *Epistolae Graecae* (Haguenau: Secerius, 1528).
208 Wolfgang Lazius, *Liber de passione Domini nostri Jesu Christi, carmine hexametro, incerto autore ad Donatum episcopum scriptus* (Basel: J. Oporinus, 1552).

— *Examerom Dei opus*[209]
— *Responsio de missa, matrimonio et iure magistratus in religione*[210]
Wolphangus Ubisembergius, theologus = Wolfgang Wissenburg (1496–1575)
— *Antilogia papae hoc est de corrupto ecclesiae statu*[211]
Victo Teodoro = Veit Dietrich, also Vitus Theodorus, (1506–1549)
— *In simples explicatio sententiarum ex Ioanne Evangelista collectarum*[212]
Urbanus Regius = Urbanus Henricus Rhegius/Urban Rieger (1489–1541)
— *Propheçie Veteris Testamenti de Christo collecte*[213]
Wolphgangus Musculus = Wolfgang Musculus (1497–1563)
— *In Psalterium comentarii*[214]
— *In Epistolam Pauli ad Romanos*[215]
— *In Genessim*[216]
— *In Evangelium Ioannis*[217]
— *In Evangelium Mathei*[218]
Otros libros que permanecen en el Secreto del Santo Oficio son:
[Other books that remain in the secret chambers of the Holy Office are:]
— *Derecho canónico con annotaciones*, de Carlo Molineo [Charles Du Moulin][219]
— *Colloquio de Damas*[220]
— *Nuevo Testamento*, en romançe, de Francisco Encinas[221]

---

209 Wrongly attributed. Wolfgang Capito, *Hexemeron Dei opus* (Strasbourg: Vu. Rihelius, 1539).
210 Wrongly attributed. Wolfgang Capito, *Responsio de missa matrimonio & iure magistratus in religionem* (Strasbourg: Vu. Rihelium, 1537).
211 Matthias Flacius [preface, Wolfgang Wissenburg], *Antilogia Papae: hoc est, de corrupto Ecclesiae statu & totius cleri papistici perversitate scripta aliquot veterum authorum; ante annos plus minus CCC & interea, nunc primum in lucem eruta & ab interitu vindicata* (Basel: J. Oporinus, 1555).
212 Theodorus Vitus, *Simplex et perspicua explicatio, insignium et iucundissimarum sententiarum ex johanne Evangelista collectarum à Vito Theodoro. Cum praefatione D. Philippi Melanthonis* (Leipzig: Günther, 1551).
213 Urbanus Regius, *Prophetiae Veteris Testamenti de Christo* (Frankfurt: P. Brubachii, 1542).
214 Wolfgang Musculus, *In sacrosanctum Dauidis Psalterium commentarij* (Basel: J. Herwagen, 1551).
215 Wolfgang Musculus, *In epistolam apostoli Pauli ad Romanos* (Basel: J. Herwagen, 1555).
216 Wolfgang Musculus, *In Mosis Genesim plenissimi Commentarii* (Basel: J. Herwagen, 1554).
217 Wolfgang Musculus, *In Divi Ioannis Apostoli Evangelium Wolfgangi Musculi Dusani Commentarii In tres Heptadas digesti, castigati, locupletati* (Basel: J. Herwagen, 1555).
218 Wolfgang Musculus, *In Evangelistam Matthaeum Commentarii* (Basel: Johann Herwagen, 1548).
219 Carolus Molinaeus, *Tractatus commerciorum et usurarum, redituumque pecunia constitutorum et monetarum, cum explicatione L. Eos. C. de usur. l periculi precium* (Paris: A. Parvus, 1555).
220 Pietro Aretino, *Colloquio de damas* (Seville, 1547; Zaragoza, 1548).
221 Francisco de Enzinas, *El Testamento Nueuo de nuestro Senor y Saluador Iesu Christo nueua y fielmente traduzido del original Griego en romance Castellano* (Venecia: Juan Philadelpho [Geneva: Jean Crespin], 1556).

— *Belial de consolación*[222]
— *Carta enviada a nuestro agustísimo señor príncipe don Felipe II, rey de España*, por Juan Pérez de Pineda[223]
— *La Primera Epístola de San Pablo a los Corintios*, en romançe, por Juan de Valdés[224]
— *Diálogo de Mercurio et Charon*, de Juan de Valdés[225]
— *Revelación de San Pablo*, en romançe

---

222 Jacobus de Theramo, *Consolatio peccatorum seu Processus Belial [French:] La consolacion des poures pecheurs, ou Le proces de Belial* (Lyons: M. Huss & J. Schabler, 1487).

223 Juan Pérez de Pineda, *Carta embiada a nuestro augustissimo senor principe Don Philippe, Rey de España, de Inglaterra, de Napoles, y de las Indias del Peru, &c. en que se declaran las causas de las guerras y calamidades presentes, y se descubren los medios y artes con que son robados los españoles, y las mas vezes muertos quanto al cuerpo, y quanto al anima.* (Geneva: J. Crespin, 1557).

224 Juan de Valdés, *Comentario ó declaracion familiar y compendiosa sobre la primera epístola de San Pablo apóstol á los Corintios, muy útil para todos los amadores de la piedad cristiana / compuesto por Juan Valdesio* (Venezia: Juan Philadelpho [Geneva: Jean Crespin], 1557).

225 Wrongly attributed. Alfonso de Valdés, *Dialogo de Mercurio y Caron* (Venice: Antonio Bruccioli, 1543).

Appendix B —
Editions and Translations of the Works of the Spanish Reformers[1]

Antonio del Corro (1527–1591)

—, *A supplication exhibited to the most mightie Prince Philip king of Spain &c. Wherin is contained the summe of our Christian religion, for the profession whereof the Protestants in the lowe Countries of Flaunders, &c. doe suffer persecution, vvyth the meanes to acquiet and appease the troubles in those partes. There is annexed An epistle written to the ministers of Antwerpe, which are called of the confession of Auspurge, concerning the Supper of our sauiour Iesus Christ. Written in French and Latine, by Anthonie Corronus of Siuill, professor of Diuinitie* (London: Henrie Bynneman, 1567; London: Coldocke, 1577).

—, *A theological dialogue. Wherin the Epistle of S. Paul the Apostle to the Romanes is expounded. Gathered and set together out of the readings of Antonie Corranus of Siuille, professor of Diuinitie* (London: Thomas Purfoote, 1575).

—, *Acta consistorii Ecclesiae Londino-Gallicae, cum responso Antonii Corrani: ex quorum lectione facile quiuis intelligere poterit statum controuersiae inter Ioannem Cusinum, eiusdem Ecclesiae Ministrum, & Antonium Corranum, Hispanorum peregrinorum Concionatorem* (London, 1571).

—, *An epistle or godlie admonition, of a learned minister of the Gospel of our sauiour Christ sent to the pastoures of the Flemish Church in Antwerp, (who name themselues of the Confession of Auspurge,) exhorting them to concord with the other ministers of the Gospell. Translated out of French by Geffray Fenton. Here may the christian reader lerne to know what is the true participation of the body of Christ, & what is the lauful vse of the holy Supper.* Translated by Sir Geoffrey Fenton (London: Henrie Bynneman, 1569, 1570).

—, *Carta a Casiodoro de Reina,* (Théobon, 24 Dec. 1563), in L. Usoz y Rio/B.B. Wiffen, eds. *Reformistas Antiguos Españoles* (Madrid: J. Martin Alegría, 1862).

—, *Carta a los pastores luteranos de Amberes; Carta a Felipe II; Carta a Casiodoro de Reina; Exposición de la Obra de Dios* (Seville: Editorial MAD, 2006).

—, *Comentario a Eclesiastés,* in E. Monjo Bellido, ed., *Obras de los Reformadores españoles del siglo XVI,* Colección Eduforma Historia, Vol. IX (Seville: Editorial MAD, 2011). Translation from the Latin by Fco. Ruiz de Pablos.

---

1 The editions and translations of Reginaldo Gonzalez de Montes's *Artes* are also included in this list.

—, *Comentario Dialogado de la carta a los Romanos,* in E. Monjo Bellido, ed., *Obras de los Reformadores españoles del siglo XVI,* Colección Eduforma Historia, Vol. VIII (Seville: Editorial MAD, 2010). Translation from the Latin by Fco. Ruiz de Pablos.

—, *Concio de Summo hominis bono, quam Hebraei Cohelet; Graeci et Latini Ecclesiasten vocant* (London, 1579).

—, *Dialogus in Epistolam D. Pauli ad Romanos, Antonio Corrano Hispalensi, Hispano, in Academia Oxonensi Professore, Theologo auctore* (Frankfurt: Nicolai Bassaci, 1587).

—, *Dialogus theologicus: Quo epistola Diui Pauli apostoli ad Romanos explanatur. Ex praelectionibus Antonij Corrani Hispalensis, sacrae theologiae professoris, collectus, & concinnatus* (London: Thomae Purfoetij, 1574).

—, *Diuinorum operum tabula. Articuli veteris Testamenti. Articuli noui Testamenti* (London: H. Bynneman, 1570).

—, *Ecclesiastes regis Salomonis: sive, de summo hominis bono concio vere regia: Exposita et nunc primum in Germania edita* (Heidelberg: Jonae Rosae, 1619).

—, *Eenen brief ende vriendelycke bewysinghe aen den herders der Duytscher gemeynten binnen Antwerpen vande Confessie van Ausborch: hun vermanende tot eendrachticheyt ende vrientschap te houden metten anderen dienaren des Evangeliums. Nu eerst overgeset* (Antwerp: Gillis Coppens van Diest, 1567).

—, *Epistola beati Pauli apostoli ad Romanos, e graeco in latinum metachpastkos versa, & in dialogi formam redacta, ut instar christian catecheseos iuuentuti esse possit Per Ant. Corranum Hispalensens, Theolgie professorem* (London: Thomas Vautrouiller, 1581).

—, *Epistre et amiable remonstrance d'un ministre de l'Évangile de nostre Redempteur Iesus Christ, envoyée aux Pasteurs de l'Eglise Flamengue d'Anvers, lesquelz se nomment de la Confession d'Augsbourg, les exhortant à concorde & amitié avec les autres ministres de l'Évangile* (Antwerp [London], 1567).

—, *Justificatio fidei, Christianae, antiquæ, catholicæ & orthodoxæ = Op Dutz, Proevesteen eñ oprechte wechtschale, van het goede olde, algemene christlicke gelove: van Godt geschapen tor salicheit* (Groningen: David Lip van Augspurch, 1618).

—, *Lettre envoyée a la majesté du roy des Espaignes, &c. Nostre Sire. Par laquelle un sien treshumble subiect lui rend raison de son departement du Royaume d'Espaigne, & presente à sa Ma. la confession des principaux poinctz de nostre Religion Chretienne: luy monstrant les griefves persecutions, qu'endurent ses subiects des Pais Bas pour maintenir ladite Religion, & le moyen duquel sa Ma. pourroit user pour y remedier* (Antwerp, 1567).

—, *Paraphrasis and Commentary on Ecclesiastes* (London: John Wolfe, 1579).

—, *Reglas Gramaticales para aprender la lengua Española y Francesa, confiriendo la vna con la otra, segun el orden de las partes de la oration Latinas* (Oxford: Joseph Barnes, 1586).

—, *Reglas gramaticales para aprender la lengua española y francesa* [1586] (Madrid: Arco Libros, 1988).

—, *Sapientissimi regis Salomonis concio de summo hominis bono, quam Hebræi Cohelet, græci & Latini Ecclesiasten vocant in Latinam linguam ab Antonio Corrano Hispalensi versa, & ex eiusdem prælectionibus paraphrasi illustrata. Accesserunt & notæ quædam in singula capita; quibus totius concionis œconomia, ac singularum ferè sententiarum dialectica connexio, simul cum rhetorica elocutione oftenditur* (London: John Wolfe, 1579).

—, *Sobre las Tentaciones de Cristo* [Frankfurt: Nicolas Bascus, 1573] (Madrid: Iglesia Española Reformada Episcopal, 1988). Notes by Carlos Lopez; translation by María Araujo Fernández.

—, *Solomon's Sermon of Man's Chief Felicitie Called in Hebrew Koheleth, in Greeke and Latin Ecclesiastes; with a Learned, Godly, and Familiar Paraphrase Vppon the Same, Gathered Out of the Lectures of A.C. [Antonio Corro] & Now Englished for the Benefit of the Unlearned*. Translated by Thomas Pye (Oxford: Joseph Barnes, 1586).

—, *Tableau de l'oeuure de Dieu* (Norwich: Anthony de Solempne, 1569).

—, *Tabula divinorum operum, in qua de humani generis creatione ac restauratione ex sacris voluminibus aphorismi continentur* (London: [J. Kingston], 1584).

—, *The Spanish Grammer: with certeine Rules teaching both the Spanish and French tongues. London: Imprinted by Iohn Wolfe. 1590 [Reglas gramaticales]; By which they that haue some knowledge in the French tongue, may the easier attaine to the Spanish, and likewise they that haue the Spanish, with more facilitie learne the French: and they that are acquainted with neither of them, learne either or both. Made in Spanish, by M. Anthonie de Corro. With a Dictionarie adioyned vnto it, of all the Spanish wordes / most necessarie for all such as desire the knowledge of the same tongue. Translated by Iohn Thorius, graduate in Oxenford* (London: John Wolfe, 1590).

— ed., *Alfonso de Valdés, Dialogo en que particularmente se tratan las cosas acaecidas en Roma: el añō de M.D. XXVII. a la gloria de dios y bien vniuersal de la republica Christiana* (Oxford: J. Barnes, 1586).

—, "Documents inédits et originaux – Lettres de divers à la duchesse de Ferrare 1564–1572," *Bulletin de la Société d'Histoire du Protestantisme Français* 30 (1881), 450–457.

Francisco de Enzinas (1518–1552)

—, "Dedicatoria del Nuevo Testamento al Emperador Carlos V". http://www.iglesiar-eformada.com/Enzinas_F_Dedicacion_NT.html

—, "Der Anfang von Francisco de Enzinas' "Historia de statu Belgico deque religione Hispanica", Eduard Böhmer (ed.). *Zeitschrift für Kirchengeschichte*, 13 (1892), 346–359.

—, trans., *El primero volumen de las Vidas de illvstres y excellentes varones griegos y romanos pareadas escritas primero en lengua griega por el graue philosophe y verdadero historiador Plutarcho & al presente traduzidas en estilo castellano. Por Francisco d'Enzinas* (Strasbourg: Augustin Frisio, 1551).

—, trans., *Las vidas de dos illustres varones, Cimon Griego, y Lucio Lucullo Romano, puestas al paragòn la una de la otra; escritas primero en lengua Griega por Plutarcho de Cheronea y al presente traduzidas en estilo castellano* (1547).

—, trans., *Las vidas de los ilustres y excellentes varones Griegos y Romanos. Traducidas en Castellano por Juan Castro de Salinas [Francisco de Enzinas]* (Cologne: sold in Antwerp at the house of Arnold Birckmann, 1562).

—, trans., *Todas las decadas de Tito Liuio Paduano: que hasta al presente se hallaron, y fueron impressas en Latin, traduçidas en romançe Castellano, agora nueuamente re-conosçidas y emendadas, y añadidas de mas libros sobre la vieja translaçion* (Cologne: sold in Antwerp at the house of Arnold Birckmann, 1553).

—, *Acta Concilij Tridentini, Anno M.D. XLVI celebrati vnà cum Annotationibus pijs, & lectu dignissimis. Item, Ratio, cur qui Confessionem Augustanam profitentur, non esse as-sentiendum iniquis Concilij Tridentini sententijs iudicarunt* (Basel: Joannes Oporinus, 1546).

—, *Bericht over de toestand in de Nederlande en de godsdienst bij de Spanjarden* (Hilversum: Verloren, 2002). Translated by Ton Osinga y Chris Heesakkers.

—, *Breve y Compendiosa Institución de la Religión Cristiana*. Marcel Bataillon, ed. (Madrid: Fundación Universitaria Española, 1977).

—, *Breve y compendiosa institución de la religión cristiana*. Serie de Disidentes Españoles del Siglo XVI, Colección Ediciones Críticas, no. 8. (Cuenca: Universidad de Castilla-La Mancha, 2008). Introduction and notes by Jonathan L. Nelson.

—, *Breve y compendiosa instituçion de la religion Christiana, necessaria para todos aquellos que con iusto titulo quieren usurpar el nombre de Christo.* Francisco de Elao [Francisco de Enzinas] (Antwerp: Adamo Corvo [Matthias Crom], 1540.

—, *Correspondencia de Francisco de Enzinas*, Charles Schmidt, ed. (Strasbourg: 1863).

—, *Denkwürdigkeiten Melanchthon gewidmet: aus dem lateinischen Manuskript* (Leipzig: Dürrsche Buchhandlung, 1897). Translated by Hedwig Boehmer.

—, *Denkwürdigkeiten vom Zustand der Niederlande und von der Religion in Spanien* (Bonn: Georgi, 1893). Translated by Edward Boehmer.

—, *Dos informaziones: Una dirijida al Emperador Carlos V. i otra, a los Estados del Imperio; obra, al parezer, de Franzisco de Enzinas. Prezede una Suplicazion a D. Felipe II, obra, al parezér, del Dr. Juan Perez. Ahora fielmente reimpresas, i seguidas de vários apéndizes*, in L. Usoz y Rio/B.B. Wiffen, eds., *Reformistas antiguos españoles*, Vol. XII (San Sebastián: Ignacio R. Baroja, 1857).

—, *El Nuevo Testamento De nuestro Redemptor y Salvador Iesu Christo. Traduzido de Griega en lengua Castellana, por Francisco de Enzinas, dedicado a la Cesarea Magestad* (Antwerp: Esteuan Mierdmanno, 1543).

—, *El Psalterio de Dauid traduzido en lengua Castellana conforme a la verdad Hebraica.* (Lyons: Sebastian Grypho [Strasbourg: Agustín Fries/Arnoldo Birckmann], 1550).

—, *El Testamento Nueuo de nuestro Senor y Saluador Iesu Christo nueua y fielmente traduzido del original Griego en romance Castellano.* (Venice: Juan Philadelpho [Geneva: Jean Crespin], 1556).

—, *Epistolario* (Geneva: Droz, 1995). Translation from the Latin and notes by Ignacio J. García Pinilla.

—, *Francisci Enzinatis Burgensis Historia de Statu Belgico deque Religione Hispanica.* Francisco Socas, ed. (Stuttgart: B. G. Teubner, 1991).

—, *Geloofsvervolgingen in Spanje* (Middelburg: Gihonbron Foundation, 2009).

—, *Histoire de l'estat du pais bas, et de la religion d'Espagne* (St. Marie: François Perrin, 1558).

—, *Historia de la muerte de Juán Diaz, por determinazión tomada en Roma, le hizo matár su hermano Alfonso Díaz, en la madrugada del sábado 27 iii. m. del año 1546*, in L. Usoz y Río/B.B. Wiffen, eds., *Reformistas antiguos españoles*, Vol. XXI (Madrid: J. Martín Alegría, 1865).

—, *Historia de statu Belgico et religione Hispanica* (Wittenberg, 1545).

—, *Historia vera de morte sancti viri Ioannis Diazii Hispani, quem eius frater germanus Alphonsius Diazius, exemplum sequutus primi parricidae Cain, velut alterum Abelem, refariem interfecit*. Per Claudium Senarclaeum [F. de Enzinas] (Basel: Joannes Oporinus, 1546).

—, *La Chasse Aux Luthériens Des Pays-Bas. Souvenirs De F. De Enzinas. Annotés by Albert Savine. D'après Les Documents D'archives Et Les Mémoires. Illustrations Documentaires* (Paris: Louis Michaud, 1910).

—, *Les Mémorables de Francisco de Enzinas traduit pour la première fois depuis le 16e siècle du texte original* (Brussels: Librairie Encyclopédique, 1963). Translated and edited by Jean de Savignac.

—, *Los Prouerbios de Salomon declarados en lengua Castellana conforme à la verdad Hebraica* (Leon [Strasbourg]: Sebastian Grypho, 1550).

—, *Mémoires anonymes sur les troubles des Pays-Bas, 1565–1580.* J-B-F. Blaes, ed. (Nendeln, Liechtenstein: Kraus, 1977).

—, *Mémoires de Francisco de Enzinas: texte latin inédit, avec la traduction française du XVIe siècle en regard, 1543–1545.* 2 vols. Charles Louis Alcée Campan, ed. (Bruxelles: Muquardt, 1862–63).

—, *Mémoires de Francisco de Enzinas* (Bruxelles: Librairie Encyclopaedique, 1963).

—, *Memorias: Historia del estado de los Países Bajos y de la religión de España* [1545]. Translated from the French [1558] (Buenos Aires: La Aurora, 1960).

—, *Memorias. Informe sobre la situación en Flandes y la religión de España* (Madrid: Ediciones Clásicas, 1992). Translation and notes by Francisco Socas Galván.

—, *Nuevo Testamento* (Buenos Aires: La Aurora, 1943).

—, *Verdadera historia de la muerte del santo varón Juan Díaz, por Claude de Senarclens.* Ignacio J. García Pinilla, ed. (Cuenca: Universidad de Castilla-La Mancha, 2008).

Reginaldo Gonzalez de Montes

—, *A Discoverie and Plaine Declaration of Sundry Subtill Practices of the Holy Inquisition of Spaine, and the Originall Thereof: with Certain Speciall Examples Set Apart by Themselves, (besides Other that are Here and There Dispersed in Their Most Convenient places,) Wherein a Man May See the Foresaid Practises of the Inquisition, as They Bee Practised and Exercised, Very Lively Described* (London: John Bellamie, 1625). Translation from the Latin by Vincent Skinner.

—, *A Discovery and playne declaration of sundry subtill practises of the holy inquisition of Spayne: Certain special examples set aparte by them selves, besides other that are here and there dispersed in their most convenient places, wherein a man may see the forsaid practises of the Inquisition, as they be practised and exercised, very lively described. Set forth in Latine, by Reginaldus Gonsalvus Montanus, and newly translated in english by V. Skinner* (London: John Day, 1568, 1569). Translation by Vincent Skinner.

—, *A full, ample and punctually discovery of the barbarous, bloudy, and inhumane practises of the Spanish Inquisition, against Protestants: with the originall thereof. Manifested in their proceedings against sundry particular persons, as well English as others, upon whom they have executed tyrannie. First written in Latin by Reginaldus Gonsaluius Montanus, and after translated into English* (London: John Bellamy, 1625). Translation from the Latin by Vincent Skinner.

—, *Artes de la Inquisición española,* David González Romero, ed. (Córdoba: Almuzara, 2010).

—, *Artes de la Inquisizion española: Primer traduczion castellana de la obra escrita en latin, por el español Raimundo Gonzalez de Montes,* in L. Usoz y Río/B.B. Wiffen, eds. *Reformistas antiguos españoles,* Vol. V (San Sebastian: Ignacio R. Baroja, 1851).

—, *Artes de la Santa Inquisición española de González Montes,* in E. Monjo Bellido, ed., *Obras de los Reformadores españoles del siglo XVI,* Vol. IV (Seville: Editorial MAD, 2008). Translated from the Latin by Fco. Ruiz de Pablos.

—, *De heylige Spaensche inquisitie, met haer loosheyt, valscheyt ende arghelisten ontdect, wtgestelt ende int licht gebracht. Alles door Reynaldo Gonsalvo Montan eerstelijk in Latijne ghaschreuen. Ende nv eerts in onser Nederlantscher sprake door M. Malvmpertum Taphaea (een liefhebber der waerheyt) uergheset* (London: Jan Day, 1569). Translation by Maulumpertus Taphaea.

—, *De Inquisitione Hispanica Oratiunculae septem ex narratione Reginaldi Gonsalvi Montani ante XXXVIII annos, divulgates collectae, et publica in Auditorio Philosophico recitatae Haidelbergae.* Simon Stenius, ed. (Heidelberg: Voegelianis, 1603).

—, *Den Grouwel der Verwoestinghe oft Grondich bericht ende ontdeckinghe, van de Gronden der Spaenshe Inquisitie. Tot Waerschouwinghe van alle goede ende oprechte Nederlanders ende Evangelishche Gheloofs ghenoten, wtghegheren door een uriendt ende Liefhebber der serlver. Hier is oock nock by ghevoecht de Spaenshe Inquisitie, beschreven door Regindaldum Gonsalvium Montanu. Comt ick sal u toonen uwen Vyandt* (s'Graven-Haghe: Aert Meuris, 1621). Translation by Johann Aventroot.

—, *Der Heiligen Hispanischen Inquisition, etliche entdeckte vnd offentliche an Tag gebrachte ränck vnd Practicken. Item, Etliche bsonders gsetzte Exempeln, vber die jenigen, so hin vnd wider im büchlein sind angezogen worden, in denem gemelte Inquisitorische ränk gleichsam in offnen tafeln, vnd in der vbung selbst mögen angeschawet werden. Hinden haben wir etlicher gottseliger märterer Christi herrliche zeugnüssen hinzugethan, welche von den Inquisitorem, durch jre falsche Practicken als meinedige vnd abtrünnige sind verleumbdet vnd außgeschrieben worden, so sie doch von wegen der bekanntnuß des waren glaubens mit Chrislicher standthafftigkeit den todt gelitten haben. Alles newlich durch Reginaldum Gonsaluium Montanum in Latein beschrieben, vnd jetzt erst der hochgelobten Teuschen Nation zu guten verteutschet* (Heidelberg: Johannes Mayer, 1569, 1574).

—, *Der heyliger Hispanischer inquisitie, etlicke listighe secrete consten ende practijcken, ontdect ende int licht ghebracht. Item, Eenighe bysondere examplelen, behalven de ghene die hier en daer int Boeck ghestelt zijn. Wy hebben oock hier by ghevoecht de ghetuyghenissen van eenighe Godsalighemartelaren. Eerst int Latijn beschreven door Reginaldum Gionsalvium Montanum, ende nu nieuwelick in onse Nederlantsche sprake overgheset. Psalm 74. vers. 22. Maeckt dy op God, ende voert wt dijn sake* (Norwich: Antonius de Solempne, 1569; s'Graven-hage: Aert Meuris, 1620).

—, *Der Tyrannischen Hispanischen Inquisition Heimlichkeiten, durch Gottes sonderbare schildung offenbaret und zu diesen lezten Zeiten der Welt entdecket: mit Exempeln und Historien bewiesen.* (Amberg: Johannes Schönfeldius, 1611). Translation by Joachim Beringer.

—, *Die praktiken der spanischen inquisition, aus dem lateinischen des Reginaldus Gonsalvius Montanus übersetzt und erläutert von Franz Goldscheider* (Berlin: Alf Häger, 1925).

—, *Háló,* Péter Kőszeghy, ed. (Budapest: Balassi Kiadó, 2000). Translation by Gáspár Heltai.

—, *Háló: Kolozsvár* [Budapest, 1570] (Budapest: Magyar tudományos akadémia, 1915). Translation by Gáspár Heltai.

—, *Hispanicae inquisitionis & carnificinae secretiora: Ubi, praeter illius originem; processus tyrannicus, in fidelium religionis reformatae confessorum, comprehensione: bonorum sequestratione: audientiis varii generis: testium publicatione, & confutatione exemplis illustrioribus tum martyrum, tum articulorum & regularum inquisitoriarum, in fine adjectis. Per Joachimum Ursinum [Joachim Beringer], Anti-Jesuitam, de Jesuitis, qui Inquisitionem Hispanicam in Germaniam et Bohemiam vicinam introducere moliuntur, praefantem* (Amberg: Johannes Schönfeld, 1611).

—, *Histoire de l'Inquisition d'Espagne: exposee par exemples pour estre mieux entendue en ces derniers temps* ([London], 1568).

—, *Historie van de Spaensche inquisitie: uutgestelt door exempelen, op datmen die te beter in dese laetste tijden verstaen mach* [Wesel, 1569] (Zug, Switzerland: Inter Documentation Co., 1995). Translation from the French by Joris de Raedt; preface by Petrus Datheen.

—, *Inquisitio Hispanica. Schrecklicher Process vnd erbermliche Exempel, wie man in Hispanien vnd anderswo mit den armen Christen vmbgehet, vnd vmb der Wahrheit willen Marter vnd Tödtet. Aus dem latein Verdeutscht Durch Wolffgangum Kauffmann* (Eisleben: Andreas Petri, 1569). Translation by Wolfgang Kauffmann.

—, *Inquisitionis Hispanicae Artes aliquot detectae, ac palam traductae (1567)*, in L. Usoz y Río/B.B. Wiffen, eds. *Reformistas antiguos españoles*, Vol. XIII (Madrid: J. Martin Alegria, 1857).

—, *Sanctae Inqvisitionis hispanicae artes aliquot detectæ, ac palam traductæ. Exempla aliquot, praeter ea quę suo quęq(ue) loco in ipso opere sparsa sunt, seorsum reposita, in quibus easdem inquisitorias artes veluti in tabulis quibusdam in ipso porrò exercitio intueri licet. Addidimvs appendicis vice piorum quorumdam Martyrum Christi elogia, qui cum mortis suppliciũ ob fidei confessionem christiana constantia tulerint, inquisitores eos suis artibus perfidiæ ac defectionis infamarint. Reginaldo Gonsalvio Montano authore. 'Exurge Deus, judica causam tuam'. Psal. 74* (Heidelberg: Michael Schirat, 1567).

—, *Sanctae Inqvisitionis hispanicae artes aliquot detectæ, ac palam traductæ*, in L. Usoz y Río/B.B. Wiffen (eds.), *Reformistas antiguos españoles*, Vol. XIII (Madrid: J. Martín Alegría, 1856).

Constantino Ponce de la Fuente (1502–1560)

—, *Beatus Vir: carne de hoguera. Exposición del Primer Salmo, de Constantino Ponce de la Fuente* (Madrid: Editora Nacional, 1978). Notes by Emilia Navarro de Kelley.

—, *Catecismo christiano: Añadiose la confession d'un pecador penitente, hecha por el mismo author* (Antwerp: Guillermo Simon, 1556).

—, *Cathecismo Christiano, compuesto por el Doctor Constantino. Añadióse la confesión de un pecador penitente, hecha por el mismo Author*, in L. Usoz y Rio/B.B. Wiffen, eds., *Reformistas Antiguos Españoles*. Vol. XIX (Madrid: J. Martín Alegría, 1863).

—, *Cathecismo Christiano, para instruir a los niños* (Seville: Juan de León, 1547; Antwerp: Guillermo Simón, 1556).

—, *Confesión de un pecador* (Madrid: Fundación Universitaria Española, 1988). Notes by María Paz Aspe Ansa.

—, *Confesión de un pecador penitente delante de Jesucristo, redemptor y juez de los hombres* (Seville: Juan de León, 1547; Évora: Andrés de Burgos, 1554; Antwerp: Guillermo Simón, 1556).

—, *Confessio hominis pecatoris coram Deo*, in Daniel Gerdes, *Scrinium Antiquarium, Sive Miscellanea Groningana Nova, Ad Historiam Reformationis Ecclesiasticam Præcipue Spectantia*. 8 vols. (Groningæ et Bremæ, 1749–65), Vol. 3, 458–483.

—, *Confession d'un pecheur devant Jesus Christ Sauver et Juge du Monde* (Geneva: Pierre Aubert, 1619).

—, *Confession d'un pour Pecheur*, in Jean Crespin, *Histoire des martyrs* (Geneva: héritiers d'Eustache Vignon, 1608), fols. 551–566.

—, *Doctrina Christiana, en que está comprehendida toda la información que pertenece al hombre que quiere servir a Dios. Parte primera. De los artículos de la fe* (Seville: Juan Canalla, 1548, 1549; Antwerp: Juan Steelsio, 1554, 1555).

—, *Doctrina Christiana. Parte primera*, in E. Monjo Bellido, ed., *Obras de los reformadores españoles del siglo XVI*. Vol. X (Seville: Editorial MAD, 2015). Introduction and notes by David Estrada Herrero.

—, *Exposición del primer psalmo de David: cuyo principio es «Beatus Vir» dividida en seys sermones* (Seville: Juan de León, 1546; Seville: Cristobal Alvarez, 1551; Antwerp: Guillermo Simón, 1556).

—, *Exposición del primer psalmo de David: cuyo principio es «Beatus Vir» dividida en seys sermones*. Eduard Böhmer, ed. (Bonn: Carlos Georgi, 1881; Madrid: Editora Nacional, 1988).

—, *Exposición del Primer Psalmo dividida en seis sermones* [1546]. Emilia Navarro de Kelley, ed. (Alicante: Biblioteca Virtual Miguel de Cervantes, 1999).

—, *Exposición del Primer Psalmo dividida en seis sermones* [1546], in E. Monjo Bellido, ed., *Obras de los reformadores españoles del siglo XVI*. Vol. V (Seville: Editorial MAD, 2008). Introduction by David Estrada Herrero.

—, *Exposición del primer salmo dividida en seis sermones*. (Nashville, TN.: Casa editorial de la Iglesia metodista episcopal del Sur, 1902).

—, *La confession d'un pécheur devant Jésus Christ rédempteur et juge des hommes, 1547: précédé de 'Le procès du doute et de la subjectivité dans l'Espagne du XVIe siècle' par Dominique de Courcelles* (Grenoble: J. Millon, 2000).

—, *Summa de doctrina Cristiana compuesta por el muy reverendo señor el Doctor Constantino en que se contiene todo lo principal y necessario que el hombre christiano deue saber y obrar* (Seville: Juan Cromberger, 1543, 1544).

—, *Summa de doctrina Cristiana. Sermón de Nuestro Redentor en el Monte* (Seville: Juan de León, 1545, 1547; Seville: Cristobal Alvarez, 1551; Antwerp: Martín Nucio, 1551).

—, *Summa de doctrina Cristiana. Sermón de Nuestro Redentor en el Monte. Catezismo Cristiano. Confesión del pecador: Cuatro libros compuestos por el Doctór Constantino Ponze de la Fuente* [1545]. *De la perfección de la vida. Del gobierno de la casa. Dos epistolas de S. Bernardo, romanzadas por el maestro Martín Navarro* [1547], in L. Usoz y Rio/B.B. Wiffen, eds., *Reformistas antiguos españoles*, Vol. XIX (Madrid: J. Martín Alegría, 1863).

—, *The Confession of a Sinner. With a biographical sketch by Benjamin B. Wiffen* (London: Bell and Daldy, 1869). Translation by John T. Betts.

Juan Perez de Pineda (1500–1567)

—, ed., *Commentario o Declaración breve y compendiosa sobre la epistola de S. Paulo apostol a los Romanos muy saludable para todo christian, compuesto por Juan Valdesio, pio y sincero theologo* (Venice: Juan Philadelpho [Geneva: J. Crespin], 1556).

—, ed., *Commentario o Declaración familiar y compendiosa sobre la epistola de S. Paulo apostol a los Corinthios, muy util para todos los amadores de la piedad christiana, compuesto por Juan Valdesio, pio y sincero theologo* (Venice: Juan Philadelpho [Geneva: J. Crespin], 1557).

—, *An excellent comfort to all Christians, against all kinde of calamities no lesse comfortable, then pleasant, pithy, and profitable: Compendiously compiled by Iohn Perez, a faithfull seruant of God, a Spaniard (in Spanish) and now translated into English by Iohn Daniel, of Clements Inne, with diuers addicions by him collected and therevnto annexed* (London: Thomas East, 1576; London/Edinburgh: Ballantine, 1871).

—, *Breve sumario de induljencias,* in L. Usoz y Rio/B.B. Wiffen, eds., *Reformistas antiguos españoles,* Vol. XIX (Madrid: J. Martin Alegría, 1862).

—, *Breve tratado de la doctrina antigua de Dios, i de la nueva de los hombres, util i necessario para todo fiel christiano* (Geneva: Jean Crispin, 1560).

—, *Breve tratado de la doctrina antigua de Dios, i de la nueva de los hombres, util i necessario para todo fiel christiano* in L. Usoz y Rio/B.B. Wiffen, eds., *Reformistas antiguos españoles,* Vol. VII (San Sebastián: Ignacio R. Baroja, 1852).

—, *Carta embiada a nuestro augustissimo senor principe Don Philippe, Rey de España, de Inglaterra, de Napoles, y de las Indias del Peru, &c. en que se declaran las causas de las guerras y calamidades presentes, y se descubren los medios y artes con que son robados los españoles, y las mas vezes muertos quanto al cuerpo, y quanto al anima* (Geneva: Juan Crespin, 1557).

—, *Catechismo* (Venice: Pietro Daniel, [Geneva: Jean Crespin] 1556).

—, *Dos informaciones muy útiles, la una dirigida a la Magestad del Emperador Carlo quinto deste nombre, la otra a los estados del Imperio. Y agora presentadas al Catholico Rey don Philipe su hijo. Que tienen muy necessarios avisos para ser instruydo todo Principe Christiano en la cause del Evangelio. Con una suplicacion a la Magestad del rey, donde se declara el oficio de los juezes y Magistrados, y a lo que es obligado todo fiel Christian, para ser salvo.* ([Geneva: Jean Crespin] 1559).

—, *El Testamento Nuevo (1556). Epístola Consolatoria (1560).* (Buenos Aires: La Aurora / México: Casa Unida de Publicaciones, 1958).

—, *El Testamento Nuevo de nuestro señor y salvador Jesu Christo* (Venice: Juan Philadelpho [Geneva: Jean Crespin], 1556).

—, *Epístola consolatoria a los fieles de Jesu Christo, que padecen persecucion por la confession de su Nombre. En que se declara el proposito y buena voluntad de Dios para con ellos, y son confirmados contra las tentaciones y horror de la muerte y enseñados como se han de regir en todo tiempo prospero y adverso.* (Geneva: Jean Crespin, 1556).

—, *Epístola consolatoria by Juan Perez, (1560), one of the Spanish Reformers in the sixteenth century, now reprinted page for page from the original with a notice of the author in English and in Spanish,* in L. Usoz y Rio/B.B. Wiffen, eds. *Reformistas antiguos españoles,* Vol. II (London: S. & J. Bentley, Wilson and Fley, 1848).

—, *Epístola consolatoria by Juan Perez, (1560), one of the Spanish Reformers in the sixteenth century, now translated froma a reprint of the edition published by Don Luis de Usoz y Rio in 1848. With notices of the author by the late Benjamin B. Wiffen.* (London: James Nisbet, 1871).

—, *Epístola consolatoria by Juan Perez* [1560] (Madrid: Librería Nacional y Extranjera, 1874).

—, *Epístola consolatoria* [1560] (London: G.M. Watts, 1866).

—, *Epístola consolatoria*, in E. Monjo Bellido (ed.), *Obras de los Reformadores españoles del siglo XVI*, Vol. II (Seville: Editorial MAD, 2007).

—, *Epístola Consolatoria*, Xavier Vilaró, ed. (Barcelona: Fundació Enciclopedia Catalana, 1994).

—, *Jehovah a free pardon, with many graces therein conteyned, graunted to all Christians by our most holy and reuerent father God almightie, the principal high priest and bishoppe in heauen and earth, first written in the Spanish tounge, and there published by a Spaniard vnknowen, (yet as it seemeth) the seruant of our sayde Holy Father; and now translated into the mother English tounge, by Iohn Danyel of Clements Inne* (London: Thomas East, for Andrew Maunsell, 1576).

—, *Los Psalmos de David con sus Sumarios, en que se declara con brevedad la contenido en cada Psalmo, agora nueva y fielmente traducidos en romance Castellano por el doctor Juan Pérez, conforme a la verdad de la lengua Sancta. Salmo LXXXV. Muéstranos, Señor, tu misericordia, y danos tu salud* (Venice: Pedro Daniel, [Geneva: Jean Crespin] 1557).

—, *Los Psalmos de David con sus Sumarios, en que se declara con brevedad la contenido en cada Psalmo, agora nueva y fielmente traducidos en romance Castellano por el doctor Juan Pérez, conforme a la verdad de la lengua Sancta. Salmo LXXXV. Muéstranos, Señor, tu misericordia, y danos tu salud* [1557] (Buenos Aires: La Aurora, 1951).

—, *Sumario breve de la Doctrina Cristiana hecho por vía de pregunta y respuesta, en manera de coloquio, para que así aprendan los niños con más facilidad, y saquen de ella mayor fruto. En que también se enseña cómo se han de aprovechar de ella los que la leyeren. Compuesta por el Doctor Juan Pérez* (Venice: Pedro Daniel [Geneva: Jean Crespin], 1556).

—, *Suplicazión a Don Felipe II*, in L. Usoz y Rio/B.B. Wiffen, eds. *Reformistas antiguos españoles*, Vol. XII (San Sebastián: Ignacio R. Baroja, 1857).

Casiodoro de Reina (1520–1594)

—, *Apología de la concordia de Wittemberg*. 1580.

—, *Biblia [del Oso], que es, los sacros libros del viejo y nuevo testamento. Trasladada en español* (Basel: Thomas Guarin, 1569).

—, *Catechismus, dat is, Corte onderwijsinghe van de voorneemste hooftstucken der christelijcker leere, op vraghe ende antwoort ghestelt: na de wijse vande straefborchse, ende andere euangelische hooch duytsche kercken, de Confessie van Ausborch toe-ge-daen sijnde, nu nieuwelijck in neder-duytscher spraken ghestelt* (Antwerp: Aernot s'Conincx, 1580). Edition by Cassiodoro de Reyna of the Strasbourg catechism, prepared by Johann Marbach

—, *Comentario al Evangelio de Juan*, in E. Monjo Bellido, ed., *Obras de los Reformadores españoles del siglo XVI*, Vol. VII (Seville: Editorial MAD, 2010). Translated from the Latin by Fco. Ruiz de Pablos.

—, *Confessio in articulo de Coena, Cassiodori Reinii, Hispani, ministri in ecclesia quae Antrerpiae se Augustanam Confessionem profiteri dicit, quam si eius symmistae sincere profitentur, sublata erit inter eos et ecclesiarum reformatorum ministros controversia* (Antwerp: Giles van den Rade, 1578).

—, *Confession de fe christiana hecha por ciertos fieles españoles, los quales, huyendo los abusos de la Iglesia Romana, y la cruedad de la Inquisición d'España, dexaron su patria para ser recebidos de la Iglesia de los fieles, por hermanos en Christo* (London, 1559).

—, *Confession de fe Christiana, hecha por ciertos fieles españoles, los qvales hvyendo los abvsos de la Iglesia Romana, y la crueldad e de la Inquisition d'España, dexaron su patria, para ser recebidos de la Iglesia de los fieles, por hermanos en Christo: Das ist Bekenntnis des Christlichen Glaubens: gestellt durch etliche Christgleubige Hispanier, welche wegen des Missbreuch der Römischen Kirchen ihr Vaterland verlassen* (Cassel: W. Wessel, 1601).

—, *Confession de fe christiana*, in A. Gordon Kinder, ed., *The Spanish Protestant Confession of Faith* [London, 1560/61] (Exeter: University of Exeter, 1988).

—, *Eclesiastés* (Barcelona: Muchnik, 1998). Prologue by Doris May Lessing.

—, *El Evangelio segun San Lúcas.* E. Reeves Palmer, ed. (Madrid: Sociedad Bíblica Británica y Extranjera, 1886).

—, *Evangelium Iohannis: hoc est, iusta ac vetus apologia pro aeterna Christi divinitate;* & *Expositio primae partis capitis quarti Matthaei* (Frankfurt: Nicolas Bassei [Bascus], 1573).

—, *Éxodo* (Barcelona: Poliedro, 2005). Prologue by Horacio Vázquez Rial.

—, *Exodo: versión de la biblia del oso* (Barcelona: Muchnik, 1998). Prologue by David Grossman, translation of the prologue by Antonio Padilla.

—, *Exposición de la Primera Parte del Capítulo Cuarto de San Mateo sobre las Tentaciones de Cristo* (Madrid: Iglesia Española Reformada Episcopal, 1988). Translation by María Araujo Fernández.

—, *Expositio primae partis capitis quarti Matthae commonefactoria ad ecclesiam Christi, de periculis piorum Ministrorum Verbi in tempore cauendis* (Frankfurt: Nicolas Bassé, 1573).

—, *Genesis* (Barcelona: Muchnik, 1998; Barcelona: Poliedro, 2005). Prologue by Juan Manuel de Prada..

—, *Je'ná, hue garabé ra'íchari ju mapurigá osári San Lúca: El Santo Evangelio según San Lucas* (México: Sociedad Bíblica Americana, 1957). Translation into Tarahumara by Kenneth S. Hilton and M. Hilton.

—, *La Confesión Española de Londres*, A. Gordon Kinder, ed., Diálogo Ecuménico 48 (1988), 365–419.

—, *The Spanish Protestant Confession of Faith* (London: Cassell, 1601).

Juan de Valdes (1505?—1541)

—, *Alfabeto christiano de Juan de Valdés: Reimpresion fiel del traslado italiano: Añádense ahora dos traducciones modernas, una en castellano, otra en inglés*, (translation by Luis de Usoz y Río); *Alfabeto christiano. A faithful reprint of the Italian of 1546: with two modern translations, in Spanish and in English* (translation by Benjamin B. Wiffen), in L. Usoz y Río/B.B. Wiffen, eds. *Reformistas antiguos españoles*, Vol. XVI (London: Eyre & Spottiswoode, 1861).

—, *Alfabeto christiano, che insegna la vera via d'acquistare il lume dello Spirito santo. In che maniera il christiano ha da estudiare nel suo proprio libro, e che frutto ha da trahere dello studio, e come la santa scrittura gli serve per interprete, o commentario* (Venice: Nicolò Bascarini, 1545; Venice: [Francesco Brucioli], 1546). Translaton from the Spanish by Marco Antonio Magno.

—, *Alfabeto christiano, scritto in lingua spagnuola*, in L. Usoz y Río/B.B. Wiffen (eds.). *Reformistas antiguos españoles*, Vol. XVI (Madrid: Martin Alegría, 1860).

—, *Alfabeto cristiano: Que enseña el verdadero camino de adquirir la luz del Espíritu Santo. Con notas biográficas y críticas sobre el autor por B. Foster Stockwell, y sobre Julia Gonzaga por Benjamín B. Wiffin* (Buenos Aires: La Aurora, 1948).

—, *Alfabeto christiano, which teaches the true way to acquire the light of the Holy Spirit* [1546], with a notice of Juan de Valdés and Giulia Gonzaga (London: Bosworth & Harrison, 1861). Translation from the Italian by Benjamin B. Wiffen.

—, *Alfabeto Cristiano*, Adriano Prosperi, ed. (Rome: Istituto storico per l'età moderna e contemporanea, 1988).

—, *Alfabeto cristiano: diálogo con Guilia Gonzaga* (Bari: Gius Laterza e Figli, 1938). Introduction and notes by Benedetto Croce.

—, *Alfabeto cristiano: Domande e risposte; Della predestinazione; Catechism*, Massimo Firpo, ed. (Turin: Giulio Einaudi, 1994).

—, *Cartas inéditas de Juan de Valdés al Cardenal Gonzaga* (Madrid: S. Aguirre, 1931). Introduction and notes by José F. Montesinos.

—, *Cartas inéditas de Juan de Valdés al cardenal Gonzaga* (Madrid: Biblioteca Nacional, 1971).

—, *Cent et dix consyderations divines de Jan de Val d'Esso. Traduites prémiérement, d'Espaignol (sic) en langue Italienne, et de nouveau mises en Francois, par C.K.P.* (Lyon: Claude Senneton et Jean d'Ogerolles, 1563). Translated by C.K.P. [Claude de Kerquefinen, Parisien].

—, *Cent et dix consyderations divines de Jan de Val d'Esso* (Paris: Mathurin Prevost, 1565).

—, *Ciento diez divinas consideraciones*, in L. Usoz y Rio/B.B. Wiffen, eds. *Reformistas antiguos españoles*, Vol. IX (San Sebastián: Ignacio R. Baroja, 1854).

—, *Cinque Trattatelli Evangelici* (Roma, 1545).

—, *Comentario a los Salmos*, Carlos López Lozano, ed. (Terrassa: CLIE, 1987).

—, *Comentario o declarazion breve i compendiosa sobre la epístola de San Pablo apóstol á los Romanos, muy util para todos los amadores de la piedad christiana*, Juan Pérez de Pineda, ed. [Venecia: Iuan Philadelpho [Genève: Jean Crespin], 1557], in L. Usoz y Rio/B.B. Wiffen, eds. *Reformistas antiguos españoles*, Vol. X (Madrid: J. Martín Alegría, 1856).

—, *Comentario ó declarazion familiar y compendiosa sobre la primera epístola de San Pablo apóstol á los Corintios, muy útil para todos los amadores de la piedad cristiana / compuesto por Juan Valdesio.* Juan Pérez de Pineda, ed. [Venezia: Juan Philadelpho [Geneva: Jean Crespin], 1557], in L. Usoz y Rio/B.B. Wiffen, eds. *Reformistas antiguos españoles*, Vol. XI (Madrid: J. Martín Alegría, 1856).

—, *Comentario o Exposición sobre 41 psalmos de David, escrito por Juan de Valdés en el siglo XVI, y ahora impreso por primera vez*, Manuel Carrasco, ed. (Madrid: Librería Nacional y Extranjera, 1885).

—, *Commentary on the First Book of the Psalms, Now for the First Time Translated from the Spanish, Having Never Before Been Published in English, by John T. Betts. [Edited by Maria Betts and Edward Boehmer.] Appended to Which Are the Lives of the Twin Brothers, Juan and Alfonso De Valdés, by Edward Boehmer.* [Extracted from the Bibliotheca Wiffeniana, with the Author's Additions on Recent Discoveries of Valdés' Works and with Introduction by the Editor, John T. Betts] (Edinburgh/London: Ballantyne, Hanson and Co, 1894).

—, *Commentary on the first book of the Psalms: now for the first time translated from the Spanish, having never been published in English* (London/Edinburgh, 1894; Madrid: Biblioteca Nacional, 1971). Translation by John T. Betts.

—, *Commentary upon our Lord's Sermon on the Mount. Reprinted from the Commentary itself.* Edward Boehmer, ed. (London: Trübner, 1882). Translation by John T. Betts.

—, *Commentary upon St. Paul's Epistle to the Romans; translated from the Spanish by John T. Betts; appended to which are The lives of the twin brothers Juán and Alfonso de Valdés by Edward Boehmer; with introduction by the editor* (London: Trübner, 1883).

—, *Commentary Upon St. Paul's First Epistle to the Church at Corinth: Now for the First Time Translated from the Spanish, Having Never Before Been Published in English.* (London: Trübner, 1883). Translation by John T. Betts.

—, *Commentary upon St. Paul's First Epistle to the Church at Corinth. Now for the first time translated from the Spanish, having never before been published in English, by John T. Betts.* Appended to which are a "Dedicatory letter by Juan Perez, to Maximilian, king of Bohemia" and "The lives of the twin Brothers, Juan and Alfonso de Valdés" by Edward Boehmer with an introduction by the editor, John T. Betts (London: Trübner, 1883).

—, *Commentary Upon the Epistole to the Romans* (London: Trübner, 1883). Translation by John T. Betts.

—, *Commentary Upon the Gospel of St. Matthew: Now for the First Time Translated from the Spanish, and Never Before Published in English* (London: Trübner, 1882). Translation by John T. Betts.

—, *Consideraciones y pensamientos*, Juan Orts González, ed. (Madrid: Editorial J. de Valdés, 1935).

—, *Diàleg de Doctrina Cristiana*, Xavier Vilaró, ed. (Barcelona: Proa, 1994).

—, *Dialog on Christian Doctrine* (forthcoming). Translation and notes Frances Luttikhuizen.

—, *Diálogo de doctrina christiana* (Venezia: [Francesco Brucioli], 1545).

—, *Diálogo de doctrina christiana y el Salterio traducido del hebreo en romance castellano,* Domingo Ricart, ed. (México: Universidad Nacional Autónoma de México, 1964).

—, *Diálogo de doctrina christiana, nuevamente compuesto por un religioso* (Alcalá: Miguel de Eguía, 1529).

—, *Diálogo de doctrina cristiana nuevamente compuesto por un religioso. Impreso en 1529 en Alcalá de Henares y publicado nuevamente con motivo del cuarto centenario,* Theodoro Fliedner, ed. (Madrid: Librería Nacional y Extranjera, 1929).

—, *Diálogo de doctrina Cristiana*, B. Foster Stockwell, ed. (Buenos Aires: La Aurora / México, DF: Casa Unida de Publicaciones, 1946).

—, *Diálogo de doctrina Cristiana*, in E. Monjo Bellido, ed. *Obras de los reformadores españoles del siglo XVI*, Vol. III (Seville: Editorial MAD, 2008).

—, *Diálogo de doctrina Cristiana*, José F. Montesinos, ed. (Madrid: Espasa-Calpe, 1953).

—, *Diálogo de doctrina Cristiana*, Miguel Jiménez Monteserín y Javier Ruiz, eds. (Madrid: Nacional, 1979).

—, *Diálogo de doctrina cristiana: reproduction en fac-similé de l'exemplaire de la Bibliothèque Nationale de Lisbonne [edition d'Alcalá de Henares, 1529]*, Marcel Bataillon, ed. (Coimbra: Imprensa da Universidade, 1925).

—, *Diálogo de la lengua* (Barcelona: Océano, 2002).

—, *Diálogo de la lengua* (México: Porrúa, 1966). Prologue by Juan M. Lope Blanch.

—, *Diálogo de la lengua (tenido ázia el A. 1533), i publicado por primera vez el año de 1737. Ahora reimpreso conforme al ms. de la Biblioteca Nazional, único que el Editór conoze. Por Apéndize va una Carta de A. Valdés,* in L. de Usoz y Río/B.B. Wiffen, eds. *Reformistas antiguos españoles,* Vol. XXII (Madrid: Martin Alegría, 1860).

—, *Diálogo de la lengua* [Madrid: Ediciones de la Lectura, 1928] (Munich: Lincom, 2014).

—, *Diálogo de la lengua escrito por Juan de Valdés hácia el año 1533 en Nápoles (reimpreso Madrid 1860).* Eduard Boehmer, ed. (Halle, 1865).

—, *Diálogo de la lengua und Refranes,* Eduard Boehmer, ed. (Bonn: Eduard Weber, 1895).

—, *Diálogo de la lengua,* A. Quilis, ed. (Barcelona: Plaza & Janés, 1984; Madrid: Libertarias-Prodhufi, 1999).

—, *Diálogo de la lengua,* Cristina Barbolani, ed. (Messina-Firenze: D'Anna, 1967; Madrid: Cátedra, 1982).

—, *Diálogo de la lengua,* Felix F Corso, ed. (Buenos Aires: Perlado, 1940).

—, *Diálogo de la lengua,* Francisco Marsá, ed. (Barcelona: Planeta, 1986).

—, *Diálogo de la lengua,* José Ardanaz, ed. (Barcelona: Orbis, 1983).

—, *Diálogo de la lengua,* José Enrique Laplana Gil, ed. (Barcelona, Critica, 2010).

—, *Diálogo de la lengua,* Jose Fernandez Monntesinos, ed. (Madrid: Editorial Espasa-Calpe, 1964).

—, *Diálogo de la lengua,* José Moreno Villa, ed. (Madrid: Biblioteca Calleja, 1919).

—, *Diálogo de la lengua,* Juan M. Lope Blanch, ed. (Madrid: Castalia, 1969).

—, *Diálogo de la lengua,* Lore Terracini, ed. (Modena/Roma: STEM, 1957).

—, *Diálogo de la lengua,* Rafael Lapesa, ed. (Zaragoza: Ebro, 1940).

—, *Diálogo de la Lengua: a Diplomatic Edition by Kormi Anipa* (Cambridge, UK: Modern Humanities Research Assocation, 2014).

—, *Diálogo de las lenguas,* Janet H. Perry, ed. (London: University of London Press, 1927).

—, *Diálogos. Escritos espirituales. Cartas,* Angel Alvala, ed. (Madrid: Fundación José Antonio de Castro, 1997).

—, *Dialogue de la langue: (1535); présentation en version bilingue espagnol et français = Diálogo de la lengua* (Paris: Champion, 2008). Translation and notes by Anne-Marie Chabrolle-Cerretini.

—, *Dialogue on Christian Doctrine,* in José C. Nieto, ed. *Two catechisms: the Dialogue on Christian Doctrine and The Christian Instruction for Children* (Lawrence, KS: Coronado Press, 1980). Translation by William Burwell Jones and Carol D. Jones.

—, *Dialogus doctrinae christianae* (Index de Venezia, 1549).

—, *Divine Considerations Treating of Those Things Which Are Most Profitable, Most Necessary and Most Perfect in Our Christian Profession* (Cambridge: Roger Daniel, 1646). Translation by Nicholas Ferrar.

—, *Divine Considerations. The English translation of Nicholas Ferrar. With George Herbert's prefatory epistle,* Frederic Chapman, ed. (London: John Lane, 1905).

—, *Ein Edel Schrifftlich Kleinath und Verehrung des Ehrwüdigen Hern Petri Pauli Vergerii. An des Durchleüchtigen Hochgebornen Fúrsten und Herrn, Herrn Christoffs Hertzogen zu Würtemberg, u. erstegebornen Son, Her Eberhartum, lateinisch geschriben* (Tübingen, 1555).

—, *El Evangelio según San Mateo,* Carlos López Lozano, ed. (Terrassa: CLIE, 1986).

—, *El Evangelio según San Mateo, declarado por Juan de Valdés, ahora por primera vez publicado,* Eduard Boehmer, ed. (Madrid: Librería Nacional y Extranjera, 1880).

—, *El Salterio: traduzido del hebreo en romance castellano, transcripción por J. d. V., ahora por primera vez impreso.* [1550], Eduard Boehmer, ed. in L. Usoz y Rio/B.B. Wiffen, eds. *Reformistas antiguos españoles,* Vol. 23 (Bonn: Carlos Georgi, 1880).

—, *Godsalige Anmerckingen uyt het Italiansche overgeset* ([Emden],1565). Translation into Dutch by Adriano Garino. Listed in Friedrich Samuel Bock, *Historia Antitrinitariorum* (Liepzig, 1774), 981.

—, *Göttliche Betrachtungen — Consideraciones divinas* (Leipzig: Justus Naumann, 1873). Translation by Otto Anger.

—, *Hundertundzehn Göttliche Betrachtungen: Aus dem Italienischen (von Eduard Böhmer). Mit einem Anhang: Ueber die Zwillingsbrüder Juan und Alfonso de Valdés von Eduard Böhmer* (Halle: Georg Schwabe, 1870).

—, *Hundred and Ten Consideracions* (London: Bernard Quaritch, 1865). Translation by John T. Betts.

—, *Il dialogo della dottrina cristiana (1529).* Teodoro Fanlo y Cortés e Anna Morisi Guerra, eds. (Torin: Claudiana, 1991).

—, *In che maniera il Christiano ha da studiare nel suo proprio libro, il Modo che si de tenere nell'insegnare et predicare il principio della religione Christiana.* (Rome, 1545; Venice: [Francesco Brucioli], 1545).

—, *In que maniera doviano esser instrutti insino dalla pueritia li figlioli delli christiani nelle cose della religiosa christiana* (Siena, Biblioteca comunale, Ms. G. VIII. 28 /folios 62v–70r).

—, *Instruccion cristiana para los niños por Juan Valdés en ocho lenguas: Christliche Kinderlehre / Juan de Valdés' Spiritual Milk: Octoglot: Christliche Kinderlehre. Die Übersetzungen des sechzehnten Jahrhunderts ins Italienische, Lateinische, Polnische, und neue aus dem Italienischen ins Deutsche, Englische, Französische, Engadinische, nebst Rückübersetzung ins Spanishche* (Bonn: J. Flittner / London: Trübner, 1883).

—, *Istruzione cristiana e comparazioni di Giovanni Valdès* (Rome/Florence, 1884).

—, *Joya cristiana del siglo XVI. Manera que se debería observar para informar desde la niñez a los cristianos en las cosas de la religión, por Juan de Valdés,* Eduard Boehmer, ed. (Madrid: Librería Nacional y Extranjera, 1882, 1884).

—, *Juan de Valdés' Minor Works: Commentary upon Our Lord's Sermon on the Mount; Commentary upon the Gospel of St. Matthew; Spiritual Milk, or Christian Instruction for Children; XVII Opuscules. Translated from the Spanish and Italian and edited by John T. Betts.* (London: Trubner & Co. 1882).

—, *La Epístola de San Pablo apóstol á los Romanos y a la I de los Corinthios,* in L. Usoz y Rio/B. B. Wiffen, eds. *Reformistas antiguos españoles,* Vol. X (Madrid: J. Martín Alegría, 1856).

—, *Lac spirituale Johannis de Valdés: institutio puerorum christiana,* Friedrich Koldewey, ed. (Braunschweig: Bruhn, 1864; Heilbronn: Henninger, 1870; Halis: G. Aemilii Barthel, 1871).

—, *Lac spirituale, proalendis ac educandis Christianorum pueris ad gloriam Dei. Munusculum Vergerii* (1556?).

—, *Las ciento diez divinas consideraciones: Recensión del manuscrito inédito de Juan Sánchez de 1558.* J. Ignacio Tellechea Idígoras, ed. (Salamanca: Centro de Estudios Orientales y Ecuménicos Juan XXIII, 1975).

—, *Latte Spirituale, col quale si debbono nutrire et allevare i figliuoli de Christiani in gloria di Dio. Proverb. 1. cap. Accio che à piccioli sia data prudentia, et à giovanetti scientia et intelletto.* Pietro Paolo Vergerio, ed. (Basel: Jakob Kündig [Giacomo Parco], 1549; Pavia: Francesco Moscheni, 1550).

—, *Le cento e dieci divine considerazioni* (Halle: Ploetz, 1860).

—, *Le cento e dieci divine considerazioni di Giovanni Valdesso (tradotte dalla Spagnuola nella Italiana lingua-Cenni biografici sui fratelli G. e A. Valdesso),* Eduard Boehmer, ed. (Halle: E. Anton/Ploetz, 1860).

—, *Le cento e dieci divine considerazioni,* Edmondo Cione (ed.). (Milan: Fratelli Bocca, 1944).

—, *Le cento e dieci divine considerazioni.* Teodoro Fanlo y Cortés, ed. (Genoa/Milan: Marietti, 2004).

—, *Le cento et dieci divine considerationi del S. Giovanni Valdesso: nelle quali si ragiona delle cose piu utili, piu necessarie, e piu perfette, della christiana professione. I Cor. ii.* C. S. Curione, ed. (Basel: J. Oporinus, 1550).

—, *Le Dialogue sur la doctrine chrétienne* (Paris: Presses univ. de France, 1995). Translation and introduction by Christine Wagner.

—, *Leche de la fee* (1556?), in *Cathaolgus librorum* (Valladolid, 1559).

—, *Les divines consyderations, et sainctes meditations de Jean de Val d'esso, Gentil-homme Espaignol. Touchant tout ce qui est necessaire, pour la perfection de la vie Chretienne. Traduites par C.K.P. Revues de nouveau et rapportées fidelement à l'Exemplaire Espaignol, el amplifiées de la Table des principales matiéres traitées par l'Aucteur* (Lyon: Pierre Picard, 1601). Translated by Claude de Kerquefinen, Parisien.

—, *Lo Evangelio di San Matteo,* Carlo Ossola and Anna Maria Cavallarin, eds. (Rome: Bulzoni, 1985).

—, *Manera que se debería observar para informar desde la niñez a los hijos de los cristianos en las cosas de la religion* (Madrid: Librería Nacional y Extranjera, 1884; Mexico: El Fénix, 1946).

—, *Modo che si dee tenere ne l'in segnare il principio della religione christiana.* (Rome, 1545).

—, *Modo di tenere nell'insegnare & predicare il principio della religione Christiana* (Rome, 1545).

—, *Psalmos de David (1537)* (Venice: Pedro Daniel [i. e. Jean Crespin], 1558).

—, *Qual maniera si devrebbe tenere a informare insino della fanciullezza i figliuoli de Christiani delle cose della religion,* in *Index of Pius IV* (Rome, 1549).

—, *Qual maniera si dovrebbe tenere a informare insino da fanciullezza I figiuoli dei christiani delle cose della religion,* in *Index de Venisa* (Venice, 1549).

—, *Spiritual milk, or, Christian instruction for children* (London: Trübner, 1882). Translated from the Italian by John T. Betts.

—, *Sul principio della dottrina cristiana. Cinque trattatelli evangelici di Giovanni Valdesso ristampati dall'edizione romana del 1545,* Eduard Boehmer, ed. (Halle: George Schwabe, 1870).

—, *The hundred and ten considerations of Signior Iohn Valdesso treating of those things which are most profitable, most necessary, and most perfect in our Christian profession. Written in Spanish, brought out of Italy by Vergerius, and first set forth in Italian at Basil by Cœlius Secundus Curio, anno 1550. Afterward translated into French, and printed at*

Lions 1563, and again at Paris 1565. And now translated out of the Italian copy into English, with notes. Whereunto is added an epistle of the authors, or a preface to his Divine Commentary upon the Romans. I Cor., ch. 2. Nowbeit we speak wisdome amongst them that are perfect, yet not the wisdome of the world (Oxford: Leonard Lichfield, 1638). Translation by Nicholas Ferrar.

—, The Spanish reformers: three opuscules reprinted from a work published by Trübner & Co. entitled XVII Opuscules (London: Hodder & Stoughton, 1883).

—, Three opuscules; reprinted from a work entitled 'XVII opuscules' (Madrid: Biblioteca Nacional, 1971).

—, Trataditos, Eduard Boehmer, ed. (Bonn: Carlos Georgi, 1880).

—, Trataditos, in L. Usoz y Rio/B.B. Wiffen, eds. Reformistas antiguos españoles, Vol. XXIV (Bonn: Carlos Georgi, 1880).

—, Two catechisms: the Dialogue on Christian Doctrine and The Christian Instruction for Children, José C. Nieto, ed. (Lawrence, KS: Coronado Press, 1980). Translation by Wm Burwell Jones y Carol D. Jones).

—, Über Christlichen Grundlehren. Fünf Evangelische Tractate, Gedruckt zu Rom 1545, Jetzt Zuerst Ins Deutsche Übersetzt, E. Boehmer (Halle: Schwabe, 1870).

—, Ziento i diez consideraziones de Juan de Valdés [1565]. Ahora publicadas por primera vez en castellano, in L. Usoz y Rio/B.B. Wiffen, eds. Reformistas antiguos españoles. Vol. IX. (San Sebastián: Ignacio R. Baroja, 1854).

—, Ziento i diez consideraziones leidas i explicadas házia el año de 1538 i 1539, por Juan de Valdés, conforme a un manuscrito castellano escrito a. 1558 existente en la biblioteca de Hamburgo, i ahora publicado por vez primera con un facsímile. Primera vez publicadas en castellano, el año 1855 por Luis de Usóz y Rio y ahora correjidas nuevamente con mayor cuidado (London: Spottiswood, G.A. Claro del Bosque, 1863).

Cipriano de Valera (1532–1602)

— [Guillermo Massan, pseud.] (trans.), Cathólico Reformado o una declaración que muestra quánto nos podemos conformar con la Iglesia Romana, tal qual es el día de hoy, en diversos puntos de la Religión: y en qué puntos devamos nunca jamás convenir, sino para siempre apartarnos della. Ítem, un Aviso a los afficionados a la Iglesia Romana, que muestra la dicha Religión Romana ser contra los Cathólicos rudimentos y fundamentos del Catecismo. Compuesto por Guillermo Perquino [William Perkins], Licenciado en Sancta Theología, y trasladado en Romance Castellano por Guillermo Massan [Cipriano de Valera], Gentilhombre, y a su costa imprimido. London: Richard Field, 1599.

— [Guillermo Massan, pseud.] (trans.). Catholicvs Reformatvs Hoc est, Expositio Et Declaratio, Praecipvarvm Aliqvot Religionis controuersiarum, quae ostendit, quatenus Ecclesiae ex Dei verbo reformatae in iis cum Ecclesiâ Rom. qualis ea hodie est, consentiunt, & quatenus ab eadem dissentiunt. Hannover: G. Antonius, 1601, 1603, 1608.

— La Biblia. Que es los Sacros Libros del Vieio y Nuevo Testamento. Segunda Edición. Revista y conferida con los textos Hebreos y Griegos y con diversas translaciones. Por Cypriano de Valera. «La palabra de Dios permanece para siempre». Esayas. 40.8. [Amsterdam: Lorenço Jacobi, 1602]. Madrid: Sociedad Bíblica. Madrid, 1990.

—, "A todos los amadores del Señor Iesu Christo", Prólogo a Juan Calvino, Catecismo, que significa forma de instruccion: que contiene los principios de la religion de Dios, util y necessario para todo fiel Christiano. Compuesta en manera de dialogo, donde pregunta *el maestro y responde el discipulo (1559)*. (trans. Juan Pérez de Pineda). London: Richard. Field, 1596.

—, "A todos los fieles de la nación española que dessean el adelantamiento del reyno de Jesu Christo. Salud". (Advertencia en Juan Calvino, *Institución de la religión Christiana*). London: Richard Field, 1597.

—, "Otra epistola al christiano lector", en G. Perquino [William Perkins], *Catholico Reformado*, (trans. Guillermo Massan [C. de Valera]). London: Richard Field, 1599.

—, (trans.), *Institución de la religión Christiana, compuesta en quatro libros y dividida en capítulos. Por Juan Calvino. Y ahora nuevamente traduzida en Romance Castellano por Cypriano de Valera*. London: Richard Field, 1597.

—, *A full view of popery, in a satyrical account of the lives of the Popes, &c, from the pretended succession of St Peter, to the present Pope Clement XI, wherein all the imposters and innovations of the Church of Rome appear in their true colours, and all their objections, cavils, &c, are fully answer'd and confuted. The whole being interspers'd with several pasquils. To this is added, a confutation of the Mass, and a vindication of reformed devotion. In two parts, written by a learned Spanish convert, and address'd to his countrymen: now faithfully translated from the second and best edition of the original* (trans. John Savage). London: Bernard Lintott, 1704.

—, *An Answere or Admonition to Those of the Church of Rome, Touching the Iubile, Proclaimed by the Bull, Made and Set Foorth by Pope Clement the Eyght, for the Yeare of Our Lord. 1600*. Translated Out of French. London: John Wolfe, 1600.

—, *Aviso a los de la Iglesia Romana sobre la indiccion del jubileo por la bulla del Papa Clemente octavo*. London: Richard Field, 1600.

—, *Dos Tratados. El Primero es del Papa i de su autoridad, colejido de su vida i dotrina. El Segundo es la Missa: el uno i el otro recopilado de la que los Dotores i Conzilios Antiguos, i la Sagrada Escritura enseñan. Ítem, un enxambre de los falsos milagros con que María de la Visitación, Priora de la Anunziada de Lisboa, engañó a mui muchos i de cómo fue descubierta i condenada. Revelación, XVII, 1. «Ven i mostrarte he la condenazión de la gran Ramera, la qual está sentada sobre muchas aguas.» Y vers. 15. «Las aguas que has visto donde la Ramera se sienta, son pueblos, compañas, gentes y lenguas»*. [Signed: C.D.V.]. London: Ricardo del Campo [i. e. Richard Field], 1599.

—, *Dos Tratados. El Primero es del Papa y de su autoridad colegido de su vida y doctrina, y de lo que los Dotores y Concilios antiguos, y la misma sagrada Escritura enseñan. El Segundo es de la Missa recopilada de los Dotores y Concilios y de la Sagrada Escritura. «Toda planta, que no plantó mi Padre celestial, será desarraygada.» Mt. XV. 13. «Caída es, caída es Babylonia, aquella gran ciudad, porque ella ha dado a bever a todas las gentes del vino de la yra de su fornicación.» Apoc. XIV. 8*. London: Arnold Hatfild, 1588.

—, *El Libro de los Salmos*. New York: Sociedad Biblica Americana, 1876.

—, *El Nuevo Testamento. Que es los Escriptos Evangélicos y Apostólicos. Revisto y conferido con el texto Griego. Por Cypriano de Valera*. Amsterdam: Henrico Lorenzi, 1625.

—, *El Testamento nuevo de nuestro señor Jesu Christo*. (trans. Casiodoro de Reina). London: Ricardo del Campo [Richard Field], 1596.

—, *Exhortacion [al cristiano lector à leer la sagrada escritura. En la cual se nuestra cuales sean los libros Canonicas o' sagrada escritura y cuales sean los libros Apochryphos]*. Amsterdam: L. Jacobi, 1602.

—, *Institución de la Religión Cristiana de Juan Calvino*. (trans. Cipriano de Valera) [Londres, 1597], Buenos Aires: La Aurora, 1952.

—, *Institución de la Religión Cristiana*. (de Juan Calvino). Rijswijk: Fundación Editorial de la Literatura Reformada, 1968.

—, *Institución religiosa escrita por Juan Calvino el año 1536 y traduzida al Castellano por Zipriano de Valera. Segunda vez, fielmente impresa, en el mismo número de páginas.* En L. Usoz y Rio y B.B. Wiffen, eds., *Reformistas antiguos españoles.* Vol. XIV, XV. [Madrid: José López Cuesta. 1858]. Barcelona: Diego Gómez Flores, 1983.

—, *Los dos tratados del Papa i de la Misa, escritos por Cipriano D. Valera; i por él publicados primero el a. 1588, luego el a. 1599: i ahora fielmente reimpresos.* En L. Usoz y Rio y B.B. Wiffen, eds., *Reformistas Antiguos Españoles.* Vol. VI. [Madrid: J. Martín Alegría, 1851]. Barcelona: Diego Gómez Flores, 1983.

—, *Sefer Torah, Nevi'im u-Khetuvim: el Libro de la Ley, los Profetas, y las Eskrituras.* (trans. William G. Schauffler). Konstantinoplah: [American Bible Society], 1905.

—, *Tabla, en la cual mui clara y suczintamente se declara, quién sea el Antichristo* [London, 1588], in: A. Gorden Kinder, "Religious Literature as an Offensive Weapon: Cipriano de Valera's Part in England's War with Spain", The Sixteenth Century Journal Sixteenth Century Journal 19.2 (1988), 223–235.

—, *Tratado del Papa.* Isabel Colón Calderón, ed., Seville: Fundación José Manuel Lara, 2010.

—, *Tratado para confirmar en la fe cristiana a los Cautivos de Berbería. Compuesto por Zipriano D. Valera i por él publicado el A. 1594*, in: L. Usoz y Rio y B.B. Wiffen, eds., *Reformistas Antiguos Españoles.* Vol. VIII. [San Sebastián: Ignacio Ramón Baroja, 1854]. Barcelona: Diego Gómez Flores, 1982.

—, *Tratado para confirmar los pobres cautivos de Berberia, en la católica y antigua fe y religion Cristiana, y para los consolar, con la palabra de Dios, en las aflicciones que padecen por el Evangelio de Jesucristo.* Miguel Ángel de Bunes Ibarra, ed., Seville: Renacimiento, 2004.

—, *Tratado para confirmar los pobres cautivos de Berbería, en la católica i antigua fe i religión cristiana i para los consolar con la palabra de Dios en las aflicciones que padezen por el Evangelio de Jesucristo. «Por tu causa, oh Señor, nos matan cada día: somos tenidos como ovejas para el degolladero. Despierta, ¿por qué duermes, Señor? Despierta, no te alejes para siempre.» Salmo 44, 23. Al fin de este tratado hallaréis un enxambre de los falsos milagros i ilusiones del demonio con que María de la Visitación, priora de la Anunziada de Lisboa, engañó a mui muchos; i de cómo fue descubierta y condenada al fin del año de 1588.* London: Peter Short, 1594.

—, *Two treatises the first, of the liues of the popes, and their doctrine. The second, of the masse: the one and the other collected of that, which the doctors, and ancient councels, and the sacred Scripture do teach. Also, a swarme of false miracles, wherewith Marie de la Visitacion, prioresse of the Annuntiada of Lisbon, deceived very many: and how she was discouered, and condemned. The second edition in Spanish augmented by the author himselfe, M. Cyprian Valera, and translated into English by Iohn Goulborne.* London: John Harrison, 1600.

Appendix C —
The Reformistas Antiguos Españoles Library

The following is a list of the books that comprise the original twenty-two volumes of the "Reformistas Antiguos Españoles" series (1847–1865), together with two extra volumes added later by Eduard Bohemer. This list is followed by the volumes published by Emilio Monjo Bellido in the series *Obras de los Reformadores españoles del siglo XVI* and which can be considered a continuation.[1]

Vol. I. "Carrascon" [1633] de Fernandes de Tejeda (San Sabastián: Ignacio R. Baroja, 1847).

Vol. II. Juan Pérez, *Epístola Consolatoria* [1560] (London: Richard Bentley, 1848).

Vol. III. Juan Pérez, *Carta a Felipe II y Imágenes del Anticristo* [1556–1557] (San Sebastián: Ignacio R. Baroja, 1849).

Vol. IV. Juan de Valdés, *Dos Dialogos* [1530, 1586] (Madrid: J. Martín Alegría, 1850).

Vol. V. Raimundo Gonzalez de Montes, *Artes de la Inquisicion Española* [1567] (San Sebastián: Ignacio R. Baroja, 1851).

Vol. VI. Cipriano de Valera, *Los dos tratados del Papa y de la Misa* [1588] (Madrid: J. Martín Alegría, 1851).

Vol. VII. Juan Pérez, *Breve tratado de doctrina* [1560] (San Sebastián: Ignacio R. Baroja, 1852).

Vol. VIII. Cipriano de Valera, *Tratado para confirmar la fe cristiana a los cautivos en Berbaria. Aviso a los de la Iglesia Romana sobre jubileos* [1594, 1600]. Juan de Nicolas, *El español reformado* [1621] (San Sebastián: Ignacio R. Baroja, 1854).

Vol. IX. Juan de Valdés, *Ciento i Diez Consideraziones* [1565] (San Sebastián: Ignacio R. Baroja, 1854).

Vol. X. Juan de Valdés, *Dos Epistolas de San Pablo: A los Romanos, y la I. de los Corintios* [1573] (Madrid: J. Martín Alegría, 1856).

Vol. XI. Juan de Valdés, *Comentario o Declarazion familiar i compendiosa, sobre la primera Epístola de San Pablo Apóstol a los Corintios* (Madrid: J. Martín Alegría, 1856).

Vol. XII. Francisco de Enzinas, *Dos Informaziones* [1559]; Juan Pérez, *Suplicazión a D. Felipe II* (San Sebastián: Ignacio R. Baroja, 1857).

---

1 For a systematic description of each of the volumes, see Mario Escobar Golderos, "Biblioteca de Reformados Antiguos Españoles," in *Historia para el Debate Digital* (November 19, 2007), http://historiaparaeldebate.blogcindario.com/2007/11/00009-biblioteca-de-reformados-antiguos-espanoles.html.

Vol. XIII. Reginaldo Gonsalvio Montano, *Inquisitionis Hispanicae* [1567] (Madrid: J. Martín Alegría, 1856).

Vols. XIV–XV Juan Calvino, *Instituzion de la Relijion Cristiana* [1536] y traduzida por Cipriano de Valera [1597] (Madrid: J. López Cuesta. 1858). 2 vols.

Vol. XVI. Juan de Valdés, *Alfabeto cristiano: añádase ahora dos traduziones modernas, una en castellano, otra en inglés* (Londres: Eyre & Spottiswoode, 1861).

Vols. XVII–XVIII. Juan de Valdés, *Ziento y Diez Consideraziones*. Publicadas en 1855, por Luis de Usoz i Rio. Ahora correjidas nuevamente (Londres: Claro del Bosque, 1863).

Vol. XIX. Juan Pérez, *Breve Sumario de Indulgencias* [1560] (Madrid: J. Martín Alegría, 1862).

Vol. XX. Constantino Ponze de la Fuente, *Suma de doctrina cristiana. Catezismo Cristiano. Confesión del pecador* [1540, 1548, 1551]. *Dos epístolas de S. Bernardo romanzadas por el Mastro Martín Navarro* (Madrid: J. Martín Alegría, 1863).

Vol. XXI. Anon., *Historia de la muerte de Juan Diaz* [1546] (Madrid: J. Martín Alegría, 1865).

Vol. XXII. Anon., *Dialogo de la lengua* [1533] publicado por primera vez en 1737. (Madrid: J. Martín Alegria, 1860).

Vol. XXIII. Juan de Valdes, *El Salterio* [1550]. Traduzido del Hebreo en romance castellano, E. Boehmer, ed. (Bonn: Carlos Georgi. 1880).

Vol. XXIV. Juan de Valdes, *Trataditos* [1545], E. Boehmer, ed. (Bonn, Carlos Georgi, 1880).

Obras de los Reformadores españoles del siglo XVI, edited by Emilio Monjo Bellido.[2]

Antonio del Corro, Carta a los pastores luteranos de Amberes; Carta a Felipe II; Carta a Casiodoro de Reina; Exposición de la Obra de Dios, in E. Monjo Bellido, ed. Obras de los reformadores españoles del siglo XVI, Vol. I (Seville: Editorial MAD, 2006). Introduction by Antonio Ribera Garcia.

Juan Perez de Pineda, Epístola consolatoria, in E. Monjo Bellido (ed.), Obras de los Reformadores españoles del siglo XVI, Vol. II (Seville: Editorial MAD, 2007). Introduction by Emillio Monjo Bellido.

Juan de Valdes, Diálogo de doctrina Cristiana, in E. Monjo Bellido, ed. Obras de los reformadores españoles del siglo XVI, Vol. III (Seville: Editorial MAD, 2008). Introduction by David Estrada.

Reginaldo Gonzalez Montes, Artes de la Santa Inquisición española de González Montes, in E. Monjo Bellido, ed., Obras de los Reformadores españoles del siglo XVI, Vol. IV (Seville: Editorial MAD, 2008). Translated from the Latin and introduction by Francisco Ruiz de Pablos.

Constantino Ponce de la Fuente, Exposición del Primer Psalmo dividida en seis sermones [1546], in E. Monjo Bellido, ed., Obras de los reformadores españoles del siglo XVI, Vol. V (Seville: Editorial MAD, 2008). Introduction by David Estrada.

---

2 At present all these volumes are out of print, but will shortly be reprinted in another format under the auspices of CIMPE. Likewise, several of them are also being translated into English.

Casiodoro de Reina, Comentario al Evangelio de Juan, in E. Monjo Bellido, ed., Obras de los Reformadores españoles del siglo XVI, Vol. VII (Seville: Editorial MAD, 2010). Translated from the Latin and introduction by Fco. Ruiz de Pablos.

Antonio del Corro, Comentario Dialogado de la carta a los Romanos, in E. Monjo Bellido, ed., Obras de los Reformadores españoles del siglo XVI, Colección Eduforma Historia, Vol. VIII (Seville: Editorial MAD, 2010). Translated from the Latin and introduction by Fco. Ruiz de Pablos.

Antonio del Corro, Comentario a Eclesiastés in E. Monjo Bellido, ed. Obras de los reformadores españoles del siglo XVI, Vol. IX (Seville: Editorial MAD, 2011). Translated from the Latin and introduction by Fco. Ruiz de Pablos.

Constantino Ponce de la Fuente, Doctrina Christiana. Parte primera, in E. Monjo Bellido, ed., Obras de los reformadores españoles del siglo XVI. Vol. X (Seville: Editorial MAD, 2016). Introduction and notes by David Estrada.

Index

Refo500 Academic Studies (R5AS)

Vol 37: Patrizio Foresta /
Federica Meloni (Hg.)
Arts, Portraits and Representation in the Reformation Era
Proceedings of the Fourth Reformation Research Consortium Conference

2016. Ca. 400 pages with ca. 120 Figures, hardcover
ISBN 978-3-525-55249-0

Vol 35: Piotr Wilczek
Polonia Reformata
Essays on the Polish Reformation(s)

2016. 145 pages, hardcover
ISBN 978-3-525-55250-6

Vol 34: Charles Raith II
After Merit
John Calvin's Theology of Works and Rewards

2016. 190 pages, hardcover
ISBN 978-3-525-552483-

Vol 33: Bo Kristian Holm /
Nina J. Koefoed (Hg.)
Lutheran Theology and the shaping of society: The Danish Monarchy as Example
2017. Ca. 392 pages, hardcover
ISBN 978-3-525-55124-0 *(12/2016)*

Alle Bände auch als eBook beziehbar

Band 32: Tobias Schreiber
Petrus Dathenus und der Heidelberger Katechismus
Eine traditionsgeschichtliche Untersuchung zum konfessionellen Wandel in der Kurpfalz um 1563

2016. Ca. 350 Seiten mit 12 Tab., gebunden
ISBN 978-3-525-55247-6

Vol 31: Matthew L. Becker (ed.)
Nineteenth-Century Lutheran Theologians
2016. 359 pages, hardcover
ISBN 978-3-525-55130-1

Vol 29: Jeff Fisher
A Christoscopic Reading of Scripture: Johannes Oecolampadius on Hebrews
2016. 268 pages with 5 fig. and 5 tables, hardcover
ISBN 978-3-525-55101-1

Vol 28: Anne Eusterschulte /
Hannah Wälzholz (ed.)
Anthropological Reformations – Anthropology in the Era of Reformation
2015. 575 pages, with 7 colored and 12 b/w-fig., hardcover
ISBN 978-3-525-55058-8

Vol 27: Gabriella Erdélyi (Ed.)
Armed Memory
Agency and Peasant Revolts in Central and Southern Europe (1450–1700)

2016. 361 pages, hardcover
ISBN 978-3-525-55097-7

V&R Academic

Verlagsgruppe Vandenhoeck & Ruprecht | V&R unipress

www.v-r.de

Refo500 Academic Studies (R5AS)

Vol 25: Karen E. Spierling (ed.)
Calvin and the Book
The Evolution of the Printed Word
in Reformed Protestantism

2015. 170 pages, hardcover
ISBN 978-3-525-55088-5

Vol 24: Arnold Huijgen (ed.)
**The Spirituality of the
Heidelberg Catechism**
Papers of the International Conference on the
Heidelberg Catechism Held in Apeldoorn 2013

2015. 287 pages, with 2 tables, hardcover
ISBN 978-3-525-55084-7

Vol 23: Herman J. Selderhuis / J.Marius
J. Lange van Ravenswaay (ed.)
**Reformed Majorities in
Early Modern Europe**

2015. 373 pages, hardcover
ISBN 978-3-525-55083-0

Vol 22: Tarald Rasmussen /
Jon Øygarden Flæten (ed.)
**Preparing for Death,
Remembering the Dead**

2015. 377 pages, with 78 figures, hardcover
ISBN 978-3-525-55082-3

Alle Bände auch als eBook beziehbar

Band 21: Jonathan Mumme
Die Präsenz Christi im Amt
Am Beispiel ausgewählter Predigten
Martin Luthers, 1535–1546

2015. 403 Seiten, gebunden
ISBN 978-3-525-55080-9

Vol 20: Wim Decock / Jordan J. Ballor /
Michael Germann / Laurent Waelkens (ed.)
Law and Religion
The Legal Teachings of the Protestant
and Catholic Reformations

2014. 278 pages, hardcover
ISBN 978-3-525-55074-8

Band 19: Jan-Andrea Bernhard
**Konsolidierung des reformierten
Bekenntnisses im Reich der
Stephanskrone**
Ein Beitrag zur Kommunikationsgeschichte
zwischen Ungarn und der Schweiz in der
frühen Neuzeit (1500-1700)

2015. 800 Seiten, mit 3 Abb., gebunden
ISBN 978-3-525-55070-0

Vol 18: Anna Vind / Iben Damgaard /
Kirsten Busch Nielsen / Sven Rune
Havsteen (Ed.)
(In)Visibility
Reflections upon Visibility and Transcendence
in Theology, Philosophy and the Arts

2016. 592 pages with ca. 51 figures, hardcover
ISBN 978-3-525-55071-7

V&R Academic
Verlagsgruppe Vandenhoeck & Ruprecht | V&R unipress

www.v-r.de